Sacred Books of the Buddhists, vol. xxxiii

THE CLARIFIER
OF THE
SWEET MEANING

TRANSLATION OF THE PALI COMMENTARIES

in

CELEBRATION OF THE CENTENARY

of

THE PALI TEXT SOCIETY

1881–1981

Publication No. 1

THE CLARIFIER OF THE SWEET MEANING

(Madhuratthavilāsinī)

COMMENTARY ON THE
CHRONICLE OF BUDDHAS
(Buddhavaṁsa)
by
BUDDHADATTA THERA

Translated by
I. B. HORNER

Published by
THE PALI TEXT SOCIETY, LONDON

Distributed by
ROUTLEDGE & KEGAN PAUL LTD.
London, Henley and Boston
1978

First published 1978

UNESCO COLLECTION OF REPRESENTATIVE WORKS

This Buddhist text has been accepted in the series of translations from the literature of Burma, India, Sri Lanka, and Thailand, jointly sponsored by the United Nations Educational, Scientific, and Cultural Organisation (UNESCO), and the National Commissions for Unesco in these countries.

ISBN 0 7100 8777 2

Printed in Great Britain by Spottiswoode Ballantyne Ltd.
Colchester and London

PREFACE

The Pali Text Society has been in existence for close on 100 years. Up to date, 1976, it has published translations of all the Pali canonical works except Paṭisambhidāmagga, Apadāna, Yamaka, and part of Paṭṭhāna. But translations of only four commentaries have been issued: those on Khuddakapāṭha[1], Dhammapada[2], Dhammasaṅgaṇi[3], and Kathāvatthu[4]. To commemorate its centenary in 1981 the Society has established a Translation of the Commentaries (Aṭṭhakathā) Project. The object is to publish as many translations of these into English as possible as and when they become ready, and not waiting for the centenary year itself. I feel it a privilege that my translation of the Buddhavaṁsa Commentary (BvA) called Madhuratthavilāsinī or Clarifier of the Sweet Meaning (CSM) should be the first to go to press under this Project. That it was nearing completion before the Project was formed gave me an advantage over the other translators.

As this is so, I am taking the opportunity to make a few general remarks as briefly as I can, first about the sources of the Commentaries, then about their function, and lastly something about their methods. I hope by this means some guide-lines may suggest themselves for future research into commentarial structure and organization as a whole, not excluding investigation of specific differences or similarities such as may be found to exist between cty and cty or between one group and another group.[5] BvA, Jātakanidāna, VvA, PvA, CpA and ApA, for example, may be said to be more concerned with expounding legendary matters than monastic regulations (Vinaya), doctrinal themes and numerous other points (Sutta), or psycho-philosophical concepts (Abhidhamma).

[1] By Ñāṇamoli Thera, Illustrator, (in MR and Ill.), 1960.

[2] By E. W. Burlingame, Buddhist Legends, 3 vols., reprinted 1969 from the original edn., H.O.S. vols. 28, 29, 30.

[3] By Pe Maung Tin, The Expositor, 2 vols., 1920, 1921, reprinted 1976.

[4] By B. C. Law, Debates Commentary, 1940.

[5] See BPE, 3rd edn., Intr. xxvi.

Because the Commentaries form a highly important branch of Pali literature, fundamental to a precise interpretation and understanding of the Teaching, they have by no means failed to attract the attention of certain reliable authorities in the field of Pali studies. Prominent in this connexion is E. W. Adikaram[1] who roughly divides his material into two groups: differences between Aṭṭhakathās and the Canon, and differences between one Aṭṭhakathā and another. Everything he says merits close study and consideration. Perspicacious and helpful too, though very much shorter, are observations made by Ñāṇamoli Thera on the exegetical apparatus[2] and on the function of a cty.[3] The less recent work of M. Winternitz[4] and of B. C. Law[5], in both cases on more general lines and of considerable length, remains valid for some of the problems connected with commentarial origin, growth, purpose and contents.[6]

In what follows I am dealing with the ctys on rather different lines, and the approaches to the commentarial methods I put forward below in Section III of this Preface are made on the whole from angles I have hitherto not seen discussed. But first, the sources of the ctys must be re-stated as, in spite of all that has been written about them, there still seems to be ignorance and misunderstanding. Secondly, the aim or object of the ctys likewise has to be stated again, principally to give due emphasis to the reasons and necessity for their compilation. Then, in Section III, some of the characteristic devices they use in the course of their clarifications are briefly examined. Not seldom these clarifications turn out to be remarkably instructive.

I *Sources of the Commentaries*

The production of the Commentaries in the form we have them now was undertaken in the main by Buddhaghosa and Dhammapāla and to a lesser extent by Buddhadatta, to whom BvA is ascribed. All were bhikkhus, all lived in C5 A.C., and all appear to

[1] EHBC, Colombo 1946, esp. p. 1–42.

[2] Illustrator, Intr. vi (in MR & Ill.).

[3] Guide, 1962, Intr. xliii.

[4] Hist. Ind. Lit., transln., Calcutta 1933, II 183–210.

[5] A Hist. of Pali Lit., London 1933, II 384–576.

[6] Mrs Rhys Davids, too, has given a few notes that, as she says, "may prove useful when the times are ready for a full inquiry into the history of the Buddhist commentaries", BPE, Intr. p. xxx.

have been Indians who came to the Mahāvihāra in Anurādhapura in Sri Lanka to pursue their translation tasks there with the consent of the resident monks. There may have been more than one Buddhaghosa and more than one Buddhadatta and it is possible there were at least four Dhammapālas.[1]

Strictly speaking, not one of these is the author of any commentary that has come down to us under his name. Rather is it the case they were translators and editors mainly engaged in reducing to a more acceptable and sophisticated order the material they found existing already in Sri Lanka as Commentaries. Probably emanating from India (perhaps even from the Buddha himself), these Commentaries had been brought to Sri Lanka by Mahinda in some form of Māgadhī, there to be put into Sinhalese. And so they remained, some of them perhaps for about nine centuries, before being rendered into the language we now call Pali, as well as being organized and edited by the so-called commentators, Buddhaghosa and the others whose names the works now carry, but who in reality were translators and editors[2], not writers and original compilers. Buddhaghosa himself, or so we may believe, tells us as much in his introductory verses to each of the voluminous ctys on the four great Nikāyas[3], also in those on VA[4] and Asl[5]. To take the Nikāya ctys first, we find that he says:

"The Commentaries, recited at the beginning (First Council[6]) by five hundred Elders and later recited again (Second and Third Councils[7]), were brought to the Island of Sīhaḷa[8] by Mahā-Mahinda and later put into the Sīhaḷa language for the benefit of the Island-dwellers. Removing the Sīhaḷa language from them (the Commentaries) and rendering them into the beautiful language[9], free from defects, suitable to the style of the canonical texts,[10] not contradicting the tradition of the Elders resident in the Mahāvihāra, lamps in the line of Elders, experts in decision, I will make the meaning clear, removing any repetitions, for the elation of good people and for the perpetuation of Dhamma."

In introducing the Pali translation of the Vinaya Commentary, Buddhaghosa has said, as recorded:

[1] DAṬ, ed. Lily de Silva, 1970, I xli ff. [2] See Ppn, Intr. xii ff.
[3] DA 1f, MA 1f, SA 1f, AA 1f. [4] VA 1f. [5] Asl 1, ver. 13–17.
[6] So DAṬ i 19. [7] Ibid. 20. [8] Sri Lanka.
[9] The language of Magadha. [10] tantinaya.

"As this Commentary has been composed in the language of the Island of Sīhaḷa, it does not render any service to the bhikkhu-population overseas, therefore now I shall begin this Commentary in conformity with the style of the canonical texts . . . In beginning this exposition I shall base it on the Mahā-aṭṭhakathā and without discarding whatever are correct meanings and rulings that are given in the Mahāpaccarī and other famous Commentaries such as the Kurundī that can be admitted to the tradition of the Elders . . . I shall therefore avoid incorrect 'readings' (scribes' errors) handed down in these. From them, giving up only a different tongue[1] and condensing protracted exegeses, not excluding any decision nor deviating from any textual tradition . . . (I shall expound the Vinaya)"[2].

Again, as noted by Mrs Rhys Davids, "Buddhaghosa himself says in the introductory verses to the Atthasālinī"[3]:

"The Commentary[4] on that Abhidhamma, at first (at the First Council) recited by Mahākassapa and other sages and again recited later (at the Second and Third Councils) by the (other) seers, had been brought by the Elder Mahinda to this superb Island and put into the language of the Island-dwellers. Removing from it (the Commentary) the language of the dwellers in Tambapaṇṇi[5], rendering it into the faultless language which is in keeping with the style of the canonical texts, elucidating the decisions of the residents in the Mahāvihāra unmixed with and uncorrupted by the views of other sects, and taking what ought to be taken also from the Nikāyas and the Commentaries, I will clarify the meaning making the proficient delighted."

It could not be more clearly stated that Buddhaghosa's great concern was to reduce the mass of the ancient Commentaries to a systematic and more rational form, more readily understandable to a greater number of bhikkhus and that, apart from banishing the redundancies he found in them, he was resolved to adhere closely

[1] Different from the language of the texts, i.e. giving up the Sīhaḷa language.

[2] See too transl. at ID, 2–3.

[3] Asl p. 1, ver 13ff. Translns. of these verses appear also at BPE Intr. xxviii, and in Expos. I. 2f.

[4] No way of telling whether sing. or pl., but on Abhidhamma is said, not on Dhs.

[5] An ancient name for Sri Lanka.

to their basic method of exegesis no less than to the teaching of the Elders, or Theravāda tradition, enshrined in them. He would then, only very rarely intruding his own opinion, translate them from Sinhalese into Pali, and that is what we have today as the Pali Commentaries.

The traditional story as given in some detail in Mhvs[1] is that on the advice of his teacher, Revata Thera at Bodh-gayā, the young brahman (later to be named Buddhaghosa) received the *pabbajjā*, or "going forth" as a necessary preliminary to going to Sri Lanka to fulfil his wish of making a deep study of the three Piṭakas together with their Commentary. For here, in Jambudīpa, as Revata Thera explained to him, "there is no Commentary", *n'atthi aṭṭhakathā idha.* Arrived at the Mahāvihāra, Buddhaghosa asked for "all the manuscripts" so that he could compose a Commentary. To test his capabilities as a textual organizer and a translator (from the Sinhalese tongue into that of the Māgadhas[2]) and to determine his comprehension of the material he longed to deal with, the resident monks, enormously impressed by his learning, gave him two verses and said: "Show your ability with these. When we have seen it we will give you all the manuscripts." The Visuddhimagga is the result of his studies of the Canonical texts and the old Sinhalese Commentaries. Though written by him, it is an original work only in so far as it is a systematization and coordination of this old commentarial material into a less diffuse and more compact form than that which apparently prevailed in them[3]. How far the other "original" work attributed to Buddhaghosa, called Ñāṇodaya, may be rightly so regarded could only be known should some Ms or other version of it unexpectedly come to light.[4]

Unfortunately none of the old pre-Pali Commentaries, those "edited" and translated by Buddhaghosa, Dhammapāla, and BvA by Buddhadatta, is extant any more. But the names of those seemingly most used by e.g. Buddhaghosa, especially in VA, have come down to us through him as Mahā- or Mūla- aṭṭhakathā, Mahāpaccarī, Kurundī, and Andhakaṭṭhakathā, and others also.[5]

[1] Mhvs xxxvii 215–248, from which the above is abbreviated.

[2] I.e. Pali.

[3] Ppn. Intr. xix.

[4] B. C. Law remarks, "It would be highly interesting if Siam preserves a text", Buddhaghosa, *Bombay Branch RAS*, 1946, p. 2. See also Ibid. p. 79. It was supposed to have been written in India, as was Asl.

[5] A list is given at BPE, Intr. xxviii.

Sometimes these are merely cited, sometimes approved of, sometimes adversely criticized by him in VA and elsewhere[1], thus showing that besides being a translator, he had editorial interests as well. The same holds good of Dhammapāla. Buddhadatta in BvA mentions none of these ancient Commentaries by name. The expression "in the manuscripts", *potthakesu*, may perhaps refer to them however.[2]

Also, and living even prior to the compilers of the old commentaries, there were the Porāṇas, scholars who were "undoubtedly revered teachers of old and they must have played an important part in the formation and stabilising of the Theravāda school".[3] Adikaram is of the opinion that even if they were not known in India by the name Porāṇa, yet their views and interpretations of the Teaching were incorporated in an old commentary (such as referred to above) which, when the Mahā-aṭṭhakathā and other commentaries came to be written, became known as Porāṇaṭṭhakathā.[4]

BvA could hardly fail to know of the existence of the Porāṇas, and it ascribes to them a verse it cites[5] as do at least eleven other commentaries. Moreover, the Burmese Chaṭṭhasaṅgāyanā edition of BvA ascribes the following verse to them also with a note that the Sinh. version omits both the verse and its attribution[6]:

> One Buddha in a Sāra-eon, in a Maṇḍa-eon the Conquerors are two,
> In a Vara-eon three Buddhas, in a Sāramaṇḍa-eon four Buddhas,
> Five Buddhas in a Bhadda-eon; there are no more Conquerors than that.

Further, in giving the eight stock reasons why the Lord is to be called Tathāgata, though BvA cites three verses[7] which other commentaries in almost identical exegeses on this same subject attribute to the Porāṇa, it does not do so. Again, there is a verse that at least four other commentaries ascribe to them, but neither BvA[8] nor UdA 403 does this. Nor have I found any prose passage that BvA ascribes to them. Is it the only cty not to do so?

[1] Ppn. Intr. xix. [2] Cf. below, p. xii. [3] EHBC, 23.
[4] Cf. Oldenberg's remarks at Dīp, p. 2. [5] BvAC, 35.
[6] Ibid. 191. [7] Ibid. 15, 16, 17. [8] Ibid. 42.

Besides knowing of the Porāṇas, the ancients who were their predecessors, the ctys are aware too of those who may have been their contemporaries, and to whom they refer sometimes merely as "they" (understood), *api paṭhanti*, "they also read"[1]; sometimes as *aññe* or *apare*[2], others; and more often as *keci*, some. Probably, in some passages these may all be different. For example, a passage on *nirāmisa* at PṭsA begins by saying "In the manuscript they (understood) write 'sāmisañ ce'. That is no better", *potthake sāmisañ ce ti likhanti, taṁ na sundarataraṁ*[3]. It then gives three dyads, in the affirmative and the negative, that should be known or understood in explanation of *nirāmisa* and *sāmisa*. This passage is preceded by interpretations of words or concepts (connected with *gotra-bhū*) made first by *aññe* and then by *keci*, both of whose interpretations appear to be rejected. Or again, for example, at UdA 116 253 428 what *keci* say, *vaṇṇeti*, *vadanti*, *paṭhanti*, is spoken of as *taṁ na sundaraṁ*, "that is not right". Their readings also appear to be rejected at UdA 34, *tan akāraṇaṁ*, and 431, *n'atth' idaṁ kāraṇaṁ* "that is mistaken", probably also at UdA 44, but not necessarily at UdA 51. Indeed, Dr Lily de Silva, finding that references to *keci* tend to be pejorative, hazards the guess that *keci* were Abhayagirins and perhaps the residents at the Uttaravihāra, provided these were not identical[4] which DPPN rightly takes them to have been[5]. It should be noted, however, that as it seems that a fair proportion of the readings (*paṭhanti*) or sayings (*vadanti*) attributed to *keci* is recorded without any criticism being made[6], these interpretations are, therefore, by no means always rejected as being untenable. But until such time as a full survey of all commentarial references to *keci* has been compiled, it is possible to extract only a few of their readings from here and there in a haphazard way.

It thus seems better to present merely a small number of occasions when BvA in ascribing a variant reading to *keci* expresses neither agreement nor disagreement, or appears to agree, or definitely disagrees. But I hope this small number will be

[1] Or "they" may perhaps refer to readings and writings in the ancient Sinhalese ctys.

[2] *apare* at UdA 245, and ibid. 374 where what they say is not to be adopted.

[3] PṭsA i 276. Text reads *ca* for *ce*.

[4] DAṬ i p. lixff.

[5] See s.v. Abhayagiri and Uttaravihāra.

[6] E.g. BvAC 13 (with, however, *pana*, but), 151, 152 (twice), 160, UdA 44, 51.

sufficient to mark the importance the ctys attach to *keci*. Belonging to the first of these three categories is the passage: *gavapānenā ti idaṁ vuttam eva, ghatapānenā ti pi paṭhanti keci*[1]. Or again, *atthamī ti atthaṅ gato, keci attham gato ti paṭhanti*[2]. And, *yasavipulo ti vipulayaso . . . keci tatth' āsi vipulo rukkho ti paṭhanti*—"widely famed . . . some read 'there was a wide tree there'"[3].

But we also get: *cando tāragaṇe yathā ti . . . keci cando paṇṇaraso yathā ti paṭhanti*—"as the moon among a host of stars . . . some read 'as the moon on the fifteenth day'". This reading seems acceptable as BvA says, *so uttānattho va*, "this meaning is quite clear"[4].

Against this there is the passage: *sabbakilesānī ti sabbakilese, liṅgavipariyāsaṁ katvā vuttaṁ. Keci tattha sabbakilesehī ti paṭhanti*—"all the defilements means all the defilements, said having made a change of gender. Some read 'there (i.e. at Nārada's Tree of Awakening) with all the defilements'"[5] which is incorrect though not noted as such. However, what *keci* say, *vadanti*, about "possessed of eight special qualities" is definitely rejected for it does not agree with or fit the text, *taṁ pāliyā na sameti*[6]. This is due to the fact that "some" mistakenly interpret these qualities with reference to a hermitage which would provide eight happinesses, whereas the happinesses should be taken to refer to a recluse's state of mind: composed, purified, clarified, without blemish, without defilement, grown soft and workable, fixed, immovable[7]—the eight.

These few words about *keci* may give some indication of the extreme care with which the ctys were written or translated. Indeed it could be added here that some (unspecified) people are objected to because they write an erroneous writing in the manuscripts: *mayi pabbajite ti mayi pabbajitabhāvaṁ upagate. Mama pabbajitaṁ santan ti potthakesu likhanti, so pamādalekho ti veditabbo*[8]—"*when I had gone forth* means when I had reached the status of one who has gone forth. They write in the manuscripts,

[1] BvAC 151.
[2] Ibid. 160.
[3] Ibid. 184.
[4] Ibid. 201.
[5] Ibid. 185.
[6] Ibid. 76.
[7] This is 'stock', often describing the mind of a person ready to enter into jhāna.
[8] BvAC 230. "In the manuscripts", *potthakesu*, perhaps means in the old MSS. of the pre-Pali ctys.

'there being my going forth'; this should be understood as an erroneous writing."[1]

II *Function of a Commentary*

The prime object of every Commentary is to make the meanings of the words and phrases in the canonical passages it is elucidating abundantly clear, definite, definitive even, "heuristic" in E. Hardy's words[2], and virtually beyond all doubt and argument. This is to preserve the Teaching of the Buddha as nearly as possible in the sense intended, and as conveyed by the succession of teachers, *ācariyaparamparā*[3]. Always there were detractors, always there were and still are "improvers" ready with their own notions. Through enemies and friends alike deleterious change and deterioration in the word of the Buddha might intervene for an indefinite length of time. The ctys are the armour and protection against such an eventuality. As they hold a unique position as preservers and interpreters of true Dhamma, it is essential not only to understand them but to follow them carefully and adopt the meaning they ascribe to a word or phrase each time they comment on it. They are as "closed" now as is the Pali Canon. No additions to their corpus or subtractions from it are to be contemplated, and no cty written in later days could be included in it. With the ṭīkās or sub-commentaries which explain points in the ctys needing "further elucidation for their correct interpretation or sometimes merely giving additional information"[4] we are not concerned here.

III *Some Methods of Exegesis*

The Commentaries are vast store-houses of a knowledge that ranges from the highest reaches of Buddhist thought, as e.g. the three Jewels, the aggregates (*khandha*), elements (*dhātu*), sense-bases (*āyatana*), dependent origination (*paṭiccasamuppāda*), the faculties (*indriya*), the Way (*magga*) and its eight components, the meditations (*jhāna*) and attainments (*samāpatti*), the marks of phenomenal existence (*lakkhaṇa*), freedom (*vimutti*), nibbāna and

[1] Cf. *pamādapāṭhā*, KhA 207, PvA 25, both connected with *pahūte*.
[2] VvA Intr. p. ix.
[3] Vin v 2f., VA 62. See ID 55.
[4] PLC 192ff.

its synonyms, through less exalted philosophical and psychological concepts to quite homely matters such as places, plants, cow-keeping, animals.

Grammar is often considered; changes of tense and gender, also the substitution of one case for another, are usually noted as they occur (BvA exercises great care in these matters), and attention is called to grammatical usages or rules, *lakkhaṇa*[1].

Telling and apposite similes and metaphors are employed, and stories not infrequently told so as to illustrate a point that has arisen and give some perspective to the whole matter. Some of these refer to a past that may be remote and legendary, or to times not so remote. The story then may take the form of a jātaka-tale. Others, supposedly real and of more recent, possibly contemporary, occurrence may deal with such matters as local government, prevailing manners and customs and ways of behaviour, pronounced to be good or bad, seemly or unseemly both in regard to their social effects and their kammic fruition as well. But it is impossible to convey in the short space of a Preface more than a broad outline of the nature of this material—often of considerable historical interest to us. No doubt all the ctys make use of it as a kind of by-product of the words and phrases they are specifically commenting on to give substance to these and invest them with unimpeachable authenticity. That these words and phrases are indeed almost inexhaustible may be seen from the Indexes to most PTS editions.

The commentators, aided no doubt by a trained memory, must have been in complete command of most, if not all, of the canonical works. How otherwise, in support of their commentarial explanation, could they draw from them so aptly and pertinently when occasion required[2] or display so well the prominent or latent teaching they contain?[3]

Naturally the contents of the ctys vary between Vinaya, Sutta and Abhidhamma. They vary also according to the nature and perhaps the main emphasis, if any, of the particular canonical work being commented on. Thus, as Ñāṇamoli says of KhA[4], "The weight of final emphasis laid by the text on Lovingkindness as a

[1] E.g. BvAC 89 114 175 258; cf. ThagA i 114.
[2] See e.g. Ñāṇamoli, Guide, Intr. xliii.
[3] Cf. E. Hardy, VvA, Intr. ix, n. 1 where he speaks of Dhammapāla's acquaintance with the sacred texts being naturally greater than his own.
[4] Illustrator (in MR & Ill), Intr. vi.

basis for attaining the bliss of nibbāna is exploited in the Commentary."

As naturally as the contents of the ctys vary, so, too, they may correspond and tally one with another especially on the inescapable, recurrent terms that are the very stuff of the Teaching. In consequence, commentarial explanations showing little or no divergence from one another may well appear not only in one or two but in several ctys as parallel or very comparable passages, though sometimes varying in length. For example, all the ctys that handle the term Tathāgata give in almost precisely the same words the eight reasons why the Lord is to be so known[1]. It is not a word of dual meaning. Similarly, there is virtually but the one explanation of *caturaṅgika-sannipāta*[2], the four-factored assembly of bhikkhus. Or one may turn to the fairly long and very similar exegesis of *pāṇātipāta*, occurring in at least five different ctys,[3] or to the explanations of various consecutive words at DA iii 1051f., AA v 7–9, or *duvidhaṁ hi kammaṭṭhānaṁ* at DA iii 721–4, MA i 275–8, or of the various kinds of *paññā* at DA iii 931–3, MA iv 82–6, SA i 119–122. Clearly these are all repetitions taken, if not from the cty that was prepared and ready first, then from some common source. On the other hand, there are occasions when exegeses of the same words may vary quite substantially. A clear example of this can be found in the exegeses on the Ābhassara, Subhakiṇha and Vehapphalā devas at BvAC 37, MA i 35 and AA iv 27. For though a few analogous expressions may be used, that is all there is in common. Or there are at least two quite different definitions of *bhikkhu*, one occurring in the Padabhājaniya[4] or Old Commentary on the Pātimokkha rules[5], and the other in Niddesa[6]. Both these works were written in Pali and though primarily ctys were admitted into the Canon before it was "closed".

Further, a canonical word may be uncommented on in its own position by its own cty, though a comment on this same word may occur elsewhere. Yet, the reliability of the transposition of an interpretation from cty to cty may well be open to question and

[1] DA i 59, MA i 45, AA i 103, UdA 129, ItA i 117, BvAC 15. The explanations of the reasons sometimes show discrepancies.

[2] BvAC 126, DA ii 418.

[3] DA i 69, MA i 198, SA ii 144, KhA 29, Asl 97.

[4] Vin iii 24 46 73 91 120 etc., cf. Vbh 245.

[5] See Vin i, Intr. xxi, n. 1, 2.

[6] Nd1 70. See too exegesis on *bhikkhave*, ItA i 38, different again.

sometimes inadmissible[1]. However, there seem to be border-line cases now and again. For example, BvAC 33 in its explanation of *deva-cakkhu* says *deva-cakkhu* means a super-knowing, *abhiññā*, arisen by an augmentation of light, *ālokavaḍḍhana*; this perhaps does not tell us much. But ItA ii 28 takes *dibba-cakkhu* to mean that, having augmented the light-kasiṇa, *kasiṇālokaṁ vaḍḍhetvā*, there is an arising of knowledge of deva-like vision, *dibba-cakkhuñāṇassa*. Though this may be so as far as It and ItA are concerned, is it legitimate to assume that BvA also is silently referring to this kasiṇa? The functions of *dibbacakkhu* are differently explained again at Nd1 355f.

Or, to take another example, the meaning which is relevant and therefore assigned to the word *dukkha* at AA ii 96, 203, 208, etc. is *vaṭṭadukkha*, the anguish of the round (of saṁsāric existence) while at AA ii 263, iii 182 *dukkha* is explained in relation to the four truths.[2] These, however, cover *vaṭṭadukkha* and the cessation of it in accordance with the third ariyan truth. BvA 63 and Asl 41, in a longer statement on the word *dukkha*, explain it in neither of these two ways. But other specified denotations[3] such as *vedanā*[4] might perhaps be subsumed under one or other of the five meanings these two works posit in order to give an indication of the prevalence of *dukkha* in human life. *Dukkha*, therefore, is an example of a word briefly explained by some ctys, more elaborately by others, even if not always very obviously bearing the same meaning. But once the Dhamma, "deep, difficult to see, difficult to understand . . . intelligible to the wise"[5] is comprehended, the relevance and correctness of this meaning becomes clear.

However much the principal contents of the ctys may vary from one another[6], the basic and invariable commentarial method as we have it today is to work through the corresponding canonical text and expound its words in their successive order of appearance. Yet, by no means are all canonical words commented on. Sometimes, when one would value commentarial help none is forthcoming. Possibly either the meaning was lost even by the time the old Commentaries were composed, or the word was

[1] See Section III. 6 below on words of multiple meaning.

[2] At S v 437 it is said that he who understands any one of the truths understands them all; see also Rāhula, What the Buddha Taught, p. 27. The AA explanations accord very well.

[3] See e.g. AA v, Index s.v. *dukkha*.

[4] E.g. KhA 80.

[5] Vin i 4.

[6] See above, p. xiv.

fully understood *then* but is no longer, or not with accuracy and certainty.

Besides this basic commentarial method followed throughout by all the ctys, they have in common a number of other means of elucidation, not necessarily in use all the time, but as need arose. It was then that they could turn to one or other, or sometimes more than one, of these devices.

Though these devices are important for our greater and more precise understanding of the commentarial structure as a whole, only a small fraction of this vast subject can be presented here, and no pretence is made for finality or comprehensiveness of any kind or in every way. Indeed, everything said below about commentarial methods of elucidation could be added to and expanded, and other methods could be discussed. But like the compiler of BvA, who on occasion expressed his fear of becoming too long[1], so too I aim at being not over-prolix in the following indications of some of the methods of exegesis used by the Commentaries.

III 1 *Canonical quotations*

Every cty, especially when trying to make its point beyond all dispute, is liable to give quotations from canonical works. Though it may mention these by name[2] more often than not it does not provide what nowadays would be thought of as an exact reference. It may introduce its quotation with the words, *vuttaṁ pi c'etaṁ*, or, *vuttaṁ* (*pi*) *h'etaṁ*, "for this was said"; or with the expression, *yath 'āha*, or *ten' āha*, "as was said", sometimes adding "by the Lord"[3] or "by the Porāṇas"[4] or by someone else, but not necessarily naming the source. Or a cty may give mere stock descriptions, as of a learned brahman, with no indication that these may occur scattered throughout the Canon[5].

III 2 *Other readings*

Other "readings", *pāṭha*, may be given in the ctys and occur not at all infrequently in BvA[6]. When the variant reading is recorded,

[1] BvAC 177, cf. 26 (3 lines from end) and 197 (top).
[2] See e.g. Index of Quotations and References, MA v 136ff.
[3] E.g. BvAC 144, UdA 405. Both of frequent occurrence in Nd.
[4] BvAC 35; see above, p. x.
[5] E.g. BvAC 67, and D i 88 120 130, A i 163 166.
[6] With this paragraph cf. above p. xiff, on *keci*.

it may be said, *ayam eva vā pāṭho*[1], "or this itself is the reading". Or it may be said, . . . *vā pāṭho*[2], "or (such and such a word) is a reading". Or, . . . *api pāṭho,* "(such and such a word) is also a reading", chiefly but not always when there is some definite variation in sense[3]. This other reading may then either be rejected as not right or correct[4], or it may be accepted. In this latter case it may be said to be "the same meaning", "the meaning is the same", *so yev' attho*, or, *ayam ev' attho*[5]. There are also occasions where a cty, after giving another reading, then states what this means and adds "This is better" or more correct, *ayaṁ sundarataro*[6].

An interesting passage at KhA 78 shows meticulous commentarial handling of this problem: "And here in the phrase 'One is what?' (*ekaṁ nāma kiṁ*) the reading is twofold as *kiṁ* and *ki ha.* Herein the Sinhalese reading is *kī ha,* for they say *kī ha* when *kiṁ* should be said. Some (*keci*) assert that *ha* is a particle, and also that this too is the very reading[7] of the Elders' tradition. However, the meaning is the same in either case and it can be read according to preference"[8]. This is not unique. Other passages, as mentioned above, say the variant gives the very meaning. Thus it is equally good.

There are two interesting occasions in UdA[9] where other readings are given: (1) *Kāya nu 'tthā ti, katamāya nu bhavatha? Kāya notthā ti pi pāli: so ev' attho. Kāya nvetthā ti pi paṭhanti: tassā katamāya nu etthā ti attho.* (2) *Na khv' etan ti, na kho etaṁ. Ayam eva vā pāṭho:- na kho tan ti pi paṭhanti, na kho etam icc' eva padavibhāgo.*

In contrast to BvA which, as already noted, gives other readings fairly copiously, it seems that MA on M Stas 51–100[10], for example, makes little if any reference to these at all. This appears to hold good too of much of the rest of MA, with but few exceptions. That

[1] BvAC 94 98 101 116.

[2] MA i 137, AA ii 114; and see AA v Index 3, s.v. pātha for more references to AA.

[3] BvAC 98f. 101 123 128 238 256, MA iv 9, SA i 327, AA ii 180 189 265 323.

[4] E.g. VA i 221, UdA 253 *taṁ na sundaraṁ*, that is not right, good, or correct.

[5] BvAC 85 173 267 269, AA ii 189 323.

[6] E.g. BvAC 256.

[7] *ayam eva pāṭho.*

[8] Ñāṇamoli's transln., Illustrator (in MR & Ill) 81f.

[9] UdA 105, 106. Cf. DA i 49 for (1).

[10] MA iii.

at MA i 137 can hardly be counted as it comes in a stock description of the meanings of *agga-sadda*, the word 'agga'[1]. Reasons behind this absence of 'other readings' can only be guessed at. Did the compiler of MA know of variants but thought it unnecessary to include them, and indeed perhaps judged it was not very feasible considering the already great size of MA? Or did he, in the main, use one source only? If so, was it the only one he had access to, even perhaps allowed access to, or was it the only one in existence? Or was there, as perhaps there may have been in another connexion, "deliberate suppression of non-orthodox views on the part of orthodoxy"?[2]

III 3 *Enumerations*

Another form of commentarial elucidation consists in enumerating different kinds of the same item, all of which may have some connexion with the canonical word. For example, at MA ii 112 the process for calming all the constructions, *sabbasaṅkhāra-samatha*, is expounded in two stages: first, by stating that by the shakings, tremblings and writhings of the *saṅkhāras*, their calming results; and secondly, by speaking of the casting aside of differing kinds of the same item, here the four *upadhi*, roughly a basis leading to rebirth. This word *upadhi* therefore occurs here four times as the final element of a compound: *khandha-upadhi*, *kilesa-*, *abhisaṅkhāra-*, and *pañcakāmaguṇa-upadhi*[3]. All these modalities (of grasping) have to be given up because they militate against the attainment of nibbāna. The *upadhis* are explained rather more fully at SA i 31 and SnA 44 in the order *kāma*, *khandha*, *kilesa*, *abhisaṅkhāra*. They are also among the three *vivekas*, detachments from, enumerated as *kāya*, *citta*, and *upadhi*[4].

Other examples where enumeration is used in explanation are of *mariyādā* at MA iv 89 where two kinds are given and then another two kinds; of fields, *khetta*, three kinds at MA iv 114, AA ii 9; of disappearances, *antaradhāna*, five kinds at AA i 87 but three kinds at MA iv 115, VbhA 431; of parinibbāna, three kinds at MA iv 116—these last two in explanation of *apubbam acarimaṁ*; of lions, *sīha*, four kinds at DA iii 827, AA iii 65, SnA 125; of lion-postures,

[1] E.g. at VA i 173, DA i 236, AA ii 114.

[2] DAṬ i, Intr. lxii.

[3] Cf. SA i 175.

[4] DA i 169, Nd1 26 140f., DhA ii 103, ItA i 146, UdA 231.

sīhaseyyā, four kinds at UdA 403; of control, *saṁvara*, five kinds at ItA i 110[1]; of the talk, *kathā*, of Buddhas, two kinds at DA ii 382, KvA 34, namely *sammuti* and *paramattha*; of (more ordinary) talk, three kinds at MA ii 258, named as *ekanālikā*, *caturassā*, *nisinnavattikā*. Then at KhA 125 still another four kinds of talk, called *catubbidhā*, four-fold, are named and examples of each kind given. There are also the three kinds of *vivekā*, detachments or seclusions, and the three kinds of world, *loka*, referred to below[2], and many another. Naturally the number is not to be taken literally but sometimes as meaning "kinds of" as in the examples just given; and sometimes as meaning "reasons for", clearly to be seen in the enumeration of the four *suttanikkhepa*, reasons for the delivery of a discourse[3]. On all occasions it is usually said which kind is intended "here", where "here" means the passage in the canonical context that is being elucidated.

Moreover, a cty can select fewer items from a larger total, or a greater number may be added to a lesser. This again bears witness both to the flexibility of the ctys and to the care bestowed on commentarial compilation. For example, as we have just seen AA i 87 counts the *antaradhāna*, 'disappearances', as five. It does so by means of adding to the three named elsewhere. In the same way KhA 120 adds two kinds of tumult, *kolāhala*, to the three that BvA 272 and SA i 130 refer to, but which would not have been compatible with their needs. Thus, for KhA *kolāhala* is five-fold, *pañcavidha*, for BvA and SA there are three *kolāhalā*.

Thus we are brought to our next Section concerning "the machinery of exegesis"[4]. But before going on it should perhaps be emphasized again that the few examples given above form no more than an insignificant fringe of enumerations whose proportions, if collected, would be vast; and moreover that such enumerations are a feature of the Canon[5] as well as of the ctys.

III 4 "*Folds*"

This is a device where it is said such-and-such a word is "x-fold". For example, at VA i 225 *saddhamma* is three-fold, *tividha*. Each

[1] Cf. below, p. xxi. [2] P. xxiii.

[3] DA i 50, MA i 15, SA ii 3, UdA 29, ItA i 35, BvAC 64.

[4] See Ill (in MR & Ill) p. 135, n. 69.

[5] All Aṅguttara, the Saṅgīti and Dasuttara Suttas of D iii, the Ekuttaraka of Vin v 115–140, for example.

of the three "folds" is succinctly stated without, apparently, giving precedence to one over the others, all being equally applicable. Of equal importance, too, are the two "folds", *duvidha*, of *vinaya* at MA i 22 (cf. ib. ii 208), SA ii 253, SnA 8, ItA i 110, Asl 351. One is the *vinaya* of control, *saṁvara*, the other of elimination, *pahāna*. These "folds" are then each divided into five "folds", *pañcavidha*, all of which are named; SnA then goes on to treat the subject at some length. All the "folds" here are wanted, thus none takes precedence over the others. At UdA 362 there is the *catubbidha ogha*, the four-fold flood of *kāma*, *bhava*, *diṭṭhi*, and *avijjā*, all equally to be crossed over so that the arahant can stand safely on the dry land of the further shore.

In other passages, however, as at UdA 233 where *sīla* is said to be two-fold, the "folds" would appear to belong to different categories, the *lokiya* and the *lokuttara*, mundane and supermundane, both necessary as the former is needed as a basis for the latter. Another subtle distinction is to be found in the four-fold faith, *catubbidhā saddhā*, of DA ii 529, iii 1028, for here each "fold" is applicable to a person at a different stage in his progress along the Way. Also of equal importance, but again referring to the different stages attained, is the *tividha viveka*[1], the three-fold aloofness or detachment from *kāya*, *citta* and *upadhi*. On the other hand, though *pavāraṇā* is called four-fold at MA i 93, this in effect signifies the word has four meanings appropriate to four different occasions, one of which is named as "the one intended here", *ayaṁ idha adhippetā*. Thus again, at SnA 74, 255 *santhava* is described as three-fold, the third "fold" being intended at p. 74 and the first two at p. 255. And in a number of ctys a question, *pucchā*, is said to be five-fold, *pañcavidhā*[2]; after describing each kind the right one is given for each context.

There is too the important word "eye" or "vision", *cakkhu*, important since the Bhagavan sometimes has the epithet *cakkhumā*, One with vision. So *cakkhu* has to be fully explained and receives lengthy analysis in the Niddesa[3], without, however, the occurrence of the word *vidha*, fold. This is introduced into the shorter exegeses at BvAC 33 and ItA i 99. Though these two passages

[1] See above p. xix.

[2] DA 68, MA ii 334, SA ii 8, AA i 101, Nd1 339, ItA i 40, BvAC 58, Asl. 55.

[3] Nd1 354–60. The word *cakkhu*, *cakkhu-sadda*, is very briefly interpreted at DA i 183.

show considerable divergence, both say vision is two-fold: *maṁsacakkhu* and *ñāṇacakkhu* (*paññācakkhu* in ItA), and that the former is two-fold and the latter five-fold. Comparable in some ways are the two folds of *kicca*[1], what has to be done. The first of these two folds, *niratthaka*, remains as one fold without subdivision; but the second, *sātthaka*, falls into a five-fold classification each having its own importance for daily monastic life.

Sometimes, perhaps only occasionally, a word may have a varying number of "folds" ascribed to it according to the canonical passage where it occurs. For example, MA i 62 cites six such passages to show that the number of "folds" in the word *āsava* runs from two, *dvedhā*, to seven, *sattadhā*, as handed down in each passage cited including the one being commented on (M i 6), where *āsava* is seven-fold, a number also arrived at by the same stages at ItA i 114f. It might be noticed here that ItA speaks of the body, *kāya*, as being of many "folds", *bahuvidha*, and sages, *munayo*, as being of many "folds", *anekavidha*[2]. BvAC 44 ascribes sixteen "folds" to *mahāpaññā*, great wisdom, but though it gives no hint of what these are, the exegeses on this word that occur elsewhere[3] make them plain.

III 5 *A sub-device*

A Commentary now and again puts forward some number perhaps from two upwards of, say, states. All would be involved in a full understanding and proper assessment of the word being commented on. Thus DA iii 1061, AA iv 118, in rather a long exegesis of *app' icchassa*[4], one who is of few or no desires, include four items which, for reasons given, might *not* be wished for: *paccaya*, *adhigama*, *pariyatti*, *dhutaṅga*, a monk's requisites, attainment of (any of the four stages of the Way and nibbāna), knowledge of the canonical texts, and ascetic practices. DA and AA add in commentarial style that the matter is fully discussed in Visuddhimagga.[5]

References to Vism, which may be called a commentarial sub-device or sub-method, are fairly constantly made both by Bud-

[1] DA 45. Referred to at AA ii 125. UdA 116 draws a distinction between *kicca* and *karaṇīya*, the former meaning small things to be done.

[2] ItA i 100, 150.

[3] DA iii 931, MA iv 82, SA i 119.

[4] See also MA ii 140, AA i 76, SnA 494.

[5] Cf. Vism 292.

dhaghosa and Dhammapāla in order that a cty need discuss only in brief what there has been said in detail. This sub-method is therefore another indication that these translators of the old Sinhaḷa Commentaries were acting here also in their capacity as editors, introducing abridgements in place of verbosity. For of course Vism, the work of Buddhaghosa himself, post-dates these old Commentaries, having been compiled at a time after he had learnt, mastered, and systematized their contents with a proficiency that justified his translating them and editing them in Pali. With this "encyclopaedia of the Buddha's teaching"[1] to hand it was only common-sense to refer to it. BvA, however, does not appear to mention Vism by name and one cannot tell if, for example, its "three worlds", *tayo lokā*[2], of *saṅkhāraloka*, *sattaloka*, *okāsaloka*, are based directly on Vism's corresponding analysis.[3]

III 6 *Multiple Meanings*

Lastly, I wish to draw attention to one other commentarial device, whose importance has, I think, been somewhat overlooked[4]. This device is concerned with canonical words of multiple meanings and is in essence an analysis of these words, *sadda*. In such contexts *sadda* is used in its meaning of "word". For example, the ancient Pali "Dictionary", Abhidhānappadīpikā, enumerates 14 different meanings of the word dhamma, *dhammasadda*, ending with *ādo*[5], "and so forth", a wise precaution, for I have been able to add three more. Whatever the word, after the ctys have stated it, they immediately give the meanings it can have, then cite canonical passages and say which of the word's several meanings is appropriate to each one. Finally, and unfailingly, they assert which one is intended "here". Thus is eliminated the possibility of a wrong meaning being substituted for the right one.

To give a brief idea of this method, I will take "this word sādhu", *ayaṁ sādhu-saddo*, or *sādhū ti ayaṁ saddo āyācana-sampaṭicchana-sampahaṃsana-sundara-daḷhīkammādisu* (omitted at

[1] DPPN s.v. Visuddhimagga.

[2] BvAC 11–12, 94, also e.g. UdA 207.

[3] Vism 204—ascribed by H to Nd.

[4] But see Grammatical Index to AA s.v. *sadda* which lists occasions of its use in AA, and Index of Grammatical Terms, ThagA iii, e.g. under *ati-*, *anu-*, *ca-sadda*. Both Indexes compiled by Dr H. Kopp.

[5] W. Rāhula, Wrong Notions of Dhammatā, *Buddhist Studies in Honour of I. B. Horner*, 1974, p. 182.

BvA, which ends *sundarādisu*) *dissati*. Indeed, these are to be "seen" like this: *āyācana*, SnA 176; *sampaṭicchana*, BvAC 47; *daḷhīkamma*, DA i 171, MA i 19, SA ii 7. As far as I know AA does not dissect *sādhusadda*, but it defines *sādhu* by one or other of these meanings according to the Aṅg. contexts where it occurs. So *āyācana* is chosen at AA ii 136; *sampahaṃsana* at AA iv 120, 167; *sundara* at AA ii 290, iv 98. Thus the five meanings of *sādhu* are accounted for, and made use of when appropriate.

I now give a list of a number of words of multiple meanings that I have come across together with commentarial passages where they are discussed. On the whole these passages are similar to one another, but not always. Naturally there is often a difference as to which of the meanings it is that is deemed to be proper to this or that canonical context. I have made no attempt to tabulate these; also I am conscious that the list certainly cannot be regarded as complete.

Some Exegeses which use sadda *as 'word'*

[Words having *sadda* attached, but not of multiple meaning, or only one meaning given, are marked by an asterisk.]

aṅgaṇa MA i 139 (no *sadda*), BvA[1] 175
agga VA 173, DA i 235, MA i 136, AA i 124 135, ii 114, ItA ii 102
ajjhatta UdA 374
attha SA i 334, SnA i 238, ItA i 81
atthi VA i 209 (no *sadda*)
*anu ItA i 168, ThagA i 114
anta DA i 103, ItA ii 112; cf. MA i 87
antarā DA i 34, AA iii 75, SnA i 20, UdA 109 164, ItA ii 95
*api UdA 278 392, ItA i 45, VvA 94
abhi VA i 20, Asl 2 20
abhikkanta VA i 170, DA i 227, MA i 139, ii 124, SA i 14, AA ii 105 375 KhA 114, SnA i 155, UdA 286, VvA 52 (shorter)
*ādi AA ii 9 BvA 65
āyatana DA i 124; cf. AA ii 272, PṭsA i 83, Asl (no *sadda*), VbhA 45f.
āram(b)bha PṭsA i 44, Asl 145, PugA 246
āsajja VvA 55
iti VA ii 442, AA iii 14, UdA 45 215, ItA i 19f. 23f.

[1] All references to BvA are to the PTS edn.

idaṁ ItA i 107
*idha VA v 1067
ukkā MA i 175 (no *sadda*), BvA 144
uposatha SnA i 199, UdA 296; cf. MA iv 74 (no *sadda*)
uppanna Asl 67
uḷāra DA iii 878, SA iii 208, VvA 10, BvA 30
eka UdA 18, ItA i 37
etaṁ ItA i 5
eva SA iii 123, UdA 392
evaṁ DA i 26, MA i 3, SA i 5, AA i 4, KhA 100, SnA i 135, UdA 6, PṭsA iii 529
kappa DA i 103, MA ii 125, SA i 15, AA ii 377, KhA 115, CpA 10, BvA 65
kāma VvA 11
kiṁ VvA 16
*kira Jā i 158, VvA 322, PvA 103
kusala BvA 49, PṭsA i 129, 205, Asl 38
kevala MA ii 125, SA i 15, AA ii 376, KhA 115
khandha ItA ii 22
*kho ItA i 54
gati MA iii 364
*gandha ItA ii 57
guṇa BvA 43 76; cf. SA i 23 (no *sadda*)
ca KhA 228, ItA i 54 93 172 178, ii 23 32, VvA 74, PvA 18, ThagA i 108 155, ii 10 125 156 249 256 273, iii 75 79, CpA 12, BvA 185, Asl 171 297
cakka MA ii 27, AA i 120, iii 9, PṭsA iii 626
cakkhu DA i 183; cf. ItA i 99, Nd1 354ff. (no *sadda*), BvA 33
channa ThagA i 25
ṭhāna MA i 102
tathāgata ItA i 117
*tu ItA ii 151, CpA 117
te VvA 9
dukkha ItA ii 5, BvA 63, Asl 41
deva VvA 18, ThagA i 27
dhamma DA i 99 (cf. DhA i 22), MA i 17, AA iv 97, ItA i 39, BvA 13, PṭsA i 18, Asl 38
pariyāya VA i 132, DA i 36, MA i 18, ItA i 151
*pasu ItA ii 70
pātimokkha ItA ii 129

puñña ItA i 73
*putta ItA ii 70
bodhi BvA 55 145; cf. VA i 139, iv 952, MA i 54, SA ii 153, UdA 27, CpA 18 (all without *sadda*)
brahma MA i 34, BvA 11
brahmacariya DA i 177, MA ii 41, ItA i 107
bhūta MA i 31, KhA 165, NdA iii 96
*matta SnA i 137; cf. DA i 35
*mama AA iii 162
maya VvA 10
mūla MA i 12, UdA 27
me DA i 28, MA i 4, SA i 5, AA i 6, KhA 101, SnA i 135, UdA 11, ItA i 22, VvA 25, ThagA i 26, ii 144, PṭsA iii 530
yaṁ BvA 52
*yathā BvA 48
rūpa AA i 21, BvA 41
loka UdA 107
vaṇṇa DA i 37, MA ii 125, SA i 14, AA ii 375–6, KhA 114, VvA 16
vā DA i 51, AA i 29 55, iii 171, iv 75, SnA i 266, UdA 211 278 321 422, ItA ii 52 104, ThagA i 57, ii 173 228, iii 12 85, CpA 130
vidhā Asl 304
vutta MA i 94, UdA 45, ItA i 4
veda BvA 68
*vedanā Asl 41
vo MA i 18, ItA i 39
saṃsaṭṭha Asl 70
saṅkhā MA i 75
saṅgaha Asl 305
sacca SA i 328, SnA i 232
sabba MA i 17, ItA i 52, CpA 18
samaya VA i 106, DA i 31, MA i 7, SA i 9, AA i 11, KhA 104, UdA 18, BvA 127, PṭsA iii 530, Asl 57
sampanna MA i 153 (no *sadda*), ItA ii 175, BvA 14 (no *sadda*)
sādhu DA i 171, MA i 18, SA ii 7, SnA i 176, BvA 47
sukha ItA i 74, ii 4, ThagA i 27, Asl 40
suta DA i 28, MA i 4, SA i 6, AA i 6, SnA i 135, UdA 11, ItA i 23, PṭsA iii 530
suvaṇṇa VvA 9
*hi PvA 103, ThagA i 77 130 171

Another parallelism, of a different kind, exists at BvAC 3 and AA ii 124. Both these passages catalogue, without any discrepancies, the places where the Buddha stayed (or spent the rains) during the first twenty years after the Awakening.

Also, there is only one other cty I know of besides BvA that speaks of the four unalterable or obligatory places for all Buddhas, *sabbabuddhānaṁ cattāri avijahitaṭṭhānāni*[1]. These are: sitting cross-legged for Awakening in one and the same place; turning the Wheel of Dhamma in a deer-sanctuary at a seers' resort; the placing of the first footstep at the gateway of Saṅkassa city after descending from the devas (having taught Abhidhamma in a deva-world); and the positions for the four legs of the bed in the Scented Chamber in Jetavana. The vihāra too does not alter whether it be large or small, only the city alters—probably it can be built at different points of the compass relative to the vihāra.

I believe there to be a growing awareness that the Dhamma of the Pali Canon is so deep, subtle, precise, comprehensive and systematic[2] that it is difficult to understand, and not easy at all as at one time seems to have been thought[3]. It is true that though the words it uses, or most of them, can be *translated* yet still the question would remain what some of them might *mean* in this context or that or in every context, if it were not for the commentaries and their precise, comprehensive and systematic methods of interpretation. The main purpose of this Preface has been to present some at least of these commentarial methods not just as they apply to BvA but as instruments and tools used throughout the entire body of the commentaries. Canon and commentary are interdependent. The latter is essential for an understanding, as exact as may be, of the former. Together they form one ordered whole to guide man in his quest for detachment and the perfection of freedom.

London 1976 I. B. Horner

[1] BvAC 131 297f., DA ii 424.
[2] Cf. Vin i 4.
[3] Cf. too Gotma's rebuke to Ānanda at D ii 55.

INTRODUCTION

As far as I know this is the first attempt to render the Madhuratthavilāsinī, the Buddhavaṁsa Commentary (BvA), into English or any European language. This translation, which I call "The Clarifier of the Sweet Meaning" (CSM), is based almost entirely on the edition I made in roman script, published by the Pali Text Society in 1946 (BvAC), an edition for which I used virtually only the Simon Hewavitarne Bequest edition, Colombo 1922. But the publication of the Chaṭṭha Saṅgāyanā edition (BvAB) in Rangoon 1959, has enabled me to note in CSM some of the differences in the readings between this and BvAC. A full record would be placed more appropriately in a new edition in roman script of this cty than in a translation of it, and has not been attempted here.

In the meantime, however, a great number of variant readings as found in the verses in five or six printed editions of the Buddhavaṁsa (Bv) itself have now been given by N. A. Jayawickrama in his edition of Bv, PTS 1974, and to a lesser extent in my translation of this work under the title "Chronicle of Buddhas" (CB), SBB 31, 1975. As most, but not all, of Bv verses appear also in BvA, anyone interested in variant readings could now consult both this recent edition and this recent translation of Bv.

For similarities in a general way between BvA and other Pali works, there is first and foremost the Jātakanidāna. Its Dūrenidāna, or Remote Antecedents, and its Avidūrenidāna, or Not So Remote Antecedents (Jā i 3–82), correspond closely, though with certain differences also, both to BvA's Sumedhakathā and to its long account of the life of the Buddha Gotama in Chronicle XXVI.[1]

In addition, ApA (pp. 1–31) narrates the Story of Sumedha in similar terms. Following this is its Dūrenidāna (pp. 31–52) where the Chronicles of former Buddhas, fully treated in Bv and BvA, appear in greatly abbreviated form. This they do too in the rather

[1] See also EHBC, p. 40.

differently worded because differently stressed version[1] given in Thūpavaṁsa (pp. 147–166).[2] ApA's Avidūrenidāna (pp. 52–81) and its Santikenidāna, or Proximate Antecedent (pp. 82–99), can also well be read in conjunction with BvA's Chronicle of Gotama the Buddha.

In its broad outlines this story can hardly be changed, of course. The amount of detail put in or left out may change, however, largely according to the needs of the account that is handling these matters. BvA had no axe to grind; there were no particular aspects either of the career of the Bodhisatta or of those of the former Buddhas that it had to adhere to and emphasize to the exclusion of other aspects.[1] It was thus in a position to give, for example, in Chronicle XXVI an unhampered wealth of detail in its narration of the Bodhisatta's last life from his birth to the Great Departure from the household state which preceded his six years of austerities.[3] So thorough is this account that even the feats of archery he had to perform to win his bride[4] almost entirely coincide with those described in practically identical terms in the Sarabhaṅga Jātaka (No. 522). In this Jātaka the archer's name was Jotipāla, which was also that of Gotama when he was the Bodhisatta under the Buddha Kassapa.[5]

The compiler, or translator, of BvA was named ācariya Buddhadatta. At the time of dealing with this cty he appears to have been residing in a monastery at Kāvīrapaṭṭana[6], probably "on the east coast of South India".[7] This was in the 5th century A.C. Probably he is to be identified with the Buddhadatta to whom also are ascribed the Vinaya-vinicchaya, Abhidhammāvatāra, Jinālaṅkāra[8], and the Dantadhātubodhivaṁsa.[9] Almost certainly a younger contemporary of Buddhaghosācariya, he "was quite familiar with the great exegetist's writings",[10] a statement made on the grounds

[1] See CB, p. xxiv, also for remarks on Mahāvastu and Jinakālamālī.

[2] Ed. N. A. Jayawickrama, SBB 28, 1971.

[3] The time needed by Gotama for the "striving" (far longer than that needed by any other Bodhisatta, see CB p. xxxvi) is ascribed by Ap p. 301, ver. 29, 30 to his having been rude in a previous birth to the Buddha Kassapa.

[4] BvA 279. [5] See Bv xxv 10ff.

[6] BvAC 299.

[7] See account of "The Author" in Buddhadatta's Manuals, ed. A. P. Buddhadatta, 1927, vol. II, p. viii.

[8] PLC 105ff.

[9] Ibid. 106, and DPPN. So far unpublished in roman script.

[10] PLC 109.

that "the commentary [BvA] follows very closely the method of Buddhaghosa's works".

It is true that BvA refers by name to Asl, a work ascribed to Buddhaghosa.[1] The introductory portion of Asl[2] gives the same verses and omits the same ones as does BvA in its Sumedhakathā and Dīpaṅkarabuddhavaṁsa. But it is only when BvA has got as far as verses 200, 201 of the Dīpaṅkara Chronicle (BvAC 126) that it says that these verses were written in the Atthasālinī, the Commentary on the Dhammasaṅgaṇi, in explanation of its antecedents: *ayaṁ gāthā Atthasāliniyā Dhammasaṅgaṇi-aṭṭhakathānidāna-vaṇṇanāya Dīpaṇkarabuddhavaṁse likhitā.*

VvA is also referred to at BvAC 284 where it says that the story of Kanthaka's rebirth as a devaputta is to be taken from Vimalattha-vilāsinī Vimānavatthaṭṭhakathā.[3] So it is not repeated here, i.e. in BvA. But VvA is ascribed not to Buddhaghosa but to Dhammapāla. The great commentator of this name is generally agreed to be posterior to Buddhaghosa. On the other hand, tradition has it that Buddhaghosa and Buddhadatta met on an occasion when both were at sea.[4] Whatever the dates at which these three commentators lived, it has to be fully realized that Buddhaghosa was not the author of the Pali commentaries, but the principal organizer of the vast amount of old Sinhaḷa commentarial material, apparently now lost, but existing in his day and without any doubt in its entirety. The presentation of this ancient material in a more acceptable form, which included translating a now unknown but obviously very great quantity of it into the language now called Pali, was the work that occupied him during his stay at the Mahāvihāra.

In all probability the old Sinhaḷa commentaries came to exist in their entire mass more or less contemporaneously with one another. Thus all, or nearly all, were known to Buddhaghosa and the other editor-translators whose names have come down to us. But it cannot be said that these editor-translators invented the names of the commentaries on this or that canonical work. For we may take it that if the mass of the ancient commentaries was in

[1] Tradition has it that Buddhaghosa "wrote Asl in India before departing for Ceylon", Winternitz, Hist. Ind. Lit. ii 190, n. 3, translation 1933.

[2] Si. edn. 44–73. This portion was not reproduced in PTS edn. of Asl.

[3] VvA 314.

[4] Saddhamma-saṅgaha, *JPTS* 1890, p. 53. The author of this work, Dhammakitti, probably belonged, according to DPPN, to the 14th Century. We cannot say, however, how old this tradition was by then.

existence all at the same time it will not have been difficult for references to be made by name to any commentary on any of the canonical collections. These editor-translators did not invent these names. They are the names they will have found and then used, preserved and handed down so that it is by these same names that the commentaries are known today. The fact that any commentary on the canon may refer to others is no guarantee that these latter were "written" earlier than the ones that refer to them; the commentarial material was "there" en bloc.

Though BvA appears to mention no more than Asl and VvA by name, it yet has parallels, some of them striking, with other ctys but which it does not name. A list of parallel or comparable interpretations of a number of words is given above in the Preface.[1] Moreover the "seven" said to have been born on the same day as the Bodhisatta appear not only at BvAC 131, 276, 298 but in other ctys also.[2] In addition to these BvA contains a few interesting passages parallels for which seem to be of very infrequent occurrence. For example, BvAC 3 enumerates the places where the Buddha Gotama spent his first twenty rains-residences as does AA ii 124. Then the account BvAC gives of the Marvel of the Double (BvAC 31) at the time of the Bodhisatta's birth is almost precisely the same as that given at DhA iii 213f.[3] when it was performed by the Buddha on another occasion. The four places considered obligatory for all Buddhas, BvAC 131, 297, have their parallel at DA ii 424, but I have not found them elsewhere.

Grammar

This Section, which for want of a better name, I have called "Grammar", is meant only to call attention to a few grammatical points that BvA appears to consider sufficiently important or instructive to remark upon, such as changes of case, tense and voice. Before presenting examples of these, it seemed advisable to me to give in as clear a form as possible the Pali names of the cases. According to traditional Pali Grammars these are seven in number and not eight, as since the vocative, *ālapana*, is included under the first case, *paṭhamā*, it has therefore no real or independent existence as an eighth or *aṭṭhamī* case.

[1] Preface, p. xxiv. [2] See below, p. xLiii.
[3] Cf. DA i 57.

Each of the seven cases is known in Pali by two classes of names: what I should like to call a "descriptive name" and used by commentators; and an "ordinal name" used by grammarians. After the ordinals the word *vibhatti*, case, is to be understood. The order and names of the cases are as follows:

1	nominative	paccatta[1]	paṭhamā[2]
2	accusative	paccatta(?)[1] upayoga[3]	dutiyā
3	instrumental	karaṇa	tatiyā
4	dative	sampadāna	catutthī
5	ablative	nissakka (apādāna)[4]	pañcamī
6	genitive	sāmin	chaṭṭhī
7	locative	bhumma (adhikaraṇa)[4] (ādhāra)[4]	sattamī
(8	vocative	ālapana[4]	aṭṭhamī[4])

Changes of case are not infrequently pointed out in BvA, as they are too in other ctys.[5] A few examples taken from BvAC now follow:

p. 37 l. 3, p. 55 l. 25 bhummatthe paccattavacanaṁ,[6] the nom. case in the sense of a loc.

p. 66 l. 16 karaṇatthe upayogavacanaṁ daṭṭhabbaṁ, the acc. case is to be understood in the sense of an instrumental.

p. 85 l. 14, p. 101 l. 8 bhummatthe karaṇavacanaṁ daṭṭhabbaṁ, the instr. case is to be understood in the sense of a loc.

p. 103 l. 15 sāmi-atthe paccattavacanaṁ, the nom. case in the sense of a genitive; cf. p. 186 l. 11.

p. 105 l. 4 we get: sāmivacanaṁ icchanti saddavidū karaṇatthe vā sāmivacanaṁ, the grammarians want a genitive case or a genitive in the sense of an instr.

[1] Intr. to Pali, p. 14 calls *paccatta* the nom. case. So transld. at MR & Ill, 237, 271. Each Index III at VA viii and ThagA iii calls it the acc. case, as does PED. Research into this seeming ambiguity would probably be lengthy.

[2] Not in this sense in PED.

[3] PED gives ellipsis or the acc. case.

[4] Given by CPD. Childers too gives most of the names of all the cases, but not PED; see Childers' art. on *kārakaṁ*.

[5] See Gram. Indexes to VA, AA, ThagA; also Indexes to SA and UdA under the Pali names of the cases; and MR & Ill under the English names in Index of Words and Subjects.

[6] As at CpA 136.

p. 116 l. 22, p. 260 l. 9 upayogatthe sāmivacanaṁ[1], the genitive case in the sense of an acc.

p. 124 l. 10 nissakkatthe[2] upayogavacanaṁ, the acc. case in the sense of an abl. Cf. p. 101 l. 13 where it is stated that paṭhaviyā is nissakkavacana, the abl. case.

p. 139 l. 30 sampadānatthe vā bhummaṁ daṭṭhabbaṁ, or the loc. should be understood in the sense of a dat.

p. 171 l. 15 sāmi-atthe bhummavacanaṁ, the loc. case in the sense of a gen.

p. 173 l. 23 sāmi-atthe upayogavacanaṁ, the acc. case in the sense of a gen.

p. 241 l. 11 karaṇatthe sāmivacanaṁ daṭṭhabbaṁ, the gen. case is to be understood in the sense of an instr.

In the above examples all the cases (excluding the vocative) are called by their commentarial or "descriptive" names and not by their ordinal names, *paṭhamā*, *dutiyā* up to *sattamī*, which mark their recognized position in the Indian order of cases and form part of the grammarians' language. There are at least two occasions, however, when BvA also uses this language: first, BvAC p. 39 l. 4, 5 where a genitive compound is spoken of as *chaṭṭhīsamāsassa . . . chaṭṭhiyā samāso*, "a sixth case compound"; and secondly at BvAC p. 267 l. 15 where we find *nimittasattamī*, the seventh case denoting cause or reason, i.e. pacified (*nibbuta*) by reason of the third fruition, namely the fruit of no-return, *anāgāmiphala*.

The abl. as *apādāna*, and the loc. as *adhikaraṇa* and *ādhāra*[3] are I think not used by our compiler who appears to prefer *nissakka* and *bhumma* respectively.

From the above it will also be seen that the cases substitute for one another in varying combinations, for example there is *upayogatthe paccattaṁ* at AA iii 389 l. 7 and *upayogatthe karaṇavacanaṁ* at SnA 266, but neither I think occurring in BvA. The mystery is why, when the case-endings differ, the right case was not used. This could not have been always for the sake of metre for AA iii

[1] As at ThagA iii 89, Asl 307.

[2] *nissakka* not given in EPD as a name for the abl. For further references see PED, s.v., and add VA 808 l. 12. Apart from *nissakka*, it seems none of the above names for cases appears in PED except *bhumma*. Intr. to Pali names all the cases except the voc.

[3] ThagA i 156 l. 24 *ādhāre* (v.l. *avadhāre*) *c'etaṁ bhummavacanaṁ*. PED cites Sn (in mistake for SnA) 211 for *ādhāra*, "name for the loc. case ('resting on')".

389 and VA 808 refer to prose passages, so it looks as if, for some reason this usage was deliberate, and almost as if grammatical science was not entirely fixed in this respect. Though case-changes appear to be considered to merit commentarial mention it is never said that the case used was an error, merely that it was to be understood in the sense of another case. Naturally the vocative is exempt from such changes. Examples of the use of *ālapana* can be found by referring to various grammatical indexes.[1]

CPD, which has not yet reached *upayoga*, gives, however, one name for the abl., two for the loc., and two for the voc., as noticed above. Childers too gives the names of all the cases under their ordinal names, and of all except three under their descriptive titles: *paccatta*, *upayoga* and *sāmin* are not in this grammatical sense there. PED pays but scant attention, a defect that, if rectified in a 2nd edition, perhaps might promote further research in this interesting theme.

We may take it that Buddhadatta or the original compiler of BvA was undoubtedly interested in grammar, *saddasattha*,[2] the science of words, and thought it important to draw attention to it so as to make the text as clear as possible.

Three times he says the (grammatical) rule, *lakkhaṇa*,[3] may be taken or understood from grammar.[4] Thus,

(1) BvAC 114, "There is nothing elsewhere means that the rule for 'elsewhere' is to be understood from grammar", *n'atthi aññatrā ti aññatra lakkhaṇaṁ saddasatthato gahetabbaṁ.*

(2) BvAC 175 on Bv viii 8: "And (of) this great seer means (of) this great seer Anomadassin. 'Of this supreme among men also' is also a reading. The meaning is: (Of) this supreme among men also. The rule is to be taken (understood) from grammar", *tassā pi ca mahesino ti tassa Anomadassissa. Tassā pi dipaduttamo ti pi pāṭho. Tassā pi dipaduttamassā ti attho. Lakkhaṇaṁ saddasatthato gahetabbaṁ.*

(3) BvAC 238 on Bv xx 5: "Eighty-four thousand who had gone forth following the example of the Self-Awakened One means it should be understood here that 'Self-Awakened One' is put into

[1] See each Index III at VA viii, AA v, ThagA iii.

[2] BvAC 25 114 175 238; see too SnA 266.

[3] Cf. ItA ii 126 *saddalakkhaṇanayena*, in accordance with the (grammatical) rule for words.

[4] BvAC 114 175 238.

the accusative case because of the prefix *anu*. The meaning is that they went forth after the Self-Awakened One. The rule is to be understood from grammar", *caturāsītisahassāni sambuddhaṁ anupabbajan ti tattha anunāyogato sambuddhan ti upayogavacanaṁ katan ti veditabbaṁ, sambuddhassa pacchā pabbajiṁsū ti attho. Lakkhaṇaṁ saddasatthato gahetabbaṁ.*

The rule is that *anu* takes the accusative case.[1] At BvAC 89 it is said: "They followed the Tathāgata means they went behind the Tathāgata. Where there is the prefix *anu* there is the accusative case in the sense of a genitive. It is the rule . . .", *anuyanti Tathāgatan ti Tathāgatassa pacchato yanti, anuyoge sati sāmi-atthe upayogavacanaṁ hotī ti lakkhaṇaṁ. Tena vuttaṁ anuyanti Tathāgataṁ.*

Another prefix said to govern the accusative case[2] is *abhi*: *abhi-sadda-yogena hi idaṁ upayogavacanaṁ*, but the meaning is to be understood as a locative, *attho pana bhummavasena ve ditabbo.*

A change of tense (from the present to the aorist), *kālavipariyāya*,[3] is also spoken of with the injunction that from now on in similar expressions the meaning is to be taken in the sense of the past, *kālavipariyāyena vuttan ti veditabbaṁ. Īdisesu vacanesu ito upari pi atītakālavasen' eva attho gahetabbo.*[4] At BvAC 103, l. 23 the present tense is referred to as *vattamānavacana*,[5] as it is again at BvAC 99, l. 39 and 252, l. 2 where, in explaining *padissanti* and *vandāmi* (present) respectively, it is said that this tense should be understood as the past tense, *atītavacana*, or in the sense of a past, *atītattha*. At BvAC 292, l. 15 it is said that though the future tense, *anāgatavacana*, should be used (and here would be *hessati*, "there will be"), the past tense, *atītavacana*, was used (*āhu*, "there was") on account of its effect on the ear, or because of a change of tense, *kālavipariyāsa*.[3]

At BvAC 25 two words are used, the one denoting the active voice of the verb, *kattukāraka*, and the other the passive, *kammakāraka*. Neither is in PED in this sense, but the former, s.v. *kattā*, is given in Childers as "a name for the active voice". Also at BvAC 204, l. 31 we get *kattukārake daṭṭhabbo, kārakavipallāsena vuttaṁ*: it should be understood to be in the active voice, it is said by means of a change of voice.

[1] Cf. ThagA i 114 ItA i 168.
[2] UdA 432.
[3] The terminations *-yāya* and *-yāsa* both appear.
[4] BvAC 123, l. 36.
[5] As at SnA 16, l. 24.

Besides changes of case, tense and voice, changes of gender are also sometimes made and duly recorded, as at BvAC 185, l. 2: *sabbakilesānī ti sabbakilese, liṅgavipāriyāsaṁ katvā*[1] *vuttaṁ*; or as at BvAC 166, l. 12: *so ca kāyo ratananibho ti so c'assa bhagavato kāyo suvaṇṇavaṇṇo*; *tañ ca kāyaṁ ratananibhan ti pi pāṭho*; *liṅgavipallāsena vuttaṁ.*[2] These examples show two words used for this grammatical practice: *liṅgavipariyāsa* and *liṅgavipallāsa*. Known of course to other ctys also,[3] a study of them with this practice in mind might possibly reveal some consistent reason or reasons for the changes in gender recorded.

Cases of elision of part of a word are also noted, as at BvAC 99, l. 36, 180, l. 5 where *vibhattilopa* signifies the dropping of the case-ending or the omission of the inflexion[4]; and as at BvAC 188, l. 7 where *lopaṁ katvā* means "having made an elision" of one word which had formed part of a compound.

Some Words not in PED

Note: the letter 'p' in the following entries refers to the page-number of BvAC.

ali, a bee, p. 160, l. 23, p. 274, 4 ll. from end (both in compounds). In Childers and CPD.

uttuṅga, "that had risen" (of waves, "high"), p. 284, last line (in a compound). Not in Childers or CPD but in M-W.

upagīyamāna, being sung, p. 179, l. 25. Childers, *upagāyati*, to sing; M-W, being celebrated, s.v. *upagai*, to sing.

kākalī, a low-toned musical instrument, p. 179, l. 24–5 (in a compound). Childers, "a soft sound in music"; M-W, "a musical instrument with a low tone". Abh, "a high tone, a bass or low tone, a minute tone".

gumugumāyamāna, murmuring, humming or buzzing, of bees (*bhamara* here), p. 95, l. 3–4, p. 179, l. 24. Not in Childers or M-W. But BHSD, s.v. *gumugumanti* says "they make a (pleasant) noise (subject, lutes)" and cites Mhvu iii 267. J. J. Jones translates this passage as "the lutes are played, giving forth their

[1] Cf. BvAC 108, l. 5, 123, l. 24, 162, l. 23.

[2] Also BvAC 193, l. 13, 208, l. 2.

[3] See e.g. AA v, Gram. Index s.v. *vipallāsa*, PED and ThagA iii, Gram. Index s.v. *liṅga-vipallāsa*.

[4] Also ItA ii 18, VvA 174 (which adds "or a change of gender"), 192, PvA 147 (both of which add that otherwise it is one case in place of another).

sweet notes". As the word is onomatopoetic it may be taken to convey both the buzzing or humming of bees and the humming of lutes.

cakkikānaṃ, turning, wheeling, revolving (?), p. 114, 4 ll. from end, in a comparison: *cakkikānaṁ mahācakkayantaṁ viya*, perhaps: like the mechanism of the big wheel turning (said of an oil-press). If so, not the gen. pl. of a diminutive, *cakkika*, but pres. part. of some verb. See note to text p. 114. Not in Childers, and not in a relevant sense in M-W or Abh.

cakkhati, he relishes, p. 33, l. 15. Also at Vism 481; Ppn, in its Pali-English glossary notes that the word is not in PED.

jaṅgama, mobile, p. 210, l. 28, of an elephant's lips. A well-attested canonical word occurring e.g. at M i 184, S i 86, v 43, A iii 364 in the simile of the elephant's footprint. KS v 34, n. 3 notes that PED omits—an omission, one would think, due only to some unfortunate oversight. The commentarial explanations are identical, *jaṅgamānan ti paṭhavītalacārīnaṁ*, "of mobile (moving, walking creatures) means of those moving (going, faring along) on the earth's surface". See too its use in a comparison at DA i 39, l. 32 and VvA 4, l. 3 where it also means "moving".

Sometimes *jaṅgama* is preceded by the word *thāvara*, immobile, stationary, as at e.g. KhA 217, l. 12. Here *nidhi*, treasure, treasure-store is said to be fourfold, the first two "folds" being *thāvara* and *jaṅgama*, translated by Ñāṇamoli[1] as "fixture" and "ambulant" respectively. The treasure that is a "fixture" consists of gold and fields and anything else that cannot change its posture. The "ambulant", on the other hand, consists of slaves of both sexes and the animals, from elephants to pigs, used by a householder for various purposes, all of which are associated with change of posture. The definitions of *thāvara-dhana* and *jaṅgama-dhana*, wealth that is stationary or immobile, and wealth that is movable or mobile, at SnA i 28 appear to be but shortened versions of *nidhi* as *thāvara* and as *jaṅgama* at KhA 217.

At p. 55, l. 13, 120, l. 29 there is the compound *thāvara-jaṅgama*, the mobile and immobile, see n. to text p. 55. Therefore PED is incorrect when, s.v. *thāvara*, it states this to be a word used "always in connection with *tasa*". Indeed, the only

[1] MR & Ill 243.

reference to *jaṅgama* I can find in PED is s.v. *tasa* where, under *tasa-thāvarā*, plural, "movable and immovable beings", attention is drawn to Mhvu i 207 for *jaṅgama-sthāvara*.

The word *jaṅgama* is given by Childers as "movable", and by M-W as "moving, movable, locomotive, that which has motion as opposed to that which is stationary, living". But plants, though living in the fields and lands, are not mobile and belong to the stationary category rather than to the mobile, moving one denoted by *jaṅgama*.

nirassāsa, without breath, suffocating, p. 209, l. 27. Not recognized in the lexicons.

maṁsarasabhojana, meal consisting of a flesh-product, p. 298, 2 ll. from end. Not in PED as a compound, though of course all 3 elements appear. The importance of the compound is that it is here said it is *dhammatā*, regulation,[1] for all Buddhas that on the day of the parinibbāna there is a partaking of, or eating, *bhojana*, a meat or flesh, *maṁsa*, product, *rasa*. The conclusion therefore seems inescapable, even if *rasa* were translated as flavour or taste, that the last meal a Buddha ate was a meat-meal or a meal in which there was meat in some form. Therefore, this passage provides evidence that *sūkara-maddava*, the Buddha Gotama's last meal, should not be translated as sometimes it has been as "truffles", but rather as tender, *maddava*, (flesh or meat) from a boar. See PED which favours Franke and Oldenberg but differs from RhD. Indeed, DA ii 568, l. 13–14 is quite clear: *sūkarassa pavatta-maṁsaṃ*, meat of a boar available (in the market). DAṬ ii 218 further explains: *vanavarāhassa mudumaṁsa*, the soft flesh of a forest boar or wild hog. UdA 399 agrees with DA ii 568 and while ascribing this interpretation to the Mahā-aṭṭhakathā, also gives different interpretations made by "some", *keci*, and by "others", *añño*,[2] both of which appear to substantiate RhD's "truffles". See also Miln 175 for Gotama's last meal before the Awakening and the last before his parinibbāna.

mahatī vipañcikā makaramukhādi vīṇā ca turiyāni ca appear to be three kind of lutes, p. 41, l. 1.

a. *mahatī*: BHSD, "presumably a kind of lute", refers to Mhvu ii 159, l. 5, iii 407, l. 19, Divy 108, l. 4. Not in Childers in

[1] See W. Rāhula, Wrong Notions of Dhammatā in *Buddhist Studies in Honour of I. B. Horner*, 1974, p. 181ff.

[2] See Preface, p. xi.

this sense; M-W, p. 753, column b, "the seven-stringed or (according to some) hundred-stringed Vīṇā or lute of Nārada."

b. *vipañcikā*: M-W, "a lute (=*vīṇā*)".[1] BHSD: "Senart's em. for *vevādikā*, q.v." Here we find "? vevādika, or -aka, some musical instrument: Mhvu ii 159, l. 6 (so mss., Senart em. vipañcikā): represents same orig. form as vādiśa, q.v." Here we find "? vādiśa, m. or nt. some musical instrument: Mhvu iii 407, l. 19; represents, probably corruptly, the same orig. as vevādika (or -aka), q.v. (both follow mahatī in the list)". At Mhvu ii 159, which gives a long list of musical instruments, only *vipañcikā* follows *mahatī* and at iii 407 in a similar but not identical list, only *vādiśa* follows. Therefore it is open to question whether "both" follow unless we are certain that these two words, *vipañcikā* and *vādiśa*, denote the same instrument.

c. *makaramukha*: I can find no other occurrence of this word. It may be a *vīṇā* with its neck shaped like a *makara*, a word usually taken to mean a kind of sea-monster; also "regarded as an emblem of Kāma".[2]

vadana, countenance, p. 208, l. 10, 209, l. 21 (in compounds). Not in this sense in PED or Childers, but in M-W.

vadhū, female, p. 179, l. 25 in *kokila-vadhū*, female cuckoos. Not in this sense in PED or Childers; but M-W, "the female of any animal".

varūtha, fender (of a chariot), p. 279, l. 21. In Abh 374, Childers, M-W.

vikhyāta, renowned, p. 184, l. 20 in *sabbaloka-vikhyāta*. Not in Childers, but in M-W.

vila, a hole, crevice, cave, p. 199, l. 4 in *pabbatavila*. Not in Childers, but in M-W.

suṇḍataṭa, sloping flank (of an elephant), p. 210, l. 24, at end of a compound. Probably = *śroṇi-taṭa*, given by M-W as "the slope of the hips".

Assonance

A feature of BvA that seems to me worthy of notice is the fascination that words and assonance, or words of similar sounds,[3] appears

[1] Macdonnell, Skt. Dict.: "vipañcī, *f.* Indian lute". [2] Ibid. s.v., makara.

[3] See too Woven Cadences 217 where E. M. Hare notes that the poetry of Sn "shows a love of alliteration and assonance, word-play, puns and puzzles", and see his Indexes, p. 218b.

to have exercised over the mind and literary style perhaps of Buddhadatta himself when he was removing the Sīhaḷa language from this cty and rendering it into the "beautiful language"[1] that has remained to this day. The list of words not in PED given above[2] is also a pointer to the wide vocabulary that was at our "author's" command. Apparently he did not consider assonance as a "blemish of detail in the book"[3], but as a homophonous enhancement, especially of proper names. Though attention is called in the footnotes to some of the occurrences, most of these and a few others are also collected below so as to give, I hope, a picture making a greater impact than could be obtained merely from scattered references. Naturally, as it is not possible to contrive anything in a translation even faintly reproducing the Pali sound-patterns, they have of necessity to be lost.

p. 6, l. 15 anilabalasamuddhutataraṅgabhaṅgaṁ asaṅgaṁ Gaṅgaṁ
p. 56, 4 ll. *from end*, anilabalacalitajalataraṅgabhaṅgasaṅghaṭṭitā
p. 284, last l. to p. 285, uttuṅgataraṅgabhaṅgaṁ asaṅgaṁ Gaṅgaṁ
p. 6, l. 26 Mandāragirisārena narasārena Bimbisārena
p. 285, 2 ll. *from end*, duranusāro Merumandārasāro sattasāro Bimbisāro
p. 182, l. 19 dasabaladharo . . . catuvesārajjavisārado vimuttisārado Nārado nāma narasattuttamo
p. 236, l. 2f. visuddhaṁ passati *vi*vaṭehi ca akkhīhi *passatī* ti Vipassī ti nāmam akaṁsu. *Vi*ceyya viceyya *passatī* ti vā Vipassī ti vadanti.
p. 247, l. 4f. s.v. Vessabhū, vijitamanobhū sabbalokābhibhū sayambhū Vessabhū
p. 253, l. 8 saccasandho Kakusandho
p. 254, l. 4 vigatabhavabandho Kakusandho
l. 16 vigatarandhaṁ Kakusandhaṁ
l. 20 appaṭisandho Kakusandho
p. 255, l. 9 Kakusandhassa viddhastabhavabandhanassa
p. 256, l. 9 adandhassa Kakusandhassa

[1] See Preface, p. vii, part of Buddhaghosa's introductory verses to the ctys on the 4 great Nikāyas.
[2] See p. xxxviiff.
[3] *ganthavitthāradosa*, BvAC 26,3 ll. from end.

p. 257, *last verse* Apetabandho Kakusandhabuddho
adandhapañño gatasabbarandho
tilokasandho kira saccasandho . . .

p. 258, l. 2 -poṇāgamano Koṇāgamano

p. 259, l. 28 -pūraṇāgamanassa Koṇagamanassa

p. 260, l. 14 -pāṇāgamanaṁ Koṇāgamanaṁ

p. 262, *last verse* Sukhena Koṇāgamano gatāsavo
vikāmapāṇāgamano mahesi
vaṇe viveke sirināmadheyye
visuddhavaṁsāgamano vasittha

p. 125, l. 18 atha so manussabhakkho sakahitanirapekkho paravadhadakkho yakkho makkhaṁ asahamāno

p. 227, l. 16 padumadalasadisanayanāya Padumanāmāya

Moreover in some of the Chronicles proper names seem handed down by attraction, giving only the minimum of variation from one another. One wonders how these names came into being and what or who determined their choice. A fairly elaborate example occurs at

p. 160, l. 21 sabbadhanadhaññavatī Sudhaññavatī nagare . . . vibhavasirisamudayenākulassa sabbasamiddhivipulassa Vipulassa nāma rañño . . . suruciramanoharaguṇagaṇavipulāya Vipulāya nāma aggamahesiyā . . .

Here Vipula and Vipulā are the names of the king and queen. In addition, both of these names and that of the city are augmented by compound elements which further describe the bearers of the names.

A further example is *samussitacārūpayodharāya Yasodharāya* (p. 171, 29). This is the case too with some of the other names occurring so copiously in BvA. For example: *asamā Asamā* (p. 177, 17), *anuttarassa Uttarassa* (142, 4), *anuttarāya Uttarāya* (258, 12), where the description is much simpler.

Finally, the various names of cities and people that are identical with or closely resemble one another when they appear in one and the same Chronicle have an interest of their own. I cannot say, however, why the nomenclature in such Chronicles manifests so little variety whereas in others, the majority, there is quite a wide range. But I do not think that BvA is the sole Pali work where the characters in one episode are the same in name, only varying according to whether they are masculine or feminine. Some examples in BvA now follow:

p. 142, l. 4 Uttara was the name of the city, also of the king, Uttarā that of the queen.
p. 166, l. 21 Sudhamma the name of the city and of the king, Sudhammā that of the queen.
p. 177, l. 29 Dhaññavatī was the name of a city, Sudhañña a banker there, his daughter's name was Dhaññavatī.
p. 197, l. 12 Sudatta was the king, Sudattā the queen.
l. 21 Nakula the name of the township, also of a banker.
p. 202, l. 31 Sirinandana the name of the city, also of a banker.
p. 219, l. 17 Saraṇa the name of the city, and of the king, described as *sabbalokasaraṇa.*
p. 227, l. 25 Vīra the name of the township, also of the banker.
p. 232, l. 16, 18 Sirivaḍḍhā gave the milk-rice, Sirivaḍḍha the 8 handfuls of grass.
p. 235, l. 23 Bandhumatī was the name of the city and also of the queen, Bandhumā that of the king.

The Co-natals

As for a long time the number seven has been regarded as a symbol of completion or perfection,[1] so seven are those held to have been of simultaneous birth, co-natal with the Bodhisatta, born on the same day as he was, *satta sahajatāni*[2]; and so, as they were also born on the same day as one another each had six co-natals, apart from the Bodhisatta, to form a set of seven. Though this set may not be intrinsically of much importance as a set, and in this respect differs from its individual members, yet, as possible quasi-history, even authentic history in some cases, and as a tradition surviving in some of the commentaries, a little investigation here may not be out of place.

The co-natals are listed three times in BvA[3] and at least seven

[1] E.g. the 7 Jewels of a universal king, 7 priceless things at Jā vi 489, and the gifts each of 700, ibid. 503.

[2] At Jā vi 512 the phrase *Mahāsatto sahajāte saṭṭhisahasse amacce . . . oloketvā* is mistranslated (Cowell vi 265) as "the 60,000 courtiers who were born when he was" instead of "who were born simultaneously (with one another)". Further, it should be noticed that *sahajā* at Cp II 4. 8 is not to be taken literally but as referring to the simultaneous "going forth" of a man and his wife, CpA 136.

[3] BvAC 131 276 298.

times in five other ctys and also in Jkm.[1] Besides this, one cty speaks of one member only of the set, another cty of another member, and still a third of a different member as being co-natal with the Bodhisatta.[2]

With one interesting and curious exception, for which there is possibly some "historical" ground if not confusion, the seven co-natals are constant throughout these lists, though they may be slightly differently arranged or described: Rāhulamātā, Ānanda, Channa, Kanthaka, nidhikumbhā, Mahābodhirukkha, Kāḷudāyin.[3] The exception is always Ānanda's name for, unlike the others, it does not occur with uniform regularity. It is found at BvAC 131, DA ii 425, ApA 58[4] 358, also at BvAB corresponding to BvAC 276 apparently as a genuine variant for BvAC's *Ājānīyo hatthirājā*[5] at this passage for it gives this reading in a footnote.

The list of the co-natals at Jā i 54, though spoken of as seven, contains only six names in Fausböll's edn. These are Rāhulamātā devī, Channo amacco, Kāḷudāyi amacco, Kanthako assarāja, Mahābodhi rukkho, cattāro nidhikumbhiyo. Here Ānanda's name is absent as is that of his substitute, the *hatthirājā*, the state-elephant of BvAC 276. But it is open to question whether it is not Fausböll who is responsible for the omission. For in the Bangkok edn. of Jātakanidāna p. 75, corresponding to Fausböll, vol. I, p. 54, Ānando rājakumāro is placed between Kāḷudāyi amacco and Kanthako assarājā.

Ānanda is also omitted at BvAC 298, but here again BvAB fills the blank, as it does that at BvAC 276, by giving his name, though it notes no other reading. One would therefore like to know whether what BvAB is giving here is a genuine reading or put in by later editors[6] to make BvA more consistent with itself. Attention has been called above to the omission of Ānanda's name at ApA 58 in the SHB edn.

[1] Jā i 54, DA ii 425, AA i 301, ThagA ii 221, ApA 58 358 531f., Jkm 26.

[2] DA i 284 (the 4 urns), SA ii 317 (Channa), VvA 314 (Kanthaka).

[3] List as at BvC 131, DA ii 425, ApA 58 358.

[4] Here n. 11 says Ānanda's name is omitted in SHB.

[5] Not found elsewhere? At Mhvu ii 25 the Bodhisatta's elephant is called Candana.

[6] EC 37 adds Kāḷudāyin to make its list come up to seven on the grounds that though it is not in Jkm, English edn. p. 26, the Bangkok edn. gives it. Here there is no omission of Ānandatthera.

This curious anomaly of the inclusion or omission of Ānanda's name would seem to suggest a certain doubt somewhere, some time, whether in fact his birth did or did not take place on the same day as the Bodhisatta's—a doubt very likely connected with conflicting views of his age when he died.[1] Else why the absence of his name almost as often as its presence? The substitution made for it so as to achieve the required "seven" is always an elephant: the elephant called *Ājānīyo hatthirājā* at BvAC 276, and *ārohaniyahatthi* at AA i 301, ThagA ii 221, ApA 532, thus describing the elephant as a riding one and not a working one. Naturally the Bodhisatta had a riding elephant while he was still leading the household life, though the part it played is in no way comparable to that played by *Kanthaka assarājā* above all on the night of the Great Departure to homelessness[2] for whose successful outcome the horse was essential.

At Vv 81. 15 Kanthaka is recorded to say, "In the superb city of Kapilavatthu of the Sakyans I was Kanthaka, co-natal with Suddhodana's son."[3] This is one of the only two canonical statements concerning co-natals in the sense being spoken of here that I have found. The other is at Ap 501, ver. 19 where Kāḷudāyin is represented as saying, *tadahe 'va ahaṁ jāto saha ten'eva vaḍḍhito*, "I was born on the same day as him (Siddhattha, ver. 18) and grew up with him." Neither of these passages concerns itself with more than one member of the seven co-natals, any more than do four commentarial passages that also treat of one member only. In the first place there is VvA 314 corroborating Kanthaka's statement. Secondly, at SA ii 317 in a brief description of Channa it is said *Tathāgatena saddhiṁ ekadivase jāto*, born on one and the same day together with the Tathāgata; and thirdly, at DA i 284 we find *Tathāgatassa pana jātadivase . . . cattāro nidhayo upagatā*, on the day of the Tathāgata's birth four treasure-urns appeared.[4]

With these four treasure-urns, *cattāro* or *catasso nidhikumbhā* or *nidhikumbhiyo* or *cattāro nidhayo*, we enter, so it seems, into a realm of fancy. Their measurements when given[5] are large: a gāvuta,

[1] See below, p. xLviif. For conflicting views concerning his birth, ordination and death see DPPN, s.v. Ānanda, and Encyclopaedia of Buddhism, fasc. 4, p. 529ff.

[2] See text p. 282ff.

[3] See also VvA 314.

[4] Also BvAC 23.

[5] Jā i 54, DA i 284, BvAC 276, DhA iv 208, ApA 58, PṭsA iii 677 (not at the Tathāgata's birth).

half a yojana,[1] three gāvutas, a yojana.[2] Their contents, recorded at least once,[3] are somewhat baffling[4]: *saṅkho*, chank or mother-of-pearl in the first urn, then *elo* (salt? water?), then *uppālo*, and finally *puṇḍarīka*, normally two kinds of water-lily or lotus. Such urns were held to come, perhaps through Sakka's intervention, at the birth of an outstanding person, Jotika for example who possessed great merit,[5] and presumably their arrival portended a momentous event. So it was only natural to include them as one of the seven of simultaneous birth.

In mentioning the four great treasures as the "shell" (*saṃkha*), the "lotus" (*paduma*), the *piṅgala*, and the *elapatra*, the Mahāvastu says[6] they are in four different localities, as does Divy 61; the former context also states that they were under the protection of Nāga-kings, and the latter that they were presided over by four great kings.[7]

In Vkn the four great treasures, *mahānidhāna*, filled with all the kinds of jewels of great potency and inexhaustible, are spoken of as the sixth of eight wonderful and marvellous things which are constantly manifest in a certain devī's abode.[8] Professor Lamotte, in an extremely interesting and informative note[9], asserts that, according to most (Sanskrit) sources the four treasures will appear on the advent of the Buddha Maitreya; and that, according to other sources, they exist already and appear of their own accord and are made use of by the local inhabitants on the seventh day of the seventh month every seven years. This is reminiscent of a passage in Miln[10] which, in speaking of the Jewel-treasure of a universal monarch, says that on the disappearance of one such monarch it lies hidden[11] and is produced for the next wheel-turning king because of his right practice, appearing as do his other six treasures, of its own accord.[12] It may not be unjustified, therefore, to assume

[1] PṭsA iii 677 reads "two gāvutas", but this is the same as half a yojana.
[2] See table of measurements at *Chronicle of the Thūpas*, p. 15, n. 38.
[3] DA i 284.
[4] DAṬ of no help.
[5] DhA iv 208, PṭsA iii 677. He is one of five persons of great merit spoken of at Vism 382f., AA i 405, DhA i 385.
[6] Mhvu iii 383, and see Jones's transln. iii 380f. and 381 n. 1.
[7] See BHSD s.v. elapatra, piṅgala, and śaṅkha.
[8] Vkn 278f.
[9] Ibid., n. 34.
[10] Miln 218.
[11] In Vepulla Mountain, Jā iv 232.
[12] D ii 175, M iii 174.

that the four treasure-urns disappeared as mysteriously as they had come once they had signalized the exceptionally rare event of the birth of a Bodhisatta in the world. For nothing more is said to indicate their further existence.

The Bodhi-tree is in a category apart. It was a real tree, a cutting from which flourishes to this day at the Mahāvihāra in Anurādhapura, and is often said to be the oldest historical tree in the world.[1] But how to establish it was of simultaneous birth with the Bodhisatta, and therefore 35 years old at the time of the Awakening, and alive when Saṅghamittā, daughter of the Emperor Asoka (273–232 B.C.)[2], went from Jambudīpa to Srī Laṅkā taking this cutting with her? Perhaps there is some traditional lore to the effect that this Assattha had been growing for 35 years at the place, always in Jambudīpa, and always the same place, where, each under a different Tree, the Awakening of Buddhas occurs. But if there is such a tradition I do not know of it.

It may not be out of place to say a little here about the length of the life-spans of the others: a woman, three men, and a horse, who are held to have been born on the same day as the Bodhisatta.

Rāhulamātā died at the age of 78 according to Ap ii 584 (ver. 3ff.) where she is called Yasodharā.[3] It is supposed she married Gotama when she was sixteen years old, and if they were co-natal he was sixteen also, but Rāhula, so it seems, was not born at all long, perhaps only a week[4] or even less than a week before Gotama, his father, left home on the Great Departure at the age of twenty-nine[5].

Ānanda's death is not mentioned anywhere in the Pali canon so far as I know. However, at DhA ii 99 he is said to have been aged 120 years when he died.[6] Therefore, if he had been born on the

[1] Though the famous plane tree at Kos, connected by popular tradition with Hippocrates, is also extremely old, there is no certain knowledge of its age.

[2] Vincent Smith, Asoka, 1920, p. 73f.

[3] See DPPN, s.v. Rāhulamātā, for the names by which Rāhula's mother and Gotama's wife appear to have been called.

[4] Jā i 62.

[5] See Lamotte, Hist. du Bouddhisme indien, p. 733ff. for some conflicting possibilities for Rāhula's age when his father both left home and also first returned to Kapilavaṭṭhu.

[6] I am grateful to Mr John Ireland for having drawn my attention to this passage. The laywoman Visākhā and 4 brahmans, Pokkharasādi, Brahmāyu (M ii 133), Sela and Bāvari (Sn 1019), are all cited at DA ii 413 as having lived for 120 years. Everyone mentioned in this passage has a part to play in the Pali Canon. Much less important was the grandmother of the girl the parents of

same day as the Bodhisatta he would have lived another 40 years after the *parinibbāna*, and hence would have been an arahant for this number of years. But at DA ii 413 another view is taken of the length of his life-span. For here it is said that Ānanda, Mahākassapa and Anuruddhatthera all died at the age of 150—and Bakkulatthera at 160. All these are called long-lived, *dīghāyuka*, though not living as much as 200 years. Neither of these passages speaks of Ānanda as a co-natal. Besides the co-natal passages mentioned at the beginning of this Section that either include or omit his name, there are other commentarial passages which, though not mentioning his age when he died, or his co-nativity, yet bring forward another aspect of this latter tradition. For they say that after being born in Tusitapura "together with our Bodhisatta", *amhākaṁ Bodhisattena saddhiṁ*, and deceasing from there he was born in the household of Amitodana, the Sakyan,[1] Suddhodana's brother. Lamotte states[2] that Ānanda died one year before Ajātasattu, whose death he gives as having taken place in 463 B.C. It is traditionally held that the Buddha died in the eighth year of this king's reign. If 462 B.C. is truly the date of Ānanda's death and if he lived to be 120 or 150, it is questionable whether he could have been born on the same day as Gotama.[3] Northern sources concerning Ānanda differ, I believe, from Pali commentarial sources, and have not been consulted.

There seems no indication of Kāḷudāyin's age when he died. After becoming an arahant and having successfully urged Gotama, very recently awakened, to return to Kapilavatthu at his father's insistent requests, he was declared pre-eminent among the disciples to gladden the clans[4], but then becomes rather a shadowy figure of whom little more is recorded.

Channa, clearly, must have outlived the Buddha who, just before his *parinibbāna*, instructed Ānanda to impose the *brahmadaṇḍa* on this former charioteer of his,[5] notable for his pride and arrogance, with the result that he attained arahantship and the chastisement

Revata of the Acacia Wood planned he should marry, at the age of seven. She was alive at 120 years old, DhA ii 189.

[1] DA ii 492, AA i 292, ThagA iii 111.

[2] Hist. du Bouddhisme indien, p. 102; see also ibid. pp. 227–8, 331.

[3] There is no consensus of opinion, however, that 563 B.C. as given in the Sinhalese tradition can be accepted for the year of Gotama's birth.

[4] A i 25.

[5] D ii 154.

or penalty automatically lapsed.[1] It has not been possible to discover the length of his life-span, but had it been 120 years presumably he would have been mentioned with the others who reached this age. As it is, an old man of eighty or so when the *brahmadaṇḍa* was imposed on him, he is likely to have died not long after the Buddha.

The co-natal Kanthaka,[2] the Bodhisatta's horse, died of a broken heart immediately after he had borne Gotama away on the Great Departure from home and luxury and Gotama had then gone on alone to seek for nibbāna leaving behind him the horse and the charioteer. As Gotama is supposed to have set out on his new life at the age of 29, therefore Kanthaka, when he died, was 29, quite a good age for a horse and in no way exaggerated. It is said he had been greatly attached to the Mahāsatta, the Great Being, in several former births.[3]

Miscellaneous

In the Introduction to CB[4] attention was drawn to the importance attaching to trees from Rg-Vedic times onward both as symbols of longevity and for their practical benefits of giving shelter from rain and sun. These are perhaps among the reasons why all Buddhas sit beneath trees during the night before the Awakening. This regard for trees persists in BvA. Apart from a list[5], and it is no more than a list, of some thirteen noble trees planted by Prince Jayasena to beautify a park, two Bodhi-Trees in particular appear so much to have fired our compiler's imagination that he was led to describe them in glowing terms: the Pāṭalī, in full and fragrant flower for Vipassin's Awakening[6], and Sikhin's Tree[7], the Puṇḍarīka, of the same dimensions and thick with fruits as well as flowers. It is difficult to know why the choice both in BvA and DA[8] fell on these two Trees while none of the others is described at all[9].

[1] Vin ii 292, VA vii 1403.
[2] At Mhvu ii 193 also said to be co-natal, "born at the same time as he."
[3] VvA 316.
[4] p. xxxvi ff.
[5] BvAC 168.
[6] Ibid. 236.
[7] Ibid. 243.
[8] DA ii 415f.
[9] A little information is given about Koṇḍañña's "Lovely Sāla" at text p. 140, but no description.

These two, however, are used as a kind of model for three others: Vessabhū's Sāla-Tree[1] and Koṇāgamana's Udumbara[2], the former said to be of the same proportions as the Pāṭalī and rich in fruits as well as flowers, the latter, of the same dimensions as the Puṇḍarīka, and "covered with a profusion of fruits"[3]. That the fruit only and not the flowers form part of this description is but another example of the care with which the ctys were compiled, for so rare is it to see flowers of an udumbara as to be almost impossible. Besides this Sāla and Udumbara, there was Kakusandha's Sirīsa Tree[4], of the same dimensions as the Pāṭalī (and therefore of the Puṇḍarīka) and, like it, sweetly scented. Of the two, therefore, the Pāṭalī seems to have been more notable for its flowers and the Puṇḍarīka for its fruits. BvA goes no further than this and does nothing to suggest, as does DA, that there was any resemblance between the Sāla tree on the one hand and the Nigrodha and Assattha on the other.[5]

It was said above that this Assattha Tree must have been 35 years old at the time of Gotama's Awakening[6]. It would be a mistake, however, to try and calculate the ages of the splendidly grown Pāṭalī, Puṇḍarīka, Sāla, Udumbara and Sirīsa. For though we may calculate the ages of the Buddhas when they awakened beneath these Trees[7], there is no tradition that any Bodhisatta other than Gotama had any co-natals. It is more likely that the size of the Trees had little to do with their age but rather was taken to conform to the longevity and giant proportions of all the former Buddhas and their contemporaries who, we may believe, included not men only but also animals, trees and plants.

Indeed the great elephant-nāga, Doṇamukha, in a vivid and detailed portrayal of all the parts of his body[8], is likened to a mountain peak. As the Buddha Piyadassin was able to stroke his head with the palm of his hand[9], and as the size of his hand must have been in proportion to his height of 80 cubits, only an elephant

[1] BvAC 248.
[2] Ibid. 258.
[3] DA ii 416 says "there were no flowers".
[4] BvAC 253.
[5] DA ii 416, probably referring to the Trees of Kassapa and Gotama.
[6] Above, p. xlvii.
[7] For example, Vipassin led the household life for 8,000 years, and engaged in striving for 8 months.
[8] BvAC 210.
[9] Ibid. 211.

of some comparable size could have been envisaged as the potential slayer of this Buddha. By the time of the Buddha Gotama, when we are well within historical times, the elephant Nālāgiri, sent by Devadatta and Ajātasattu in an attempt to kill him, must have had the dimensions of a present-day elephant. For the Buddha Gotama is recorded to have stretched forth his right hand and stroked the animal's forehead.[1]

That this episode finds no place in BvA is no reflexion upon the compiler's remarkable powers as a story-teller. For Devadatta's attempts to murder the Buddha are "ascribed to the 37th year after the Enlightenment: when, in other words, the Buddha was 72 years old".[2] And BvA's long, fascinating, and extremely detailed account of the Bodhisatta's last birth,[3] when he had come from his abode in Tusita after deceasing from his individuality as Vessantara, goes no further, naturally, than the Turning of the Wheel of Dhamma. For it is an account solely of Gotama in his final appearance as the Bodhisatta. As such it is clearly meant to be the grand climax of the 24 lives, spread over a hundred thousand eons and four incalculable periods, in each of which lives he had made his aspiration for Buddhahood under 24 different Buddhas, all the time maturing himself for Buddhahood. It is indeed a great and moving story, wonderfully told.

This seems to make it all the more a pity that our compiler, no doubt due to his determination not to let his book become too long, gave no time or place to other stories apart from recounting six legendary tales from by-gone days.[4] The curious thing is that all these centre on the taming by the relevant Buddha of an extremely powerful and hostile nonhuman adversary, all, except one *devarāja*, being man-eating *yakkhas*, two of whom bore the name Naradeva, used of course in an unfavourable sense.[5] The aim of all these dramatic stories, told with such immense verve, is to show a Buddha's powers to be pre-eminent and impossible to rival in all circumstances.

In conclusion, there are a number of verses in BvA that are not attributed to any source, either the Porāṇas, the Porāṇatthakathā

[1] Vin ii 195.
[2] Ñāṇamoli, *Life of the Buddha*, Kandy 1972, p. 258.
[3] BvAC 270–91.
[4] Ibid. 125f., 185f., 198f., 209f., 253f., 265.
[5] At S i 5, Pv iv 3. 50 in a favourable sense and not as a personal name but as a generic term.

or the Pali canon. As far as I can discover, they have no parallel in other ctys. Whoever was responsible for them evinces no trifling skill as a versifier. Perhaps on one occasion at least it was Buddhadatta himself, for in introducing a set of 17 verses[1], it is said: *tasmā mayā pākaṭattā Dīpaṅkarakumārassa jātiyaṁ dassitāni*, "therefore the customary state of affairs is shown by me in regard to Prince Dīpaṅkara's birth", that is to say, the portent-signs at the time of his birth are given in agreeable verse followed by their symbolism in prose.

Again, there is a set of 8 verses "ascribed" to the Buddha Piyadassin and said to be addressed by him to the lordly elephant he had subdued by thoughts of loving-kindness. Who knows what this Buddha may have said a hundred thousand eons ago? Equally, who knows who in fact composed these verses? But this is of no consequence; above everything, they are an adornment to this commentary, with their burden of refraining from harming or killing any living thing and, instead, developing loving-kindness and compassion all the time. Nor have we any means of knowing who was the author, or authors, of the other unascribed verses found throughout BvAC, or how far the compiler was himself responsible for them. These unascribed verses are numbered at the right-hand side of the page. Verses that are quotations or variant readings or that are taken from Bv for some special purpose have no number at right-hand side. Verses numbered at the left-hand side are Bv verses in their consecutive order of appearance.

Throughout the work the compiler has shown himself as a proficient grammarian, as accomplished in the use of words, often choosing unusual ones, as a lover of the sounds of words, as an excellent story-teller, and possibly also as an elegant and imaginative versifier. All this, together not only with the picturesque similes and metaphors but also with the ready agreement with the traditional assessment of words, contributes to the charm and instructiveness of this interesting and, in various ways, unusual commentary.

I acknowledge with gratitude the help I have received in the preparation of this volume from Ven. Dr W. Rāhula and from Mr K. D. Somadasa.

London, 1976. I. B. Horner

[1] BvAC 79.

ABBREVIATIONS

A	Aṅguttara-nikāya
AA	A cty
Ap	Apadāna
ApA	Ap cty
Asl	Atthasālinī
Be	Burmese edn. of Bv
Bv	Buddhavaṁsa
BvA	Bv cty
BvAB	Bv cty, Burmese edn.
BvAC	Bv cty, Ceylon edn.
Cp	Cariyāpiṭaka
CpA	Cp cty
D	Dīgha-nikāya
DA	D cty
DAṬ	ṭīkā to DA
Dh	Dhammapada
DhA	Dh cty
Dhs	Dhammasaṅgani
Dīp	Dīpavaṁsa
Divy	Divyāvadāna
It	Itivuttaka
ItA	It cty
Jā	Jātaka
Jkm	Jinakālamālī
Kh	Khuddakapāṭha
KhA	Kh cty
Kkvt	Kaṅkhāvitaraṇī
KvA	Kvu cty
Kvu	Kathāvatthu
M	Majjhima-nikāya
MA	M cty
Mhbv	Mahābodhivaṁsa
Mhvs	Mahāvaṁsa

Mhvs-ṭ	Mhvs-ṭīkā
Mhvu	Mahāvastu
Miln	Milindapañha
Moha	Mohavicchedanī
Nd	Niddesa
Pṭs	Paṭisambhidāmagga
PṭsA	Pṭs cty
Pug	Puggalapaññatti
PugA	Pug cty
Pv	Petavatthu
PvA	Pv cty
S	Saṁyutta-nikāya
SA	S cty
Smp (and VA)	Vin cty
Sn	Suttanipāta
SnA	Sn cty
Thag	Theragāthā
ThagA	Thag cty
Thīg	Therīgāthā
ThīgA	Thīg cty
Thūp	Thūpavaṁsa
Ud	Udāna
UdA	Ud cty
UJ	Upāsakajanālaṅkāra
VA (and Smp)	Vin cty
Vbh	Vibhaṅga
VbhA	Vbh cty
Vin	Vinaya-piṭaka
Vism	Visuddhimagga
Vv	Vimānavatthu
VvA	Vv cty

Abh	*Abhidhānappadīpikā* (Moggallāna), 3rd edn. 1900
BD	*Book of the Discipline* (I. B. Horner), 1938–67
BHSD	*Buddhist Hybrid Sanskrit Dictionary* (Franklin Edgerton), 1953
BPE	*Buddhist Psychological Ethics* (Mrs Rhys Davids), 3rd edn. 1974
CB	*Chronicle of Buddhas* (I. B. Horner), 1973
Childers	*A Dictionary of the Pali Language*, 1872, 1875

CPD	*Critical Pali Dictionary*, Copenhagen, 1924–
cty, comy	commentary
DBK	*The Birth-Stories of the Ten Bodhisattas and the Dasabodhisattuppattikathā* (H. Saddhatissa), 1975
DPPN	*Dictionary of Pali Proper Names* (G. P. Malalasekera), 1938
EC	*Epochs of the Conqueror* (N. A. Jayawickrama), 1968
EHBC	*Early History of Buddhism in Ceylon* (E. W. Adikaram), 1946
EPD	*English-Pali Dictionary* (A. P. Buddhadatta), 1955
EV	*Elders' Verses* I, II (K. R. Norman), 1969, 1971
Expos	*Expositor* (Pe Maung Tin), 1920, 1921
GS	*Book of Gradual Sayings* (F. L. Woodward), 1932–6
H	*see* SHB
ID	*Inception of Discipline* (N. A. Jayawickrama), 1962
JPTS	*Journal of the Pali Text Society*, 1882–1923
Min Anth	*Minor Anthologies of the Pali Canon*, 1931, 1935, 1974, 1975
MLS	*Middle Length Sayings* (I. B. Horner), 1954–9
MR and Ill	*Minor Readings and Illustrator* (Ñāṇamoli), 1961
MQ	*Milinda's Questions* (I. B. Horner), 1963, 1964
M-W	*A Sanskrit-English Dictionary* (Monier-Williams), 1872
PED	*Pali-English Dictionary* (T. W. Rhys Davids and W. Stede), 1921–5
PLC	*Pali Literature of Ceylon* (G. P. Malalasekera), 1928
Ppn	*Path of Purification* (Ñāṇamoli), 3rd edn. 1975
PTC	*Pali Tipitakaṁ Concordance* (F. L. Woodward and others), 1952–
SBB	Sacred Books of the Buddhists
SHB	Simon Hewavitarne Bequest
Sta	Sutta
Vkn	*Vimalakīrtinirdeśa* (Et. Lamotte), 1962

CONTENTS

		PAGE
Preface		v
Introduction		xxix
Abbreviations		liii

CLARIFIER OF THE SWEET MEANING

	Story of the Book's Beginning	1
Exposition of		
I	The Section on the Jewel-Walk	8
IIA	The Account of Sumedha	96
IIB	The First Chronicle: the Lord Dīpaṅkara	170
III	The Second Chronicle: the Lord Koṇḍañña	189
IV	The Third Chronicle: the Lord Maṅgala	203
V	The Fourth Chronicle: the Lord Sumana	220
VI	The Fifth Chronicle: the Lord Revata	231
VII	The Sixth Chronicle: the Lord Sobhita	239
VIII	The Seventh Chronicle: the Lord Anomadassin	247
IX	The Eighth Chronicle: the Lord Paduma	255
X	The Ninth Chronicle: the Lord Nārada	263
XI	The Tenth Chronicle: the Lord Padumuttara	274
XII	The Eleventh Chronicle: the Lord Sumedha	285
XIII	The Twelfth Chronicle: the Lord Sujāta	292
XIV	The Thirteenth Chronicle: the Lord Piyadassin	300
XV	The Fourteenth Chronicle: the Lord Atthadassin	309
XVI	The Fifteenth Chronicle: the Lord Dhammadassin	315

		PAGE
XVII	The Sixteenth Chronicle: the Lord Siddhattha	320
XVIII	The Seventeenth Chronicle: the Lord Tissa	326
XIX	The Eighteenth Chronicle: the Lord Phussa	332
XX	The Nineteenth Chronicle: the Lord Vipassin	336
XXI	The Twentieth Chronicle: the Lord Sikhin	346
XXII	The Twenty-first Chronicle: the Lord Vessabhū	353
XXIII	The Twenty-second Chronicle: the Lord Kakusandha	360
XXIV	The Twenty-third Chronicle: the Lord Koṇāgamana	368
XXV	The Twenty-fourth Chronicle: the Lord Kassapa	375
XXVI	The Twenty-fifth Chronicle: the Lord Gotama	387
	Differences between the Buddhas	425
	Envoi	430

Indexes

Index of Words 433

Index of Pali Proper Names 446

The Clarifier of the Sweet Meaning called the Commentary on the Chronicle of Buddhas

Homage to that Lord, Arahant, Perfect Buddha

STORY OF THE BOOK'S BEGINNING

[1] I do homage to the Buddha of infinite knowledge, the abode of compassion, the extinction of stain, well concentrated and benevolent; to the glorious Dhamma which restrains existence; and to the Community, the mine of virtues and devoid of
blemishes. 1

The General of the Dhamma (i.e. Sāriputta), the greatest in wisdom among the Conqueror's disciples, asked (about the Chronicle of Buddhas) in the assembly of his (the Buddha's) relatives, the King of the Dhamma, the teacher who had gone
from this to the other shore and was devoid of blemishes. 2

Here, the Chronicle of Buddhas was declared (explained) by the Tathāgata, who was in the line of supreme Buddhas, who came from an extremely pure line, the excellent leader, free from the accumulation of kamma[1], and who dwelt in concentration.[2] 3

Down to this day, the sons of the Wellfarer have transmitted it

[1] hatāvakāsa as at Dh 97. Explained at DhA ii 188 as the destruction of the seed of skilled and unskilled action. This means arahantship is attained.

[2] BvAC samācitaṁsena, BvAB samādhivāsena.

(the *Buddhavaṁsa*) just as they had heard it, without corrupting the mode of the text and the meaning of the text as well as the sequence of the narration. 4

Since the Commentary of that same lineage of the perfect Buddhas, which has always been a nectar to the people's ears, producing serene joy and wisdom, has been handed down in succession; 5

And as I had been duly requested for a long time by Buddhasīha[1] who delights in the sublime Dhamma and in whom such virtues as morality are developed, therefore I will begin its Commentary. 6

[2] For the perpetuation of the Conqueror's Dispensation which always destroys people's evil, also for the rise and growth of my own merit and for the serene joy of the multitude, 7

There will be this Commentary on the Chronicle of Buddhas, devoid of the fault of corruption, based on the textual course (tradition) transmitted in the Mahāvihāra, and containing the essential matter in brief. 8

As there is nothing here worthy of hearing other than the narration of the Chronicle of Buddhas which produces serene joy for those delighting in the virtuous qualities of the Buddhas and washes away the great dirt of evil (sin), 9

Therefore, (you) who are duly concentrated, abandoning dispersion (perplexity), with minds undivided, listen, lending your ears respectfully to (me) who am explaining this Commentary which is sweet and well lettered (composed). 10

Now, this narration, which is very rare, should always be respectfully listened to and related by an intelligent[2] man, leaving aside all other activity (work). 11

Herein, as was said (ver. 8 above), "There will be this Commentary on the Chronicle of Buddhas containing the essential matter in brief", so first the Chronicle of Buddhas should be defined. This is the definition. From here onwards the Chronicle of Buddhas should be understood to mean talk in detail on the line of the twenty-five Buddhas who have arisen already in four incalculable (periods) and a hundred thousand eons according to demarcation by uprising, by eon and so on.

[1] A pupil of Buddhadatta to whom he dedicated the Vinaya-vinicchaya.

[2] Read budhena, m.c. for buddhena, and also for better meaning.

Thus there is demarcation by eon, demarcation by name, demarcation by clan, demarcation by birth, demarcation by city . . . father . . . mother . . . Tree of Awakening . . . turning the Wheel of Dhamma . . . penetrations[1] . . . assemblies of disciples . . . chief disciples . . . (monastic) attendants . . . chief women disciples . . . retinue of monks . . . rays . . . height of the physical frame . . . acts of merit[2] while (still) the Bodhisatta . . . by declaration . . . by the Bodhisatta's strivings . . . by life-span, demarcation by (the attainment of) final nibbāna . . . by these twenty-two demarcations which have come down in the texts "demarcating" is defined. And several sections not incorporated in the text should be brought forward here too: defined, they are tenfold: demarcation by (the time spent) living the household life . . . by the three palaces . . . by (the number of) dancing-women . . . chief consort . . . son . . . vehicle . . . [3] Departure . . . striving[3] . . . (lay-)attendants, demarcation by vihāra.[4]

> Having pointed out the several sections (each) according to its place, we will go[5] here and there in an orderly way[6]. 12

And this is defined thus:

> By whom was it spoken, where and for whose sake was it spoken? For the sake of what, when, whose was the utterance, and by whom was it conveyed?[7] 13
> First saying all this clearly in an orderly way, afterwards I will make a Commentary on the Chronicle of Buddhas. 14

Herein, "By whom was it spoken?" means by whom was this Chronicle of Buddhas spoken? It was spoken by Him whose

[1] abhisamaya, penetration, arrival at, attainment of—here usually of Dhamma. Two kinds at Vism 216: that consisting in development (of the Way), and that consisting in realization (of nibbāna).

[2] adhikāra, also meaning homage, sacrifice, honour, and referring to that paid by the Bodhisatta to whichever Buddha it was under whom he was making his aspiration.

[3] This means as a Buddha, as the Bodhisatta's striving has been referred to already.

[4] Cf. text p. 130.

[5] gamissāma, with v. l. kathessāma.

[6] samāsato, by group, in combined form; cf. KhA 228, Vism 82.

[7] Cf. Vin v 1f.

knowledge moves unobstructed[1] in all states, by Him of the Ten Powers, by Him who is confident in the four confidences, by the king under Dhamma, by the lord under Dhamma, by the Tathāgata, by the omniscient fully Self-Awakened one.

"Where was it spoken?" It was spoken in the Great Vihāra in Nigrodha's park in the great city of Kapilavatthu while he was walking up and down on the Jewel-Walk which was extremely beautiful to behold, a cynosure of the eyes of devas and mankind.

"And for whose sake was it spoken?" It was spoken for the sake of eighty-two thousand relations and countless crores of devas and men.

"For the sake of what was it spoken?" It was spoken for the sake of crossing over the four floods.

"When was it spoken?" means the Lord was without a regular dwelling for the first twenty years after the Awakening[2]; going wherever he was comfortable, he stayed there. How was that? Having turned the Wheel of Dhamma in the seers' resort[3] during the first rains and caused crores of brahmans to drink of the drink of deathlessness, he stayed in the deer-sanctuary in the seers' resort near Bārāṇasī; during the second rains he was in the Great Vihāra in the Bamboo Grove near Rājagaha, and during the third and fourth likewise; during the fifth he was in the Hall of the Gabled House in the Great Grove near Vesālī; during the sixth on Mount Maṅkula[4]; during the seventh in the abode of the Thirty-Three; during the eighth in the Bhesakalā Grove near the Crocodile Hill (in the land) of Bhagga; during the ninth at Kosambī; during the tenth in the forest-thicket in Pārileyyaka[5]; during the eleventh in the brahman village of Nālā; during the twelfth at Verañjā; during the thirteenth on Mount Cāliya[6]; during the fourteenth at the Great Vihāra in the Jeta Grove; during the fifteenth in the great city of Kapilavatthu; during the sixteenth, having tamed Āḷavaka and caused eighty-four thousand breathing things to drink of the drink of deathlessness, he was at Āḷavī; during the seventeenth again at Rājagaha; during the eighteenth again on Mount

[1] appaṭihatañāṇacāra; cf. UdA 28.

[2] AA ii 125; the whole passage occurs in fuller detail at Jkm 29–35.

[3] isipatana.

[4] Not identified with precision, see DPPN. Called Makula in BvAB and at Jkm 33.

[5] BvAB Pāli-.

[6] Or Cālikā. Jkm 34 reads Pāliya. Near Rājagaha.

Cāliya; likewise during the nineteenth; but during the twentieth rains he stayed again near Rājagaha.

[4] Therefore it was said: "The Lord was without a regular dwelling for the first twenty years after the Awakening; going wherever he was comfortable, he stayed there". But from then on[1] he stayed near Sāvatthi in the Great Vihāra in Jeta's Grove or in the Eastern Park because there was a constant supply of requisites[2]. But when the teacher had become Awakened and had spent the first rains in the deer-sanctuary in the seers' resort near Bārāṇasī, he went to Uruvelā when the rains were over and he had "invited". Staying there for three months, he tamed the three matted-hair ascetic brothers, and conducting the "Invitation" with a thousand monks on the full-moon day of Phussa, he went to Rājagaha and stayed there for two months. Then five months had gone by since he left Bārāṇasī, the whole of the cold season had passed, and seven or eight days had elapsed since the day that the Elder Udāyin[3] had arrived. In the month of Phagguna[4], he[5] thought, "The cold season has passed, spring has come; it is the occasion for the Tathāgata to go to the city of Kapila." Thinking he should go to his relations' city he praised going in sixty verses[6].

Then the teacher, having heard his[7] words and being anxious to show goodwill to his relations, left Rājagaha surrounded by ten thousand inhabitants of Aṅga and Magadha and ten thousand inhabitants of Kapilavatthu—in all by twenty thousand whose cankers were destroyed. Travelling a yojana each day, he arrived in two months at the city of Kapila[8], a distance of sixty yojanas from Rājagaha. There he performed the Marvel of the Double[9] so as to have homage paid by his relations. Then this Chronicle of Buddhas was taught.

"Whose was the utterance?" It was the utterance of the Fully

[1] Jkm 35, in saying "from then on for 25 years", thus correctly spreads the Teaching over 45 years.

[2] paribhoga, use, things used; 4 kinds at Vism 43.

[3] This was Kāḷudāyin, see Jā i 86, also DPPN. Supposed to have been born at the same time as the Buddha.

[4] BvAB Phaggunapuṇṇamāsiyaṁ, on the full-moon day of Phagguna.

[5] I.e. Udāyin.

[6] So BvAB and Bv, p. x; BvAC differs: thinking thus, he first praised going in these verses.

[7] Udāyin's.

[8] BvAB Kapilavatthupura.

[9] See text p. 31.

Self-Awakened One only and was not shared by disciples or by buddhas by and for themselves.

"And by whom was it conveyed?" It was conveyed by an unbroken succession of teachers. It should be understood that, beginning with the Elder Sāriputta, Bhaddaji, Tissa, Kosiyaputta, Siggava, Moggaliputta, Sudatta, Dhammika, Dāsaka, Sonaka and Revata[1] thus conveyed it down to the time of the Third Council, and after that it was thus conveyed to contemporary times simply by a succession of their pupils.

It is in respect of this that that verse was spoken:

> "By whom was it spoken, where, and for whose sake was it spoken? For the sake of what, when, whose was the utterance, and by whom was it conveyed?" 1

COMMENTARY ON THE ANTECEDENTS

The Commentary on this conveying is now thus: And inasmuch as this Commentary, having shown these three antecedents: the Remote Antecedent[2], the Not-So-Remote Antecedent[3], the Proximate Antecedent[4], is called explained, well explained [5] and is understood, well understood by those who hear it from the beginning, therefore, having shown these Antecedents, we will explain them.

Herein, the demarcation of these antecedents must be understood from the beginning. Herein, this is an illustration of the matter in abridged form. After the Great Being had made his resolve at the feet of Dīpaṅkara of the Ten Powers till the time when he deceased from his individuality as Vessantara and was reborn in Tusita-abode, the course of existence is spoken of as the Remote Antecedent. After his decease from Tusita-abode till the attainment of omniscience on the dais round the Tree of Awakening, the course of existence is spoken of as the Not-So-Remote Antecedent. When it is said "At one time the Lord was staying in Anāthapiṇḍika's Park in the Jeta Grove near Sāvatthi", and "He was staying at the squirrels' feeding-ground in the Bamboo Grove near Rājagaha", and "He was staying in the Hall of the Gabled

[1] Cf. Asl. 32.
[2] Jā i 2–47.
[3] Ibid. 47–77.
[4] Ibid. 77–94.

House in the Great Grove near Vesālī", in the interval between the attainment of omniscient knowledge on the dais round the Tree of Awakening till the time when he was on the couch of final nibbāna, wherever the Lord stayed that is to be understood as the Proximate Antecedent. To this extent, by means of an abridged form only, the commentary on the External Antecedent is completed in regard to the three Antecedents: the Remote, the Not-So-Remote, and the Proximate.

I. THE SECTION ON THE JEWEL-WALK

And now comes the Commentary on the Inner Antecedent based on the method that begins thus:

I 1 Brahmā Sahampati, chief in the world, his hands clasped, requested Him who was unexcelled: "There are beings here who by nature have little dust (of defilements) in them; teach Dhamma out of compassion for this generation."

Herein[1] "At that time the Lord was staying in the squirrels' feeding-ground in the Bamboo Grove near Rājagaha" is as in the Suttantas when they begin "At one time the Lord was staying in Nigrodha's Park near Kapilavatthu among the Sakyans. Then the venerable Sāriputta approached the Lord; having approached, he questioned the Lord on the Chronicle of Buddhas." Not having spoken of an Antecedent in the way beginning thus, why is an Antecedent meant in the way beginning:

> "Brahmā Sahampati, chief in the world, his hands clasped, requested Him who was unexcelled"?

It should be said: When Brahmā was requesting the Lord for the teaching of Dhamma it was spoken for the purpose of showing the true mode of teaching the whole Dhamma. It should be said:

> "When was this Conqueror asked by Brahmā for the teaching of Dhamma? When, where, and by whom was this verse uttered?"[2] 1
>
> (and ver. 17)

[6] Now in the eighth week after the Lord had become awakened, the teacher was asked, was requested by Brahmā for the teaching of Dhamma. This is the consecutive narrative:

The Great Man, his resolve made, having seen on the day of the Great Departure the dancing-women sitting and lying down[3] (looking) disgusting, unclothed, uncovered, was exceedingly stirred at heart. He addressed Channa, who filled a special posi-

[1] BvAC tattha with v l. ettha as in BvAB.
[2] See text p. 11.
[3] This whole narrative is repeated in greater detail at text p. 281ff.

tion[1], saying, "Bring the glorious steed Kanthaka[2], the noble slayer for glorious men[3]." He mounted the glorious steed when he had been brought and, with Channa as companion, issued forth from the city when the city-gates had been opened by the devatās who haunted the city-gates. Passing through three territories during the remainder of the night, the perfect being[4], standing on the bank of the Anomā river, spoke thus to Channa[5], "Channa, taking Kanthaka, the glorious steed, and these other trinkets of mine, no longer lovely,[6] go back to Kapila city." Having dismissed Channa, he cut off the dark hair on his chest and his topknot with a sword so sharp that it resembled blue lotuses and threw it up into the air. Then, taking a bowl and robe given by devas, he went forth by himself and walking gradually on tour and crossing the river Ganges which was untrammelled[7]—for the waves that had risen through the force of the wind had subsided—he entered the city called Rājagaha, the King's[8] residence shining and aglow from the rays of a host of gems. There, as though deriding[9] the people who were elated by pride and authority, and as though arousing shame in a person who was wearing grand garments, and as though binding the hearts of the citizens to himself by his pleasing youthfulness, and as though a cynosure of the eyes of all the people because of the splendour of his appearance shining with the thirty-two glorious Marks of a Great Man, as though an accumulation of merit (made) a passage for his lovely feet, and walking along[10]

[1] pāṭekkadesāvacchanna, obviously a play on Channa's name, probably invented by BvA compiler. It could be variously translated. I have chosen the above rendering since Channa was not only the Bodhisatta's special charioteer but a close friend as well.

[2] BvAB Kaṇṭaka.

[3] arinaravaramanthaka, a play on the name Kanthaka. Cf. text p. 282. If this is what this compound means, "slayer", crusher, manthaka, should not be taken literally, but as a slayer of e.g. the defilements, a task in which Kanthaka would help by carrying his master away from the household life; cf. Vv No. 81. 15ff. See M. Palihawadana, A New Approach to the Interpretation of Ṛgvedic *Ari*, p. 88 in Añjali, a Felicitation Volume presented to Prof. O. H. de A. Wijesekera, Peradeniya, 1970, who suggests that ari can have the meaning of "noble", or something comparable, besides signifying "non-friend, foe." Ari again in compounds below, text pp. 8, 210, 245, 282, 288.

[4] anomasatta.

[5] Cf. Jā i 64.

[6] BvAB asādhāraṇāni (not to be shared), with v. l. asubharāni as in BvAC.

[7] asaṅga. Note play on words: -taraṅgabhaṅgaṁ asaṅgaṁ Gaṅgaṁ. Cf. text p. 284–5.

[8] Bimbisāra.

[9] parihāsayanto, BvAB parihāyento.

[10] The v. l. gamana seems preferable to text's gagaṇa.

unimpeded, he was like a rock, his sense-faculties tranquil, his mind tranquil, looking ahead no more than a plough's length. When he had walked in Rājagaha for almsfood and taken only enough rice to keep himself going, he departed from the city. Sitting down in a secluded place in the open air on a slope of Mount Paṇḍava[1] in a very delightful stretch of well levelled ground that had both shade and water, he partook of food of a mixed nature by the power of reflexion.

The great king of Magadha, Bimbisāra, the elect of Mandāra Hill, the elect of men[2], went into the presence of the Great Man. When he had asked his name and clan[3], he offered him his kingdom and said with joy in his heart, "Do take part of my kingdom." "No, sire, I have no need of a kingdom. I have got rid of a kingdom and am intent on striving for the welfare of the world. I will become a Buddha, one who lifts the veil from the world[4]". When he was departing having spoken thus, the king said, "Well then, when you have become a Buddha, you must propound it in my kingdom first of all." "Very well," he said, and when he had given him the assurance he approached Āḷāra and Uddaka. But as he did not find in them the essence of the teaching of Dhamma, he left them. Though engaging in austerities for six years at Uruvelā, but unable to arrive at deathlessness, he refreshed his physical frame by taking coarse food.

[7] Then near Uruvelā in the market town of Senānī[5], Sujātā, the daughter of a landowner of Senānī[6], a young girl attained to years of discretion, made a vow at a banyan tree: "If I went to my clan's house, being of the same caste, and were to become pregnant for the first time I would make an oblation". Her vow was successful. On the full-moon day of Visākha she thought "I will make the oblation today", and early in the morning offered milk-rice, smooth[7] and very sweet. On that same day the Bodhisatta, having attended to his physical frame, while he was waiting for the time of walking for alms early in the morning, went to the root of that

[1] Cf. Jā i 66, DhA i 85.

[2] Mandāragirisāra narasāra are epithets of Bimbisāra. Cf. text p. 285. BvAB reads Paṇḍavagirisārena.

[3] gotta, i.e. descent, ancestry.

[4] vivittacchado; or, free of mental and spiritual coverings in the world.

[5] BvAC Senānīnigame, BvAB Senānigame with v. l. as in BvAC.

[6] BvAC Senānikuṭumbikassa, BvAB Senānigamaku-.

[7] anāyāsa, free from trouble.

banyan tree and sat down. Then as a slave-woman named Puṇṇā, her wet-nurse, was going to prepare the ground at the root of the tree, she saw the Bodhisatta, the sun who was a sage, sitting down near the glorious tree surveying the eastern quarter of the world. The splendour of his physical frame was like the glorious golden tinge of the radiant glow of sunset over mountain-peaks, making a mock of the deep darkness, and making it to shine like a grove of lotuses when the sun reaches a cleft in a massive rock[1].

And as the lustre issued forth from his physical frame and she saw that that entire tree was the colour of gold it occurred to her, "Our devatā has come down from the tree today and is sitting there anxious to accept the oblation with his own hand." Swiftly she went to Sujātā and told her of this matter.

Then Sujātā, full of faith, adorned herself with all her ornaments and filling a golden bowl to the brim[2] with the sweet milk-rice, a very sweet drink, she uncovered the golden bowl, placed it on her head and went along towards the banyan. As she was going along, from afar she saw the Bodhisatta, sitting there like a tree-devatā, making that entire tree the colour of gold from the lustre of his physical frame, beautiful as an accumulation of merit. Taking him to be the tree-devatā, Sujātā was filled with joy and happiness, and going along from the place where she had first seen him and constantly stooping down, she took the golden bowl from off her head and, placing it in the Great Being's hands, she revered him by means of the fivefold prostration[3]; and saying, "Inasmuch as my desire is accomplished, so may yours be accomplished too", she departed.

Then the Bodhisatta accepted the golden bowl[4] and went to the bank of the river Nerañjarā, placed the golden bowl on the bank of a ford called Suppatiṭṭhita, and bathed. When he had come out of the water he made forty-nine balls of almsfood and after partaking of the milk-rice he thought: "If I become[5] a Buddha today, let this golden bowl go upstream," and he threw it in. That bowl went upstream, entered the abode of a nāga-king called Kāla and, pushing up the little bowls of three (previous) Buddhas, it came to rest beneath them.

[1] BvAC ghanavivaragataṁ, BvAB -vivaram upagataṁ with v. l. as in BvAC.

[2] satasahassaghanika.

[3] pañcapatiṭṭhita, apparently a commentarial expression (see PED s.v. pañca): by the forehead, waist, elbows, knees and feet.

[4] Cf. Jā i 70–71. [5] BvAC bhavāmi. BvAB bhavissāmi with v. l. as in BvAC.

The Great Being spent the day-sojourn in a forest-thicket just there. Towards evening he was given eight handfuls of grass by a grass-cutter named Sotthiya who was carrying grass and knew the aspect of a Great Man. He accepted them, ascended to the dais round the Tree of Awakening and stood at the southern side. But this locality trembled like a drop of water on a lotus leaf. The Bodhisatta[1] thought: "This (place) is unable to bear my special quality", [**8**] and he went to the western side. That trembled exactly the same. He again went on, to the northern side. That trembled exactly the same. Again he went on, to the eastern side. Here was a steady place of a (suitable) size for a cross-legged position. The Great Man, coming to the conclusion, "This place is the place for shattering the defilements", grasped those grasses by the tips and scattered them. They divided as though by the weight of their tips. The Bodhisatta, thinking: "I will not leave this cross-legged position without having attained Awakening", and resolutely determining on the fourfold energy[2], sat down cross-legged facing eastwards with his back against the trunk of the Tree of Awakening.

At that very moment Māra, offering the whole of the world, having created a thousand arms (by supernormal power), mounted[3] a noble[4] elephant named Girimekhala, a glorious elephant a hundred and fifty yojanas in height, and resembling a mountain-peak. Surrounded by a very strong force, Māra's force[5] (extending for) nine yojanas and consisting of bows, knives, axes, arrows and swords, and as though enveloping the mountain slope all round[6], (Māra) came to the Great Being who was as though attained to greatness. While the sun was still up the Great Man routed Māra's forces in utter confusion.

As though he were being honoured with joy by the shoots of the Tree of Awakening which, like sprigs of red coral lovely to behold, were falling down on his robe which thus resembled the flowers of "victory's joy"[7] when in full bloom, and having acquired the

[1] BvAB mahāpurisa with v. l. as in BvAC.

[2] caturaṅgaviriya, see MA i 124, 257, referring according to MAA to the phrase kāmaṁ taco *ca* nhāru *ca* aṭṭhī *ca* maṁsalohitañ *ca* avasissatu, as at Jā i 71; see also S ii 28, A i 50.

[3] BvAC āruyha, BvAB abhirūyha.

[4] Girimekhala is again called arivāraṇa at text p. 288; and gajarāja, elephant-king, at Mhbv 31. On ari, see text p. 6.

[5] BvAB adds Mārabalena.

[6] BvAC samantato, BvAB samantā, with v. l. as in BvAC.

[7] jayasumana, name of a plant; cf. Vism 174.

knowledge of the recollection of former habitations during the first watch (of the night), purified the knowledge of deva-like vision during the middle watch, and entering on the knowledge of dependent origination during the last watch, reflecting on the perpetual round[1] (of births), and becoming a Buddha as dawn was breaking, he uttered this solemn utterance:

> "Seeking but not finding the house-builder, I travelled through countless births in saṁsāra. Anguish is birth again and again. House-builder, you have been seen now; you shall not build the house again. All your rafters are broken down, your ridge-pole demolished too. Now my mind has attained what is without constructions, and reached the destruction of cravings,"*

and he passed seven days enjoying the bliss of freedom. Emerging from that attainment[2] on the eighth day, and knowing the devatās' doubt, he rose up into the air so as to dispel their doubt and, having displayed the Marvel of the Double and dispelled their doubt, he stood at the northern side facing slightly towards the east of where he had been sitting cross-legged. He thought, "Indeed, omniscient knowledge has been pierced by me when I was in this crossed-legged position", and he passed seven days surveying with steadfast gaze the place of the cross-legged position as well as the Tree of Awakening for it was the place of his arrival[3] at the fruits of the perfections that he had fulfilled during the four incalculables and the hundred thousand eons. That place received the name Animisacetiya[4] "Cetiya of the Steadfast Gaze".

Then, between the place where he had stood and that where he had sat in the cross-legged position, he passed seven days walking up and down on the Jewel-Walk which stretched from west to east. That place received the name Ratanacaṅkamanacetiya "Cetiya of the Jewel-Walk". **[9]** Thereupon devatās created Ratanaghara "Jewel-House" to the western quarter. Seated there cross-legged, he passed seven days thinking out the Abhidhamma-piṭaka in detail including the whole of the Paṭṭhāna in its infinite methods.

* As at Dh 153–4, Thag 183–4, Ja i 76. Referred to at UdA 208; quoted VA 17, DA 16, KhA 12, Asl 18. See BD iv Intr. p. vii for further references.

[1] vaṭṭavivaṭṭa, evolution and devolution, expansion and contraction.
[2] Cf. VA 957 for following passage, also below text p. 289f.
[3] adhigama, explained at AA i 87. Five kinds given at Netti.
[4] See also Jā i 77.

That place received the name Ratanagharacetiya "Cetiya of the Jewel-House".

Thus, having passed exactly four weeks near the Tree of Awakening, in the fifth week he approached Ajapāla's Banyan from the root of the Tree of Awakening. Thinking out Dhamma there and also experiencing the bliss of freedom, he spent seven days at Ajapāla's Banyan. After the seven days he sat down at the Mucalinda (tree). Hardly had the Lord sat down than there arose a great storm-cloud out of season filling the whole interior of the range of mountains (that encircled the world[1]). When it had arisen Mucalinda, the nāga-king, thought: "This great storm-cloud is rising just as the teacher has come into my abode. I must provide a room for him to stay in[2]". (Using the) seven kinds of gems he was able to create a deva-like mansion resembling a mansion of the devas. When he had done this he thought: "There will be no great fruit for me unless I render a physical service to Him of the Ten Powers". So, making (of himself) a very large individuality, he stood wrapping his coils seven times round the teacher and made a great hood above[3]. Then the Lord, sitting cross-legged in the pavilion made of all the jewels inside the great space of the enclosure, while the canopy above was pouring down a variety of fragrant flowers endued with a variety of fragrant scents, stayed there as though dwelling in the Scented Chamber. The Lord, having thus spent that week there, sat down afterwards for a (further) week at the Rājāyatana (tree). There too he experienced the bliss of freedom. Up to now seven weeks had been completed. The Lord spent the time here between the bliss of meditation and the bliss of the fruits.

Then when the seven weeks had passed, the thought arose in him: "I would rinse my mouth." Sakka, lord of devas, bringing some healthful myrobalan, gave it to him. Then Sakka gave him tooth-wood from an iron-wood tree and water for rinsing his mouth. Then the Lord, having chewed the tooth-wood and rinsed his mouth with water from Lake Anotatta, sat down at the root of the Rājāyatana (tree). At that time the four guardians of the world offered him a beautiful bowl made of crystal, and after he had accepted and partaken of rice-cakes and honey-balls from the

[1] cakkavāḷagabbha.

[2] vasāgāra.

[3] Cf. Vin i 3, Jā i 80, Ud II 1, Asl 35, 100f. See also MA i 385.

merchants Tapassu and Bhallika, he went back and sat down at the root of the Ajapāla Banyan.

No sooner had he sat down there and was reviewing the profound nature of the Dhamma he had arrived at of himself alone, than there arose to him the reasoning common to all Buddhas and reached when they do not wish to teach Dhamma to others: "This Dhamma arrived at by me is deep, difficult to see, difficult of discovery, peaceful, excellent, inaccessible by discursive thought, subtle, to be known by the wise."*

[**10**] Then Brahmā Sahampati, knowing with his mind the reasoning in the mind of Him of the Ten Powers, exclaiming: "Indeed, sir, the world is lost"†, and surrounded by a host of Brahmās from the ten-thousand world-systems, came along followed by Sakka, Suyāma, Santusita and by the (devas) who have power over the creation of others[1] and appeared before the Lord. Fashioning the earth as a support for himself, putting his right knee to the earth, he brought together his clasped hands which were shining like stainless unspoiled lotus-buds, their ten fingers touching one another[2], and raising them to his head, he said: "Revered sir, let the Lord teach Dhamma, let the Wellfarer teach Dhamma. There are beings who by nature have little dust (of defilements) and are declining from not hearing Dhamma, but they will be learners of Dhamma."

> "There has appeared in Magadha before you an unclean Dhamma by (minds) with stains devised. Open this door of deathlessness; let them hear Dhamma awakened to by the stainless one.
> As on a crag on crest of mountain standing a man might watch the people all around, even so do you. O Wisdom fair, O Seer of all, ascending the terraced heights that consist of Dhamma, look down, from grief released, upon the peoples sunken in grief, oppressed with birth and age.
> Arise, O hero, Conqueror in the battle, leader of the caravan,

* Vin i 4.
† Ibid. 5.

[1] paranimmitavasavatti.
[2] See UJ Intr. p. 85 and Ch.I § 49. The reading above is: jalamānāmalāvikalakamalamakula-sadisaṁ (with v. l. as at BvAB: jalajāmalāvikalakamalamakula-sadisaṁ) dasa nakhasamodhānasamujjalam añjaliṁ sirasmiṁ katvā. See also text 147, 250.

without a debt, walk in the world. May the Lord teach Dhamma. There are those who will understand."[1]

Thinking: "Now should not the One awakened by you awaken others, the one crossed over help others across, the one who is freed free others?"[2] he (the Buddha) said:

What is the use while I (remain) unknown of realizing Dhamma here? Having reached omniscience I will help the world together with the devas to cross over.[3]

(Brahmā) thinking, "He has made the aspiration, fulfilled the perfections and attained the state of omniscience", said: "If Dhamma is not taught by you who else will teach Dhamma, who else will be the refuge, shelter, shield and resting-place for the world?" And he asked the Lord for the teaching of Dhamma in a variety of ways beginning thus. Accordingly it was said: [11] "When the Lord had become Awakened, the teacher was asked by Brahmā in the eighth week for the teaching of Dhamma".[4]

Now, "When, where and by whom was this verse uttered?"[5] The occasion for answering these questions has (now) been reached. Herein, "When was it said?" It was said at the time of the First Great Council. This First Great Council should be understood according to the method spoken of in the Khandhaka on the Council[6]. Herein, "By whom was it said?" It should be understood that this verse, "And Brahmā, chief in the world" (I 1) was spoken by the venerable Elder Ānanda after he had taken his seat for the Dhamma in the pavilion, the choicest to be seen like the orb of the moon at the full, which after the Lord's final nibbāna had been made by Ajātasattu, the great king of Magadha, vanquisher of all beings, for the recital of Dhamma near the doorway to the Sattapaṇṇa Cave on a flank of Mount Vebhāra near the city of Rājagaha. This is the connection[7] with this verse. So far as here this verse too has the meaning as spoken:

When was this Conqueror asked by Brahmā for the teaching of
Dhamma? When, where, and by whom was this verse uttered?[8] 17
(and ver. 16)

[1] Vin i 5, D ii 39, M i 168, S i 137. [2] Cf. text p. 90.

[3] Cf. IIA. 55, reading Buddho hessaṁ, as also at Jā i 14, for tārayissaṁ above and at DA 466, MA ii 176.

[4] Cf. text p. 5f. [5] See text p. 5

[6] Vin ii 284. [7] sambandha, tying together. [8] See text p. 5.

But though it was spoken thus by means of this connection, I will give an explanation of its words that are not clear.

I 1 Therein[1] *Brahmā* means developed[2] by means of the eminence of various special qualities: Brahmā. And this word Brahmā is seen in such contexts as Mahābrahmā, brahman, Tathāgata, parents, the best, and so on. For example, in such contexts as "a thousand Brahmās"* Brahmā stands for a Mahābrahmā. Herein it is brahman:

> "Dispeller of darkness, Buddha, seer of all, gone to world's end, all becomings overpassed, cankerless, all anguish cast out, whose name is truth, him I follow, brahman"†.

"Brahmā, monks, is a synonym for Tathāgata"‡—herein it is Tathāgata. "Brahmā are parents called, teachers of old"§—herein it is parents. "He turns the Brahma-wheel"‖—herein it stands for the best. But here it stands for a Mahābrahmā, one who, having developed the first meditation in the highest degree, reborn in the domain of the first meditation, having a life-span enduring for an eon.

1 The word "and" has the meaning of a conjunction[3]: Brahmā and others in the ten-thousand world-systems and a brahman is the meaning. It is merely for filling up the line.[4]

1 *Chief in the world* means: herein the world means three worlds:[5] the world of constructions, the world of beings, the world of location. [**12**] Among these the world of beings is meant here. The lord and chief of this is "chief in the world". The chief over one region of the world is also called "chief in the world". It is like "chief of devas", "chief of men".

* M iii 101, quoted MA i 34 where cf. the definitions of Brahmā with above. BvAB reads dvisahasso which at M iii 101 follows sahasso.

† Sn 1133.

‡ Cf. A iv 340.

§ A i 132.

‖ A ii 9.

[1] Comy on Bv verses may be said to begin here.

[2] brūhita, increased, practised, cultivated.

[3] sampiṇḍanattha as at KhA 228.

[4] padapūraṇamatta, cf. ibid. 219. The word "and", ca, is placed in ver. 1 between Brahmā and the next word, "chief in the world", lokādhipati.

[5] As at SnA 442, and Vism 204 where explained in detail. The three are repeated at text p. 94. Three other kinds at Netti p. 11.

1 *Sahampati* means: it is said that during the Dispensation of the Lord Kassapa an Elder named Sahaka, having achieved the first meditation, and the meditation not waning away, at the close of his life was reborn as a Mahābrahmā in the domain of the first meditation, having a life-span enduring for an eon. But they knew him there as Sahampatī Brahmā. He should be called Sahakapati, but they say Sahampatī, adding the nasal sound[1] in accordance with tradition.

1 *Hands clasped* means: one with his hands clasped. The meaning is that having made a hollow between his palms (he raised them) to his head.

1 *Who was unexcelled* means: no other is so absolutely glorious or excels him: he is unexcelled. Or, there is nothing glorious excelling him: he is unexcelled. The meaning is: supreme, he who was unexcelled.

1 *Requested* means: having requested[2], he asked. He now requested the Lord to show the meaning of that matter spoken of beginning, "There are beings here".

1 Therein *there are* means: there exist, are to be got at, there are coming within the Awakened One's range of vision.

1 *Here*[3] means: this particle is a designation of location. It is sometimes said in reference to this Dispensation, as when he said: "Monks, just here is a recluse, here a second recluse, here a third recluse, here a fourth recluse; void of recluses are other (systems teaching) alien views".* Sometimes to a location as when he said:

> "Living just here as one who has become a deva, I am mindful that a new life-span was obtained by me. Know it thus, sir"†.

Sometimes it[4] is merely for filling up a line, as when he said: "Here I, monks, may have eaten and been satisfied".‡ Sometimes it refers to the world, as when he said: "Here a Tathāgata arises in the world for the weal of the manyfolk, for the happiness of the manyfolk"§. Here too it should be understood that it was said in reference to the world. Therefore the meaning is "in this world of beings".

* M i 63. See MLS i 85 for explanation and further references.
† D ii 285, quoted MA ii 199, Asl 348.
‡ M i 12.
§ Cf. M i 179, A i 22.

[1] anussara; cf. text pp. 71, 164.
[2] BvAC āyācitvā, BvAB āyācittha.
[3] Cf. Asl 348.
[4] idha, here.

1 *Beings* means that breathing things are called held, gripped[1], clinging, sticking, adhering, attained to[2], and reached by[3] desire for and attachment to the categories beginning with material shape. But in ordinary speech this term of common usage is applied also to those without attachment.

1 *Little dust* (*of defilements*) means in an eye made of wisdom the dust of attachment, hatred, confusion is a small amount, a trifle; these and the particular nature of these is: by nature having little dust (of defilements); those whose particular nature it is to have little dust (of defilements) are those who by nature have little dust (of defilements): "of those beings who have little dust (of defilements)" [**13**] is a class. Making a change, saying "Teach Dhamma", the meaning is to be understood by making a connection with this.

1 *Teach*: this is an expression for asking; the meaning is "teach, speak, point out".

1 *Dhamma* means[4]: herein this word Dhamma can be seen in such passages as: the teaching[5], concentration, wisdom, the normal, the particular nature, voidness, merit, offence, what can be known, the four true things and so on.—As he said: "Here, monks, they master Dhamma: the discourses in prose, in prose and verse, the expositions . . . the miscellanies"*—in such passages the teaching is to be seen. "These lords were the stuff of their own being (evaṁ-dhammā)"†—in such passages referring to concentration.

> "By whomsoever, monkey-king, as by you, these four things[6] are seen: Truth, Dhamma[7], steadfastness, self-sacrifice—he passes beyond them."‡

* At e.g. M i 133, A iii 177.

† D ii 10 54. Cf. evaṁ-dhammatā at Vism 585, trans. Ppn 676 "ineluctable Regularity". Concentration may be said to be the stuff of a Buddha's being; all Buddhas practise it regularly.

‡ Jā i 280, quoted CpA 230.

[1] Vism 310.

[2] Vism 310 lagitā pattā, BvAB lagitā ti sattā.

[3] BvAC, Vism sampattā, BvAB sattā ti.

[4] Cf. following passage with MA i 17, ItA i 37, PṭsA i 18.

[5] pariyatti. Three kinds at DA 21, MA ii 107, Asl 23.

[6] dhammā, at Jā i 280 called guṇā, special qualities.

[7] Ibid. explains as vicāraṇapañña, the wisdom of attention, investigation.

—in such passages referring to wisdom. "Liable to (dhamma) birth, liable to old age, then liable to dying"*—in such passages referring to the normal. "Skilled states of mind (dhammā), unskilled states of mind, states of mind that are indeterminate"†—in such passages referring to the particular nature. "Now at that time there were mental states (dhammā), there were categories"‡—in such passages referring to voidness. "Dhamma pursued brings happiness"§—in such passages referring to merit. "Two Undetermined rules"‖—in such passages referring to offences. "All things (dhammā) in every mode come within the range of the path of knowledge of the Buddha, the Lord"¶—in such passages referring to what can be known. "Having seen Dhamma, known Dhamma, attained Dhamma"**—in such passages referring to the four true things. Here too the four true things are to be understood.

1 *Out of compassion* means: be compassionate, merciful.

1 *This* means: he spoke designating the generation.

1 *Generation* means: generation because of being generated: that generation.[1] The intention is: Deliver the mass of beings from the anguish of saṁsāra. But some read:

> "The Lord, chief of the world, supreme among men, was asked by a host of Brahmās, their hands clasped".

So far as here this verse in every respect has the meaning as spoken.

Then when the Lord had heard Brahmā Sahampati's words of request, a great compassion arose in Him of the Ten Powers, in him of a power of compassion which had been cultivated for an illimitable period, in him who was surpassing in doing services for the welfare of others by way of giving them opportunity[2]. And at

* Cf. M i 162, A i 147.

† Dhs in Mātikā, p. 1; cf. Vin v 120, 207.

‡ Dhs 121. These are taken here to illustrate voidness for there is no eternal self or being to be got at, Asl 155.

§ Sn. 182.

‖ Vin iii 187. For dhamma as rule see Indexes to BD iv, v, s.v. Rule (*dhamma*); and as offence see Kkvt 17.

¶ Nd1 451. Cf. Sn 868. BvAC reads ñāṇapathe, BvAB -mukhe as at Pṭs ii 194.

** Vin i 12, etc.

[1] As at AA i 287.

[2] To make merit.

the time of the Council this verse was established by the recensionists to show the arising of that compassion in the Lord:

[14] I 2 In him possessed of knowledge-and-right-conduct, in the steadfast one, the bringer of light, bearer of his last body, Tathāgata, matchless person, there arose pitifulness towards all beings.

2 Therein *possessed of knowledge-and-right-conduct*: possessed of means it is called threefold in respect of being rich in, provided with, sweet.[1] Therein,

"(I am) possessed of irrigated rice-fields[2] which parrots are consuming, Kosiya: I declare to you, brahman, I cannot make them stop*"

—this is called possessed of as being rich in. "Furnished with this control of the Pātimokkha, he is well furnished, come to it, well come to it[3], possessed of it, endowed with it"†—this is called possessed of as being provided with. "The under surface of this great earth is fertile[4], revered sir, even as a flawless honeycomb"‡ —this is called possessed of as being sweet. Here it is to be construed as possessed of as being rich in as well as possessed of as being provided with.

2 *Knowledge*[5] means: knowledge in the sense of penetrating inimical states of mind and in the meaning of what is to be known. Now these knowledges are three, and six, and knowledges are eight. The three knowledges should be understood simply according to the method handed down in the Bhayabherava Discourse§; the eight as in the Ambaṭṭha Discourse‖, for eight knowledges are spoken of there comprised of the knowledge due to insight and the

* As at Jā iv 278.
† Vbh 246, Vism 7.
‡ Vin iii 7.
§ M Sta 4.
‖ D Sta 3; DA 268.

[1] Same explanation given at MA i 153 of "possessed of", sampanna.
[2] sālikedāra, referring to the Jātaka of this name (No. 484) where two parrots devoured a crop of rice.
[3] BvAB inserts upāgato samupāgato, cf. Vism 16, MA i 153.
[4] sampanna, full.
[5] Cf. VA 116, Vism 202.

psychic potency of making by mind together with the six super-knowings.

2 *Right-conduct*[1] means: these fifteen things should be understood: control over moral habit, guarding the doors of the sense-faculties, moderation in eating, intentness on vigilance, faith[2], conscience, shame, much learning, the putting forth of energy, the arousing of mindfulness, the endowment with wisdom, the four meditations in the sphere of form. For inasmuch as the ariyan disciple conducts himself[3] precisely by these fifteen things he proceeds to the deathless realm. Therefore it is called right-conduct. As he said, "Herein, Mahānāma, an ariyan disciple is moral"*—all should be understood simply according to the method spoken of in the Middle Fifty†. Knowledge and right conduct are knowledge-and-right-conduct. Possessed of, rich in knowledge-and-right-conduct is he by whom knowledge-and-right-conduct are possessed and completed. Or, possessed of, provided with, endowed with knowledge-and-right-conduct means possessed of knowledge-and-right-conduct.

And the meaning of both is to be construed like this: of him who is possessed of knowledge-and-right-conduct.

2 *In the steadfast one* means steadfast as to the liked, steadfast as to the disliked. Steadfast one is handed down in a passage in the Mahāniddesa‡ (where) "in the steadfast one" is (explained) by characteristic mark, the meaning being: of one who is steadfast, unaffected by what is liked and what disliked.[4]

[15] 2 *In the bringer of light* means in brilliance. The meaning is that the mass of light of the physical frame was even more (brilliant) than the sun rising over Yugandhara[5]. "In the bringer of the light of wisdom" can also be said. For this was said:

> "Four lights there are in the world, a fifth does not exist: the sun that shines by day, the moon that brightens the night, then by day and night a fire gives light now here, now there; the Self-Awakened One, best of shining things—this is radiance unsurpassed"§

* M i 355.
† M Stas 51–100.
‡ Ndl 459.
§ S i 15, 47.

[1] Cf. VA 116, Vism 202.
[2] From here to wisdom constitute the 7 excellent things of M i 356, etc.
[3] carati, fares, moves, progresses.
[4] Cf. M i 299f.
[5] BvAC and BvAB differ somewhat.

Therefore the meaning of the bringer of a mass of light refers both to the physical frame and to wisdom.

2 *Bearer of his last body* means: bearer of the last of all his physical frames. The meaning is: not of again-becoming.

2 *Of the Tathāgata* means herein that for eight reasons the Lord is called Tathāgata[1]. For what eight? He is Tathāgata because he has come (āgata) thus (tathā). He is Tathāgata because he has gone (gata) thus (tathā). He is Tathāgata because he has come (āgata) to the characteristic mark of truth (tatha). He is Tathāgata because he is fully Self-Awakened in accordance with true things (tathadhamma). He is Tathāgata for seeing truth (tatha). He is Tathāgata for speaking thus (tathā). He is Tathāgata for acting thus (tathā). He is Tathāgata in the sense of vanquishing.

How is the Lord Tathāgata because he has come thus? In accordance with that resolve,[2] he fulfilled the perfection of giving, fulfilled the perfections of moral habit, renunciation, wisdom, energy, patience, truth-speaking, resolute determination, loving-kindness, equanimity. These are the ten perfections, the ten higher perfections, the ten ultimate perfections. Having fulfilled the full thirty[3] perfections by the sacrifice of a limb, the sacrifice of (his own) life, the sacrifice of wealth, kingdom, child-and-wife—having sacrified these five in great sacrifice, so, as the Fully Self-Awakened Ones beginning with Vipassin have come thus, so too has our Lord come thus—Tathāgata. As was said:

> "Just as in the world, beginning with Vipassin, sages have come to omniscience here, so too has come this Sakyamuni, called therefore Tathāgata, one with vision."[4]

How is he Tathāgata because he has gone thus? As, beginning with Vipassin, when they have just come to birth, standing on the earth with even feet and facing north, by taking seven strides[5], they have gone thus; so too our Lord has gone thus—Tathāgata. As was said:

[16] "The very moment he was born, like a lordly bull[6] he touched

[1] From here to end of exegesis on Tathāgata cf. DA i 59ff., MA i 45ff., AA i 103ff., UdA 129ff.

[2] abhinīhāra, made at Dipaṅkara's feet, see text p. 5.

[3] See text p. 59. The thirty are mentioned at MA iii 22, DhA 84.

[4] H refers this stanza to the Porāṇaṭṭhakathā, the ancient Comy.

[5] Cf. D ii 15, M iii 123.

[6] gavampati, lord of herds.

the earth with even feet. Gotama stepped out for seven paces while deities held up a white parasol.
Having gone the seven paces, Gotama investigated the quarters equally all round; like a lion standing on a mountain-top he uttered words endowed with eight qualities.[1]*

How is he Tathāgata because he has come to the characteristic mark of truth? He has come infallibly by the courses of knowledge to the characteristic mark of all things of form and formlessness, to the characteristic mark of recluseship, and to truth, not untruth. Gone so[2], one who has understood, is Tathāgata.

Inasmuch as he has come (āgata) to the characteristic mark of all things, his own recluseship and to truth itself, therefore is the teacher Tathāgata.[3]

How is he Tathāgata because he is fully Self-Awakened in accordance with true things? The true things are called the four ariyan Truths. In brief, as he said, "These four are truths, monks, not untruths, they are not otherwise. What four? 'This is anguish'—this is a truth, monks, this is not an untruth, this is not otherwise'"† And the Lord was fully Self-Awakened to these, therefore he is called Tathāgata because of full Self-Awakening to the truths. Herein the word "gone" (gata) has the sense of full Self-Awakening.

The leader awakened of himself fully to the truths[4] having the names of truth[5]. Therefore is he Tathāgata because of awakening
of himself to the truths[6] (having the names of) truths[7]. 18

How is he Tathāgata for seeing truth? Now, the Lord said, "By all modes a Tathāgata knows and sees the objective support of material shapes, sounds, smells, tastes, touches, and mental states

* Verses attributed to Porāṇa, the ancients, at DA 61, MA i 46, AA i 105 .
† S.v. 430, cf. Pṭs ii 104.

[1] Cf. D ii 211, 227, M ii 140 for the 8 qualities.
[2] BvAC va gato, BvAB patto with v. l. as at BvAC.
[3] H ascribes this stanza to the Ancients. Not in DA, MA, or AA exegeses which agree with each other, but their treatment of this reason for being a Tathāgata differs from that in BvA.
[4] saccāni.
[5] tathanāmāni.
[6] saccānaṁ.
[7] tathānaṁ.

coming within the range of the door of the eye, ear, nose, tongue, body, and mind (respectively) of numberless beings in the illimitable world-systems[1]—thus he is Tathāgata because of seeing truth. Or, whatever is truth in the world that truth of the world he sees. For this too the Lord is Tathāgata. Herein the origin of the word Tathāgata is to be understood in the sense of one who sees truth.

> Whoever knows, beholds things by the method of truth is a Self-Awakened One, one who sees truth. Therefore he is called Tathāgata[2].

[17] How is he Tathāgata for speaking thus? In the time extending for forty-five years between the Self-Awakening and the parinibbāna, the ninefold composition beginning with Suttas in prose was spoken, was uttered by the Tathāgata. All that, as though gauged with one gauge, was truth itself, not untruth. Because of that it was said, "And, Cunda, from the night the Tathāgata completely awakened to full Self-Awakening to the night when he attained parinibbāna in the element of nibbāna that is without clinging—in that interval all that he said[3], uttered[4], demonstrated[5], is just so and not otherwise. Therefore he is called Tathāgata."* But, herein since the word "gone" (gata)[6] has the meaning of speech (gada) thus is he Tathāgata for speaking thus. The word[7], the talk[7] means utterance. Tathāgata means his talk (āgada) is truthful, definite. It is said after having made the syllable *da* represent the syllable *ta*.

> Inasmuch as the Conqueror speaking thus is one making known the true things, and his talk is truth, therefore the Awakened One is Tathāgata.[8]

* D iii 135, A ii 24, It p. 121–2, etc.

[1] Longer exegesis at ItA ii 188ff.

[2] Ascribed to Porāṇaṭṭhakathā by H.

[3] bhāsati, referring to the ninefold classification.

[4] lapati—usual meaning is to mutter. According to ItA ii 190 here it means on account of demonstrating or pointing out.

[5] niddisati, he demonstrated by means of a summary, uddisana.

[6] Text's reading gadasadda perhaps should be corrected to gata- in accordance with other commentarial readings, e.g. MA i 50, ItA ii 190.

[7] āgadanam āgado.

[8] H attributes this to the Porāṇaṭṭhakathā.

How is he Tathāgata for acting thus? With his body the Lord acts exactly as he speaks. His body tallies with his speech and his speech with his body. So it was said, "As the Tathāgata speaks, monks, so he acts; as he acts so he speaks. Thus, because as he speaks so he acts, as he acts so he speaks, he is called Tathāgata."* As goes his speech[1] so goes his body too, as goes his body so goes his speech too. So he is Tathāgata for acting thus.

> As goes his speech so goes his body. Because the Self-Awakened One, the teacher is one speaking thus, therefore is he Tathāgata."†

How is he Tathāgata in the sense of conquering? He conquers all creatures across the illimitable world-systems to the height of existence above and making Avīci the boundary below by means of moral habit and concentration and wisdom and freedom and the knowledge and vision of freedom. He has no gauge or measure, so he is ungauged, immeasurable, unsurpassed. Therefore it was said, "Monks, in the world with the devas the Tathāgata is vanquisher, unvanquished, absolute seer, having self-mastery. Therefore is he called Tathāgata."‡

Thus is the derivation[2] of the words to be understood: *agada*[3] is like *agada*. What is this? The elegance of teaching[4] as well as the elegance of merit. He vanquishes the world with the devas and all those holding other tenets as a powerful physician by means of this deva-like antidote (vanquishes) snakes. Thus for vanquishing all the world the antidote consists in the elegance of teaching [**18**] and it also consists of merit. (The word) Tathāgata should be understood having made the syllable *da* represent the syllable *ta*. Thus is he Tathāgata in the sense of vanquishing.[5]

> Whatever teacher's self-mastery is like the correct antidote, that
> teacher is therefore Tathāgata. 19

2 *In the matchless person* means: in a person without anyone to

* D iii 135, A ii 24, It p. 121–2, etc.
† H attributes this to the Porāṇaṭṭhakathā.
‡ D iii 135, A ii 24.

[1] yathā vācā gatā—as goes his speech.
[2] Or, establishment, siddhi. Cf. MA i 51, ItA ii 191.
[3] agada also means antidote.
[4] As at Vism 524, 541.
[5] As at A i 22, AA i 116.

match him. There is no person other than a matchless person who is able to give the acknowledgement thus, "I am Buddha"*: in this matchless person.

2 *Arose* means arisen, originated.

2 *Pitifulness* means a state of pity, pitifulness.

2 *All beings* means that it is a designation given to groups of beings without exception. The meaning is: entire classes of beings.

So far as here this verse too has the meaning as spoken.[1]

Then when the Lord had been requested by Brahmā for the teaching of Dhamma and had aroused pity for creatures, anxious to teach Dhamma he addressed Mahā-Brahmā in a verse:

> "Opened for them are the doors of deathlessness. Let those with ears to hear renounce (their former) faith. Thinking of useless fatigue, Brahmā, I did not speak Dhamma sublime and excellent for men."†

Then Brahmā Sahampati, knowing, "The opportunity for the Lord to teach Dhamma was made by me", bringing his ten resplendent fingers together to his head in salutation, having greeted the Lord he departed surrounded by a host of Brahmās keeping his right side towards him. Then when the teacher had given an assurance to that Brahmā he thought, "To whom should I first teach Dhamma?" Thinking, "Āḷāra is learned, he will understand Dhamma quickly", but, arousing his thoughts and surveying again he knew that he had done his (kammic) time a week ago and that Uddaka had done his (kammic) time the previous night. Again, thinking, "Where is the group of five monks staying at present?" and adverting his mind to the group of five, he knew they were near Bārāṇasī in the deer-sanctuary. At day-break (on the full-moon day[2]) in the month of Āsāḷha he took his bowl and robe and when he had gone eighteen yojanas along the road, on seeing a Naked Ascetic named Upaka on the highway, he explained to him his own Buddha-status, and arrived at the seers' resort in the evening of that same day. There he made known his own Buddha-status to the group of five and, addressing the group

* A ii 39.
† Vin i 7, M i 169, S i 138.

[1] See text pp. 11, 13.
[2] This should be inserted, cf. text p. 291.

of five from the glorious Buddha-seat that had been made ready, he taught the Discourse on the Turning of the Wheel of Dhamma.*

[**19**] Of these the Elder Aññā-Koṇḍañña put forth knowledge in accordance with the teaching and at the conclusion of the Discourse was established in the fruit of stream-entry together with eighteen crores of Brahmās. The Teacher, who had gone there for the rains, on the next day established the Elder Vappa in the fruit of stream-entry. Having established them all in the fruit of stream-entry by this same means, he gathered together the five Elders on the fifth day of the bright half of the month and taught the Discourse on the Marks of Non-self.† At the conclusion of the Discourse the five Elders were established in arahantship.

Then the Teacher, seeing the qualifications of Yasa, a young man of family, and seeing him departing and leaving his house, summoned him, saying, "Come, Yasa", and in that very same night established him in the fruit of stream-entry, and on the following day in arahantship. After that when he had let fifty-four people who were his friends go forth by the "Come, monk" (formula for) going forth, he established them in arahantship. Thus the Teacher, when he had kept the rains, "inviting" with the sixty-one arahants who thus were now in the world, addressing the monks, spoke thus:

Making this earth for the welfare of others and for your own,
fare along, monks, speaking Dhamma to men. 20
Dwell in lonely places, on mountain-slopes and in forests,
constantly making known to the world my True Dhamma. 21
Set forth, monks, explaining Dhamma's message. There are
good practices for the welfare of creatures: (such is) my word. 22
Close every door to states of woe; cankerless, without equal,
open the door of the way to liberation in heaven. 23
The Teaching with the practices is the abode of special qualities
such as compassion. Increase enlightenment and faith throughout the world. 24
To those householders who are supporters from their constant
giving of material things, render a service in return by the giving
of Dhamma. 25
When you are teaching True Dhamma, raise aloft the banner of

* Vin i 10.
† Ibid. 13.

seers. With everything done that should be done, fare along for
the good of others.[1] 26

When he had spoken thus, the Lord sent out those monks to the districts, and when he was himself going to Uruvelā he instructed a group of thirty young men on the way in the Kappāsiya forest-thicket. The least one of these was a stream-entrant, and the best of all a non-returner. There was neither one arahant nor one average person. Having let them all go forth by the "Come, monk" (formula for) going forth and, having himself arrived at Uruvelā, he displayed three thousand five hundred marvels and tamed three brothers who were matted-hair ascetics, beginning with Kassapa of Uruvelā, and their followers numbering one thousand matted-hair ascetics. Having let them go forth in the status (of monk by the formula) "Come, monk", [**20**] he made them be seated at Gayā's Head and established them in arahantship by means of the Discourse on Burning.*

Surrounded by these thousand arahants, the Lord thought, "I will redeem my assurance to King Bimbisāra"[2], and he arrived in the Laṭṭhivana-park on the outskirts of the city of Rājagaha. The keeper of the park told the king. When he had heard that the Teacher had come the king, surrounded by twelve crores of brahman householders, approached Him of the Ten Powers, the glorious sun of seers who was cleaving through the forest[3], like the sun cleaving through a dense fissure. Having inclined his head, which was resplendent with the array of jewels shining on his crest, to the feet of Him of the Ten Powers, the soles of which were adorned by the wheels and by glowing, stainless, blossoming lotus-buds[4], he sat down at a respectful distance together with his company.†

Then it occurred to those brahman householders, "Now, does the great recluse fare the Brahma-faring under Kassapa of Uruvelā or Kassapa of Uruvelā under the great recluse?" Then the Lord,

* Ibid. 34.
† Vin i 36, Jā vi 220.

[1] Verses at UJ 133f.
[2] See text p. 6.
[3] vana, here probably in its figurative sense of taṇhā; cf. KhA 111.
[4] Cf. text p. 10.

knowing with his mind the reasoning in their minds, addressed the Elder[1] in verses:

> "What have you seen, dweller in Uruvelā, that you, known as emaciate, have abandoned the sacred fire? I ask you about this matter, Kassapa: Have you abandoned the fire-instruments?"*

The Elder, knowing the Lord's intention, said:

> "The sacrifices speak of forms and sounds, also of tastes, sense-pleasures and women. Knowing that this is dross among clingings, I delighted therefore neither in sacrifice nor offering."*

When he had spoken this verse, to make clear his own status as a disciple he inclined his head to the Tathāgata's feet and said, "Revered sir, the Lord is my teacher, a disciple am I".* Having said this, he rose above the ground seven times to the height of one palm-tree . . . to the height of seven palm-trees, and having performed the marvel, descending from the sky, he praised the Lord and sat down at a respectful distance.

Then when the populace had seen that marvel of his, they said, "Indeed, those called Awakened are of great majesty; thus Kassapa of Uruvelā, in whom false views had become strong and had imagined of himself, 'I am an arahant', bursting the net of false views, was tamed by the Tathāgata", and they talked a talk about the special qualities of Him of the Ten Powers.† When the Teacher heard that, he said, "It is not only now that I have tamed Kassapa of Uruvelā; in the past too he was similarly tamed by me". Then the populace, rising from their seats, greeting the Lord and raising their clasped hands to their heads, spoke thus, "Lord, we see that this one was tamed now. But how was he tamed by the Lord in the past?" Then the Lord, requested by the populace, [21] having told the Mahānāradakassapajātaka‡ that had been concealed by other (previous) existences, expounded the four truths.

Then, after King Bimbisāra had heard the teacher's talk on Dhamma he was established in the fruit of stream-entry together with eleven myriad brahman householders. One myriad declared the state of lay-followers. When the king had gone for refuge, and

* Vin i 36, Jā vi 320. † Jā i 83, vi 220. ‡ Jā vi 220ff., No. 544.

[1] thera, called Kassapa of Uruvelā at Vin i 36.

had invited the Lord together with the Order of monks for the following day, circumambulating the Lord three times keeping his right side towards him, he paid homage and departed.

On the next day, surrounded by the thousand monks, as the deva-king of a thousand eyes is surrounded by a host of deities (or) as Mahābrahmā is surrounded by a host of Brahmās, the Lord entered Rājagaha. The king gave dāna[1] to the Order of monks with the Awakened One at the head, and at the end of the meal spoke thus to the Lord, "I shall not be able to go on, revered sir, without the Three Jewels; in season and out of season I shall come into the Lord's presence. The Laṭṭhivana is too far away, but this Bamboo Grove of ours, a pleasure-park, is neither too near (to a village) nor too far (from one) for those who desire solitude. It is suitable for coming and going, free from the crowding of people, ideal for solitude, possessed of shade and water, embellished with cool, flat stones, a piece of ground to be utterly delighted in, always with fragrant flowers and glorious trees[2], adorned with delightful long houses, roofless inner chambers[3], mansions, dwelling-places, curved houses[4], pavilions and so on. May the Lord accept this from me." And taking water, which was the colour of pearls and as though scented with fragrant flowers, in a golden ceremonial vessel which was as though it had just been warmed over embers, he poured the water over the hands of Him of the Ten Powers while he was bestowing the Bamboo Grove Park. On the acceptance of this park, the great earth thinking, "Planted[5] are the roots of the Awakened One's Dispensation", trembled as though dancing for joy. In Jambudīpa, except at the Great Monastery in the Bamboo Grove, there was no other occasion when the earth trembled at a lodging's being accepted. Then the Teacher, having received the Bamboo Grove Park, made a benediction for the king for the gift of the monastery:

> Though he be furnished with a myriad mouths, who is the man able to tell the advantage of giving a residence, except Awakened Ones, protectors of the world? 27
> Long life and beauty and happiness and strength are for

[1] This word is known to Westerners as meaning gifts of food, clothing and so on.

[2] taru, as at Mhvs. 15. 79, explained at Mhvs-ṭ. p. 351, as bodhirukkha.

[3] See BD ii 16, n. 5, 6.

[4] See BD iv 75, n. 4.

[5] otiṇṇa, a troublesome word, meaning e.g. set down, put down, descended.

whatever man gives a monastery to the Order. He is to be
called one who grants a boon that is extolled with perspicuity. 28
The giver of a residence that is for warding off dangers to life
by its coolness and so on protects his (own) life-span; therefore the wise say of him that he is of long life-span.[1] 29
[22] There is no strength, beauty nor perspicuity for one dwelling
in a residence that is too warm or too cool. Therefore he who
is the giver of a monastery gives strength and beauty, perspicuity too. 30
From constant protection in various ways against the arising
of anguish in the world, from cold, heat, creeping things and
wind and sun, the giver of a monastery is very happy. 31
Cold, heat, wind, sun, bites and rain, creeping things, beasts
of prey and so forth are anguish. Inasmuch as the giver of a
residence[2] wards (them) off, he therefore knows the welfare of
others. 32
Whoever with his thoughts at peace, joyous, gives a monastery
that because it is an enjoyment in a becoming is a delight to
the mind, is to be called a giver of all lofty qualities beginning
with moral habit. 33
Getting rid of the stain of avarice and of greed, he gives a
habitation, an abode of special qualities. As one blown out[3]
there, in heaven beyond he is surely born, griefless. 34
If a man should construct a lovely, charming, superb monastery and monks should live therein, he should give them food
and drink and clothing, respectfully, constantly, with his
thoughts at peace. 35
Therefore, sire, in enjoyment in becomings, in delight repeatedly experienced, through the fruit of the gift of a
monastery, there is peace, happiness, and afterwards he goes
on griefless. 36

So when the king of sages had given thanks to Bimbisāra, the king of men, for the gift of the monastery, he rose from his seat surrounded by the Order of monks. With the lustre[4] of his own physical frame which was of the greatest loveliness making the cities, groves, mansions and so on (look) as though they had been

[1] āyuppada.
[2] BvAC nivāsa, BvAB vihāra.
[3] khitta.
[4] pabhā; 4 kinds at A ii 139.

sprinkled with gold-dust[1], he entered the Great Monastery in the Bamboo Grove with the peerless grace of an Awakened One, with the illimitable splendour of an Awakened One.

> In the restful monastery in the Bamboo Grove, there the Tathāgata's mind delighted. The wise one dwelt in divers monasteries beholding those who were accessible to instruction. 37

[**23**] Then while the Lord was staying there, King Suddhodana heard, "My son has practised austerities for six years, attained the supremely highest Self-Awakening, and turned the glorious Wheel of Dhamma; he has reached Rājagaha and is staying in the Great Monastery in the Bamboo Grove". He sent for a chief minister and said, "Come, my good man, when you have arrived[2] at Rājagaha in the company of a thousand men, say on my behalf, 'Your father, King Suddhodana, wants to see you'. Come back bringing my son." He answered the king in assent, saying, "Very good, your majesty," and having gone along the road for sixty yojanas in company with the thousand men, he entered the monastery at a time when Dhamma was being taught. He thought, "Let be the message sent by the king", and stood still surrounded by his company; on hearing the Teacher's teaching of Dhamma, he attained arahantship as he stood there together with the thousand men. He asked for the going forth. The Lord, saying, "Come, monks", stretched forth his hand. At that very moment all those, becoming bearers of bowls and robes made by psychic power and being suitably attired like Elders of a hundred years' standing, surrounded the Lord.

The king, thinking, "Neither does he come back nor is a message from him heard", nine times sent messengers in a similar manner. Not even one of these nine thousand men told the king or delivered a message: all, attaining arahantship, went forth. Then the king thought, "Who will do my bidding?" and, surveying all the royal forces, he saw Udāyin[3]. It is said that he was a minister who effected everything for the king, an intimate friend on very confidential terms who, born on the same day as the Bodhisatta[4] had been his playfellow and friend. Then the king addressed him,

[1] Jā i 93.
[2] BvAC patvā, BvAB gantvā.
[3] This is Kāḷudāyin. See also ThagA 221, CpA 4, ApA 358, 538 for accounts of Suddhodana trying to see his son.
[4] See below, text pp. 131, 276, 298.

saying, "My dear Udāyin, anxious to see my son, I sent out nine thousand men, but not even one man came back or even delivered a message. It is difficult to understand. Is it not possible that as I am coming to the end of my life you could show me my son whom I wish to see while I am still alive?" "I should be able to do so, your majesty, if I am allowed to go forth", he said. "My dear, whether you have gone forth or not, show me my son". He said, "Very good, your majesty", and took the king's message.

On reaching Rājagaha he heard the Teacher's teaching on Dhamma and, attaining arahantship together with a thousand men, was established in the status (of monk by the formula) "Come, monk". On the full-moon day of Phagguna he thought, "The cold season has passed, the rainy season has come, the forest-thickets are in full bloom, the road is fit for travel, it is the time to arrange a meeting with his relations for Him of the Ten Powers". Having approached the Lord, he praised travelling in more than sixty verses[1] so that the Lord would travel to his family's city:

> Now crimson glow the trees, revered one[2], casting their foliage, questing for fruit, like crests of flame they shine. It is time, great hero, for the Sakyans[3].*

[24] It is not too cool, it is not too hot, there is not much dearth of almsfood, the ground is green and grassy: this is the time, great sage.†

Then the teacher said to him, "Why are you praising a journey Udāyin?"

"Revered sir, your father, King Suddhodana, wants to see you. Arrange a meeting with your relations."

"It is well, Udāyin. I will arrange a meeting with my relations. Therefore tell the Order of monks and they will fulfil the observances for a journey".

"Very well, revered sir", and the Elder told the Order of monks.

The teacher departed from Rājagaha surrounded by ten thousand

* Thag 527, quoted ApA 359, 535.
† Jā i 87, both verses.

[1] BvAB gives 64, BvAC the first and the last of these.

[2] bhadante.

[3] The reading above, Bhagīrathānaṁ, is admitted at ThagA. ii 223, which explains that Bhagīratha was a king of old to whose lineage the Sakyan Bhagīrathā belong, and (the Buddha) has a duty towards them. Reading at BvAB, Jā i 87, ThagA is bhagī rasānam. See EV I, notes on v. 527.

young men of family who lived in Aṅga-Magadha and by ten thousand who lived in Kapilavatthu—by twenty thousand monks whose cankers were destroyed. Walking a yojana a day, he reached Kapilavatthu in two months. Just as the Lord arrived some Kāsiyans said, "We will see the best relation of ours", and finding the place where the Lord was staying and observing that the Park of Nigrodha the Sakyan was delightful, they arranged for every kind of attention: going out to meet the Lord holding perfumes and flowers, all their limbs adorned with ornaments, and honouring him with the perfumes, flowers and scented powders and revering him, they went to Nigrodha's Park itself. There the Lord, surrounded by the twenty thousand whose cankers were destroyed, sat down on the Buddha-seat that had been made ready. But the Sakyans were conceited by nature, stiff with conceit, and thinking, "Prince Siddhattha is younger than we are, our junior brother, a sister's son, a nephew", they said to many young princes, "Do you pay homage, we will sit very close to you". As they were sitting thus the Lord, perceiving their intention, thought, "These relations do not pay homage to me because of their having grown old in vain[1] nor do they know of what kind is a Buddha, of what kind a Buddha's power, nor that a Buddha is of this kind, a Buddha's power of this kind. Come, showing them my own Buddha-power and power of psychic potency, I shall perform a marvel. Creating in the sky a Walk consisting of all the jewels[2] spanning the ten-thousand world-system, pacing up and down there, and perceiving the intention of the populace, I could teach Dhamma." Accordingly it was said by the recensionists to show the Lord's reasoning:

I 3 As these men with devas do not know of what kind is this
Buddha, supreme among men, nor of what kind is his
power of psychic potency, power of wisdom, of what kind
is the power of a Buddha, benevolent towards the world—

[25] 4 As these men with devas do not know that of this kind is
this Buddha, supreme among men, and of this kind is his
power of psychic potency, power of wisdom, of this kind
is the power of a Buddha, benevolent towards the world—

5 Come, I will display the unsurpassed power of a Buddha:
in the zenith I will create a Walk adorned with jewels.[3]

[1] moghajiṇṇa as at Dh 260. [2] Cf. DhA iii 163. [3] Quoted CpA 5.

3 Therein *as these do not*[1] *know* means as these do not[1] know. The syllable *na* is for negation; the syllable *hi* is a particle intimating cause. Inasmuch as devas and mankind beginning with these relations of mine do not know my powers of psychic potency nor the Buddha-powers which have not been manifested, that a Buddha is of this kind, a Buddha's power of this kind, therefore I will display my Buddha-power and power of psychic potency. That is the meaning.

3 *Men with devas*: herein *devas* intend devas by rebirth[2]. With devas means together with devas. Who are these? Men, men and those belonging to devas (are) men with devas. Or, a deva is a deva by convention[2], for example King Suddhodana, so that, saying, "With his majesty (devena) King Suddhodana" means that "men with devas" are the people who are (his) relations. With devas, men with Suddhodana, men with devas, with kings—these relations of mine do not know my power is the meaning. Moreover the remaining devas[3] are included, for all devas are called devas according to the meaning of deva. Enjoyment and so on is the aim in the natural condition[4] of devas. Or, devas and men are devas-and-men, men together with devas are men with devas. Who are these? "Worlds[5]" should be understood as a remaining expression.

3 *Buddha*[6] means awakened[7], thoroughly awakened to the four true things. As was said:

> Thoroughly known by me is what was to be thoroughly known, and developed is what was to be developed, got rid of is what was to be got rid of, therefore, brahman, I am Buddha.*

And herein the grammatical construction of the word Buddha should be regarded as being in the active voice.[8] Indeed that Lord is fully self-awakened, thus he is recognized and known by devas

* M ii 145, Sn 558, Thag 828, quoted VA 115, UdA 84, Vism 201, etc.

[1] na h'ete . . . na hi ete.

[2] These two categories of devas, with the third category (not mentioned here, but see text p. 30), are briefly explained at Vbh 422, MA i 33, KhA 123, VbhA 518.

[3] Probably referring to the third category, see preceding note.

[4] dhātu-attha, taking attha as aim.

[5] loka can mean people, mankind, see text p. 11f.

[6] Cf. long exegesis of Buddha at KhA 14ff.

[7] buddha.

[8] kattukāraka, not in PED.

and men who have arrived at eminent attainments[1]. Herein the grammatical construction of the word Buddha should be regarded as being in the passive voice:[2] he is awakened in the sense "There is awakening for him". That means he is one having awakening. All this should be understood in accordance with grammatical science.

3 *Of what kind* means: what kind, being like what, equal to what, of what colour, of what (physical) form, tall or short?

3 *Supreme among men* means supreme among men is of men or among men the supreme, the best.

3 *Power of psychic potency*[3] means herein in the sense of succeeding, the psychic potency produced, and psychic potency in the sense of attainment. Or, psychic potency means beings succeed with it, thus they are successful, enriched, excellent. [**26**] And it is tenfold as is said*: Ten kinds of psychic potency. What ten? The psychic potency of resolute determination, the psychic potency of transformation . . . of mind-made (body) . . . by the intervention of knowledge . . . by the intervention of concentration, the psychic potency of ariyans, the psychic potency born of the fruition of kamma, the psychic potency of the meritorious, the psychic potency consisting in lore, the psychic potency in the sense of succeeding due to right exertion (applied) here or there.

This is a difference between these: normally one, he adverts his mind to a manifold; having adverted it to a hundred or to a thousand, he resolutely determines with knowledge: I am a manifold. Thus the psychic potency shown after exposing (the above summary) is called the psychic potency of resolute determination because it is produced by resolute determination.

This is its meaning: having entered on the fourth meditation as a support for the super-knowings and having emerged from it, if he wishes to be a hundredfold, he says, "I am a hundredfold, I am a hundredfold"; and having done the preliminary work with thoughts of the preliminary work in the sensual sphere, having entered again on the meditation as a support for the super-knowings, and emerging from that but adverting again, he resolutely determines. Thus with a kind of resolute determination he

* Pṭs ii 205, Vism 378ff.

[1] E.g. fruits of the Way.

[2] kammakāraka, not in PED.

[3] iddhibala. Iddhi is explained at some length at Vism 378ff.

is a hundredfold and a thousandfold and so on. This is the purport. Therein a mind (set on) meditation as a support takes a sign for its objective support, thoughts of preliminary work have a hundred objective supports or certain objective supports from among a thousand. And these are due to appearance, not due to description. The mind of resolute determination has a hundred objective supports, but that mind in absorption is like a state of consciousness[1] that, belonging to the fourth meditation in the corporeal sphere, arises immediately as one.

Herein, a monk, abandoning his normal form, shows himself in the form of a boy or shows himself in the form of a nāga or shows himself in the form of a bird or shows himself as a diverse military array—thus the psychic potency of transformation is so called because it is a psychic potency for the abandoning and alteration of the normal form.

Herein, a monk creates from this body another body having visible form, mind-made, complete in all limbs with no defect in the sense-faculties[2]. In this way the psychic potency of the mind-made (body) is so called because it is a psychic potency occurring as the production of another mind-made physical frame inside the physical frame.

A distinction brought about by reaching the knowledge of arahantship that is to be acquired either before the knowledge has arisen or after or at the moment is called the psychic potency of the intervention of knowledge. There was the psychic potency of the intervention of knowledge in regard to the venerable Bakkula[3] and in regard to (the venerable) Saṅkicca,[4] and their story should be told here.

A distinction brought about by reaching serenity either before or after or at the moment of concentration is called the psychic potency of the intervention of concentration. There was the psychic potency of the intervention of concentration in the venerable Sāriputta[5] . . . in the venerable Sañjīva[6] . . . in the venerable

[1] gotrabhū. On this term see D. Seyfort Ruegg, "Pali gotta/gotra and the term gotrabhū" in *Buddhist Studies in Honour of I. B. Horner*, 1974, p. 199ff.

[2] D i 77.

[3] Story given at Vism 379, MA iv 190, ThagA ii 83. BvAB reads Bākula.

[4] See DhA ii 240, ThagA ii 254, Vism 379. These two, Bakkula and Saṅkicca, with Bhūtapāla are given as examples at Pṭs ii 211.

[5] See Ud 39.

[6] M i 333

Khāṇukoṇḍañña[1] . . . in the laywoman follower Uttarā[2] . . . in the laywoman follower Sāmavatī.[3] Their stories should be told here. But not in detail by me as there is benefit in omitting the blemish of detail in a book.

What is the psychic potency of ariyans? As to this, if a monk desires, "May I abide perceiving the unrepulsive in the repulsive" [27] he abides perceiving the unrepulsive. If he desires, "May I abide perceiving the repulsive in the unrepulsive" he abides perceiving the repulsive. He abides there with equanimity, mindful and clearly conscious[4]. This is called the psychic potency of ariyans from its occurring only in ariyans who have achieved mastery over their minds.

What is the psychic potency born of the fruition of kamma? Beginning with going above ground, the psychic potency born of the fruition of kamma is that of all birds, of all devas, and of some men belonging to the beginning of the eon and of inhabitants of the states of suffering.[5]

What is the psychic potency of the meritorious? A wheel-turning king goes above ground with his four-factored army. A golden mountain-slope eighty cubits high was produced for the householder Jaṭilaka[6]: this is the psychic potency of the meritorious. The householder Ghosita's safe survival when in seven places attempts were made to kill him[7] is the psychic potency of the meritorious. The appearance to the merchant Meṇḍaka of rams consisting of the seven jewels in a place that was a small area of land[8] is the psychic potency of the meritorious.

What is the psychic potency consisting in lore? The psychic potency consisting in lore begins in these ways: experts in the lore (sorcerers), having pronounced the lore (spells), go above ground and show an elephant in space, in the air . . . and they show a diverse military array.[9]

Having done this or that work when variously reborn is psychic

[1] Cf. DhA ii 254.
[2] AA i 451.
[3] AA i 418, ItA 29. These five are given as examples at Pṭs ii 212, Vism 380.
[4] Pṭs ii 212, Vism 381–2.
[5] Pṭs ii 213, Vism 382.
[6] DhA iv 216, Vism 383 cite five meritorious people of whom three appear above. Cf. AA i 415.
[7] DhA i 174, reading Ghosaka.
[8] Ibid. iii 364.
[9] Pṭs ii 213.

potency in the sense of succeeding due to right exertion and it is called psychic potency in the sense of succeeding due to right exertion. The power of this tenfold psychic potency is called the power of psychic potency. The meaning is that *they do not know this power of psychic potency* of mine.

3 *Power of wisdom* means: the intention is that bestowing the advantage of all worldly and supermundane special qualities is the power of wisdom of the way to arahantship. Neither do they know that. Some say that the power of wisdom is a synonym for the six knowledges that are not shared (by Buddhas) with others.[1]

3 *The power of a Buddha*: here an Awakened One's power means an Awakened One's might or the knowledges of Him of the Ten Powers[2]. Therein the knowledges of Him of the Ten Powers means the knowledge of what is and what is not causal occasion, the knowledge and cognizance of past, future and present fruition of deeds, the knowledge of the courses leading everywhere[3], the knowledge and cognizance of the world with its various and divers features, the knowledge of the divers characters (of beings), the knowledge of inclinations and proclivities, the knowledge as it really is of the defilements in, purification of, emergence from the attainments of meditation, of the deliverances and of concentration, the knowledge and recollection of former habitations, the knowledge of the deceasing (hence) and uprising (elsewhere of beings), the knowledge of the destruction of the cankers—these ten. A Buddha's power is a synonym for these ten knowledges.

4 *Of this kind* means of this kind[4], or this itself is the reading.

5 *Come* is a particle for starting (the line).[5]

5 *I* demonstrates oneself. What is that to say? It is to say that inasmuch as these relations of mine know neither a Buddha's power nor a Buddha's special qualities [**28**] and because they have grown old in vain and, through conceit, do not pay homage to me who am the eldest in all the world, there is therefore in them a sign of conceit; having broken this, it is said a Buddha's power could be shown in the sense of paying homage.

[1] asādhāraṇañāṇa, referred to at SnA 605, Miln. 285, Nāmarūpaparicchedа 123, and below, text p. 185.

[2] Cf. M i 169ff., A v 32ff. where these ten powers are given slightly differently and in greater detail.

[3] I.e. to all bourns.

[4] edisan ti īdisaṁ.

[5] Jā vi 188; cf. DA 237.

5 *I will display* means I could display[1]; or, "I will display[2]" is a reading; the meaning is the same.

5 *Power of a Buddha* means the might of an Awakened One or the eminence of an Awakened One's knowledge.

5 *Unsurpassed* means not surpassed[3].

5 *A Walk* means a place that could be walked in.

5 *I will create* means I could create[4]. "I am creating a Walk" is also a reading; the meaning is the same.

5 *In the zenith* means in the sky.

5 *Adorned with* all the *jewels* means adorned, ornamented in the sense of producing delight with all the ten (kinds of) jewels: with pearls, gems, beryl, mother-of-pearls, quartz, corals[5], silver, gold, cat's eyes, rubies[6]. That is: adorned with all the jewels. Some read, "In the zenith adorned with jewels"[7]. Then as the Lord was thus considering, the earth-devas and so forth who lived in the ten-thousand world-system, joyful at heart, gave their approval.

It is to be understood that the beginning of the (next) verse was established by the recensionists for making this matter clear.

I 6 Devas of earth, those belonging to the Great Regents, the Thirty-Three, and Yama's devas, and the Happy Ones, those who rejoice in creating, those too with power over others' creatings, and those of Brahmā's retinue, blissful, made a far-flung clamour[8].

6 Therein (devas of) *earth* means those who are on the earth. They are in palaces[9], mountain-slopes, woods and trees.

6 *Those belonging to the Great Regents* means associated with the Great Regents[10]. The devas who are in the sky, having heard the sound of the devas on the earth, then the cloud-devas of

[1] dassayissāmī ti dasseyyaṁ.

[2] dassessāmi.

[3] anuttaran ti niruttaraṁ.

[4] māpayissāmī ti māpeyyan ti.

[5] To here as at Miln 380.

[6] Cf. the ten at Vin ii 238, also see Miln 267.

[7] As in the verse. Apparently the commentator prefers "with all the jewels".

[8] Quoted at CpA 5.

[9] Perhaps pāsāda, temples, palaces, terraces, should read pāsāṇa, stone, rock, which at VbhA 64 is compared in size with pabbata, mountain slope, here the next word. But at Vin v 171 we find both pāsāṇa and pāsāda.

[10] Many of these devas occur, with some exegesis, at VbhA 519f. See also M Sta. 120.

thunder[1], then the cloud-devas of warmth, then the cloud-devas of cold, then the cloud-devas of rain, then the cloud-devas of wind, then the four Great Regents, then the Thirty-Three, then Yama's (devas), then the Happy Ones, then the devas who enjoy creating, then those devas with power over others' creatings, then those in Brahmā's retinue, then the Brahmapurohitā, then the Great Brahmās, then the devas of Limited Radiance, then those of Boundless Radiance, then those of Light, then those of Limited Lustre, then those of Boundless Lustre, then the Lustrous devas, then the Vehapphala[2] devas, then the Avihā devas, then the Atappā, then the Sudassā, then the Sudassī, then the Akaniṭṭha devas, having heard the sound, made a mighty sound. The meaning is that, except for those without consciousness and beings in the immaterial spheres, all devas, mankind, nāgas and so on in the places where the news was heard shouted out their acclamation, their hearts given over to zest.

6 *Blissful* means being joyous at heart, full of zest and happiness.

6 *Far-flung* means widespread.

Then the Teacher, immediately after he had considered, having entered upon the attainment of the white kasiṇa[3], resolutely determined "Let there be light in the ten-thousand world-systems." [29] Through the resolute determination of his mind there was light at once from the earth as far as the Akaniṭṭha abode. Accordingly it was said:

I 7 Illumined were the earth, together with the worlds of the devas and the numerous baseless spaces between the worlds, and the dense gloom was dissipated when they saw the wonderful marvel.

7 Therein *illumined* means made clear.

7 The *earth* means: herein this earth is fourfold:[4] the earth that has characteristic marks, the earth with its constituents, earth as a (meditational) sign, the earth so-called. When it is said in such

[1] For this and the next four groups of cloud-devas cf. S iii 254ff., also DPPN s.v. Valāhakāyikādevā.

[2] Francis Story, *Gods and the Universe*, Buddhist Publication Society, Kandy, 1972, p. 12–13, translates this and the next five classes, taking these devas as Brahmās, respectively as Greatly Rewarded, Immobile, Serene, Beautiful, Clear-Sighted, Supreme Brahmās.

[3] See A v 46.

[4] Cf. MA i 25.

contexts as, "What, your reverence, is the internal earth-element? Whatever is internal, referable to an individual, hard, solid"*, this is the earth that has characteristic marks. "Whatever monk should dig the earth or get it dug"† means the earth with its constituents; and the hair of the head and so on, and the twenty parts of iron and copper and so on that are external and the earth together with the constituents of colours and so on is called the earth with its constituents. "One comprehends the earth-kasiṇa"‡ means the earth as a (meditational) sign and the earth as an objective support for meditation. One who attains meditation by the earth-kasiṇa, reborn in a deva-world, on returning acquires the name of a deva of earth; thus it is said, "The devas of water and earth"§—among these this is the earth so-called, and what is called earth should be understood as a description. But here the intention is the earth with its constituents.

7 *Worlds of the devas* (sadevakā) means worlds with devas. "With devatās" (sadevatā) is also a reading if it is better. The meaning is that the world of men together with that of the devas was illumined.

7 *Numerous* (puthu) means many (bahu)[1].

7 *Spaces between the worlds* means that this is a synonym for the Nirayas[2] and spheres of asuras. And that between the three world-systems is one space between the worlds. It is like the space in the middle of three cart-wheels when they are standing knocking against one another. Each space between the worlds measures eight thousand yojanas[3].

7 *Baseless* means without support from beneath[3].

7 *And the gloom* means the darkness.

7 *Dense* means thick, solid, permanently dark for lack of light from the sun or moon.

7 *Dissipated* means destroyed.

7 *When* means when the Lord out of pitifulness for creatures diffused light so as to work the marvel, then the dense gloom in the space between the worlds was lost and destroyed.

7 *Wonderful* means worthy of a finger's snap, worthy of snapping one's fingers in astonishment.

* M i 185. † Vin iv 33. ‡ M ii 14. § D ii 259.

[1] Cf. Nd1 11 puthū kāme ti bahū kāme.
[2] naraka. Lists of purgatories at Divy 67, Mhvu i 5.
[3] Cf. DA 433, MA iv 177.

7 *Marvel* (*pāṭihīra*) means a marvel from the removing of opponents, or it is a marvel that one works (paṭiharati) thinking that the thoughts of creatures **[30]** are overcome by false views and conceit, or it is a marvel that one works against (paṭi-āharati) the composure of creatures of little faith. *Paṭihera* is also a reading; the meaning is the same. Herein this is a synonym for the eminence of producing light.

7 *When they saw the wonderful marvel*: herein the meaning is to be understood by introducing this phrase: devas, men and beings arisen in the spaces between the worlds, having seen this wonderful marvel of the Lord's, came to extreme zest and satisfaction. Otherwise neither does the end fit the beginning nor the beginning the end. There was now not only light in all the worlds of men and of devas, but there was light too everywhere in the threefold world that is regarded as constructions, beings, location.[1] Showing the meaning, this verse was spoken:

I 8 Among devas, heavenly musicians, men, demons, a magnificent far-flung radiance appeared in both this world and that beyond, below and above, across and around.

8 Therein *devas* means devas by convention, devas by rebirth, devas by purification[2]. All these devas are included here. Devas and heavenly musicians and men and demons are *devas*, *heavenly musicians*, *men*, *demons*. Together with (saha) devas, heavenly musicians, men, demons means with (sa[3]) devas, heavenly musicians, men, demons. But what is that world? In that world with (sa) devas, heavenly musicians, men, demons.

8 *Radiance* means light.

8 *Magnificent* means herein that this word magnificent appears in passages as sweet, best, far-flung in measure[4]. So it appears as sweet in passages such as "They eat and partake of magnificent (uḷārāni) solid foods and magnificent (uḷārāni) soft foods",* and as best in such passages as "The revered Vacchāyana praises the recluse Gotama with magnificent (uḷārāya) praise",† and as far-

* M i 238. † M i 175.

[1] See text p. 11f.
[2] See text p. 25.
[3] Trans. in verse "among".
[4] DA iii 878, SA iii 208. VvA 10–11 ascribes three meanings to uḷāra: great, excellent, best.

flung in such passages as "The measureless magnificent (uḷāro) effulgence surpassing the deva-majesty of devas"*. Here this is to be understood as best.

8 *Far-flung* means measureless.

8 *Appeared* means originated, arose, was produced.

8 *In this world and that beyond* means in this world of men and in the deva-world beyond.

8 *In both* means in both of these. It should be understood as if in what is internal and external in both.

8 *Below* means in the Nirayas beginning with Avīci.

8 *And above* means from the height of becoming and above in the open sky.

8 *Across* means and from across in the ten-thousand world-systems.

8 *And around*: the meaning is that having dispelled the wide-spread darkness, [31] a radiance was manifested flooding the worlds and the regions in the way said. Or the meaning is that the radiance remained after having suffused the huge measureless region from across all round.

Then when the Lord had suffused light throughout the ten-thousand world-systems, entering on the fourth meditation as a basis for the super-knowings, emerging from that and adverting (his mind) by a mental act of resolute determination, he rose up into the sky and displayed the Marvel of the Double in the midst of a vast company of devas and men as though he were showering the dust of the feet over the heads of those relations (of his).

From the text this should be understood thus:

What is the Tathāgata's knowledge in regard to the Marvel of the Double? As to this the Tathāgata works the Marvel of the Double[1] that is not shared by disciples: from the upper part of the body a flame of fire proceeded, from the lower part of the body a stream of water proceeded; from the lower part of the body a flame of fire proceeded, from the upper part of the body a stream of water proceeded; from the front of his body . . . from the back of

* D ii 12, M iii 120.

[1] DhA iii 214f. explains how this was done as does our text, with some variations; cf. Jā i 77, 88, Pṭs i 125, DA 57.

his body . . . from the back of his body . . . from the front of his body . . .; from his right eye, from his left eye . . . from his left eye, from his right eye . . .; from his right ear, from his left ear . . . from his left ear, from his right ear . . .; from his right nostril, from his left nostril . . . from his left nostril, from his right nostril . . .; from his right shoulder, from his left shoulder . . . from his left shoulder, from his right shoulder . . .; from his right hand, from his left hand . . . from his left hand, from his right hand . . .; from his right side, from his left side . . . from his left side, from his right side . . .; from his right foot, from his left foot . . . from his left foot, from his right foot . . .; from each finger, from the spaces between the fingers . . . from the spaces between the fingers, from each finger . . .; from the pore of the skin of every hair of his body a flame of fire proceeded, from the pore of the skin of every hair of his body a stream of water proceeded; rays of the six colours proceeded: blue, yellow, red, white, crimson and opaque brilliant. The Lord walked up and down, a counterpart (of him) stood or sat or lay down. The Lord stood, the counterpart walked up and down or sat or lay down. The Lord sat, the counterpart walked up and down or stood or lay down. The Lord lay down, the counterpart walked up and down or stood or sat. The counterpart walked up and down, the Lord stood or sat or lay down. The counterpart stood, the Lord walked up and down or sat or lay down. The counterpart sat, the Lord walked up and down or stood or lay down. The counterpart lay down, the Lord walked up and down or stood or sat. This is to be understood as the Tathāgata's knowledge of the Marvel of the Double.

Because of the Lord's attainment of the heat-kasiṇa the flame of fire proceeded from the upper part of his body. Because of his attainment of the water-kasiṇa the stream of water proceeded from the lower part of his body. The words "From the upper part of his body a flame of fire proceeded and from the lower part of his body a stream of water" are to be taken to show that from the part (of the body) from which the stream of water proceeded, from that part the flame of fire proceeded; and from that part from which the flame of fire proceeded, from that part the stream of water proceeded. This is the method also in the other expressions. But the flame of fire was not mixed with the stream of water, nor the stream of water with the flame of fire. But among the rays each second ray proceeded at the same moment as the first ray as though they were pairs, yet there was no procedure of two mental acts at one moment. For, owing to the buoyancy of the sub-consciousness of Buddhas these rays are as though they proceed in five ways at one moment from a dweller by mental acts. But the adverting (of the mind), the preparation, and the resolute determination for producing these rays are separate. Thus, for the blue ray [32] the Lord attained the blue-kasiṇa, for the yellow ray and so on he attained the yellow-kasiṇa and so on. It is thus that, while the Lord was performing the Marvel of the Double, it was a time of adorning the entire ten-thousand world-system. Accordingly it was said:

I 9 The superb being, unexcelled, guider away, teacher, was honoured by devas and men; of great might, with the mark of a hundred merits, he displayed the wonderful marvel.

9 Therein *superb being*[1] means superb, glorious, best among all beings with his own special qualities of morality and so forth, it means superb being. Or, a superb being is the superb of beings where being is a name for consciousness.[2] Best, superb, because he is a being with the ten powers, the four confidences, the knowledges not shared (by disciples) means superb being;[1] by virtue of there being a "container"[3] a being[4], superb[4], superb being[1]. If it is a being who is superb[5] it is to be taken thus from a reading of the word superb[6] as the first part of the compound; this is not a defect.[7] From the absence of a fixed order and from there being a number of (ways of) expression it should be understood as words like superb man[8], superb individual, glorious man, and so forth. Or he of whom the being[9] is superb is a superb being[10]. And here too

[1] sattuttamo.

[2] sattan ti viññāṇassa (BvAB ñāṇassa) nāmaṁ, where sattan, neuter, perhaps, means life, life-principle; cf. PvA 40 gatasattan ti vigatajīvitaṁ, of an ox that was dead.

[3] samānādhikaraṇavasena. See MR & Ill 114 on this meaning of adhikaraṇa at KhA. 106, MA i 9. Taken as "locality" at Expos i 82 (Asl 61) as adhikaraṇa also has the meaning of locative case.

[4] satto uttamo.

[5] uttamasatto.

[6] uttama.

[7] BvAC dosa, BvAB bheda.

[8] naruttama as in I.10.

[9] sattan, neuter again, see n. above.

[10] sattuttamo.

if the first word in the compound becomes superb[1], saying, being who is superb[2] according to the reading where it is the first in the compound means a master of the mind, a master of words[3]—as it is said herein; this a not a defect. Or, from the attributes of the two, the first reading should be regarded as (one who has) "kindled fire."[4]

9 *Guider away*[5] means guider away in that he restrains[6] and tames beings in regard to many a wrong practice of discipline[7].

9 *Teacher* means teacher in that he instructs beings in a fit and proper way in respect of matters belonging to the here-now and to a future state.

9 *Was* means was[8].

9 *Honoured by devas and men*[9] means devas amuse and enjoy themselves with the five deva-like kinds of sense pleasures; men because there is a fulness of mind; devas and men are devas-and-men. Honoured by devas and men is honoured by devas and men[10]. He is honoured by being honoured with flowers and so forth, and he is honoured with requisites; the meaning is "esteemed". But why is choice made only of devas and men? Was not the Lord honoured also by animals such as the nāgas Āravāla*, Kāla†, Apalāla*, Dhanapāla,‡ Pārileyyaka§, and other nāgas; and by Sātāgiri||, Āḷavaka, Hemavata¶, Sūciloma**, Khara**, and other yakkhas whose bourns were the downfall? This is true. It must be understood that this was said as a comprehensive demarcation[11] and as a demarcation of individuals who were capable[12] (of reaching the higher achievements).

* References to all these nāgas (serpents or elephants) given in DPPN.
† Is this Kālahatthi?
‡ Part of this elephant's story under his name of Nālāgiri is told at Vin ii 194f.
§ Story of this elephant at Vin i 352f., Ud 41.
|| See Sn 153–180. DPPN. gives accounts of these yakkhas, and references.
¶ D ii 256, iii 204.
** S i 207f., Sn p. 47f. Khara is called Kharaloma in BvAB.

[1] uttamo. [2] uttamasatto. [3] cittagū padvagū.
[4] āhitaggi, one who has placed the sacred fire upon the altar, a sacrificer, M-W., but the meaning could also be "a fire provided with fuel".
[5] vināyaka, one who disciplines.
[6] vineti. [7] vinaya. [8] ahū ti ahosi.
[9] BvAB and BvAC differ in some respects in this paragraph. Mostly I follow BvAB.
[10] devamanussehi pūjito devamanussapūjito.
[11] ukkaṭṭhaparicchedа as at SnA 229, 231.
[12] bhabbapuggalaparicchedа. I can find no other reference to this compound.

9 *Of great might* means possessed of the great might of a Buddha.

9 *Mark of a hundred merits* means that in the unending world-spheres all beings may each one perform a deed of merit a hundred times. The Bodhisatta was reborn after he had by himself alone performed the deed a hundredfold done by all these other people. Therefore he is called one having the mark of a hundred merits[1]. But some say that for every hundred deeds of merit the marks appear one by one. This being so "anyone may become a Buddha" is rejected[2] in the Commentaries.

[33] 9 (*He*) *displayed* means he displayed the Marvel of the Double to the great astonishment of all devas, men and so forth.

When the Teacher had performed the Marvel of the Double in the sky and had surveyed the mental character of the populace, being anxious to teach them a suitable teaching of Dhamma as he walked up and down, he created the Jewel-Walk consisting of all the jewels and extending over the ten-thousand world-systems. Accordingly it was said:

I 10 Requested by the glorious deva, he, one with vision, supreme among men, leader of the word, reflecting on the matter then created a well-wrought Walk there with all the jewels.

10 Therein *he* means that teacher.

10 *Requested*: the meaning is requested for a teaching of Dhamma on the first (day) itself in the eighth week.

10 *By the glorious deva* means by Brahmā Sahampati.

10 *One with vision*: herein the meaning is he relishes; the even and the uneven of vision are turned to account[3]. But this vision is twofold: the eye of knowledge and the bodily eye. Therein the eye of knowledge is fivefold: the Buddha-eye, vision of Dhamma, seer of all, deva-like vision, eye of wisdom.[4] Of these the Buddha-eye is called knowledge of (others') inclinations and underlying tendencies as well as knowledge of the higher or lower state of the

[1] Referred to at Vism 211.

[2] BvAC reads pakkhitta, inserted; BvAB paṭikkhitta, rejected.

[3] Cf. Vism 481 for cakkhati (relishes) and vibhāveti (turns to account) in exegesis of cakkhu. Cakkhu is eye, eyesight, vision. See also ItA ii 26.

[4] Cf. Nd2 235 MA ii 179, Mhvs i 158–60.

faculties of others; it has been handed down in the phrase "He surveyed the world with the Buddha-eye"*.

Vision of Dhamma is called the three lower ways and the three fruits, as has been handed down in the phrase "There arose vision of Dhamma, dustless, stainless"†.

Seer of all means what has been handed down in the phrase "As, O Wisdom fair, Seer of all, ascending the terraced heights that consist of Dhamma"‡.

Deva-like vision[1] means a super-knowing that has arisen by means of augmentation of light[2], knowledge associated with thought, as has been handed down in the phrase "By purified deva-like vision"§.

Eye of wisdom[1] means "vision arose, knowledge arose"|| as has been handed down in the phrase "The eye of wisdom is knowledge of former habitations and so on".

Bodily eye[1] is called "Because of eye and material shape"¶ which here is spoken of as bodily eye[3]. But it is twofold: vision with accessories and vision as sensitivity. Where this lump of flesh is obstructed from reaching the eye in the eye-cavity there are the four elements and colour, scent, taste, nutritive essence[4], production, life-principle, being, sensitivity of vision, [34] sensitivity of body: in brief, there are thirteen accessories. In detail—when beings are arising there are four originations, thirty-six sensitivities of the life-principle, being, vision and sensitivities of body; and these four originations by kamma make forty accessories. This is called vision with accessories.[5] But it is called vision as sensitivity when, consisting of sensitivity, able to see material shapes, it is fixed on the circle of perception which is encompassed by a dark circle by means of having determined a white circle. But all these are onefold as to impermanence, as to being constructed; twofold

* Vin i 6.
† Vin i 11 16, D i 110, ii 288, S iv 47, A iv 186, etc.
‡ As at text p. 10.
§ M i 183, etc.
|| Vin i 11, etc.
¶ M i 111, etc.

[1] One of the three cakkhūni given at D iii 219, It 52.
[2] Light-kasiṇa, ItA ii 28.
[3] Cf. Vism 20 444.
[4] Asl 82 306.
[5] Cf. ibid. 306–7.

as to having cankers or not, as to the mundane and supermundane; threefold as to plane, as to a triad of grasping;[1] fourfold as to an objective (meditational) support not determined in regard to the extremely small and the immeasurable; fivefold in respect of material shapes, nibbāna, non-material shapes, and all that are and that are not objective (meditational) supports; sixfold they are in respect of the Buddha-eye and so on—so that as these quotations refer to the eyes of the Lord, the Lord is called One with vision.

10 *Reflecting on the matter* means that the intention is that after creating the Walk, which was a sign for the teaching of Dhamma, having investigated and considered the welfare and good of devas and mankind.

10 (He) *created* (māpayi) means he created (māpesi).

10 *Leader of the world* means a leader in that he leads the world towards deliverance and heaven.

10 *Well-wrought* means well-wrought[2] and finished.

10 *With all the jewels* means consisting of the ten kinds of jewels.[3]

And now, in order to show the Lord's success in the three kinds of marvels, it was said:

I 11 The Lord was master of the three marvels: psychic potency, the speaking of suitable discourses, and instruction[4]. The leader of the world created a well-wrought Walk with all the jewels.

11 Herein *psychic potency* means the kinds of psychic potency are the marvel of psychic potency, such as having been one one becomes manifold and having been manifold one becomes one, as occurs in the contexts.

11 *Speaking of suitable discourses* means knowing the mental character of another (person); the speaking of suitable discourses is a marvel constant in the teaching of Dhamma by disciples and by Buddhas.

11 *Instruction* means that instruction is a marvel in the sense that it is exhortation that is suitable to the disposition of this (person) or that. These are the three marvels.

[1] after kāma rūpa arūpa.
[2] suniṭṭhitan ti suṭṭhu niṭṭhitaṁ, happily concluded.
[3] See text p. 28.
[4] As at D i 212ff., A i 170f.

Herein the marvel of instruction by means of the marvel of psychic potency was habitual to Mahā Moggallāna, the marvel of instruction by means of the marvel of the speaking of suitable discourses to the Captain under Dhamma[1]. But the marvel of instruction is the constant teaching of the Dhamma of the Buddhas.

[35] 11 *Of the three marvels*: the meaning is, among these three marvels.

11 *The Lord* is a term signifying respect and veneration (accorded to him who is) the supreme being and distinguished by all special qualities[2]. And this was said by the Ancients:

"Lord" is the best word, "Lord" is the supreme word. He, deserving respect and veneration, is therefore called Lord.

11 *Master*: the meaning is that in this threefold marvel he had attained mastery, reached mastery. Masteries mean five masteries named as: adverting, attaining, resolutely determining, emerging, reviewing.[3] Herein, he adverts to whatever meditation (he chooses) where, when and for as long as he wishes; he has no difficulty in adverting; ability to advert quickly is called mastery in adverting. Likewise he attains whatever meditation (he chooses) where . . . he likes; he has no difficulty in attaining; ability to attain quickly is called mastery in attaining. Ability to remain (in meditation) for a long time is called mastery in resolutely determining. Ability to emerge buoyantly in the same way is called mastery in emerging. But the reviewing impulsions are simply mastery in reviewing. If they arise immediately after adverting they are also called masteries in adverting. Mastery is so-called from the reaching of mastery in these five masteries. Therefore it was said "The Lord was master of the three marvels".

Now, to show how the Jewel-Walk was disposed, verses were spoken beginning:

I 12 In the ten-thousand world-system he displayed like a course of pillars on (each) supreme mountain Sineru, Walks made of jewels.

12 Therein *In the ten-thousand world-system* means among the ten-thousand world-spheres.

[1] Sāriputta.

[2] As at Vism 209. See DA 33, MA i 10 both of which refer to Vism, and also supply the word "all".

[3] Cf. Pṭs 99f., Vism 154f.

12 *On* (*each*) *supreme mountain Sineru* means on the mountain called Great Meru[1].

12 *Like pillars* means making those Mount Sinerus in the ten-thousand world-spheres stand like a course of golden pillars and, creating a Walk above them, he displayed it[1].

12 *Made of jewels* means made of jewels[2].

13 *Spanning the ten-thousand* means: when the Lord was creating the Jewel-Walk he created it making one end stand spanning the brim of the eastern world-sphere and one end (spanning) the brim of the western world-sphere. Therefore it was said:

I 13 The Conqueror created a Walk spanning the ten-thousand; all golden were the sides of that Walk which was made of jewels.

13 Therein *Conqueror* means Conqueror by conquering the enemies that are the defilements.

13 *All golden were the sides* means that the Walk that was fashioned thus [36] was made of gold at both sides, the confines being exquisitely charming. The intention is that it was made of jewels in the middle.

14 *The junction of* (*each pair of*) *beams* should be understood as beams in pairs consisting in a variety of jewels.

14 *Symmetrical*[3] means conformable.

14 *The floor-boards covered with gold* means covered with golden slabs[4]. Above the junctions of the beams were covering planks made of gold.

14 *All golden were the railings* means that the railings too consisted of gold, so that the railing which surrounded the Walk was not mixed with any other jewel.[5]

14 *Well-fashioned on both sides* means fashioned on both sides.[6] The syllable *da* makes a liason between the words.

15 *Strewn over with sand* (*consisting*) *of jewels and pearls* means strewn over with sand consisting of jewels and pearls. Or, "jewels and pearls and sand" means jewels-and-pearls-and-sand—these were strewn over, spread over with jewels, pearls, sand.

15 *Fashioned* means fashioned, made in these ways.

15 *Made of jewels* means the Walk consisted of all the jewels.

[1] Following BvAB.
[2] ratanāmaye ti ratanamaye.
[3] anuvagga, conforming, similar (to each other).
[4] sovaṇṇaphalakatthatā ti sovaṇṇaphalakehi atthatā.
[5] Gold is counted as one of the ten jewels.
[6] d-ubhato passe sunimmitā.

15 *It illumined all the quarters* means it illumined, it lit up even all the ten quarters.

15 *Like him of the hundred rays* means as him of the thousand rays, like the sun.

15 *When he has risen*[1] means is high[2]; for he of the thousand rays, when he has risen high[3], illumines even all the ten quarters, in like manner even one Walk consisting of all the jewels illumined (them).

16 But now, when the Walk was finished, in order to show the Lord's processing there, the verse beginning "Walking up and down in that, the wise one" was spoken.

16 Therein *wise one* means intent on wisdom.

16 *He of the thirty-two glorious Marks* means possessed of the thirty-two Marks of a Great Man[4], with feet of a level tread and soles of the feet (showing wheels) and so forth.

17 *Deva-like* means come into being, born in a deva-world.

17 *Flowers of the Coral Tree* means that among the devas of the Thirty-Three the Coral Tree of the utmost loveliness, a hundred yojanas in circumference all round, is produced as a result of the Koviḷāra tree[5]. When it is blossoming the whole of the deva-city waits for each stage of its fragrant scent; the mansions (of the devas), strewn over with the pollen from its coral-coloured flowers, resemble untarnished gold[6]; and the flowers of this Coral Tree are called the Coral Tree.

17 (They) *showered down on the Walk* means they poured down flowers on to that Jewel-Walk and honoured the Lord with them as he was walking in that Walk in the way described.

17 *All the devas* means the devas of the sensual spheres and so forth.

[37] 18 *The company of devas saw him* means as it was said: even from their own abodes they saw that Lord as he was walking in the Jewel-Walk.

18 *Ten-thousand*: the nominative case in the sense of the locative. Companies of devas in the ten-thousand saw (him) is the meaning.

18 *Joyous*[7] means joyous.[7]

[1] uggata.
[2] udita, risen, high.
[3] abbhuggata.
[4] See D Sta 30, M Sta 91.
[5] DhA i 273; also A iv 117.
[6] navakanaka.
[7] pamoditā . . . pamuditā.

18 *They assembled* means they assembled together.

18 *Elated, exultant* means elated and exultant through zest.

18 *Joyous:*[1] the connexion should be shown now between what is to be said and the devas of the Thirty-Three and so on, otherwise one is not free of the defect of redundancy.[2] Or else, the meaning is: *joyous*, they see that Lord; *elated, exultant, joyous* they assembled together here and there.

Now, in order to show that those who saw and those who assembled together there, were the same, the verse beginning [**I 19**] "The Thirty-Three[3] and Yama's[3] (devas)" was spoken.

19 Therein *minds uplifted* means minds elated through zest and happiness.

19 *Happy* means the state of mind is elated, is happy.

20 *Compassionate for the world's welfare* means compassionate for the world and the world's welfare. Or, compassionate in regard to the world's welfare, compassionate for the world's welfare.[4]

20 *Like*[5] *the orb of the moon high aloft in the zenith*: the meaning here is that they saw the leader, the giver of bliss, brilliant with a Buddha's splendour like the orb of the moon in autumn, newly risen in the sky, full, free from all adversity.[6]

21 (Devas of) *Light*[7] is said as a demarcation of excellence; the (devas of) Limited Splendour, Boundless Splendour, Light should be understood through a division into limited, middle and excellent; all, reborn by means of (experience of) the second meditation, are included.

21 *Lustrous* (devas): here too it is said as a demarcation of excellence. Therefore the (devas of) Limited Lustre, Boundless Lustre, Lustrous (devas) should be understood through a division into limited and so on; all, reborn by means of (experience of) the third meditation, are included.

21 *Vehapphala* (devas): Vehapphala means abundant fruit.[8]

[1] pamoditā.

[2] punarutta dosato; also at text pp. 46, 85; and MA iii 97.

[3] As at text p. 28.

[4] Merely a difference in Pali phraseology here: lokahitena vā anukampakaṁ lokahitānukampakaṁ.

[5] Reading va with Bv against ca in BvA.

[6] upaddava, accident, distress, affliction, risk. Cf. the four upakkilesā, "stains" afflicting the sun and moon at Vin ii 295, A ii 53, and the four roga, "illnesses", disturbances, at Miln 274.

[7] See text p. 28 for these and the following devas; also MA i 35, AA iv 27f.

[8] "Greatly rewarded".

These, reborn by means of (experience of) the fourth meditation, are dwellers on one plane with non-perceiving beings. But above they were shown as belonging to Brahmā's retinue[1], reborn by means of (experience of) the first meditation. Therefore they are not shown here; they are not pointed to here as formless and non-perceiving beings due to the absence of eyes and ears.

21 *And Akaniṭṭha devas* here also are so called because of a demarcation of excellence. Therefore it is to be understood that the five Pure Abodes named Avihā, Atappā, Sudassā, Sudassī, and Akaniṭṭha[2] are included.

21 *Garments and raiment that were very pure and bright* means beautifully pure, very pure, bright, white; the garments they were dressed in[3] and had put on[3] were very pure and bright; [**38**] the meaning is that those very pure and bright garments and raiment they were clothed in were perfectly pure white[4]. "Very pure and bright raiment" is also a reading.

21 *Clasped hands* means having clasped the hands like lotus buds *they stood raising* clasped hands to their heads.

22 *They let fall* means they poured down on.

22 *And flowers*[5] means and blossoms. Or, "flowers"[5] is also a reading. A change of expression is understood but its meaning is the same.

22 *The five-hued* means having five colours. Five colours in respect of the colours green, yellow, red, white and crimson.

22 *Mixed with sandal-wood powder* means mixed with powder from sandal-wood.

22 *They waved wearing apparel* means garments were waved.

22 *Ah, the Conqueror, compassionate for the world's welfare* means Ah, the Conqueror, friendly to the world and Ah, (He who is) compassionate to the world, Ah, the merciful one; and, chanting such words of praise, they let fall the flowers while wearing apparel was being waved.

To show now the words of praise used with these (gestures) the verse was spoken:

I 23 Thou, the teacher, flag and banner, and the sacrificial post

[1] Text p. 28.
[2] See D iii 237.
[3] For nivāseti and pārupati see BD ii 32, n. 2, 3.
[4] paṇḍara, pure white.
[5] pupphaṁ . . . pupphāni, i.e. sing. and pl.

for breathing things, the resting-place, support, and lamp (and island), supreme among men![1]

23 Herein *teacher* means he teaches for the welfare and benefit of this world and the world beyond.

23 *Flag* means like a flag in the sense that homage should be paid to flags; a flag.

23 *Thou, the banner* means Thou art a banner like Indra's banner[2] in the sense of having a (complex) form[3] and in the sense of being good to look upon. Or, as when one has seen in the world the banner of anyone whomsoever this banner is evident as the banner of so-and-so who is the flag-owner, even so the Lord is for arrival at wisdom and nibbāna; having seen the Lord, arrival at nibbāna is evident. Because of this it was said *banner and the sacrificial post*. The meaning is: Thou, a sacrificial post, art erected for the sacrificing of all sacrificial acts beginning with giving to the culmination in the knowledge of the destruction of the cankers, as in the words of the Kūṭadanta-sutta.[4]

23 *Resting-place* means mainstay.

23 *Support* means that as the great earth is the support and foundation for all breathing things because of being what holds them up, so Thou too art a support.

23 *And lamp* means a light. As in the fourfold gloom[5] a light set up shows the shapes of existing beings, so in the darkness of ignorance Thou art a light showing the highest truth to existing beings. Or, as an *island*[6] in the sea is a support for beings shipwrecked in the great sea, [39] so too Thou art like an island for breathing things who are sinking in the ocean of saṁsāra where support is not obtainable.[7]

23 *Supreme of men*[8] means the supreme of men[9], supreme

[1] This ver. also at Ap 20, ver. 79, 422, ver. 9.

[2] The only reference CPD gives to indadhaja is to this passage.

[3] samussaya, a body.

[4] D i 127ff.

[5] Caturaṅge tamasi as at SA i 170; cf. Nd1 355, UdA 354 for explanation of caturaṅga andhakāra.

[6] dīpa is both island and lamp. Here, clearly island is meant. Lamp is glossed as light, padīpa, at the beginning of this paragraph.

[7] alabbhaneyya-patiṭṭhā; cf. MA i 55, Asl 22.

[8] dipaduttama, supreme of bipeds. I think this should be as here, and not "among" as at this ver. in CB. Except in the exegesis that follows, I have used "men" for the less acceptable "biped" which includes birds and some devas as well as men.

[9] dipadānam uttamo, supreme of bipeds.

among men. But here, because there is no exclusive[1] sense, there is no impediment[2] (to using) a compound in the genitive.[3] Hence indeed the construction of the genitive compound in the exclusive sense. And the fully Self-Awakened One is supreme of those having no feet, two feet, four feet, many feet, form, no form, perception, no perception, neither-perception-nor-no-perception. But why is he spoken of here as supreme of bipeds? Because he is quite the best[4]. But in this world the best, when arising, does not arise among the footless, those having four feet or many feet, but arises only among bipeds. Among which bipeds? Among human beings as well as among devas. Arising among human beings, he is reborn as a Buddha able to keep mastery over the thirty thousand and the great thousand world-systems.[5] Arising among devas, he is reborn as Great Brahmā dwelling as master over the ten-thousand world-system. That (Brahmā) becomes the legitimate provider (of a monk's material needs)[6] or the monastic attendant of this one (the Buddha). Thus too he is called supreme among bipeds because he is the best.

24 *Of the ten-thousand world-system* means the world-systems as ten thousand.

24 *Great in psychic potency* means great majesty coupled with great psychic potency.

24 *Attending on* means encircling the Lord all round.

26 *Believing* means they were full of faith.

25 *The bull of men* means the chief of men.

27 *Ah, wonderful*, means herein it is not permanent like the climbing of a mountain for one who is bewildered—that is wonderful; or, as that which happens without a moment's delay is wonderful: "Ah, this is a surprise"—the meaning is that it is connected with a snap of the fingers.[7]

[1] niddhāraṇa, not in PED, but in Childers. Cf. KhA 224.

[2] paṭisedha, prohibition, prevention.

[3] chaṭṭhīsamāsa. [4] seṭṭhatara.

[5] Cf. Nd1, 356 for enumeration of the world-system(s) from one to, finally, thirty thousand and the great thousand.

[6] kappiyakāra, -kāraka, someone whom a monk may legitimately ask for any allowable or permissible (kappiya) material thing he needs, see Vin i 206, iv 90, also e.g. MA ii 209. As monks are not allowed to obtain any thing from their supporters (dāyaka) by hinting or intimating, much less than by asking them outright, it is necessary for them to have a kind of confidant (man or woman) who is allowed to ask them about their needs and arrange with the dāyakas to give anything wanted so long as it is something permissible for monks to have.

[7] Cf. DA 43, MA iii 2, AA i 113, UdA 127.

27 *Astonishing* means unprecedented; what is without precedent is astonishing. This is an expression for both surprise and consternation.[1]

27 *Astounding*[2] means making the hair rise up erect.

27 *Such (as this) never before* means that having quoted the phrase it should be taken as "I have not seen an astonishing thing like this before".

27 *Wonder* means a wonderful thing.[3]

28 *Each in his own abode* means each in his own abode.[4]

28 *Remaining* means dwelling in.

28 *Devatās*: this phrase should be understood as an inclusive phrase for devas and female devas.[5]

28 *These laughed* means these *devatās laughed a mighty laugh*; they laughed a loud laugh, not merely smiling, because their hearts were overcome by zest.

28 *In the zenith* means in the sky.

29 *In the sky* means in mansions and so forth in the sky; this too is the method for those *on the earth*.

[40] 29 *Dwellers in grass and on paths* means dwellers on blades of grass and on paths.

30 *Meritorious* means (having) great merit.

30 *Great in psychic potency* means great majesty.

31 *They sent forth chants* means they sent forth chants to be used by deva-dancers[6] for honouring the Tathāgata.

31 *In the air* means in the sky. [7]

31 *Down the aery paths* (anilañjase) means: on aery paths. Because (the word) 'air' (ambara) has many meanings[8] anilañjase is used. It is a synonym of the preceding (word).

31 *Drums* means covered with hides[9]; or this itself is the reading; the meaning is the drums[10] of the devas.

31 *They played* means they made to sound[11].

[1] Cf. DA 43, MA iii 3.

[2] "Horrific" would be the correct transl. of lomahaṅsana if it did not carry so many overtones of dread and terror and fear which I think are not intended here.

[3] accheran ti acchariyaṁ.

[4] sakaṁ sakamhi bhavane ti attano attano bhavane.

[5] devadhīta, deva-daughters.

[6] devanāṭaka.

[7] ambare ti ākāse.

[8] Besides antalikkha, ākāsa, gagana, etc., it means cloth.

[9] BvAC cammāvanaddhānī ti cammavinaddhāni; Bv, BvAB cammanaddhāni. Cf. Vin i 194.

[10] dundubhiyo.

[11] vādentī ti vādayanti.

32 *Conches*[1] means conches that are blown.

32 *Cymbals*[1] means a specific musical instrument, slender in the middle.

32 *Kettle-drums*[1] means they are called tam-tams, small drums.

32 *They played* means they made to sound.[2]

33 *Surely one who is astonishing* means surely one who is wonderful.

33 *Has arisen* means is arising.

33 *Astounding* means making the hair rise up erect.

33 *Constant* means that inasmuch as this is an astonishing thing that this teacher is arising in the world, we are obtaining therefore the fulfilment of (our) aim which has been unfailingly[3] constant.

33 *We are obtaining* means we shall obtain.

33 *The moment* means that apart from their eight untimely periods the ninth period is intended.[4]

33 *For us* means to us.[5]

33 *Has come about* means is obtained.

34 Hearing these say "*A Buddha*" means that on hearing this expression "a Buddha" the zest that arose in these devas was of the five kinds.[6]

34 *At once* means at that time.

35 *Cheering*[7] means that at the time they were delighted they made sounds and so on with the sounds of cheering.

35 *Applauding* means they sent forth sounds of applause.

35 *Acclamation* means sounds of acclamation and sounds of shouting.

35 *Beings*[8] has the intention of devas and so on. Some read "they waved a variety of flags[9] in the heavens".

36 *They sang* means they sang songs connected with the special qualities of Buddhas.

36 *They cried out exultingly* means they made sounds of exultant crying out with their mouths.

[41] 36 *They played* means they played on and used musical

[1] saṅkhā paṇavā deṇḍimā; cf. D i 79.

[2] vajjayantī (Bv vajjanti) ti vādayanti.

[3] avassaṁ as at MA ii 67.

[4] Nine are given at D iii 263, eight at A iv 225, the ninth being the timely, favourable or opportune period for leading the brahmacariya.

[5] no ti amhākaṁ.

[6] Each kind defined at Vism 143f.

[7] Bv bhiṅkāra, BvA hiṅ-.

[8] pajā.

[9] paṭāka.

instruments and lutes[1] such as the mahatī[2], the vipañcikā[3], the makaramukha,[4] so as to do homage to the Tathāgata.

36 *They clapped their hands* means they clapped[5] their hands. A change in gender is to be understood[6].

36 *And they danced* means others were dancing and they themselves danced.

37 *Inasmuch, great hero, as the Wheel-mark is on your feet* means that herein *inasmuch* means in this manner: *great hero*[7] from association with great energy[8]. *Wheel-mark on the feet* means that the Wheel-mark adorns the soles of both feet complete in every way with a thousand spokes, with tyre and hub. But this word wheel is to be seen as prosperity, part of a vehicle, a posture, giving, jewel, Dhamma, the chest, the Wheel-mark and so on.[9] In such passages as "Monks, there are these four wheels, possessed of which for devas and mankind",* prosperity is to be seen. In such passages as "As the wheel the foot of the draught (-animal)"†, it is part of a vehicle. "The four-wheeled, nine-doored"‡—herein it is a posture. "Give and partake of and be not negligent, the Wheel is turning for all living creatures"§—herein it is giving. "The deva-like wheel-jewel has appeared"||—herein it is the Wheel-treasure. "The Wheel that has been set turning by me"¶—

* A ii 32, quoted Asl 58, VbhA 399. Cf. D iii 276, GS ii 35, n. 1.

† Dh 1. This is probably the wooden wheel referred to at DA 1058.

‡ S i 16, 63. This refers to the 4 types of bodily deportment, and the body's 9 orifices for which cf. Thag 1150–52. Cf. DA 1058, SA i 58.

§ Cf. Jā iii 412.

|| Cf. D ii 172, iii 61, M iii 172. According to Jā iv 232 it originates in Cakkadaha.

¶ Sn 557, M Sta 92.

1 vīṇā, the usual word for a lute.

2 At Mhvu ii 159, iii 407, Divy 108, l. 4, in a long compound. BHSD says "Skt. id., of Nārada's 'seven-stringed' lute". In the Guttila Jā (ii 252) Guttila's seven-stringed instrument, sattatanti, is merely called a vīṇā, also at VvA 139; referred to at AA i 28.

3 Mhvu ii 159.

4 I can find no other mention of this word, presumably also a kind of lute. Lit. shark's face or head.

5 bhujāni poṭhentī ti bhuje appoṭhenti. Striking the upper arms with the hands in their exaltation. Apphoṭhenti defined at text p. 98.

6 From masc. to neut.

7 vīra.

8 viriya.

9 Cf. MA ii 27, AA i 120, iii 9, PṭsA 626, VbhA 399 for various meanings of cakka, wheel.

herein indeed it is the Wheel of Dhamma. "The wheel spins round at the head of a man of insatiate greed"*—here the meaning is the wheel on the chest[1], a wheel that strikes.[2] "There are wheels on the soles of the feet"†—herein it is a Mark; here too the Wheel as a Mark should be understood.

37 *The flag, the thunderbolt, the banner, with the decorative marks of the vaddhamāna*[3] *and the elephant-hook* means the Mark of the wheel on the feet is overspread, adorned, surrounded by a flag and a thunderbolt and a banner and a vaddhamāna and an elephant-hook. When the Wheel-Mark is adopted the remaining Marks are adopted too, likewise the eighty lesser characteristics and the fathom-long halo. Therefore, the Lord's body, being adorned with these thirty-two Marks of a Great Man, with the eighty lesser characteristics and the fathom-long halo was like a lotus-grove in full bloom, it was as though ornamented with manifold jewels, it was as though an untarnished golden portal was shining like star-light; and while he was emitting the six-hued rays it was exceedingly resplendent as they streamed and wreathed from side to side in the vault of the heavens.

Now, to show the Lord's excellence in the body of form and the body of Dhamma,[4] it was said, beginning:

I 38 So are you unique in form, in morality, concentration and wisdom, equal to the unequalled in freedom, in setting the Wheel of Dhamma turning.

38 Therein *in form* means this word form is to be seen in the aggregates, existence[5], sign[6], condition, [42] physical frame, appearance, configuration and so on.[7] As it was said, "Whatever material form, past future, present"‡—herein it is to be seen as the aggregate of material form. "He develops the Way by the up-

* Jā i 414, iv 4, quoted VbhA 372.
† D iii 143 148, M ii 136.
‡ M i 38, Vism 607, etc.

[1] A kind of punishment or torture.
[2] paharaṇacakka. Used in explanation of khurapariyanta at MA ii 27, AA iii 9, PṭsA 627, VbhA 399.
[3] vaddhamāna, meaning doubtful, perhaps cuṇṇa, perfumed bath powder; cf. VA 75, Mhvs xxiii 33, Mhvs-ṭ i 304.
[4] dhammakāya as at D iii 84, Miln 73, ThagA i 205.
[5] bhava; cf. rūpabhava as opposed to kāma- and arūpabhava.
[6] nimitta, see rūpanimitta at Pṭs i 92.
[7] Cf. AA i 21.

rising of fine materiality"*—herein as fine-material existence. "Perceiving the immaterial within himself, he sees external material forms†—herein as a sign of kasiṇa (meditation). "Evil, unskilled states arise, monks, with material form, not without material form"‡—herein as condition. "A space that is enclosed is reckoned as material shape"§—herein as physical frame. "Because of the eye and material forms visual consciousness arises"||—herein as appearance. "He is one who measures by material form and is satisfied with material form"¶—herein as configuration. Here it should be understood simply as configuration.

38 *In morality* means simply in the fourfold morality.[1]

38 *In concentration* means simply in the threefold concentration.[2]

38 *In wisdom* means in supermundane wisdom.

38 *Unique* means matchless[3], incomparable.

38 *In freedom* means in the freedom of the fruits.[4]

38 *Equal to the unequalled* means unequalled former Buddhas; equal in morality and so forth to these unequalled Buddhas means "equal to the unequalled". To this extent is shown the Lord's excellence in the body of form and the body of Dhamma.

Now, to show the Lord's physical strength and so forth it was said:

I 39 The natural strength of your body is as the strength of ten elephants; you are without an equal in the power of psychic potency, in setting the Wheel of Dhamma turning.

39 Therein *the strength of ten elephants* means the strength of ten six-tusked elephants. The strength of the Tathāgata is twofold: physical strength and power of knowledge. Here physical strength

* Dhs 160, Vbh 171 263f. 299; cf. Vism 557.
† A i 40, Dhs 204ff.; cf. D ii 110, iii 260.
‡ A i 83.
§ M i 190.
|| M i 111, S iv 32.
¶ A ii 71, Pug 53.

[1] Jā iii 195, Vism 15, Asl 168; also Miln 243 (control by the Pātimokkha, control over sense-organs, purity of mode of livelihood, reliance on the knowledge of conditions, paccaya).

[2] D ii 219 (2 sets), M iii 162, and see MLS iii 207, n. 1 for further references.

[3] asādiso ti asadiso.

[4] Five kinds of freedom, vimutti, at MA iv 168. See also Pṭs ii 143ff.

is to be understood in accordance with the elephant-families. How is that?

> Kālāvaka and Gaṅgeyya, Paṇḍara, Tamba, Piṅgala, Gandha,
> Maṅgala, Hema, Uposatha and Chaddanta—these ten.[1]

These are to be understood as the ten elephant-families. Kālāvaka is the family of ordinary elephants. The strength of each Kālāvaka elephant is as the physical strength of ten men. The strength of each Gaṅgeyya is that of ten Kālāvakas. In this way it is to be taken up to the Chaddantas[2]. The strength of one Tathāgata is that of ten Chaddantas. It is this that is called the strength of radiance[3], the strength of diamond. This is the strength of a thousand crores of elephants; by a counting of men [43] it is the strength of ten thousand crores of men. Such is the physical strength of the Tathāgata. But the power of knowledge is the boundless knowledge of One of the Ten Powers[4], the knowledge of the four confidences[5], the knowledge of not trembling in the eight companies[6], the knowledge of demarcation by the four modes of birth[7], the knowledge of the demarcation by five bourns[8], the fourteen knowledges of a Buddha[9]—thus it is called the power of knowledge. But here physical strength is intended.

39 *The natural strength of your body*: the meaning is: and the natural strength of your body is that (strength of ten elephants). Therefore the strength of ten elephants has the meaning of the strength of ten six-tusked elephants. Now, for showing the power of knowledge it was said, *you are without an equal in the power of psychic potency, in setting the Wheel of Dhamma turning*. Therein without an equal, *in the power of psychic potency unequalled* means without an equal, unique, incomparable in assuming different

[1] Verse ascribed to the Porāṇas at MA ii 25, SA ii 43, PṭsA iii 625, VbhA 397; verse also at UdA 403 and subsequent passages to be compared with BvA.

[2] And is so taken elephant-family by family, at MA ii 26, SA ii 43f., Pṭs A 625, VbhA 397.

[3] nārāyana. See DPPN, "a certain measure of physical strength . . . equivalent of the strength of ten Chaddanta elephants"; and see BHSD s.v. Nārāyana.

[4] M i 69ff.

[5] Ibid. 71.

[6] Ibid. 72.

[7] Ibid. 73.

[8] Ibid. 98.

[9] Briefly explained at text p. 185. Referred to at Miln 285. For the six Buddha-knowledges, not shared by others, see MQ ii 9, n. 6.

forms, resolute determination and so forth through the power of psychic potency.

39 *In setting the Wheel of Dhamma turning* means without an equal in the knowledge of teaching. Now, that Teacher who is thus possessed of ancient[1] special qualities is the sole leader in all the world. Pay homage to this Teacher. So as to show the suitability of obeisance to the Tathāgata it was said:

I 40 Pay homage to the great sage, one with pity, protector of the word(s), who is furnished thus with all the special qualities, endowed with all (their) factors.[2]

40 Therein *thus* is a particle in evidence of what is said.

40 *Furnished with all the special qualities*: 'all" means this is a word for inclusiveness; special quality (guṇa) means that this word "special quality" appears in various meanings. Such as: "I allow you, monks, when garments are unsoiled a double (di-guṇa) outer cloak"*–here in the sense of a covering.

> Times pass away, days are hurrying on, the stages of life (vayo-guṇa) gradually wane.†

—here in the sense of a quantity. "It is to be expected that the offering yields a hundredfold (sata-guṇa)"‡—here in the sense of advantage.[3] "Entrails (anto-guṇa)"§, "one may make many garland-wreaths (mālā-guṇa)"||—here in the sense of joining together.[4] "I gained power in the super-knowings that is possessed of eight special qualities[5] (guṇa)¶—here in the sense of prosperity. Here too prosperity is to be understood as the meaning. Therefore the meaning is: Furnished with, possessed of all mundane and supermundane special qualities, with all prosperities.

* Vin i 290, quoted DA 403.
† S i 3, Jā iv 487, quoted DA 403.
‡ M iii 255, quoted again text p. 76 and DA 403. See MA v 71, and cf. A iii 42.
§ S ii 270, Kh 2.
|| Dh 53.
¶ Bv IIA 30, quoted Jā i 6.

[1] ādi, initial, first, primeval.
[2] Cf. Thag 1251 evaṁ sabbaṅgasampannaṁ muniṁ.
[3] Cf. text p. 76.
[4] Cf. SA i 23.
[5] Detailed at text p. 76.

40 *Endowed with all (their) factors* means endowed with, possessed of all the special qualities of a Buddha and with the factors of the special qualities.

40 *To the great sage*: a great sage means a sage surpassing in greatness other sages beginning with buddhas by and for themselves.

[44] 40 *One with pity* means one with pity because of a connexion with the special quality of pity.

40 *Protector of the world(s)* means the sole protector of the whole world and all the worlds. The meaning is that it is to be expected that he is a striker against, one who comes to grips with, our torment and anguish.

Now, to show that Him of the Ten Powers was worthy of all humility, the verses were spoken beginning:

I 41 You are worthy of all respect, praising, reverence and laudation, homage and honour.

41 Therein *respect* means giving one's own respect to others.

41 *Praising* means praising in one's absence.

41 *Reverence* means obeisance.

41 *Laudation* means laudation in one's presence.

41 *Homage* means clasping the hands in salutation or paying homage with the mind.

41 *Honour* means honouring with garlands, perfumes, unguents and so forth.

41 *All* means all; this is a word for inclusiveness.

41 *You are worthy*: the meaning is: you are suitable.

42 *Those who should be reverenced in the world* means those who in the world are to be reverenced, ought to be reverenced, *are worthy of reverence. Those* means those in the world are worthy of reverence; this is a synonym only for the first word.

42 *Best of all* means: you are the best, the highest of all these, *great hero*; *like you* no one *exists* in the world.

Then when the Lord had displayed the Marvel of the Double and had created the Jewel-Walk and was walking up and down there, the venerable Sāriputta was staying in Rājagaha on Mount Vulture Peak surrounded by five hundred monks. Then the Elder, looking round for the Lord, saw him in the sky over Kapilapura walking up and down on the Jewel-Walk. Accordingly it was said:

I 43 Even as he was standing on the Vulture Peak, Sāriputta, of great wisdom, proficient in concentration and meditation, saw the leader of the world.

43 Therein *Sāriputta* means the son of the brahman lady Rūpasārī: Sārī's son.

43 *Great wisdom* means possessed of the great sixteen-fold wisdom.[1]

43 *Proficient in concentration and meditation*: herein *concentration* means that he places the mind evenly and fixes it on the objective (meditational) supports. It is a threefold concentration: with initial and sustained thought, without initial but with sustained thought, without initial and without sustained thought.[2] *Meditation* means the first meditation, the second meditation, the third meditation, the fourth meditation; [45] included in these: the first meditation and so forth, the meditation on loving-kindness and so forth. Meditation too is twofold:[3] reflexion on mark, reflexion on objective (meditational) support[4]. Therein, saying "He reflects on the mark of impermanence and so forth" is called reflexion on mark that is insight and knowledge. But in regard to the first meditation and so forth it is called meditation (jhāna) because of lighting up (reflecting, upanijjhāna) the objective (meditational) support and because of burning up (jhāpana) opposition.[5] *Proficient* in the concentrations and in the meditations means proficient in concentration and meditation, skilled in concentration and meditation.

43 *On the Vulture Peak* means as he was standing on the mountain so named.

43 *Saw* means he saw.[6]

44 *Like a king of sāla trees in full bloom* means: as at a king of sāla trees covered with blossoms[7], the trunk evenly rounded,[8] the

[1] Cf. MA iv 82–87, AA ii 81–86.
[2] See text p. 42.
[3] Cf. MA ii 348.
[4] Jā v 251, DhA i 230, VvA 213.
[5] Pṭs i 49, Vism 150.
[6] passatī ti passi, present tense explained by the aorist.
[7] sabbapāliphulla as at DA 40; sabbaphāli- at M i 212, 218.
[8] An allusion to one of the 32 Marks of a Great Man.

branches well adorned with an abundance of fruits, shoots and sprouts, so he *looked at* Him of the Ten Powers, the "king of sāla trees", as having the root of morality, the trunk of concentration, the branch of wisdom, the flower of super-knowing, the fruit of freedom: thus is the connexion with the word "looking at"[1].

44 *Like the moon in the heavens* means as on the moon[2] at the full in autumn-time surrounded by a host of stars, freed from dense cloud, snow-clouds, smoke and dust, and from attack by Rāhu[3], so he looked at the glorious moon, the sage, the one who brings destruction of all defilements to the dark multitude and makes accessible to people a blossoming mass of white lotuses. *Like* (yathā) is merely a particle.

44 *Like the sun at midday* means shining as the sun[4] at noon-tide garlanded with bright and effulgent rays.

44 *Bull of men* (narāsabha) means bull of men (narava-sabha)[5].

45 *Blazing* means resplendent, glorious, beautiful and lovely (like) the moon at the full in autumn-time, (so was) shining with superlative Buddha-majesty his glorious physical frame adorned with the Marks and the minor characteristics.

45 *Like a tree of lamps* means like a tree for lamps on which the lamps have been placed.[6]

45 *Like the newly risen sun* means blazing with loveliness like the freshly risen sun[7]. And the youthful stage of a man is so called because it is upward[8] and is not like the waxing and waning of the moon.

45 *Illuminated by a halo extending for a fathom* means coloured by the halo which extended for a fathom.

45 *He saw the wise one, the leader* means he saw the sole wise one, leader of all the world.

Then as the venerable General under Dhamma was standing on the peak where many dark waters are held and flow down, on the

[1] *ulloka.*
[2] rajanikara, night-maker.
[3] Cf. Vin ii 295, A ii 53, Miln 273 and see notes at MQ ii 94.
[4] aṁsumālin, the one garlanded with rays or sunbeams.
[5] See SnA 40 on usabha.
[6] Cf. text p. 129; see too DhA iv 120.
[7] ādicca.
[8] udaya.

peak scented with various fragrant[1] flowers and trees, on the peak exceedingly pleasing to the heart, on Mount Vulture Peak, he saw the Lord, surrounded by a host of ten thousand devas and brahmans who had come to the mountain-range, walking up and down on **[46]** the Walk made of all the jewels with the supreme majesty of a Buddha, with the unexcelled grace of a Buddha, and he thought, "Look, I, having approached the Lord, would entreat him for an elucidation of the special qualities of Buddhas, for a teaching on the Buddhavaṁsa", and he assembled five hundred monks who were staying there with him. Accordingly it was said, beginning:

I 46 In an instant he had gathered together five hundred monks, their tasks done, steadfast ones, the cankers destroyed, stainless.

46 Therein *five hundred monks*[2] means the genitive is to be understood in the sense of an accusative: five hundred monks.[3]

46 *Tasks done* means the sixteen tasks quite concluded (connected) with the four tasks (each) referring to the four Ways by reason of comprehension, eradication, realization and development.[4]

46 *Cankers destroyed* means that the four cankers were utterly destroyed.

46 *Stainless* means devoid of stains because of the cankerless state, or the continuity of stainless, highly and utterly purified thought.

46 *In an instant* means at that very instant.

46 *He had gathered together* means he caused to gather together.

Now, to show the reason for the gathering together and coming of these monks it was said:

I 47 He displayed the marvel called Making the Worlds Bright (and said) "We too, going there, we will reverence the Conqueror.

[1] surabhi. See note at MQ ii 219.

[2] In the genitive.

[3] Accusative.

[4] These are the functions of the disciple in regard to each of the four Ways or Truths respectively. See Vism 689ff., also MQ ii 184, n. 3.

48 Come, all of us will go, we will question the Conqueror. When we have seen the leader of the world we will dispel doubt."

47 Therein *called Making the World Bright* means the marvel is said to be making the world bright[1] because of a brightening of the world. 'Pleasing to the world[2]' is also a reading. Its meaning is his marvel of unveiling the world[3]. For, having made it one in light from the Akaniṭṭha abode above to the intervals between Avīci below, it is called the basis for all beings to see one another in this interval.

47 *He displayed* means he displayed.[4]

47 *We too* means we too.[5]

47 *There* means *going there* where the Lord is.

47 *We will reverence* means "we will reverence the Lord's feet with our heads". And here (again) we means we[5]. A connection between these two words is to be understood: the first as the action of going, the second as the action of reverencing; otherwise it is not free from the defect of redundancy.[6]

48 *Come* means come along[7].

[47] 48 *We will dispel doubt* means: as those whose cankers are destroyed have no doubt, why did the Elder speak thus? He spoke like this of extirpation to those going by the first Way to the truth: "How many states are to be got rid of by vision? The four arisings of thought with recourse to views, arising of thought accompanied by perplexity, greed, hatred, stupidity, conceit leading to states of woe, and the defilements connected with each one"[8]. But these are not considered as perplexities and doubts. So is not the description ignorant? It should be understood that as the Elder was anxious to question the Lord about the Buddhavaṁsa and also about the range of the Buddhas[9], but not about that of the buddhas by and for themselves nor about that of disciples of Buddhas he therefore spoke thus without the subject of range.

[1] lokappasādaka.
[2] lokappasādana, the reading at Bv.
[3] lokavivaraṇa, itself a marvel. See MQ ii 204 for references and add CpA 4.
[4] nidassayī ti nidassesi.
[5] amhe pī ti mayam pi.
[6] punaruttadosato, as at text p. 37.
[7] ethā ti āgacchatha.
[8] Cf. Dhs 1011.
[9] Buddhavisaya, see MQ ii 6, n. 7.

48 *We will dispel* means we will dispel.[1]

When these monks had heard the Elder's bidding each one, taking his own bowl and robe as though well clad in armour, great nāgas, defilements broken, bonds cut through, of few desires, well pleased, aloof, ungregarious, endowed with morality, concentration, wisdom, freedom and the knowledge and vision of freedom, assembled very quickly. Accordingly it was said:

I 49 These assented, saying "It is good"; prudent, the faculties controlled, taking bowl and robe, they went up (to him) quickly.

49 Therein *it is good*[2] means that this word good (sādhu) is to be found in such contexts as imploring, receiving, approval and well. Such as: "It were good, revered sir, if the Lord were to teach me Dhamma in brief"*—in such contexts imploring is to be seen. "Saying, 'It is good, revered sir', that monk was delighted with and rejoiced in the Lord's words"†—in such contexts it is receiving. "It is good, it is good, Sāriputta"‡—in such contexts it is approval.

> "It is good that a king have a liking for Dhamma, it is good that a man be sensible, it is good there be no treachery among friends; happy is the non-doing of evil"§

—in such contexts it is well. Here it is receiving, so the meaning is that they said, "It is good, it is well" when they had received the Elder's bidding.

49 *Prudent* means clever, wise.

49 *Faculties controlled* means the doors of the faculties guarded, possessed of control over the faculities.

49 *They went up to* means they approached the Elder.

[48] 50 Now the recensionists, to show that the General under Dhamma came forward, spoke the verse beginning "With those whose cankers were destroyed, stainless."

50 Therein *with the tamed* means with the tamed in body and thought.

* e.g. S iii 35.
† M iii 16, S iii 100, A ii 178.
‡ S ii 49, v 221.
§ Jā v 222.

[1] vinodayissāmā ti vinodessāma.

[2] Cf. DA 171, MA i 18, SnA 176, for exegesis of sādhu. All give one more meaning than does BvA.

50 *In the supreme taming* means arahants. The locative case is to be understood in the meaning of an attribute.

51 *By these monks* means by the five hundred monks.

51 *Leading the great host* means he had a host great both in morality and so forth, and in regard to number: leading the great host. In respect of the different words a host great in the special qualities of morality and so forth is a great host. He had means: leading the great host.

51 *Blazing*[1] *like a deva in the heavens* means that, like a deva splendid[2] with the splendour of psychic potency, he approached the Lord in the vault of the heavens.

52 Now these, being thus, *approached* means that so as to show the method of approach *clearing the throat and*[3] begins the beginning (of the verse).

52 *And*[3] *sneezing* means and of the sound of sneezing.

52 *Carefully avoiding* means that the intention is avoiding, not doing those two (things).

52 *With reverence* means with ascetic qualities quite without stains.

52 *With deference*: the meaning is bearing themselves with humility.

53 *The self-become*[4] means having fulfilled the perfections by himself alone without another's instruction, he arrived at the status of a Buddha.

53 *High aloft* means newly arisen high.

53 *Like the moon* means like the moon in the zenith, they saw the Lord blazing in the heavens like the moon. Thus the connexion of words is to be understood. Here too[5] the word "like" (yathā) is merely a particle.

54 *Like lightning*[6] means like a volume of lightning. Were there lightning[7] which lasted long he would be like that. That is the meaning.

54 (*Like*) *in the heavens* means as in the sky. Here too the word "like" (yathā) is merely a particle. From here onwards the word "like" in such places is to be regarded as merely a particle.

[1] jalanto: Bv, Be laḷanto, sporting, singing.

[2] vijalanto means both shining forth and playing, dallying.

[3] ca is repeated though it is needed only once.

[4] sayambhū, cf. Pṭs I 174, Nd1 143, KhA 14, Miln 214 227 236.

[5] Probably referring back to ver. 44.

[6] vijju.

[7] acirappabhā, meaning lightning, so Abh.

55 *Like* (iva) *a clear pool* means undisturbed and clear like (viya) a large pool, very deep and wide.

55 *As* (yathā) *a lotus in full bloom*[1] *on the water* means that the meaning is to be regarded as: like a lotus-grove[2] in full bloom on the pool. "As a lotus in full bloom" is also a reading. The meaning is that because of his loveliness he was (like) a lotus-grove[3] in full bloom.

Then these monks headed by the General under Dhamma, having raised their clasped hands to their heads, fell down at the feet of Him of the Ten Powers, the soles of which were adorned with wheels. That is the meaning. Accordingly it was said, beginning:

56 *Holding up their clasped hands, elated, exultant, joyous, they fell down* there means they fell down[4], they honoured.

[49] 56 *To the Mark of the Wheel* (loc.) means the wheel, the mark (acc.); that foot on which there is a Wheel-mark is said to be a foot that has a Wheel-mark by reason of birth.

56 *At the teacher's* means they fell down at his feet the soles of which were adorned with wheels.

57 Now the verses *Sāriputta, of great wisdom, like and similar to a koraṇḍa*[5] *(flower)* were spoken for explaining some of these Elders by name. There *like and similar to a koraṇḍa (flower)* means in colour like and similar to the flower of a koraṇḍa. So, if it is to be understood thus: either as like (sama) a koraṇḍa (flower) or as similar to (sādisa) a koraṇḍa (flower), what is the twofold, like and similar to, that is spoken of? This is not a blemish; such a likeness to a koraṇḍa (flower) is just because of similarity to a koraṇḍa (flower); there is no intention apart from this phrase.

57 *Skilled in concentration and meditation*: here the word "skilled" (kusala)[6] is to be seen in different contexts as health, blameless, clever, of happy fruition. It is to be seen as health in contexts such as this: "I hope the revered one is well (kusala), I hope the revered one is in good health."* In contexts thus it is

* J iv 427, etc.

[1] suphullapadumaṁ. Bv suphullaṁ padumaṁ yathā as is the other reading referred to here.

[2] padumavana.

[3] kamalavana.

[4] nipatiṁsu, glossing nipatanti; at p. 37 this is glossed by sannipatanti.

[5] A shrub, yellow amaranth; in one of its meanings a mythical plant that never fades.

[6] See Asl 38.

blameless: 'But what, revered sir, is bodily conduct that is skilled (kusala)? Whatever bodily conduct is blameless, sire."* It is clever in the contexts: "You are skilled (kusala) in all the parts of a chariot."† In (other) contexts it is (productive of) happy fruition: "By the act of doing, by the act of accumulating a good (kusala) kamma."‡ But here it is to be regarded as clever (cheka).

57 *He reverences* means he reverenced.

58 *Thundering* means: he thunders, means thundering.[1]

58 *Like a black storm-cloud* means thundering like a dark-blue bearer of waters, the intention being in the range of psychic powers.

58 *Like and similar to a dark blue lotus* means in colour similar to a dark blue water-lily. The meaning here should be taken also according to the method spoken of above.

58 *Moggallāna* means Kolita, so called by reason of his clan.

59 *And Kassapa the Great too*: compared with Uruvelā-Kassapa, Nadī-Kassapa, Gayā-Kassapa, Kassapa the Boy, lesser and minor Elders, this one was Great; hence he is called Kassapa the Great. *And too* in the sense of conjunction of the particle (pi ca).

59 *Resembling molten gold* means that the colour of his skin was similar to glowing gold.

59 *Ascetic quality* means here that by shaking off the defilements[2] the state that is ascetic is called ascetic state, is called ascetic quality[3]. And what is called ascetic state? Fewness of wishes, contentment, submissiveness, detachment, this being desirous of—these five states that go with volition for ascetic practice are called ascetic states[4] from the expression: Just because of fewness of wishes[5]. Or by shaking off the defilements the shaking off is called knowledge: in this ascetic quality.

[50] 59 *Proclaimed chief* means placed as chief, best, topmost, with the words: "This is the chief, monks, of my disciples that are monks who are preachers of asceticism, that is to say Kassapa the Great"§. The meaning is that he was placed in that place.

And this word chief[6] (agga) is to be seen in such contexts as:

* M ii 115.
† M i 395.
‡ Dhs 431.
§ A i 23.

[1] gajjītā ti gajjatī ti gajjitā.
[2] Cf. Vism 61.
[3] Cf. Sn 385, SnA 373.
[4] Cf. Vism 81, Miln 348ff.
[5] A iii 219.
[6] As at VA 173, DA 235–6, MA 136–7, AA i 124, ii 114.

beginning, tip, portion, best. Thus: "From today forth, good door-keeper, I am barring the door to Jain men and Jain women"*—in contexts such as these beginning (ādi) is to be seen. In such contexts it is tip: "Well then, one should rub the tip (agga) of that finger with the tip of (another) finger"†, "a tip of sugar-cane[1], a tip of bamboo[1]."‡ In such contexts it is portion: "I allow you, monks, to distribute a portion (agga) of (something) sour in taste or sweet in taste with a portion of a monastery or with a portion of cells§." In such contexts it is best: "Compared, monks, with creatures, footless, bipeds . . . of these the Tathāgata is pointed to as chief‖". Here it is to be understood as best (seṭṭha) and is also right as tip (koṭi). As the Elder was best and also topmost in his own place, it was said "placed as chief", meaning he was placed as chief, best, topmost.[2]

59 *Lauded* means applauded by devas and mankind and so forth.

59 *Commended by the teacher* means commended, praised by the teacher, saying: "Kassapa, monks, like the moon, approached families modestly drawing back both in body and in thought, ever unobtrusive among the families".¶ Commended and praised thus in various ways in the Suttas, he too honours the Lord.

60 *Of those of deva-like vision*: the meaning is: of those who are monks of deva-like vision the deva-like vision is the chief, the best. Accordingly it was said: "He is chief, monks, of my disciples that are monks of deva-like vision, that is to say Anuruddha**". The Elder Anuruddha was the son of the Lord's uncle named Amitodana the Sakyan; he was the younger brother of Mahānāma, and was of great merit, most excellent and lovely[3]. He, with six others, leaving home for homelessness, went forth.[4] The manner of his going forth is handed down in the Khandhaka on Schism in the Order.[5]

* M i 380.
† Cf. Kvu 315.
‡ Untraced.
§ Cf. Vin ii 167.
‖ A ii 34, v 21.
¶ S ii 197–8, quoted Miln 389, ThagA iii 135.
** A i 23.

[1] Both these words at Vism 172 in the "air-kasiṇa".
[2] agga seṭṭho koṭibhūto.
[3] Cf. AA i 189–90.
[4] pabbajita, referring to the preliminary ordination.
[5] Vin ii 180–206.

60 *Near* means in the Lord's presence.

61 *In what is an offence and what is not an offence* means *proficient* in what is an offence and what is not an offence.

61 *In what is curable*[1]: the meaning is in what has a remedy and what has no remedy. There (the class of offences) that has a remedy is sixfold, that without remedy is an offence involving Defeat.[2] The reading is: proficient in what is an offence and what is not, in what is curable—and that is the meaning.

[51] 61 *In the Vinaya* means in the Vinaya-piṭaka.

61 *Proclaimed chief* means: Saying, "He is chief, monks, of my disciples that are monks who are experts in Vinaya, that is to say Upāli"—the meaning is he was placed in the chief place.

61 *Upāli* is the Elder Upāli.

61 *Commended by the teacher* means commended, extolled by the teacher. The Elder, having learnt the Vinaya-piṭaka in the presence of the Tathāgata, gave these three decisions, combining them together by means of omniscient knowledge: the decision for (the monk of) Bharukaccha,[3] the decision for Ajjuka,[4] the decision for Kassapa the Boy.[5] Therefore, saying: "The Elder is chief of Vinaya experts",* it is said he was commended by the teacher in the way beginning thus.

62 *Penetrated to meanings delicate and subtle* means: a meaning that was delicate and subtle was penetrated, a meaning that was difficult to see and subtle was penetrated.

62 *Very glorious among speakers* means best of speakers on Dhamma. Saying: "He is chief, monks, of my disciples that are monks who are speakers on Dhamma, that is to say Puṇṇa, Mantānī's son",† he, put in the chief line, was therefore called very glorious among speakers.

62 *Having a following* means with an Order. It is said five hundred young men of family went forth in the presence of the Elder, and all of them were of the native district[6] of Him of the

* A i 25.
† A i 23.

[1] Reading satekicchāya against sati- of Bv.
[2] See Vin v 115.
[3] Vin iii 39.
[4] Ibid. 66.
[5] Jā i 148, DhA iii 144, MA ii 129, AA i 284, and ThagA ii 101 which mentions these three decisions.
[6] jātabhummakā; cf. jātabhūmakā at M i 145, A iii 366.

Ten Powers, residents in this native territory; the cankers of all were destroyed, all were possessed of the ten (good) themes of Discourse[1]—therefore "having followers" was said.

62 *Seer* means a seer looks for, seeks skilled states.

62 *Mantānī's son* means he was the son of the brahman woman Mantānī; Puṇṇa was his name.

62 *Widely famed* means widely famed for his special qualities and fewness of wishes and so forth.

Now, after the Teacher had attained full Self-Awakening, had turned the glorious Wheel of Dhamma, the Elder Aññakoṇḍañña had gone on gradually and was staying at Rājagaha. Then he arrived at Kapilavatthu and let his own nephew, the brahman youth Puṇṇa, go forth. Having honoured the Lord and asked his permission he went to Chaddanta Lake to stay there. But Puṇṇa came together with the Elder to see the Lord, thinking, "Now that I have carried through the duties of one who has gone forth, I will go to Him of the Ten Powers".[2] So, having left Kapilapura and henceforth giving reasoned attention he soon attained arahantship and approached the Lord. And these two Elders, the Elder Anuruddha and the Elder Upāli, having entered Kapilapura on the day of the gathering of the Lord's relations there, appeared like those gone forth. But this agrees neither with the text of the Khandhaka nor with the Commentary and should be accepted (only) after examination. Then the Teacher **[52]** knowing the mental character of the five hundred monks headed by the Elder Sāriputta, began to speak of his own special qualities.

I 63 Knowing the minds of these, the sage skilled in similes, cutter off of doubt, great hero, spoke of his own special qualities.

63 There *skilled in similes* (opammakusalo) means skilled in similes (upamāya kusalo).

63 *Cutter off of doubt* means the cutter off of uncertainty for all beings. Now, to speak about those special qualities that he showed were his own, it was said:

I 64 These are the four incalculables of which the extent is not

[1] See M i 145, iii 113, A v 67, 130, Miln 344, etc., and cf. AA i 203 for these standard headings of Dhamma-talk.

[2] For this paragraph see too AA i 202–3.

known: the aggregation of beings, and space, and the infinite world-spheres, and the immeasurable knowledge of a Buddha—it is impossible to ascertain these[1].

64 *Four* means a delimitation by reckoning.

64 *These* means that he now pointed out the matters to be spoken of.

64 *Incalculables* means that because of their being impossible to calculate, the meaning is that they are incalculable, passing beyond reckoning.

64 *Extent* means the beginning or the end or the boundary.

64 *Of which* means of these four incalculables.

64 *Is not known* means is not discernible. Now *these* in the way spoken are to intimate the four incalculables.

64 *Aggregation of beings* was said first. Aggregation of beings means a multitude of beings. The aggregation of beings is infinite, measureless, immeasurable. Likewise *space*, for neither is there an end to space. So too are the *world-spheres* infinite.

64 *Knowledge of a Buddha* means omniscient knowledge is immeasurable.

64 *It is impossible to ascertain these* means: inasmuch as these are infinite it is not possible to ascertain them.

Now, the teacher in the display of his own psychic potency said, "Of the wonders and marvels that have arisen for devas and mankind and so forth, what is this wonder called? There is a wonder, a marvel superior to this. Listen to me thereon". Increasing the teaching of Dhamma, he spoke beginning:

I 65 What is this wonder in the world that consists of my display of psychic potency? There are many other wonders, astonishing, astounding.

65 Herein *what* is an expression (implying) a contrary (assertion).

65 *This* means he spoke referring to this display.

65 *That*: this word "that" (yaṁ) is shown in the accusative case in such passages as "That (yaṁ) which we asked you have

[1] Verse appears again, without the first line, at text p. 135. See also Asl 160f. where these 4 incalculables are explained.

declared. I ask you another (question). Please tell me this."*
[53] "This is impossible, monks, it cannot come to pass that (yaṁ) two arahants, fully Self-Awakened Ones should arise simultaneously in one world-system"†—here it is in the instrumental case. "In that (yaṁ) eon when the Lord Vipassin arose"‡—here it is in the locative. "That which (yaṁ) was received by me, revered sirs, in the presence of the Three and Thirty devas, I related that to the Lord, revered sirs"§—in such passages it is in the nominative case. Here too it is to be understood as in the nominative case.

65 He pointed out, saying, "*Many other wonders* of mine are *astonishing*, *astounding*, eminent."

Now, explaining these wonders, he spoke beginning:

I 66 When I was in the Tusita group I was called Santusita then. The (inhabitants of the) ten-thousand, having gathered together, clasping their hands, requested me:

66 Therein *when* means at that time.

66 *I* demonstrates oneself.

66 *In the Tusita group* means in the class of devas called Tusita (Happy). When I had fulfilled all the thirty perfections[1], had made the five great sacrifices[2], and from the conduct on behalf of kinsmen, from the conduct for the sake of the world, had reached the summit of the (various kinds of) conduct—wisdom[3], and had given great gifts for hundreds for a week[4], and the earth had quaked seven times[5], I, deceasing from individuality as Vessantara, was reborn for a second time in Tusita-abode. There too I was a deva-king named Santusita.

66 *The* (inhabitants of the) *ten-thousand*, *having gathered*

* Sn 1052.
† M iii 65, A i 27, Vbh 336, Miln 236.
‡ D ii 11.
§ D ii 220.

[1] See text p. 59.
[2] Cf. DhA iii 441, the sacrifice of wife, children, kingdom, life, limb.
[3] These three "kinds of conduct", cariyā, also at DhA iii 441, as lokatthacariyā ñātatthacariyā buddhicariyā ti tisso cariyā. Above reading is ñātatthacariyā lokatthacariyā buddhicariyānaṁ koṭiṁ patvā. Of six cariyā at Vism 101 buddhicariyā is the fifth; the rest are different from our context.
[4] sattasatakamahādānāni. Great gifts of special offerings of food and presents to monks made by lay-people to the Buddha and his disciples as gifts of merit, cf. Mhvs xxvii 46.
[5] Cf. Miln 113ff.

together: the meaning is: the devas of the ten-thousand world-systems having assembled.

66 *Clasping their hands, requested me* means: having approached me, they requested me, saying "Good sir, owing to your fulfilling the ten perfections and not having been filled with longing for the splendour of Sakka or for the splendour of Māra, Brahmā or a universal monarch, but, for the sake of ferrying beings[1] across, you are filled with longing for Buddhahood. It is now the time, dear sir, for Buddhahood, it is the occasion, dear sir, for Buddhahood."* Accordingly it was said:

I 67 This is the time for you;[2] great hero, arise in the womb of a mother. Helping men with the devas[3] to cross over, may you awaken to the undying state.[4]

67 Therein *time for you* means: your time,[5] or this itself is the reading.

67 *Arise* means: take on relinking; "descend" is also a reading.

67 *Men with the devas*[3]: the meaning is the world (of men) with the devas.

67 *Helping to cross over*: herein, fulfilling the perfections is called: he helps to cross over, and bringing the perfections to the summit is also called: he helps to cross over. [54] Having deceased from individuality as Vessantara, having taken on relinking in Tusita city and remaining there for sixty hundred thousand years and fifty-seven crores of years is also called: he helps to cross over. On the day that Rāhula, the bond, was born he mounted Kanthaka, and setting out with his friend Channa, passing over three territories and "going forth" on the bank of the river Anomā is also called: he helps to cross over. Engaging in striving for six years, and ascending the dais round the Tree of Awakening on the full-moon night of Visākha, having routed Māra's forces, having recollected former habitations during the first watch (of the night), purified the deva-vision during the middle watch, in the last watch

* Cf. Jā i 48.

[1] loka, of which people, beings, creatures is one of the meanings. Ferrying them across the ocean of saṁsāra.

[2] kālo 'yaṁ te, Bv kālo deva.

[3] sadevakaṁ.

[4] Quoted text p. 79, 142, 273, DhA i 84, UdA 149, UJ 127.

[5] kālo tava.

having reflected on the twelve factors of dependent origination in forward and reverse order, piercing the way of stream-attainment is also called: he helps to cross over. At the moment of the fruit of stream-attainment . . . and at the moment of the way of once-return and at the moment of the fruit of once-return and at the moment of the way of no-return and at the moment of the fruit of no-return is also called: he helps to cross over. When he gave the drink of the undying to the group of five with the eighteen thousand crores of devas, from then on it is to be said: he helps to cross over. Accordingly it was said: Helping men with the devas to cross over, may you awaken to the undying state.

Then the Great Being, being requested by the devatā, but not giving them an assurance, investigated the fivefold great investigation[1] according to the demarcations by time, continent, district, family, and (length of) the mother's life-span.

As to this, first he investigated the time: "Is it the time or is it not the time?" It is not the time if the time of the life-span exceeds a hundred thousand years. Why? When the rounds of birth, ageing, dying and so forth do not mature and there is no teaching of the Dhamma of Buddhas that is freed from the three characteristic marks, so that when they are talking about impermanence, anguish and no-self these (people), not having faith, say, "Whatever is this they are talking about?" Consequently there is no penetration. This being so it is a dispensation not leading out[2]. Therefore it is not the (right) time. Nor is it the (right) time when the duration of the life-span is less than a hundred years. Why? Then beings are abounding in defilements. Exhortation given to those who are abounding in defilements does not persist after the occasion of the exhortation. Therefore this too is not the (right) time. The (right) time is when the duration of the life-span is less than a hundred thousand years and more than a hundred years. Thinking, "Men are now of life-spans of about a hundred years", so the Bodhisatta saw that it was the time when he should be reborn.

Then investigating the continent, he thought, "Buddhas are reborn only in Jambudīpa", and he saw the continent. As the

[1] mahāvilokana; again at text p. 273. Not uncommon in the Comys., sometimes eight. Referred to at Miln 193, see MQ i 278, n. 1 for references.

[2] anīyānika, from saṁsāra to nibbāna.

continent was ten thousand yojanas in extent[1], he thought, "In which district are they reborn?" Investigating the district he saw that it was the Middle District.

Next, investigating the family, and thinking, "Buddhas are reborn in a family held in high repute by the world. The warrior-noble family is now held in high repute by the world, I will be reborn therein. The king named Suddhodana will be my father", and he saw the family.

Next, investigating the mother, he thought, "A Buddha's mother is not a wanton or a drunkard, the five moral habits are untorn. And this queen named Mahāmāyā is such a one. She shall be my mother. What is the extent of her life-span?" And so considering, he saw it would be for ten months and seven days.

So when he had investigated this fivefold investigation in this way, he said, "It is time, dear sirs, for my Buddhahood", and after giving an assurance to the devatās and having remained there[2] for as long as his life-span lasted, [55] he took on relinking in the womb of Queen Māyā in the family of the Sakyan king. Accordingly it was said:

I 68 When I, deceasing from the Tusita group, descended into the womb, then the earth and the ten-thousand world-system quaked.

68 There *I descended* means I descended, I entered.

68 *Into the womb* means into the mother's womb.

68 *The ten-thousand world-system quaked* means: now the Bodhisatta, mindful and clearly conscious, descending into the mother's womb, took on relinking at the full-moon of Āsāḷha under the asterism of Uttarāsāḷha. And, among the nineteen relinking thoughts[3] loving-kindness was under the influence of a highly potent thought-moment associated with knowledge concomitant with joy and of a thought-moment of unprompted[4] skill. Thereupon the ten-thousand world-system, shaking, quaked and trembled.

68 *Earth* (dharaṇī) means the supporter (dharaṇī), the earth (paṭhavī) supports everything that is stationary and mobile.[5]

[1] As at SnA ii 437, UdA 300.

[2] In Tusita abode.

[3] Explanation at Vism 457f., 545ff.

[4] asaṅkhārika; cf. Vism 452, and see Ppn Index s.v. prompted.

[5] thāvara-jaṅgama, as at text p. 120. Thāvara is stationary, steady, firm and usually refers to the vegetable and mineral worlds. Jaṅgama, its opposite, not in

69 *When I, clearly conscious, issued forth* herein means: when I, mindful, clearly conscious, was coming down from my mother's womb, from the Dhamma-seat, like a speaker on Dhamma, it was like a man coming down from a ladder; having stretched forth both my hands and my feet, standing I issued forth without stain or soil from when I was in being[1] in my mother's womb.

69 *Approval* means approval.[2]

69 *Sending forth* means they themselves sent forth, they gave approval.

69 *Shook* means quaked. When he was descending into and when he was issuing forth from his mother's womb the ten-thousand (world-system) shook. Then when the Lord had just descended into his mother's womb, not seeing (another) descent equal to his own, he spoke this verse so as to show his own wonder, (I 70) "There is no descent equal to mine".

70 Therein *descent* means descending into a womb. The nominative case in the sense of a locative (is used) in the phrase "in taking on relinking".

70 *To mine* (me) means mine (mayā).

70 *Equal* means there is no like.

70 *As to birth*: here it means he was born from this mother; the mother is said to be the genetrix. Hence, from the genetrix, from the mother, is the meaning.

70 *As to issuing forth*: the meaning is as to the issuing forth, the bringing forth from the mother's womb.

70 *As to Self-Awakening*: herein, praised and lovely is Awakening, Self-Awakening. And this word Awakening[3] is to be seen in such contexts as tree, way, nibbāna, omniscient knowledge. In passages handed down thus: "At the root of the Tree of Awakening being recently fully Self-Awakened",* and "Between the Tree of Awakening and Gāyā",† the Tree is spoken of as Awakening. [56] In passages handed down thus: "Awakening is spoken of as knowledge of the four ways"‡ it is Way. In passages handed down

* Vin i 1, Ud 1. † Vin i 8, M i 170. ‡ Nd1 456, 481, Nd2 114.

PED, is the animal world of living beings; also said of an elephant's lips at text p. 210. Cf. DA i 39, KhA 217, SnA i 28, VvA 4. See Intr. p. xxxviii.

[1] sambhavana, as at Netti 28f. where called the footing for birth.

[2] sādhukāran ti sādhutāraṁ.

[3] bodhi. Cf. BvA 145f., VA i 139, MA i 54, SA ii 153, UdA 27, CpA 18.

thus: "Having attained Awakening, the undying, the unconstructed"*, it is nibbāna. In passages handed down thus: "Glorious, supreme of intellect, he gains Awakening"† it is omniscient knowledge. But here the Lord's knowledge of the way to arahantship is intended. Others say "omniscient knowledge". The meaning is "In regard to perfect Self-Awakening, I am the best in this." But why did the Lord praise himself in respect of Self-Awakening? Because of the bestowal of all special qualities the Lord's Self-Awakening is a bestower of all special qualities and it gives in full all the special qualities of a Buddha. But not to others. But on some of the others it bestows the way to arahantship, also the fruit of arahantship; on some the three knowledges; on some the super-knowings; on some the four analytical insights; on some it bestows a disciple's knowledge of the perfections or the knowledge of a buddha-by-and-for-himself. But on Buddhas it bestows the achievement of all special qualities. Therefore the Lord, because of its bestowal (on him) of all special qualities, praised himself, saying "I am the best". Moreover, when he reached Self-Awakening the earth shook. Therefore he said "As to the Self-Awakening I am the best."

70 *As to turning the Wheel of Dhamma:*[1] herein, turning the Wheel of Dhamma is twofold: the knowledge of penetration, the knowledge of teaching.[2] Here the knowledge of penetration bringing the noble fruit for himself was promoted by wisdom. The knowledge of teaching bringing the noble fruit for disciples was promoted by even-mindedness, without initial thought, without sustained thought. The knowledge of teaching is mundane, indeterminate; and neither is in common with the other. Here, the intention is knowledge of teaching.

Now as the Lord was descending into the womb, and while they were hearing the earth quaking and so forth, this verse was spoken by devatās:

I 71 "Ah, the wonder in the world!"

71 Therein *greatness of the special qualities of Buddhas* means:

* Untraced.
† D iii 159.

[1] Cf. MA ii 28.
[2] Cf. SA ii 288.

Ah, how great are the special qualities of Buddhas, ah, the great might of Buddhas!

71 *In six ways the ten-thousand world-system shook* means that among the ten-thousand world-spheres the great earth shook, trembled in six ways. How? It bent up from the east, bent down from the west; it bent up from the west, bent down from the east; it bent up from the north, bent down from the south; it bent up from the south, bent down from the north; it bent up from the centre, bent down from the edge; it bent up from the edge, bent down from the centre. Thus in six ways like a ship agitated by the force of the winds and struck by the breaking of waves and waters, did this great earth, four myriad and two hundred thousand yojanas thick[1]—the earth bounded by the waters that are its support—even though incognizant being as though cognizant, quake as though dancing for joy.

[57] 72 *And great was the radiance*[2] means the radiance was superb, surpassing the deva-majesty of devas.

72 *Astounding the wonder* means there was a wonder and an astounding (event).

72 Now were spoken the verses beginning *For at that time the Lord* so as to show from the earthquake the occurrence of the wonderful happenings when the Lord was appearing in the world and so forth.

72 *Eldest in the world* means best in the world.

73 *With devas*[3] means of the world with devas. The accusative case is to be understood in the sense of the genitive.

73 *Displaying* means showing a marvel.

73 *Even as he walked* means that having spanned the ten-thousand world-systems and while he was standing in that Walk made of jewels he *talked even as* he was walking up and down.

73 *Leader of the world* means: then thundering like a lion, roaring a lion's roar from the surface of a flat rock, or like a storm-cloud pouring down rain and as it were bringing down the River of the Sky[4], the Teacher talked a talk on Dhamma connected with the four truths and bright with different methods and

[1] As at text p. 135, Jā i 25 (iii 42, different measurement), Vism 205.

[2] obhāsa, see MLS iii 202, n. 2.

[3] sadevakaṁ, acc. case. The context is: showing it to men with the devas; but the closer meaning is: by (the) making (of) men with the devas see it.

[4] ākāsagaṅgaṁ otārento; simile at Jā i 95, DA iii 973, MA iii 25, SA i 306, AA i 165, UdA 419.

stamped with the three characteristic marks (of phenomena) in a deep and beautiful voice with the eight fine qualities, pleasant to the ear and lovely.

73 *Nor did he turn back on the way as though he were on a walk of (only) four cubits* means: when the teacher was creating that Walk, one end had its outer rim at the eastern edge of the world-sphere, the other had its outer rim at the western edge of the world-sphere. The teacher, walking up and down on this Jewel-Walk which was thus steadfast, turned back after he had reached one or other of the ends, but he did not turn back on the way till he had reached both ends. While he was walking up and down in the Walk as though it were a measure of (only) four cubits, he turned back quickly only when he had reached both the ends. The meaning *nor did he turn back on the way* is thus.

But how did the Lord make the Walk short when the measure of its extent was the ten-thousand? Or did he fashion it as a great individuality? He did not do that. A Buddha's majesty of Buddhas is unthinkable. From the abode of the Akaniṭṭha (devas) as far as Avīci it was one open space.[1] And across the ten-thousand world-spheres was one open space. Devas and men saw as all devas and men see (anyone) walking up and down as usual. Thus they saw the Lord walking up and down. And while the Lord was walking up and down he taught Dhamma, and in the meantime attained the attainments.

Then the venerable Sāriputta, thinking "He is embellished with the thirty-two glorious Marks produced by the power of unlimited and vast heaped-up skill", and having seen the Lord's glorious body resplendent with the eighty minor characteristics like the full-moon at autumn time and like the Coral Tree in full and abundant bloom and a hundred yojanas in height, with his halo extending to the height of eighteen ratanas, glorious in contour like a noble mountain of molten gold, walking with the unexcelled grace of a Buddha, and walking up and down surrounded by a company of ten thousand devas, he thought: "The whole ten-thousand world-system must be assembled here for a great teaching on Dhamma. And a teaching by the Lord on the Buddhavaṁsa will be very helpful, bringing satisfaction. Suppose now I were to question Him of the Ten Powers [**58**] about the Buddhavaṁsa from the resolve onwards?" Having determined on this, he

[1] Cf. text p. 46, one in light.

arranged his robe over one shoulder, approached the Lord, brought together his clasped hands which were shining like stainless unspoiled lotus-buds, their ten fingers touching one another, and raising them to his head[1], he asked the Lord, beginning: "Of what kind, great hero, was your resolve?" Accordingly it was said:

I 74 Sāriputta, of great wisdom, proficient in concentration and meditation, attained to the perfection of wisdom, asked the leader of the world:

75 Of what kind, great hero, supreme among men, was your resolve? At what time, wise one, was supreme Awakening aspired to by you?[2]

Now, what is this sequence of meanings? It is a sequence of meanings based on a question asked. There are three sequences of meanings[3]: a sequence of meanings based on a question asked, a sequence of meanings dictated by another's mental disposition, a sequence of meanings dictated by the natural course of Dhamma. Herein, "When this had been said, Nanda the cowherd spoke thus to the Lord: 'Now, what, revered sir, is the hither bank, what the further bank?'*"—a sequence of meanings based on a question asked should be understood thus in respect of a discourse given by the Lord to those who asked. "Then there arose a reasoning in the mind of a certain monk, thus: 'It is said, sir, that material shape is not self, that feeling, perception, the habitual tendencies, consciousness is not self. What is the self that deeds affect that are done by not-self?' Then the Lord, knowing by mind the reasoning in the mind of this monk, addressed the monks saying: 'What do you think about this, monks? Some foolish man here, not knowing, ignorant, with his mind in the grip of craving, may deem to go beyond the teacher's instruction thus: 'It is said, sir, that material shape is not self . . . What is the self that deeds affect that are done by not-self?' What do you think about this, monks? Is material shape permanent or impermanent?"†—a sequence of meanings dictated by another's mental disposition should be understood thus in respect of a discourse spoken by the Lord when he knew the

* Cf. S iv 180f.
† M iii 19.

[1] See text, p. 10.
[2] Quoted text p. 65, CpA 6, DAṬ ii 16.
[3] Cf. DA 122–3, MA i 175, UdA 4 to end of this paragraph.

mental disposition of others. By whichever Dhamma a teaching has begun, because of that Dhamma being conformable to Dhamma, because of its not being opposed to it[1], among these Discourses a further teaching comes—on account of these a sequence of meanings dictated by the natural course of Dhamma should be understood. On account of this it was said: sequence of meanings based on a question asked.

74 Therein *attained to the perfection of wisdom* means attained to the height of a disciple's knowledge of the perfection.

74 *Asked* means asked.[2]

Therein, a question means: a question illuminating what has not been seen, a question referring to what has been seen, a question cutting off perplexity, a question of inference, a question that is a longing to converse—it is fivefold.[3] Which was the Elder's question? Inasmuch as this Buddhavaṁsa is not the sphere of buddhas-by-and-for-themselves **[59]** (though) having accumulated the accessories of merit for an incalculable and more than a hundred thousand eons, nor of the two chief disciples (though) having accumulated the accessories of merit for an incalculable and a hundred thousand eons, nor of other great disciples (though) having accumulated the accessories or merit for a hundred thousand eons, but as it is the sphere of omniscient Buddhas only, therefore it should be understood that the Elder's questions are ones illuminating what has not been seen.

75 *Of what kind* means the method of asking is a "what?" method.

75 *Your* means your.[4]

75 *Resolve* means applying his mind to Buddhahood and thinking: "I will not rise without obtaining the Buddha's declaration", lying down having resolutely determined on energy.[5] Accordingly it was said:

I 75 Of what kind, great hero, supreme among men, was your resolve?

75 *At what time*? means in which time?

[1] Read apaṭipakkha-.
[2] pucchatī ti āpucchi.
[3] DA 68, MA ii 334f., SA ii 8f., AA i 101f., ItA 40f., Asl 55f.
[4] te ti tava.
[5] This refers to the Bodhisatta as Sumedha lying in the mire at the feet of the Buddha Dīpaṅkara, see IIA. 52ff.

75 *Aspired to* means wished for, longed for. "The Awakened One should awaken, the freed one should free". So thinking, he asked when the aspiration for Buddhahood had been made.

75 *Awakening* means perfect Self-Awakening; it is a synonym for knowledge of the Way to arahantship and of omniscient knowledge.

75 *Supreme* means that it is called supreme because of its being the best for the awakening of disciples. The 'm' between the two (bodhi and uttama) makes a liaison between the two (words). Now, asking about the things making a Buddha he said:

I 76 Of what kind were giving, morality, renunciation, wisdom and energy? And of what kind were patience, truth-speaking, resolute determination, loving-kindness, equanimity?

77 Of what kind, wise one, leader of the world, were your ten perfections? How were the higher perfections fulfilled, how the ultimate perfections?

76 Therein, concerning the perfection of *giving*: as the sacrifice of external possessions it is a perfection; the sacrifice of any of one's limbs is a higher perfection; the sacrifice of one's life is an ultimate perfection.[1] This is also the method for the remaining perfections. Thus there are exactly thirty perfections: ten perfections, ten higher perfections, ten ultimate perfections.[2] Therein there is no measure to the fulfilment of the Bodhisatta's perfection of *giving*. And, certainly, in the words of the Sasapaṇḍita Birth-story:

> When I saw one approaching for alms, I sacrificed my own self. There was no one equal to me in giving—this was my perfection of Giving.*

Thus, in making a sacrifice of (one's) life in this way the perfection of *giving* is classed as an *ultimate perfection*.

Similarly, there is no measure to the fulfilment of the perfection of *moral habit*. And, certainly, in the words of the Saṅkhapāla Birth-Story:

[60] Though pierced by stakes, though hacked about by knives, I

* Jā. No. 316, Cp I 23; quoted Jā i 45, ApA 49.

[1] BvAB gives the right reading and is followed here. Cf. text p. 113.
[2] Cf. Jā i 25; also DhA i 84.

was not angry with the hunter-boys—this was my perfection of Morality.*

Thus, in making a sacrifice of (one's) self the perfection of *moral habit* is classed as an *ultimate perfection*:

Similarly, there is no measure to the fulfilment of the perfection of *renunciation* through giving up a great kingdom. And, certainly, in the words of the Cūḷasutasoma Birth-Story:

The great kingdom that I possessed I threw away as if it were spittle; sacrificed, there was no clinging (to it)—this was my perfection of Renunciation.†

Thus, having thrown away the kingdom without attachment (to it), the perfection of *renunciation* when he was departing (from home) is classed as an *ultimate perfection.*

Similarly, in the time of Wise Mahosadha[1] and so forth there was no measure to the fulfilment of the perfection of *wisdom*. And, certainly, in the words of the Sattubhattaka Birth-Story when I was Wise Senaka:[2]

I, investigating by wisdom, released the brahman from sorrow. There was no one equal to me in wisdom—this was my perfection of Wisdom.‡

The perfection of *wisdom* when he was showing that the snake had gone inside the sack is classed as an *ultimate perfection.*

Similarly, there was no measure to the fulfilment of the perfection of *energy*. And, certainly, in the words of the Mahājanaka Birth-Story:

All men are lost indeed if, in the midst of waters, they see no

* Jā. No. 524, Cp II 10 7; quoted Jā i 45, ApA 50.
† Jā. No. 525; quoted Jā i 46, ApA 50.
‡ Jā No. 402; verse not in Fausböll.

[1] Jā No. 546. The Bodhisatta was born as minister to King Vedeha.

[2] Jā No. 402, called Sattubhasta-jātaka. Our text reads Sattubhattakapaṇḍitakāle. Ja i 46, which I follow, Sattubhattajātake Senakapaṇḍitakāle. Cf. ApA 50 for Sattubhasta- (v. l. Satthubhatta-) Senakapaṇḍitakāle. All the following verses are quoted at Jā i 46f., ApA 50f.

shore. There was no contrariety of mind[1]—this was my perfection of energy.*

Thus while he was crossing the great sea the perfection of *energy* is classed as an *ultimate perfection.*

Similarly, in the Khantivāda Birth-Story:

Even though they were cutting me, incognizant, with sharp swords I was not angry with the King of Kāsi—this was my perfection of patience.†

Thus, experiencing great strength (even) though in an incognizant state, the perfection of *patience* is classed as an *ultimate perfection.*

In the Mahāsutasoma Birth-Story:

Protecting truth-speaking, having sacrificed my life, I set free a hundred warrior-nobles—this was my perfection of truth-speaking.‡

Thus, having sacrificed life while protecting truth, the perfection of *truth* is classified as an *ultimate perfection.*

In the Mūgapakkha Birth-Story:

[61] Mother and father were not disagreeable to me, nor was the great retinue disagreeable to me. Omniscience was dear to me, therefore I resolutely determined on that itself.§

Thus, again having sacrificed life while resolutely determining on that itself, the perfection of *resolute determination* is classed as an *ultimate perfection.*

In the Ekarāja Birth-Story:

No one was frightened of me, nor did I fear anyone; sustained by the power of loving-kindness, I delighted in the forest then.‖

* Jā No. 539.
† Jā No. 313.
‡ Jā No. 537. Cf. Cp III 12 6.
§ Jā No. 538. Cf. III 1 6; 3 10; 6 18.
‖ Jā No. 540. Called Sāmajātaka there and at ApA 51. Cf. Cp. III 13 and III 14, the former, where this verse occurs, being called Suvaṇṇasāmacariya, and the latter Ekarājacariya as also at Jā i 47.

[1] cittassa aññathā, same expression at Cp I 8 15. See CPD s.v. aññathā.

Thus, not recking even of life, in showing loving-kindness the perfection of *loving-kindness* is classed as an *ultimate perfection.*

In the Lomahaṁsa Birth-Story:

> I lay down in a cemetery leaning against a skeleton; crowds of rustic children approached and displayed a great deal of derisive behaviour.*

Thus, an even-mindedness was not overwhelmed nor was happiness or suffering when the rustic children were spitting (on him) and so forth as well as when (others) were offering garlands and perfumes, the perfection of *even-mindedness* was classed as an *ultimate perfection.* This is in brief here and is to be taken in detail from the Cariyāpiṭaka.†

Now, to show the Lord's answers when he was being questioned by the Elder, it was said by the recensionists:

I 78 Asked by him, he of the voice sweet as the karavīka's made answer cooling to the heart, rejoicing the world with the devas.

79 What was taught, what was celebrated concerning past Buddhas, Conquerors, what was the traditional account of their teaching and activities, he expounded for the welfare of the world with the devas from his discernment going back to his former habitations.

78 Therein *asked by him, he made answer* means: being asked by the General under Dhamma, he answered him and spoke all the Buddhavaṁsa from (the time of) his own resolve to the culmination in full Self-Awakening.

78 *Voice sweet as a karavīka's*[1]: the meaning is a sweet voice like the karavīka bird's: he whose voice is as sweet as the karavīka's, sweet as the karavīka's in sound. As to this sweetness of the sound of karavīkas: they say karavīka birds, **[62]** having tapped a mango of sweet taste with the point of a claw, having drunk the juice of the fruit as it trickled out, knocking it with their wing like intoxicated quadrupeds going crooked, they begin to sing. And crowds of quadrupeds, intent on fodder, ejecting even the grass they had

* Jā No. 94. Verse at Cp III 15 1; cf. M i 79.

† Cp III 15.

[1] Cf. MA iii 382f. for following passage.

taken in their mouths, listen to that loud sound; beasts of prey who had been chasing small animals, not going forward[1] on the foot they had raised, stand still like a painting[2]; and animals that were being chased and were afraid of dying, also stand still; and birds flying in the sky having spread their wings, also stand still; and fish in the water, not moving the membrane of the ears, hearing that sound, also stand still. Thus are sweet voiced karavīkas.

78 *Cooling to the heart* means: leading the mind of all people who have been burned by the fires of the defilements to a cool state by means of understanding the flow of talk on Dhamma.

78 *Rejoicing* means gladdening.

78 *With the devas* means the world with the devas.

79 *Concerning past Buddhas* means that before our Lord's resolve, the Buddhas Taṇhaṅkara, Medhaṅkara, Saraṇaṅkara and Dīpaṅkara[3] had arisen in a single eon. After these there were the Buddha Koṇḍañña and the others, in all twenty-four Buddhas counting Dīpaṅkara and the others, here called past Buddhas. Concerning these past Buddhas.

79 *Concerning Conquerors* is merely a synonym for that.

79 *Taught* means Dhamma-talk about the twenty-four Buddhas, associated with the four truths, was spoken.

79 *Celebrated* means the career of these beginning with demarcation by eon, birth, clan, life-span, Tree of Awakening, male disciples, female disciples, assemblies, attendants, parents, son, wife, is called celebrated.

79 *What was the traditional account of their teachings and activities:* the meaning is that the traditional account of their teachings and activities as celebrated has been taught from Dīpaṅkara, Him of the Ten Powers, to Kassapa.

79 *From his discernment going back to former habitations* means: thinking "One birth, two births", though detailed thus as formerly they inhabited them, they come to, arrive at a former habitation regarded as a continuity of the aggregates—from his discernment going back to these former habitations, by his recollection and knowledge of former habitations.

79 *He expounded* means he answered.

79 *Welfare of the world* means the Buddhavaṁsa is for the welfare of all the world(s).

[1] anatikkamitvā. MA's anukkhipitvā seems preferable.

[2] cittakatā viya.

[3] Cf. CpA 12–13.

79 *With the devas* means for people with the devas.

Then the Lord, his heart tempered with compassion, urging people with the devas to listen, spoke beginning, "Productive of zest and joyousness."

80 Therein *productive of zest and joyousness* means causing zest and joyousness. Through previous zest there is joyousness. Productive of the five kinds of zest.[1]

80 *Removal of the darts of sorrow* means the removal, shattering of the darts considered as sorrow.

[63] 80 *The acquiring of all the attainments* means that by this they acquire even all the attainments and so forth of devas and men: acquirement of all the attainments, the meaning being that this Dhamma-teaching of the Buddhavaṁsa is the acquiring of all the attainments.

80 *Keeping in mind* means keeping in mind,[2] honouring the recollection of the Buddhas.

80 *Listen* means listen[3], attend to.

80 *To me* means to me.[4]

81 *The crushing of pride*[5] means the crushing of all prides beginning with pride of birth[6].

81 *The driving away of sorrow* is called the mental torment of affliction through the loss of relations and so on.[7] From whatever cause there is melancholy—when there is the mark of inner brooding on it, the considering of its nature with the mind, the manifestation of grief—(if) he drives away that sorrow, it is the driving away of sorrow.

81 *The complete delivering from saṁsāra* means making for a complete delivering from the shackles of saṁsāra. The "overpassing of saṁsāra" is also a reading; its meaning being making for an overpassing of saṁsāra.

81 *The destruction of all anguish* means that herein this word anguish[8] is to be seen in contexts such as: painful feelings,

[1] Vism 143, Asl 115.
[2] cittīkatvā ti citte katvā.
[3] suṇothā ti suṇātha.
[4] me ti mama.
[5] madanimmadana as at A ii 34, Vism 143.
[6] Three kinds at A i 146, and see PED s.v. mada.
[7] Five kinds of vyasana, loss, misfortune, at Vin v 129, D iii 235, A iii 147, Miln 196. Cf. Vbh 99f.
[8] dukkha. Cf. Asl 41 for this paragraph.

painful bases (for sensations), painful objective (meditational) supports, conditions for pain, painful manifestations. "This is getting rid of anguish"*—in such contexts painful feelings are shown. "Birth is anguish and ageing is anguish"†—in such contexts it is among the painful bases (for sensations). "But inasmuch, Mahāli, as material shape is painful, fallen on pain, beset by pain"‡—in such contexts it is objective (meditational) support. "The accumulation of evil is anguish"§—in such contexts it is a condition for anguish. "But this is not easy to describe in full, monks, so many are the anguishes of Niraya"||—in such contexts it is painful manifestations. But here it is to be understood as painful bases (for sensations) and condition for pain. Therefore the meaning is: making for the destruction of all anguishes beginning with birth.

81 *Way* (acc.) means: herein the Way is called the teachings of the Buddhavaṁsa for it is being tracked by those desirous of what is skilled, or they go along slaying the defilements.[1] This teaching of the Buddhavaṁsa has become the way to nibbāna.

81 *Respectfully* means respectfully keeping in mind, being attentive.

81 *Fare along* means: be resolutely determined on, listen. Or, having heard this teaching of the Buddhavaṁsa which is for producing zest and joyousness, for removing the darts of sorrow, and is the cause of acquiring all the attainments, now bringing about the special qualities for crushing pride and so on, for the destruction of all anguish, and the way to Buddha's state, saying *Fare along*, **[64]** he produced the power for an aspiration for Buddhahood for all devas and men.

Thus is finished the Exposition of the Section on the Jewel-Walk, of the Clarifier of the Sweet Meaning, the Commentary on the Chronicle of Buddhas

Finished as to all methods is the Commentary on the Inner Antecedent

* From formula for fourth meditation (jhāna).
† Vin i 10.
‡ S iii 70.
§ Dh 117.
|| M iii 167.

[1] Cf. VbhA 114, Moha 34.

IIA ACCOUNT OF SUMEDHA[1]

Now:

IIA 1 A hundred thousand eons and four incalculables ago there was a city named Amara, good to look upon, delightful.[2]

The occasion has arisen for the Commentary on the Chronicle of Buddhas handed down by the method such as this (verse) and the following. Inasmuch as after examining the delivery of Discourses, so this Commentary on the Chronicle of Buddhas becomes clear from the examination of the delivery of Discourses when it is being spoken. Delivery of discourses is of four kinds[3]: according to the speaker's inclination, according to the inclination of others, as the result of a question, on account of need arisen. Those discourses which the Lord spoke unasked by others and according to his own inclination only, such as the Ākaṅkheyya Discourse,[4] the Vatthu Discourse[5]—the delivery of these is according to one's own inclination. But those that were spoken according to the inclination of others and after he had considered the inclination of others, their patience, mentality and state of awakening, thinking, (for example): "Mature now in Rāhula are the things bringing freedom to maturity. Suppose I were to train Rāhula further in the destruction of the cankers?"*—discourses such as this Exhortation to Rāhula,[6] the Discourse on the Turning of the Wheel of Dhamma[7]—the delivery of these is according to the inclination of others.

Having approached the Lord, these devas and men asked a question. And questioned thus, the delivery of those discourses that were spoken by the Lord such as the Devatāsaṁyutta[8] and the Bojjhaṅgasaṁyutta[9] was as the result of a question. And the delivery of those that were taught because of a reason that had arisen,

* M iii 277, S iv 105.

[1] For the Sumedhakathā cf. Jā i 3f, ApA 2–31, Mhbv 2ff.
[2] Jā i 3, quoting Bv.
[3] Cf. DA 50, MA i 15, AA i 19, UdA 29, ItA i 35.
[4] M Sta 6.
[5] M Sta 7.
[6] Cūḷarāhulovādasutta, M Sta 147; Mahā-, M Sta 62.
[7] Vin i 10, S v 420.
[8] S i 1.
[9] S v 63.

such as the Heirs of Dhamma[1] and the Simile of the Child's Flesh[2] was on account of a need that had arisen[3]. Thus of these four kinds of delivery of a discourse, the delivery of this Chronicle of Buddhas was as the result of a question. For it was delivered by the Lord as a result of a question. As the result of whose question? The Venerable Sāriputta's. So in reference to this it was said, beginning:

[65] Sāriputta, of great wisdom, proficient in concentration and meditation, attained to the perfection of wisdom, asked the leader of the world: Of what kind, great hero, supreme among men, was your resolve?*

So this teaching of the Chronicle of Buddhas should be understood as being the result of a question.

1 Therein *A hundred thousand eons* (kappa): here this word kappa is to be seen in various contexts[4] as believing, allowable, time, designation, cutting off, interpretation, pretext, completeness, duration of the life-span, great eon, and so forth. Thus, "This is to be believed (okappaniya) of the good Gotama inasmuch as he is an arahant, Perfect Buddha"†—in such contexts "believing" is to be seen. "I allow you, monks, to make use of fruit that in five ways is allowable (kappa) to recluses"‡—in such contexts it is "allowable". "In which I ever constantly (niccakappa) abide"†—in such contexts it is "time". "The Venerable Kappa said"§ and "They say Kappa of the Banyan was the name the Lord gave to this brahman"||—in such contexts it is "designation". "Adorned, hair and beard trimmed (kappita)"¶—in such contexts it is "cutting off". "Is the practice (kappa) concerning two finger-breadths allowable (kappati)?**—in such contexts it is

* Bv I 74, 75 quoted CpA 6.
† M i 249.
‡ Vin ii 109.
§ Sn 1092.
|| Ibid. 344.
¶ Jā vi 268.
** Vin ii 294, 300.

[1] M Sta. 3.
[2] S ii 97.
[3] So too was the Vessantara-jātaka, see text p. 295.
[4] Cf. MA ii 125f., SA i 15, AA ii 377, KhA 115f., CpA 10. Of these only CpA includes "great eon", mahākappa.

interpretation (vikappa). "There is good reason (kappa) for lying down"*—in such contexts it is "pretext". "Having illumined the whole (kevalakappa) of Jeta Grove"†—in such contexts it is "completeness". "Let the Lord remain for a span (kappa), let the Well-farer remain for a span"‡—in such contexts it is "life-span". "Of what kind, revered sir, is an eon (kappa)?"§—here it is a "great eon". By the word "and so forth"—"Indeed we, discussing together with a disciple did not know he was one resembling (kappena) the teacher"||—here it is "resemblance" "If what is allowable (kappa) is destroyed, if the occasion for making allowable becomes worn away"¶—here it is "allowable" through Vinaya. But here it should be understood as "great eon". Therefore *a hundred thousand eons* means a hundred thousand great eons.

1 *And four incalculables* means that the remaining phrase should be understood as "on the conclusion of the four incalculables". The meaning is: on the conclusion of the four incalculables in addition to the hundred thousand eons.

1 *A city named Amara* means that the city was called both Amara and Amaravatī. But some[1] explain it even here in another way. How can they when this was the name of this city?

1 *Good to look upon* means good to look upon because of its being adorned with well laid-out carriage-roads, crossroads, gateways, squares, places where three or four roads meet, walls, enclosures, palaces, large residences, abodes[2].

1 *Delightful* means it was delightful to devas and mankind and so forth because the extremely charming districts were equally clean, [**66**] because it was full of shade and water, because food was easily obtainable, because it was suitable for all means of existence, because it was prosperous.

2 *Resounded with the ten sounds*: with the sound of elephants, with the sound of horses, with the sound of chariots, with the sound of drums, with the sound of chanks, with the sound of lutes, with the sound of singing, with the sound of cymbals, with

* D iii 256, A iv 333, Vbh 386.
† S i 1, etc., A i 278.
‡ Vin ii 294, 289, D ii 104, 115, S ii 276, A iv 309, Ud 62.
§ S ii 181.
|| M i 150.
¶ Vin iv 121.

[1] *keci*.
[2] Cf. Miln 1, 330.

the sound of gongs, and with the tenth sound (which was) "Partake of, drink, eat."[1] It resounded with these ten sounds. The meaning is: uninterrupted merry-making, festivities, sports.

2 *Well provided with food and drink* means it was well provided with food and drink, was well stocked with food, and with the four kinds of nutriment[2], and with drink. Thus is shown its good conditions for almsfood. The meaning is: it was furnished with plentiful food and drink. Now, so as to show examples of these ten sounds, it was said:

IIA 2 The sound of elephants, the sound of horses, and of drums, chanks, and chariots.
3 as well as of "Eat, drink" shouted out for victuals and drink.

2 *The sound of elephants* means with the sound of the trumpeting of elephants; the accusative case should be understood in the sense of an instrumental. This is also the method in the remaining lines.

2 *And of drums, chanks, and chariots* means with the sound of drums and with the sound of chanks and with the sound of chariots, said with a change of gender.[3]

3 "*Eat, drink*" means: by using the former method thus, the meaning is said to be here *shouted out*, called loudly for what was connected with food and drink. But of these sounds only one kind (of each) is shown, not all, but all the tenfold (sounds) are shown, not (merely) one. The sound of the tabour is included in the sound of drums; the sounds of lutes, singing, cymbals, and gongs are included in the sound of chanks. Showing all the ten, praising the city's success thus by the one procedure, yet to show this again it was said:

IIA 3 The city was complete in all respects. It engaged in every industry,
4 was possessed of the seven kinds of treasures, crowded with all kinds of people; prosperous as a deva-city, it was a dwelling-place for doers of merit.

[1] Cf. D ii 147, Jā i 3.

[2] Perhaps the four kinds given at A iii 30, KhA 207: what can be eaten, drunk, chewed, savoured.

[3] From masc. to neut.

3 Therein *complete in all respects* means: possessed of all the constituent parts of a city, with city gateways, halls and so forth, replete with all sources of wealth,[1] treasures, and grain[1], grass, wood and water.

3 *Engaged in every industry*: the meaning is that it engaged in, engaged well in every occupation, having every occupation.

[67] 4 *Possessed of the seven treasures* means replete with the seven kinds of treasures beginning with pearls[2]; or that it was possessed of the seven kinds of treasures beginning with the elephant in the region where is the dwelling of a universal monarch.

4 *Crowded with all kinds of people* means: crowded with people of different kinds, districts and dialects.

4 *Prosperous* means prosperous, opulent in all means of human support and enjoyment.

4 *As a deva-city* means it was said it was prosperous like a deva-city, like Ālakamanda,[3] like Amaravatī.[4]

4 *A dwelling-place for doers of merit* (āvāsaṁ puññakamminaṁ) means: a dwelling-place (āvāso) in the sense that doers of merit dwelt here. It should be known that āvāso is to be understood as āvāsaṁ after a change in gender has been made. Merit means that one becomes conspicuous by that ('nena); the meaning is that he becomes conspicuous by reason of family, beauty, intelligence, wealth, importance. Or merit means it cleanses away all unskill, stains and dust. It is work (kamma): those who have it are doers of merit. It means the dwelling-place for those doers of merit.

The brahman named Sumedha lived there[5]. He was of good birth on both sides and of pure descent from mother and father back through seven generations, unchallenged, irreproachable in respect of birth[6], lovely, good to look upon, charming, possessed of the utmost beauty of complexion; he was master of the three Vedas, versed in the vocabularies and rituals with the phonology and exegesis, and the legendary tradition as the fifth; he was learned in idioms, a grammarian, proficient in popular philosophy and the Marks of a Great Man[6]. But when he was young his parents died. Then an official who was the treasurer, bringing a

[1] Cf. D i 134, S i 71, iv 324.
[2] See Ml ii 251.
[3] A city of the devas, see DPPN.
[4] Sakka's city.
[5] CpA 13 has almost the same description of Sumedha.
[6] Stock, as at e.g. text p. 148, D i 88, M ii 165, A i 163, see MLS ii 317.

ledger, opened rooms which contained a variety of treasures, gold, silver, jewels, pearls and so forth, and said: "One of these, young man, is your mother's property, one your father's property, one your grandfather's and great-grandfather's." When he had pointed out the treasure as far as the seventh generation back, he said: "Take good care of it", and made him sit down. He assented, saying, "It is good", and doing (deeds of) merit, lived as master in the house. Accordingly it was said:

IIA 5 In the city of Amaravatī the brahman named Sumedha, accumulating countless crores, was rich in plentiful crops.

6 A repeater[1], expert in mantras, master of the three Vedas, he had reached perfection in the (science of) Marks, the legendary tradition, and the obligatory duties (of a brahman).

5 Therein *In the city of Amaravatī* means in the city called Amaravatī.

5 *Named Sumedha*: here wisdom (paññā) is called intelligence (*medha*), lovely (*su*-dhara) in him, it was extolled, so he was known as Sumedha (lovely intelligence).

5 *Brahman*[2] means: a brahman intones the prayer, repeats mantras. **[68]** But the grammarians say a brahman is the offspring of Brahma. And the ariyans say one is a brahman because evil is warded off.

5 *Accumulating countless crores* means the accumulating of crores (gen. pl.), accumulating crores (compound word), and accumulating crores that are countless. That accumulating of countless crores by him means accumulating countless crores of wealth.

5 *Rich in plentiful crops*: it is said first in respect of the rich crops in the ground and in the granary; this is to be understood as said in respect of the rich crops permanently needed for food.

6 *A repeater* (ajjhāyaka) means he is a repeater, he does not meditate (na jhāyati), is lacking in the development of the meditations. As it was said, "These do not meditate now, these do not meditate now, Vāseṭṭha, they are repeaters. This is how the second phrase came into use."* There thus arose an expression of reproof

* D iii 94 which reads tatiyaṁ akkharaṁ, the first it gives being brahmaṇā, the second jhāyakā, and the third ajjhāyakā. See also DA 247, AA ii 261 for this passage. Akkhara, among other meanings, is a phrase or a letter of the alphabet.

[1] Of Vedic texts.

[2] See DA 244, MA i 109, UdA 58, and cf. Nd2 464.

for brahmans who, in the time of the first world-cycle, were lacking in meditation. But now, saying "he repeats that" means he is a repeater; saying "he recites mantras" means that, in giving an expression of praise, they define him in this way. Experts in the mantras[1] means that they carry the mantras in mind.

6 *Of the three Vedas* means of the three Vedas: the Rig Veda, the Yajur Veda, the Sāma Veda. But this word "veda" is to be seen as knowledge, joy, texts. In contexts such as "That brahman whom I saw[2] as Veda-master, man-of-naught, not attached to the sphere of sense-desires"* it is to be seen as knowledge. In contexts such as "Who, thrilled (vedajāta), roam the world"† it is to be seen as joy. In the contexts "Master of the three Vedas, versed in the vocabularies and rituals"‡ as texts. Here too it is texts.

6 *Master* means being perfect in enunciating the three Vedas with the lips.[3]

6 *In the* (*science of*) *marks*: marks are the marks on a woman, the marks on a man[4], the Marks of a Great Man and so on.

6 *In the legendary tradition* means saying "Thus indeed it has been" in various texts considered to be old connected with expressions of this kind.[3]

6 *In the obligatory duties* means in the own obligatory duties of brahmans or according to their own teachers.[5]

6 *Had reached perfection* means he was a widely famed teacher who had reached perfection.

Then one day he, the wise Sumedha, happy and wise with the group of ten special qualities, was sitting cross-legged in seclusion, his back straight, on the upper storey of a palace, and he thought: "Anguish it is to take on relinking in again-becoming, so is the breaking up of the physical frame on the repeated occasions of rebirth. So I, because I am liable to birth, liable to ageing, liable to disease, liable to dying, must seek for the unborn, unageing, undiseased, undying, for nibbāna, blissful and cool[6]. [**69**] Released

* Sn 1059; also 176, 1091.
† A ii 63, Vv 34 27, Kvu 554, etc.
‡ See text p. 67.

[1] On Vedic mantras see e.g. s.v. mantra, MLS ii Index.
[2] Reading here addasāmi; Sn 1059 ābhijaññā.
[3] DA i 247, AA ii 261.
[4] See D i 9, where these are part of the low art of fortune-telling.
[5] Cf. SnA ii 585.
[6] Cf. Ariyapariyesanasutta, M Sta 26.

without fail from the prison of becoming[1], the way leading to nibbāna should be developed by the one (sole) way[2]." Accordingly it was said:

IIA 7 Sitting in seclusion, I thought thus then: Again-becoming is anguish, also the breaking up of the physical frame.

8 Liable to birth, liable to ageing, liable to disease am I then; I will seek the peace that is unageing, undying, secure.

9 Suppose I, casting aside this putrid body filled with various ordures, should go on indifferent, unconcerned?

10 There is, there must be that Way; it is impossible for it not to be. I shall seek that Way for the utter release from becoming.

And now, having given the sequence of the verses and the meaning of the obscure lines, we will go on.

7 Therein *in seclusion* means in private.

7 *I thought thus* means that a method of thinking is to be seen by this (expression); I thought thus.

7 *Then* means in the time of that wise Sumedha.

7 *I thought thus* means the Lord now identified himself with the wise Sumedha. Therefore, explaining, "I myself was this Sumedha then", the Lord spoke as the supreme among men, saying, "I thought thus then."

8 *Liable to birth* means the condition of birth. This is the method for the remaining words also.

8 *Peace* means nibbāna.

9 *Suppose* is a particle in the sense of thinking about[3]. The meaning is "but if I".

9 *Putrid body* means a body become putrid.

9 *Filled with various ordures*[4] means carrying various ordures: urine, faeces, pus, blood, bile, phlegm, saliva, mucus and so forth[5].

9 *Indifferent* means without desire.

10 *There is* means it will be got at without fail.

10 *There must be* (hehiti) means there must be (bhavissati). This is a phrase for thinking about.

[1] bhavacāraka; cf. saṁsāracāraka, Vism 495.
[2] See M i 55f.
[3] Cf. PvA 282.
[4] kuṇapa, lit. a corpse.
[5] Defined at Vism 259ff.

10 *It is impossible for it not to be* means it is impossible for it not to be by reason of the one Way. But "that Way to be (hetuye)"[1] means through the existence of cause, not it is not. Simply to be (hetuye) is the meaning.

10 *For the utter release from becoming* means for freedom from the shackles of becoming.

11 In order that the meaning of what he was thinking about should be clear, he now spoke, beginning, *Even as*. For as there is happiness as the opposite to anguish in the world, so as there is becoming there must be non-becoming as its opposite; [**70**] and as there is heat there is also what is cool for allaying it, so there must be (something) also for allaying and quenching the fires of attachment and so forth; and as there is too the lovely blameless Dhamma as the opposite of an evil, miserable dhamma, so too as there is evil birth, from the throwing away of all births, there must be the unborn that is considered to be nibbāna. Accordingly it was said:

IIA 11 Even as anguish exists, happiness exists too, so as becoming exists non-becoming also is to be desired.

12 Even as heat exists, coolness exists too, so as the threefold fire exists nibbāna is to be desired.

11 *Even as* is a particle with the sense of simile.

11 *Happiness* means happiness well destroys bodily and mental anguish.

11 *Becoming* means producing.

11 *Non-becoming* means non-producing. While becoming exists what is liable to non-becoming also is to be desired.

12 *The threefold fire exists*: the meaning is that when the threefold fire of attachment and so forth exists.

12 *Nibbāna* means the quenching, allaying of this threefold fire of attachment and so forth; so *nibbāna is to be desired.*

13 *Evil* means unskilled, wretched.

13 *Loveliness too* means skill also.

13 *So* means just so.

13 *As birth exists* (jāti vijjante) means as birth is existing (jātiyā vijjamānāya). It was spoken making an error in gender and omitting the inflection.

13 *The unborn also* means throwing away births, the unborn nibbāna is to be desired too.

[1] Cf. kātuye, Thīg 418, and marituye, ibid. 426.

Then I thought still further: "As a man who has fallen down on a heap of filth, sees from afar a stainless pool adorned with clusters of red, blue and white lotuses, and thinks: 'Now, by what way can one get there?' he is intent on searching for that pool. A non-searching for it by him is not a defect in that pool, it is a defect in that man only. Thus, as there exists a washing away of the stains of the defilements[1], so the non-searching by him for the great pool of the Undying is not a defect in the great pool of the Undying, of the great nibbāna, it is a defect in that man only.[2] And as too there exists for a man who is surrounded by thieves a path for escape, but if he does not escape there is no defect in that path, the defect is in that man only. Even so there exists for the man who has been gripped by the thieves of the defilements an auspicious great way leading to the great city of nibbāna. **[71]** The non-searching for that way is not a defect in the way, it is a defect in that man. And as for the man who is hard pressed by a disease there exists a doctor for curing disease, but if he, having sought that doctor, does not get himself cured of that disease, the defect is not in the doctor, the defect is in that man only.[3] Even so, for one who is hard pressed by the diseases of the defilements[4] and there exists a way proficient in allaying the defilements, but if he does not seek a teacher, the defect is in him only, the defect is not in the teacher for guiding away the diseases of the defilements. Accordingly it was said:

IIA 14 Even as a man fallen into filth, though seeing a brimming pool does not seek that pool, that is not a defect in the pool.

15 So, though the pool of the Undying[5] exists for washing away the stains of the defilements, if one does not seek that pool, the defect is not in the pool of the Undying.[5]

16 Even as that man who is beset by enemies, while there exists a path for escape does not flee away, that is not a defect in the direct way.

[1] Cf. Miln 353.
[2] Cf. ibid. 246f.
[3] Cf. M ii 257, Miln 247.
[4] Cf. Miln 354.
[5] amatantale. Usually tala is dry land, but below the text suggests it is a pool, taḷāka. Probably -taḷa would be the better reading as an abbreviation of -taḷāka, pond or lake.

17 So, the one who is beset by the defilements, while there exists a safe path does not seek that way, the defect is not in the safe direct way.

18 And even as a man who has a disease, while there exists a physician does not get that disease cured, the defect is not in the physician.

19 So, (if) the one who is anguished, hard pressed by the diseases of the defilements does not seek that teacher, that is not a defect in the guider away.

14 Therein *fallen into filth* means got into filth or fallen into, soiled with filth.

15 *Washing away the stains of the defilements* (nom.) means in the washing away of the stains of the defilements (loc.[1]). The nominative case in the sense of the locative.

15 *In the pool of the Undying* (loc.) means of the pool regarded as the Undying. The locative case should be understood in the sense of a genitive. It is said (thus) including the nasal sound[2].

16 *By enemies* means by opponents.

16 *Beset* means completely obstructed.

16 *Path for escape* (gamanaṁ pathe) means path for escape (gamanapathe). Making the augment of the nasal sound for the sake of not upsetting the metre.

16 *Does not flee away* means: if he should not flee away.

16 *That man* means that man who is beset by thieves.

[72] 16 *In the direct way* means in the Way. And there are many names for the Way:

> Way, road, track, course, direct way, path, walk, boat, bridge for crossing over, and raft and float, causeway[3].

Here it is spoken of by the name "direct way".

17 *Safe* means safe from the absence of all distresses.

17 *In the safe direct way* (siva-m-añjase) means of the safe direct way's (sivassa añjasassa).

18 *In the physician* means in the doctor.

18 *If he does not get cured* means if he should not get cured.

[1] As in Bv II 15.

[2] anussāra, the nasal sound -ṁ, here amata-n-tale. The term anussāra occurs again at text p. 164. Buddhaghosa and Dhammapāla are inclined to use anunāsika, and the classical grammarians niggahīta.

[3] DA iii 743, MA i 229, SA iii 177, SnA i 34, Nd2 485.

18 *The defect is not in the physician* means it is not a defect of the physician's: the defect is the diseased man's only.

19 *Anguished* means bodily and mental anguish have been produced.[1]

19 *Teacher* means teacher of the Way to release.

19 *In the guider away* means in the teacher.

Then I, having thought thus, further thought thus: "As a man fond of dressing, having thrown aside a corpse that was tied to his neck[2], would go along happily, so, when I have thrown aside this putrid body, I could enter the great city of nibbāna with indifference just as men and women who have defecated on a dung-hill[3] do not go along taking it on their hip or taking it along wrapped up in the end of their cloth. Having thrown it aside, they go along simply indifferent, hating it and averse from seeing it. So when I have thrown aside this putrid body, I must be able to enter the undying city of nibbāna with indifference. And just as boatmen, having thrown aside an old leaky boat, go on simply indifferent, even so, when I have thrown aside this putrid body that oozes from the nine openings[4], indifferent will I enter the city of nibbāna. And just as a man taking various kinds of gems with him: pearls, crystals, emeralds and so forth, and going along a way together with thieves, takes a safe road through fear of losing his own gems, even so, this putrid body is like a thief plundering gems and if herein I do not create desire the gems of the skilled Dhamma of the ariyan Way will perish for me. Therefore, having thrown aside this body of mine that is born of producing and is like a great thief, I must be able to enter the great city of nibbāna." Accordingly it was said:

IIA 20 And even as a man, having discarded a loathsome ordure tied to his neck, would go on at ease, independent, his own master,

21 So, casting aside this putrid body, a conglomeration of various ordures, I would go on indifferent, unconcerned.

[73] 22 Even as men and women, casting aside excrement in a place for defecation, go on indifferent, unconcerned,[5]

[1] sañjāta; or, are from the same origin.
[2] Cf. A iv 377.
[3] Cf. Jā i 146, Vism 196.
[4] Cf. Miln 74, and see MQ i 101 for further references.
[5] Cf. Bv II A 9.

23 so too I, casting aside this body filled with various ordures, will go on as one having eased himself (leaves) a privy.
24 And even as the owners, having cast aside an old, broken-down and leaking boat, go on indifferent, unconcerned,
25 so too I, casting aside this body of nine constantly streaming apertures, will go on as its owners (leave) a worn-out boat.
26 And even as a man, who, taking goods with him, is going along with robbers, but seeing a danger of the goods being plundered goes on casting them aside,
27 so too I, getting rid of this body which resembles a great thief, will go on without danger of plundering what is skilled.

20 *And as a man an ordure* means: and as a man, young, in the prime of life, fond of adornment, would be revolted, ashamed, disgusted if the ordure of a snake or dog or human being were tied around his neck[1], would go on having discarded that ordure.

20 *At ease* means feeling ease.

20 *Independent* means abiding as he likes.

21 *A conglomeration of various ordures* means it is a heap of countless kinds of ordures. "Filled with various ordures" is also a reading.

22 *In a place for defecation* means that here they defecate and urinate—so, defecation. The defecation and the place are called "place for defecation." Or, one passes water means that this is a name for urine; the place for that is a privy—in this place for defecation: the meaning is in the place for excrement.

23 *As one having eased himself* (*leaves*) *a privy* means as men and women (leave) a privy when they have eased themselves.

24 *Old* means worn-out.

24 *Broken-down* means breaking down, falling to pieces.

24 *Leaky* means taking in water.[2]

24 *Owners* means the owners of the boat.

25 *Nine apertures* means the nine apertures because of being connected with the apertures which are the nine openings of the eyes, ears, and so forth.

[1] Cf. Vin iii 68, M i 119–120, A iv 376.

[2] udakagāhinin ti udakāgāhiniṃ.

25 *Constantly streaming* means constantly discharging. The meaning is perpetually oozing what is impure.

26 *Taking goods* means taking no matter what goods beginning with gems.

[74] 26 *Seeing a danger* means seeing a danger of the goods being divided into portions.

27 *So* means like the man going along taking the goods.

27 *This body* means this body (kāya) is the (place of) origin (āya) for extremely detestable, vile things.[1] Origin is the place of arising. Origin means the body is the (place of) origin for vile (things) such as vile head-hairs and so forth.

27 *Resembles a great thief* means like a great thief who plunders all that is good, making onslaught on creatures, taking what has not been given and so forth out of infatuation for alluring objects of sight and so forth. Therefore the construing of the meaning is to be understood as: as that man who was taking gems and goods was going along together with the thieves (but then) went along after he had got rid of the thieves, even so I too, getting rid of this body that is like a great thief, will go along to seek for myself the Way making for safety.

27 *Without danger of plundering what is skilled* means without danger of pillaging the skilled Dhamma.

Then the wise Sumedha, thinking of a reason for the "departure" by means of these various similes, thought still further: "Though my father, grandfather and so forth had collected this great heap of wealth, they did not go on to the world beyond taking even one kahāpaṇa.[2] But I have taken it and I must give a reason for going away", and having gone to the king, he informed him: "I, great king, with my heart oppressed by birth, ageing and so on, would go forth from home into homelessness. I have wealth to the value of countless hundreds and thousands of crores. Let the king accept it." The king said: "I have no need of your wealth, you do as you like with it." He said, "Very well, sire", and having had a drum beaten in the city, giving gifts to the populace, and getting rid of desire for property and desire for defilement, he departed alone from the city of Amara, similar to the glorious city of Amara.[3]

[1] Cf. KhA 38.
[2] Cf. M ii 71, 73.
[3] So called because it was inhabited by men like devas, Mhbv 2.

Near a mountain called Dhammaka in the Himavant, the home of various herds of deer, he made a hermitage. Having a leaf-hut constructed there, having a place for pacing up and down constructed that was clear of the five defects, giving up his outer cloak that was endowed with the nine defects, and clothing himself in a bark garment that was endowed with twelve special qualities, he went forth to gain the power of the super-knowings that is endowed with eight special qualities. But, when he had gone forth thus, giving up the leaf-hut that was filled with eight defects, approaching the root of a tree that was possessed of ten special qualities, giving up all grain products and partaking of wild fruits, striving the striving whether he were lying down, standing or pacing, he was an attainer of the eight attainments within a week, and of the five super-knowings.[1] Accordingly it was said:

IIA 28 So I, having thought thus, giving away countless hundreds of crores of wealth to rich and poor, went up to the Himavant.

29 On the mountain named Dhammaka close to the Himavant my hermitage was well made, well constructed was my leaf-hut.

[75] 30 I created a walk there that was clear of the five defects; I gained power in the super-knowings that was possessed of eight special qualities.

31 There I gave up my outer cloak that was endowed with nine defects and clothed myself in a bark-garment that was endowed with twelve special qualities.

32 I gave up the leaf-hut that was filled with eight defects and approached the root of a tree that was endowed with ten special qualities.

33 I completely gave up sown and planted grain and ate wild fruits that were possessed of countless special qualities.

34 I strove the striving there, whether sitting, standing, pacing. Within a week I reached power in the super-knowings.

28 Therein *So I* means thus I. Above the meaning is: having thought by the methods spoken of.

[1] Cf. CpA 13.

28 *To rich and poor*[1] means to those with protectors and those without protectors; both the well-to-do and to the poverty-stricken. Saying, "Take what you need", he gave it together with his granaries.

29 *Close to the Himavant* means near, close to the Himavant, king of mountains.

29 *The mountain named Dhammaka* means the mountain so named. And why is it called Dhammaka? Because generally Bodhisattas have gone forth in the going forth of seers and when they have produced the super-knowings they carry out the Dhamma for recluses near that mountain. Because of its being a support for the Dhamma for recluses it was commonly known therefore as Dhammaka.

29 *My hermitage was well made* means: spoken thus it is as though the hermitage, leaf-hut and walk were created by Sumedha the Wise with his own hands. But they were not created with his own hands. Were they not fashioned by the devaputta Vissakamma on receiving a message from Sakka, and then (did not) the Lord, referring to his birth through his own might of merit, begin by saying: "Sāriputta, on that Dhammaka mountain

My hermitage was well made, well constructed was my leaf-hut,
I created a walk there that was clear of five defects".

29 Therein *leaf-hut* means a hut roofed with leaves.

30 *There* means in that place for the hermitage.

30 *Clear of five defects* means clear of the five defects of a walk. What are the five defects in a walk? Being uniformly hard[2], trees inside it, densely covered, too narrow, too wide. Clear of these [**76**] five defects, it is called a walk when its size is limited to sixty ratanas[3] in length and one and a half ratanas in width. Or, clear of five defects means clear of, lacking the defects of the five hindrances.

30 *I gained power in the super-knowings* means a connexion is thus to be seen with this further clause.

30 *Possessed of eight special qualities* means possessed of eight special qualities spoken of thus: with the mind thus composed, quite purified, quite clarified, without blemish, without defilement, grown soft and workable, fixed, immovable, I gained, I procured

[1] nāthānāthā, the protected (or, protectors) and the unprotected.
[2] thaddhasamatā. Jā i 7 thaddhavisamatā, and says it hurts the feet.
[3] A measure of length, see e.g. VbhA 343. Probably a cubit.

power in the super-knowings. But some say: "Endowed with the eight happinesses of recluses; and that these eight happinesses of recluses are:[1] not appropriating wealth and grain, seeking blameless almsfood, eating almsfood emancipated[2], not oppressing the country (like) a king's men who oppress the country by taking wealth and grain, being without desire for or attachment to a livelihood, being without fear of being plundered by thieves, not associating with a king or a king's ministers, being unimpeded in regard to the four quarters[3]." These[4] say, "Endowed with, possessed of these eight happinesses of recluses I created a hermitage"—thus making a connexion with the hermitage. This does not agree with the text.

31 *Outer cloak* means a garment.

31 *There* means in that hermitage.

31 *Endowed with nine defects* means: Sāriputta, while I was living there, I gave up, I abandoned the very valuable outer cloak in which I was clothed and dressed. He explained, saying, "Giving up the outer cloak, I gave it up when I had seen nine defects therein." For nine defects in an outer cloak of those who have gone forth as ascetics are expounded. What are the nine? He explained, saying: "The high value of the outer cloak; the being dependent on others; that it is soon soiled through use and when it is soiled it has to be washed and dyed again; it gets worn out through use and when it is old it must be mended or stitched again; again it is difficult to handle when one is on quest (for alms); it is not suitable for the going forth of ascetics; it is in common with (the outer cloaks of) opponents so, lest opponents take it, it must be guarded; when it is put on it takes the place of an adornment; one who takes it when he is walking (for alms) has great desires. So I gave up, I abandoned the outer cloak which is endowed with these nine defects. He explained: Giving up the outer cloak when I had seen

[1] Cf. Jā v 252 for eight fortunate states of a homeless monk who is without wealth.

[2] nibbutapiṇḍapāta. According to Jā v 253 this appears to mean he eats as owner but hopes that the food given to him is in accordance with the rule for ordinary monks. But almsfood for one who is canker-free is called almsfood for the emancipated, nibbutapiṇḍa, to be partaken of when he is no longer a slave to desire, and is neither negligent nor hindered by defilement. Cf. Vism 43.

[3] catūsu disāsu appaṭihatabhāva. He can go in whatever direction he likes, Jā v 254. Cf. the five qualities of a cātuddisa monk at A iii 135, and see AA iii 280 in explanation: catūsu disāsu appaṭihatacāro.

[4] "These" are the "some" referred to at the beginning of the last sentence.

the defects therein I clothed myself in a bark-garment on giving up the outer cloak.

31 *Bark-garment*: the meaning is, having cut muñja grass into small pieces and fastening them together I took a garment made of cut up bark so as to clothe and dress (myself).

31 *Endowed with twelve special qualities* means endowed with twelve advantages. Herein the word "special quality" (guṇa) has the sense of advantage[1] in contexts such as, "It is to be expected that the offering (yields) a hundredfold (sataguṇa).*" The syllable "ma" makes a liason between the (two) words[2].

[77] There are twelve special qualities in a bark-garment: it is of no value; there is no dependence on others; it is possible to make it with one's own hands; when it gets worn through use there is no need to mend it; there is no fear of thieves; it is easily got ready when one is going on quest (for almsfood); it is perfectly suitable for the going forth of ascetics; it is not regarded as an adornment for one who is resorting to places (of resort for alms); one has few desires (such as are) caused by robe-material; it is comfortable to use; bark is easily obtained; and if a bark-garment is lost it is a matter of indifference. It is possessed of these twelve special qualities.

32 Then Sumedha the Wise, while he was living there in the leaf-hut, getting up early in the morning and reviewing his own reason for "departure", reflected thus: "Abandoning the household life like a ball of spittle and the tinkling sounds of the new golden anklets mingled with the sweet and merry things that are delightful to people, and the riches and prosperity that, attributes of a dwelling, shine, are splendid and lovely, I, from content with detachment, have entered Tapovana[3] (Tapa Grove) which carries away the evil of all people. But life here in the leaf-hut is like a second life in a house. Come, I would live at the root of a tree." Accordingly it was said, *I gave up the leaf-hut which was filled with eight defects.*

32 *Filled with eight defects* means filled with, connected with eight defects. With what eight? In what has to be accomplished after great preparation with grass, leaves and clay and so forth; what

* M iii 255; according to MA v 71 a hundred advantages; cf. A iii 42.

[1] Cf. text p. 43.
[2] Between guṇa and upāgataṁ: guna-m-upāgataṁ.
[3] Not in DPPN.

is called the lodging becomes old by constantly being attended to; it must be reconditioned but there is no one-pointedness of mind if it is reconditioned at a wrong time; there is no reason for a lovely body by warding off cold and heat; thinking, 'With entry into a house it is possible to do any evil whatsoever', it is a reason for concealing what is blamable (in conduct); thinking, 'This is for me', there is appropriation[1]; in a house, there is living with a companion; and it is much shared being shared with lice, fleas, house-lizards and so forth. Seeing these eight perils thus, the Great Being gave up the leaf-hut.

32 *Endowed with ten special qualities*: the meaning is that: having rejected a roof *I approached the root of a tree that was endowed with ten special qualities*. With what ten? The smallness of the preparations; it is just here for the going to it; the blamelessness of obtaining it easily; the arousing of the perception of impermanence through constantly seeing the changes in the leaves of the tree; the absence of envy in regard to a lodging[2]; the unworthiness of doing evil, for one is ashamed of doing evil there; the absence of appropriation; dwelling together with devas; the rejection of a roof; happiness in the use of it; indifference because of easily obtaining a lodging at the root of a tree in whatever place one goes to. Having seen these ten special qualities, he spoke, saying, "I approached the root of a tree", and said:

> Reliance is spoken of and praised by the best of Buddhas.
> Where is the dwelling equal to the root of a tree for aloofness? 38
> With devatās watching over envy in regard to a dwelling-
> place, living at the root of a tree is a good custom for aloofness. 39
> [78] Seeing the leaves of the tree, crimson, green, yellow and
> fallen, one dispels the perception of permanence. 40
> Therefore a man of sense should not disdain a Buddha's
> inheritance, aloofness at the root of a tree, an abode for
> developing delight. 41

Then Sumedha the Wise, being one who had seen defect in a leaf-hut, living with the advantage gained from a lodging at the root of a tree, reflected further: "Anguish is the quest for food and my going to a village for the sake of food. Not having 'departed'

[1] saparigghabhāva; cf. D i 247, where it means marriage.

[2] senāsanamacchera; cf. D iii 234, Vism 683 where āvāsamacchariya is the first of five kinds of envy or stinginess or dog-in-the-manger behaviour.

because of any poverty, I have not gone forth for the sake of food; and there is no measure of the anguish of the quest for food. Suppose that I should subsist on wild fruits?" Showing this by a factual addition, he said:

IIA 33 I completely gave up sown and planted grain and ate wild fruits that were possessed of countless special qualities.[1]

33 Therein *sown* means coming up after sowing.

33 *Planted* means coming up after planting. The resulting harvest is twofold according to whether there was sowing or planting. Because of his small desire for that twofold (crop), giving it up he subsisted on wild fruits.

33 *Wild fruits* means fruit fallen of its own accord.

33 *Ate* means partook of.

Living independent of others, content with wild fruits, avidity
for food given up, he is a sage of the four quarters. 42
And his way of life is purified who gives up desire for tastes;
therefore indeed one should not disdain the eating of fallen
fruits. 43

Sumedha the Wise, proceeding thus, in no long time, within a week, reached the eight attainments and the five super-knowings. For making this matter clear, it was said, beginning:

34 "I strove the striving there."[2]

34 Therein *there* means in that hermitage.

34 *The striving* means he put forth energy.

34 *Whether sitting, standing, pacing* means sitting and standing and pacing.

And Sumedha the Wise, refusing a bed and passing the nights and days in sitting, standing and pacing only, within a week reached power in the super-knowings. When Sumedha the ascetic had attained power in the super-knowings thus and was passing the time in the bliss of the attainments, the teacher Dīpaṅkara arose in the world giving protection to all people, bringing fear to Māra's forces and giving the light of knowledge. This, in brief, is his

[1] This verse has appeared already, text p. 75.

[2] This verse, II A 34, has appeared at text p. 75.

previous history[1]: It is said that the Great Being named Dīpaṅkara, having fulfilled all the thirty perfections in an individuality similar to Vessantara's, and while the individuality lasted giving great gifts while an earthquake occurred[2], **[79]** was reborn on the completion of the life-span in Tusita city, and remained there for the length of that life-span.

Then the devatās of the ten thousand world-system, having assembled, said:

> This is the time for you; great hero, arise in the womb of a mother. Helping men with the devas to cross over, may you awaken to the undying state.[3]

When he had heard the bidding of the devatās and had investigated the five great investigations, deceasing from there he took on relinking at Rammavatī city on the full-moon day of Āsāḷha under the asterism of Uttarāsāḷha in the womb of queen Sumedhā in the family of king Sudeva who had subdued Vāsudeva[4] by his own glory and splendour. Being very carefully carried in the womb of the chief queen and staying there for ten months like a jewel on a finial unsullied by any impurity[5], he issued forth from her womb like the moon at autumn time making a fissure in the clouds. At the moment of prince Dīpaṅkara's relinking and at the moment of his birth there appeared the marvels of the thirty-two portent-signs. It is said that these thirty-two marvels occur on these four occasions only: when all omniscient Bodhisattas are descending into the mother's womb, issuing forth from it, attaining awakening, and turning the Wheel of Dhamma. Therefore the customary course of affairs is shown by me in regard to prince Dīpaṅkara's birth:

> When Dīpankara, the lovely prince was born, bringing blessings, bringing peace, then the ten-thousand world-
> system shook and quaked all round.[6] 44

[1] ānupubbikathā; cf. MA ii 19, iii 328.
[2] See Vessantara Jā. (No. 547), and Jā i 74, Miln 113ff.
[3] As at text p. 53.
[4] See DPPN.
[5] Cf. DA 438, MA iv 183.
[6] For the following description of events accompanying the birth of a Buddha, cf. DA ii 440ff., MA iv 186ff.

Then the devatās in every ten thousand world-spheres gathered together in one world-sphere. 45

Devatās first received the Bodhisatta, the Great Being, as soon as he was born and afterwards human beings (received) him. 46

Drums, kettle-drums and skins of drums that no one was beating, and lutes with strings no one was plucking, at that moment sounded forth sweetly all round. 47

And shackles were burst everywhere, all illnesses disappeared of themselves, and those born blind saw material shapes; the deaf heard sound all round. 48

Men, backward at birth, obtained mindfulness, the lame went on foot as though in a vehicle. Of themselves boats going to distant parts rapidly reached port. 49

[80] And all gems, whether in the sky or on earth, shone all round of their own accord; extinguished was fire in the terrible Niraya, and in rivers the water did not even dry up. 50

In the spaces between the worlds, even in (those where there was) continual anguish, there was glorious wide-spread lustre. Likewise the great ocean then was all frothy on the surface and the water was sweet. 51

No wind blew, rough or harsh; the trees were in full blossom. The moon shone brilliantly with the stars, nor was the sun too hot. 52

Birds[1] from the trees and the mountains were happy on the earth below; and a great cloud covering the four continents rained down sweet moisture all round. 53

Companies of devas, happy at heart, remaining in their own deva-like abodes, danced, sang and made music, shouted and frolicked. 54

At that time great door-panels opened of their own accord; neither hunger nor thirst oppressed the populace anywhere in the world. 55

And those breathing things, constantly at enmity, achieved a mind of utmost loving-kindness—crows associated with owls[2] and dogs frolicked with wild boars. 56

And fierce poisonous snakes willingly frolicked with mongooses; lice and house-mice confidently took hold of cats. 57

[1] khagā, sky-goers; a rare word(?) also at p. 288 in a long compound.

[2] One of the things said to be impossible of occurrence, Jā iii 477 (ver. 8).

In the interval between Buddhas, though there was no water in the pisāca-world, it was devoid of thirst; the hump-backed were upright and charming in body; and the dumb uttered sweet speech. 5

[81] And breathing things, happy at heart, spoke to one another affectionately; and horses neighed with delight, splendid elephants in rut trumpeted thunderously.[1] 5

Filled with delectable[2] perfumes and powders, scented with flowers, saffron[3] and incense, garlanded gaily all round with a beautiful large banner was the ten-thousand (world-system). 6

The quaking of the ten-thousand world-system was the portent-sign of the acquisition of omniscient knowledge. The gathering together of the devatās in one world-system and their having gathered together simultaneously at the time of the turning of the Wheel of Dhamma was the portent-sign of the receiving of Dhamma. The receiving first by devatās was the portent-sign of the acquisition of the four jhānas of the fine-material sphere. The receiving afterwards by human beings was the portent-sign of the acquisition of the four jhānas of the sphere of formlessness. The beating of the drums and the kettle-drums of their own accord was the portent-sign of the proclamation of the great drum of Dhamma. The plucking of the lute-springs of their own accord was the portent-sign of the gradually (ascending stages) in abiding (in meditation). The bursting of the shackles of their own accord was the portent-sign of the bursting of the conceit "I am". The disappearance of all illnesses among the populace was the portent-sign of the acquisition of the four truths. The seeing of material shapes by those born blind of the acquisition of deva-like vision. The hearing of sound by the deaf of the acquisition of the element of deva-like hearing. The arising of mindfulness in those backward at birth of the acquisition of the arousings of mindfulness. The going on foot by the lame of the acquisition of the four bases of psychic potency. The arrival at port of boats going to distant parts of the penetration of the four analytical insights. The shining of the gems of their own accord of the effulgence of Dhamma. The

[1] gajjati; usually said of a thunder-cloud, to roar.

[2] surabhi means belonging to the suras, "gods", as opposed to the asura, non-gods.

[3] kuṅkuma, sweet-smelling. See MQ i, Intr. p. lii.

extinguishing of the fires in Niraya of the extinguishing of the eleven fires[1]. The non-drying up of the water in rivers of the acquisition of the four confidences. The light in the spaces between the worlds of the vision of the light of knowledge after having dispelled the darkness of ignorance. The sweetness of the water in the great ocean of the one flavour that is the flavour of nibbāna. The non-blowing of the wind of the breaking of the sixty-two (sectarian) views. The blossoming of the trees of the blossoming with the flowers of freedom. The brilliant shining of the moon of the support of the populace.[2] The sun's being stainless and not too hot of the arising of bodily and mental happiness. The coming to earth of the birds from the mountains and so forth of the going for refuge of the great populace among breathing things when they had heard an exhortation. The raining of the great cloud that covered the four continents of the great rain of Dhamma. The devatās' dancing and frolicking while they remained in their own abodes of the breathing forth of the solemn utterance on the attainment of Buddhahood. The opening of the door-panels of their own accord of the opening of the door of the eightfold Way. The absence of oppression from hunger of the acquisition of deathlessness through mindfulness of body. The absence of oppression from thirst of the happy state through the bliss of freedom. The acquisition of loving-kindness among enemies of the acquisition of the four Brahma-abidings. [**82**] The garlanding of the ten thousand world-systems with one banner was the portent-sign of garlanding with the ariyan Dhamma. The remaining characteristics are to be known as portent-signs of the acquisition of a Buddha's remaining special qualities.

Then Prince Dīpaṅkara, amusing himself with the great property, gradually coming to radiant youth and experiencing, like bliss in a deva-world, the bliss of the kingdom in three palaces suitable to the three seasons, saw successively as he was going to frolic in the pleasaunce the three deva-messengers known as ageing, disease and death. When the thrill of seeing them had receded, he entered Rammavatī city which in beauty and opulence was like Sudassana city[3]. When he had entered the city he had the

[1] Eleven mentioned at Jā iii 411, beginning with rāga; enumerated at Pṭs i 129 to make ten, but making eleven if jarā and maraṇa are taken separately.

[2] bahujanakattatāya. I am doubtful of my rendering.

[3] A deva-city.

mahout summoned for the fourth time, and spoke thus: "I, my dear, would go out to see the pleasaunce. Have riding elephants made ready." Answering "Very well, sire" in assent, he had eighty-four thousand elephants made ready. It is said that the devaputta called Vassakamma then adorned the Bodhisatta with clothes and garments of various hues, with bangles embellished with jewels and pearls, with charming rings of new gold, with earrings and a crest, and adorned the hair of his head with most fragrant flowers and garlands.

Then Prince Dīpaṅkara, like a deva-prince, mounted a splendid elephant from among the eighty-four thousand elephants surrounding him and, surrounded by a large number of troops, entered the pleasaunce as ascetic people were leaving it[1]. Dismounting from the elephant's back, he walked about the pleasaunce and sat down on a stone of charming appearance and calming to his heart, and turned his thoughts to going forth. At that very moment a great Brahmā, cankers destroyed in the Pure Abodes[2], bringing the eight requisites for recluses, appeared in the Great Being's range of vision. On seeing him, the Great Being asked "What is that?" When he heard that it was recluses' requisites, taking off the things he was adorned with and giving them into the hands of the royal keeper of ornaments, he took the sword of state and, cutting off his hair with the crest[3], threw it up into the sky, into the air. Then Sakka, king of devas, taking that hair and the crest in a golden casket, built on the summit of Sineru Makuṭacetiya "Crest Cetiya"[4] three yojanas in extent and made of sapphires.

Then the Great Man, putting on the yellow robes, the banner of arahants given by devas, threw his pair of cloths into the sky. When Brahmā had received them he built a cetiya in the Brahma-world made of all the gems and (extending for) twelve yojanas. And as Prince Dīpaṅkara was going forth a crore[5] of men went forth following him. Surrounded by this crore of men, the Great Being engaged in striving for ten months. Then on the full-moon day of

[1] yatijananīyyāna could also mean the way out, the release, the outlet for people who were yatis, monks or ascetics; cf. Vism 79.

[2] Suddhāvāsakhīṇāsava does not appear to be a personal name, cf. DA ii 437 where khīṇāsavā Suddhāvāsa-Brāhmāno received the Bodhisatta first before human beings did. At the same time there is no return from the Pure Abodes.

[3] makuṭa, crest, diadem. Cf. CpA 223 rājamakuṭaṁ sīse paṭimuñcitvā. See too Divy 411.

[4] Makuṭa-cetiya seems mentioned here only.

[5] Given as four hundred thousand at ApA 13, Jkm 10.

Visākha he entered a city for alms. It is said that on that day in that city they were cooking milk-rice without water as an offering to devas. People gave it to the Great Being with his company when he entered for alms. There was enough for all the monks numbering a crore. And the devatās infused a deva-like nutritive essence[1] into the Great Being's bowl. When he had partaken of it [83] and had spent the day-sojourn there in a sāla grove, he emerged from his solitary meditation towards evening. Dismissing the crowd and accepting eight handfuls of grass given to him by a Naked Ascetic named Sunanda, he went to the root of a pipphali[2] Tree of Awakening. Spreading a grass spreading ninety cubits in extent, he sat down cross-legged at the root of the Tree of Awakening with his back against the trunk of the Tree of Awakening, his back erect, having resolutely determined on the four-factored energy.[3]

Thereupon, having routed Māra's forces, recollecting former habitations during the first watch of the night, purifying deva-like vision during the middle watch, and during the last watch reflecting on the mode of conditions[4] in regard to their forward and reverse (order), and having attained the fourth jhāna by means of in-breathing and out-breathing, he emerged therefrom. He interpreted the five categories seeing the full fifty marks[5] in respect of rise and fall[6]. Increasing insight into the knowledge of cognizance[7], and at dawn penetrating the whole of a Buddha's special qualities by means of the ariyan Way, he roared a Buddha's lion-roar.

Spending seven weeks near the Tree of Awakening itself, and agreeing to Brahmā's (request for the) teaching of Dhamma, he turned the Wheel of Dhamma in Sunanda Monastery enabling a hundred crores of devas and men to drink of the nectar of Dhamma. Then, raining down the rain of Dhamma like a great storm-cloud covering the four continents, and liberating the multitude from bonds, he set out, it is said, for an almstour of the country. Then, because Sumedha the wise was spending the time in the

[1] Apparently this oja would be taken in through the pores of the skin, see M i 245 where the Bodhisatta Gotama refused the devas' offer to give him this dibba-oja.

[2] Ficus religiosa.

[3] caturaṅgaviriya; see text p. 8.

[4] paccayākāra, referring to paṭiccasamuppāda, dependent origination.

[5] sammapaññāya to read samapaññāsa, as in the other passages.

[6] See explanation at Vism 631 where each of the five categories (khandha) is said to have ten marks or characteristics. Repeated below, text pp. 133, 184, 190.

[7] gotrabhū.

bliss of the attainments, he noticed neither the quaking of the earth nor those signs. Accordingly it was said:

IIA 35 While I was thus attaining accomplishment and becoming a master in the teaching (for ascetics), the conqueror named Dīpaṅkara arose, leader of the world.

36 Rapt in the delight of meditation, I did not see the four signs of arising, of being born, of being awakened, of teaching Dhamma.[1]

35 Therein *thus* means that now what is to be said is demonstrated.

35 *I* (me, gen.) means for me (mama, dat.).

35 *Attaining accomplishment* means attaining accomplishment in the five super-knowings.

35 *Becoming a master* means become a master, the meaning being arriving at mastery.

35 *In the teaching (for ascetics)* means in the teaching for illuminating ascetics.[2] The genitive case is to be understood in this context.[3]

35 *Conqueror* means conqueror through conquering the enemies that are the defilements.

36 *Arising* means taking on relinking.

36 *Being born* means issuing forth from the mother's womb.

36 *Being awakened* means being fully self-Awakened with the supreme and perfect Self-Awakening.

36 *Teaching Dhamma* means turning the Wheel of Dhamma.

[**84**] 36 *The four signs* means the four signs.[4] The meaning is that the signs were the quakings and so forth in the ten-thousand world-system on the four occasions: the relinking, birth, awakening and turning the Wheel of Dhamma of Dīpānkara, Him of the Ten Powers. As to this it was said, "But as there were these many signs, why are (only) four signs mentioned? Is it not unsuitable?" "It is not unsuitable if, of these many signs, the occurrence on four occasions only is spoken of as the four signs."

[1] Besides Jā i 11 this verse is found at Asl, Se p. 56.

[2] Reading with Se vikāsentānaṁ tāpasānaṁ for text's vemānasatāpasānaṁ.

[3] anādaralakkhaṇe sāmivacanaṁ daṭṭhabbaṁ. Cf. DA 284, MA ii 170, UdA 382, CpA 191. See CPD, s.v. *anādara*.

[4] caturo nimitte ti cattāri nimittāni.

36 *I did not see* means I did not see.[1] Now, to demonstrate the reason why he did not see these four signs, he said:

36 *Rapt in the delight of meditation.* The delight of meditation is a synonym for the bliss of attainment. The meaning is: "I did not see these signs because of the concentration on, because of the possession of the delight of meditation."

Then at that time[2] Dīpaṅkara, Him of the Ten Powers, surrounded by a hundred thousand canker-waned ones, walking on almstour gradually reached the extremely charming city called Ramma, and stayed in the Great Sudassana Monastery. The inhabitants of Ramma city heard: "They say Dīpaṅkara, Him of the Ten Powers, attained the incomparable perfect Self-Awakening and turned the glorious Wheel of Dhamma. Walking on almstour, he has gradually reached the city of Ramma and is staying in the Great Sudassana Monastery." After breakfast they brought clarified butter and fresh butter as well as medicines, and together with upper robes, flowers, incense, perfumes in their hands, they approached the Buddha. Reverencing the teacher, honouring him with the flowers and so on, and listening to an excessively sweet talk on Dhamma, they invited the Lord for the morrow. Rising from their seats they departed keeping their right sides towards Him of the Ten Powers.

On the next day, having prepared the Unparalleled Great Gift[3] and built a pavilion, they roofed it with stainless lotuses and blue water-lilies. Making a flooring using the four kinds of scents[4] they strewed the five articles of honouring with puffed rice[5] as the fifth. They had jars full of cool water placed in the four corners of the pavilion covering them with plantain leaves, fastening awnings that were extremely lovely to behold like the flowers of victory's joy[6] on the top of the pavilion, arranging sparkling gold, pearls and silver, and hanging out there ropes of perfumes, ropes of flowers, ropes of leaves, ropes of jewels and burning incense. At that

[1] nāddasan ti nāddasiṁ.

[2] Cf. CpA 13f., also DA i 83.

[3] asadisamahādāna, the gift each Buddha receives once in his life. See MQ ii 121, n. 3.

[4] See MQ i, Intr. li ff.

[5] White mustard, powdered rice, jasmine buds, thistle (or, panic) grass, and puffed rice. Also at text p. 277. See Thūp, ed. N. A. Jayawickrama, p. 35, n. 35.

[6] jayasumana, name of a plant. Again at text p. 86.

charming clean Ramma city, they placed plantains and their fruits in the full jars adorned with flowers. Raising aloft banners and flags of various hues, they surrounded both sides of the great road with screen-walls adorning the way by which Dīpaṅkara, Him of the Ten Powers, would come. Throwing down soil at the places eroded by water, making what was uneven even, they strewed it with sand like pearls, they strewed it with the articles of honouring with puffed rice as the fifth and set up plantains with the fruits and the buds.

Then at that time Sumedha the ascetic, coming out from his own hermitage-ground and going through the sky above those inhabitants of Ramma city, saw them exultingly clearing and adorning the way. Thinking, "What is the reason for this?" and **[85]** descending from the sky in full view of them all, he stood at a respectful distance and asked these people: "Sirs, for whom are you clearing this way?" Accordingly it was said:

IIA 37 (The people in) the border-country, having invited the Tathāgata, cleared the way for his coming, their minds delighted.

38 I, at that time, departing from my own hermitage, rustling the bark-garments, went through the air then.

39 Seeing the delighted populace elated, exultant, joyous, I descended from the heavens and immediately asked the people:

40 "Elated, exultant, joyous is the great populace. For whom is the way being cleared, the direct way, the path and road?"

37 *In the border-country* means in what is called the border-country as it is to one side of the Middle Country.[1]

37 *The way for his coming* means the way by which he must come.

38 *I, at that time* means I, at that time.[2] This instrumental case is to be understood in the sense of a locative.

38 (*My*) *own hermitage* means leaving (his) own hermitage.[3]

38 *Rustling* means shaking off.[4]

[1] Cf. AA ii 36, v. 64.

[2] ahaṁ tena samayenā ti ahaṁ tasmiṁ samaye.

[3] sakassamā ti attano assamato nikkhamitvā.

[4] dhunanto ti odhunanto. The second word scarcely justifies the translation

38 *At that time* and *then*: the meaning of these two words is unified. The former is for the action of leaving, the latter is for the action of going, and together the connexion should be understood. Otherwise it[1] is not free from the defect of redundancy.[2]

38 *Then* means at that time.

39 *Delighted* means full of happiness.

39 *Elated, exultant, joyous*: these three words are synonyms of one another, illustrative of each other's meaning. Or, elated with pleasure, exultant with zest, joyous with joyousness.

39 *Descended* (lit. descending) means coming down.

39 *I asked the people* means I asked the people[3], or this is itself the reading.

39 *Immediately* means then, at that very moment.

40 Now to show that meaning it was said, beginning: *Elated, exultant, joyous*. This great populace was clearing the way there, elated, exultant, joyous at heart. Why was it being cleared? Or for whom was it being cleared? Quoting the words "Is being cleared" thus, the meaning can be understood. Otherwise it is not construable.

40 *Being cleared* means being made clear.

40 *Way, the direct way, the path and road*: these are simply synonyms for the way.

When these people[4] were thus asked by Sumedha the ascetic, they said, [**86**] "Revered Sumedha, do you not know that the Buddha named Dīpaṅkara has attained the incomparable perfect Self-Awakening and has turned the glorious Wheel of Dhamma? Walking through the country he has gradually reached our city and is staying in the Great Sudassana Monastery. We have invited this Lord and are clearing the way that this Buddha, the Lord is to take." When he had heard this Sumedha the ascetic thought, "They say 'Buddha', but this very sound is difficult to come by, how much more the arising of a Buddha. Well then, I too together with these people must clear the way to be taken by Him of the Ten

"shaking off". The first word therefore probably means "shaking about, tossing about". Sumedha later (II A 52) had his bark-garment spread over the mire, so had not yet shaken it off.

[1] Presumably the passage.

[2] As at text p. 37.

[3] mānuse pucchī ti manusse pucchiṁ.

[4] Cf. Thūp 4, CpA i 4.

Powers." He spoke to these people thus, "If, good sirs, you are clearing this way for a Buddha, give me just one section, and I too will clear the way for the Buddha together with you." Thereupon these answering "Very well" in assent and saying "This Sumedha the wise is of great psychic potency, great might", knowing that there was one section that was hard to clear, eroded by water and extremely uneven, they remarked "You clear this section and decorate it", and gave it to him. Thereupon Sumedha the wise, having aroused zest through meditation on the Buddha, thought, "Certainly through psychic potency I am able to make this section exceedingly beautiful, but it would not satisfy me to do that. Today I must do menial physical tasks", and bringing soil he began to fill that part. But before he had finished clearing that part, the inhabitants of Ramma city announced the time to the Lord, saying, "The meal is ready, revered sir."

When they had announced the time thus He of the Ten Powers dressed himself in a double-fold robe in colour like flowers of victory's joy and covered the three circles[1]. Then he fastened his waistband, radiant like a flash of lightning, as though tying up a bouquet of flowers with a golden chain, and wearing as his outer garment a red and lovely robe of rags gathered from a dust-heap in colour like flowers of the kiṁsuka tree[2] smeared with the essence of lac, as though sprinkling the essense of lac on the crest of a mountain's golden peak, or encircling a golden cetiya with a net of coral, or encasing a golden festooned column in a red woollen blanket, or covering the moon at autumn time with a red cloud, and issuing forth from the door of the Scented Chamber like a lion from a golden cave, he stood facing the Scented Chamber. Then all the monks, taking each one his bowl and robe, surrounded the Lord, and as they stood surrounding him the monks were of this kind:

> Of few wants, content, speakers of gentle words, aloof, ungregarious, trained, censuring evil.
> And all were possessed of morality, were proficient in concentration and meditation, possessed of wisdom and freedom, possessed of and furnished with (right) conduct.

[1] See Sekhiya 1 (Vin iv 185) where monks have to cover the nābhimaṇḍala and jānumaṇḍala, the circles of the navel and two knees.

[2] "Flame of the forest", Butea monosperma or frondosa.

Cankers destroyed, attained to mastery, of psychic potency, splendid, sense-faculties tranquil, attained to taming, pure, again-becoming destroyed. 63

[87] Thus the Lord, his own attachment, hatred, confusion gone, shone exceedingly surrounded by those whose attachment, hatred, confusion were gone. Then the teacher, surrounded by the four hundred thousand who were of great majesty, their cankers destroyed (and won to) the six super-knowings, like him of a thousand eyes[1] surrounded by a host of deities, and like Great Brahmā surrounded by a host of Brahmās, with the peerless grace of a Buddha which produces an accumulation of skill and strength in an unlimited mass (of people) he followed along that adorned and prepared way like the moon at autumn-time in the vault of the heavens surrounded by a host of stars.

The wise one with golden coloured lustre, making golden coloured the trees on the way among what was golden coloured, golden coloured he followed along the way. 64

Sumedha the ascetic, opening his eyes, surveyed the bodily form of the Lord Dīpaṅkara as he was coming along by that adorned and prepared way. He was of the most perfect beauty, embellished with the glorious thirty-two Marks, characterized by the eighty lesser characteristics, splendidly encircled by a halo measuring a fathom, flashing like multitudes of sapphires in the sky, emitting the six-hued rays. And he (Sumedha) thought, "Today I must make sacrifice of my life for Him of the Ten Powers. Do not let the Lord tread in the mire, let him come treading on my back together with the four hundred thousand whose cankers are destroyed as though he were treading on a jewelled plank for a bridge—for long that will be for my welfare and happiness." Loosening his hair and spreading the antelope's hide, his matted hair and bark-garments over the dark-coloured mire, he lay down there on top of the mire. Accordingly it was said:

IIA 41 Asked by me, these declared that an incomparable Buddha had arisen in the world, the Conqueror named Dīpaṅkara, leader of the world, and that it was for him that the way, the direct way, the path and road was being cleared.

[1] Sakka.

42 When I heard "Buddha", zest arose immediately. Saying "Buddha, Buddha" I expressed my happiness.
43 Standing there elated, stirred in mind, I reasoned: "Here will I sow seeds; indeed, let not the moment pass:
44 If you are clearing for a Buddha, give me one section. I myself will also clear the direct way, the path and road."
[88] 45 They gave me a section of the direct way to clear then. Thinking "Buddha, Buddha", I cleared the way then.
46 Before my section was finished, the great sage Dīpaṅkara, the Conqueror, entered upon the direct way with four hundred thousand steadfast ones who had the six super-knowings, whose cankers were destroyed, stainless.
47 Many were those who, beating drums, were going forward to meet him. Men and deities, rejoicing, made applause.
48 Devas saw the men and the men saw the devatās, and both, their hands clasped, followed the Tathāgata.
49 The devas with deva-like musical instruments, the men with man-made ones, both playing on these, followed the Tathāgata.
50 Deities in the zenith of the sky poured down in all directions deva-like mandārava flowers, lotuses, flowers of the Coral Tree.
51 The men on the surface of the earth threw up in all directions flowers of campaka, saḷala, nīpa, nāga, punnāga and ketaka.
52 Loosening my hair, spreading my bark-garments and piece of hide there in the mire, I lay down prone.
53 "Let the Buddha go treading on me with his disciples. Do not let him tread in the mire—it will be for my welfare."

41 Therein (*these*) *declared* means they answered.

41 *The Conqueror named Dīpankara*, (it was) *for him* (*that* the way) *was being cleared*: "path" is also a reading.

42 *I expressed happiness*: the meaning is that I experienced happiness.

43 *Standing there* means standing just there in that place where he came down from the sky.

43 *Stirred in mind* means there was zest in (my) astonished mind.

43 *Here* means in this Dīpaṅkara, a field for merit.

43 *Seeds* means the seeds of skill.

43 *I will sow* means I will myself sow.[1]

43 *Moment*: exempt from the eight inopportune moments[2] the ninth is a concurrence (of events producing) the opportune moment.[3] What was exceedingly difficult to obtain was obtained by me.

43 *Indeed* is only a particle.

43 *Let not pass*: the meaning is, do not let it go past, do not let it pass by.

[89] 44 *Give* means give.[4]

45 *They*: the meaning is, those men who were asked by me.

45 *I cleared then* means I cleared then.[5]

46 *Was (not) finished* means not cleared, imperfectly executed.

46 *Whose cankers were destroyed*; herein there are four cankers: the canker of sense-pleasures, the canker of becoming, the canker of view, the canker of ignorance. In whom these four cankers are destroyed, got rid of, rooted out, tranquillized, not liable to arise again, burnt up by the fires of knowledge—these cankers are destroyed; (they are) *stainless* for the very reason that their cankers are destroyed.

48 *Devas saw the men*: herein in the men's seeing of the devas it was not through ordinary seeing, but inasmuch as the men, standing here, saw, so too did the devas see the men.

48 *Devatās* means devas.

48 *And both* means and both devas and men.

48 *Hands clasped* means making the hands clasped, putting both hands to the head.

48 (*They*) *followed* (anuyanti) *the Tathāgata* means they went behind the Tathāgata. Where there is the prefix *anu* there is the accusative case in the sense of a genitive. It is the rule.[6] So it was said: anuyanti Tathāgataṁ (acc).

49 *Playing on* means making sound.

50 *Mandārava* means flowers of the mandārava.

50 *Poured down* means poured down over.

50 *In all directions* means in all quarters.

[1] ropessan ti ropayissāma.
[2] akkhaṇe, see A iv 225, D iii 287 and 263 where there are nine.
[3] This one "Moment", eko khaṇo, is described at A iv 227.
[4] dadāthā ti detha.
[5] sodhem’ ahaṁ tadā ti sodhemi ahaṁ tadā.
[6] lakkhaṇa. Cf. text pp. 114, 175, 238.

50 *In the zenith of the sky* means in the zenith of what is known as the sky[1]. Or, in the sky, as in the heaven(s). For the zenith is called heaven.

50 *Deities* means non-dying.[2]

51 *Saḷala* means blooms of the sarala tree.

51 *Nīpa* means flowers of the kadamba.

51 *Nāga, punnāga and ketaka* means the perfume of nāga and flowers of punnāga and ketaka.

51 *On the surface of the earth* means on the earth.

52 *Loosening my hair . . . I* means I, loosening my hair which was in braids, tawny, wavy, matted; the meaning is strewing it over.

52 *There* means in the section given to me.

52 *Piece of hide* means portion of hide.

52 *In the mire* means in the swamp and the mud.

52 *Prone* means being face downwards.

52 *I lay down* means I lay down.[3]

53 *Do not let him*: *do not let* is a negative in sense; *him* is a particle for filling the line.[4] The meaning is: do not let the Buddha tread in the mire.

53 *It will be for my welfare* means: his not treading in the mire will be for long for my welfare. "It will be for my happiness" is also a reading.

[**90**] Thereupon as he was lying in the mire Sumedha the wise considered thus: "Should I so wish, having burnt up all the defilements and being newly ordained in the Order, I could enter Ramma city. But having burnt up my defilements while I am unknown is not a function for one attaining nibbāna. Suppose now that I, like Dīpaṅkara, Him of the Ten Powers, having attained the utmost full Self-Awakening, embarking in the ship of Dhamma and pulling out the populace from the sea of saṁsāra, afterwards should attain parinibbāna myself? This would be suitable in me." Therefore, making the eight things concur[5] he lay down making the resolve for Buddha-status. Accordingly it was said:

IIA 54 While I was lying on the earth it was thus in my mind:
If I so wished I could burn up my defilements today.

[1] ākāsanabhagatā ti akāsasankhāte nabhasi gatā.
[2] marū ti amarā.
[3] nipajj° ahan ti nipajjim ahaṁ.
[4] padapūraṇatthe, in the meaning of filling the foot of a verse.
[5] See explanation below, text p. 92.

55 What is the use while I (remain) unknown of realizing Dhamma here? Having reached omniscience, I will be a Buddha in the world with the devas.

56 What is the use of my crossing over alone, being a man aware of my strength? Having reached omniscience, I will cause the world together with the devas to cross over.

57 By this act of merit of mine towards the supreme among men I will reach omniscience, I will cause many people to cross over.

58 Cutting through the stream of saṁsāra, shattering the three becomings, embarking in the ship of Dhamma, I will cause the world with the devas to cross over.

54 Therein *While I was lying on the earth* means while I was lying on the earth[1], or this is itself the reading.

54 *In (my) mind*[2]*:* the meaning is that it was a reflexion in the mind. "It was thus in my mind"[3] is also a reading.

54 *Wishing* means desiring.

54 *Defilements* means that the defilements defile, will torment—the ten beginning with attachment[4].

54 *I could burn up* means I could burn up.[5] The meaning is, I could burn up my defilements.

55 *What is the use* means an expression for opposing[6].

55 *While I (remain) unknown* means: while I am not distinguished (from others), not understood, concealed. What is the use of having, like the monks here, made destruction of the cankers? The intention is that, having fulfilled the things that make a Buddha, the great earth having trembled at the (time of the) relinking, the birth, the Awakening, the turning of the Wheel of Dhamma, he (then) thought: "One who is awakened should be an awakener, one who has crossed over should be a helper across, one who is freed should be one who frees."[7]

55 *In the world with the devas* means in the world with the devas.[8]

56 *Being a man aware of my strength* means seeing his own strength and power.

[1] paṭhaviyaṁ . . . puthuviyā.
[2] cetaso.
[3] cetanā.
[4] Cf. Dhs 1548, Vbh 341, Vism 683.
[5] jhāpaye . . . jhāpeyyaṁ.
[6] paṭikkhepavacana, or rejection, refusal. Cf. PvA 189.
[7] Cf. text p. 10.
[8] sadevake ti sadevake loke.

56 *I will cause to cross over* means I will cause to cross over.[1]

[91] 56 *The world together with the devas* means classes of beings with the devas, people with the devas.

57 *By this act of merit* means by this very outstanding action; the meaning is: sacrificing my life to the Buddha by the act of merit of lying down on the mire.

58 *The stream of saṁsāra* (saṁsārasota) means: saṁsāra is the circling on (saṁsaraṇa) from here and from there in modes of births, bourns, stations of consciousness, and in the nine abodes of beings on account of kamma and the defilements. As it was said:

> The endless chain of aggregates, of elements, of bases too that carries on unbrokenly is what is called saṁsāra.*

If it is said: saṁsāra and stream (sota), the stream of saṁsāra (saṁsārasota) is meant: that stream of saṁsāra. Or, the stream of saṁsāra (saṁsārassa sotaṁ) is the stream of saṁsāra (saṁsārasota). That is the cause of saṁsāra (saṁsārakāraṇa). The meaning is: cutting through the stream of craving.

58 *The three becomings* mean the three becomings are intended as the defilements due to kamma-producing-becoming in the sensuous, fine-material and non-material becomings.

58 *The ship of Dhamma* is the ariyan eightfold Way. Indeed it is called the ship of Dhamma in the sense of crossing over the four floods.

58 *Embarking* means mounting up into.

58 *I will cause to cross over* means I will cause to cross over.[2] And because of his longing for Buddhahood, he said:

IIA 59 Human existence, attainment of the (male) sex, cause, seeing a teacher, going forth, attainment of the special qualities, an act of merit, and will-power—by combining these eight things the resolve succeeds.[3]

59 Therein *human existence* means: the aspiration of one who is aspiring to Buddhahood succeeds only when he is in human status, not of those born as nāgas and so forth. And why is that? Because of the absence of the (three skilled) root-causes.[4] Even if he is

* Vism 544 (translated at Ppn), AA iii 206, SnA ii 426, UdA 270, Asl 10.

[1] santāressan ti santāressāmi. [2] See ver. 56.

[3] Jā i 14, 44, MA iv 122, SnA 48, ItA i 121, ApA 16, 48, 140, UJ p. 345, etc.

[4] ahetukabhāva, the three being absence of greed, hatred, confusion: without these. Cf. Vbh 402 417 419, Vism 456.

existing in human status the aspiration succeeds only for one who is of the male sex. It does not succeed for women or for eunuchs, the sexless or hermaphrodites. And why is that? Because there is no completeness of characteristics. Accordingly it was said in detail: "It is impossible, monks, it cannot come to pass that a woman who is an arahant can be a perfect Buddha."* Therefore for one of female sex even though she be of human birth the aspiration does not succeed.

59 *Cause* means that only for a man in this individuality who is endowed with a cause for attaining arahantship does the aspiration succeed, but not for another.

59 *Seeing a teacher* means that, if one aspires in the presence of a living Buddha the aspiration succeeds; but the aspiration does not succeed if (made) near a cetiya of a Lord who has attained final nibbāna, nor before an image at the root of a Bodhi-Tree, nor in the presence of buddhas by and for themselves or of disciples of Buddhas. Why? Though knowing (those beings who are) fit and unfit,[1] [92] though demarking by the knowledge concerned with the demarcations of kamma and its fruitions, (yet) because there is incapacity to "declare" the aspiration succeeds only in the presence of a Buddha.

59 *Going forth* means: for one aspiring in the presence of a Buddha, a Lord, the aspiration succeeds only for one who has gone forth among ascetics who promulgate the efficacy of kamma, or among monks, not for a householder.[2] Why? Only Bodhisattas who have gone forth arrive at Self-Awakening, not those leading a household life. Therefore, in the beginning, at the time of (making) the aspiration,[3] one should be one who has gone forth.

59 *Attainment of the special qualities* means: this succeeds only for one who has gone forth and has obtained the eight attainments and the five super-knowings, and not for one who has given up these attainments of the special qualities. Why? Because of this deficiency in one who is devoid of the special qualities.

59 *Act of merit* is the sacrifice by one possessed of the special

* M iii 65, A i 28.

[1] bhabbābhabbake, explained at Vbh 341f. as those who are and those who are not obstructed by bad deed, defilements, bad resultant (or fruition of deeds) and so on.

[2] na gihiliṅge ṭhitassa.

[3] paṇidhāna here; cf. VvA 270.

qualities even of his own life for Buddhas. It succeeds only for one possessed of this act of merit, not for another.

59 *Will-power* means: only for him who is possessed of the resolve does great will-power succeed, great exertion and endeavour and search for the things making a Buddha, not for another. Now this is a simile for the greatness of will-power: Whoever, by the power of his own arms has crossed over the whole interior of the Cakkavāḷa sphere that had become one mass of water and is capable of getting to the further shore, he achieves Buddhahood. And if he does not deem this a difficult task for himself but thinks: "I, having crossed over this, will get to the further shore", and if he is thus possessed of great will-power and endeavour, the aspiration succeeds for him, not for another.

And when the wise Sumedha had combined these eight things and had made the resolve for Buddha-status, he lay down. And the Lord Dīpaṅkara came and stood near the wise Sumedha's head. When he saw the ascetic Sumedha lying on the mire, he thought: "This ascetic is lying down having made a resolve for Buddhahood. Will his aspiration succeed or not?" And while he was reflecting he precipitated his perception into the future and knowing: "When a hundred thousand eons and four incalculables from now have passed, he will be the Buddha named Gatoma", and standing erect in the midst of the assembly, he declared:

"Do you not see, monks, this severe ascetic lying on the mire?"

"Yes, revered sir."

"He is lying down after having made a resolve for Buddhahood. His aspiration will succeed. After a hundred thousand eons and four incalculables from now he will be the Buddha named Gotama. And when he is in that individuality the dwelling will be the city named Kapilavatthu, the mother the queen named Mahāmāyā, the father the king named Suddhodana, the two chief disciples Upatissa and Kolita, the attendant Ānanda, and the two chief women disciples will be Khemā and Uppalavaṇṇā. [**93**] When his knowledge is fully matured, departing on the Great Departure, striving the great striving, and accepting from Sujātā a gift of milk-rice at the root of a banyan tree, and partaking of it on the banks of the Nerañjarā, mounting the dais of the Bodhi-Tree,[1] he will be fully Self-Awakened at the root of an Assattha[2] tree."

[1] Cf. DhA i 86.

[2] Ficus religiosa, pipal (peepul) tree, the Bo-tree.

Accordingly it was said:

IIA 60 Dīpaṅkara, knower of the world(s), recipient of offerings, standing near my head, spoke these words:

61 Do you see this very severe ascetic, a matted hair ascetic? Innumerable eons from now he will be a Buddha in the world.

62 Having departed from the delightful city of Kapila, the Tathāgata will strive the striving and perform austerities.[1]

63 After sitting at the root of the Ajapāla (Goatherd's) tree and accepting milk-rice there, the Tathāgata will go to the Nerañjarā.

64 When he has partaken of the milk-rice on the bank of the Nerañjarā that Conqueror will go to the root of the Tree of Awakening by the glorious way prepared.

65 Then, having circumambulated the dais of the Tree of Awakening, the unsurpassed one of great renown will awaken at the root of an Assattha tree.

66 His genetrix and mother will be named Māyā, his father Suddhodana; he will be named Gotama.

67 Kolita and Upatissa, cankerless, attachments gone,[2] tranquil in mind, concentrated, will be the chief disciples.

68 Ānanda will be the attendant who will attend on that Conqueror. Khemā and Uppalavaṇṇā will be the chief women disciples,

69 cankerless, attachments gone,[2] tranquil in mind, concentrated. That Lord's Tree of Awakening is said to be the Assattha.

70 Citta and Hatthāḷavaka will be the chief (lay) attendants; Uttarā and Nandamātā will be the chief women (lay) attendants.

60 Therein *knower of the world(s)*[3] means: knower of the world because of the world being known in every way. For the Lord knew the world in every way, knew it profoundly and penetrated it as to its individual nature, its arising, cessation, and the

[1] Cf. Miln 244, 284. According to Bv all Buddhas practise austerities but for varying lengths of time.

[2] vītarāgā, Vv vītamalā.

[3] See Vism 204.

means for its cessation. [94] Therefore he is said to be knower of the world. As it was said:

> Therefore truly the knower of the world, very wise, gone to the world's end, one who has brought the Brahma-faring to a close, calmed, knowing the end of the world, hopes neither for this world nor for another.*

Further, there are three worlds: the world of the constructions, the world of beings, the world of location.[1] Herein, the things beginning with the earth that have arisen (dependent) on conditions are called the world of the constructions. Conscious, not conscious, neither-conscious (-nor-not-conscious) beings are called the world of beings. The place of the habitation of beings is called the world of location. And these three worlds were known by the Lord according to their individual nature. Therefore he is called knower of the worlds.

60 *Recipient of offerings*[2] means a recipient of offerings because of his being worthy, because of his being deserving of receiving offerings.

60 *Standing near my head* means standing near my head.[3]

60 *These*[4]: the meaning is that *spoke the words* is now to be said.

61 *Matted hair ascetic* means: a matted hair ascetic has matted hair—that matted hair ascetic.

61 *Very severe* means severe ascetic.

62 *There was* means: there was[5]; the meaning is then[6], or this is itself the reading.

62 *Named Kapila* means named Kapila.[7]

62 *From the delightful* means from what is possessed of delight.[8]

62 *The striving* means energy.

63 *Will go* means will go.[9]

* S i 62, A ii 49f.; quoted Vism 204.

[1] See also text pp. 11, 30.

[2] As at Thag 566.

[3] ussīsake maṁ ṭhatvānā ti mama sīsasamīpe ṭhatvā.

[4] idaṁ, sing., to agree with vacanaṁ, for which, however, the plural "words" seems better here.

[5] ahū ti ahani; both are aorist, 3rd pers. sing. of the verb hoti.

[6] atha, as at Bv II 62.

[7] Kapilavhayā ti Kapila-avhayā.

[8] rammā ti rammaṇīyato.

[9] ehitī ti essati. BvAB reads essati gamissati.

The rest of the verses are quite clear.

Then the wise Sumedha thinking "My aspiration will succeed", was full of happiness. When the great populace had heard the words of Dīpaṅkara, Him of the Ten Powers they were exultant and joyous thinking, "The ascetic Sumedha is a sprout of the Buddha-seed." And it occurred to them thus: "It is like a man crossing a river, but being unable to cross over by the direct ford, he goes across by one lower down.[1] Even so, we, though not obtaining the fruit of the Ways in the Dispensation of Dīpaṅkara, Him of the Ten Powers, will be capable of realizing the fruit of the Ways in the future face to face with you when you are the Buddha," and they made an aspiration. Dīpaṅkara, Him of the Ten Powers, having commended the Bodhisatta, the Great Being, and honoured him with eight handfuls of flowers, departed keeping his right side towards him. And those four hundred thousand whose cankers were destroyed also honoured the Bodhisatta with flowers and perfumes, and departed keeping their right sides towards him. And men with the devas, having honoured and revered him likewise, departed keeping their right sides towards him.

Then Dīpaṅkara, the surpassing light-bringer (atidīpaṅkaro) to the whole world, surrounded by the four hundred thousand whose cankers were destroyed, being honoured by the inhabitants of Ramma city, being joyfully greeted by the devas, was like a splendid golden mountain-crest shining in the evening light **[95]** as he went along the way that had been adorned and prepared while countless[2] marvels were in progress. He entered the extremely delightful Ramma city, resplendent like Amara city, dark with incense, scented with various fragrant blossoms, perfumes, and aromatic powders; flags and banners were hoisted; and the pleasantly murmuring[3] swarms of bees[4] had their hearts enchained by the perfumes. The sun of the Ten Powers sat down on the summit of Yugandhara. He was like a beautiful autumn moon, making

[1] In this sentence are three verbs with similar but not identical meanings: taranto, uttaritum̐ and otarati. I do not know what shades of difference in the meanings may be intended.

[2] Between viya, like, and anekesu, countless, BvAB interpolates jaṅgamamāno.

[3] BvAC 95 gumugumāyamānaṁ. BvAB gumbagumbāyamānaṁ, and noticing BvAC's reading. Cf. text p. 179. In both passages it would seem that the word is onomatopoetic. See BHSD. s.v. gumugumunti and reference to Mhvu iii 267.

[4] bhamaragaṇa as at UdA 291; said to be of five colours at Jā i 52.

mock of the hosts of darkness; he was like the sun causing the lotuses in a grove to open wide their flowers. (Each monk in) the Order of monks sat down in succession as he reached his own seat. And the lay-followers, the inhabitants of Ramma city, who were possessed of the special qualities of faith and so forth gave to the Order of monks with the Buddha at its head gifts of many and various kinds of solid foods and so forth, decorated and endowed with colour, perfume and flavour, the source of unparalleled happiness.

Then the Bodhisatta, having heard the declaration of Him of the Ten Powers, as though deeming that Buddha-status was within his grasp, glad at heart for all who had come, rising from his prostrate posture and thinking "I will examine the perfections", sat down cross-legged, his back erect, on a heap of flowers. While the Great Being was seated thus the devatās of the entire ten-thousand world-system gave applause, saying, "Master Sumedha the ascetic, seated in the cross-legged position of Bodhisattas of old, you thought, 'I will examine the perfections'. When you were sitting down all those former portents that had been manifested appeared too today. Undoubtedly you will become a Buddha. We know this: He for whom these portents are manifested will certainly be a Buddha. Therefore do you exert yourself making firm your own energy." And they eulogized the Bodhisatta with many and various praises. Accordingly it was said:

IIA 71 When they had heard these words of the great seer who was without an equal, men and deities, rejoicing, thought "Sprout of the Buddha-seed is this."

72 The sounds of acclamation went on; the (inhabitants of the) ten-thousand (world-system) with the devas clapped their hands, laughed, and paid homage with clasped hands.

73 (Saying) "If we should fail of the Dispensation of this protector of the world, in the distant future we will be face to face with this one.

74 As men crossing a river but, failing of the ford to the bank opposite, taking a ford lower down cross over the great river,

75 even so, all of us, if we miss (the words of) this Con-

queror, in the distant future will be face to face with this one."

[96] 76 Dīpaṅkara, knower of the world(s), recipient of offerings, proclaiming my kamma, raised his right foot.

77 All the sons of the Conqueror who were there went round me keeping their right sides towards me; devas, mankind and non-gods[1] (then) departed, saluting respectfully.

78 When the leader of the world with the Order had passed beyond my sight, rising from my prostrate posture, I sat cross-legged then.

79 I was happy with happiness, joyful with joyousness, and flooded with zest as I sat cross-legged then.

80 Sitting cross-legged I thought thus then: "I have come to mastery in the meditations, gone to perfection in the super-knowings.

81 In the (ten) thousand worlds there is no seer equal to me; without an equal in the states of psychic potency I obtained happiness of this kind."

82 While I was sitting cross-legged eminent denizens of the ten-thousand sent forth a great shout: Assuredly you will be a Buddha.

83 Those former portents that were manifest when Bodhisattas were sitting cross-legged are manifest today:

84 Cold was dispelled and heat allayed: these are manifest today. Assuredly you will be a Buddha.

85 The ten-thousand world-system was silent and undisturbed: these are manifest today. Assuredly you will be a Buddha.

86 Great winds did not blow, streams did not flow: these are manifest today. Assuredly you will be a Buddha.

87 Flowers arisen on dry land and arisen in the water all flowered then; all these are flowering too today. Assuredly you will be a Buddha.

88 As creepers and trees were fruit-bearing then, all these are fruiting too today. Assuredly you will be a Buddha.

89 Treasures of the sky and of the earth were shining then;

[1] In CB a-sura appears wrongly as "demons".

all these treasures are shining too today. Assuredly you will be a Buddha.

90 Man-made and deva-like musical instruments were played then; both these are sounding too today. Assuredly you will be a Buddha.

[97] 91 Various flowers rained down from the heavens then; these are manifest too today. Assuredly you will be a Buddha.

92 The great sea receded, the ten-thousand quaked; both these are sounding too today. Assuredly you will be a Buddha.

93 Even the ten-thousand fires in the Nirayas were extinguished then; these fires are extinguished too today. Assuredly you will be a Buddha.

94 The sun was stainless, all the stars were visible; these are manifest too today. Assuredly you will be a Buddha.

95 Though it had not rained, water gushed from the earth then; it is gushing from the earth too today. Assuredly you will be a Buddha.

96 Hosts of stars and constellations are shining in the vault of the heavens. Visākhā is in conjunction with the moon. Assuredly you will be a Buddha.

97 (Animals) having lairs in holes, lairs in caves, came forth each from its lair; these lairs are rejected too today. Assuredly you will be a Buddha.

98 There was no tedium among beings, they were contented then; all are contented too today. Assuredly you will be a Buddha.

99 Illnesses were allayed then and hunger abolished; these are manifest today. Assuredly you will be a Buddha.

100 Attachment was slight then, hatred and confusion done away with; all these are gone too today. Assuredly you will be a Buddha.

101 Fear did not exist then; this is manifest too today. By this sign we know: Assuredly you will be a Buddha.

102 Dust did not fly up; this is manifest too today. By this sign we know: Assuredly you will be a Buddha.

103 Unpleasing smells went away, a deva-like scent was wafted round; that scent is blowing too today. Assuredly you will be a Buddha.

104 All the devas except the formless ones were manifest; all these are visible too today. Assuredly you will be a Buddha.

105 As far as the Nirayas everything was visible then; everything is visible too today. Assuredly you will be a Buddha.

[98] 106 Walls, doors and rocks were no obstacle then; they are as space too today. Assuredly you will be a Buddha.

107 At that moment deceasing and arising did not exist; these are manifest too today. Assuredly you will be a Buddha.

108 Firmly exert energy; do not turn back, advance. We discern this too: Assuredly you will be a Buddha.

71 Therein *had heard these words* means that the Bodhisatta had heard the words of the Lord Dīpaṅkara's declaration.

71 *Without an equal* means without an equal owing to the absence of an equal of one like him. As it was said:

I have no teacher; one like me does not exist.
In the world with the devas I have no rival.*

71 *Of the great seer* means the great seer searched and quested in the great categories of morality, concentration, wisdom: of that great seer.

71 *Men and deities* means men and deities.[1] This is an exhaustive description, for all nāgas, yakkhas and so forth in the ten-thousand world-system were as though *rejoicing*.

71 *Sprout of the Buddha-seed is this*: the meaning is *rejoicing*, thinking, "Indeed, this Buddha-sprout has arisen."

72 *The sounds of acclamation* means that the sounds of shouting *went on*.

72 *Clapped their hands* means that they struck their arms with their hands.

72 *The ten-thousand* means the ten-thousand world-system.

72 *With the devas* means with the devas; with the devas[2] has the meaning that the ten-thousand *paid homage*.

* Vin i 3, M i 171, quoted Miln 235. Cf. Mhvu iii 326.

[1] naramarū ti narā ca amarā ca.
[2] sadevakā ti saha devehi sadevakā.

73 *If of this* means if of this,[1] or this itself is the reading.

73 *If we should fail* means if we should not meet with.

73 *In the distant future* means in a future time.

73 *We will be* means we will come to be.[2]

73 *Face to face with this one*[3] means being face to the face of this one[4]—the accusative case in the sense of the genitive.

74 *Crossing a river* means people crossing a river; "crossing over a river" is also a reading.[5]

74 *Ford to the bank opposite* means the ford facing.

74 *Failing of* means having failed of.[6]

75 *If we miss* means: the meaning is that if we miss (the words of) this Lord we shall be (those whose) duties are not done.

76 *Proclaiming my kamma* means declaring my aim that had developed.

[99] 76 *Raised his right foot* means lifted his right foot. "Circumambulating (me) keeping me on (his) right" is also a reading.

77 *The sons of the Conqueror* means the disciples of the teacher Dīpaṅkara.

77 *Devas, mankind and non-gods (then) departed, saluting respectfully* means: all these devas and so forth, circumambulating him thrice with their right sides towards him, honouring him with flowers and so forth, reverencing him with the five-fold prostration,[7] returned and, surveying him again and again, extolling him with praises and various preparations of sweet curries and condiments, (then) departed. "Then[8] nāgas and gandhabbas, saluting respectfully, departed" is also a reading.

78 *Had passed beyond my sight* means: when the Lord had passed beyond my range of sight. "When access by sight had been lost" is also a reading.

78 *With the Order* means together with the Order, with the Order.

[1] yad'imassā ti yadi imassa. Asl (Ke) p. 59 yadi p'assa.

[2] hessāmā ti bhavissāma.

[3] imaṁ, acc.

[4] imassa, gen.

[5] nadiṁ tarantā ti nadī taranakā; naditarantā ti pi pāṭho—and is so at Asl (Ke) p. 59.

[6] virajjhiyā ti virajjhitvā.

[7] Cf. text p. 7.

[8] tadā, but narā, men, at Jā i 17, ApA 19, Asl (Ke) p. 59.

78 *Rising from my prostrate posture* means getting up from the place where I had been lying on the mire.

78 *Sitting*[1] *cross-legged* means I sat down having crossed my legs on a heap of flowers. "Joyful, with a joyful mind, I got up from the seat then" is also a reading. The meaning is just as clear.

79 *Flooded with zest* means thoroughly pervaded with zest.

80 *Come to mastery* means attained to a state of mastery.

80 *In the meditations* means in the meditations relating to the fine-material sphere and the immaterial sphere.

81 *In the thousand* means in the ten thousand.

81 *Worlds* means world-system.

81 *Equal to me* means like unto me. Saying, without specification, "There is none equal to me", now, exemplifying this precisely, he said, "*Without an equal in the states of psychic potency.*"

81 Therein, *in the states of psychic potency* means in the five psychic potencies.

81 *I obtained* means I acquired.

81 *Happiness of this kind* means mental bliss[2] of this kind.

Then when the ascetic Sumedha had heard the declaration of Him of the Ten Powers, deeming that Buddha-status itself was within his grasp, he was joyful at heart. In the ten-thousand world-systems the Great Brahmās in the Pure Abodes had seen Buddhas in the past displaying marvels arising (at the time of their) declaration to sure Bodhisattas. Making known the correctness of the Tathāgata's words, (Sumedha) spoke the verse beginning "*While I was sitting cross-legged*" showing that "These verses they spoke are very pleasing to me."

82 Therein *while I was sitting cross-legged* means while I was sitting cross-legged.[3] Or this itself is the reading.

82 *Eminent denizens of the ten-thousand* means denizens in the ten-thousand[4], Great Brahmās.

83 *Those former* means those former.[5] It should be understood that it (yā) was said omitting the inflection.

83 *Were sitting cross-legged* means sitting cross-legged.[6]

[1] Here ābhujitvā, but in ver. at BvAC 96 ābhujiṁ.
[2] Cf. D ii 214 sukhā bhīyo somanassaṁ, mental bliss is more than happiness.
[3] pallaṅkābhujane mayhan ti mama pallaṅkābhujane.
[4] dasasahassādhivāsino ti dasasahassīvāsino.
[5] yā pubbe ti yāni pubbe.
[6] pallaṅkavaraṁ ābhuje ti pallaṅkābhujane.

83 *Portents that were manifest*: the meaning is portents were manifested.[1] Spoken in the present tense (padissanti) it is to be understood to be in the past tense (padissiṁsu). And the meaning of whatever is said (in the following verses) is to be taken as referring to the past.

83 *Those are manifest today* means those former portents which arose when sure Bodhisattas were sitting cross-legged, [**100**] these portents are manifest today. Therefore, the meaning is "Assuredly you will be a Buddha." It is to be understood that it is not those self-same portents that arose, but *those* that are similar to them *are manifest today*.

84 *Cold* means coldness.

84 *Was dispelled* means was gone, gone away.

84 *These* means the going away of cold and the allaying of heat.

85 *Silent* means soundless, noiseless.

85 *Undisturbed* means unconfused,[2] or this itself is the reading.

86 *Did not flow* means did not proceed, did not move.

86 *Streams* means rivers.

86 *These* means the non-blowing, the non-flowing.

87 *Arisen on dry land* means arisen on the earth, on mountain slopes, among trees.

87 *Arisen in the water* means water-flowers.

87 *Flowered*[3] means they flowered for former Bodhisattas. The present tense is to be understood in the sense of the past in accordance with the method spoken of above.[4]

87 *These are flowering too today*: the meaning is that these flowers are flowering today.

88 *Fruit-bearing* means fruit-carrying.

88 *These too today* means these too today.[5] "These too" is in the masculine gender because *creepers*[6] *and trees* are spoken of.

88 *Are fruiting* means producing fruits.

89 *Of the sky and of the earth* means in the sky and on the earth.

89 *Treasures* means treasures that are pearls and so forth.

[1] nimittāni padissantī ti nimittāni padissiṁsu.

[2] nirākulā ti anākulā.

[3] pupphanti, present tense.

[4] Text p. 99.

[5] te p'ajjā ti te pi ajja.

[6] latā is fem., but the demonstrative pronoun would follow the gender of the final word in a compound, here rukkha, masc.

89 *Were shining* means were effulgent.

90 *Man-made* means pertaining to men, man-made.

90 *Deva-like* means pertaining to devas, deva-like.

90 *Musical instruments* means there are five kinds of musical instruments: ātata, vitata, ātatavitata, susira, ghana.[1] Therein ātata means a kind of drum covered with leather on one side of the instrument; vitata means on both sides; ātatavitata means completely covered such as the great Indian lute and so forth; susira means bamboo-pipe[2] and so forth; ghana means cymbal[3] and so forth.

90 *Were played*[4] means were played.[5] According to the method spoken of above[6] the present tense should be understood in the sense of the past. This is also the method for phrases of this kind below.

90 *Are sounding* means they are sounding there as though with their own sweet[7] music emitted with skill. The meaning is they are resounding.

91 *Various flowers* means various flowers of different scents and colours.

91 *Rained down*[8] means rained down.[9] The meaning is they fell down.

91 *These*[10] *too* means these[11] divers flowers that were raining down are manifest too, the intention being that they were being poured down by hosts of devas and Brahmās.

92 *Receded* means drew back.

[**101**] 92 *Both these too today* means both these too today: the great sea and the ten-thousand.

92 *Are sounding* means are resounding.

93 *The ten thousand in the Nirayas* means countless tens of thousands.

[1] See e.g. DA ii 617, MA ii 300, SA 191, VvA 37, Mhvs -ṭ 518. See also VvA 161 for the musical instruments vīṇā, muraja, etc.

[2] vaṁsa, see Miln 31.

[3] sammatāla as at Thag 893, 911 (both -tāḷa).

[4] Present tense.

[5] Aorist.

[6] Text p. 99.

[7] suppatālitā.

[8] Present tense.

[9] Aorist.

[10] te.

[11] tāni.

93 *Are extinguished* means are quenched; they are come to peace.

94 *Stars* means constellations.

94 *These are manifest too today* means the stainlessness of the sun, and the stars today are manifest by day.

95 *Though it had not rained*[1] means though it had not rained.[2] The instrumental case is to be understood in the sense of a locative. Or, "though it had not rained"[3] also means though it had not rained down.[4] 'Na'[5] is only a particle as in such contexts as "having heard[6] the messenger's speech."*

95 *It is gushing from too today*: the meaning is that that water too today having gushed from, is rising.

95 *From the earth*[7] means from the earth;[8] ablative case.

96 *Hosts of stars* means all the hosts of stars including those in eclipse and the constellations.

96 *Constellations* means constellations and stars.

96 *In the vault of the heavens* means they are illuminating the entire vault of the heavens.

97 (*Animals*) *having lairs in holes* means: (those) having lairs in holes are snakes, mongooses, crocodiles, lizards and so forth.[9]

97 *Having lairs in caves*[10] means having lairs by rivers,[11] or this itself is the reading.

97 *Each from its lair* means from its own lair; "from that lair" is also a reading, the meaning being that then at that time from its lair, from a hole.

97 *Came forth* means came forth.[12]

* Sn 417.

[1] anovaṭṭhena, instrumental.
[2] anovaṭṭhehi, loc.
[3] anovaṭṭhe.
[4] anabhivaṭṭhe.
[5] Referring to the termination na in anovaṭṭhena.
[6] sutvāna for sutvā.
[7] mahiyā. Mahī, lit. "the great one", occurring only, accord. to PED., in late Pali literature.
[8] paṭhaviyā.
[9] Cf. SA ii 285, AA iii 68.
[10] As at Cp III 7 1.
[11] jharāsayā for darīsayā. Jhara not in PED. but M-W gives cascade, waterfall and (fem. -*ī*) a river. It perhaps corresponds to dakāsaya of S and A, the Comys. exemplifying by fish and turtles.
[12] nikkhamantī ti nikkhamiṁsu, i.e. present tense and aorist.

97 *Rejected* means well rejected; the meaning is well withdrawn from.

98 *Tedium* means dissatisfaction.[1]

98 *Contented* means contented with the highest contentedness.

99 *Were abolished* means they disappeared.

100 *Attachment* means attachment to sense-pleasures.

100 *Slight then* means it was trifling; by this is shown absence of obsession.

100 *Are gone* means are lost.

101 *Then* means when former Bodhisattas were sitting cross-legged.

101 *Did not exist* means was not.[2]

101 *This too today*: the meaning is: even today still sitting cross-legged; but this is not that.[3]

101 *By this sign we know* means for this very reason we all know that you will be a Buddha.

102 *Did not fly up* means did not go up high, did not exist, was not.

103 *Unpleasing smells* means evil smells.

103 *Went away* means disappeared.

103 *Was wafted round* means was wafted round.[4]

103 *That too today* means that *deva-like scent* too today.

[**102**] 104 *Were manifest* means were manifest.[5]

104 *These too today* means all these devas too today.

105 *As far as*[6] is a particle in the sense of demarcating; the meaning is as far as.[6]

106 *Walls* means walls.[7]

106 *Were no obstacle* means they were not makers of an obstacle.

106 *Then* means formerly.

106 *As space*: the meaning is that these doors, walls, mountain-slopes, not being able to make an obstacle across it, were like unentangled (open) space.

[1] ukkaṇṭhā. Cf. Vbh 352, SnA ii 469.

[2] na bhavatī ti na hoti.

[3] etaṁ h'ayaṁ na hoti; perhaps this refers to the similarity of the posture, not to its unbroken continuity.

[4] pavāyatī ti pavāyi.

[5] Present and aorist tenses, as usual.

[6] yāvatā ti . . . yāvatakā ti.

[7] kuḍḍā ti pākārā. Both defined by the same three words at Vin iv 266.

107 *Deceasing* means dying.

107 *Arising* means relinking birth.

107 *At* (*that*) *moment* means at the moment when former Bodhisattas were sitting cross-legged.

107 *Did not exist* means was not.

107 *These too today* means these too today;[1] words for arisings is the meaning.

108 *Do not turn back* means do not go back.

108 *Advance* means go forward. The remainder herein is quite clear.

Thereupon the wise Sumedha, having heard the words of Dīpaṅkara, Him of the Ten Powers, and of the devatās of the ten-thousand world-spheres, becoming filled with abundant strength, reflected: "Indeed, the utterance of Buddhas is not false, there is no unreliability in the talk of Buddhas. Inasmuch as there is the falling down of a clod of earth that has been thrown into the sky, the dying of what has been born, the rising of the sun after it has set, the lion's roaring his lion's roar on issuing forth from his den, the delivery, assuredly, of the heavy burden a pregnant woman has been carrying, even so indeed is the utterance of Buddhas assuredly not false. For certain I will be a Buddha." Accordingly it was said:

IIA 109 When I had heard the utterance both of the Buddha and of the ten-thousand, elated, exultant, joyous, I thought thus then:

110 The utterance of Buddhas is not of double meaning, the utterance of Conquerors is not false, there is no untruth in Buddhas. Assuredly I will be a Buddha.

111 As a clod of earth cast into the sky assuredly falls to the ground, so is the utterance of the best of Buddhas assured and eternal. There is no untruth in Buddhas. Assuredly I will be a Buddha.

112 As too the dying of all creatures is assured and eternal. so is the utterance of the best of Buddhas assured and eternal. There is no untruth in Buddhas. Assuredly I will be a Buddha.

[**103**] 113 As on the waning of the night the rising of the sun is assured, so is the utterance of the best of Buddhas

[1] tāni p'ajjā ti tāni pi ajje. Cf. text p. 100.

assured and eternal. There is no untruth in Buddhas. Assuredly I will be a Buddha.

114 As the roaring of a lion when he leaves his den is assured, so is the utterance of the best of Buddhas assured and eternal. There is no untruth in Buddhas. Assuredly I will be a Buddha.

115 As the delivery of a pregnant woman is assured, so is the utterance of the best of Buddhas assured and eternal. There is no untruth in Buddhas. Assuredly I will be a Buddha.

109 Therein *when I had heard the utterance both of the Buddha and of the ten-thousand* means having heard the utterance of Dīpaṅkara, the Fully Self-Awakened One, and of the devatās of the ten-thousand world-spheres. *Both* means of both;[1] or the word "both" is a nominative in the sense of a genitive.

109 *I thought thus* means I thought thus.[2]

110 *Not of double meaning* means a dual utterance does not occur. The meaning is an utterance that is definite. "A reliable utterance" is also a reading. Its meaning is a faultless utterance.

110 *The utterance is not false* means the utterance is not untrue.

110 *Untruth*: the meaning is there is no utterance of an untruth.

110 *Assuredly I will be a Buddha* means "Quite definitely I will be a Buddha." It must be understood that the present tense is used because it is sure, because it must be.

113 *The rising*[3] *of the sun* means the coming up[4] of the sun, or this itself is the reading.

113 *Assured and eternal* means absolutely inevitable as well as eternal.

114 *As he leaves his den* means as he is leaving his den.

115 *Delivery of a pregnant woman* means (the delivery) of those heavy in the womb of pregnant women.

115 *Delivery* means delivery,[5] meaning the delivery of a child. The syllable "ma" makes a liaison between the words. And the rest herein is quite clear.

[1] ubhayan ti ubhayesaṁ.
[2] evaṁ cintes' ahan ti evaṁ cintesiṁ ahaṁ.
[3] uggamana.
[4] udayana.
[5] bhāra-m-oropanaṁ.

Indeed, he thought, "I will be a Buddha" and, being convinced, in order to reflect on the things making a Buddha, he thought, "Where then are the things making a Buddha? Are they above, below, in the quarters, in the intermediary quarters?" Gradually examining the entire ideational element[1] and seeing that the first perfection, that of Giving, was followed and resorted to by former Bodhisattas, he exhorted himself thus:

"Wise Sumedha, you, from now onward should fulfill the first perfection, that of Giving. For as a jar of water that has been overturned discharges all the water and takes none of it back, even so, recking of neither wealth nor fame [**104**] nor wife and children nor any of the limbs,[2] but giving completely of everything wished for for the prosperity of all supplicants, while seated at the root of the Tree of Awakening and thinking, 'you will be[3] a Buddha,'" he firmly and resolutely determined on the first perfection, that of Giving. Accordingly it was said:

IIA 116 Come, I will examine the things making a Buddha, here and there, above, below, in the ten quarters, as far as the ideational element.

117 Examining, I saw then the first perfection, that of Giving, the great path pursued by the great seers of old.

118 You, having made firm, undertake and go on to this first perfection, that of Giving, if you wish to attain Awakening.

119 As a full jar overturned by whatever it may be discharges the water completely and does not retain it there,

120 so, seeing supplicants, low, high or middling, give a gift completely like the overturned jar.

116 Therein *Come* is a particle in the sense of beginning (this group of verses).

116 *The things making a Buddha* means the things making for Buddhahood. The things making for Buddhahood are the ten things beginning with the perfection of Giving.

116 *I will examine* means I will examine;[4] the meaning is that I will ascertain.

[1] dhammadhātu, defined at MA iii 113 in terms of omniscience; differently defined at Vbh 89.

[2] aṅgapaccaṅga, lit. limb after limb, any or all of the limbs.

[3] bhavissatī ti where BvAB reads bhavissasī ti.

[4] vicināmī ti vicinissāmi, pres. and fut.

116 *Here and there* means here, there,[1] or this itself is the reading. The meaning is "I (will) examine all places."[2]

116 *Above* means in the deva-world.[3]

116 *Below* means in the human world.[3]

116 *The ten quarters* means in the ten quarters. The intention is to say, "Where then are these things making a Buddha, above, below, across, in the quarters, in the intermediary quarters?"

116 *As far as the ideational element* means that herein "as far as" is an expression for demarcating. "The ideational element" should be understood as the remainder of the phrase (and) meaning the occurrence of the individual character of a thing (dhamma). What is this called? It means "I will examine as far as there is an occurrence of the individual character of the things that are things of sense-pleasure, of fine materiality and of immateriality".

117 *Examining* means testing, ascertaining.

117 *By . . . of old* means by ancient Bodhisattas.

117 *Pursued* means practised, followed.

118 *Undertake* means make the undertaking. The meaning is: "From today onwards this perfection of Giving is to be fulfilled by me."

118 *Go on to the perfection*[4] *of Giving* means: go on to the perfection[5] of Giving; the meaning is: fulfil it.

[105] 118 *If you wish to attain Awakening* means: if, having gone up to the root of the Tree of Awakening, you wish to attain the incomparable Self-Awakening.

119 *By whatever it may be* means by water or milk or whatever it may be. Or, as there is a union with the word "full" the grammarians want a genitive or a genitive in the sense of the instrumental—the meaning is "by means of anything".

119 *Overturned* means made facing down.

119 *Does not retain it there* means does not retain it in that (jar).

119 *(Or) discharges*: the meaning is: or discharges the water completely.

120 *Low, high*[6] *or middling* means low, middling, excellent; the syllable 'ma'[6] makes a liaison between the words.

[1] ito c'ito ti ito ito.
[2] tattha tattha.
[3] Cf. text p. 30.
[4] pāramitā.
[5] pāramī.
[6] hīna-m-ukkaṭṭha.

120 *Like the overturned jar* means like what is made facing down.

On seeing supplicants approach, he thus of himself exhorted himself: "Do you, Sumedha, not leaving a remnant of yourself, fulfil the perfection of Giving by the sacrifice of all your wealth, the higher perfection by the sacrifice of any of your limbs, the ultimate perfection by the sacrifice of your life."

Then it occurred to him: "Not so few only can be the things making a Buddha." And reflecting further and seeing the second perfection, that of Morality, he thought: "Wise Sumedha, you, from now onward should fulfil the second perfection, that of Morality. As a yak-cow, not recking even of her own life, protects only her tail,[1] even so you too, from now onward, not recking even of your own life but protecting only your morality, will be a Buddha." And he firmly and resolutely determined on the second perfection, that of Morality. Accordingly it was said:

IIA 121 But not these few only can be the Buddha-things. I will examine other things too that are maturing for Awakening.

122 Examining, I saw then the second perfection, that of Morality, followed and practised by the great seers of old.

123 You, having made firm, undertake and go on to this second perfection, that of Morality, if you wish to attain Awakening.

124 And as a yak-cow if her tail is caught in anything, does not injure her tail, but goes to death there,

125 so, fulfilling the moral habits in the four planes, protect morality continuously like the yak-cow her tail.

121 *But not these* means but not just these.

121 *Maturing for Awakening* means bringing the Way to maturity or bringing omniscient knowledge to maturity.

[106] 122 *The second perfection, that of Morality*, means that the foundations of all skilled states are in morality. Founded in morality one does not deteriorate as to skilled states, one acquires all the mundane and supermundane special qualities. Therefore

[1] A yak's tail is a beautiful object, and fans made of it were used for fanning royalty.

the perfection of Morality should be fulfilled. The meaning is that he saw the second perfection, that of Morality.

122 *Followed and practised* means followed as well as made much of.

124 *Yak-cow* means a female yak animal.

124 *In anything* means there wherever among various trees, creepers, thorns, and so forth.

124 *Caught* means caught.[1]

124 *There* means remaining just there where it was caught,[2] she goes to her death.

124 *Does not injure* means does not destroy.

124 *Tail* means: she does not go along destroying her tail but comes to death just there.

125 *Moral habits in the four planes* means: moral habits are distributed into four kinds: the meaning is in respect of control by the Pātimokkha, control over the sense-organs, complete purity of mode of livelihood, and relying (only) on the requisites (of a monk's daily life).[3] But in respect of the planes, that indeed and also skill itself are included in merely two planes.

125 *Fulfilling* means fulfilling by the absence of tearing, cutting, spotting and so forth.

125 *Continuously* means all the time.

125 *Like the yak-cow* means as the yak-cow.[4] The rest herein is quite clear.

Then it occurred to him: "Not so few only can be the things making a Buddha." And reflecting further and seeing the third perfection, that of Renunciation, he thought: 'Wise Sumedha, you, from now onward should fulfil the third perfection too, that of Renunciation. As a man who has been in a prison-house for a long time has no affection for it but, on the contrary, is fretting and wanting not to be (there), even so do you too see every becoming as a prison-house; then fretting and wanting to be free of all the becomings, be one who is turned toward renunciation. Thus you will be a Buddha." And he firmly and resolutely determined on

[1] pativilaggitan ti pativilaggaṁ.
[2] Here laggitaṁ.
[3] These are the first four categories of moral habits at Miln 336.
[4] camarī iva. BvAB reads camarī migo viya.

the third perfection, that of Renunciation. Accordingly it was said:

IIA 126 But not these few only can be the Buddha-things. I will examine other things too that are maturing for Awakening.

127 Examining, I saw then the third perfection, that of Renunciation, followed and practised by the great seers of old.

128 You, having made firm, undertake and go on to this third perfection, that of Renunciation, if you wish to attain Awakening.

129 As a man who for long has lived painfully afflicted in a prison does not generate attachment there but seeks only freedom,

[107] 130 so do you see all becomings as a prison. Be one turned toward renunciation for the utter release from becoming.

129 Therein *in a prison* means in a prison-house.
129 *For long has lived* means has lived for a long time.
129 *Afflicted* means oppressed by suffering.
129 *There* means in the prison.
129 *Attachment* means affection.
129 *Does not generate* means does not arouse. Thinking, "On being freed from this prison I will go elsewhere" he does not generate attachment there. What does he do?
129 *Seeks only freedom*: the intention is that he seeks only freedom, only deliverance.
130 *One turned toward renunciation* means: be one turned toward renunciation.[1]
130 *From becoming* means from all becomings.
130 *For the utter release* means for the sake of utter deliverance. "Being turned toward renunciation he will attain Self-Awakening" is also a reading. The meaning of the rest is quite clear.

Then it occurred to him: "Not so few only can be the things making a Buddha." And reflecting further and seeing the fourth perfection, that of Wisdom, he thought: "Wise Sumedha, you, from now onward should fulfil the fourth perfection, that of Wisdom. Not avoiding anyone among the low, middling or high,

[1] nekkhammābhimukho ti nikkhamanābhimukho hohi.

also approaching all wise men you should ask questions. Just as a monk who walks for alms-food, not avoiding any family among those divided into 'low' and so forth, but walking for almsfood in a successive order quickly acquires enough for his sustenance, so too will you, approaching all wise men and questioning them, become a Buddha." And he firmly and resolutely determined on the fourth perfection, that of Wisdom. Accordingly it was said:

IIA 131 But not these few only can be the Buddha-things. I will examine other things too that are maturing for Awakening.

132 Examining, I saw then the fourth perfection, that of Wisdom, followed and practised by the great seers of old.

133 You, having made firm, undertake and go on to this fourth perfection, that of Wisdom, if you wish to attain Awakening.

134 And as a monk, looking for alms, not avoiding low, high or middling families, acquires sustenance thus,

[108] 135 so you, questioning discerning people all the time, going on to the perfection of Wisdom, will attain Self-Awakening.

134 Therein *looking for alms* means walking for almsfood.

134 *Low, high, middling*: the meaning is low, high, middling families. A change in gender is made.[1]

134 *Not avoiding* means not evading. If while he is walking he misses the successive order of the houses, this is called: he avoids. The meaning is: not acting thus.

134 *Sustenance* means enough for sustenance. The meaning is: he acquires life-supporting nutriment.

135 *Questioning* means: having approached distinguished wise people in various places and questioning them in the way beginning, "What, sir, is skill, what is unskill, what is blameable, what is blameless?"*

135 *Discerning people*[2] means wise people. "Discerning people"[3] is also a reading.

* M iii 205.

[1] From masc. to neut.

[2] buddhaṁ janaṁ (where buddha does not have its technical sense of Awakened). BvAB budhaṁ janaṁ. PED does not give budha.

[3] buddhe jane.

135 *Perfection of Wisdom*[1] means "Going to the perfection of Wisdom"[2]. The meaning of the rest is quite clear.

Then it occurred to him: "Not so few only can be the things making a Buddha." And reflecting further and seeing the fifth perfection, that of Energy, he thought: "Wise Sumedha you, from now onward should fulfil the perfection of Energy. Just as a lion, the king of beasts, is firm in energy in every mode of behaviour, so too you, being firm in energy, not laggard in energy in every becoming, in every mode of behaviour, will be a Buddha." And he firmly and resolutely determined on the fifth perfection, that of Energy. Accordingly it was said:

IIA 136 But not these few only can be the Buddha-things. I will examine other things too that are maturing for Awakening.

137 Examining, I saw then the fifth perfection, that of Energy, followed and practised by the great seers of old.

138 You, having made firm, undertake and go on to this fifth perfection, that of Energy, if you wish to attain Awakening.

139 And as a lion, the king of beasts, whether he is lying down, standing or walking, is not of sluggish energy but is always exerting himself,

140 so you too, firmly exerting energy in every becoming, going on to the perfection of Energy, will attain Self-Awakening.

139 *Not of sluggish energy* means not laggard in energy.

[109] 140 *In every becoming*[3] means in a becoming of birth upon birth; the meaning is: in all becomings.[4] "Having stirred up energy you will attain Self-Awakening" is also a reading. The meaning of the rest is quite clear.

Then it occurred to him: "Not so few only can be the things making a Buddha." And reflecting further and seeing the sixth perfection, that of Patience, he thought: "Wise Sumedha, you, from now onward should fulfil the perfection of Patience and be

[1] paññāya pāramī.
[2] paññāpāramitaṁ.
[3] sabbabhave, sing.
[4] sabbesu bhavesu, pl.

patient both of respect and disrespect. Just as the earth has neither affection nor repugnance for what one throws on to it, whether this be pure or impure, but is patient, endures it and bears with it, so you too, being patient of all forms of respect and disrespect, will be a Buddha." And he firmly and resolutely determined on the sixth perfection, that of Patience. Accordingly it was said:

IIA 141 But not these few only can be the Buddha-things. I will examine other things too that are maturing for Awakening.

142 Examining, I saw then the sixth perfection, that of Patience, followed and practised by the great seers of old.

143 You, having made firm, undertake this sixth; with mind unwavering therein you will attain Self-Awakening.

144 And as the earth endures all that is thrown down on it, both pure and impure, and shows no repugnance (or) approval,

145 so you too, patient of all respect and disrespect, going on to the perfection of Patience, will attain Self-Awakening.

143 *With mind unwavering* means single-mindedly.

144 *Both pure* means the pure is sandal (wood or powder), saffron, perfumes, garlands and so forth.

144 *And impure* means the impure is the ordure, dung, urine, spittle, mucus and so forth of snakes, dogs and human beings.

144 *Endures* means is patient, bears with.

144 *Thrown down on* means put down on.

144 *Repugnance* means anger.

144 *Approval*[1] means of that usage, of that placing on. "Repugnance, kindness"[2] is also a reading. Its meaning is that it has no repugnance for or satisfaction in what is thrown down on it.

145 *Patient of respect and disrespect* means: be you one who endures all respect and disrespect [**110**] They also read: "Likewise you too, patient of respect and disrespect in every becoming." "Having gone to the perfection of Patience" is also a reading. The meaning is: having gone to the perfection of that Patience by means of fulfilling it. The meaning of the rest is quite clear.

[1] tayā.

[2] dayā as at Bv II 144, Asl (Ke) reads dvayaṁ, for both.

Not saying even so much henceforward, we will go on and wherever there is a distinguishing property, speaking of that only (and) showing it among the readings.

Then it occurred to him: "Not so few only can be the things making a Buddha". And reflecting further and seeing the seventh perfection, that of Truth(-speaking), he thought: "Wise Sumedha, you, from now onward should fulfil the seventh perfection, that of Truth(-speaking). Even if a thunderbolt[1] were falling on your head, not for the sake of wealth and so forth, not because of desire and so forth, must you tell an intentional lie. Just as the star called Osadhī, not leaving its own course, does not go by another course, but goes on its own course during all the seasons, even so too, you, capable of not speaking a lie having abandoned the truth, will be a Buddha." And he firmly and resolutely determined on the seventh perfection, that of Truth(-speaking). Accordingly it was said:

IIA 146 But not these few only can be the Buddha-things. I will examine other things too that are maturing for Awakening.

147 Examining, I saw then the seventh perfection, that of Truth(-speaking), followed and practised by the great seers of old.

148 You, having made firm, undertake this seventh; by speech without double-meaning therein you will attain Self-Awakening.

149 And as Osadhī[2] is balanced for devas and mankind in (all) times and seasons, does not deviate from her course,

150 so you too must not deviate from the course of the Truths; going on to the perfection of Truth(-speaking), you will attain Self-Awakening.

148 Therein *therein* means in the perfection of Truth (-speaking).

148 *Speech without double-meaning* means speech that is not untrue.

149 *Osadhī* means the star Osadhī. When gathering medicinal

[1] asanī, nine kinds at DA 569.

[2] The star of healing; a sign of constancy and dependability. Cf. MA ii 372, iii 274.

herbs (osadha) they take the medicinal herbs on seeing that Osadhī the star has risen. Therefore it is said to be Osadhī the star.

149 *Balanced* means become the measure.[1]

149 *For devas and mankind* means for the world with the devas.

149 *In times*[2] means in the time of the rains.

149 *In seasons*[3] means in the cold weather and the hot. "In (every) time in the cycle of the seasons"[4] is also a reading. Its meaning is: In times means in the hot weather. In the cycle of the seasons means in the cold weather and in the rains.

[111] 149 *Does not deviate from her course* means: whatever the season she does not deviate, does not depart from her own course of motion.[5] . . .[5] She travels for six months in an easterly direction and for six months in a westerly direction. Or *osadhī* means healing herbs: ginger, long pepper, black pepper and so forth. *Does not deviate* means: whatever is a little gift of fruit is a medicinal herb through being a gift of fruit; not giving a fruit of herself she does not turn back, deviating. *From her course* means from her course of motion. As bringing up bile is a bringing up of bile, as bringing up wind is a bringing up of wind, as bringing up phlegm is a bringing up of phlegm is the meaning. The meaning of the rest is quite clear.

Then it occurred to him: "Not so few only can be the things making a Buddha." And reflecting further and seeing the eighth perfection, that of Resolute Determination, he thought: "Wise Sumedha, you, from now onward should fulfil the perfection of Resolute Determination. You should be stable in that resolute determination you resolutely determine on. Just as a mountain does not even tremble or move when the wind is striking it in all directions but remains in precisely its own place, even so you too, being stable in your own resolute determination, will be a Buddha." And he firmly and resolutely determined on the eighth perfection, that of Resolute Determination. Accordingly it was said:

IIA 151 But not these few only can be the Buddha-things. I will

[1] tulābhūtā ti pamāṇabhūtā. Cf. text p. 113; and PvA 110 atulan ti appamāṇaṁ.

[2] samaye.

[3] utuvasse.

[4] utuvaṭṭe.

[5] I have here omitted the sentence yaṁ yaṁ phaladānamattaṁ osadhaṁ taṁ taṁ phaladānena, and inserted it lower under *Does not deviate*, with BvAB. But wherever it should come, this whole passage seems somewhat obscure.

examine other things too that are maturing for Awakening.

152 Examining, I saw then the eighth perfection, that of Resolute Determination, followed and practised by the great seers of old.

153 You, having made firm, undertaking this eighth, being stable therein, will attain Self-Awakening.

154 And as a mountain, a rock, stable and firmly based, does not tremble in rough winds but remains in precisely its own place,

155 so you too must be constantly stable in resolute determination; going on to the perfection of Resolute Determination, you will attain Self-Awakening.

154 Therein *a rock* means made of stone.

154 *Stable* means unmoving.

154 *Firmly based* means it has stability, is also well based. "Just as a mountain, stable, safe and sound"[1] is also a reading.

154 *In rough winds* means in strong winds.

154 *In precisely its own place* means in precisely its own place,[2] in precisely the place where it is standing. The meaning of the rest is quite clear.

Then it occurred to him: "Not so few only can be the things making a Buddha." And reflecting further and seeing the ninth perfection, that of Loving-kindness, [**112**] he thought: "Wise Sumedha, you, from now onward should fulfil the perfection of Loving-kindness, should be of like mind[3] towards friends and enemies. Just as water pervades, giving coolness to evil people and good people alike,[4] even so you too, being of like mind with loving-kindness towards all beings, will be a Buddha." And he firmly and resolutely determined on the ninth perfection, that of Loving-kindness. Accordingly it was said:

IIA 156 But not these few only can be the Buddha-things. I will examine other things too that are maturing for Awakening.

[1] BvAB adds suppatiṭṭhito, firmly based.

[2] sakaṭṭhāne yevā ti attano ṭhāne yeva.

[3] ekacitta.

[4] ekasadisa.

157 Examining, I saw then the ninth perfection, that of Loving-kindness, followed and practised by the great seers of old.

158 You, having made firm, undertaking this ninth, be without an equal in Loving-kindness if you wish to attain Awakening.

159 And as water pervades with coolness good and evil people alike and carries away dust and dirt,

160 so you too, by developing loving-kindness for foe and friend equally, going on to the perfection of Loving-kindness, will attain Self-Awakening.

158 Therein *be without an equal* means be with no-one like you in the development of loving-kindness.

159 *Alike* means equal.

159 *Pervades* means reaches.

159 *Carries away* means cleanses.

159 *Dust* means adventitious dust.

159 *Dirt* (rajo) means the dirt of sweat and so forth produced on the physical frame. "Dust (rajan), dirt" is also a reading. This is the very meaning.

160 *For foe and friend*[1] means for foe and for friend. The meaning is for a friend[2] and for a rival.[3]

160 *By developing loving-kindness* means increase loving-kindness by development. The meaning of the rest is quite clear.

Then it occurred to him: "Not so few only can be the things making a Buddha." And reflecting further and seeing the tenth perfection, that of Equanimity, he thought: "Wise Sumedha, you, from now onward should fulfil the perfection of Equanimity, you should be indifferent towards happiness and suffering. Just as the earth is indifferent whether what is being thrown on to it is pure or impure, so too you, being indifferent toward happiness and suffering, will be a Buddha." [**113**] And he firmly and resolutely determined on the tenth perfection, that of Equanimity. Accordingly it was said:

IIA 161 But not these few only can be the Buddha-things. I will

[1] BvAC both in ver. 160 and the Comy. reads ahitahite. Bv, BvAB read hitāhite.

[2] Here mitta for the earlier hita.

[3] BvAC sapatte; BvAB amitte, not-friend.

examine other things too that are maturing for Awakening.

162 Examining, I saw then the tenth perfection, that of Equanimity, followed and practised by the great seers of old.

163 You, having made firm, undertaking this tenth, being balanced, firm, will attain Self-Awakening.

164 And as the earth is indifferent to the impure and the pure thrown down on it and avoids both anger and courtesy,

165 so you too must be balanced always in face of the pleasant and unpleasant and, going on to the perfection of Equanimity, you will attain Self-Awakening.

163 Therein *balanced*[1] means remaining in a state of indifference. As the beam of a balance that is weighted evenly remains even and neither bends down nor rises up, even so you too, being weighted evenly against happinesses and sufferings, will attain Self-Awakening.

164 *Avoids anger and courtesy* means avoids repugnance and satisfaction. "Avoiding kindness and anger" is also a reading. That is the very meaning. The remainder is to be understood according to the method set out for the perfection of Patience.

Then when the wise Sumedha had examined these ten perfection-things, he further thought: "The things maturing for Awakening and making a Buddha that can be fulfilled by Bodhisattas in this world are so few only and are not more than this. But these perfections are neither in the sky above nor in the earth below, nor are they in the eastern quarter and so forth, but only within the very flesh of my heart are they founded." Thus seeing that the foundation of these was in his own heart, making all of them firm, reflecting on them again and again with resolute determination, he reflected on them in forward and in reverse order; taking them at the limit he went back to the beginning; taking them at the beginning he arrived at the limit; taking them in the middle he brought them to a finish at both (of the ends); taking them at both of the ends he brought them to a finish in the middle. Thinking: "The perfections are truly a sacrifice of external possessions, the higher perfections are truly a sacrifice of any of one's limbs,

[1] Cf. text p. 110.

the ultimate perfections are truly a sacrifice of one's life," he reflected on the ten perfections, the ten higher perfections, the ten ultimate perfections[1] as though he were gliding up and down a pair of palm trees.

While he was reflecting on the ten perfections, this great earth, extending for four myriad (yojanas) and two hundred thousand yojanas thick, roaring a great roar because of the incandescence of Dhamma, trembled, quaked and shook violently as though it were a bunch of reeds being trodden on by an elephant or as though it were a sugar-cane mill that was being pressed hard, [**114**] and it whirled round like a potter's wheel and like the wheel in an oil-press. Accordingly it was said:

IIA 166 So few as these only are those things in the world maturing for Awakening. There is nothing elsewhere beyond these. Be established firmly in them.

167 While I was reflecting on these things with their intrinsic nature, traits and characteristic marks, the earth and the ten-thousand quaked because of the incandescence of Dhamma.

168 The earth moved and squealed like a sugar-cane mill on being pressed; the earth shook thus like the wheel in an oil-press.

166 Therein *so few only* means it was said to show there were neither less nor more than the ten perfections that have been designated.

166 *Beyond these* means there is nothing beyond the ten perfections.

166 *There is nothing elsewhere* means that the rule for "elsewhere" (aññatra) is to be adopted from grammar. The meaning is that beyond the ten perfections there is no other thing making a Buddha.

166 *In them* means in these ten perfections.

166 *Be established* means stand firm. The meaning is: stand firm while fulfilling them.

167 *On these things* means on these perfection-things.

167 *While I was reflecting on*[2] means while I was ascertaining. The genitive case is to be understood in the sense of a locative.[3]

[1] Cf. text p. 59. [2] sammasato. [3] Cf. text p. 83.

167 *With their intrinsic nature, traits and characteristics* means while he was reflecting on what is agreed on as the intrinsic nature with the traits and characteristic marks.

167 *Because of the incandescence of Dhamma* means because of the incandescence of the knowledge of consolidating the perfections.

167 *The earth*[1] means: wealth[2] is said to be treasure; it supports that or it is contained herein, so it is the supporter of wealth, the friendly one.[3]

167 *Quaked* means quaked.[4] While the wise Sumedha was examining the perfections the ten-thousand quaked because of the incandescence of his knowledge.

168 *Moved* means shook in six ways.[5]

168 *Squealed* means roared, sang.

168 *Like a sugar-cane mill on being pressed* means as a pressed sugar-cane mill. "Like a pressed mill for molasses" is also a reading. That is the very meaning.

168 *In an oil-press* means in a press for pressing oil.[6]

168 *Like the wheel* means like the mechanism of the big wheel turning.[7]

168 *Thus* means: as the wheel for pressing oil whirls round and shakes, *thus* this *earth shook.* The rest is quite clear in meaning.

While the great earth was shaking thus, the people, the inhabitants of Ramma city, [**115**] unable to restrain themselves while they were waiting on the Lord, fell down fainting like great sāla trees blasted by a whirlwind.[8] Water-jars and so on and potters'

[1] vasudhā.

[2] vasu.

[3] vasudhā medinī. Medinī also means the fat one. See Vism 125 for six names for the earth, paṭhavī, including these two.

[4] pakampathā ti pakampittha.

[5] I follow BvAB and BvAC's v. l., reading chappakāra. rather than BvAC's cakkākāra (noted as a v. l. by BvAB). The six ways are probably E–W, W–E, N–S, S–N, up and down, down and up.

[6] telayante ti telapīḷanayante.

[7] cakkikānaṁ mahācakkayantaṁ viya; or, like the mechanism of the big wheel among the little wheels; or, again: among those that are turning, wheeling, cakkikānaṁ. Skt. lexicons know caksika tenatively, in the sense of a juggler or twister; BHSD "perh. a juggler who does tricks with wheels or discs". See Mhvu Transl. iii p. 110, n. 6, 443.

[8] yugantavātabbhā as at Jā i 26. yugandharavāta- at BvAB.

wares, moving and striking against one another, were smashed to smithereens. The great populace, terrified and alarmed, approached the teacher and asked him: "Now, what is this, Lord? Is it the twisting round of a serpent or is it some twisting round among spirits, yakkhas or devatās? Certainly we do not know what it is, but all this great populace is disturbed. Could it be something evil for this world, or something good? Tell us the reason for this."

When the teacher had heard what they said he replied: "Do not you be afraid, do not worry. You have nothing to fear on this account. The wise Sumedha of whom I declared today: 'In the future he will be the Buddha called Gotama' is now reflecting on the perfections, and while he is reflecting on them the entire ten-thousand world-system is shaking and squealing in unison because of the incandescence of Dhamma." Accordingly it was said:

IIA 169 As many as comprised the company at the alms-giving to the Buddha, they lay there fainting on the ground, trembling.

170 Countless thousands of water-jars and many a hundred pitchers were shattered and crushed there striking against one another.

171 The great populace anxious, alarmed, terrified, staggered, their minds in confusion, having gathered together approached Dīpaṅkara:

172 "What will happen, good or evil, to the world? The whole world is disturbed. One with Vision, remove this."

173 Dīpaṅkara, the great sage, assured them then: "Have confidence, have no fear of this earthquake.

174 He of whom I declared today that he will be a Buddha in the world is reflecting on the Dhamma that was followed by former Conquerors.

175 The Dhamma reflected on by him is the entire plane of Buddhas. It is for this reason that the earth of the ten-thousand with the devas and men is shaking."

169 Therein *as many as* means so many as.[1]

[116] 169 *Was* means was.[2] "That company was then" is also a reading. Therein the meaning is: that company that was standing there.

[1] yāvatā ti yāvatikā.

[2] āsī ti ahosi. Translated in the verse as "comprised."

169 *Trembling* means shaking.

169 *They* means that company.

169 *Lay* means lay.[1]

170 *Water-jars* means of water-jars: the nominative case in the sense of a genitive. The meaning is: countless thousands of water-jars.

170 *Shattered*[2] (*and*) *crushed* means broken up[3] as well as crushed. The meaning is crushed-and-shattered.

170 *Striking against one another* means beating against one another.

171 *Anxious* means fearful at heart.

171 *Alarmed* means full of terror.

171 *Terrified* means terrified with fear.

171 *Staggered* means staggered in mind. The meaning is the thoughts were unsteady. But all these are synonyms for one another.

171 *Having gathered together* means having gathered together,[4] or this itself is the reading.

172 *Disturbed* means impaired, frightened.

172 *Remove this* means remove this disturbance and fear. The meaning is: destroy it.

172 *One with Vision* means One with Vision, with the five kinds of vision.[5]

173 *Them*[6] *then* means these people then; the genitive case in the sense of an accusative.

173 *Assured* means informed, made known.

173 *Have confidence* means thoughts of confidence.

173 *Have no fear* means have no fear.[7]

174 *He of whom I* means the wise Sumedha of whom I.

174 *Dhamma* means Dhamma of the perfections.

174 *Former* means ancient.[8]

174 *Followed by Conquerors*: the meaning is: followed by Conquerors at the time they were Bodhisattas.

[1] setī ti sayittha, pres. and aorist.
[2] saṁcuṇṇa.
[3] cuṇṇa, perhaps powdered.
[4] samāgammā ti samāgantvā.
[5] See text p. 33.
[6] tesaṁ.
[7] mā bhāthā ti mā bhāyatha.
[8] Cf. text p. 104.

175 *Plane of Buddhas* means the perfection of Buddhas.
175 *For this* means for the reason that he was reflecting on this.
175 *Is shaking* means is moving.
175 *With the devas* means in the world with the devas (and men).

When the great populace had heard the Tathāgata's words, exultant, elated, they issued forth from Ramma city taking garlands, perfumes, unguents and approached the Bodhisatta. When they had approached him and had honoured and reverenced him with the garlands and so forth, keeping their right sides towards him, they entered Ramma city again. Then the Bodhisatta, having reflected on all the ten perfections making (them) firm with resolute determination, rose from the seat where he was sitting. Accordingly it was said:

[**117**] IIA 176 Having heard the Buddha's words, their minds were calmed at once. All, approaching me, greatly reverenced me again.

177 Having undertaken the special qualities of Buddhas, having made firm my purpose, I paid homage to Dīpaṅkara and arose from my seat then.

176 *Minds were calmed* means when the great populace who had been anxious at heart when the earth was shaking had heard the reason for it, their minds were calmed. The meaning is: they came to peace. "The people were calmed" is also a reading. It is quite clear.
177 *Having undertaken* means having taken rightly. The meaning is undertaken.
177 *Special qualities of Buddhas* means the perfections. The rest is quite clear.

Then as the Bodhisatta, the being merciful to all, was rising from his seat the devas of the entire ten-thousand world-system assembled together and honoured him with deva-like perfumes and garlands and so forth, and proclaimed praises and blessings in phrases such as these: "Master Sumedha the ascetic, today you have made a great aspiration at the feet of Dīpaṅkara, Him of the Ten Powers. May that succeed without a stumbling-block for you, may there be no fear or horror for you there, may no illness, however trifling, arise in your physical frame. Fulfilling the perfections forthwith, penetrate perfect Self-Awakening. As trees flower and fruit at the time for bearing flowers and bearing fruit, likewise do you too, not letting that time go by, forthwith reach Self-Awakening." When they had proclaimed thus and had saluted the Bodhisatta, they returned each to his own deva-abode. Even as the Bodhisatta was being highly praised by the devatās, he thought: "I, having fulfilled the perfections, will be a Buddha a hundred thousand eons and four incalculables from now." And making energy firm with resolute determination, he ascended into the sky and went to Himavant itself, the abode of a host of seers. Accordingly it was said:

IIA 178 As he was rising from the seat both devas and men showered down deva-like and earthly flowers.

179 And these pronounced a safety-blessing, both devas and men: Great is your aspiration, may you obtain what you wish.

180 May all calamities be avoided, grief, illness be done away with, may there be no stumbling-block for you. Quickly reach supreme Awakening.

181 As flowering trees flower when the season has come, so do you, great hero, flower with a Buddha's knowledge.

[118] 182 As they whoever that were Self-Awakened Ones fulfilled the ten perfections, so may you, great hero, fulfil the ten perfections.

183 As they whoever that were Self-Awakened Ones awakened on the dais of a Tree of Awakening, so may you, great hero, awaken in a Conqueror's Awakening.

184 As they whoever that were Self-Awakened Ones set turning the Wheel of Dhamma, so may you, great hero, set turning the Wheel of Dhamma.

185 As the moon shines clear on a full-moon night, so do you shine fully in the ten-thousand.

186 As the sun, freed from Rāhu, blazes with splendour, so do you, freed of the world, shine with glory.

187 As whatever are those rivers that flow into the great ocean, so may the world with the devas flow into your presence.

188 Praised and lauded by these, he, undertaking the ten things, fulfilling those things, entered the forest then.

178 Therein *deva-like* means mandārava (flowers and flowers of the) Coral Tree. The meaning is: the devas holding deva-like blossoms and the men earthly flowers.

178 *They showered down* means they showered around.

178 *As he was rising* means when he had risen.

179 (*These*) *pronounced* means they announced, they made known.

179 *Safety-blessing* means state of safety.

179 Now the phrase beginning *Great is your aspiration* was said in order to show the method in which it was spoken: "Though you, wise Sumedha, aspire to a great position *may you obtain* according to your aspiration."

180 *All calamities* (sabbītiyo): it comes (eti), thus are calamities (īti); all calamities (sabbā ītiyo) (is) all calamities (sabbītiyo), misfortunes.

180 *May . . . be avoided* means may they not be.

180 *May grief, illness*[1] *be done away with* means: may the grief reckoned as grieving, the illness reckoned as paining come to be done away with.

180 *For you* means for you.[2]

180 *May there be no stumbling-block* means may there be no stumbling-block.[3]

180 *Reach* means arrive at, attain.

180 *Awakening* means one proceeds to knowledge of the Way to arahantship and to omniscient knowledge.

181 *When the season*: the meaning is: when this or that tree's season for flowering *has come*.

[**119**] 181 *Flowering* means flowering ones.

181 *With a Buddha's knowledge* means with the eighteen Buddha-knowledges.[4]

181 *Do you flower* means may you flower.

182 *Fulfilled* means they fulfilled.[5]

182 *Fulfil* means fulfil thoroughly.

[1] BvA reads soko rogo here and in the verse; Bv sabbarogo.

[2] te ti tava.

[3] mā bhavatv' antarāyo ti mā bhavatu antarāyo.

[4] Cf. text p. 185, Miln 285 where spoken of as 14.

[5] pūrayun ti pūrayiṁsu.

183 *Awakened* means they awakened.

183 *In a Conqueror's Awakening* means: in the Awakening of Conquerors, of Buddhas. The meaning is: at the root of the Tree of Awakening to omniscience.

185 *On a full-moon night* means on a full-moon night.[1]

185 *Fully* means fulfilled is what was desired.

186 *Freed from Rāhu* means freed from Rāhu, not lacking any deficiency.[2]

186 *With splendour* means with ardour, with light.

186 *Freed of the world*: the meaning is: being unsmeared by worldly things.

186 *Shine* means shine.[3]

186 *With glory* means with a Buddha's glory.

187 *Flow into* means enter the great sea.

187 *May (they) flow* means may they approach.

187 *Into your presence* means close to you.

188 *By these* means by the devas.

188 *Praised and lauded* means praised as well as lauded. Or, lauded with praises by Dīpaṅkara and so forth.

188 *The ten things* means the ten perfection-things.

188 *Forest* means a great wood. He entered the great wood on Mount Dhammaka[4] is the meaning. The rest of the verses are very clear.

Concluded is the Account of Sumedha in the Clarifier of Sweet Meaning, the Commentary on the Chronicle of Buddhas

IIB THE EXPOSITION OF THE CHRONICLE OF THE BUDDHA DĪPAṄKARA

The inhabitants of Ramma city who were lay-followers gave a great gift to the Order of monks with the Buddha at the head and again honoured and reverenced him with garlands, perfumes and so forth. When he had eaten and had withdrawn his hand from the bowl, they sat down near him anxious to hear the benediction for

[1] puṇṇamāye ti puṇṇamāsiyaṁ.

[2] sobbhānunā; this seems to mean not lacking the deep hole (sobbha) that is made in the sun at the time of an eclipse, i.e. when Rāhu seizes the sun (or moon) in his mouth and appears to bite off a piece.

[3] virocā ti virāja.

[4] BvAB Dhammika.

the gift. Then the Teacher gave them a benediction of the utmost sweetness, going to the heart:

"A gift is deemed the highest source of happiness and so forth, and is said to be a stairway, a support for the deva-like.[1] 65
A gift is a man's shelter, a gift is a succour for relations, a gift is the utmost bourn of beings afflicted by suffering. 66
[120] A gift is designated a boat in the sense of ferrying (people) across suffering; and a gift, by guarding one from fear, is praised as a city. 67
And a gift is spoken of as a poisonous snake in the sense that it is difficult to attack; a gift is a lotus from being unsmirched by the stains of greed and so forth. 68
In the world there is no help for a man like unto a gift; therefore practise that course with active inclination. 69
Wise gifts here are sources of (rebirth in) a heaven-world. Who is the man in the world, delighting in welfare, who would not give? 70
Who is the man who, when he hears that a gift produces attainment among the devas, would not give a gift, a cord of happiness, a joy to the mind? 71
As he is faring along by giving he can find delight for a very long time, surrounded by nymphs, in Nandana, Nandana of the gods.[2] 72
A giver finds sublime zest; he walks respected in this world, and a giver goes on to unending renown,[3] and a giver is to be trusted. 73
That man, having given a gift, goes on to prosperity and riches[4] and long life; he has too a comely body; he sports together with devas in heaven, staying in mansions that resound with the various cries of peacocks. 74
The wealth of thieves, enemies, kings, water, fire is not shared; but that gift one gives is verily in the plane of the knowledge of disciples, in the plane of (buddhas) by and for themselves, in the plane of Buddhas." 75

[1] An explanation of various of the terms in the first five verses occurs at MA iii 90, AA iv 99, UdA 281.

[2] suranandana. Nandana is a lovely grove in Tāvatiṁsa.

[3] khyāti. See KhA 101 for this and khyāta; also see MR & Ill., p. 108, n. 14 which notes khyāta replaces the synonymous vissuta at DA 28, AA 6, UdA 12.

[4] Two kinds of wealth or riches, bhoga, at A i 92: of worldly things and of Dhamma.

When he had given the benediction for the gift in the way beginning thus and had explained the advantage in giving, he at once talked a talk on moral habit,[1] this moral habit which verily is the root of the attainments[2] in this world and the world beyond:

> "Morality is the highest source of happinesses; the moral man advances by morality to the (Three and) Thirty, for morality is a shelter and a cave and a succour for one who has come into saṁsāra.
> And where, here or beyond, is there other help for people equal to morality? Morality is the chief support for special qualities as is the earth for what is stationary and what is mobile.[3]
> Lovely indeed is morality, morality is supreme in the world. He is called a moral man whose conduct is a practising of the ariyan life."[4]

[**121**] There is no adornment equal to the adornment of morality. There is no perfume equal to the perfume of morality. There is no (way of) cleansing away the stains of the defilements equal to morality. There is no (way of) allaying the burning fever (of passion and so forth) equal to morality. There is no (way of) generating fame equal to morality. There is no stairway for mounting up to heaven equal to morality. And there is no doorway for entering into the city of Nibbāna equal to morality. As it was said:

> [5]Kings decked with pearls and jewels shine not as shine those restrained ones who are decked with the deckings of morality.
> Where could be a perfume like the perfume of morality that is wafted with the wind and equally against the wind?
> The perfume of flowers goes not against the wind, neither sandal nor incense nor jasmine; a good man pervades all the quarters and always the perfume goes against the wind.*

* Dh 54, A i 226, Jā iii 291, Miln 333, DA 56.

[1] This progressive talk on giving, morality and heaven occurs often in the Pali Canon. For some references see BD iv 23, n. 1.

[2] No doubt meaning successful attainments in meditation.

[3] See text p. 55.

[4] ariyavuttisamācāro yena vuccati sīlavā. Cf. Jā iv 42 sīlavante ariyavuttine.

[5] Nine of these eleven verses are also at Vism 10 but in a different order.

Sandal or incense and lotus, also the double-jasmine[1]—among these kinds of perfume the perfume of morality is supreme.*

Neither the Ganges nor Jumnā, the Sarabhū nor Sarassatī, the deeply flowing Aciravatī nor even the great river Mahī[2] is able to cleanse away here that stain for breathing things. For only the water of morality can cleanse away that stain for living things.

Neither the wind bringing rain-clouds, nor yet yellow sandal, neither necklaces nor gems nor the effulgence of moon-beams avail[3] here for the fever of living beings as does avail this well guarded ariyan morality that is perpetually cool.

Morality entirely dispels fear of self-reproach, and to the moral man always brings fame and gladness.

Where is there another stairway equal to morality for mounting up to heaven, or where indeed a doorway for entering into the city of Nibbāna?

Thus it may be known of morality that it is of supreme advantage, at the root of (all) special qualities, and stealing away the strength of (all) defects.

When the Lord had explained thus the advantages in morality, he said, "Depending on[4] this morality is this heaven obtained", and so as to explain this he at once talked a talk on heaven: "This heaven is constantly agreeable, pleasant, liked, entirely happy; there is enjoyment here and they constantly obtain bliss. The devas of the four Great Kings receive deva-like happiness, deva-like bliss for ninety hundred thousand years,[5] the devas of the Thirty-Three for three crores of years and sixty hundred thousand years".[6] Thus he talked a talk beginning with what is connected with the special qualities of heaven. [**122**] Again, having tempted (them) with the talk on heaven thus, he said: "Yet this heaven is impermament, not everlasting, there should be no desire and attachment herein", and expounding the peril, the vanity, the depravity

* Dh 55, and as above omitting A i 226.

[1] vassikā or vassikī, jasminum sambac, chief of flowers for its scent, M iii 7, S iii 156, A iv 22, Miln 182.

[2] Cf. A iv 101.

[3] samayanti; sameti basically means to come together, to unite.

[4] Cf. DA 472, MA iii 91, etc. for this paragraph.

[5] As at DA 647, but see Kvu 208.

[6] Cf. DhA i 365.

of sense-pleasures and the advantage in renouncing them,[1] he talked a talk on Dhamma, the culmination of which is, the undying.

When he had taught Dhamma to the great populace thus and had caused some to be established in the refuges, and some in the five moral habits, and some in the fruit of stream-attainment, and some in the fruit of once-returning, and some in the fruit of nonreturning, also some in the four fruits, some in the three knowledges, some in the six super-knowings, some in the eight attainments, rising from his seat he departed from Ramma city and entered Sudassana monastery. Accordingly it was said:

IIB 189 Then they, having entertained the leader of the world with the Order, approached the teacher, Dīpaṅkara, for refuge.

190 The Tathāgata established some in going for refuge, some in the five moral habits, others in the ten-fold morality.

191 To some he gave recluseship in the four supreme fruits; to some he gave the analytical insights, things without equal.

192 To some the bull of men gave the eight glorious attainments; he bestowed the three knowledges on some and six super-knowings.

193 In this fashion the great sage exhorted the multitude. By this means the Dispensation of the protector of the world was wide-spread.

194 He, named Dīpaṅkara, mighty in jaw, broad of shoulder, caused many people to cross over, he freed them from a bad bourn.

195 Seeing people who could be awakened even though they were a hundred thousand yojanas away, in a moment that great sage, going up to them, awakened them.

189 Therein *they* means the lay-followers who were inhabitants of Ramma city.

189 *Refuge*[2] should be understood here as refuge, the going for refuge, the one going for refuge.[3] It crushes, combats, ruins, thus it is a refuge. What is that Triple Gem? When people have

[1] As at Vin i 15 etc.
[2] Cf. MA i 131f., KhA 10ff.
[3] saraṇaṁ saraṇāgamanaṁ saraṇassa gantā ca veditabbā.

gone to it for refuge, by that very going for refuge, it destroys and crushes fear, anguish, bad bourn and the defilements. Thus it is called a refuge. And this was said:

> Whoever may go to the Buddha for refuge shall not go to a state of woe; getting rid of the human frame they shall fill up a class of devas.[1]
>
> [123] Whoever may go to Dhamma for refuge . . .[2]
>
> Whoever may go to the Order for refuge . . . shall fill up a class of devas.[2]

The arising of mentality which occurs in the modes of support by the Triple Gem is called going for refuge. The man possessing this is called one going for refuge. Thus should these three be understood: refuge, going for refuge, the one going for refuge.[3]

189 *That* means that Dīpaṅkara. The genitive case (tassa) is to be understood in the sense of an accusative. "They went there for refuge" is also a reading.

189 (*To* the) *teacher* means to the teacher.[4]

190 *Some in going for refuge*: the meaning is he established some individuals in going for refuge. The meaning should be taken as referring to a past time though spoken as referring to the present. This is also the method for the rest (of the verses). "Some[5] in going for refuge" is also a reading. And this is its very meaning.

190 *Some in the five moral habits* means he *established* some individuals in the five habits of abstention from.

190 *Others in the tenfold morality* means he established other individuals in the tenfold morality. "Some in the ten skilled (things)" is also a reading. The meaning of this is that he caused some individuals to undertake the ten things that are skilled.[6]

191 *To some he gave recluseship* means: herein, according to ultimate truth the Way is called recluseship. As it was said: "And what, monks, is recluseship? It is this ariyan eightfold way itself,

[1] At e.g. D ii 255, S i 27, Jā i 97, quoted DA 233, KhA 16. Cf. Divy 195, also Sikshāsamuccaya, Eng. trans. p. 172, citing the Sūkarikāvadāna.

[2] Jā i 97, Divy 196.

[3] Cf. KhA 16.

[4] satthuno ti satthāraṁ, gen. sing. and acc. sing.

[5] kassaci for the verse's kañci.

[6] Right conduct in body (3 ways), speech (4 ways), thought (3 ways), see M i 286.

that is to say right view . . . right concentration. This, monks, is to be called recluseship."*

191 *The four supreme fruits*: the meaning is the four supreme fruits.[1] The particle 'ma' makes a liaison between the words. It was said with a change of gender. The meaning is that he gave some the four Ways, the four fruits of recluseship according to (his) qualifications.[2]

191 *To some things without an equal* means that to some he gave the four unique things that are the analytical insights.

192 *To some the glorious attainments* means: and to some he gave the eight attainments that come to be by striving for the disappearance of the hindrances.

192 *The three knowledges on some* means that according to their qualifications (he bestowed) on some individuals the three knowledges consisting of the knowledge of deva-like vision, the knowledge and recollection of former habitations, the knowledge of the destruction of the cankers.

192 *Bestowed the six super-knowings* means he gave the six super-knowings to some.

193 *In this fashion* means by this method, by this order.

193 *The multitude* means the mass of people.

193 *Exhorted* means exhorted.[3] It must be understood that it was spoken with a change of tense. In similar phrases the meaning from now on must be taken as referring to a past time only.

193 *By this (it) was wide-spread* means that by this exhortation and instruction the Dispensation of the Lord Dīpaṅkara was wide-spread, broad, extensive.

[**124**] 194 *Mighty in jaw* means: it is said that both jaws of Great Men are full, similar to the moon on the twelfth day in the bright half of the month. He who has mighty jaws is mighty in jaw; it is to be called a lion's jaw.[4]

194 *Broad of shoulder* means he whose shoulders are like a

* S v 25, quoted DA 158.

[1] caturo phala-m-uttame ti cattāri uttamāni phalānī ti attho.

[2] upanissaya; three kinds at Vism 536, but I think not applicable here.

[3] ovadatī ti ovadi, present and aorist.

[4] sīhahanu as at D ii 18, iii 144, 175, M ii 136. See DA 450 where a Great Man's lower jaw, like a lion's, is relatively fuller than the upper. The "fullness" must refer to the shape of the jaws, due no doubt to the twenty teeth in each, which is another Mark of a Great Man.

bull's is broad of shoulder;[1] the meaning is that when the shoulders are evenly rounded[2] the shoulders are lovely like well looked after golden drums.

194 *Named Dīpaṅkara* means with the name Dīpaṅkara.[3]

194 *Caused many people to cross over* means helped many people to cross over[4] who could be guided out by a Buddha.

194 *He freed* means he freed.[5]

194 *From a bad bourn* means from a bad bourn[6]—the accusative case in the sense of an ablative.

195 Now, showing the implication of a mode of causing to cross over and freeing, the verses say "people who could be awakened." Therein *people who could be awakened* means "a generation that could be awakened," or this itself is the reading.

195 *Seeing* means seeing either with a Buddha's vision or with the vision of (a seer of) all.[7]

195 *Even a hundred thousand yojanas away* means living even countless hundreds of thousands of yojanas away. And this must be taken as spoken also in reference to the ten-thousand (world-system).

It is said that after he attained Buddhahood the teacher Dīpaṅkara passed seven weeks at the root of the Tree of Awakening. In the eighth week, acceding to the Great Brahmā's entreaty for Dhamma, he turned the wheel of Dhamma in the Sunanda monastery and caused one hundred crores of devas and men to drink of the nectar of Dhamma. This was the first penetration (of Dhamma). Then the teacher, knowing the maturity of the knowledge of his own son, Samavattakkhandha Usabhakkhandha,[8] making that son of his loins the foremost and teaching Dhamma

[1] usabhakkhandha.

[2] Another Mark of a Great Man, see e.g. D ii 18, M ii 136, DA 449.

[3] Dīpaṅkarasanāmako ti Dīpaṅkarasanāmo.

[4] tārayatī ti . . . tāresi.

[5] parimocetī ti parimocesi. Though the commentator has said that in such contexts as this verbs in the present tense must be taken as in the past tense, he still makes a statement to this effect.

[6] duggatin ti duggatito.

[7] See text p. 33.

[8] BvAC here calls him only by the former of these two names. BvAB adds the latter, which he is called at Bv II 209. Together these different readings thus call him by two of the epithets of a Great Man.

similar to the Exhortation(s) to Rāhula, brought ninety crores of devas and men to a penetration of Dhamma.[1] This was the second penetration. Again, the Lord, after he had performed the Marvel of the Double at the root of a great acacia tree at the gateway to the city of Amaravatī and had freed the great populace from the bonds, sat down, surrounded by a host of devas like the brilliant light of the sun, on the ornamental stone[2] in lovely shade at the root of the Pāricchattaka[3] in the abode of gods, in the abode of the Thirty-Three. Making his own mother foremost, the lady Sumedhā who was the bearer of zest to all the host of devas, the Lord Dīpaṅkara, deva of devas, known to all the world as a deva by purification,[4] teaching the Abhidhammapiṭaka in its seven parts, caused ninety thousand crores of devas to drink of the nectar of Dhamma. This was the third penetration of Dhamma. Accordingly it was said:

IIB 196 At the first penetration the Awakened One awakened a hundred crores; at the second penetration the protector awakened ninety crores.

197 And when the Awakened One had taught Dhamma in a deva-abode there was the third penetration by ninety thousand crores.

[**125**] And the Lord Dīpaṅkara had three assemblies of disciples. The first assembly of a hundred thousand crores was there in Sunanda monastery.

IIB 198 The teacher Dīpaṅkara had three assemblies; the first gathering was of a hundred thousand crores.

And then Him of the Ten Powers, surrounded by four hundred thousand[5] monks, progressing through villages, market-towns and cities and helping the great populace, gradually reached in a certain district a most delightful mountain named Nārada Peak. It was worshipped by the great populace, renowned in all the world, haunted by non-human beings who were exceedingly frightening, a peak which was the habitat of a variety of fragrant trees and flowers, a peak frequented by many herds of wild animals. It is

[1] BvAC dhammābhisamayaṁ pāpesi, BvAB dhammāmataṁ pāyesi which would give uniform expression to the three occasions of the penetrations.

[2] paṇḍukambalasilātala, Sakka's throne.

[3] The Coral Tree.

[4] visuddhideva; cf. text p. 30.

[5] Following BvAB. BvAC reads four thousand.

said the whole of it was haunted by a yakkha named Nārada, and that the great populace offered a human sacrifice there to that yakkha once a year.

Then the Lord Dīpaṅkara, seeing the attainment of the qualifications by that great populace, sent forth the Order of monks from there to the four quarters. Alone, without a companion, he climbed Mount Nārada, his heart compact of deep compassion, in order to guide out[1] that yakkha. Then that man-eating yakkha, indifferent to his own welfare, dextrous at slaughtering others, not conquering his rage,[2] his mind pervaded by[3] anger, wanting to drive away Him of the Ten Powers by terrifying him, made that mountain tremble. But while that mountain was being made to tremble by him, through the Lord's majesty[4] it was as though it were falling down on his own head. Thereupon he was frightened and thought, "Come now, I will kindle a fire", and he produced a great mass of fire exceedingly alarming to behold. That mass of fire, as though thrown against[5] the wind, only brought anguish to himself for it was unable to burn even a minute shred of the Lord's robe. But the yakkha thought: "Is the recluse burnt or is he not burnt?"[6]

Looking round he saw Him of the Ten Powers like a stainless autumn moon bringing delight to all people (and on seeing) the Lord as though he were seated in the pericarp of a lotus on the surface of cool waters, he thought: "Ah, this recluse is of great majesty. Whatever harm I do him, it only rebounds on me.[7] But apart from this recluse I have no other mainstay or succour. Those stumbling on the earth yet stand up (again) supported only by the earth. Come, I will go for refuge to this very recluse"

When he had thought thus, he lay down with his head towards the soles of the Lord's feet, soles that were adorned with the (Marks of the) Wheel, and saying, "Revered sir, a transgression overcame me", he went to the Lord for refuge.

[1] vinetuṁ, with the meaning of to guide out or away from ignorance, etc. It also means to discipline.

[2] In this sentence five *kkh* sounds are assembled: manussabhakkho sakahitan-irapekkho paravadhadakkho yakkho makkhaṁ.

[3] -pharita-; BvAB -pareta-, overcome, affected by.

[4] The majesty of his psychic potency is to be understood.

[5] pakkhitta; BvAB khitta. Cf. S i 13 = 64 = Sn 662 = Dh 125.

[6] BvAB supplies the second part of the question.

[7] Lit. it only falls on me, mam'ūpari yeva patati.

Then the Lord talked a progressive talk to him. On the conclusion of the teaching he was established in the fruit of stream-entry together with ten thousand yakkhas. It is said that on that day the human inhabitants of the whole of Jambudīpa [**126**] each brought one individual from each village as an offering to him, and they also brought much sesamum, husked rice, vetches, kidney-beans and beans, and ghee, fresh butter, oil, honey, molasses and so forth. Then on that day the yakkha bestowed on Him of the Ten Powers what the people had brought by way of an offering and gave (back) to them all the sesamum and so forth that had been conveyed.

Then the teacher, having let these men go forth by the "Come, monk" (formula for) going forth, caused them to be established in arahantship within only seven days. On the full-moon night of Māgha the Lord, in the midst of a hundred crores of monks recited the Pātimokkha in an assembly possessing the four factors.[1] The four factors are called: All are "Come, monks"[2]; all have the six super-knowings; all are come without any previous announcement; and the Observance day is on the fifteenth (day in the bright fortnight).[3] These are the four factors. This was the second assembly. Accordingly it was said:

IIB 199 Again, when the Conqueror had gone into aloofness on Mount Nārada, there came together one hundred crores whose cankers were destroyed, stains gone.

199 Therein *had gone into aloofness* means had gone after getting rid of the crowd (of monks).

199 *Came together* means assembled.

And when the human inhabitants of Jambudīpa were holding an annual festival on a mountain top[4] it was then that Dīpaṅkara, leader of the world, went for the rains-residence to the mountain named Sudassana. It is said that the people who had assembled for

[1] caturaṅgasamannāgata sannipāta as also at text pp. 204, 249, or caturaṅgikasannipāta as at text pp. 163, 169, 298. Same explanation as above at Jkm 31; also at DA 418 except that here the second item reads "their bowls and robes were provided by psychic potency." I have also seen caturaṅgikasannipāta explained (Friendly Way, Feb-Mar. 1967) in relation to the Buddha Gotama as: "the monks came without previous announcement, all had been ordained by the Buddha, all were arahants, and it was the full-moon day of the month of Māgha."

[2] I.e. Ordained by a Buddha with the words "Come, monk".

[3] See Vin i 104.

[4] Cf. Vin iv 85 and BD ii 335, n. 4.

that festival, on seeing Him of the Ten Powers, heard a talk on Dhamma, found satisfaction in it and went forth. On the day of the Great Invitation[1] the teacher talked a talk on insight to them suitable to their mental dispositions. When they had heard it and all had reflected on the constructions[2] they attained arahantship by a gradual insight and a gradual way. Then the teacher "invited" together with ninety thousand crores. This was the third assembly. Accordingly it was said:

IIB 200 During the time the great hero was on Sudassana mountain the great sage "invited" with ninety thousand crores.

201 I at that time was a matted-hair ascetic, severe in austerity, moving through mid-air, expert in the five super-knowings.

This verse was written in explanation of the antecedents[3] in the Chronicle of the Buddha Dīpaṅkara in the Atthasālinī, the commentary on the Dhammasaṅgaṇī.[4] But in *this* Chronicle of the Buddha there is no reason why that is more suitable. Why is this? It was spoken of above in the Accounts of Sumedha.[5]

While the Lord Dīpaṅkara was teaching Dhamma there were penetrations (of Dhamma) by tens of thousands and twenties of thousands. There was no end to the penetrations beginning with one (person), two, three and four.[6] Therefore the Dispensation of the Lord Dīpaṅkara was widely famed among many people. Accordingly it was said:

[127] IIB 202 There was penetration of Dhamma by tens and twenties of thousands. Penetration by ones and twos was incalculable by computation.

202 Therein *by tens and twenties of thousands* means by tens of thousands and twenties of thousands.

[1] mahāpavāraṇā. The pavāraṇā is a monastic function held at the end of the rains. See Vin i 157ff.

[2] saṅkhāra.

[3] nidāna, cf. text pp. 4, 5.

[4] Asl 71 (Ke).

[5] See IIA., esp. text pp. 78, 92f.

[6] BvAB, which I follow, reads . . . vīsatisahassānañ ca dhammābhisamayo ahosi yeva. ekassa pana dvinnaṁ tiṇṇaṁ catunnan ti ca ādivasena abhisamayānaṁ anto n'atthi.

202 *Penetration of Dhamma* means a piercing of the Dhamma of the Four Truths.

202 *By ones and twos* means by one as well as by two. The meaning is that in the way beginning thus (penetration) by threes, fours, tens was incalculable. Thus, because the penetrations were incalculable (in number), and the greatness attained was widely famed, and the outlet[1] was known among many learned devas and men, there was success in training in the higher morality and so forth and prosperity in mindfulness and concentration and so forth. Accordingly it was said:

IIB 203 The well purified Dispensation of the Lord Dīpaṅkara was widely famed then among the populace; it was successful, prosperous.

203 Therein *well purified* means beautifully purified by the Lord, made pure.

Four hundred thousand monks who had the six super-knowings and were of great psychic potency surrounded Dīpaṅkara the teacher all the time. At that time when those who were initiates did their kammic time they were despised—the intention being that only those whose cankers were all destroyed attained complete nibbāna. Therefore this Lord's Dispensation, fully flowering, very successful, shone exceedingly with monks whose cankers were destroyed. Accordingly it was said:

IIB 204 Four hundred thousand having the six super-knowings, having great psychic potency, continuously surrounded Dīpaṅkara, knower of the world(s).

205 Despised were those initiates who at that time departed this life as human beings without having attained their purpose.

206 The fully flowering Word shone forth continuously with arahants who were steadfast ones, their cankers destroyed, stainless.

204 Therein *four hundred thousand* means were seen by number; to show that these monks were thus a number that was seen, *having the six super-knowings, having great psychic potency* was

[1] nīyanika.

said—the meaning is to be taken thus. Or the nominative case[1] is to be understood in the sense of the genitive[2]: of (those having) the six super-knowings, (of those) of great psychic potency.

204 *Continuously* means perpetually. The intention is that they *surrounded* Him of the Ten Powers and did not miss the Lord no matter where they went.

205 *At that time* means at that time.[3] For this word 'samaya' (time, etc.) is seen in nine meanings beginning with samavāya (event). As it was said:

[**128**] As event, moment, time, multitude, as causes, and views, acquisition, and as abandonment, and as piercing it is to be seen.*

Here it is to be understood as time: the meaning is: at that time.

205 *As human beings* means as human beings.[4]

205 *Without having attained* (*their*) *purpose* means: those who have not attained, have not arrived at their purpose—by those who have not attained their purpose. "Purpose" (mānasa) is a designation of attachment and of thought and of arahantship. As it was said: "Purpose is a snare that goes going through the air"†; here purpose is spoken of as attachment. Herein it is thought: "Thought, mentality, purpose, heart, lucence"‡. Herein it is arahantship: "How, renowned among people, may an initiate do his kammic time without having attained his purpose?"§. But here only arahantship is intended. Therefore the meaning is: the fruits of arahantship not attained.[5]

205 *Initiates:* in what sense initiates? Initiates in the sense of acquiring Dhamma for initiates. And this was said: "To what extent, revered sir, is one an initiate? Monks, here a monk is

* VA i 106f., DA 31, M i 7, SA i 9, AA i 11, KhA 104, UdA 19, Pṭs A iii 530, Asl 57.

† Vin i 21, S i 111, quoted UdA 367, Ita 61, Asl 140, etc.

‡ Dhs 6, Vbh 87.

§ S i 121, quoted DhA i 432, Asl 140. The reference is to Godhika who committed suicide before he had gained arahantship, but he attained parinibbāna nevertheless.

1 chaḷabhiññā mahiddhikā.

2 chaḷabhiññānaṁ mahiddhikānaṁ.

3 tena samayenā ti tasmiṁ samaye.

4 mānusaṁ bhavan ti manussabhāvaṁ, i.e. human status.

5 For this para. cf. MA i 40f. which reads "arahantship" for "the fruits of arahantship".

possessed of an initiate's right view . . . is possessed of right concentration for an initiate. To this extent, monks, is a monk an initiate."* Moreover, initiates train themselves. And this was said: "He trains himself, and so, monk, he is one who trains himself. Therefore he is called an initiate. And what does he train in? He trains in the higher morality and he trains in the higher thought and he trains in the higher wisdom. He trains himself, monk. Therefore he is called an initiate."†[1]

206 *Fully flowering* means blossoming beautifully.

206 *Word* (pāvacana) means the extolled word (vacana). Or the word (pavacana) is the word (vacana) come to growth. Word (pāvacana) is simply word (pavacana). The meaning is the Dispensation.

206 *Shone forth* means shone brightly, shone exceedingly.[2]

206 *Continuously* means perpetually. "Shone forth in the world with the devas" is also a reading.

The city of this Lord Dīpaṅkara was called Rammavatī; his father, a warrior-noble king, was named Sudeva, his mother Sumedhā; Sumaṅgala and Tissa were the two chief disciples; the attendant was called Sāgata; the two chief women disciples Nandā and Sunandā; that Lord's Tree of Awakening was a Pipphalī[3]. He was eighty cubits in height; the life-span was a hundred thousand years.[4]

But what is the purpose of showing the cities and so forth where they were born? It is to be said: Of whom neither the city of his birth nor his father or mother could be known, then, if neither the city of his birth nor his father or mother was known, devas or Sakka or a yakkha or Māra or Brahmā or other devas, **[129]** deeming: A marvel such as this is quite natural,[5] might deem he was not to be listened to. Thence there would be no penetration

* S v 14.
† A i 231.

[1] For this para cf. MA i 40. A clear definition of sekha, initiate, is given at AA ii 331.

[2] upasobhatī ti abhirājati atirocati. These two words appear to have the meaning of out-shining, dimming other lights.

[3] This is another name for Assattha, the Bodhi Tree, hence the Anglo-Indian pipul (peepul) tree for the Bo. See note to IIB 214 in CB.

[4] The Buddhas and their contemporaries had approximately the same length of life-span.

[5] anacchariya; meaning doubtful lit. not wonderful.

(of Dhamma); if there were not a penetration a Buddha's words would be useless and the Dispensation would not be one leading out. Therefore the demarcation by the city of the birth and so forth of all Buddhas should be set forth. Accordingly it was said:

IIB 207 Rammavatī was the name of the city, Sudeva[1] the name of the warrior-noble, Sumedhā the name of the mother of Dīpaṅkara, the teacher.

213 Sumaṅgala and Tissa were the chief disciples, Sāgata was the name of the attendant on Dīpaṅkara, the teacher.

214 Nandā and Sunandā were the chief women disciples. That Lord's Tree of Awakening is said to be the Pipphalī.

216 The great sage Dīpaṅkara was eighty cubits in height. He shone like a tree of lights, like a king of sāla trees in full bloom.

217 That great seer's life-span was a hundred thousand years. Living so long he caused many people to cross over.

218 After illuminating the True Dhamma and causing the populace to cross over, blazing like a mass of fire, he, with the disciples, waned out.

219 And that psychic potency and that great retinue and those treasures of the Wheel on his feet have all disappeared. Are not all constructions void?

207 Therein *Sudeva the name of the warrior-noble* means Sudeva was the name of his father, a warrior-noble king.

207 *The mother* means the genetrix.[2]

214 *Pipphalī* means the Tree of Awakening was a kind of Ficus religiosa.[3]

216 *Eighty cubits in height* means eighty cubits tall.

216 *Like a tree of lights* means like a tree of lights ablaze with convolutions[4] of lights and garlands. He was endowed with a figure (perfect) in height and girth, his physical form was adorned with the thirty-two glorious Marks and the lesser characteristics.

[1] Bv Sumedha.

[2] janikā ti janetti, the mother who bore him.

[3] pilakkhakapitthana. This may not mean two trees, but a kind of kapitthana called pilakkhakapitthana. Again, see CB IIB 214, note.

[4] ākula, entangled, twisted.

While the Lord was alive he *shone*, meaning: he shone,[1] like a resplendent host of stars with multitudinous flames and vibrating rays in the vault of the heavens.

216 *Like a king of sāla trees in full bloom* means: like a king of sāla trees flowering with all the flowers in blossom and like the Coral Tree, a hundred yojanas in height, with all the flowers in blossom, so did the Lord, eighty cubits in height, shine exceedingly.

217 *A hundred thousand years* means his life-span was a hundred thousand years.

217 *Living so long* means living just so long a time.

[130] 217 *People* means a multitude of people.

218 *Causing the populace to cross over* means himself having caused the populace to cross.[2] "Causing men with devas to cross over" is also a reading. Its meaning is: the world with the devas.[3]

219 *And that psychic potency* means: and that splendour, majesty.

219 *Retinue* means entourage.[4]

279 *Have all disappeared:* the meaning is that these splendours that have been spoken of have disappeared, vanished.

219 *Are not all constructions void*? means: are not all constructed things void, empty? The meaning is: they are permanently devoid of essence and so forth.

Herein, though demarcation by city and so forth is handed down in the text, yet several subjects are not handed down. Bringing them forward they should be elucidated, that is to say demarcation by son, demarcation by wife, demarcation by palaces, demarcation by the household life, demarcation by dancing women, demarcation by the Departure, demarcation by the striving, demarcation by the monastery, demarcation by the attendant(s).[5] And the reason for elucidating these is just as was spoken of above.[6]

And that Dīpaṅkara had a hundred thousand wives of whom

[1] sobhatī ti sobhittha.

[2] santāretvā mahājanan ti tārayitvā mahājanaṁ.

[3] sadevakaṁ lokaṁ.

[4] yaso ti parivāro. On this meaning of yasa see also PED s.v., and text pp. 152, 160, 257 (mahāyaso ti mahāparivāro).

[5] Cf. text p. 2–3.

[6] See text p. 128f.

the chief consort was named Padumā, and his son was named Usabhakkhandha. Accordingly it was said:

His wife was named Padumā[1]—her mouth was lotus-shaped.
Usabhakkhandha was the son of Dīpaṅkara the teacher. 79
And the three palaces were known as Haṁsā, Koñcā, Māyūrā.
He lived the household life for ten thousand years.
Having departed mounted on an elephant, the Conqueror dwelt 80
in Nanda-park.[2] Nanda,[3] bringing bliss to the world, was the
name of his attendant.
81

There are five differences among all Buddhas:[4] difference in (the length of the) life-span, difference in height, difference in family, difference in (the time required for) the striving (before Awakening), difference in (the extent of) the rays.

Therein, difference in (the length of the) life-span means some were of long life-span, some of short life-span; for example, the measure of the life-span of the Lord Dīpaṅkara was a hundred thousand years, of our Lord it was one hundred years. Difference in height[5] means that some were tall, some short; for example, Dīpaṅkara was eighty cubits tall, and our Lord eighteen cubits tall. Difference in family means that some were born in a warrior-noble family, some in a brahman family; for example, Dīpaṅkara and others were born in a warrior-noble family, Kakusandha, Koṇāgamana and others in a brahman family. Difference in (the time required for) the striving means that for some the striving was only brief as for the Lord Kassapa, [**131**] for some, as for our Lord, it was for a long time. Difference in (the extent of) the rays means that the rays of the physical form of the Lord Maṅgala remained suffusing the ten-thousand world-system, of our Lord merely a fathom. Difference in (the extent of) the rays was dependent on the inclination—to the extent that one (Buddha) wished, to that extent the lustre of his physical frame suffused. Maṅgala's intention was: "May it suffuse the ten-thousand world-system."

[1] Lotus.
[2] Cf. Bv IIB 207–12.
[3] Sāgata at Bv IIB 213.
[4] Eight are given at text, p. 296, and a somewhat different eight at SnA 407. Miln 285 recognizes four differences between Bodhisattas, all coinciding with the differences between Buddhas as stated in our passage and at DA 424.
[5] pamāṇa, measure.

But there is no difference between any of them in the special qualities acquired.

And for all Buddhas there are four unalterable places[1]: unalterable is the cross-legged position in one place only; the turning of the Wheel of Dhamma in a seers' resort in a deer-sanctuary is also unalterable; the placing of the first footstep at the gateway of the city of Saṅkassa at the time of descending from the devas[2] is also unalterable; and the positions for the four legs of the bed in the Scented Chamber in Jetavana are also unalterable. And the vihāra also does not alter whether it be small or large.[3]

But[4] there is a further divergency for our Lord only in respect of the demarcation of those of simultaneous birth and in respect of the demarcation of asterisms. These seven were of simultaneous birth together with our omniscient Bodhisatta: Rāhula's mother, the Elder Ānanda, Channa, Kanthaka, the treasure-urns, the great Tree of Awakening, Kāḷudāyin.[5]

It is said that the Great Being descended into the mother's womb, departed on the Great Departure, turned the Wheel of Dhamma and performed the Marvel of the Double under the asterism Uttarāsāḷha; that he was born, was fully Self-Awakened and attained final nibbāna under the asterism of Visākha, and that the (one) assembly of his disciples, and the relinquishment of the concomitants of the life-span were in the asterism of Māgha. Having cited so much it must be explained that the descent from the devas was under the asterism of Assayuja. This is a demarcation by many matters.

The rest of the verses are very clear.

So the Lord Dīpaṅkara, having carried out the duties of all Buddhas, in due course attained final nibbāna in the element of nibbāna that has no clinging (to rebirth) remaining.

In the eon in which Dīpaṅkara, Him of the Ten Powers, arose there were also three other Buddhas; Taṇhaṅkara, Medhaṅkara,

[1] avijahitaṭṭhāna. See text p. 297f., DA 424, DAṬ ii 19, MA ii 166.

[2] After teaching Abhidhamma in a deva-world. See also text p. 232.

[3] See DA 423, MA ii 166 for measurements of the vihāras of the last seven Buddhas.

[4] This para occurs at DA ii 425.

[5] The conatal ones, sahajātāni, are listed again at text pp. 276, 298 and also e.g. at Jā i 54, AA i 301, ThagA ii 221, sometimes showing variations. See Intr. xlv ff.; and on the "four great treasures" see Lamotte, Vkn 278, n. 34, who refers to Divy 60f. and Mhvu iii 383.

Saraṇaṅkara. They are not discussed here as there was no declaration to the Bodhisatta in their presence. But in order to show in the Commentary all the Buddhas who have arisen since the beginning of that eon this is said:

Taṇhaṅkara, Medhaṅkara and then Saraṇaṅkara,
and the Self-Awakened Dīpaṅkara, Koṇḍañña supreme among men,
Maṅgala and Sumana and Revata, Sobhita the sage,
Anomadassin, Paduma, Nārada, Padumuttara,
Sumedha and Sujāta and Piyadassin of great renown,
Atthadassin, Dhammadassin, Siddhattha leader of the world,
Tissa and the Self-Awakened Phussa, Vipassin, Sikhin, Vessabhū,
Kakusandha, Koṇāgamana, and too the leader Kassapa,
[132] These were the Self-Awakened Ones, attachment gone, concentrated.
Having arisen like him of the hundred rays, dispelling the great darkness,
Blazing like a mass of fire they, with the disciples, waned out.[1]

Concluded to this extent and not made with excessive abridgement or expansion is the Exposition of the Chronicle of the Buddha Dīpaṅkara in the Clarifier of Sweet Meaning, the commentary on the Chronicle of Buddhas.

Concluded is the First Buddha-Chronicle.

III THE EXPOSITION OF THE CHRONICLE OF THE BUDDHA KOṆḌAÑÑA

After the Lord Dīpaṅkara had attained final nibbāna his Dispensation continued for a hundred thousand years. And his Dispensation only disappeared on the disappearance of the disciples who had been followers of the Buddha.[2] Subsequently to him after one

[1] Jā i 44, CpA 15.

[2] buddhānubuddhānaṁ sāvakānaṁ; cf. text p. 141, under Maṅgala, buddhānubuddhasāvakānaṁ, and buddhānubuddho yo thero at Thag 679, 1246 referring to the Elder Aññā-Koṇḍañña. ThagA iii 5 explains: buddhānubuddho ti buddhānaṁ anubuddho, sammāsambuddhehi bujjhitāni saccāni tesaṁ

incalculable had passed there arose in the one eon[1] the teacher named Koṇḍañña. This Lord, having fulfilled the perfections during sixteen incalculables and a hundred thousand eons and having thoroughly matured the knowledge of Awakening, remained in an individuality resembling Vessantara's. Deceasing from there and being re-born in Tusita city he remained there for the duration of the life-span.[2] Giving his agreement to the devas, having deceased from Tusita city, he took on relinking in the womb of Sujātā, a queen in the household of King Sunanda in the city of Rammavatī. At the moment of his relinking there appeared the thirty-two marvels as spoken of in the Chronicle of the Buddha Dīpaṅkara.[3] Cared for and protected by devatās, he issued forth from his mother's womb after ten months. The supreme among all beings, facing north, took seven strides, investigated all the quarters, and uttered the majestic phrase: "I am the foremost in the world, I am the eldest in the world, I am the best in the world, this is my last birth, now there is not again-becoming."*

When giving a name to the boy on the name-giving day, they gave him the name of Koṇḍañña. For this Lord was of the Koṇḍañña clan. He had three extremely delightful palaces called Rāma, Surāma, Subha. In these three hundred thousand dancing women skilled in dance, song and music were in attendance on him all the time. His chief consort was called Rucīdevī, [133] Vijitasena was the name of his son. He led the household life for ten thousand years. But when he had seen an old man, a sick man, a corpse, and one who had gone forth, departing in a chariot drawn by thoroughbreds, he went forth and engaged in striving for ten months. And as Prince Koṇḍañña was going forth ten crores of people went forth following his example. Surrounded by these, and after he had engaged in striving for the ten months, he, on the full-moon day of Visākha in the village of Sunanda partook of an extremely sweet meal of milk-rice and honey given by Yasodharā, a merchant's daughter whose breasts were even and firm. Having spent[4]

* D ii 15, M iii 123.

desanānusārena bujjhatī ti attho, he had been awakened to the truths that had been awakened to by the Self-Awakened ones by following their teaching.

[1] No other Buddhas arose in this eon, a Sāra-eon, see text p. 191.

[2] The length is determined by kamma.

[3] IIA 83ff.

[4] BvAC katvā, BvAB vītināmetvā.

the day-sojourn in a sāla grove beautifully adorned with fruits, sprouts and shoots, and sending away the crowd towards evening he accepted eight handfuls of grass given (to him) by Sunandaka, a Naked Ascetic. He circumambulated a lovely sāla tree three times, surveyed the eastern quarter, and with his back towards the Tree of Awakening[1] spread a grass spreading fifty-eight cubits in extent. Sitting down cross-legged, resolutely determining on the four-factored energy[2], he routed Māra's forces. Purifying the knowledge and recollection of former habitations during the first watch of the night, purifying deva-like vision during the middle watch, and during the last watch reflecting on the mode of conditions, emerging from the fourth meditation by in-breathing and out-breathing, he interpreted the (five) categories seeing the full fifty marks in respect of rise and fall.[3] Having increased insight into the knowledge of consciousness[4] he penetrated precisely with a Buddha's knowledge[5] all the knowledges of the four ways and the knowledges of the four fruits, the four analytical insights, the knowledge of demarcation by the four modes of birth[6], the knowledge of demarcation by the five bourns[6], the six knowledges not shared (by others).[7] His intention fulfilled, even as he was seated at the root of the Tree of Awakening he uttered the solemn utterance thus:

> Through many a birth in saṁsāra have I run seeking but not finding the housebuilder; anguish is birth again and again. Housebuilder, you are seen, you will not build a house again. All your rafters are broken, the ridge-pole is shattered; the mind has attained the Unconstructed, I have arrived at the destruction of cravings.*

> Just as the bourn of a blazing spark of fire struck from the anvil, gradually fading, cannot be known,

* Dh 153, 154, Jā i 76; quoted VA 17, DA 16, KhA 12–13, SnA ii 392, UdA 208, Asl 18. Cf. Thag 183, 184.

[1] BvAC bodhitaruṁ, BvAB -rukkhaṁ.
[2] See text p. 83.
[3] See explanations at Vism 631, AA iii 18. Cf. text pp. 83, 184, 190.
[4] gotrabhūñāṇa.
[5] buddhañāṇena as at text pp. 52, 119, 185. BvAB reads buddhaguṇe, special qualities of a Buddha, see text p. 117.
[6] M i 73.
[7] See Jā i 78; also MQ ii 9, n. 6.

so no bourn can be pointed to of those who are rightly freed through wisdom, have crossed over the bonds and floods of sense-desires and reached a happiness that moves not.*

Having spent exactly seven weeks at the root of the Tree of Awakening in the bliss of the attainment of the fruits, in the eighth week owing to Brahmā's entreaty, he thought, "Now, to whom should I first teach Dhamma?"[1] While he was thus reflecting, he saw the ten crores of monks who had gone forth together with him, and he thought, "Indeed, these young men of family who had accumulated the roots of skill **[134]** went forth following me when I went forth, they engaged in striving together with me, and they attended on me. Come, I will teach them Dhamma first of all." Having reflected thus, he thought, "But where are they living now?" and looking round and seeing that they were living eighteen yojanas from there in the Deva-grove near the city of Amaravati[2], he thought, "I will go to teach them Dhamma." Taking his bowl and robe, even as a strong man might stretch out his bent back arm or bend back his outstretched arm, even so, disappearing from the root of the Tree of Awakening did he appear in the Deva-grove.

And at that time these ten crores of monks were living in the Deva-grove close to the city of Amaravatī. Then these monks, having seen Him of the Ten Powers coming from afar, their minds satisfied, went to meet the Lord, received his bowl and robe, prepared a Buddha-seat, and paying their respects to the teacher, and honouring the Lord they sat down at a respectful distance surrounding him. Seated there on the Buddha-seat surrounded[3] by hosts of sages, surrounded[4] by hosts of the (Three and) Thirty, Koṇḍañña, Him of the Ten Powers, shone forth like him of the thousand eyes[5], like the autumn sun in the stainless vault of the heavens, like the moon at the full surrounded[4] by hosts of stars. Then the teacher, having spoken to these the incomparable Discourse on the Turning of the Wheel of Dhamma with the three

* Ud 93, Ap p. 543, quoted text p. 236; for similar sentiment cf. Sn 1074.

[1] Vin i 7.
[2] BvAB and two Sinh. MSS read Arundhavatī here and below.
[3] parivārita, also meaning honoured.
[4] parivuta.
[5] One of Sakka's epithets.

sections and the twelve modes[1] in accordance with the practice of all Buddhas, caused a hundred thousand crores of devas and men headed by the ten crores of monks to drink of the nectar of Dhamma. Accordingly it was said:

III 1 After Dīpaṅkara was the leader named Koṇḍañña, of infinite incandescence, with a boundless following, immeasurable, difficult to attack.
2 In patience he was like the earth, in morality like the ocean, in concentration similar to Meru, in knowledge like the heavens.
3 For the welfare of all breathing things the Buddha constantly explained the truths of the cardinal faculties, the powers, the constituents of Awakening, the Ways.
4 When Koṇḍañña, leader of the world, was turning the Wheel of Dhamma there was the first penetration by a hundred thousand crores.

1 Therein *after Dīpaṅkara* means subsequently to the Lord Dīpaṅkara.

1 *Named Koṇḍañña* means it was the name assigned to him in accordance with his own clan.

1 *Leader* means guider out.

1 *Infinite incandescence* means an infinite incandescence through the incandescence of his own morality, special qualities and merit. From Avīci below to the topmost existence above, from across the spaces in between the infinite world-elements [**135**] there was not even one individual able to live once he had looked on his face. Accordingly: infinite incandescence was said.

1 *Boundless following* means an infinite entourage.[2] For the space of this Lord's hundred thousand years to the time of his final nibbāna there was no limitation to computing the monks in his company of monks. Therefore "boundless following" is said. "Boundless following" is also said to be "boundless renown and special qualities."

1 *Immeasurable* means immeasurable in respect of the measure of the host of special qualities: immeasurable. As it was said:

Even a Buddha should speak praise of a Buddha
Even if he is not speaking of another eon.

[1] Vin i 10.

[2] amitayaso ti anantaparivāro.

In a long intermediate period an eon might waste away.
Praise of a Tathāgata should not waste away.*

Therefore immeasurable is said because the host of special qualities is immeasurable.

1 *Difficult to attack* means hard of being approached. Difficult to attack from its not being possible to approach (him) hitting, striking[1] (him). The meaning is: difficult to overcome.

2 *Like the earth* means similar to the earth.

2 *In patience* means: in patience.[2] He is said to be "like the earth" from not shaking with all that he acquires whether pleasant or unpleasant[3] and so on just as the great earth, four myriad and two hundred thousand yojanas thick,[4] (is not shaken) by an ordinary wind.

2 *In morality like the ocean* means that by the control of morality he is similar to the ocean by reason of not passing beyond the margins. For it was said: "The great sea, monks, is stable, it does not overflow its margins."†

2 *In concentration similar to Meru* means: similar to glorious Mount Meru in not shaking when states of mind are produced that are inimical to concentration. The meaning is: like that. Or it means that, like Mount Meru, the physical form is very firm.

2 *In knowledge like the heavens* means that herein a simile for the infinite nature of the Lord's knowledge is made with infinite space. Four infinites have been spoken of by the Lord. As it was said:

The aggregation of beings, and space, and the infinite world-spheres,
And the immeasurable knowledge of a Buddha it is impossible to ascertain these.‡

Therefore a simile of the Buddha's infinite knowledge was made by means of infinite space.

* DA 288, UdA 336, CpA 8.
† Vin ii 237, A iv 198, Ud 53.
‡ I 64.

1 āsajja ghaṭṭetvā, see PED s.v. āsajja.
2 khamanenā ti khantiyā.
3 M i 423.
4 As at text p. 56.

3 *Explanation of the truths of the cardinal faculties, the powers, the constituents of Awakening, the Ways* means that by means of apprehending the truths of these cardinal faculties, the powers, the constituents of Awakening, the Ways, also apprehended are the applications of mindfulness, right striving, bases of psychic potencies. Therefore he *explained* means he taught Dhamma by explanation of the thirty-seven things pertaining to Awakening by means of the four groups of cardinal faculties and so forth.

3 *For the welfare* means for the sake of the welfare.

[136] 4 *Was turning*[1] *the Wheel of Dhamma* means was himself bestowing[2] the knowledge of the teaching.

Subsequently to that, devatās of the ten-thousand world-systems, in a gathering for (hearing) the Mahāmaṅgala-sutta[3], having created subtle individualities, assembled together in this world-system. There, it is said, a certain devaputta asked a question of Koṇḍañña, Him of the Ten Powers. The Lord spoke about the blessings[4] to him. Ninety thousand crores attained arahantship there. There was no limit to the computation of stream-entrants and so forth.[5] Accordingly it was said:

III 5 After that, when he was teaching in a gathering of men and deities, there was the second penetration by ninety thousand crores.

5 Therein *after that* means subsequently to that.

5 *When he was teaching* means when the Lord was teaching Dhamma.

5 *Of men and deities* means of men as well as of undying ones.[6]

And while the Lord was performing the Marvel of the Double in the vault of the heavens for crushing the pride and conceit of the sectarians he taught Dhamma. Eighty thousand crores attained arahantship then. Those who were established in the three fruits exceeded the ways of computation. Accordingly it was said:

[1] pavattente.

[2] pavatteti has this meaning as well as that of to turn, in the sense of to turn on and on, to make arise.

[3] The Discourse on the Great Blessings, or Great Good Omens, Kh v, Sn 258ff. Five are referred to at VA 1008. See also text pp. 174, 217, 228, 233, 292.

[4] maṅgalāni.

[5] Cf. KhA 155.

[6] naramarūnan ti narānañ ca amarānañ ca.

III 6 When he taught Dhamma, crushing the sectarians, there was a penetration of Dhamma[1] by eighty thousand crores.

[2] It is said that after the teacher Koṇḍañña had attained complete Self-Awakening he stayed for the first rains in Canda monastery close to the city of Candavatī. There the son of a rich brahman named Sucindhara was called Candamāṇava[3], and the son of the brahman Yasodhara was Subhaddamāṇava. When they had heard a teaching on Dhamma face to face with the Buddha Koṇḍañña, devout in mind, they went forth in his presence together with ten thousand[4] brahman youths and attained arahantship. Then Koṇḍañña the teacher, surrounded by a hundred thousand crores with the Elder Subhadda at the head, recited the Pātimokkha on the full-moon day of the month of Jeṭṭha. That was the first assembly. Subsequently to that when Vijitasena, the son of Koṅḍañña the teacher, had attained arahantship, the Lord recited the Pātimokkha in the midst of a thousand crores with him at the head. That was the second assembly. Then, after a time, while He of the Ten Powers was touring the country-side he let go forth together with that company the king Udena who had a retinue of ninety crores of people. The Lord, surrounded by the ninety crores of arahants with Udena at their head after he had attained arahantship, recited the Pātimokkha. That was the third assembly. Accordingly it was said:

III 7 The great seer Koṇḍañña had three assemblies of steadfast ones whose cankers were destroyed, stainless, tranquil in mind.

8 The first gathering was of a hundred thousand crores, the second of a thousand crores, the third of ninety crores.

[137] It is said that our Bodhisatta, then a universal monarch named Vijitāvin, lived in the city of Candavatī. And he, surrounded by countless glorious men, guarded by Dhamma, not by the stick nor by the sword, the watery treasure-stores with Meru and

[1] dhammābhisamayo. Bv, Be, BvAB tatiyābhisamayo, the third penetration.

[2] BvAB adds: "when the Lord was teaching Dhamma, then there was a penetration of Dhamma by eighty thousand crores", and gives a note that elsewhere this is omitted.

[3] BvAB Saddamāṇava, with v. l. as above. Māṇava is a usual word for brahman youth; it may thus be an epithet here or part of his name, as too with his friend Subhaddamāṇava.

[4] BvAB ten hundred thousand.

Yugandhara (and) the unlimited earth bearing riches.[1] And at that very time the Buddha Koṇḍañña, surrounded by the hundred thousand crores of those whose cankers were destroyed, walking on tour through the country-side, reached the city of Candavatī in due course.

King Vijitāvin heard it said, "The fully Self-Awakened One has arrived in our city." After setting forth to meet the Lord and preparing a place for him to stay in, he invited him for the morrow together with the Order of monks. On the following day he had a beautiful meal arranged and to the Order of monks numbering a hundred thousand crores with the Buddha at the head he gave a great gift. When the Bodhisatta had given to the Lord to eat, he said after the benediction, "Revered sir, stay here for three months giving help to the populace," and when he had asked him he immediately bestowed the Unparalleled Great Gift on the Order of monks with the Buddha at the head.

Then the teacher declared of the Bodhisatta, "In the future he will be the Buddha named Gotama", and he taught Dhamma. When he (the Bodhisatta) had heard the teacher's talk on Dhamma, he renounced the kingdom, went forth, mastered the three Piṭakas, obtained the eight attainments and the five super-knowings and, his meditation unbroken, was reborn in a Brahma-world. Accordingly it was said:

III 9 I at that time was a warrior-noble named Vijitāvin. I held sway from end to end of the sea.

10 I refreshed with superb food the hundred thousand crores of stainless great seers together with the highest protector of the world.

11 And that Buddha Koṇḍañña, leader of the world, also declared of me: "Innumerable eons from now this one will be a Buddha in the world.

12 Having striven the striving, carried out austerities, the Self-Awakened One of great fame will be awakened at the root of an Assattha.

13 His genetrix and mother will be named Māyā, his father Suddhodana, and he will be named Gotama.

14 Kolita and Upatissa will be the chief disciples. Ānanda

[1] aparimitavasudharaṁ vasundharaṁ.

is the name of the attendant who will attend on that Conqueror.

15 Khemā and Uppalavaṇṇā will be the chief women disciples. That Lord's Tree of Awakening is said to be the Assattha."

[138] 17 When they had heard the words of the great seer who was without an equal, men and deities, rejoicing, thought, "Sprout of the Buddha-seed is this".

18 The sounds of acclamation went on: the (inhabitants of the) ten-thousand with the devas clapped their hands, laughed, and paid homage with clasped hands.

19 (Saying) "If we should fail of the Dispensation of this protector of the world, in the distant future we will be face to face with this one,

20 As men crossing a river but, failing of the ford to the bank opposite, taking a ford lower down cross over the great river.

21 even so, all of us, if we miss (the words of) this Conqueror, in the distant future will be face to face with this one".

22 When I had heard his words all the more did I incline my mind. For effecting that very aim I gave the great kingdom to the Conqueror. Having abandoned the great kingdom, I went forth in his presence.

23 Having learnt thoroughly the Suttanta and Vinaya and all the ninefold Dispensation of the teacher, I illumined the Conqueror's Dispensation.

24 Living diligent therein, whether sitting, standing or pacing, after reaching perfection in the super-knowings to the Brahma-world went I.[1]

9 Therein *I at that time* means I in that time.[2]

9 *Named Vijitāvin* means that the universal monarch was so called.

9 *From end to end of the sea* herein means: making the mountains at the rim of the world the boundary, the limit, making the enduring sea the end, *I held sway*. So far it is not obvious.

They say that the king, the universal monarch, by the majesty

[1] Cf. text p. 151, 200, 234.

[2] ahaṁ tena samayenā ti ahaṁ tasmiṁ samaye.

of the Treasure of the Wheel, keeping Sineru on his left side, went over the sea to Pubbavideha which is eight thousand yojanas in extent.[1] The king, the universal monarch, gave an exhortation there, saying, "Breathing things should not be killed, what has not been given should not be taken, wrong behaviour among sense-pleasures should not be indulged in, lies should not be spoken, intoxicating liquor should not be drunk, you should eat in moderation."[2] When he had thus given the exhortation,[3] the Treasure of the Wheel, rising up above the ground, plunged into the eastern sea; and to the extent it plunged in, to that extent there was a contraction of the movement of the waves; while the waters of the great sea, receding, had receded to the depth of a yojana **[139]** it stood still, like a wall of beryl on both sides within the sea, very lovely to behold. When it had gone thus to the bounds of the eastern ocean the Treasure of the Wheel turned back. And while it was turning back that company was at the top, the king, the universal monarch, was in the middle, the Treasure of the Wheel was at the end. And those waters, as though unable to endure the separation due to the water's boundary[4], flowed back to the shore just touching the edge of the rim (of the Wheel). Thus the king, the universal monarch, having vanquished Pubbavideha to the bounds of the eastern sea, wanting to vanquish Jambudīpa to the bounds of the southern sea, went along facing the southern sea by the way shown by the Treasure of the Wheel. Having conquered Jambudīpa, which is ten thousand yojanas in extent,[5] turning his back on the southern sea, and going along in the manner just described to vanquish Aparagoyāna, which is seven thousand yojanas in extent[5], and vanquishing the bounds of that ocean too and crossing over from the western sea, going along as before to vanquish Uttarakuru which is eight thousand yojanas in extent[5], and vanquishing the bounds of that sea as before, he turned his back on the northern sea. To this extent the sway of the king, the universal monarch, was attained over the earth bounded by the

[1] SnA 443, Vism 207 say seven thousand.

[2] yathābhutta—not the usual expression. See PED s.v. bhutta. As at D ii 173, M iii 173.

[3] To almost the end of this para. cf. DA 622f., MA iv 222f.

[4] jalantena, taken here as jala + anta, the end, ending, side of the waters, referring to the trough or chasm made in the sea between the two walls of beryl. Alternatively, jalanta could mean the shining one, referring to the Wheel-treasure.

[5] SnA 443, Vism 207.

ocean. Accordingly it was said, *I held sway from end to end of the sea.*

10 *A hundred thousand crores* means a hundred thousand crores.[1] Or this is itself the reading.

10 *Of stainless* means of those whose cankers were destroyed.

10 *With the highest protector of the world* means: the hundred thousand crores together with Him of the Ten Powers.

10 *With superb food* means with sumptuous food.

10 *I refreshed* means I refreshed.[2]

11 *Innumerable eons from now* means: in a Bhadda-eon[3] when a hundred thousand eons and three incalculables from now have passed.

12 *The striving* means energy.

22 *For effecting that very aim* means fulfilling, effecting, accomplishing that very aim making for Buddhahood, the perfection of Giving.

22 *The great kingdom* means the universal monarch's kingdom.

22 *To the Conqueror* means to the Lord. Or the locative (jine) should be understood in the sense of a dative.

22 *I gave* means I gave.[4] "Effecting the aim thus" means a connexion with this (giving) should be understood. Some read: "I gave[5] the great kingdom to the Conqueror".

22 *Having abandoned* means having given.

23 *Suttanta* means the Suttapiṭaka.

23 *Vinaya* means the Vinayapiṭaka.

23 *Ninefold* means the ninefold beginning with the Suttas, mixed prose and verse.[6]

23 *Illumined the Conqueror's Dispensation* means I adorned (it) with the widely-known[7] traditions and spiritual realizations.[8]

24 *Therein* means in that Lord's Dispensation.

[1] koṭisatasahassānan ti koṭisatasahassāni, gen. pl. and nom. pl.

[2] tappayin ti tappesiṁ.

[3] bhaddakappa, an auspicious eon in which five Buddhas arise, text p. 191, DA ii 410.

[4] adan ti adāsiṁ.

[5] dadiṁ.

[6] The nine constituent parts of the teaching are given in full at M i 133, Miln 263.

[7] lokiya, also meaning mundane. This sentence could also be translated "I adorned it with a mundane approach to what had been handed down"—mundane as opposed to supermundane.

[8] adhigama, arrival; see Netti 91, AA i 87.

24 *Diligent* means possessed of mindfulness.

[140] 24 *To the Brahma-world went I* means to the Brahma-world went I.[1]

And the city of this Buddha Koṇḍañña was named Rammavatī, his father was the warrior-noble named Sunanda, Sujātā was the name of the queen his mother, Bhadda and Subhadda were the chief disciples, the attendant was named Anuruddha, Tissā and Upatissā were the chief women disciples, the Tree of Awakening was a lovely sāla, his physical frame was eighty-eight cubits in height, the length of the life-span was a hundred thousand years, his wife was named Rucī, his son was named Vijitasena,[2] the king who was the (lay) attendant was named Canda; it is said he lived in Canda-monastery. Accordingly it was said:

III 25 Rammavatī was the name of the city, Sunanda the name of the warrior-noble, Sujātā the name of the mother of Koṇḍañña, the great seer.

30 Bhadda and Subhadda were the chief disciples, Anuruddha was the name of the attendant on Koṇḍañña, the great seer.

31 Tissā and Upatissā were the chief women disciples. The Tree of Awakening of Koṇḍañña, the great seer, was a lovely Sāla.

33 That great sage was eighty-eight cubits tall. He shone like the sun at midday, as the king of heavenly bodies.

34 The (normal) life-span lasted then for a hundred thousand years. Living so long he caused many people to cross over.

35 The earth was ornamented with those whose cankers were destroyed, stainless. As the heavens with heavenly bodies, so did he shine forth.

36 And those countless nāgas of great renown, imperturbable, difficult to attack, waned out showing themselves like a flash of lightning.

37 And that Conqueror's psychic potency which was not to be gauged, and the concentration fostered through knowledge have all disappeared. Are not all constructions void?

31 *A lovely Sāla*[3] means a lovely Sāla tree. It comes into being

[1] Brahmalokam agañch'ahan ti Brahmalokaṁ agañchiṁ ahaṁ.

[2] Here BvAC calls him Jinasena.

[3] sālakalyāṇika.

only in the time of a Buddha and in the time of a universal monarch, not at another. They say it rises up in one day only.

35 *The earth was ornamented with those whose cankers were destroyed, stainless* means that this earth was very lovely to look upon ornamented with the single glow of the yellow robes of those whose cankers were destroyed.

35 *As* means: it is a particle in the sense of a simile.

[141] 35 *With heavenly bodies* means with constellations. As the vault of the heavens with a host of stars this earth shone forth ornamented with those whose cankers were destroyed.

36 *Imperturbable* means unperturbed, unaffected by the eight things of the world.[1]

36 *Showing themselves*[2] *like a flash of lightning* means showing themselves[3] like a flash of lightning. "Flash of lightning"[4] is also a reading. It is said that in the time of the Buddha Koṇḍañña when monks were attaining final nibbāna they rose up into the air to the height of seven palm-trees, completely illuminating, like the lightning, the dark rents in the clouds and, entering on the element of heat, they waned out completely,[5] like fire, without any basis (for rebirth) remaining.[6] Accordingly it was said: *Showing themselves like a flash of lightning*.

37 *Not to be gauged* means not to be gauged,[7] unique.

37 *Fostered through knowledge* means increased through knowledge.

In regard to the method spoken of above the remaining verses are quite clear.

Koṇḍañña the Self-Awakened One waned out in the delightful Canda-park; a cetiya built for him was seven yojanas in extent.[8]
For they did not disperse this teacher's relics; these, remaining in one solid piece, were like a golden image.[9]

[1] aṭṭha lokadhammā, see D iii 260, A iv 156, Netti 162, etc.; also Jā iii 169.

[2] dassetvā.

[3] dassayitvā.

[4] vijjuppātaṁ for vijjupātaṁ.

[5] In the simile of the fire, "waned out" has to be used for parinibbāyiṁsu while just above parinibbāyamānā could equally well be "while they were waning out" or "while they were attaining final nibbāna".

[6] Here too nirupādāna means both as trans. above and without fuel.

[7] atuliyā ti atulyā.

[8] Thūp 9, and cf. Bv iii 38.

[9] Thūp 8, but said of Dīpaṅkara.

The people[1] inhabiting the whole of Jambudīpa gathered together and completed (the cetiya), seven yojanas in extent, consisting of the seven kinds of gems, and they made the plaster-work with yellow and red powder of arsenic and the binding-work with sesame oil and clarified butter.

Concluded is the Exposition of the Chronicle of the Buddha Koṇḍañña

Concluded is the Second Buddha-Chronicle

IV THE EXPOSITION OF THE CHRONICLE OF THE BUDDHA MAṄGALA

After the teacher Koṇḍañña had attained final nibbāna his Dispensation continued for a hundred thousand years. His Dispensation disappeared on the disappearance of the disciples who had been followers of the Buddha.[2] And subsequently to Koṇḍañña after one incalculable had passed four Buddhas were born in one and the same eon, Maṅgala, Sumana, Revata, Sobhita.[3] Therein, Maṅgala,[4] leader of the world, having fulfilled the perfections during sixteen incalculables and a hundred thousand eons, was born in Tusita city, remaining there for the duration of the life-span. A Buddha-tumult[5] arose on the arising of the five portent-signs.[6] Thereupon the devatās of the ten-thousand world-systems, assembling together in one world-system, requested him, saying:

[142] This is the time for you: great hero, arise in the womb of a mother. Helping men with the devas to cross over, may you awaken to the undying state.[7]

Requested thus by the devas, he deceased from the Tusita

[1] Cf. text p. 270.
[2] See first note under Koṇḍañña above.
[3] A Sāramaṇḍa eon, see text p. 191.
[4] A story of Maṅgala is given at Mhvu i 248–252.
[5] Three kinds of kolāhala, tumult, given at BvAC 272, five at KhA 120.
[6] See It 76, Asl 33. When a deva is about to decease from a group of devas these five signs appear: his garlands fade, his clothes become soiled, etc. Cf. Divy 193.
[7] As at text p. 53, etc.

group after he had made the five investigations.[1] He took on re-linking in the womb of the queen named Uttarā in the household of the incomparable (anuttara) king named Uttara in the city of Uttara, superior to (uttara) all cities. Then countless marvels appeared—to be understood exactly as in the method spoken of in the Chronicle of the Buddha Dīpaṅkara.[2]

From the time when the Great Being Maṅgala, of good omen (maṅgala) to all the world, took on re-linking in the womb of the great Queen Uttarā, the lustre of her physical frame, suffusing the region day and night to an extent of eighty cubits, remained undimmed by the light of the sun and the moon. And that lustre of her own physical frame, completely dispelling the darkness without any other light, moved about when she was being cared for by sixty-eight foster-mothers. They say that with the protection given by devatās she gave birth at the end of ten months to the Great Man Maṅgala in Uttara-madhurā pleasaunce. As soon as he was born the Great Being, investigating all the quarters and taking seven strides facing towards the north, uttered the majestic phrase.[3] At that moment the devatās in the entire ten-thousand world-systems standing there with their physical frames visible and their limbs adorned with deva-like garlands, emitted words of victory, good omen and praise. And the marvels were as already spoken of.[2] And on his name-taking day the readers of his marks, saying, "He is born with all the splendour of good omen", gave the boy the name of Maṅgala (Good Omen).

His three palaces were Yasavā, Sucimā, Sirimā. There were thirty thousand dancing-women with the lady Yasavatī at the head. For nine thousand years the Great Being experienced happiness there, similar to deva-like happiness. He begot a son named Sīlava by Yasavatī, his chief consort. When he had seen the four signs and had departed on the Great Departure mounted on the beautiful, glorious and adorned steed named Paṇḍara, he went forth. On his going forth three crores of men went forth following his example. Surrounded by these the Great Being engaged in striving for eight months.

Then, after he had partaken of sweet milk-rice containing a deva-like nutritive essence that had been given to him on the full-

[1] Cf. text pp. 54, 273.
[2] Bv IIA 83ff.
[3] See text p. 132.

moon day of Visākha by Uttarā, the daughter of the merchant Uttara in the village of Uttara, he spent the day-sojourn in a sāla grove. Accepting eight handfuls of grass given to him by Uttara, a Naked Ascetic, and going along like a glorious elephant in rut, circumambulating a Nāga (iron-wood) Tree of Awakening, he stood to the north-east side and spread a grass spreading fifty-eight cubits in extent. Sitting down cross-legged there, resolutely determining on the energy possessed of four factors,[1] he shattered Māra with his forces. Acquiring the knowledges of former habitations and of deva-like vision, reflecting on the conditional modes, [143] interpreting the categories in respect of impermanence and so forth, in due course he attained the incomparable full Self-Awakening and uttered the solemn utterance:

"Through many a birth in saṁsāra have I run . . .
I have arrived at the destruction of cravings".[2]

The lustre of the physical frame of Maṅgala, the Fully Self-Awakened One, exceeded that of other Buddhas. For, as the lustre of the physical frame of other Buddhas measured eighty cubits or a fathom all round, it was not thus with him. For the lustre of this Lord's physical frame remained perpetually suffusing the ten-thousand world-element. Trees, hills, rocks, thick walls, solid doors and so forth were as though shrouded in a cloth of gold. His life-span was ninety hundred-thousand years. For all that time the lustre of the moon, the sun and the stars and so forth was not apparent, nor was the demarcation between night and day.[3] By day beings went about doing all their work by the perpetual light of the Self-Awakened One as though by the light of the sun, and men realized the demarcation between night and day by the blooming of flowers in the morning and the cries of birds in the evening. But did not other Buddhas have this majesty? They did not. Though these were desirous of suffusing the ten-thousand world-element or beyond with light, it was only the lustre of the physical frame of the Lord Maṅgala that remained perpetually suffusing the ten-thousand world-element even as the lustre of the halo of others was a fathom's lustre on account of a former aspiration.

It is said that at the time when he was the Bodhisatta in an

[1] See text p. 83, 133, 161, 172, 177, 236.
[2] As at text p. 133.
[3] Cf. DBK, Ch. I §4, of Metteyya.

individuality resembling Vessantara's he lived with his wife and children on a mountain resembling Mount Vaṅka.[1] Then a very powerful man-eating yakkha[2] named Kharadāṭhika who harassed all the people, having heard of the Great Man's inclination for giving, approached the Great Being in the guise of a brahman and asked for his two children. The Great Being thinking, "I am giving the little children to a brahman", joyfully and cheerfully gave the two children, the earth quaking to its ocean limits. Then that yakkha, while he was yet in the Great Man's sight, giving up the guise of the brahman, seized those children and crunched them up as if they were a bundle of the edible roots of lotuses. His hideous red eyes were insatiate and glowing, his terrible teeth uneven, hideous, crooked, his hideous nose flattened, his tawny hair coarse and long, his body like the trunks of eight and a half palm-trees. When the Great Being surveyed the yakkha and saw his empty mouth dripping with blood like flames from a fire, not even then did the slightest[3] grief arise in him.[4] On the contrary, being of the opinion that his gift had indeed been well given, great zest and happiness arose in his physical frame. He made the aspiration, "As a result of this may rays issue forth from me in this same way in the future". Consequent upon that aspiration of his, rays issued forth from his physical frame after he had become a Buddha and suffused the region to that extent (already spoken of).

And there had been a further former event[5] for him. It is said that when he was the Bodhisatta, on seeing the cetiya of a Buddha[6] **[144]** he thought, "I must sacrifice my life for him". Wrapping round his whole body in the way the handles of little lamps are wrapped round, and filling with sweet-smelling clarified butter a golden vessel studded with jewels and worth a hundred-thousand (kahāpaṇas?), he lit a thousand wicks in it, and setting fire to his whole physical frame beginning with his head, he spent the entire night circumambulating the cetiya. But, striving thus till dawn, not even a pore of his skin became warm. It was as though

[1] Where Vessantara lived.

[2] Cf. text p. 125 for play on the akkha sound: here, manussabhakkha mahesakkha yakkha.

[3] appamatta. A v. l. and BvAB read kesaggamatta, slight (as) a tip of hair.

[4] Perhaps the incident referred to at Jā iv 13.

[5] pubbacariya, cf. text p. 147.

[6] ekassa Buddhassa, the Buddha who "declared" of him(?).

at that time he had entered the womb of a lotus.[1] For truly this Dhamma protects him who protects himself. Consequently the Lord said:

"Dhamma verily protects the Dhamma-farer.
Dhamma well practised brings happiness.
This is an advantage in well practised Dhamma—
The Dhamma-farer goes not to a bad bourn".*

And as the outcome of that deed the effulgence of the Lord's physical frame remained suffusing the ten-thousand world-element. Accordingly it was said:

IV 1 After Koṇḍañña the leader named Maṅgala carried aloft the torch of Dhamma annihilating the gloom in the world.
2 His lustre was unrivalled, excelling that of other Conquerors; dimming the lustre of the sun and moon, he shone over the ten-thousand.

1 Therein *gloom* means the darkness[2] of the world and the gloom of the heart.

1 *Annihilating* means overcoming.

1 *Torch of Dhamma:* now, this word "torch" (ukkā) is to be seen in various meanings, as in the goldsmith's crucible[3] and so forth. As it was said, "Having taken hold of the gold with pincers he thrusts it into the smelting-pot (ukkā-mukhe)"†—in the passage handed down the furnace (ukkā) is to be understood as the crucible of goldsmiths. In the passage handed down: "One should prepare the furnace (ukkā); having prepared the furnace he should put a fire to the smelting-pot (ukkā-mukha)",† it is the goldsmiths' pan. In the passage handed down: "As the goldsmiths' furnace (ukkā) burns inside, not outside",‡ it is the smiths' forge. In the passage handed down: "Thus the fruition will be a fall of meteors (ukkā-pāta)",§ meteor (ukkā) signifies the force of the wind.[4] In

* Thag 303, quoted Jā iv 54, 496. Cf. Mhvu ii 81.
† M iii 243, A i 257. This para. also at MA i 175.
‡ Jā vi 189, 437.
§ D i 10, 68; cf. Jā i 374, vi 476, SnA 362, Miln 178.

[1] Cf. Jā iii 55 in the Sasajātaka which exemplifies the perfection of Giving.
[2] tama . . . andhakāra are synonyms; both imply mental blindness as well as ordinary darkness.
[3] mūsā.
[4] vātavego. See CPD s.v. ukkā: 'vātavega (?, can only mean "meteor")'.

the passage handed down: "As they were carrying torches (ukkā)"* torch (ukkā) is said to be a lamp. Here too torch (ukkā) signifies a lamp. Therefore here *he carried aloft the torch* (ukkā, or lamp) consisting *of Dhamma*. The meaning is: he carried the torch consisting of Dhamma for covering over the darkness of the ignorance of a world overcome by the darkness of ignorance.

[145] 2 *Was unrivalled* means unrivalled,[1] or this itself is the reading. The meaning is that it was unequalled by other Buddhas.

2 *Of other Conquerors* means of other Conquerors.[2]

2 *Dimming the lustre of the sun and moon* means greatly dimming the lustre of the sun and moon.[3]

2 *Shone over the ten-thousand* means he shone over the ten-thousand simply by a Buddha's light without the light of the sun or moon.

After Maṅgala the fully Self-Awakened One had arrived by himself at the knowledge of Awakening, he spent seven weeks at the root of the Tree of Awakening itself. Having acceded to Brahmā's request for Dhamma, and reflecting "To whom should I first teach this Dhamma?" he saw that the three crores of monks who had gone forth with him were endowed with the qualifications.[4] Then it occurred to him: "These sons of respectable families, endowed with the qualifications, gone forth when I went forth, but sent away by me at the full-moon of Visākha for the sake of aloofness, are living near Sirivaḍḍha city in Siri woodland-grove. Come, going there I will teach them Dhamma". Taking his own bowl and robe, soaring up into the vault of the heavens like a royal ruddy goose, he descended in the Siri woodland-grove. And when those monks had greeted the Lord and had done the duties of pupils,[5] they sat down surrounding the Lord. The Lord spoke the Discourse of Turning the Wheel of Dhamma to them in accordance with the practice of all Buddhas. Thereupon those

* D i 49. Cf. DhA i 42, 205.

DAṬ i 167 takes it as the brilliance of numerous meteors colliding owing to the strength of the wind.

[1] atul'āsī ti atuly'āsi.

[2] jineh' aññehī ti jinehi aññehi.

[3] candasuriyappabhaṁ hantvā ti candasuriyānaṁ pabhaṁ abhihantvā.

[4] upanissaya; threefold at Vism 535f.

[5] Vin i 61.

three crores attained arahantship. There was a penetration of Dhamma by a hundred thousand crores of devas and men. Accordingly it was said:

IV 3 This Buddha too expounded the four supremely glorious truths. All those who had drunk of the juice of the truths removed the great gloom.

4 After he had reached the unrivalled Awakening there was at the first teaching of Dhamma the first penetration by a hundred thousand crores.

3 Therein *four* means four.[1]

3 *Supremely glorious truths* means the truths and the glories are the glorious truths. The meaning is that the truths are supreme. "The four supremely glorious truths" is also a reading. The meaning is that his four glorious truths are supreme.

3 *All those*[2] means those devas and men who were guided out by the Buddha, the Lord.

3 *Juice of the truths* means they *had drunk* of the juice of deathlessness on penetration of the four truths.

3 *Removed the great gloom* means they removed, they dissipated the gloom of confusion that is to be got rid of in this way and that.

4 *Had reached* means had penetrated.

4 *Awakening:* now herein this word Awakening (bodhi) means:

In way, in fruit, and in nibbāna, in tree, in designation likewise, and in omniscient knowledge the word *bodhi* is indeed handed down.[3] 84

[**146**] [4]In such contexts as "Awakening (bodhi) is said to be the knowledge of the four ways"* it is handed down as way. "It conduces to tranquillity, super-knowing, Self-Awakening (sambodhāya), nibbāna"† herein it is fruit. "Having attained Awakening (bodhi), the undying, the unconstructed"‡—herein it is

* Nd1 456. Cf. MA iii 326.
† Vin i 10, S iv 331, A i 30, etc.
‡ (?) Cf. Ap 388, ver. 13.

[1] caturo ti cattāri. For this passage I follow BvAB as it is clearer than BvAC.
[2] te te.
[3] As I do not see this ver. in other ctys on the word bodhi, I have very tentatively numbered it as if it were peculiar to BvA.
[4] For this para. cf. above text p. 55.

nibbāna. "Between Bodhi and Gayā"*—herein it is the Assattha Tree. "Prince Bodhi reverenced the Lord's feet with his head"†—herein it is a designation. "Glorious, supreme of intellect, he gains Awakening (bodhi)"‡—herein it is omiscient knowledge. Here too omniscient knowledge is to be understood. "Knowledge of the Way to arahantship" is right too.[1]

4 *Unrivalled* means lacking a rival, beyond measure; the meaning is: measureless. The meaning is to be taken as: After the Lord had attained Self-Awakening and was teaching Dhamma at the first teaching of Dhamma.

And when (the Buddha) was staying near the city of Citta at the root of a champak tree—like our Lord at the root of the Gaṇḍamba tree[2]—he performed the Marvel of the Double for crushing the pride and conceit of the sectarians. (Then,) seated on the ornamental stone slab at the root of the Coral Tree in the abode of the Thirty-Three, in a glorious abode consisting of glowing gold and silver, in a delightful abode of young gods and non-gods[3], he talked a talk on Abhidhamma. Thereupon there was a penetration of Dhamma by a hundred thousand crores of devatās. This was the second penetration.

And when in Surabhi[4] city the universal monarch named Sunanda had fulfilled the duties of a universal monarch, he acquired the Treasure of the Wheel. It is said that when Maṅgala, Him of the Ten Powers, arose in the world, King Sunanda saw the Treasure of the Wheel drawing back from its place. His bliss impaired, he questioned brahmans, saying: "Why has this Treasure of the Wheel that was produced by my skill and power drawn back from its place?" So they explained to that king the reason for its drawing back, saying: "On the destruction of the life-span of a universal monarch or on his undertaking the going forth or on the appearance of a Buddha the Treasure of the Wheel draws back from its place." When they had spoken thus they said: "But, sire, it is not the destruction of your life-span, you are of an

* Vin i 8, M i 170.
† M ii 91.
‡ D iii 159.

[1] As at text p. 56 which, with MA i 54, add "But others also say 'omniscient knowledge'".
[2] See e.g. DA 57.
[3] surāsurayuvati.
[4] Not in DPPN.

exceedingly long life-span. It is because Maṅgala, the fully Self-Awakened One, has arisen in the world that your Treasure of the Wheel has drawn back."[1]

When he had heard this Sunanda, the universal monarch, with his people honouring that Treasure of the Wheel with his head, implored it saying, "As long as I, by means of your majesty, reverence Maṅgala, Him of the Ten Powers, please do you not disappear." Then that Treasure of the Wheel stood still just where it was.

Then Sunanda, the universal monarch, again blissful, surrounded by a company extending for thirty-six yojanas, approached Maṅgala, Him of the Ten Powers, a Good Omen (maṅgala) for all the world. He refreshed the teacher with his Order of disciples with a great gift, gave saffron garments to the hundred thousand crores of arahants and gave all the requisites to the Tathāgata, paying a respect to that Lord that astounded the entire world. Having approached Maṅgala, the protector of all the world, honouring him, [147] bringing together his clasped hands which were shining like stainless unsoiled lotus-buds, their ten nails touching each other[2], he raised them to his head and sat down at a respectful distance so as to hear Dhamma. And his son, named Prince Anurāja, sat down too.

Then the Lord talked a graduated talk to them with Sunanda, the universal monarch, at their head. Sunanda, the universal monarch, together with the company, reached arahantship with the analytical insights. Then the teacher, surveying their former faring[3] and seeing the qualification of bowl and robe made by psychic potency, stretched out his right hand which was adorned with glowing wheels[4] and said "Come, monks". At that very moment all of them had their hair two finger-breadths (in length),[5] were carrying bowls and robes made by psychic potency like

[1] Cf. Miln 218, 285, 327 for the Treasures acting of their own accord when conditions are right.

[2] Cf. text p. 10. The above reading is dasanakhasamodhānasamujjalaṁ vimala-kamalamakulasamaṁ añjaliṁ sirasi katvā.

[3] pubbacariya, former conduct and so former births or farings (in saṁsāra).

[4] cakkajāla. Jāla can mean both a net as in jālahatthapāda (one of the 32 Marks of a Great Man: netted hands and feet), and glowing. From the construction of the words and because of the tradition that Maṅgala's body was always lustrous, it would seem that the latter meaning is intended.

[5] This length, or a two months' growth, allowed to monks at Vin ii 107, cf. ibid. 133.

Elders of a hundred years standing, and were suitably clothed. Having honoured the teacher, the Lord, they surrounded him. This was the third penetration. Accordingly it was said:

IV 5 When the Buddha taught Dhamma in the deva-abode of the chief of devas there was the second penetration by nine thousand crores.[1]

6 When Sunanda, the universal monarch, approached the Self-Awakened One, then the Self-Awakened One smote the supremely glorious drum of Dhamma.

7 The multitude that followed Sunanda then was ninety crores. And[2] all these without exception were 'Come, monk' ones.[3]

5 Therein *in the deva-abode of the chief of devas* has again the meaning: in the abode of the chief of devas.[4]

5 *Dhamma* means Abhidhamma.

6 *Smote* means struck.[5]

6 *Supremely glorious* means glorious is the Lord, supreme is the *drum of Dhamma.*

7 *That followed* means followers ready to serve[6].

7 Were means *were.*[7] "*Was* then[8] ninety crores" is also a reading. The multitude was[9] his. How great was that multitude? The meaning is it was ninety crores.

Then, it is said that while Maṅgala, protector of the world was staying in Mekhala city, Sudeva and Dhammasena, surrounded by ten thousand brahmans[10], went forth in that same city by the 'Come, monk' (formula for) going forth in that Lord's presence.

[1] Bv reads yadā buddho pakāsayi tadā koṭisahassānaṁ. BvAC reads buddho dhammam adesayi navakoṭisahassānaṁ, and BvAB buddho dhammam adesayi koṭisatasahassānaṁ, a hundred thousand crores.

[2] Bv, BvAB pi, above va.

[3] ehi bhikkhukā; above, etha bhikkhavo.

[4] surindadevabhavane ti puna devindabhavane ti attho.

[5] As at text p. 193.

[6] baddhacarā for which PED refers us to paddhacara. BvAB reads nibaddhacarā, sure, steady followers.

[7] āsun ti ahesuṁ.

[8] tadāsi for tadāsuṁ.

[9] āsi.

[10] BvAB reads māṇavakā mānavakasahassaparivāro, brahmans, their entourage (being) a 1000 brahmans. BvAC: dasamāṇavakasahassehi parivutā.

When the two chief disciples and their retinues had attained arahantship on the full-moon day of Māgha, the teacher recited the Pātimokkha in the midst of a company of a hundred thousand crores of monks. This was the first assembly. Again, in the incomparable Uttarārāma in a gathering of (his) relations, he recited the Pātimokkha to a gathering of a thousand crores[1] who had gone forth. This was the second assembly. In a gathering of monks (surrounding?) Sunanda, the universal monarch, he recited the Pātimokkha in the midst of ninety (thousand)[2] crores of monks. This was the third assembly. Accordingly it was said:

[148] IV 8 The great seer Maṅgala had three assemblies: the first was a gathering of a hundred thousand crores,

9 The second of a thousand crores[3], the third was then a gathering of ninety crores of those whose cankers were destroyed, stainless.

Our Bodhisatta was then the brahman Suruci in the brahman village of Suruci. He was master of the three Vedas[4], versed in the vocabularies and rituals together with the phonology and exegesis, and the legendary tradition as the fifth; he was learned in idioms, a grammarian, proficient in popular philosophy and the Marks of a Great Man. He approached the teacher, heard a talk on Dhamma, and found satisfaction in the Lord and his Orders of disciples. After he had gone for refuge he invited the Lord with the Order of disciples, saying, "Take your meal with me on the morrow". The Lord said, "Brahman, how many monks can you invite?"[5] He asked, "But how many monks, revered sir, are in your retinue?" It was then as at the first assembly, therefore he said, "A hundred thousand crores". He invited, saying, "If it be thus, revered sir, take your meal with me together with all of them." The teacher consented.

When the brahman had invited the Lord for the morrow and was going to his own house, he thought, "I am able to give milk-rice, rice and garments to all these monks, but how can there be a

[1] BvAB, a hundred thousand crores.

[2] It looks as if the "thousand" had crept in by error.

[3] Be a hundred thousand crores.

[4] Stock description of a learned brahman, see text p. 67.

[5] kittakehi te bhikkhūhi attho, perhaps, more literally: with how many monks is there advantage (good) for you? Or, more colloquially: how many monks can you do with?

place for them to be seated?" They say this thought of his caused the ornamental stone of the king of devas who had a hundred thousand eyes to become warm in its place on the summit of Mount Meru which is eighty-four yojanas in extent. Then Sakka, king of devas, on noticing the warm condition of his seat thought, "Now, who wants to make me descend from this place?" Reasoning about what had happened, he surveyed the world of men with deva-like vision and on seeing the Great Man he thought, "This Great Man, having invited the Order of monks with the Awakened One at its head thought about the benefit to him concerning a place where they could be seated. I should go there too and take a share of the merit". Assuming the guise of a carpenter, he appeared, hatchet and axe in hand, before the Great Man, and said "Has anyone carpentry to be done for hire?" On seeing him, the Great Being said, "What kind of work are you able to do?" "There is no craft unknown to me. Whatever anyone wants: a pavilion or a palace or any other dwelling, that I am competent to build for him". "Well then, I do have some work". "What is it, sir?" "Invited by me for the morrow are a hundred thousand crores of monks. You are to build a pavilion where they can be seated." "I will do that if you are able to give me wages." "I am able, my dear." "Very well, I will build it", he said and looked round for a site. There was a perfectly delightful site, twelve yojanas in extent, its surface as level as a kasiṇa-circle[1]. Looking again, he thought "In a part of this place let there rise up the choicest pavilion to be seen, consisting of the seven kinds of gems". **[149]** Thereupon a pavilion immediately rose up splitting the earth's surface to a (size) equal to the pavilion. There were silver capitals on golden pillars, golden on silver, coral (capitals) on jewelled pillars, jewelled on coral (pillars), there were capitals made of the seven kinds of gems on (pillars) made of the seven kinds of gems.

Thereupon he looked and thought, "Let the pavilion have a little net of tinkling bells hanging down at intervals". While he was looking a net of tinkling bells hung down, from which, when it was stirred by a gentle breeze a perfectly lovely sweet sound came forth resembling that of the five kinds of instrumental music. It was like a time a deva-like recital was taking place. He thought, "At intervals let there hang down festoons of deva-like perfumes, festoons of flowers, festoons of leaves, festoons of gems". At the

[1] Used in the kasiṇa meditative practices.

thought the festoons hung down. He thought, "Let seats and benches with suitable and very costly spreadings for the monks who amount to a hundred thousand crores rise up bursting through the earth." They rose up immediately. He thought, "Let a water-vessel rise up in each corner". At that very moment water-vessels rose up, their mouths covered by plantain-leaves and filled with beautifully cool, sweet, well-purified, well-perfumed, suitable water. He of the thousand eyes, having created all this, went to the brahman and said: "Come, sir, when you have seen the pavilion, give me the wages". The Great Man went to that pavilion and surveyed it, and as he did so his entire physical frame was completely suffused with the five kinds of zest.[1]

Then, as he was looking at the pavilion it occurred to him: "This pavilion has not been made by a human being. By my intention, my special quality indeed, the abode of Sakka, king of devas, became warm. So this pavilion has been created by Sakka, lord of devas. It would not be right of me to give a gift for one day only in a pavilion such as this. I will give for a week".

But the giving of external things, however great they be, cannot make exultant the heart of Bodhisattas. The exultation of Bodhisattas depends on the sacrifice they make at the time of giving—whether it be cutting off their adorned head or plucking out their collyriumed eyes or tearing out their heart's flesh.[2] While our Bodhisatta, in the Sivijātaka,[3] daily disbursed five hundred thousand kahāpaṇas at the four gateways and in the middle of the city, that gift was not able to arouse in him the exultation of sacrifice when he was giving the gift. But, on the other hand, when Sakka, king of devas, came in the guise of a brahman and asked for his eyes, then plucking out his eyes he gave each eye. Joy arose even as he was giving and there was no contrariety of mind even of as much as a hair's tip. Thus Bodhisattas have no satiety in giving.

Therefore when the Great Man also thought he must give a gift to the monks who amounted to a hundred thousand crores, he made them be seated for a week in that pavilion and gave them a gift called gavapāna.[4] Gavapāna [150] means that, having filled

[1] See Vism 143.
[2] Cf. DhA i 5; also DA ii 465.
[3] Jā No. 499; cf. Cp I 8.
[4] Lit. drink from cows.

great jars with milk and taken them up to the ovens and added husked rice-grains little by little to the milk that was thickening as it cooked, the meal was prepared by adding to it a cooked mixture of honey, palm-sugar, (rice-)flour, and clarified butter. It is also simply called "the meal of the four sweet things".[1] Men alone were not able to wait on them; devas too, one beside each (monk), waited on them. But that place, even though it was twelve yojanas in extent, could not alone accommodate those monks; yet these monks sat down each by means of his own (psychic) majesty. On the final day he (Suruci) had the bowls of all the monks washed and after filling them with clarified butter, butter, honey, molasses and so forth for use as medicines, he gave (to each monk) together with three robes. Monks who were newly ordained in the Order were the recipients there of robes and outer cloaks worth hundreds of thousands[2] (of kahāpaṇas).

When the teacher was giving the benediction he thought, "Now, who can this man be who has given such a great gift?" While he was considering he saw him and thought, "In the future after a hundred thousand eons and two incalculables he will be the Buddha named Gotama". Addressing the Great Being, he declared, "You, when that length of time has elapsed, will be the Buddha named Gotama." When the Great Man had heard the Lord's declaration, rejoicing at heart he thought, "As it is said that I will be a Buddha I have no use for the household life; I will go forth". And getting rid of all that property like a blob of phlegm, he went forth in the teacher's presence. Having learnt the word of the Buddha, and obtaining the super-knowings and the eight attainments, remaining for the duration of his life-span, his meditation unbroken, he was re-born in a Brahma-world[3]. Accordingly it was said:

IV 10 I at that time was a brahman named Suruci, a repeater, expert in the mantras, master of the three Vedas.[4]

11 Approaching him, going to the teacher for refuge, I honoured the Order with the Self-Awakened One at the head with perfumes and garlands. When I had honoured them with the perfumes and garlands I refreshed them with the gavapāna.

[1] Cf. ThīgA 68 where, in reference to a meal placed in a begging bowl, it is called catumadhura, the four sweet things, as above.

[2] Or, a hundred thousand.

[3] Cf. text p. 137.

[4] Cf. II A 6.

12 And that Buddha Maṅgala, supreme among men, also declared of me: "Innumerable eons from now this one will be a Buddha.

13 When he has striven the striving, carried out austerities . . ." ". . . we will be face to face with this one".

Eight verses to be expanded.[1]

14 When I had heard his words too, all the more did I incline my mind. I resolutely determined on further practice for fulfilling the ten perfections.

[151] 15 Increasing[2] zest then for the attainment of the glorious Self-Awakening, I gave my worldly wealth to the Buddha and went forth in his presence.

16 Having learnt[3] thoroughly the Suttanta and Vinaya and all the ninefold Dispensation of the teacher, I illumined the Conqueror's Dispensation.

17 Living diligent therein, developing the Brahma-development, after reaching perfection in the super-knowings to the Brahma-world went I.[4]

11 Therein *with perfumes and garlands*[5] means with perfumes[6] as well as with garlands[6].

11 *With the gavapāna:* This has just been spoken of[7]; some just read ghatapāna.[8]

14 *I refreshed* means I refreshed.[9]

14 *I resolutely determined on further practice* means all the more I resolutely determined on practice.

14 *For fulfilling the ten perfections* means for the sake of the fulfilling of the ten perfections.[10]

15 *Zest* means heart's elation.

15 *Increasing*[11] means making to grow.

15 *For the attainment of the glorious Self-Awakening* means for the attainment of Buddhahood.

[1] See iii 12–15, 18–21.
[2] anubrūhanto, also at BvAB. But see CPD. s.v. anubrūheti.
[3] Cf. iii 23, 24.
[4] Ver. 16, 17 also at xiii 18, 19, xix 12, 13. Cf. iii 23, 24, xii 16, 17.
[5] gandhamālena, in sing.
[6] gandhehi . . . mālehi, in pl.
[7] Text p. 150.
[8] ghata is a word for clarified butter.
[9] tappayin ti tappesim.
[10] dasapāramipūriyā ti dasannaṁ pāramīnaṁ pūraṇatthāya.
[11] Here anubrūhento.

15 *I gave to the Buddha* means I sacrificed for the Buddha.

15 *My worldly wealth* means my worldly wealth.[1] The meaning is: having sacrificed all property for the Buddha, the Lord, for the sake of the four requisites.

17 *Therein* means in that Buddha's Dispensation.

17 *Brahma* means *developing* the development of the Brahma-abidings.

And the Lord Maṅgala's city was named Uttara, and his father was the warrior-noble king also named Uttara, his mother too was named Uttarā. Sudeva and Dhammasena were the two chief disciples, the (lay) attendant was named Pālita; Sīvalā and Asokā were the two chief women disciples; the Tree of Awakening was a Nāga[2]. The physical frame was eighty-eight cubits tall, the life-span[3] ninety thousand years; and his wife was named Yasavatī, his son was named Sīlava[4]; he departed on horseback, stayed in Uttara-monastery, and his (monastic) attendant was named Uttara. The Lord lived[5] for ninety thousand years, and when he attained final nibbāna the ten-thousand world-systems in just one instant became one in darkness, and in all the world-systems there was a great lamenting and grieving among men. Accordingly it was said:

IV 18 Uttara was the name of the city, Uttara the name of the warrior-noble, Uttarā the name of the mother of Maṅgala, the great seer.

23 Sudeva and Dhammasena were the chief disciples. Pālita was the name of the attendant on Maṅgala, the great seer.

24 Sīvalā and Asokā were the chief women disciples. That Lord's Tree of Awakening is said to be the Nāga.

[1] Maṁ gehan ti mama gehaṁ. The word geha means house, but the Comy makes it clear this is not to be taken literally.

[2] Ironwood tree, Mesua ferrea.

[3] BvAB reads āyuparimāṇaṁ for āyu above.

[4] Bv, BvAB read Sīvala.

[5] tasmiṁ navutivassasahassāni ṭhatvā. There is something wrong here. The length of the life-span has been given just above, but probably it should have been the length of time that he lived the household life, namely 9,000 years (see ver 19). The tasmiṁ too probably should be followed by some noun, or it could be interpreted to mean he lived (or remained) in the Uttarārāma for 90,000 years—other Buddhas are reputed not only to have toured the country-side but to have paid at least one visit to a deva-world.

[152] 26 The great sage was eighty-eight ratanas tall. There streamed forth from him countless hundreds and thousands of rays.

27 The (normal) life-span lasted then for ninety thousand years. Living so long he caused many people to cross over.

28 Just as it is not possible to count the waves of the ocean so it was not possible to count his disciples.

29 For as long as the leader named Maṅgala, the Self-Awakened One, was alive there was no dying then with defilements (present) in his Dispensation.

30 Having carried the torch of Dhamma and caused the great populace to cross, he, of a great retinue, blazing like a column of fire waned out.

31 Having shown devas and men the essential nature of the constructions, blazing like a mass of fire, as the setting sun,

26 Therein *from him* means from this Maṅgala's physical frame.

26 *Streamed forth* means streamed forth. A change of "number"[1] is to be understood.

26 *Rays* means rays[2].

26 *Countless hundreds of thousands* means countless hundreds of thousands.[3]

28 *Waves* means billows, cross-waves.[4]

28 *To count* means to count,[5] to estimate. As there are such a quantity of waves in the ocean that it is not possible to count them, so too it was not possible to count this Lord's disciples. So, the meaning is: having passed beyond the ways of counting.

29 *For as long as* means for as much time as.

29 *Dying then with defilements (present)* means: with defilements (saṅkilese) is: with defilements (saha kilesehi) (present in them); dying (maraṇa) with the defilements (present) is the dying (of

[1] From sing. to plural, referring to the verb niddhāvatī ti niddhāvanti, it streams forth, they stream forth.

[2] raṁsī ti rasmiyo, sing. and pl., accounting for the sing. and plural forms of the verb.

[3] anekasatasahassiyo ti anekasatasahassā.

[4] These 3 words are ūmī vīciyo taraṅgā.

[5] gaṇetuye ti gaṇetuṁ.

someone) with the defilements (present). That was not (to be found at that time). That is to say, all the disciples in that Lord's Dispensation attained final nibbāna then after reaching arahantship, and did not die as ordinary people or stream-entrants and so forth. Some read, "Dying then with confusion (present)".

30 *Torch of Dhamma*[1] means lamp of Dhamma.

30 *Column of fire*[2] is said to be fire. But here lamp is to be understood. Therefore the meaning is: blazing like a lamp he waned out.

30 *Of a great retinue*[3] means (having) a great entourage. Some read, "he with the disciples, waned out."

31 *Of the construction* means of the things that are constructed, of things (that arise) from conditions.

[153] 31 *Essential nature* means the marks of impermanence and so forth (recognized in) recluseship.

31 *As the setting sun* means as the thousand rayed sun[4], dispelling all gloom[5], blazing and making all the world effulgent, goes to its setting, thus the sun Maṅgala, making even a grove of lotuses come into full bloom, dispelling all gloom internal and external, blazing with the lustre of his own physical frame, went to his setting.

The remaining verses are quite clear in every respect.

Concluded is the Exposition of the Chronicle of the Buddha Maṅgala

Concluded is the Third Buddha-Chronicle

V THE EXPOSITION OF THE CHRONICLE OF THE BUDDHA SUMANA

The ten-thousand world-element was thus made one in darkness in just one instant[6] on that Lord's (Maṅgala's) attainment of final nibbāna. Subsequently to him men's life-spans gradually dwindled from ninety thousand years to ten years, then gradually increased between the eons to as much as life-spans lasting for one incalcul-

[1] Cf. text p. 144.
[2] dhūmaketu, banner of smoke.
[3] mahāyasa, cf. text pp. 160, 257; also see amitayasa, text p. 135.
[4] sahassakiraṇo divasakaro.
[5] tamagata, BvAB tamagaṇa with v. l. -gata.
[6] See text p. 151.

able. When they had dwindled (again) to life-spans of ninety thousand years[1] the Bodhisatta named Sumana, having fulfilled the perfections, was born in Tusita city. Deceasing from there he took on relinking in the womb of the queen named Sirimā in the household of the king named Sudatta in the city of Mekhala. The marvels were exactly as those spoken of already.[2] When in due course he had grown up in the three palaces which had the names of Nārivaḍḍhana, Somavaḍḍhana and Iddhivaḍḍhana[3] where he had been waited on by eighty-three thousand dancing women like a deva-prince being waited on by heavenly maidens, (and) experiencing the happiness of the realm for a thousand years, he begot an incomparable (nirupama) son named Anupama by Queen Vaṭaṁsikā.

When he had seen the four signs and had departed mounted on an elephant, he went forth. On his going forth thirty crores went forth following his example. Surrounded by these he engaged in striving for ten months. After he had partaken of milk-rice into which a deva-like nutritive essence had been infused and given to him on the full-moon day of Visākha by Anupamā, the daughter of the merchant Anupama in the market-town of Anoma, he spent the day-sojourn in a sāla grove. Accepting eight handfuls of grass given to him by Anupama, a Naked Ascetic, approaching a Nāga Tree of Awakening and circumambulating it, he made a grass-spreading of the eight handfuls of grass thirty cubits in extent and sat down cross-legged there. Then, [154] having routed Māra's forces and pierced omniscient knowledge, he uttered the solemn utterance:

"Through many a birth in saṁsāra . . .
I have arrived at the destruction of cravings."

Accordingly it was said:

V 1 After Maṅgala was the leader named Sumana, without an equal in all things, supreme among all creatures.

1 Therein *after Maṅgala* means subsequently to Maṅgala.

[1] Bishop Bigandet, *Legend of the Burmese Buddha*, 4th edn., London 1911, p. 22, n. 18 gives an interesting account of these greatly varying lengths of life-span, depending on man's virtue or wickedness. A Buddha's teaching to wicked men of short life-spans would be in vain.

[2] See text p. 96ff., IIA 83–108.

[3] All three names are different at Bv and below, ver 22.

1 *Without an equal in all things* means without an equal, unique in all the morality-concentration-wisdom-things.

It is said that the Lord Sumana after spending seven weeks near the Tree of Awakening itself, having acceded to Brahmā's request that he should teach Dhamma, reflecting, "To whom should I first teach Dhamma?" he saw that the thirty crores who had gone forth with him, also the boy Saraṇa, his own younger half-brother, and the son of a brahman priest, the brahman youth Bhāvitatta, were endowed with the qualifications. Thinking, "It is to these that I should first teach Dhamma", like a royal ruddy goose, he descended into Mekhala-pleasaunce by a mountain-path.[1] Sending for the guardian of the pleasaunce he had him summon his own half-brother, the boy Saraṇa, and the son of the brahman priest, the boy Bhāvitatta, and the thirty-seven crores who had come to be surrounding them and the thirty crores who had gone forth together with himself and many crores of other devas and men. Thus at the turning of the Wheel of Dhamma he caused a hundred thousand crores to drink of the nectar of Dhamma. Accordingly it was said:

V 2 In Mekhala city, he too smote[2] the drum of deathlessness then, accompanied by the conch of Dhamma, the ninefold Dispensation of the Conqueror.

2 Therein *drum of deathlessness* means the drum for arriving at deathlessness, for arriving at nibbāna.

2 *He smote* means he sounded. The meaning is: he taught Dhamma. This drum of deathlessness is called the ninefold Buddha-word whose culmination is deathlessness. Accordingly it was spoken of like this: *accompanied by the conch of Dhamma, the ninefold Dispensation of the Conqueror.*

2 Therein *accompanied by the conch of Dhamma* means accompanied by what is known as the ninefold talk on the Dhamma of the four truths.

And Sumana, leader of the world, having attained full Self-Awakening, going along[3] in accordance with his promise[4] to free

[1] pavanapatha, also meaning "woodland path".
[2] Bv ahani, BvAC ahaṇī, BvAB āhanī.
[3] BvAB adds paṭipadaṁ, course or way.
[4] paṭiññā; this must refer to his undertaking to Brahmā.

the populace from the bonds of becoming, built the glorious city of deathlessness as a safeguard (consisting) of the jewel of skill against the plundering[1] by the defilement-thieves[2]. The extensive walls were the moral habits, the encircling moats were concentration, the gateway was the knowledge of insight, the solid door was mindfulness and clear consciousness, the pavilions and so forth were decorated with the attainments, and the people who filled (the city) were the qualities helpful to Awakening.[3] Accordingly it was said:

[155] V 3 Having conquered[4] the defilements he attained supreme Self-Awakening. The teacher built a city, a supremely glorious city of True Dhamma.[5]

3 Therein *having conquered* means having vanquished, having overcome. The meaning is: having shattered the Māras who are sons of devas[6] and who render the defilements effective.

3 *He* means he, Sumana. "Having triumphed over the defilements"[7] is also a reading. Therein the syllable *hi* is only a particle in the line (of the verse).

3 *Attained*[8] means arrived at; "attained"[8] is also a reading.

3 *City* (nagara) means city of nibbāna.

3 *Supremely glorious city* (*pura*) *of True Dhamma* means: among glorious cities that known as True Dhamma is supreme, best, existing as a basic principle[9]. Or, supreme among glorious cities consisting of True Dhamma—supremely glorious city of True Dhamma. As an alternative, "city" (nagara) is to be understood simply as a synonym for it (pura)[10]. The city (nagara) is said to be nibbāna in the sense that it is the resort and abode of initiates, non-initiates and ariyan individuals who stand firm

[1] viluppamānassa; PED only vilumpa-.

[2] Cf. Miln 332 for entry into the city of nibbāna once the defilements have been slain.

[3] Cf. Ap p. 44, ver 95, 96, Miln 332.

[4] nijjinitvā, Bv jinitvāna.

[5] saddhamma-, Bv dhamma-; cf. Dhammanagara at Miln 341ff.

[6] There was perhaps an actual, even if legendary, "devaputta, named Māra, also called Vasavatti", see DPPN ii 618f. where more information about Māra-devaputta can be found.

[7] jinitvā kilese hi.

[8] patvā . . . patto. Bv reads patto.

[9] padhānabhūta. See Vism 511, and Ppn 584, n. 23 on this meaning of padhāna.

[10] I.e. nagara, city, is a synonym for pura, city.

having penetrated the essential nature of Dhamma. And in this glorious city of True Dhamma he, the Teacher, built this main-street, the applications of mindfulness, uninterrupted, not crooked, straight, wide and extensive. Accordingly it was said:

V 4 He built a main-street, continuous, not crooked, straight, large and extensive: the supremely glorious applications of mindfulness.

4 Therein *continuous* means continuous from its being ready at hand for moving to skilled impulsion.[1]

4 *Not crooked* means not crooked because it is without defects making for crookedness.

4 *Straight* means straight simply from being not crooked. This expression is simply an explanation of the meaning of the foregoing word.

4 *Large and extensive* means wide and extensive in length and breadth, to be understood in reference to the width and extensiveness of mundane and supermundane applications of mindfulness.

4 *Main street* means great way.

4 *Supremely glorious applications of mindfulness* means both the application of mindfulness and that it is supreme among glorious (things): the supremely glorious applications of mindfulness. Or the meaning is: the glorious application of mindfulness is this superb street. Now, on both sides of the street of those applications of mindfulness in this great city of nibbāna he laid out costly treasures in the shop in Dhamma[2]: the four fruits of recluseship[3], the four analytical insights[4], the six super-knowings, and the eight attainments.[5] Accordingly it was said:

V 5 There, in the street, he laid out the four fruits of recluseship, the four analytical insights, the six super-knowings, the eight attainments.

[1] javana, impulsion, the culminating phase in the process of consciousness; here volition, skilled or unskilled (i.e. kamma) is produced. See Ñyāṇatiloka, Bud. Dict., s.v. javana. It is a member of the cittavīthi, the cognitive series in the occurrence of sonsciousness. The "main street" of this verse is mahāvīthi.

[2] Cf. Miln 336ff. for "the Buddha's jewel-shop".

[3] The fruitions of the four ways of stream-entry and so forth, see D iii 227, S v 25, A iii 272, Miln 344, 358.

[4] See e.g. Miln 339.

[5] See Miln 214 etc. for these categories.

[156] Now the Lord saying, "Those who obtain these jewels and goods are diligent, mindful, wise, possessed of conscience, shame, energy and so forth"; and showing the means of procuring these jewels he said:

V 6 Those who are diligent, without (mental) barrenness, endued with conscience and energy, these obtain whichever of these glorious special qualities they please.

6 Therein *those* (ye) is an indefinite pronoun.

6 *Diligent* means that by being opposed to negligence they are possessed of the characteristic mark of non-separation from mindfulness.

6 *Without (mental) barrenness* means devoid of the five barrennesses of the mind.[1]

6 *Endued with conscience and energy:* conscience[2] means he has conscientious scruples about bodily misconduct and so forth[3]; it is a synonym for modesty. Energy is the state of one who is vigorous[4]. Its characteristic mark is being active. Qualified individuals[5] are endued with and possessed of this conscience and energy.

6 *These* (te): this is a definite pronoun for the earlier one.

6 Again *these* (te)[6] means that these sons of respectable families *obtain*, acquire, arrive at distinction in the jewels of the special qualities in the manner spoken of.

And the Lord Sumana, making known his mind to all, having smote the drum of Dhamma and built the city of Dhamma, by this very method awakened first a hundred thousand crores. Accordingly it was said:

V 7 Thus, by this earnest application, the teacher, carrying across the populace, awakened first a hundred thousand crores.

7 Therein *carrying across* means himself carrying across from the ocean of saṁsāra by means of the ship of the ariyan Way.

[1] See M Sta 16, Cetokhilasutta; also D iii 237, A iii 248, iv 400, v 17.

[2] hiri defined at Vism 464 in same terms as here.

[3] "And so forth" refers to misconduct in speech and thought.

[4] Again see Vism 464.

[5] bhabbapuggala has a kind of technical meaning.

[6] The verse reads te te ime. The second te is translated with ime as "(whichever of) these".

7 *A hundred thousand crores:* the meaning is: crores of a hundred thousand[1] expressed by a reversal (of the terms).

And when Sumana, leader of the world, for crushing the pride and conceit of the sectarians had performed the Marvel of the Double at the root of a mango-tree in the city of Sunandavatī, he made a thousand crores of beings to drink of the nectar of Dhamma. This was the second penetration. Accordingly it was said:

V 8 At the time of the second teaching of Dhamma, when the great hero exhorted groups of sectarians, a thousand crores penetrated (it).

8 Therein *groups of sectarians* means groups who had become sectarians and[2] groups of sectarians. Some read, "The Buddha taught Dhamma quite crushing the sectarians."

And when the devatās of the ten-thousand world-systems and the people had assembled in this world-system they set on foot a talk on cessation: How do they enter on cessation? How are they entered on cessation? [157] How do they emerge from cessation? Being unable to differentiate between entering on, resolutely determining on, emerging from and so forth, the devas in the six deva-worlds of the sensuous-desires spheres with the men and the Brahmās in the nine Brahma-worlds, were two parts, (both) in doubt. Thereupon, towards evening, together with the king named Arindama, lovely among men, they approached Sumana, Him of the Ten Powers, protector of all the world(s). When they had approached, Arindama the king asked the Lord a question about cessation. Then, because of the Lord's explanation of the question about cessation, there was a penetration of Dhamma by ninety thousand crores of breathing things. This was the third penetration. Accordingly it was said:

V 9 When devas and men, one in mind, met together they asked a question about cessation and about the doubt in their minds.

10 And then when he was teaching Dhamma,[3] on the eluci-

[1] koṭisatasahassiyo ti satasahassakoṭiyo.
[2] BvAC ca, BvAB vā, or.
[3] BvAC dhammaṁ desente; Bv, BvAB dhammadesane.

dation[1] of cessation, there was a penetration of Dhamma[2] by ninety thousand crores.

And the Lord Sumana had three assemblies of disciples. At the first assembly after he had spent the rains near Mekhala city, the Lord at the first "Invitation" invited with a thousand crores of arahants together with those who had gone forth by the 'Come, monk' (formula for) going forth. This was the first assembly. After a time when King Arindama was seated on Golden Mountain which through the power of his skill had sprung up a yojana's distance from the city of Saṅkassa, the glorious sun, the sage, like a beautiful autumnal sun on Mount Yugandhara, taming ninety thousand crores of men who on arrival had surrounded King Arindama, let them all go forth by the 'Come, monk' (formula for) going forth. Surrounded by those who had gained arahantship that very day he recited the Pātimokkha in an assembly possessed of the four factors[3]. This was the second assembly. And when Sakka, king of devas, approached so as to see the Wellfarer, then the Lord Sumana recited the Pātimokkha surrounded by eighty thousand crores of arahants. This was the third assembly. Accordingly it was said:

V 11 The great seer Sumana had three assemblies of steadfast ones whose cankers were destroyed, stainless, tranquil in mind.

12 When the Lord had kept the rains, the Tathāgata on the proclamation of the "Invitation", "invited" with a hundred thousand crores.

13 Following on that, in a stainless assembly on Golden Mountain there was the second gathering of ninety thousand crores.

14 When Sakka, king of devas, came to see the Buddha, there was the third gathering of eighty thousand crores.

[158] 12 Therein *on the proclamation of the "Invitation"*[4] means a change in gender is to be understood. The meaning is: on the proclamation of the "Invitation".[4]

[1] BvAC -paridīpanaṁ; Bv, Be -dīpane.

[2] BvAC dhammābhisamayo, Bv, BvAB tatiyābhisamayo, the third penetration.

[3] caturaṅgasamannāgata, see text p. 126.

[4] abhighuṭṭhe pavāraṇe, masc.; but pavāraṇā is fem., so the feminine form is given: abhighuṭṭhāya pavāraṇāya.

13 *Following on that* means subsequently to that.

13 *On Golden Mountain* means on the mountain consisting of gold.

14 *Came to see the Buddha* means came so as to see the Buddha[1].

It is said that our Bodhisatta was then a nāga-king called Atula, of great psychic potency, of great majesty. He, hearing that a Buddha had arisen in the world, issued forth from his own abode surrounded by hosts of kinsfolk. Having had an offering made with deva-like instrumental music to the Lord Sumana who was surrounded by the hundred thousand crores of monks,[2] bestowing a great gift and giving each one a pair of robes, he was established in the refuges. That teacher too declared of him, "In the future he will be a Buddha" Accordingly it was said:

V 15 I at that time was a nāga-king of great psychic potency, Atula by name, abounding in an accumulation of skill.

16 Then I, issuing forth with my kinsfolk from the nāga-abode, attended on the Conqueror and his Order with the deva-like instrumental music of nāgas.

17 After I had given the hundred thousand crores one pair of robes each and had refreshed them with food and drink, I went to him for refuge.

18 That Buddha Sumana, leader of the world, also declared of me: "Innumerable eons from now this one will be a Buddha.

19 When he has striven the striving . . . " " . . . we will be face to face with this one."

Eight verses to be expanded as in the Chronicle of the Buddha Koṇḍañña.

20 When I had heard his words too all the more did I incline my mind. I resolutely determined on further practice for fulfilling the ten perfections.

And Mekhala was the name of the city of that Lord Sumana, his father was named Sudatta, his mother was named Sirimā; Saraṇa and Bhāvitatta were the chief disciples. Udena was his (monastic)

[1] buddhadassanupāgamī ti buddhadassanattham upāgami.

[2] Probably referring to those mentioned on text p. 154.

attendant, Soṇā and Upasoṇā[1] were the chief women-disciples; the Tree of Awakening was a Nāga. The physical frame was ninety cubits tall, the extent of the life-span was exactly ninety thousand years. Vaṭaṁsakā[2] was the name of his queen, Anupama the name of his son; he departed mounted on an elephant, Aṅgarāja was his (lay) attendant, he lived in Aṅgārāma. Accordingly it was said:

[159] V 21 Mekhala[3] was the name of the city, Sudatta the name of the warrior-noble, Sirimā the name of the mother of Sumana, the great seer.

22 He lived the houshold life for nine thousand years. The three superb palaces were Canda, Sucanda, Vaṭaṁsa.[4]

23 There were eighty-three thousand beautifully adorned women. His wife was named Vaṭaṁsikā, his son was named Anupama.

24 After he had seen the four signs he departed mounted on an elephant; the Conqueror strove the striving for not less than ten months.

25 Sumana, leader of the world, great hero, on being requested by Brahmā, turned the Wheel in the superbly glorious city[5] of Mekhala.

26 Saraṇa and Bhāvitatta were the chief disciples. Udena was the name of the attendant on Sumana, the great seer.

27 Soṇā and Upasoṇā[6] were the chief women disciples. And that Buddha of boundless fame awakened at the root of a Nāga.

28 Varuṇa and Saraṇa were the chief attendants; Cālā and Upacālā[7] were the chief women attendants.

29 That Buddha, standing ninety cubits in height[8], shone like a golden festooned column over the ten-thousand.

[1] BvAC Sonā Upasonā.
[2] BvAC reads -sakā here; at p. 153 -sikā.
[3] Jā i 34 Khema.
[4] BvAC 153 gives other names; the first is called Sirivaḍḍhana at BvAB.
[5] puravaruttame; Bv puravuttame.
[6] Above, Sonā Upasonā.
[7] Bv Cāḷā Upacāḷā.
[8] Bv, BvAC hatthasamuggato, Be, BvAB hatthamuggato.

30 The (normal) life-span lasted then for ninety thousand years. Living so long he caused many people to cross over.

31 After causing those to cross over who could be caused to cross over and awakening those who could be awakened, the Self-Awakened One, setting like the king of heavenly bodies, attained final nibbāna.

32 Those who were monks whose cankers were destroyed, of great renown, and that unique Buddha who had displayed unrivalled lustre, (all) waned out.

33 And that unrivalled knowledge and those unrivalled treasures have all disappeared. Are not all constructions void?

34 The renowned Buddha Sumana waned out in Aṅgārāma-park. A Conqueror's thūpa to him there was four yojanas high.[1]

[160] 29 Therein *like a golden festooned column* means the beautiful radiance was as though a golden festooned column was ornamented with a diversity of gems.

29 *Shone over the ten-thousand* means even the ten-thousand world-element shone with his lustre. The meaning is: it shone out.

31 *Could be caused to cross over* means could be caused to cross over.[2] The meaning is: all who could be guided out by the Buddha.

31 *King of heavenly bodies* means like the moon.

31 *Setting* means going to (its) setting[3]. Some read "to (its) setting gone".[4]

32 *Unique* means unique[5].

32 *Of great renown:* means great renown, a great reputation, a great retinue.

33 *And that knowledge* means that omniscient knowledge.

33 *Unrivalled* means unrivalled[6], unique.

The rest is quite clear.

Concluded is the Exposition of the Chronicle of the Buddha Sumana

Concluded is the Fourth Buddha-Chronicle

[1] Quoted Thūp 10.
[2] tāraṇīye ti tārayitabbe.
[3] atthamī ti atthaṅgato.
[4] atthaṁ gato.
[5] asādiso ti asadiso (asadiso at Bv).
[6] atulan ti atulyaṁ. The verse, p. 159, and Bv read atuliyaṁ.

VI THE EXPOSITION OF THE CHRONICLE OF THE BUDDHA REVATA

Subsequently to the Lord Sumana and on the disappearance of his Dispensation, men, having gradually dwindled from life-spans of ninety thousand years[1] to life-spans of ten years, gradually increasing again to life-spans of an incalculable, and dwindling again were of life-spans of sixty thousand years.

Then the teacher named Revata arose. When he had fulfilled the ten perfections he was born in Tusita-abode, an abode which was resplendent with[2] countless gems. Deceasing from there he took on relinking in the womb of Vipulā who abounded in charming qualities—her sweet face was a lotus-pond beautified by full-blown blue water-lilies which were her eyes surrounded by a row of bees[3] —the (cynosure of the) eyes of all people. In the city of Sudhaññavatī which had all kinds of wealth and grain she was chief consort in the household of the king named Vipula. He was surrounded by a huge retinue which was brightly adorned with all the adornments, he had a great deal of revenue from his prosperity and riches; he abounded (vipula) in every success. After ten months he (the Bodhisatta) issued forth from his mother's womb like a golden royal ruddy goose from Cittakūṭa mountain.[4] The marvels on his relinking and birth were as those spoken of before.[5]

And his three palaces were named Sudassana, Ratanagghi, Āvela.[6] There were thirty-three thousand women waiting on him with the lady Sudassanā at the head. Surrounded by these as a deva-prince is surrounded by heavenly maidens, he lived the household life for six thousand years experiencing the bliss of the realm.[7] [**161**] After the birth[8] of his offspring, Varuṇa, by the lady Sudassanā, he saw the four signs. Indifferent towards his various fine garments and glorious dwellings, taking off the jewelled earrings he had worn, the glorious bangles, crests and rings, the extremely fragrant perfumes and blossoms he was adorned with,

[1] As in Sumana's time.
[2] samujjotita which BvAB, reading samujjalita, gives as a variant.
[3] ali, see Childers.
[4] Famed as the abode of golden ruddy geese.
[5] See IIA 83ff.
[6] Bv Avela, BvAB Āveḷa.
[7] Cf. text p. 153.
[8] Cf. the following account with text p. 183.

then, like an extremely brilliant sun, like an autumnal moon, like the moon surrounded by a host of stars, as though surrounded by hosts of the (Three and) Thirty, like the thousand-eyed one surrounded by a host of Brahmās and (like) the great Brahmā Hārita[1] surrounded by a great four-factored army, he departed on the Great Departure in a chariot drawn by thoroughbreds.

Unfastening all his ornaments, giving them into the hands of a store-keeper, he cut off his hair and crest with a sharp sword so well whetted it resembled the petal of a blue lotus, stainless though arisen in water, and flung them up into the sky. Sakka, king of devas, receiving them in a golden casket, took them to the abode of the Thirty-Three and built a cetiya consisting of the seven kinds of gems on the summit of Sineru.

And the Great Man, putting on saffron robes given by devas, went forth. One crore of men went forth following his example. Surrounded by these he engaged in striving for seven months. On the full-moon day of Visākha he partook of sweet milk-rice given to him by Sādhudevī, the daughter of a merchant. Spending the day-sojourn in a sāla-grove, towards evening he accepted eight handfuls of grass given to him by Varuṇindhara, a Naked Ascetic, and walking towards a glorious Nāga-tree, and circumambulating the Nāga-Tree of Awakening with his right side towards it, he spread the grass to the extent of fifty-three cubits. Resolutely determining on the four-factored energy[2], routing Māra's forces, and penetrating omniscient knowledge, he uttered the solemn utterance:

"Through many a birth in saṁsāra have I run . . . the destruction of cravings".

Accordingly it was said:

VI 1 After Sumana was the leader named Revata, incomparable, unique, unrivalled, supreme, Conqueror.

It is said that Revata the teacher, after spending seven weeks near the Tree of Awakening itself, having acceded to Brahmā's request that he teach Dhamma, reflecting, "To whom should I first teach Dhamma?" and seeing the crores[3] of monks who had

[1] See D ii 261, DA ii 693. [2] See text p. 83.

[3] The plural koṭiyo refers to the devas and men as well as to the monks, as only one crore of men went forth with him.

gone forth with him and other devas and men endowed with the qualifications, he went through the air, descended in Varuṇā-park and displayed many marvels surrounded by these. Having turned the unsurpassed Wheel of Dhamma, which is deep, subtle, with three sections[1], not to be turned back by anyone, the crore of monks was established in arahantship. There was no limit to the computation of those established in the three fruits of the Ways.

Accordingly it was said:

VI 2 He too, earnestly requested by Brahmā, expounded Dhamma, the defining of the aggregates and elements, non-occurrence in various becomings.[2]

[162] 2 Therein the *defining of the aggregates and elements* means making classifications of the five aggregates and the eighteen elements by means of definitions beginning with name-and-form. The defining of the aggregates and elements is called the discerning of the states of form and formlessness by means of the characteristic marks of recluseship which are essential characteristic marks. Or, "form is like unto a ball of foam"* because it will not stand squeezing and because it is full of holes. "Feeling is like a bubble of water"* because it can be enjoyed for an instant only. "Perception is like a mirage"* because it causes illusion. "The constructions are like the trunk of a plantain-tree"* because it has no hard-wood. "Consciousness is like conjuring"* because it causes deception. In the way beginning thus the defining of the aggregates and elements should be understood as the contemplation of impermanence[3] and so forth.

2 *Non-occurrence in various becomings* means: herein becoming is growth, non-becoming decline; becoming is the eternalist view, non-becoming the annihilationist view; becoming is a small existence[4], non-becoming a great existence; becoming is existence (in the mode) of sensual pleasures[5], non-becoming is existence (in

* Cf. S iii 145, quoted Vism 479, VbhA 32ff.

[1] See Vin i 10.

[2] bhavābhava, on the analogy of phalāphala, various kinds of fruit. But perhaps it should be becoming and non-becoming and appears so to be taken below and in a number of other ctys.

[3] Cf. Vism 290.

[4] bhava, meaning becoming and existence: bhavo ti khuddakabhavo.

[5] I.e. with all five indriya, faculties, beginning with that of sight.

the mode) of form and formlessness[1]. In the way beginning thus the meaning of "various becomings" should be understood. The meaning is that he expounded the existent Dhamma for the non-occurrence of these various becomings. Or becoming means it becomes by means of this. In the three becomings the kamma-process (becoming) precedes the rebirth-process (becoming); the rebirth-process (becoming) is called non-becoming. He teaches Dhamma for the non-occurrence, for getting rid of longing for both.

And under this Buddha Revata there were three penetrations. The first was beyond the way of computation. Accordingly it was said:

VI 3 When he was teaching Dhamma there were three penetrations. Not to be told by computation was the first penetration.

3 Therein *three* means three.[2] A change of gender is made. This was the first penetration.

After a time in the city of Uttara, a supreme (uttara) city, the king was called Arindama, queller of all enemies (sabbārindama). It is said that when he heard that the Lord had arrived in his own city, then, surrounded by three crores of people, he went out to meet the Lord and invited him for the morrow. After arranging a great gift for seven days for the Order of monks with the Buddha at the head, he paid honour by means of lamps extending for three gāvuta, approached the Lord and sat down. Then the Lord taught Dhamma in a variety of ways suitable to his mind.[3] There was there the second penetration by a thousand crores of devas and men. Accordingly it was said:

VI 4 When the sage Revata instructed king Arindama then there was the second penetration by a thousand crores.

This was the second penetration.

[**163**] After a time the teacher Revata, when living near the market-town of Uttara, was sitting down for seven days attaining

[1] Cf. MA iii 223, SA iii 295, UdA 164, CpA 20, etc.
[2] tīṇī ti tayo.
[3] manonukūla.

the attainment of cessation. It is said that the people who inhabited the market-town of Uttara, bringing conjey, rice, solid foods, medicines and beverages and giving a great gift to the Order of monks, inquired of them, "Where, revered sirs, is the Lord?" Thereupon the monks said to them, "The Lord, sirs, is attaining the attainment of cessation." Then, after those seven days, seeing that the Lord had emerged from the attainment of cessation and that, like the autumnal sun he was glowing with his own peerless beauty, they asked what was the advantage in the special qualities of the attainment of cessation. The Lord spoke to them of the advantage in the special qualities of the attainment of cessation. Then he established a hundred crores of devas and men in arahantship. This was the third penetration. Accordingly it was said:

VI 5 Having emerged after seven days from solitary meditation, the bull of men instructed a hundred crores of men and deities in the supreme fruit.

The first assembly in the city of Sudhaññavatī at the first recital of the Great Pātimokkha was of arahants beyond the range of computation who had gone forth by the 'Come, monk' (formula for) going forth. The second assembly, in the city of Mekhala, was of arahants estimated at a hundred thousand crores who had gone forth by the 'Come, monk' (formula for) going forth. But Varuṇa, a chief disciple and follower of the Lord Revata's Dhamma-Wheel, chief of those of wisdom, became ill. Teaching Dhamma, explaining the three marks (of phenomena) to the populace who had arrived to inquire about his illness, and letting a hundred thousand crores of men go forth by the 'Come, monk' (formula for) going forth, causing them to be established in arahantship, he recited the Pātimokkha in a four-factored assembly.[1] This was the third assembly. Accordingly it was said:

VI 6 The great seer Revata had three assemblies of steadfast ones whose cankers were destroyed, stainless, well freed.

7 Those who gathered together at the first were beyond the range of computation. The second gathering was of a hundred thousand crores.

8 One who was without an equal in wisdom, a Wheel-follower of his, was ill then, his life in doubt.

[1] See text p. 126.

9 The third gathering was of a hundred thousand[1] crores of arahants, those sages who approached then to inquire about his illness.

8 Therein *Wheel-follower* means follower of the Wheel of Dhamma.

8 *Life in doubt*[2]: herein doubt as to his life is life in doubt. [**164**] "Is he coming to destruction of life or is he not?" is thus life in doubt.[2] "Is he dying, is he not dying because of the seriousness of the illness?" is life in doubt.[2]

9 *Those sages who approached then:* this means that if (the vowel) is long[3] the reference is to monks[4]; if it is short[5] together with a nasal vowel[6] (supplied, the word muni refers) to Varuṇa.[7]

Then our Bodhisatta, being a brahman named Atideva in the city of Rammavatī, had complete mastery in the obligatory duties of brahmans. On seeing Revata, the fully Self-Awakened One, and hearing his talk on Dhamma, being established in the refuges, and extolling Him of the Ten Powers with a thousand praises, he paid homage to the Lord with an upper robe worth a thousand. That Buddha too declared of him: "A hundred thousand eons and two incalculables from now he will be the Buddha named Gotama." Accordingly it was said:

VI 10 I at that time was a brahman named Atideva. Having approached Revata the Buddha, I went to him for refuge.

11 Having lauded his morality, concentration and incomparable special quality of wisdom[8] according to my ability[9], I gave him (my) outer cloak.

12 That Buddha Revata, leader of the world, also declared

[1] Be sahassa, a thousand.

[2] patto jīvitasaṁsayaṁ . . . jīvitasaṁsayaṁ patto . . . jīvite saṁsayaṁ patto. Different shades of meaning seem to be intended.

[3] I.e. *ī* in munī, sages.

[4] Long at Be, BvACB: ye tadā (Varuṇaṁ) upagatā munī, those sages who approached (Varuṇa) then.

[5] As at Bv.

[6] anussarena saddhiṁ; cf. note to text p. 71 where the word anussāra also occurs; also at text p. 12.

[7] ye tadā muni(ṁ) (=Varuṇaṁ) upagatā, these approached the sage (Varuṇa) then.

[8] paññāguṇam anuttamaṁ; Be reads paññāguṇavaruttamaṁ.

[9] yathāthāmaṁ above; yathā thomaṁ at Bv.

of me: "Innumerable eons from now this one will be a Buddha.

13 When he has striven the striving . . ." ". . . we will be face to face with this one."

Eight verses to be expanded.[1]

14 When I had heard his words all the more did I incline my mind. I resolutely determined on further practice for fulfilling the ten perfections.

15 Then too, remembering that[2] Buddha-thing, I increased it (thinking), "I will obtain that thing that I ardently long for."

10 *I went to him for refuge* means: I went to him for refuge[3]—the genitive case in the sense of an accusative.

11 *Special quality of wisdom* means the splendour of wisdom.

11 *Incomparable* means best. "The incomparable special quality of freedom through wisdom"[4] is also a reading. It is just as clear.

11 *Having lauded* means having lauded,[5] having praised.

11 *According to my ability* means according to my power.

[165] 11 *Outer cloak* means upper robe.

11 *I gave* means I gave[6].

15 *Buddha-thing* means: thing making for Buddha-status. The meaning is a thing that is a perfection.[7]

15 *Remembering* means recollecting.

15 *I increased* means I made grow.

15 *I will obtain* means I will procure.

15 *That thing* means that Buddahood.

15 *That I ardently long for* means: I will obtain that Buddahood that I ardently long for.

And that Buddha Revata's city was named Sudhaññavatī, his father was the warrior-noble named Vipula, his mother was named Vipulā; Varuṇa and Brahmadeva were the chief disciples; Sambhava was the attendant; Bhaddā and Subhaddā were the chief

[1] See III 11–15, 17–19.

[2] Bv taṁ, BvAC maṁ.

[3] saraṇaṁ tass° agacch° ahan ti taṁ saraṇaṁ agañchim ahaṁ.

[4] paññāvimutti is a mark of arahantship.

[5] thomayitvā ti thometvā.

[6] adās° ahan ti adāsim ahaṁ.

[7] Cf. text p. 104, on II 116.

women disciples; the Tree of Awakening was a Nāga; the physical frame was eighty cubits tall; the life-span was sixty thousand years.[1] His chief consort was named Sudassanā, his son was named Varuṇa. He departed in a chariot drawn by thoroughbreds.

The unsurpassed glow of lustre emanating from his body constantly suffused a yojana then whether by day or by night.[2]
That Conqueror, great hero, compassionate toward all beings, resolutely determined, "May all my relics be dispersed."
And in Mahāsāra pleasaunce[3] a yojana from the great city, Revata, honoured by the elect of men, attained final nibbāna.

Accordingly it was said:

VI 16 Sudhaññavatī was the name of the city, Vipula the name of the warrior-noble, Vipulā the name of the mother of Revata, the great seer.

21 Varuṇa and Brahmadeva were the chief disciples; Sambhava was the name of the attendant on Revata, the great seer.

22 Bhaddā and Subhaddā were the chief women disciples. And that Buddha, equal to the unequalled, awakened at the root of a Nāga (tree).

23 Paduma and Kuñjara were the chief attendants; Sirimā and Yasavatī were the chief women attendants.[4]

24 That Buddha, standing eighty cubits in height, illumined all the quarters like a rainbow on high.

25 The unsurpassed garland of lustre emanating from his physical frame suffused a yojana all round whether by day or by night.

[**166**] 26 The (normal) life-span lasted then for sixty thousand years. Living so long he caused many people to cross over.

27 After displaying the power of a Buddha and expounding deathlessness to the world, he waned out without

[1] BvAC reads sixty hundred thousand.

[2] Cf. vi 25 below.

[3] BvAB mahānāgavanuyyāne. Some other readings in this verse are rather uncertain.

[4] This verse is given at BvAB which recognizes that it is sometimes omitted, as at BvAC. But the omission conforms to the general rule regarding the commentarial inclusion of the verse.

grasping (after renewed existence) like a fire on the consumption of the fuel.

28 And that gem-like body and that unique Dhamma have all disappeared. Are not all constructions void?

24 Therein *illumined* means made clear.

24 *In height* means tall.

25 *Garland of lustre* means measure of lustre[1].

27 *Like a fire* means as a fire.

27 *On the consumption of the fuel* means on the consumption of the firing.[2]

28 *And that gem-like body*[3] means: and that Lord's body was the colour of gold. "And that gem-like body[4]" is also a reading, said (thus) through a change of gender. But its meaning is the same.

The rest of the verses are quite clear everywhere.

Concluded is the Exposition of the Chronicle of the Buddha Revata

Concluded is the Fifth Buddha—Chronicle

VII THE EXPOSITION OF THE CHRONICLE OF THE BUDDHA SOBHITA

Subsequently to him[5] and on the disappearance of his Dispensation, the Bodhisatta named Sobhita, having fulfilled the perfections during a hundred thousand eons and four incalculables, was born in Tusita city, remaining (there) for the duration of the life-span. On being requested by devas, deceasing from Tusita city, he took on relinking in the womb of King Sudhamma's queen named Sudhammā in Sudhamma city. After ten months, pure golden like a full moon he issued forth from his mother's womb in Sudhamma

[1] pabhāmālā ti pabhāvelā, referring to the rays or halo.

[2] upādānasaṅkhayā ti indhanasaṅkhayā. Both upādāna (in one of its senses) and indhana mean fuel. To make a distinction, "firing" (or firewood) seems preferable to "combustibles" for indhana. This word occurs also at text pp. 219, 247 and Vism 505, VbhA 110.

[3] So ca kāyo ratananibho, masc.

[4] tañ ca kāyaṁ ratananibhaṁ, neuter.

[5] I.e. Revata.

pleasaunce. The marvels at his relinking and birth were as have been described already.[1] When he had lived the household life for nine thousand years,[2] his son named Sīhakumāra arose in the womb of queen Makhilā, the head of seventy thousand dancing-women and the chief consort.

When he had seen the four signs, filled with an emotional thrill[3] he went forth in the palace itself and having there developed concentration on mindfulness of in-breathing and out-breathing and acquired the four meditations, for seven days he engaged in striving there. Then, after he had partaken of the extremely sweet milk-rice given to him by the great queen Makhilā, he formed the intention for the Departure, thinking, "While the great populace is looking on may this palace, adorned and prepared, [**167**] go through the air and descend on the earth with the Tree of Awakening in the centre, and may these women, while I am seated at the root of the Tree of Awakening, depart from the palace entirely of their own accord." With the forming of his intention King Sudhamma's abode, flying up from there, soared into the sky resembling black collyrium.

The terrace of the palace, adorned with a combination of fragrant blossoms and wreaths and adorning the whole vault of the heavens like multitudes of beautiful showers of brilliant gold, shining like the sun and like the autumnal moon, a net of tinkling bells hanging downward whose sound was like the five-fold instrumental music stirred by the wind (or) played by highly skilled people, was pleasant and delightful and charming. When from afar beings, standing in the houses, courtyards or at cross-roads, were listening and giving ear to the sweet sound, (the palace) as though desiring to be not too low and not too high for the people, and not too far from the tops of the glorious trees, as though pulling out people's eyes by the colour of the branches of the trees, resplendent with a mass of shining gems, and as though proclaiming the majesty of merit, went up into the vault of the heavens.[4] The dancing-women sang[5] with sweet voices and played[6] the five-fold instrumental music. And it is said that, like the earth so very beautiful to see,

[1] IIA 83ff.
[2] Reading above is ten thousand, but see text p. 170.
[3] sañjātasaṁvega.
[4] BvAB gaganatalaṁ, BvAC gaganaṁ.
[5] BvAC uggāyiṁsu, BvAB upagāyiṁsu.
[6] BvAC vipaliṁsu, BvAB vilapiṁsu, with v. l. uggāyiṁsu.

his four-factored army too went through the vault of the heavens surrounding the palace like a glorious army of deities, splendid in the finery of their raiment and fragrant blossoms, ablaze with the light of divers colours and the finery of the adornments.

Thereupon, the palace, going along, descended and rested on the ground with, in the centre, the Nāga-Tree, eighty cubits tall, its trunk straight, broad, round, and adorned with blossoms, sprouts and buds. And of their own accord those dancing-women descended from the palace and went away.

And the Great Man Sobhita, resplendent (sobhita) with countless special qualities, his retinue consisting of the great populace, obtained the three knowledges during the three watches of that very night. Māra's forces[1] came to him as though coming simply through the power of natural law[2]. But the palace remained just there. And Sobhita, having attained Self-Awakening and uttered the solemn utterances[3], spent seven weeks near the Tree of Awakening itself. When he had agreed to Brahmā's entreaty for Dhamma and had thought, "To whom should I first teach Dhamma?" he looked round with the Buddha-eye and saw his own two younger step-brothers, Prince Asama and Prince Sunetta. Thinking, "These two princes are endowed with the qualifications. They are capable of piercing the deep, subtle Dhamma. Come, I will teach Dhamma first to them", he went through the air and descended in Suddhamma pleasaunce. And he had the two princes summoned by the guardian of the pleasaunce and, surrounded by these and their retinues, he turned the Wheel of Dhamma in the midst of the great populace. Accordingly it was said:

VII 1 After Revata was the leader named Sobhita, concentrated, tranquil in mind, without an equal, matchless.

[168] 2 When in his own house that Conqueror had turned away[4] his mind, on attaining full Awakening he turned the Wheel of Dhamma.

3 At the teaching of Dhamma there was one assembly in the spaces as far as (the region) upwards of Avīci (from

[1] BvAC balaṁ, BvAB Mārabalaṁ.

[2] dhammatābalena. Usually dhammatā is 'regulation', 'as it ought to be'. Perhaps all that is meant is that Buddhas were assailed by Māra at this stage in their careers, thus a "regulation" event.

[3] BvAB adds anekajāti, and so on.

[4] Bv, Be vinivattayi, BvAC viniṭṭayi.

below) and downwards from the height of becoming (from above).

4 The Self-Awakened One turned the Wheel of Dhamma in that assembly. That was the first assembly, not to be told by computation.

2 Therein *in his own house* means in precisely his own abode. The meaning is: on the terrace inside the palace itself.

2 *Turned away*[1] *his mind* means he made his thoughts revolve. Remaining in his own house for the inside of a week, having turned away his thoughts from the state of an ordinary person, he attained Buddhahood.

3 *From the height of becoming* means from the abode of the Akaniṭṭha (devas).

3 *From below* means from below.[2]

4 *In that assembly* means in the midst of that assembly.

4 *Not to be told by computation* means beyond the range of computation.

4 *First penetration* means the first penetration of Dhamma.

4 *Was:* the meaning is that the assembly was not to be told by computation. "They penetrated at the first itself" is also a reading. The meaning is that those people who could not be told by computation penetrated at his first teaching of Dhamma.

After a time, having performed the Marvel of the Double at the root of a variegated trumpet-flower (tree)[3] at the gateway to Sudassana city, he sat down on the ornamental stone at the root of the Coral Tree in the abode of the Thirty-Three, in an abode consisting of glowing gold and gems, and taught Abhidhamma. At the conclusion of the teaching there was a penetration of Dhamma by ninety thousand crores. This was the second penetration. Accordingly it was said:

VII 5 Subsequently, as he was teaching in a gathering of men and deities, there was the second penetration by ninety thousand crores.

After a time there was a prince named Jayasena in Sudassana

[1] Here BvAC reads vinivaṭṭayi.

[2] heṭṭhā ti heṭṭhato.

[3] cittapāṭalī.

city. Having had a vihāra built a yojana in extent and having planted the park with an array of glorious trees; with the *asoka*,[1] the horse-ear,[2] the *champak*[3], the iron-wood[4], the *punnāga*[5], the *vakula*[6], the *cūta*[7], the jak-fruit[8], the *asana*[9], the *sāla*[10], the *kakudha*[11] the fragrant mango[12], the oleander[13] and so forth, he dedicated it to the Order of monks with the Buddha at the head. When the Lord had given the benediction for the gift and had praised the offering he taught Dhamma. There was then a penetration of Dhamma by an assemblage of a thousand crores of beings. This was the third penetration. Accordingly it was said:

VII 6 And again, a warrior-noble, Prince Jayasena, having planted a park, dedicated it to the Buddha then.
[169] 7 Lauding his offering the One with Vision taught Dhamma. Then was the third penetration by a thousand crores.

Again, the king named Uggata, having had a vihāra named Surinda[14] built in Sunandavatī[14] city, gave it to the Order of monks with the Buddha at the head. At that giving there was an assembly of a hundred crores of arahants who had gone forth by the 'Come, monk' (formula for) going forth. In the midst of these the Lord Sobhita recited the Pātimokkha. This was the first assembly.

Again, having had a vihāra built in a glorious park named Dhammagaṇa Park in Mekhala city, giving it to the Order of monks with the Buddha at the head, he gave the gift together with all the requisites. Then, in that gathering he recited the Pātimokkha in an assembly of ninety crores of arahants who had gone

[1] Jonesia Asoka.
[2] assakaṇṇa, Vatica Robusta. CPD probably not right, Shorea robusta, which is the sāla. But sāla could be Shorea [Vatica] robusta.
[3] campaka, Michelia champaka.
[4] nāga.
[5] Callophyllum inophyllum, Alexandrian or Alexandra laurel; a large tree with beautiful white fragrant blossoms.
[6] Mimusops elengi.
[7] Mango-tree, Mangifera Indica, according to M-W.
[8] panasa, Artocarpus integrifolia.
[9] Pentaptera (Terminalia) tomentosa.
[10] Shorea robusta.
[11] Terminalia Arjuna. BvAB reads kunda, jasmine.
[12] sahakāra.
[13] karavīra, Nerium odorum.
[14] BvAB Sunanda.

forth by the 'Come, monk' (formula for) going forth. This was the second assembly.

And when the Lord had spent the rains in a city of him of a thousand eyes[1] he descended for the Invitation surrounded by glorious devas[2]. He then invited in a four-factored assembly[3] together with eighty crores of arahants. This was the third assembly. Accordingly it was said:

VII 8 The great seer Sobhita had three assemblies of steadfast ones whose cankers were destroyed, stainless, tranquil in mind.

9 The king named Uggata gave a gift to the supreme among men. At that giving a hundred crores of arahants gathered together.

10 And again, a host of townspeople gave a gift to the supreme among men. Then was the second gathering of ninety crores.

11 When the Conqueror descended after staying in the deva-world, then was the third gathering of eighty crores.

It is said that our Bodhisatta was then a eminent[4] brahman named Sujāta in Rammavatī city. Having heard the Lord Sobhita's teaching of Dhamma and being established in the refuges he gave a great gift to the Order of monks with the Buddha at the head. He too declared of him, "In the future he will be the Buddha named Gotama." Accordingly it was said:

VII 12 I at that time was a brahman named Sujāta[5]. Then I refreshed the Buddha and the disciples with food and drink.

13 That Buddha Sobhita, leader of the world, also declared of me, "Innumerable eons from now this one will be a Buddha.

[170] 14 When he has striven the striving . . ." " . . . we will be face to face with this one."

[1] dasasatanayanapura must be a deva-city over which Sakka (him of a thousand eyes) held sway.

[2] sura.

[3] See text pp. 126, 163.

[4] BvAC uggata, BvAB ubhata, and perhaps meaning "pure" in descent from both parental sides, as his name, Sujāta, well or purely born, implies. Cf. udita at text p. 190.

[5] Ajita at Jā i 35.

15 When I had heard his words, exultant, stirred in mind,
I made strenuous endeavour for attaining that very aim.

15 Therein *for attaining that very aim* means that his aim was the attaining of Buddhahood. When he had heard the words of Buddha Sobhita, "In the future he will be the Buddha named Gotama", thinking "The words of Buddhas are not untrue", the attaining of Buddhahood was the aim.

15 *Strenuous* means keen, terrible.

15 *Endeavour* means energy.

15 *I made* means I made[1].

And that Lord Sobhita's city was named Sudhamma, his father was the king named Sudhamma, and his mother was named Sudhammā. Asama and Sunetta were the chief disciples; the attendant was named Anoma; Nakulā and Sujātā were the chief women disciples. The Tree of Awakening was a Nāga. The physical frame was fifty-eight cubits in height; the length of the life-span was ninety thousand years. His chief queen was named Makhilā, the son was named Sīhakumāra; there were seventy thousand dancing-women. He lived the household life for nine thousand years. He departed by palace. The king named Jayasena was the attendant. He lived, it is said, in Sotārāma (monastery). Accordingly it was said:

VII 16 Sudhamma was the name of the city, Sudhamma the name of the warrior-noble, Sudhammā the name of the mother of Sobhita, the great seer.

21 Asama and Sunetta were the chief disciples; Anoma was the name of the attendant on Sobhita, the great seer.

22 Nakulā and Sujātā were the chief women disciples. And that Buddha, awakening, awakened at the root of a Nāga (tree).

24 The great sage was fifty-eight ratanas in height. He illumined all the quarters like him of a hundred rays on high.

25 Just as a forest in full bloom is perfumed with divers scents, so his words were perfumed with the scent of moral habit.

26 And just as the ocean cannot satiate one who is looking

[1] akās'ahan ti akāsim ahaṁ.

at it, so his words could not satiate one who was hearing them.

[171] 27 The (normal) life-span lasted then for ninety thousand years. Living so long he caused many people to cross over.

28 After giving exhortation and instruction to the rest of the people, burning out like fire, he with the disciples waned out.

29 That Buddha, equal to the unequalled, and those disciples who had attained powers[1] have all disappeared. Are not all constructions void?

24 Therein *like him of a hundred rays* means like the sun. The meaning is that he illumined all the quarters[2].

25 *Forest* means a great wood.

25 *Perfumed* means smelling, scented.

26 *Cannot satiate* not making satiation, not producing satiation.

27 *Then* means at that time; the meaning is: for such a time.

27 *He caused to cross over* means he caused to cross over.[3]

28 *Exhortation* means one's own words are called exhortation.[4]

28 *Instruction* means speech repeated is called instruction.[5]

28 *To the rest of the people* means to the remaining people[6] who had not attained to penetration of the truths—the locative case in the sense of a genitive.

28 *Burning out like fire* means "burning out like a fire"[7] or this itself is the reading. The meaning is that the Lord attained final nibbāna on the destruction of the fuel[8] (for renewed existence).

The rest of the verses are quite clear everywhere.

Concluded is the Exposition of the Chronicle of the Buddha Sobhita

Concluded is the Sixth Buddha-Chronicle

[1] Explanation at text p. 202. [2] Cf. text p. 36.

[3] tāresī ti tārayi. [4] Cf. text p. 193, on xi 7.

[5] punappuna vacanam anusiṭṭhi nāma. Cf. NdA i 114 anusiṭṭhin ti punappunaṁ sallakkhāpanavacanaṁ.

[6] sesake jane.

[7] hutāsano va tāpetvā ti aggi viya tappetvā. Hutāsana is "oblation-eater", the altar of sacrifice. Cf. Vism 171 where this word is given as an example of the names for fire.

[8] Fuel and grasping are both upādāna, cf. text p. 166.

VIII THE EXPOSITION OF THE CHRONICLE OF THE BUDDHA ANOMADASSIN

And when the Buddha Sobhita had attained final nibbāna, subsequently to him there was one incalculable devoid of Buddhas.[1] But when that incalculable had passed three Buddhas came into being in one and the same eon[2], Anomadassin, Paduma, Nārada. Of these, Anomadassin[3], having fulfilled the perfections during sixteen incalculables and a hundred-thousand eons, was reborn in Tusita city. Requested by devas, deceasing from there, he took on relinking in the womb of Yasodharā, the charming and high-minded chief consort in the household of King Yasavā in the capital city named Candavatī[4]. It is said that while Prince Anomadassin was in Queen Yasodharā's womb her light remained suffusing the region for a distance of eighty cubits owing to the power of her merit. **[172]** And it could not be dimmed by the lustre of the moon or sun. After ten months she gave birth to the Bodhisatta in Sunanda[5] pleasaunce. The marvels were as in the manner spoken of already.[6]

On the name-taking day while they were choosing his name, because the seven (kinds of) jewels had fallen from the sky at his birth they therefore gave him the name of Anomadassin owing to the appearance (dassin) of the flawless (anoma) jewels. Growing up in due course he lived the household life for ten thousand years, as though amusing himself with deva-like kind of sense-pleasures. They say his three palaces were Siri, Upasiri, Sirivaḍḍha.[7] Twenty-three thousand women were in attendance on him with Queen Sirimā at the head. When Queen Sirimā had given birth to a son named Upavāna, and he (the Bodhisatta) had seen the four signs, having departed on the Great Departure by palanquin, he went forth. Three crores of people went forth following his example. Surrounded by these the Great Man engaged in striving for ten months.

Then on the full-moon day of Visākha when he had walked for

[1] Buddhapāda. M-W says pāda is "sometimes added in token of respect to proper names or titles of address".

[2] A Vara-kappa, see text p. 191; so called at Jkm 13.

[3] Cf. AA i 149, DhA i 105.

[4] DhA i 105 Bandhumatī, with v. ll. Candavatī, Candavārī, and Bhandavatī.

[5] BvAB Sumanda, with v. l. Sunanda.

[6] IIA 83ff.

[7] Bv Vaḍḍha.

alms in the brahman village of Anupama and had partaken of sweet milk-rice given to him by the daughter of the merchant Anupama, he spent the day-sojourn in a sāla-grove. Accepting eight handfuls of grass given to him by Anoma, a Naked Ascetic, he circumambulated an Ajjuna[1] Tree of Awakening and spread a grass-spreading thirty-eight cubits in extent. Resolutely determining on the four-factored energy,[2] sitting cross-legged he shattered Māra's forces together with Māra. Causing the three knowledges to arise during the three watches (of the night), he uttered the solemn utterance:

"Through many a birth . . . the destruction of cravings".

Accordingly it was said:

VIII 1 After Sobhita was Anomadassin, the Self-Awakened One, supreme among men, of boundless fame, incandescent, difficult to overcome.

2 He, having cut through all bonds, having shattered the three becomings, taught for devas and mankind the Way going to the no-turn-back.

3 As the ocean he was imperturbable, as a mountain hard to attack, as the sky unending, as a king of sāla trees he was full of bloom.

4 Living things were gladdened by the mere sight of that Buddha. Those who heard his voice as he was speaking attained deathlessness.

1 Therein *Anomadassin* means peerless to behold or boundless to behold.

1 *Boundless fame* means boundless entourage or boundless renown.

1 *Incandescent* means possessed of the incandescence of moral habit, concentration, wisdom.

1 *Difficult to overcome* means overwhelmed by difficulty; the meaning is he was not able to be overcome by a deva or by Māra or by anyone.

[173] 2 *He, having cut through all bonds* means having cut off all the ten fetters.

[1] Pentaptera (Terminalia) Arjuna.

[2] Text p. 83.

2 *Having shattered the three becomings:* the meaning is having shattered the kamma leading to the three becomings by means of knowledge making for the destruction of kamma; having made inexistent.

2 *The Way going to the no-turn-back* means that the no-turn-back is said to be nibbāna, which has become the opponent of turning back, of turning forward. "By this one goes to that no-turn-back" means going to the no-turn-back; the meaning being that *he taught* the eightfold *Way* going to that no-turn-back. "He showed"[1] is also a reading; it is the very meaning.

2 *For devas and mankind* means for devas and men[2]. The sense of the genitive is to be understood as the accusative case.

3 *Imperturbable* means as it was not possible to perturb, to shake (him) he could not be perturbed. Just as the sea, eighty-four thousand yojanas deep and the abode of countless thousands of creatures a yojana (in length), cannot be perturbed[3], thus he cannot be perturbed is the meaning.

3 *As the sky unending*[4] means as there is no end to the sky and therefore it is unending, immeasurable, having no beyond[5], even so was the Lord unending too in regard to the special qualities of Buddhas, immeasurable, having no beyond.[5]

3 *He* means he, the Lord.

3 *As a king of sāla trees he was full of bloom* means he shone like a king of sāla trees when it is full of bloom because his physical frame was adorned with all the Marks and the full (eighty) minor characteristics.

4 *By the mere sight of that Buddha:* the meaning is even by the seeing of that Buddha. Grammarians use the genitive case itself for these (two words)[6].

4 *Gladdened* means utterly gladdened, pleased.

4 *As he was speaking* means (of him) as he was speaking[7]—the accusative case having the sense of a genitive.

[1] dassesi for desesi.

[2] devamānuse ti devamanussānaṁ.

[3] But see Miln 260 for opposite view. Our commentator may have in mind the depths of the ocean where "all is still", Sn 920, but more probably thinks of the ocean as indifferent to whatever is thrown into it. Cf. text p. 141.

[4] Cf. Miln 278.

[5] apāra, endless, or, more usually, what is not beyond; probably meaning here that the Buddha had arrived at the not-beyond.

[6] tassa Buddhassa in the explanation for taṁ Buddhaṁ.

[7] vyāharantan ti vyāharantassa.

4 *Deathlessness* means nibbāna.

4 *Attained* means they arrived at.

4 *Those*: the meaning is that those who heard his voice at a teaching of Dhamma attained deathlessness.

And when the Lord had spent seven weeks at the root of the Tree of Awakening, on being requested by Brahmā for a teaching of Dhamma, surveying the world with the eye of a Buddha he saw the people, three crores in number, who were possessed of the qualifications and had gone forth together with himself. Reflecting "Now, where are these living at present?" he saw that they were staying in Subhavatī city in the Sudassana pleasaunce. Surrounded by these, he turned the Wheel of Dhamma in the midst of a company of devas and men. The first penetration by hundreds of crores was there. Accordingly it was said:

VIII 5 Penetration of his Dhamma was successful and prosperous[1] then. At the first teaching of Dhamma hundreds of crores penetrated.

5 Therein *prosperous* means because many people attained benefit.

5 *Hundreds of crores* means hundreds of crores[2]. "Hundreds of crores"[3] is also a reading. The meaning is crores of a hundred.[4]

[174] At a later time when he had performed the Marvel of the Double at the root of an asana tree[5] at the gateway of Osadhī city, sitting on the ornamental stone in the abode of the Thirty-Three, an abode it was difficult for the enemies of the devas to overpower[6], he caused the rain of Abhidhamma to rain down for three months. Then eighty crores of devas penetrated. Accordingly it was said:

VIII 6 In the penetration following on that, while (the Buddha) was raining the showers of Dhamma, at the second teaching of Dhamma eighty crores penetrated.

6 Therein *was raining* means while the Buddha's great raincloud[7] was raining.

[1] iddho phīto, often said of a rich and opulent man or city. Here, not in a worldly sense if course.

[2] koṭisatānī ti koṭīnaṁ satāni. [3] koṭisatayo. [4] satakoṭiyo.

[5] Pentaptera tomentosa. BvAB gives v. l. amba-.

[6] surāripurābhibhavane, noticed as a v. l. at BvAB.

[7] Buddhamahāmegha; cf. dhammamegha at Miln 346.

6 *Showers of Dhamma* means showers of the rains of a talk on Dhamma.

At a later time seventy-eight crores penetrated at a detailed exposition of a question on the Maṅgala (sutta).[1] That was the third penetration. Accordingly it was said:

VIII 7 Following on that, while he was raining (the Dhamma) and refreshing (them), there was the third penetration of seventy-eight crores of living things.

7 Therein *while he was raining* means while the shower of the water[2] of the talk on Dhamma was raining.

7 (*Refreshing them*) means refreshing (them) by means of the nectar of Dhamma. The meaning is: while the Lord was doing what was refreshing.

The Lord Anomadassin had three assemblies of disciples. There in the city of Soreyya[3] when he was teaching Dhamma to king Isidatta and had pleased him, he recited the Pātimokkha in the midst of eight hundred thousand arahants who had gone forth by the 'Come, monk' (formula for) going forth. This was the first assembly. In the city of Rādhavatī when he was teaching Dhamma to King Madhurindhara, he recited the Pātimokkha in the midst of seven hundred thousand monks who had gone forth by the 'Come, monk' (formula for) going forth. This was the second assembly. Again in the same city of Soreyya the Lord recited the Pātimokkha in the midst of six hundred thousand arahants who, together with the king of Soreyya, had gone forth by the 'Come, monk' (formula for) going forth. This was the third assembly. Accordingly it was said:

VIII 8 And this great seer also had three assemblies of those who had attained power in the super-knowings and were blossoming through freedom.

9 There was an assembly of eight hundred thousand then of steadfast ones who had got rid of pride and confusion, were tranquil in mind.

[1] Maṅgalapañhaniddesa. Cf. text p. 136.

[2] saliladhāra as at Miln 117.

[3] Mentioned also at text p. 249. It was on the direct route between Verañjā and Payāgatittha, Vin iii 111. There was also a caravan route between Soreyya and Takkasilā, DhA i 325ff. It was thus an important place of considerable antiquity.

10 The second gathering was of seven hundred thousand of steadfast ones who were without taints, stainless, calm.
11 The third gathering was of six hundred thousand of those who had attained power in the super-knowings, were waning out, were "burners-up".

[175] 8 Therein *and this great also* means this great seer[1] Anomadassin. "This supreme among men also"[2] is also a reading. The meaning is: this supreme among men also.[3] The rule[4] is to be understood from grammar.[5]

8 *Had attained power in the super-knowings* means had attained power in the super-knowings.[6] The meaning is: had attained stability in the super-knowings through mastery of the practice by means of a peaceful state for quick intuition.

8 *Blossoming* means had attained exceeding prosperity by all being in full bloom.

8 *Through freedom* means through the freedom of[7] the fruit of arahantship.

10 *Without taints* (anaṅgana): herein this word taint (aṅgana) is at some (passages) to be seen among the defilements. As it was said[8]: "Therein what are the three taints? Attachment is a taint, hatred is a taint, confusion is a taint"* and "Your reverences, this, that is to say 'taint' is a synonym for being occupied with evil, unskilled wishes"†. In some passages it is stain (mala). As it was said, "He exerts himself for getting rid of that dust or taint"‡. In some places or districts it is an open space round a cetiya (cetiyaṅgana), an open space round a Tree of Awakening (bodhiyaṅgana), a royal courtyard (rājaṅgana). But here it should be understood as among the defilements, therefore the meaning is "without defilements".

10 *Stainless* is simply a synonym for that.

* Vbh 368.
† M i 27.
‡ Ibid. 100.

[1] BvAC omits.
[2] tassā pi dipaduttamo.
[3] tassā pi dipaduttamassa.
[4] lakkhaṇa as at text pp. 89, 114, 238.
[5] saddasattha, as at text p. 114, 238.
[6] abhiññābalapattānan ti abhiññānaṁ balappattānaṁ.
[7] Or, due to. Cf. below p. 178, MA v 59.
[8] For the following cf. MA i 139.

11 *Of those who were "burners-up"* means: there is for those who are burners-up a burning-up known as the ariyan Way making for the destruction of the defilements. The meaning is: of those burners-up whose cankers were destroyed.

Our Bodhisatta was then a very powerful yakkha-general of great psychic potency, of great majesty, ruler over countless hundreds and thousands of crores of yakkhas. Having heard that a Buddha had arisen in the world, coming along and creating a very lovely pavilion like the orb of the moon and consisting of the seven (kinds of) gems, extremely lovely to behold, for seven days he gave a great gift there to the Order with the Buddha at the head. Then, at that time when the Lord was giving him the benediction for the meal[1] he declared: "In the future when a hundred thousand eons and one incalculable have passed[2] he will be the Buddha named Gotama". Accordingly it was said:

VIII 12 I at that time was a yakkha of great psychic potency, a chief with highest power over countless crores of yakkhas.

13 Then, having approached that glorious Buddha, the great seer, I refreshed the leader of the world and the Order with food and drink.

14 That sage, of purified sight, also declared of me then: "Innumerable eons from now this one will be a Buddha.

15 When he has striven the striving . . ." ". . . we will be face to face with this one".

[176] 16 When I had heard his words, exultant, stirred in mind, I resolutely determined on further practice for fulfilling the ten perfections.

16 Therein *I resolutely determined on further practice* means: even all the more did I make (my) endeavour firmer for fulfilling the perfections.

And the city of that Lord Anomadassin was named Candavatī[3]; his father, the king was named Yasavant, his mother was named Yasodharā. Nisabha[4] and Anoma were the two[5] chief disciples;

[1] BvAC bhutta, BvAB bhatta. [2] BvAC atīte, BvAB atikkante.

[3] See text p. 171.

[4] AA i 149 Visabhatthera, with v. l. Nissa-; but at AA i 152f. called Nisabhatthera.

[5] BvAC omits.

the attendant was named Varuṇa; Sundarī[1] and Sumanā were the two[2] chief women disciples. The Tree of Awakening was an Ajjuna. The physical frame was fifty-eight cubits in height. The life-span was a hundred thousand years. The chief consort was named Sirimā; the son was named Upavāraṇa[3]. He lived the household life for ten thousand years. He departed by means of a palanquin—and going by means of a palanquin is to be understood exactly as in the method spoken of in the Exposition of the Chronicle of the Buddha Sobhita for 'going by palace'. The attendant was the king named Dhammaka. It is said that the Lord stayed in Dhammārāma. Accordingly it was said:

VIII 17 Candavatī was the name of the city, Yasavā the name of the warrior-noble, Yasodharā the name of the mother of Anomadassin, the teacher.

22 Nisabha and Anoma were the chief disciples. Varuṇa was the name of the attendant on Anomadassin, the teacher.

23 Sundarī and Sumanā were the chief women disciples. That Lord's Tree of Awakening is said to be the Ajjuna.

25 The great sage was fifty-eight ratanas tall. His lustre streamed forth like him of the hundred rays on high.

26 The (normal) life-span lasted then for a hundred thousand years. Living so long he caused many people to cross over.

27 The words (of the Buddha) blossomed fully by means of arahants, steadfast ones without attachment, stainless; and the Dispensation of the Conqueror shone.

28 But that teacher of boundless fame, those unrivalled pairs have all disappeared. Are not all constructions void?

25 Therein *lustre streamed forth* means lustre issued forth from his physical frame. And the lustre of his physical frame all the time remained suffusing the district for a distance of twelve yojanas[4].

28 *Those pairs* means the pairs, the couples[5] that are the pairs of chief disciples and so forth.

[1] AA i 149, DhA i 105 Sundarā.
[2] BvAC omits.
[3] BvAB Upavāna, as at text p. 172.
[4] AA i 149, DhA i 106.
[5] BvAC yugalakāni, BvAB yugalāni.

[177] 28 *Have all disappeared:* the meaning is: all that have been spoken of have entered the mouth of impermanence[1]. "Are not constructions merely void?"[2] is also a reading. The meaning of this is: are not all constructions merely void, vain[3]? The syllable *ma* is a syllable for liaison between the words (sa and antarahitaṁ)[4]. The rest of the verses are quite clear in every way.

And in the presence of the Lord Anomadassin these two chief disciples made the aspiration for becoming the chief disciples Sāriputta and Moggallāna.[5] And the story of these Elders should really be told here, but I have not undertaken it for fear lest the book became too long.[6]

Concluded is the Exposition of the Chronicle of the Buddha Anomadassin

Concluded is the Seventh Buddha-Chronicle

IX THE EXPOSITION OF THE CHRONICLE OF THE BUDDHA PADUMA

And subsequently to the Lord Anomadassin when men's life-spans had dwindled gradually from a hundred thousand years to a life-span of ten years, increasing again they were of a hundred thousand years. Then the teacher named Paduma (Lotus) arose in the world. When he had fulfilled the perfections he was reborn in Tusita-abode.[7] Deceasing from there, he took on relinking in the city of Campā[8] in the household of the king named Asama in the womb of the chief consort named Asamā (Unequalled), unequalled in beauty and so forth. After ten months he issued forth from his mother's womb in Campaka pleasaunce. As he was born a rain of

[1] aniccamukha, not in PED or CPD. In view of the verb 'entered' I have taken mukha in its sense of mouth or opening.

[2] rittakam eva saṅkhārā, where the grammar is faulty.

[3] rittakā tucchakā. I do not know what is the exact force here of the suffix *ka*.

[4] sa-m-antarahitaṁ. I do not know why this is mentioned now as the word has appeared already.

[5] See AA i 152ff., DhA i 106ff.

[6] mayā ganthavitthārabhayena na uddhaṭan ti.

[7] BvAC 177 bhavane, BvAB pure, city.

[8] BvAB, Jkm 13 Campaka.

lotuses fell from the sky over the whole of sea-girt Jambudīpa. So on his name-taking day soothsayers and relations, choosing the name, gave him the very name of Prince Great Lotus.

He lived the household life for ten thousand years. The names of his three palaces were Uttara, Vasuttara, Yasuttara.[1] Thirty thousand women were in attendance on him with the lady Uttarā at the head. Then when Prince Ramma had been born to the chief queen Uttarā the Great Being, after seeing the four signs, departed on the Great Departure by a chariot drawn by thoroughbreds. On his going forth a crore of men went forth following his example. Surrounded by these for eight months he engaged in striving.

On the full-moon day of Visākha he partook of sweet milk-rice given to him by Dhaññavatī, the daughter of the merchant Sudhañña in Dhaññavatī city. Spending the day-sojourn in a fragrant-mango-grove[2], towards evening he accepted eight handfuls of grass given to him by Titthaka, a Naked Ascetic, and approaching a great Soṇa Tree of Awakening he laid down a grass spreading thirty-eight cubits in extent. Seated cross-legged, resolutely determining on the four-factored energy,[3] **[178]** routing Māra's forces, and realizing the three knowledges during the three watches (of the night) he uttered the solemn utterance: "Through many a birth . . ." When he had spent seven weeks near the Tree of Awakening itself, he consented to Brahmā's request for the teaching of Dhamma. Examining individuals by divisions[4] he saw the monks, numbering a crore, who had gone forth together with himself. In that very moment, descending from an aery path in Dhanañjaya pleasaunce near the city of Dhaññavatī, surrounded by these he turned the Wheel of Dhamma in their midst. There was then a penetration by a hundred crores. Accordingly it was said:

IX 1 After Anomadassin was the Self-Awakened One named Paduma, supreme among men, without an equal, matchless.

2 His moral habit was without equal and his concentration unending, his glorious knowledge incalculable and his freedom incomparable.

[1] Bv ix. 17 Nandā Suyasā Uttarā; Be Nandā Vasubhā Yasuttarā; BvAB Nanduttara Vasuttara Yasuttara.

[2] BvAC sahakāravane, BvAB mahāsālavane (great-sāla-grove) with v. l. with BvAC's reading. Sahakāra also at KhA 53.

[3] See text p. 83.

[4] bhājanabhūte.

3 When he of unrivalled incandescence was turning the Wheel of Dhamma there were three penetrations washing away the great gloom.

2 Therein *moral habit was without equal* means that, compared with the moral habit of others,[1] it was unique, supreme, best.

2 *And concentration (was) unending* means: and (his) concentration was immeasurable. Its unending nature should be seen among the Marvels of Unveiling the World and of the Double and so forth.

2 *Glorious knowledge* means glorious omniscient knowledge, or the knowledges that are not shared (by others).

2 *And (his) freedom* means: and the Lord's freedom due to the fruit of arahantship.[2]

2 *Incomparable* means without comparison.

3 *Of unrivalled incandescence* means of unrivalled incandescence of knowledge. "Incandescence (was) unrivalled"[3] is also a reading. "He had three penetrations" means that by this further word[4] a connection is to be understood.

3 *Washing away the great gloom* means dispelling great confusion.

At a later time the Lord Paduma, having let his own younger brothers, Prince Sāla and Prince Upasāla, go forth with their retinues in a gathering of relations and was teaching them Dhamma, he caused ninety crores to drink of the nectar of Dhamma. And when he taught Dhamma to the Elder Ramma then was the third penetration by eighty crores. Accordingly it was said:

IX 4 At the first penetration the Awakened One awakened a hundred crores; at the second penetration the wise one awakened ninety crores.

5 And when the Buddha Paduma exhorted his own son there was then the third penetration by eighty crores.

[1] aññasīlena, perhaps "other moral habit."

[2] See text p. 175.

[3] atulatejā.

[4] tassa repeated. So the verse would read: tassā pi atulatejassa dhammacakkappavattane tassa tayo abhisamayā, instead of: tassā pi . . . abhisamayā tayo. The connection would be between his incandescence and the number of penetrations taking place under him.

[179] And when the king named Bhāvitatta[1] who was well self-developed went forth by the 'Come, monk' (formula for) going forth in the presence of the Buddha Paduma—the Buddha called after the lotus—the Lord recited the Pātimokkha in that assembly surrounded by a hundred thousand crores. And this was the first assembly.

At a later time the Great Paduma, bull of sages, the bull with an even gait, went to spend the rains near the city of Usabhavatī.[2] The people who lived in the city approached the Lord, anxious to see him. The Lord taught them Dhamma. And many people there, pure with minds of faith, went forth. Then Him of the ten Powers invited at a purified "Invitation" with those and with another three hundred thousand monks. This was the second assembly.

But those who did not go forth there, having heard of the advantages of the kaṭhina robe-material, on the first day of the lunar fortnight[3] gave kaṭhina robe-material for five months, a bestowing having five advantages.[4] Then the monks, having requested that General under Dhamma who was a chief disciple, the Elder Sāla, of broad mind[5], for the formal spreading out of the kaṭhina robe-material, they gave kaṭhina robe-material to him. While the monks were making up the Elder's kaṭhina robe-material there were companions at the sewing. And Paduma, the Fully Self-Awakened One, gave threads strung through the eye of a needle. And when the robe was finished the Lord set forth on tour with the three hundred thousand monks. And at a later time the Buddha-lion, like a lion among men, a heroic lion-goer[6], arrived for the rains-residence in an extremely delightful, remote and lovely forest favourable for earnest endeavour. It was like Gosiṅga Sāla-wood, a thicket where the branches bent down with the weight of the extremely fragrant blossoms and the fruits; it was filled with beautiful sweet water[7] adorned with stainless lotuses and water-lilies; it was frequented by various herds of wild

[1] BvAB omits, so his name appears as Subhāvitatta, the next word.

[2] usabha, a bull. "Bull of sages" and similar expressions merely mean "greatest, noblest sage", etc.

[3] pāṭipade. This could also mean "following the right path".

[4] No doubt this refers to Vin MV VII I 3. See also Vin v 172.

[5] visālamati, a play on the Elder's name.

[6] sīhavikkantagāmī; cf. Miln 400 sīho vikkantacārī.

[7] vārivāha, the water-bearer. Here more likely to be pools and streams than clouds.

creatures such as deer, antelope, lions, tigers, elephants, horses, gayals, and buffaloes; and humming[1] everywhere were young female bees, the honey-makers[2] and experienced frequenters of the fragrant blossoms and scents, the fruits and juices enchaining their hearts; and the sweet cries of the female[3] cuckoos were being sung[4] like a low-toned musical instrument.[5] People seeing Him of the Ten Powers, Tathāgata, king under Dhamma, staying there with his following, shining with a Buddha's splendour, on hearing his Dhamma and having confidence in it, went forth by the 'Come, monk' (formula for) going forth. Then he "invited," surrounded by two hundred thousand monks. This was the third assembly. Accordingly it was said:

IX 6 The great seer Paduma had three assemblies: the first gathering was of a hundred thousand crores.

7 When kaṭhina robe-material had accrued at the time of the formal spreading out of the kaṭhina-cloth monks sewed a robe for the General under Dhamma.

8 Then those three hundred thousand stainless monks, having the six super-knowings, of great psychic potency, unconquered, gathered together.

[180] 9 And again, that bull of men entered upon the (rains-) residence in a forest; there was then a gathering of two hundred thousand.

7 Therein *at the time of the formal spreading out*[6] *of the kathina-cloth* means at the time of the formal spreading[6] of the kaṭhina robe-material.

7 *For the General under Dhamma* means for the Elder Sāla, the General under Dhamma.

8 *Unconquered* means not conquered; a dropping of the case-ending[7] is to be understood.

9 *That* means that Great Paduma.

9 *In a forest* means in a great wood.

[1] Or, murmuring. BvAC 179 gumugumāyamāne, BvAB gumbu-, with v. l. gumu-. See too text p. 95.

[2] bhamaramadhukara; madhukara alone at Vism 136.

[3] vadhū, the female of any animal, M-W; not in PED in this sense.

[4] upagīyamāne, see M-W. Not in PED.

[5] kākali, not in PED; see M-W.

[6] atthāra . . . attharaṇa.

[7] vibhatti-lopa as at ItA ii 18, etc.

9 *Residence* means rains-residence.

9 *Entered upon* means having entered upon[1].

9 *Of two hundred thousand* means of two hundred thousand[2]. "Then there was a gathering"[3] is also a reading if the sense[4] should be better.

Then as the Tathāgata was spending the rains in that woodland thicket, our[5] Bodhisatta who had become a lion saw him seated (there) for seven days attaining the attainment of cessation. Having a mind of faith, reverencing[6] him and circumambulating him with his right side towards him, filled with zest and happiness, he three times roared a lion's roar. For seven days he did not relinquish his zest due to thoughts of the Buddha and remained paying homage, sacrificing his (own) life since because of that very zest and happiness he did not go off in search of prey. Then at the end of those seven days, the teacher, the lion of men, emerging from the attainment of cessation, surveying the lion, thought, "May he have confidence of mind also in the Order of monks", and he formed the intention, "Let the Order come." Countless crores[7] of monks came immediately. The lion inclined his mind towards the Order. Then the teacher, having surveyed his (the lion's) mind, declared, "In the future he will be the Buddha named Gotama." Accordingly it was said:

IX 10 I at that time was a lion, overlord of wild creatures. I saw the Conqueror in the forest increasing aloofness.[8]

11 I reverenced his feet with my head, circumambulated him, roared loudly three times, and attended on the Conqueror for a week.

12 After the week the Tathāgata emerged from the glorious attainment. Thinking with purpose in his mind he brought together a crore of monks.

13 Then that great hero too declared in their midst: "Innumerable eons from now this one will be a Buddha.

[1] BvAC upāgato ti *upāgami*; BvAB *upāgamī* ti upāgato.

[2] dvinnaṁ satasahassinan ti dvinnaṁ satasahassānaṁ.

[3] tadā āsi samāgamo for verse's tadā samāgamo āsi.

[4] Reading attho for atthi.

[5] BvAC omits.

[6] BvAC vanditvā, BvAB sutvā.

[7] BvAC bhikkhū only; but see ver 12.

[8] paviveka, detachment, withdrawal from.

14 When he has striven the striving . . ." ". . . face to face with this one".

15 When I had heard his words all the more did I incline my mind. I resolutely determined on further practice for fulfilling the ten perfections.

[**181**] 10 Therein *increasing aloofness* means possessing the attainment of cessation.

11 *Circumambulated* means making circumambulation three times.

11 *Roared loudly* means thrice roared a lion's roar.

11 *Attended on* means attended on[1], or this is itself the reading.

12 *From the glorious attainment* means having *emerged from* the glorious attainment of cessation.

12 *Thinking with purpose in his mind* means simply intending in his mind, "Let all monks come here".

12 *Brought together* means got together[2].

And that Lord Paduma's city was named Campaka. The king, his father, was named Asama[3], his mother too was named Asamā. Sāla and Upasāla were the two[4] chief disciples. The attendant was named Varuṇa. Rādhā and Surādhā were the two[5] chief women disciples. The Tree of Awakening was a Great Soṇa. The physical frame was fifty-eight cubits in height, the life-span was a hundred thousand years. The name of his chief consort was Uttarā, incomparable[6] in the qualities of beauty and so forth. Prince Ramma was the name of his extremely charming[7] offspring.[8] Accordingly it was said:

IX 16 Campaka was the name of the city, Asama[9] the name of the warrior-noble, Asamā the name of the mother of Paduma, the great seer.

21 Sāla and Upasāla were the chief disciples. Varuṇa was the name of the attendant on Paduma, the great seer.

22 Rādhā and Surādhā[10] were the chief women disciples. That Lord's Tree of Awakening is said to be the Great Soṇa.

[1] upaṭṭhahan ti upaṭṭhahiṁ. The latter is the reading at Bv.
[2] samānayī ti samāhari.
[3] BvAB adds ahosi.
[4] BvAB adds tassa.
[5] So BvAB.
[6] anuttarā.
[7] atiramma.
[8] tanaya.
[9] Paduma at Jā i 36.
[10] Ibid. Rāmā and Uparāmā.

24 The great sage was fifty-eight ratanas tall. His lustre, without an equal, streamed forth over all the quarters.

25 The lustre of the moon, the lustre of the sun, the lustre of jewels, a festooned column[1], gems—all these were dimmed by the Conqueror's supreme lustre.

26 The (normal) life-span lasted then for a hundred thousand years. Living so long he caused many people to cross over.

27 Having awakened the beings whose minds were thoroughly mature omitting none, having instructed the remainder, he and the disciples waned out.

28 As a snake sheds its worn-out skin, as a tree its old leaves, so, burning up all the constructions, he waned out like a fire.

[**182**] 25 Therein *the lustre of jewels, a festooned column, gems* means the lustre of jewels and the lustre of fire[1] and the lustre of gems.

25 *Dimmed* means overcome by.

25 *The Conqueror's supreme lustre* means they were dimmed by the lustre of the Conqueror's physical frame which had become supreme.

27 *Whose minds were thoroughly mature* means that he could guide away *beings* whose faculties were thoroughly mature.

28 *Old leaves* means ancient leaves.

28 *As*[2] *a tree* means like[2] a tree.

28 *All constructions*[3] means having slain precisely all the constructions, inner and outer. "Every construction"[3] is also a reading. The meaning is the same.

28 *Like a fire* means that like a fire he had gone, had well gone to waning out without fuel (for renewed existence).

According to the method spoken of above the remainder in the verses is quite clear in meaning.

Concluded is the Exposition of the Chronicle of the Buddha Paduma

Concluded is the Eighth Buddha-Chronicle

[1] Bv reads -agghi-, BvAC -aggi-, fire. Agghi is a shortened form of agghiya. In v 29, x 26 it is a festooned column, golden in colour.

[2] va . . . viya.

[3] sabbasaṅkhāre . . . sabbasaṅkhāraṁ.

X THE EXPOSITION OF THE CHRONICLE OF THE BUDDHA NĀRADA

After the Buddha Paduma had attained final nibbāna and his Dispensation had disappeared people, gradually dwindling from a life-span of a hundred thousand years, were of a life-span of ten years. The life-spans, increasing again to an incalculable, (then) dwindling, were life-spans of ninety thousand years. Then the teacher named Nārada, supreme among men and beings, arose in the world, bearer of the Ten Powers[1], having the three knowledges, confident with the four confidences[2], giver of the essence of freedom[3]. Having fulfilled the perfections for four incalculables and a hundred thousand eons, he was reborn in Tusita-abode. Deceasing from there he took on relinking in Dhaññavatī city in the womb of the queen named Anomā, who was without compare, the chief consort in the household of the king named Sudeva, a lord of wealth[4] gained by his own energy. After ten months he issued forth from his mother's womb in Dhanañjaya pleasaunce. On his name-taking day while his name was being given there fell from the sky over the whole of Jambudīpa trinkets suitable for the indulgence of men's enjoyment, wish-fulfilling trees[5] and so forth. Because they thought, "He gave trinkets worthy of men"[6], they gave[7] him the name Nārada[8].

He lived the household life for nine thousand years. His three palaces suited to the three seasons were Vijita, Vijitāvī, Jitābhirāma[9]. They made the extremely wealthy warrior-noble maiden named Vijitasenā the chief consort of this Prince Nārada; she was endowed with good family, morality, right behaviour, beauty and was compliant in mind[10]. [183] Making her the head, there were a hundred and twenty thousand women under her.[11] After the birth

[1] M i 69ff. [2] Ibid. 71.

[3] vimuttisāra is the last of the 4 sāras at A ii 141; see also ibid. 244, iv 339. Here -sārada in assonance with Nārada.

[4] vāsudeva, see text p. 114 vasū ti ratanaṁ vuccati. The play on the name of Sudeva is apparent.

[5] kapparukkha. [6] narānaṁ.

[7] BvAC kariṁsu, BvAB akaṁsu. [8] nāra with da, giver to mankind.

[9] Bv x 19 Jitāvijitābhirāma. Text p. 188 calls the third palace Vijitābhirāma, as does BvAB with v. l. Jitābhirāma.

[10] manonukūla; anukūla is compliant, faithful, willing.

[11] BvAB vīsatisahassādhikaṁ itthīnaṁ satasahassaṁ ahosi; BvAC vīsativassādhikaṁ itthisatasahassaṁ ahosi.

to this Queen Vijitasenā of the prince named Nanduttara, bringing bliss to the whole world[1], he (the Bodhisatta) saw the four signs[2]. Surrounded by a four-factored army, going to the pleasaunce on foot, indifferent towards his various fine garments and glorious dwellings, taking off all his adornments, the jewelled earrings he had worn, the glorious bangles, crests and rings, the extremely fragrant perfumes and blossoms he was adorned with, giving them into the hands of a storekeeper, with his own sharp sword so well whetted it resembled the petal of a blue lotus, stainless though arisen in the water, he cut off his hair and crest, the most lovely jewel he was adorned with, and flung them up into the vault of the heavens. Sakka, king of devas, receiving them in a golden casket, took them to the abode of the Thirty-Three and built a cetiya three yojanas high and consisting of the seven kinds of gems on the summit of Sineru.

And the Great Man, putting on saffron robes given by devas, went forth then and there in the pleasaunce. A hundred thousand men went forth following his example. Then and there he engaged in striving for seven days. On the full-moon day of Visākha he partook of milk-rice given to him by the chief consort, Vijitasenā. Spending the day-sojourn in that self-same pleasaunce he accepted eight handfuls of grass[3] given to him by Sudassana, the park-keeper, and circumambulating a Great Soṇa Tree of Awakening he spread a grass spreading fifty-eight cubits in extent. Seated (there), having routed Māra's forces, making the three knowledges arise in the three watches (of the night) and penetrating omniscient knowledge, he uttered the solemn utterance:

"Through many a birth in saṁsāra . . .
. . . the destruction of cravings".

There in the Dhanañjaya pleasaunce, surrounded by the hundred thousand monks who had gone forth together with himself, he turned the Wheel of Dhamma. Then there was a penetration of Dhamma by a hundred thousand crores. Accordingly it was said:

X 1 After Paduma was the Self-Awakened One named Nārada, supreme among men, without an equal, matchless.

[1] sabbalokānanda-kara. [2] Cf. the following account with text p. 161.
[3] "Towards evening", sāyaṇhasamaye, omitted.

2 That Buddha, the eldest and cherished own son of a wheel-turning king, adorned with garlands and trinkets, went to a pleasaunce.

3 There was a tree there, widely famed, beautiful, tall and pure; hastening towards it he sat down under the Great Soṇa.

4 In him glorious knowledge arose, unending, like diamond, by means of which he examined the constructions upwards and downwards.

[184] 5 There he washed away all the defilements so that none remained; he attained full Awakening and the fourteen knowledges of a Buddha.

6 Having attained Self-Awakening he turned the Wheel of Dhamma. The first penetration was by a hundred thousand crores.

2 Therein *of a wheel-turner* means of a wheel-turning king[1].

2 *Eldest* means first-born.

2 *Cherished own* means cherished and own[2] son. When taken from the breast a son who is cherished and fondled is called cherished own (son).

2 *Adorned with garlands and trinkets* means adorned with pearl necklaces, bangles, rings, crests, earrings, garlands.

2 *To a pleasaunce* means he went to the pleasaunce[3] called Dhanañjaya outside the city.

3 *There was a tree there* means: it is said that in that pleasaunce there was one tree called a Crimson Soṇa. It is said it was ninety cubits in height, its trunk quite round, possessed of many forks and branches; the dense and abundant foliage was dark green, it gave deep shade; because it was inhabited by devatās it was not the resort for manifold flocks of birds; it was an ornament[4] on the face of the earth being made like a kingdom of trees, extremely delightful to behold, all the branches fully adorned with crimson blossoms, a cynosure of the delighted eyes[5] of devas and mankind.

[1] Adopted in the translation of the verse.

[2] In the translation I have taken orasa to mean "own son". The Comy., oraso putto, makes this abundantly clear.

[3] BvAC uyyāna, BvAB ārāma, with v. l. uyyāna.

[4] tilaka, see M-W for the meaning of the ornament made of coloured powders that women put on the forehead.

[5] nayanarasāyana.

3 *Widely famed* means famed widely. The meaning is: renowned[1] in all the world, well known, heard of everywhere for its own attainment. Some read "There was a wide tree there".[2]

3 *Tall* means great. The meaning is that it resembled the Coral Tree of the devas.

3 *Hastening towards it* means having reached, come to, approached that Soṇa tree.

3 *Under* means under that tree.

4 *Glorious knowledge arose* means glorious knowledge arose.[3]

4 *Unending* means immeasurable, boundless.

4 *Like diamond* means sharp as a diamond[4]; it is a synonym for the knowledge of insight of contemplating impermanence and so forth.

4 *By means of which he examined the constructions* means: by means of the knowledge of insight he examined the constructions beginning with form.

4 *Upwards and downwards* means: he examined the rise and fall of the constructions. Therefore, having reflected on[5] the mode of conditions, emerging from the fourth meditation by in-breathing and out-breathing, he interpreted the five aggregates, seeing the full fifty marks in relation to rise and fall. Having increased insight into the knowledge of cognizance, he acquired the entire special qualities of a Buddha by means of following the ariyan Way.

[185] 5 *There* means at the Soṇa tree.

5 *All the defilements* means all the defilements,[6] said having made a change in gender. Some read "there with all the defilements".[7]

5 *None remained* means without remainder.

5 *He washed away* means he washed away all the defilements to the extent of the Way(s) and to the extent of the defilements; the meaning is he brought (them) to ruin.

5 *Awakening* means knowledge of the Way to arahantship.

5 *And the fourteen knowledges of a Buddha* means the fourteen

[1] vikhyāta, not in PED.
[2] BvAC vipulo rukkho, BvAB rukkho vipulo.
[3] ñāṇavar° uppajjī ti ñāṇavaraṁ udapādi.
[4] Cf. A i 124.
[5] For this passage cf. text pp. 83, 133, 190.
[6] sabbakilesānī ti sabbakilese.
[7] tattha sabbakilesehi.

knowledges of a Buddha.[1] What are these? The knowledges of the fruits and the Ways are eight, six are the knowledges not shared (by others)[2]—these fourteen are thus called knowledges of a Buddha.[3] The word 'and' (ca) has the meaning of a conjunction. The meaning is that *he attained* other (knowledges) also: the four analytical insights[4], the knowledges of the four confidences, the knowledges that are demarcations of the four modes of birth and the five bourns[5], the knowledges of the ten powers, and the entire special qualities of a Buddha.

Having thus attained Buddhahood and agreed to Brahmā's request, he turned the Wheel of Dhamma in Dhanañjaya-pleasaunce in the presence of the hundred thousand monks who had gone forth together with himself. Then was the first penetration by a hundred thousand crores.

It is said that then, in Mahādoṇa city, nāga-king named Doṇa lived in a bank[6] in the Ganges. He was of great psychic potency, of great majesty, revered, venerated, reverenced and honoured by the populace. If the country people who lived in that region did not make him an offering of food he ruined their region by a drought or by excessive rain or by saṅkhara[7] rain. Then the teacher Nārada, looking at the bank, seeing the qualifications of many breathing things in the instruction[8] of Doṇa the nāga-king, and surrounded by a great Order of monks, went to the nāga-king's dwelling-place. Thereupon, on seeing him people spoke thus: "Lord,[9] living here is a nāga-king, terribly venomous, of fiery heat, great psychic potency and great majesty. By his great majesty he can harm people. He should not be approached." But the Lord went on as though not hearing their words; and having arrived he sat down there on an extremely fragrantly scented spreading of flowers which had been arranged for the sake of revering that nāga-king. It is said that the great populace assembled thinking to see a fight between the two: Nārada, king of sages, and Doṇa, king of nāgas.

[1] Buddhañāṇe ca cuddasā ti Buddhañāṇāni cuddasa.
[2] See MQ ii 9, n. 6.
[3] See text p. 43, Miln 216, 285.
[4] BvAB adds ñāṇāni.
[5] BvAB catuyoniparicchedakañāṇāni pañcagatiparicchedakañāṇāni.
[6] BvAC rahade, pool, BvAB tīre, bank, as also a few lines below.
[7] Meaning?
[8] vinayana, removal, instruction, setting an example.
[9] bhagavā, a vocative and not a common form of address.

Then the snake-nāga seeing the sage-nāga[1] so seated, not conquering his rage, his body being visible, blew forth smoke. Him of the Ten Powers also blew forth smoke. Again, the king of nāgas blazed up. The king of sages also blazed up. Then that nāga-king, his physical frame exceedingly wearied by the smoke and the blaze that had streamed forth from the physical frame of Him of the Ten Powers, not conquering his anguish, thought: "I will kill him with strong venom", and he discharged venom. The strength of that venom could have ruined even the whole of Jambudīpa, but it was not able to cause even a single hair on the physical frame of Him of the Ten Powers to quiver. Then the nāga-king thought: "Now, what is the recluse's course of existence?"[2] Surveying and seeing the Lord bright and splendid shining with the six-hued Buddha-rays like the autumnal sun and like the moon at the full, and thinking: "This recluse is certainly of great psychic potency and I have made a mistake through not knowing my own strength", he sought protection [**186**] and indeed approached the Lord for refuge. Then Nārada, king of sages, having guided out that king of nāgas, performed the Marvel of the Double for gladdening the minds of the great populace who were assembled there. Then ninety thousand crores of breathing things were established in arahantship. This was the second penetration. Accordingly it was said:

X 7 The great sage, taming Mahādoṇa the nāga-king, then performed a Marvel displaying it to the world with the devas.

8 Then, at that expounding of Dhamma, ninety thousand crores of devas and men crossed over all doubt.

7 Therein *then performed a Marvel:* the meaning is "he performed the Marvel of the Double" or this is itself the reading. "Just devas and men then" is also a reading.[3]

8 Therein *of devas and men* means that each has the sense of a genitive; the meaning therefore is: ninety thousand crores of devas, of men.

8 *Crossed over* means they overpassed.

And when he exhorted his own son, Prince Nanduttara, then

[1] Cf. Vin i 24f. for this passage.

[2] pavattī, cf. Vism 546.

[3] tadā devamanussā vā presumably in place of tadākāsi . . . sadevake of the verse. See BHSD for this meaning of vā.

was the third penetration by eighty thousand crores. Accordingly it was said:

X 9 At the time when the great hero exhorted his own son there was the third penetration by eighty thousand crores.

And when, in Thullakoṭṭhita city two brahman friends, Bhaddasāla and Vijitamitta[1], were seated together seeking the pool of the Undying, they saw Nārada, the fully Self-Awakened One, generous giver of the essence[2]. Seeing the thirty-two Marks of a Great Man on the Lord's body they came to the conclusion that this Fully Self-Awakened One was one who draws away the veil from the world. They were filled with confidence in the Lord and with their retinues went forth in the Lord's presence. When they had gone forth and had attained arahantship, the Lord recited the Pātimokka in the midst of a hundred thousand crores of monks. That was the first assembly. Accordingly it was said:

X 10 The great seer Nārada had three assemblies; the first was a gathering of a hundred thousand crores.

On the occasion when Nārada, the Fully Self-Awakened One, spoke the Chronicle of Buddhas, beginning with his own resolve in a gathering of (his) relations, there was then the second assembly of ninety thousand crores of monks. Accordingly it was said:

X 11 When the Buddha expounded the special Buddha-qualities with their source, ninety thousand crores of stainless ones gathered together then.

[187] 11 Therein *stainless ones* means those devoid of stains, cankers destroyed.

Then, after the guiding out of the nāga-king Mahādoṇa, a pious nāga-king named Verocana, having created a pavilion near the river Ganges measuring three gāvutas and consisting of the seven kinds of gems[3], he and his retinue invited the people of the district to see his store-house of gifts. Having had snake-dancers assembled and musicians wearing a variety of garments and adornments, with

[1] Jitamitta in ver. 23.

[2] BvAC ativiya sāradaṁ, BvAB ativisārada with v. l. as at BvAC. See text p. 182 "giver of the essence of freedom."

[3] BvAB adds saparivāraṁ bhagavantaṁ tattha nisidāpetvā, having made the Lord with his entourage sit down there.

great reverence he gave the great gift to the Lord with his retinue. On the meal's coming to an end the Lord, as though going down to the Great Ganges, gave the benediction. Then the Lord recited the Pātimokkha in the midst of eighty hundred thousand monks who, believing, had gone forth by the 'Come, monk' (formula for) going forth after they had heard Dhamma at the benediction for what had been eaten[1]. This was the third assembly. Accordingly it was said:

X 12 When the nāga Verocana gave a gift to the teacher, eighty hundred thousand sons of the Conqueror gathered together then.

12 Therein *eighty hundred thousand* means of eighty hundred thousand.[2]

Then the Bodhisatta, having gone forth in the going forth of seers, constructing a hermitage on a flank of Himavant, lived there having come to mastery in the five super-knowings and the eight attainments. And out of compassion for him the Lord Nārada went to that hermitage-site surrounded by eighty crores of arahants and ten thousand lay-followers who were established in the fruit of no-return. As soon as the ascetic saw the Lord, joyous at heart, constructing a hermitage for the Lord to dwell in with his retinue, he extolled the teacher's special qualities all night. Hearing the Lord's talk on Dhamma, he went to Uttarakuru the next day, brought back nutriments from there, and gave a great gift to the Awakened One with his retinue. Having thus given a great gift for seven days, he brought back priceless red sandalwood[3] from Himavant and honoured the Lord with that red sandalwood. Then Him of the Ten Powers, surrounded by deities and men, having talked a talk on Dhamma to him, declared, "In the future he will be the Buddha named Gotama". Accordingly it was said:

X 13 I at that time was a very severe ascetic, a matted-hair ascetic, a mover through mid-air was I[4], master of the five super-knowings.

14 And when I had refreshed with food and drink the

[1] BvAC bhuttānumodana, BvAB bhatt-.
[2] asītisatasahassiyo ti satasahassānaṁ asītiyo.
[3] lohitacandana; cf. Dh 55, Miln 321.
[4] Cf. xiii 11.

equal to the unequalled with his Order and his following, I honoured him highly with (red) sandal-wood.

15 And that Buddha Nārada, leader of the world, also declared of me: "Innumerable eons from now he will be a Buddha in the world.[1]

16 When he has striven the striving . . ." ". . . we will be face to face with this one"

[188] 17 When I had heard his words, all the more gladdened[2] in mind, I resolutely determined on the strenuous practice for fulfilling the ten perfections.

14 Therein *and when I* means and when I.[3]

14 *Equal to the unequalled* means that the unequalled are past and future[4] Awakened Ones. Equal to the unequalled is equal to, rivalling these unequalled ones. Or, the unequalled are without equals; equals are not without equals. An eminent one, equal to these unequalled and equalled ones should be spoken of as "equal to the unequalled and equalled ones". It should be understood that it[5] is said having made an elision of the one word "equalled". The meaning is: equal to the unequalled (and) the not without equals.

14 *With his following* means with the people who were lay-followers. "He, the one with Vision, also declared of me in the midst of men and deities"[6] is also a reading. This meaning is quite clear.

17 *All the more gladdened*[7] *in mind* means gladdening[7] it still further, satisfied at heart.

17 *I resolutely determined on the strenuous practice* means on the strenuous practice I resolutely determined.[8] "I resolutely determined on further practice for fulfilling the ten perfections" is also a reading.

[1] BvA buddho loke bhavissati, Bv ayaṁ buddho bhavissati.

[2] Bv hāsetvā, BvAC bhāvetvā.

[3] tadā p'ahan ti tadā pi ahaṁ.

[4] BvAB "past" only; AA i 116 also "past and future" in definition of "equal to the unequalled".

[5] Presumably asamasama for asamasamasama.

[6] The prose narrative, just before ver. 13, reads amaranaraparivuto while the above reading is naramarūnaṁ.

[7] Though I think bhāvetvā, developing, of BvAC is better, I have followed Bv, Be, BvAB hāsetvā. BvAB notes the reading bhāvetvā. See ver. 17 above.

[8] adhiṭṭhahiṁ vatam uggan ti uggaṁ vataṁ adhiṭṭhāsiṁ.

That Lord's city was named Dhaññavatī, the warrior-noble his father was named Sudeva, his mother was named Anomā. The chief disciples were Bhaddasāla and Jitamitta. The attendant was named Vāseṭṭha. The chief women disciples were Uttarā and Phaggunī. The Tree of Awakening was a Great Soṇa. The physical frame was eighty-eight cubits in height, the lustre of his physical frame constantly suffused a yojana. The life-span was ninety thousand years. And his chief consort was named Vijitasenā[1], his son was named Prince Nanduttara. The three palaces were Vijita, Vijitāvī, Vijitābhirāma.[2] He lived the household life for nine thousand years. He departed on the Great Departure simply on foot. Accordingly it was said:

X 18 Dhaññavatī was the name of the city, Sudeva[3] the name of the warrior-noble, Anomā the name of the mother of Nārada, the great seer.

23 Bhaddasāla, Jitamitta were the chief disciples. Vāseṭṭha was the name of the attendant on Nārada, the great seer.

24 Uttarā and Phaggunī were the chief women disciples. That Lord's Tree of Awakening is said to be the Great Soṇa.

26 The great sage was eighty-eight ratanas tall. The ten-thousand was brilliant like a golden festooned column.

27 Lustrous rays extending for a fathom streamed forth from his body in every direction, constantly, day and night, and suffused a yojana then.[4]

[189] 28 At that time none of the people within the circuit of the yojana lit torches or lamps as they were overspread with the Buddha's rays.[5]

29 The (normal) life-span lasted then for ninety thousand years. Living so long he caused many people to cross over.

30 As the heavens look beautiful when ornamented with stars, so did his Dispensation shine with arahants.

31 After making firm the bridge of Dhamma so that the remainder who had entered on the Way[6] could cross over the stream of saṁsāra, that bull of men waned out.[7]

[1] Bv x 20 Jitasenā.
[2] Jitābhirāma at text p. 182.
[3] Sumedha at Ja i 37.
[4] tadā, Bv disā.
[5] BvAC -raṁsena, BvAB -raṁsīhi.
[6] paṭipannaka; cf. MA ii 137, where 4 kinds are mentioned.
[7] BvAC reverses order of this verse and the next.

32 Both that Buddha, equal to the unequalled, and those whose cankers were destroyed, of matchless incandescence, have all disappeared. Are not all constructions void?

26 Therein *like a golden festooned column* means beautiful and lovely as though the column were made of gold ornamented with manifold jewels.

26 *The ten-thousand was brilliant* means because of his lustre even the ten-thousand world-system was brilliant. The meaning is that it was resplendent. Explaining this very matter the Lord said: "Lustrous rays extending for a fathom streamed forth from his body in every direction."

27 Therein *lustrous rays extending for a fathom* means like lustrous rays extending for a fathom: lustrous rays extending for a fathom. The meaning is: like our Lord's lustrous rays extending for a fathom.

28 *None* (na keci) means that herein the syllable 'na' has the sense of exclusion. It is to be understood that its connection is with the further meaning[1] of the word '(they) lit.'

28 *Torches* means little lamps with handles: *torches or lamps; some people* indeed *did not light*[2], they did not make burn. Why was that? Because of the effulgence of the lustre of the Buddha's physical frame.

28 *With the Buddha's rays* means with the Buddha's rays.[3]

28 *Overspread*[4] means reached by.

30 *With heavenly bodies* means with stars.[5] As the vault of the heavens shines when it is ornamented with stars, *so did his Dispensation shine* forth when it was ornamented *with arahants.*

31 *Could cross over the stream of saṁsāra* means the welfare of crossing over the ocean of saṁsāra.

31 *The remainder who had entered on the Way:* the meaning is that, setting aside the arahants, the remaining individuals who were initiates together with "lovely"[6] ordinary people.

[1] uttarattha, not in BvAB.

[2] Reading here keci pi janā na ujjālenti for na keci . . . janā . . . ujjālenti of the verse.

[3] buddharaṁsenā ti buddharasmīhi.

[4] BvAC adds otthaṭā va before adhigatā; the meaning of the gloss therefore would be, "reached by as though overspread".

[5] uḷūhī ti tārāhi.

[6] kalyāṇa.

31 *The bridge of Dhamma* means the bridge of the Way. The meaning is that after setting up the bridge of Dhamma to help the remaining individuals to cross over saṁsāra, being one who had done all the duties, he attained final nibbāna. The remainder, from what is stated above, is quite clear everywhere.

Concluded is the Exposition of the Chronicle of the Buddha Nārada

Concluded is the Ninth Buddha-Chronicle

XI THE EXPOSITION OF THE CHRONICLE OF THE BUDDHA PADUMUTTARA

[**190**] After the Buddha Nārada's Dispensation had continued for ninety thousand years[1] it disappeared. And that eon came to an end. After that for incalculable eons[2] Buddhas did not arise in the world, it was void of Buddhas, without the light of Buddhas. Then when eons and incalculables had passed there arose in the world in one eon a hundred thousand eons ago one Buddha named Padumuttara who had conquered Māra, laid down the burden, was (as) the essence of Meru,[3] was without saṁsāra, the choicest of beings, supreme in all the world.[4]

When he had fulfilled the perfections he was reborn in Tusita city. Deceasing from there, he took on relinking in the city of Haṁsavatī in the womb of the Queen Sujātā[5], who came of a very high family,[6] and was the chief consort of a king named Ānanda[7], giver of bliss[8] to all people. She, after ten months gave birth to Prince Padumuttara in Haṁsavatī pleasaunce. The marvels at his relinking and birth were as those spoken of above[9]. They say that

[1] So BvAB with v. l. as in BvAC pañcanavutivassāni, 95 years.

[2] See explanation at Jkm 14 (EC 19f.).

[3] Mt. Meru was the symbol of strength and unshakeability. This and the next two words read Merusāra, asaṁsāra, sattasāra.

[4] sabbalokuttara, a play on the name of this Buddha.

[5] Sumedhā at SA ii 89, AA i 287.

[6] BvAB udito-ditakule jātāya, BvAC uditakule jātāya. Cf. uggata at text p. 169, and see text p. 36, uggato ti udito.

[7] Ānanda at Bv, BvAC 192f., 196 and DPPN, Nandana above, Nanda at BvAB, SA ii 89, AA i 287, Sunanda at DhA i 417.

[8] ānandanakara.

[9] IIA 83ff.

at his birth a rain of lotuses (paduma) rained down. For this reason his relations gave him the name of Prince Padumuttara on his name-taking day.

He lived the household life for ten thousand years. His three palaces, suitable to the three seasons, were called Naravāhana, Yasavāhana, Vasavattī. There were a hundred thousand and twenty thousand women in attendance on him with the lady Vasudattā at the head. After a son, Prince Uttara[1], unsurpassed[2] in all qualities, had been born to the lady Vasudattā he, (the Bodhisatta), having seen the four signs thought he would depart on the Great Departure. Even as he was thinking this, the palace named Vasavattī soared up into the sky like a potter's wheel and going through the vault of the heavens like a deva-mansion and like the moon at the full descended on the ground, like the palace spoken of in the Exposition of the Chronicle of the Buddha Sobhita[3], with the Tree of Awakening in the centre. The Great Man, they say, descending from that palace, [4]clothing himself in saffron garments, the banner and ensign of arahantship, which had been given to him by devas, went forth then and there. And when the palace had arrived it remained precisely its own place. Excepting the women, the whole company that had come with the Great Being, went forth. Together with these the Great Man engaged in striving for seven days.[4] After he had partaken of sweet milk-rice given to him on the full-moon day of Visākha by Rucinandā,[5] the daughter of a merchant in the city of Ujjeni, he spent the day-sojourn in a sāla grove. Towards evening he accepted eight handfuls of grass given to him by Sumitta, a Naked Ascetic, and approached a Salala[6] Tree of Awakening, circumambulated it keeping his right side towards it and spread a grass-spreading thirty-eight cubits in extent. Sitting down cross-legged, resolutely determining on the fourfold energy, routing Māra's forces together with Māra, he recollected his former habitations during the first watch (of the night), purified the deva-like vision during the second watch, reflected on[7] the mode of the conditions during the

[1] SnA i 341 Uparevata.
[2] anuttara.
[3] Text p. 167.
[4]...[4] BvAC omits this sentence down to "for 7 days" as BvAB notices.
[5] BvAB Rucānandā.
[6] See IIA 51.
[7] For this passage cf. text pp. 83, 133, 184.

third watch and emerging from the fourth meditation by in-breathing and out-breathing, he interpreted the five aggregates, seeing the full fifty marks in relation to rise and fall. Having increased insight into[1] the knowledge of cognizance, he penetrated the entire special qualities of a Buddha by means of the ariyan Way, [**191**] and uttered the solemn utterance obligatory on all Buddhas,

> "Through many a birth . . .
> . . . the destruction of cravings".

They say that then a rain of lotuses rained down as though adorning even all the interspaces in the ten-thousand world-systems. Accordingly it was said:

XI 1 After Nārada was the Self-Awakened One, the Conqueror named Padumuttara, supreme among men, imperturbable as the ocean.

2 It was like a Maṇḍa-eon in which this Buddha was born. In this eon people of outstanding merit were born.

1 Therein *as the ocean* means being deep like the ocean[2].

2 *It was like a Maṇḍa-eon* means: that eon in which two[3] Buddhas arise is called a Maṇḍa-eon. An eon is twofold[4]: a Void eon and a Non-void eon. Therein Buddhas, buddhas by and for themselves, universal monarchs do not arise in a Void eon, therefore it is said to be a Void eon because it is void of individuals having the special qualities. A Non-void eon is fivefold: Sāra-eon, Maṇḍa-eon, Vara-eon, Sāramaṇḍa-eon, Bhadda-eon. Therein a Sāra-eon is so called by reason of the appearance of one Fully Self-Awakened One producing the essence of the special qualities, generating the essence of the special qualities in an eon that had been void of the special qualities, lacking them. And in whatever eon two leaders of the world arise, that is to be called a Maṇḍa-eon. And in whatever eon three Buddhas arise, the first of these declares the second a protector of the world, the second (declares)

[1] vipassanā, probably to be inserted here as in the parallel passages.

[2] Cf. M i 487f., the Tathāgata is deep like the ocean.

[3] BvAC adds sambahulā vā, "or several".

[4] This exegesis on the kappas appears briefly at Jkm 20f. At ibid. 14 Padumuttara is rightly assigned to a Sāra-eon which, as explained below, had the qualities of a Maṇḍa-eon.

the third. That wherein men are joyous at heart because each by himself has caused the wish to be made for a longed-for aspiration[1], is to be called therefore a Vara-eon. And in whatever eon four Buddhas arise, that is to be called a Sāramaṇḍa-eon on account of its being even more eminent than the foregoing eon. In whatever eon five Buddhas arise, that is to be called a Bhadda-eon,[2] but it is very difficult to obtain. And in this (kind of) eon creatures as a rule are rich in goodness and happiness; as a rule, having three root-conditions,[3] they bring destruction to the defilements; those having two root-conditions[4] go to a good bourn; those without a root-condition acquire a root-condition. Therefore this (kind of) eon is to be called a Bhadda-eon. Accordingly it was said: "A Non-void eon is fivefold". And this was said by the Ancients:[5]

> One Buddha in a Sāra-eon; in a Maṇḍa-eon the Conquerors are two; in a Vara-eon three Buddhas; in a Sāramaṇḍa-eon four Buddhas; five Buddhas in a Bhadda-eon—there are no more Conquerors than this.

But in the eon in which Padumuttara, Him of the Ten Powers, arose, even though being a Sāra-eon, yet because, through the attainment of special qualities, it had a resemblance to a Maṇḍa-eon it was called a Maṇḍa-eon.

2 The word *va* (like) is to be understood in the sense of likeness.

2 *Outstanding merit*[6] means merit[7] accumulated.

2 *People* means an abundance of people.

When the Lord Padumuttara[8], supreme among men, had spent seven days[9] sitting cross-legged near the Tree of Awakening, he thought: "I will put one foot on the ground", **[192]** and he

[1] vārayanti, a causative. Such aspirations are usually to the effect that some high monastic position might be achieved in the future, such as that of a chief disciple.

[2] Auspicious-eon.

[3] Cf. VbhA 17 for tihetukā, du- and ahetukā. To have 3 of these hetu is to have no lobha, dosa or moha, no greed, hatred or confusion. Such a being can be found only among men. See Ñyāṇatiloka, Bud. Dict. p. 130.

[4] Non-greed, non-hatred.

[5] BvAB notes that this verse and its attribution are omitted in BvAC.

[6] kusala, lit. skill or goodness.

[7] puñña.

[8] Cf. this paragraph with SnA ii 89f.

[9] So BvAB, SA ii 89, AA i 287; 7 weeks at BvAC.

stretched forth his right foot. Then cleaving the earth[1] there rose up, whether arisen in the water or not, the filaments and pericarps of stainless lotuses, the widespread foliage unstained though arisen in the water. Indeed their leaves were ninety cubits, the filaments thirty cubits, the pericarps ten[2] cubits and the pollen of each was the measure of nine water-pitchers. And the teacher was fifty-eight cubits in height. There were eighteen cubits between his two arms, his forehead was five cubits, and his hands and feet were each eleven cubits. If the pericarps of ten[2] cubits were so much as touched by one of his feet of eleven cubits, the pollen reached up to the height of nine water-pitchers coming up to the complete fifty-eight cubits of his physical frame, covering him as with finely ground red powder. The Saṁyutta reciters say "It is for this reason that the teacher Padumuttara is thus known to the world".*

Then the Lord Padumuttara, supreme in all the world, having acceded to Brahmā's request for the teaching of Dhamma, surveying the divisions among creatures, saw in Mithilā city the two princes, Devala and Sujāta, possessed of the qualifications; going at that very moment by an aery path, he descended in Mithilā-pleasaunce and had the two princes summoned by the keeper of the pleasaunce. These, saying, "Our aunt's son, Prince Padumuttara, having gone forth and achieved full Self-Awakening, has arrived in our city. Come, We will approach him so as to see him." And with their retinues they approached the Lord Padumuttara and sat down surrounding him. Then Him of the Ten Powers, surrounded by these and shining like the full moon surrounded by a host of stars, turned the Wheel of Dhamma there. Then was the first penetration of Dhamma by a hundred thousand crores. Accordingly it was said:

XI 3 At the Lord Padumuttara's first teaching of Dhamma there was a penetration of Dhamma by a hundred thousand crores.

At a subsequent time, at a meeting with the ascetic Sarada, when he was teaching Dhamma to the populace who had been tortured

* SA ii 90.

[1] As at AA i 287.

[2] BvAB twelve.

by the tortures of Niraya, he caused beings numbering thirty-seven hundred thousand to drink of the nectar of Dhamma. This was the second penetration of Dhamma. Accordingly it was said:

XI 4 Following on that, while (the Buddha) was raining (Dhamma) and refreshing living things there was the second penetration by thirty-seven hundred thousand (crores).

And then the great king, Ānanda, together with twenty thousand men and twenty thousand ministers, appeared in Mithilā city in the presence of Padumuttara, the fully Self-Awakened One. And the Lord Padumuttara let all these go forth by the 'Come, monk' (formula for) going forth. Going along, surrounded by these, [**193**] doing a kindness to his father, he stayed in Haṁsavatī, the capital. There, like our Lord at Kapila city, pacing up and down in the vault of the heavens he spoke the Chronicle of Buddhas. Then there was the third penetration of Dhamma by fifty hundred thousand. Accordingly it was said:

XI 5 At the time when the great hero approached Ānanda, as he came into his father's presence he smote the kettle-drum of deathlessness.

6 When the drum of deathlessness had been smitten and the rain of Dhamma was raining down, there was the third penetration by fifty hundred thousand.

5 Therein *having approached*[1] *Ānanda* means his father was known by the name, King Ānanda.

5 *Smote* means he struck.

6 *Had been smitten* means was being smitten.

6 *When the drum of deathlessness* means when the drum of deathlessness[2]—a change of gender is to be understood. "Assiduously repeated" (āsevito) is also a reading. Its meaning is that it was being assiduously repeated.

6 *The rain of Dhamma was raining down* means it was raining down the rain of Dhamma.[3]

Showing now the means causing the penetration it was said:

XI 7 The Buddha, an exhorter, and instructor, a helper across

[1] upasaṁkamitvā for upasaṁkami of the verse.

[2] amatabherimhī ti amatabheriyā.

[3] vassante dhammavuṭṭhiyā ti dhammavassaṁ vassante.

of all breathing things, skilled in teaching, caused many people to cross over.

7 Therein *exhorter* means an exhorter in that he exhorted with expositions on the special qualities and advantages of undertaking the refuges, moral habits, ascetic practices[1].

7 *Instructor* means an instructor, awakener, in that he instructed as to the four Truths.

7 *Helper across* means a helper across the four floods.

And when the Teacher, his face[2] like the moon at the full,[3] recited the Pātimokkha in Mithilā pleasaunce in Mithilā city in the midst of a host of a hundred thousand crores of monks on the full-moon day of Māgha, that was the first assembly. Accordingly it was said:

XI 8 The teacher Padumuttara had three assemblies; the first was a gathering of a hundred thousand crores.

And when the Lord had spent the rains-residence on Vebhāra Mountain Peak[4] teaching Dhamma to the populace who had come to see the Mountain, and letting ninety thousand crores go forth by the 'Come, monk' admission[5] (to the Order), he recited the Pātimokkha surrounded by these. That was the second assembly. Accordingly it was said:

XI 9 When the Buddha, equal to the unequalled, was staying on Mount Vebhāra there was the second gathering of ninety thousand crores.

[194] Again, when the Lord, having the special qualities, protector of the three worlds, was touring the countryside for delivering the populace from the bonds there was an assembly of eighty thousand crores of monks. Accordingly it was said:

XI 10 Again, when he set forth on tour, there was the third gathering of eighty thousand crores from villages, market-towns, districts.

[1] See Miln 351.
[2] vadana, countenance.
[3] This refers to bindussara, one of the 8 qualities of a perfect voice, attributed to a Great Man at SnA 349 and enumerated at D ii 211, 227. Bindu may be translated as full, close, compact (so PED s.v. bindu).
[4] One of the 5 hills surrounding Rājagaha.
[5] ehibhikkhubhāva.

10 Therein *from villages, market-towns, districts* means "through villages, market-towns, districts"[1] or this itself is the reading. The meaning is: of those who had gone forth having departed from villages, market-towns, districts.

Then our Bodhisatta who was a district governor named Jaṭika[2] and had countless crores of wealth, gave a glorious gift with robe-material to the Order with the Buddha at the head. And on the occasion[3] of the benediction for the meal he too declared of him: "In the future, a hundred thousand eons from now, he will be the Buddha named Gotama." Accordingly it was said:

XI 11 I at that time was a district governor named Jaṭika[4]. I gave cloth with food to the Order with the Self-Awakened One at the head.

12 And then he too[5], as he was sitting in the midst of the Order, declared of me: "A hundred thousand eons from now this one will be a Buddha.

13 When he has striven the striving, carried out austerities . . ." ". . . in the distant future we will be face to face with this one."

14 When I had heard his words I resolutely determined on further practice and made strenuous endeavour[6] for fulfilling the ten perfections.

11 Therein *to the Order with the Self-Awakened One at the head*[7] means to the Self-Awakened One at the head, to the Order[8]; the accusative case in the sense of a genitive.

11 *I gave cloth with food* means I gave food with robe-material.

14 *Strenuous* means very strenuous.

14 *Endeavour* means I made energy.[9]

And in the time of the Lord Padumuttara there were no

[1] gāmanigamaraṭṭhehi, with or through.
[2] BvAB Jaṭila.
[3] BvAC samaya, BvAB avasāna, end.
[4] Be, BvAB, Jā i 37 read Jaṭila, Bv Jaṭiḷa.
[5] tadā, Bv buddho.
[6] akāsiṁ uggaṁ (Bv aggaṁ) daḷhaṁ, Be uggadaḷhaṁ.
[7] acc. case.
[8] gen. case.
[9] Cf. text p. 170.

sectarians. All devas and men simply went to the Buddha for refuge. Accordingly it was said:

XI 15 Stamped out were all sectarians, distracted and downcast then. No one looked after them. They threw them out from the district.

[195] 16 All (of them) gathering together there, went into the Buddha's presence and said: "Great hero, you are our protector, may you be our refuge, One with vision."

17 Compassionate, having pity, seeking the welfare of all breathing things, he established all the assembled sectarians in the five moral habits.

18 It was thus uninvolved with and empty of sectarians; it was ornamented with arahants, steadfast ones who had come to mastery.

15 Therein *stamped out* means arrogance and conceit rent asunder.

15 *Sectarians* (titthiyā) means that herein "ford" (tittha) is to be understood, "ford-maker" (titthakara) is to be understood, "those that ford" (titthiyā, sectarians) is to be understood. Therein when it is said "Herein they cross over by means of the views of eternalism and so forth", the heretical belief is the ford. The producing of this heretical belief is the ford-maker.[1] From being in the ford they are those that ford (sectarians). But it is said that at the time of the Lord Padumuttara there were no sectarians. It should be understood that the words beginning "*Stamped out were sectarians*", were to show that even those who were such-like were (stamped out).[2]

15 *Distracted* means the minds disturbed.

15 *Downcast* is just a synonym for that.

15 *No one looked after them* means no men at all did a service to these other sectarians nor gave almsfood, nor reverenced nor revered nor honoured them, nor rose from their seats, nor made the gesture of clasped hands.

15 *From the district* means even from their own district.[3]

[1] Cf. AA ii 272.

[2] ye pana santi te pi īdisā ahesun ti.

[3] BvAC sakaraṭṭhato, from their own district, province or territory; BvAB sakala-, the entire, with v. l. saka- noted. Saka- may well be the better reading.

15 *They threw out* means they drove out, turned away. The meaning is that they did not give them habitation.

15 *Them* means the sectarians.

16 *Went into the Buddha's presence* means that on being turned away thus by these people who lived in the district, even all the other sectarians, gathering together, simply went for refuge to Padumuttara, Him of the Ten Powers. The meaning is that they went for refuge after they had spoken thus: "You are our teacher, protector, bourn, resting-place, refuge."

17 He is compassionate means *compassionate.*

17 He fares with pity means *having pity.*

17 *Assembled* means the sectarians who gathered together and went for refuge.

17 *He established in the five moral habits* means he caused them to be established in the five moral habits.[1]

18 *Uninvolved* means non-involved, unmixed with those others holding heretical beliefs.

18 *Empty* means empty[2], void of those sectarians.

18 *It* means that the rest of the phrase is to be regarded as (relating) to "that Dispensation of the Lord."

18 *Ornamented* means richly ornamented.[3]

18 *With ones who had come to mastery* means with ones who had attained mastership.

[**196**] That Lord Padumuttara's city was named Haṁsavatī, and his father was the warrior-noble named Ānanda, his mother was the queen named Sujātā; Devala and Sujāta were the two[4] chief disciples, the attendant was named Sumana, Amitā and Asamā were the two[4] chief women disciples; the Tree of Awakening was Salala. The physical frame was fifty-eight cubits in height, and the lustre of his physical frame filled twelve yojanas all round. The life-span was a hundred thousand years. The chief consort was named Vasudattā, the son was named Uttara. The Lord named Padumuttara is said to have attained final nibbāna in the exceedingly delightful Nanda-park, and his relics were not dispersed. The people who lived in the whole of Jambudīpa, gathering

[1] For the commentator's meticulous use of the causative, cf. the sentiment expressed e.g. at Dh 276, "Yours is the ardour for the task; Tathāgatas are showers (of the Way)".

[2] suññatan ti suññaṁ.

[3] vicittavicitta.

[4] Om. at BvAC.

together, built a cetiya consisting of the seven kinds of jewels, twelve yojanas in height. Accordingly it was said:

XI 19 Haṁsavatī was the name of the city, Ānanda the name of the warrior-noble, Sujātā the name of the mother of Padumuttara, the great seer.

24 Devala[1] and Sujāta were the chief disciples. Sumana was the name of the attendant on Padumuttara, the great seer.

25 Amitā and Asamā were the chief women disciples. That Lord's Tree of Awakening is said to be the Salala.[2]

27 The great sage was fifty-eight ratanas tall. The thirty-two glorious Marks resembled a golden festooned column.

28 For twelve yojanas all round ramparts, doors, walls, trees, mountain-crags were no obstruction to him.

29 The (normal) life-span lasted then for a hundred thousand years. Living so long he caused many people to cross over.

30 After causing the populace to cross over and cutting through all doubt, he, blazing like a mass of fire, waned out with the disciples.

28 Therein *mountain-crags* means mountain, reckoned as crags.[3]

28 *Obstruction* means producing concealment beyond.

28 *For twelve yojanas* means day and night the lustre of the Lord's physical frame remained suffusing regions for twelve yojanas all round.

The remainder of the verses are clear in every respect. From here onward, abridging the meaning(s) that have repeatedly occurred beginning with the fulfilment of the perfections, I will proceed by speaking only of the remaining meanings. [**197**] For if we should say over and over again what has been said already when would this Explanation come to an end?

Concluded is the Exposition of the Chronicle of the Buddha Padumuttara

Concluded is the Tenth Buddha-Chronicle

[1] As at Ap i 106; Revata at SA ii 90, ThagA i 115ff.

[2] salalarukkho ti vuccati. Bv salaḷo ti pavuccati.

[3] nagasiluccayā ti nagasaṅkhātā siluccayā. See PED, s.v. naga for a confusion between tree (forest) and mountain.

XII THE EXPOSITION OF THE CHRONICLE OF THE BUDDHA SUMEDHA

And after the fully Self-Awakened One Padumuttara had attained final nibbāna and his Dispensation had disappeared no Buddhas arose for seventy hundred thousand eons[1]; they were void of Buddhas. But thirty thousand eons ago from now the two fully Self-Awakened Ones Sumedha and Sujāta arose in one and the same eon[2].

Therein the Bodhisatta named Sumedha who had wisely attained[3], having fulfilled the perfections was reborn in Tusita-city. Deceasing from there he took on relinking in the womb of the queen named Sudattā, chief consort of the king named Sudatta in the city of Sudassana. After ten months, like the newly risen sun breaking through rents in the clouds[4], he issued forth from his mother's womb in Sudassana-pleasaunce. He lived the household life for nine thousand years. It is said that his three palaces were named Sucanda[5], Kañcana[6], Sirivaḍḍha[7]. There were forty-eight thousand women with the great queen Sumanā at the head.

When he had seen the four signs after queen Sumanā had given birth to a son named Punabbasumitta, departing on the Great Departure mounted on an elephant he went forth. And a hundred crores of men went forth following his example. Surrounded by these he engaged in striving for eight months[8]. On the full-moon day of Visākha he partook of sweet milk-rice given to him by Nakulā, the daughter of a merchant in the market-town of Nakula, and having spent the day-sojourn in a sāla grove he accepted eight handfuls of grass given to him by Sirivaḍḍha, a Naked Ascetic, and spread a grass-spreading twenty cubits in extent at the root of a Nīpa[9] Tree of Awakening. Having routed Māra's forces, he

[1] DA 411 "an incalculable", Jkm 14 gives 69,000 eons.
[2] Therefore a Maṇḍa-eon.
[3] adhigatamedha, a play on his name.
[4] BvAC jaladharavivaragata, BvAB saliladhara-.
[5] BvAC Sucandanaka; BvAB Sucandana.
[6] BvAC Koñca.
[7] BvAB -vaḍḍhana.
[8] BvAC aṭṭha māse, 8 months, also at p. 296. The reading aḍḍhamāsa, half a month, Bv, Be, BvAB (which notices BvAC's reading at p. 296) is probably erroneous. See EC p. 21, n. 2.
[9] nimba at Bv xii 24, Jkm 15 (see EC p. 21, n. 3).

attained complete Self-Awakening[1] and uttered the solemn utterance in the way beginning. "Through many a birth". After spending seven weeks near the Tree of Awakening itself, in the eighth week he acceded to Brahmā's request for Dhamma. Surveying the fortunate people, he saw that his own younger brothers, Prince Saraṇa and Prince Saccakāli, and the hundred crores of monks who had gone forth together with himself were capable of piercing the Dhamma of the four truths[2]. **[198]** Going through the air and descending in Sudassana pleasaunce near Sudassana city he had his own brothers summoned by the keeper of the pleasaunce and turned the Wheel of Dhamma in the midst of these and their retinues. There was penetration of Dhamma then by a hundred thousand crores. Accordingly it was said:

XII 1 After Padumuttara was the leader named Sumedha, hard to attack, of intense incandescence, supreme sage in all the world.

2 He was clear-eyed, full-mouthed, of tall stature, upright, majestic. He sought the welfare of all beings and released many from bondage.

3 When the Buddha had attained the full supreme Awakening, he turned the Wheel of Dhamma in the city of Sudassana.

4 Under him there were three penetrations when he was teaching Dhamma. The first penetration was a by hundred crores.

1 Therein *of intense incandescence* means of a very high degree of incandescence.[3]

2 *Clear-eyed* means his eyes were beautifully clear. His eyes were clear like a string of pearls hung up after it had been washed and polished. Therefore it is said "he was clear-eyed." The meaning is that his fine clear eyes were soft, affectionate, blue[4], stainless, furnished with[5] fine eyelashes. It is also fit and

[1] Here abhisambodhi for the more usual sammāsam-.

[2] Or, the 4 true things, catusaccadhamma. In BvA however, piercing or penetrating Dhamma is not seldom specifically mentioned.

[3] A play on words: uggatejo ti uggatatejo. The same at SA iii 8 (on S iv 172) with the addition of the word balava-tejā.

[4] nīla. At e.g. M ii 137 one of the Marks of a Great Man ascribed to Gotama is that his eyes were dark or intense blue, abhinīla.

[5] BvAC āvuta, BvAB ācita.

right to say that the five (colours of the) eyes were beautifully clear.[1]

2 *Full-mouthed* means his countenance was like the autumn moon at the full.[2]

2 *Tall stature* means a tall stature, large, because the physical frame was eighty-eight cubits in height. The meaning is that the height of the physical frame was not shared by others.[3]

2 *Upright* means having divinely straight limbs[4]; the physical frame was as tall as it was straight, a glorious physical frame resembling a golden portal erected in a deva-city.

2 *Majestic* means the physical frame was shining forth.

2 *He sought the welfare* means he searched for the welfare.

4 *Three penetrations* means three penetrations[5]. A change in gender is made.

And when the Lord got under his power the man-eating yakkha named Kumbhakaṇṇa whose majesty resembled that of Kumbhakarṇa[6] and whose terrifying physical frame could be seen as he was prowling in the forest-tracks leading into the great forest. Early one morning (the Lord) having entered on to the attainment of great compassion[7], emerged from it and surveyed the world. Seeing what was happening he went alone with no companion to that yakkha's abode, entered and sat down on a state-couch that was made ready. Then that yakkha, not conquering anger[8], furious as a terribly venomous poisonous snake that had been thrashed with sticks, wanted to terrify Him of the Ten Powers. Making his own individuality more terrible, [**199**] making his head to resemble a mountain, creating eyes like the orb of the sun, making his teeth long and broad and sharp like ploughshares[9], his

[1] Defining this word, pasannanetta, SnA 453 uses the expression pañcavaṇṇa, the 5 colours. This refers to a Buddha's bodily eye, maṁsacakkhu, for which see above, text p. 33, and Nd2 § 235.

[2] Cf. SnA 453: the face being like the orb of the full moon. Cf. text p. 193.

[3] This must refer to his contemporaries as 3 other Buddhas were the same height (see text p. 296) and Sumana was 90 cubits tall.

[4] Cf. SnA 453. One of the Marks of a Great Man.

[5] abhisamayā tīṇi . . . tayo.

[6] Though this name is spelt here in the Pali form, I can only suppose the reference is to the rākṣasa Kumbhakarṇa, a gigantic brother of Rāvaṇa, described in the Rāmāyaṇa.

[7] See DhA i 26, 367.

[8] Cf. text p. 185.

[9] naṅgalasīsa, see S i 104.

stomach pendulous, blue, distended, uneven, his arms to resemble palm-tree trunks, his nose flattened, hideous, crooked, his mouth distended and reddened like a hole[1] in a mountain-side, and his hair unkempt, tawny, shaggy, rough, he came dreadfully frightening in appearance and stood before the Lord Sumedha. Though breathing forth flames and blazing up, and though raining down the ninefold downpours[2]: rocks, mountains, blazing fire, water, mud, ashes, weapons, burning charcoal and sand, they were unable to stir even a tip of the Lord's hair. So (the yakkha) thought: "When I have asked the Lord a question I will kill him." And he asked a question as Ālavaka did.[3] Then while the Lord was answering that question he led that yakkha to guiding out[4]. It is said that on the following day the people who lived in his district brought a prince and gave him to the yakkha together with food they had brought in carts. But the yakkha gave the prince to the Buddha. Men who had been standing at the entrance to the forest approached the Lord. Then while Him of the Ten Powers was teaching Dhamma suitable to that yakkha's mind, vision of Dhamma arose to ninety thousand crores of living beings in that gathering. That was the second penetration of Dhamma. Accordingly it was said:

XII 5 And again, when the Conqueror was taming the yakkha Kumbhakaṇṇa, there was the second penetration by ninety thousand crores.

And when he taught the four truths in the Sirinanda pleasaunce in the city of Upakāri, then there was the third penetration of Dhamma by eighty thousand crores. Accordingly it was said:

XII 6 And again, when he of boundless fame expounded the four truths, there was the third penetration by eighty thousand crores.

The Lord Sumedha also had three assemblies of disciples. In the first assembly at Sudassana city there were a hundred crores of those who had destroyed the cankers. Again on Mount Devakūṭa when the kaṭhina-cloth was being formally spread out there were ninety crores at the second (assembly). Again, at the third

[1] vila, not in PED; see M-W.

[2] Named also at SnA 224, three being the same as and six different from the above. Cf. text p. 289, also p. 209 for nava vidha-āyudhavassa.

[3] Another yakkha; see SnA 225f.

[4] taṁ yakkhaṁ vinayam upanesi.

(assembly) when the Lord was walking on tour there were eighty crores. Accordingly it was said:

XII 7 The great seer Sumedha had three assemblies of steadfast ones whose cankers were destroyed, stainless, tranquil in mind.

8 When the Conqueror went to Sudassana, the glorious city,[1] there gathered together then a hundred crores of monks whose cankers were destroyed.

9 And again, on Devakūṭa at the (time of the) formal spreading out of the kaṭhina (robe-material) for monks, there was then the second gathering of ninety crores.

[200] 10 And again, when Him of the Ten Powers was walking on tour, there was then the third gathering of eighty crores.

Then our Bodhisatta[2] being a brahman youth named Uttara, superior to[3] all people, bestowed the eighty crores of riches he had accumulated and gave a great gift to the Order of monks[4] with the Buddha at the head. Hearing his[5] Dhamma then[6] and being established in the refuges, having "departed", he went forth. And at the end of the meal that Teacher too, while giving the benediction,[7] declared of him: "In the future he will be the Buddha named Gotama." Accordingly it was said:

XII 11 I at that time was a brahman youth named Uttara. Eighty crores of riches were stored in my house.

12 Giving the whole of it to the leader of the world with the Order, I approached him for refuge and found delight in the going forth.

13 That Buddha too, while he was giving the benediction, declared of me: "After thirty thousand eons this one will be a Buddha.

14 When he has striven the striving, carried out austerities . . ." ". . . in the distant future we will be face to face with this one".

[1] BvAC nagaravaraṁ, Bv nagaraṁ varaṁ, BvAB nāma nagaraṁ.
[2] BvAC reads only Bodhisatta.
[3] uttara, a play on his name.
[4] BvAB reads Order only.
[5] BvAC tassa, BvAB dasabalassa.
[6] BvAC omits.
[7] BvAC bhojanāvasāne anumodento; BvAB bhojanānumodanaṁ karonto.

The verses on the declaration are to be expanded.[1]

15 When I had even heard his words all the more did I incline my mind. I resolutely determined on further practice for fulfilling the ten perfections.

16 Having learnt thoroughly the Suttanta and Vinaya and all the ninefold Dispensation of the teacher, I illumined the Conqueror's Dispensation.

17 Living diligent therein, whether sitting, standing, pacing, after reaching [2] perfection in the super-knowings[3] to the Brahma-world went I.

11 Therein *stored* means laid down[4] because it was treasure.

12 *The whole* means the entire.

12 *All*[5] means giving without remainder.

12 *With the Order* means with his Order.

12 *I approached* means I approached him; the genitive case in the sense of an accusative.[6]

12 *Found delight* means I went forth.

13 *After thirty thousand eons* means when thirty thousand eons have passed.

[**201**] And the name of the city of that Lord Sumedha was Sudassana, the king his father was named Sudatta, his mother was named Sudattā. The two chief disciples were Saraṇa and Sabbakāma, the attendant was named Sāgara, the two chief women disciples were Rāmā and Surāmā. The Tree of Awakening was a Great Nīpa. The physical frame was eighty-eight cubits in height, the life-span was ninety thousand years. He led the household life for nine thousand years. His chief consort was named Sumanā, his son was named Punabbasumitta, he departed mounted on an elephant. The rest is to be seen in the verses. Accordingly it was said:

XII 18 Sudassana was the name of the city, Sudatta the name of the warrior-noble, Sudattā the name of the mother of Sumedha, the great seer.

[1] See IIA 62–70.

[2] BvAC patvā, Bv, BvAB gantvā, going to. Cf. text p. 138, 151, 234.

[3] BvAC, Bv, Be abhiññāsu pāramiṁ, BvAB abhiññapā-.

[4] BvAC nihitaṁ, BvAB nidahitaṁ.

[5] Not translated in the verse as after kevala, the whole, sabba, all, seems superfluous.

[6] (tassa upagañchiṁ in the verse). BvA reads upagañchin ti taṁ upagañchiṁ.

23 Saraṇa and Sabbakāma were the chief disciples. Sāgara was the name of the attendant on Sumedha, the great seer.

24 Rāmā and Surāmā were the chief women disciples. That Lord's Tree of Awakening is said to be the Great Nīpa[1].

26 The great sage was eighty-eight ratanas tall. He illumined all the quarters as the moon in a host of stars.

27 As a universal monarch's gem shines over a yojana, so did his jewel suffuse a yojana all round.

28 The (normal) life-span lasted then for ninety thousand years. Living so long he caused many people to cross over.

29 With steadfast ones who had attained the three knowledges, the six super-knowings, the powers—with such arahants was this thronged.

30 And when all of these, of boundless fame, well freed, devoid of clinging, had displayed the light of knowledge, they, of great fame, waned out.

26 Therein *as the moon in a host of stars* means as a full moon in the heavens makes effulgent and illumines in a host of stars even so did he make effulgent all the quarters. Some read "as the moon on the fifteenth (day)". This meaning is quite clear.

27 *A universal monarch's gem* means as the Jewel-treasure of a universal monarch is spoken of as equal in extent to the nave of a cart four cubits in length and is surrounded by eighty-four thousand gems, so it is said to be like the beauty of the splendour of the rising autumnal moon at the full surrounded by a host of stars. [**202**] When the Jewel-treasure, extremely delightful to behold, comes from a massive mountain[2], even as it is coming its radiance suffuses the district for the distance of a yojana all round.[3] So did the radiance from the physical frame of this Lord Sumedha suffuse the measure of a yojana all round.

29 *The three knowledges, the six super-knowings* mean the three knowledges and the six super-knowings.[4]

[1] Anthocephalus cadamba. Bv calls this Tree mahānimba, a great Neem tree, Azadirachta Indica. See EC p. 21, n. 3.

[2] See Miln 218.

[3] See M iii 174, Miln 118.

[4] tevijja-chaḷabhiññehī (instrumentive to agree with tādihi, "with steadfast ones") ti tevijjehi chaḷabhiññehi cā ti attho.

29 *Attained the powers* means attained the powers of psychic potency.

29 *With steadfast ones* means with (those) attained to a steadfast state.

29 *Was thronged* means crowded, glowing with a single (kind of) yellow robe[1].

29 *This* is said in reference to the Dispensation or to the surface of the earth.

30 *Of boundless fame* means of a boundless retinue or of a renown and fame without gauge.

30 *Devoid of clinging* means without the four clingings.[2]

In the remaining verses the meaning is quite clear everywhere.

Concluded is the Exposition of the Chronicle of the Buddha Sumedha

Concluded is the Eleventh Buddha-Chronicle

XIII THE EXPOSITION OF THE CHRONICLE OF THE BUDDHA SUJĀTA

Subsequently to him[3] in that same Maṇḍa-eon[4] when beings had gradually come to be of unlimited life-spans, but in due course dwindling so that life-spans were of ninety thousand years, the teacher Sujāta, well-born,[5] comely in body, of perfectly pure birth, arose in the world. When he had fulfilled the perfections he was reborn in Tusita city. Deceasing from there and taking on re-linking in Sumaṅgala city in the womb of Pabhāvatī, chief consort of the king named Uggata, he issued forth from his mother's womb after ten months. When he was being given a name on the name-taking day, because his birth brought happiness to all beings in the whole of Jambudīpa they gave him the name of Sujāta. He led the

[1] Cf. Vbh 247, Miln 19.

[2] upadhi, given at e.g. MA iii 169 as clinging to the aggregates (khandha), the defilements (kilesa), the determinations (abhisaṅkhāra), and to the sense-pleasures (kāmaguṇa).

[3] Sumedha, the preceding Buddha.

[4] See text p. 191.

[5] sujāta, purely born, not of mixed parentage.

household life for nine thousand years. Siri, Upasiri and Nanda were his three palaces. There were twenty three thousand women in attendance on him with Queen Sirinandā at the head.

When he had seen the four signs and the son named Upasena had been born to Queen Sirinandā, departing on the Great Departure mounted on the glorious thoroughbred steed named Haṁsavaha, he went forth. On his going forth a crore of men went forth following his example. When he, surrounded by these, had engaged in striving for nine months, and on the full-moon day of Visākha had partaken of very sweet honey and milk-rice given to him by the daughter of the merchant Sirinandana in the city of Sirinandana, he spent the day-sojourn in a sāla grove. Towards evening he accepted eight handfuls of grass given to him by Sunanda, a Naked Ascetic, **[203]** and approaching a Bamboo Tree of Awakening he spread a grass spreading thirty-three cubits in extent. Even while the sun was still up he routed Māra's forces together with Māra. Piercing through to full Self-Awakening, he uttered the solemn utterance conformably with all Buddhas, and spent seven weeks near to the Tree of Awakening itself.

Requested by Brahmā and seeing that his own younger brother, the boy Sudassana, and a priest's son, the boy Deva, were capable of piercing the Dhamma of the four truths[1], he went through the air and, descending in the Sumaṅgala pleasaunce near Sumaṅgala city had his own brother and the priest's son summoned by the keeper of the pleasaunce. Seated in the midst of these with their retinues he turned the Wheel of Dhamma. There was a penetration of Dhamma there by eighty crores. This was the first penetration. And when the Lord had performed the Marvel of the Double at the root of a great sāla tree at the gateway of the Sudassana pleasaunce, he went for the rains to the devas of the Thirty-Three; then there was a penetration of Dhamma by thirty-seven thousand[2]. This was the second penetration. And when Sujāta, Him of the Ten Powers, went into his father's presence then there was a penetration of Dhamma by sixty hundred thousand. This was the third penetration of Dhamma. Accordingly it was said:

XIII 1 In that same Maṇḍa-eon the leader was named Sujāta,

[1] See note to text p. 197 above.

[2] Be, BvAB read 37 hundred thousand here and in ver. 5.

lion-jawed, broad of shoulder[1], immeasurable, difficult to attack.

2 Stainless as the moon, pure,[2] majestic as him of the hundred rays—so shone the Self-Awakened One, always[3] blazing with splendour.

3 The Self-Awakened One, having attained full supreme Awakening, turned the Wheel of Dhamma in the city of Sumaṅgala.

4 While Sujāta, leader of the world, was teaching the glorious Dhamma eighty crores penetrated at the first teaching of Dhamma.

5 When Sujāta, of boundless fame, was spending the rains with the devas, there was the second penetration by thirty-seven thousand.

6 When Sujāta, equal to the unequalled, went into his father's presence, there was the third penetration by sixty hundred thousand.

1 Therein *in that same Maṇḍa-eon* means that the Lord Sujāta arose in the self-same Maṇḍa-eon as that in which the Lord Sumedha arose.

[**204**] 1 *Lion-jawed* means that his jaws were like a lion's; and as a lion's lower jaw is full but not the upper one, so the Great Man's lower jaw was like that of a lion; and the two were full resembling the moon on the twelfth (day) in the bright half (of the month).

1 *Broad of shoulder* means that the shoulders were evenly rounded like a bull's,[4] the shoulders were like well looked after golden drums.[5]

2 *As him of the hundred rays* means like the sun.

2 *With splendour* means with a Buddha's splendour.

3 *Supreme Awakening* means supreme Self-Awakening.

When in the city of Sudhammavatī he had taught Dhamma in Sudhamma pleasaunce to the people who had come and when he had let the sixty hundred thousand go forth by the 'Come, monk'

[1] Cf. IIB 194.

[2] suddha at Bv, Be; buddha at BvACB.

[3] BvAC sadā, Bv pabhā.

[4] Hence the descriptive term usabhakkhandha, "bull's shoulder", here translated "broad of shoulder".

[5] Cf. text p. 124.

method[1] he recited the Pātimokkha in their midst. This was the first assembly. Following on that, when the Lord descended from a heaven[2] there was the second assembly of fifty hundred thousand. Again, when four hundred thousand men who had come and had heard that Prince Sudassana had gone forth in the Lord's presence and had attained arahantship, they thought, "We too will go forth". The Elder Sudassana, taking them, approached Sujāta, the bull of men. Having taught them Dhamma and let them go forth by the 'Come, monk' (formula for) going forth, the Lord recited the Pātimokkha in an assembly possessing the four factors.[3] This was the third assembly. Accordingly it was said:

XIII 7 Sujāta, the great seer, had three assemblies of steadfast ones whose cankers were destroyed, stainless, tranquil in mind.

8 They, among the sixty hundred thousand (of those) who had attained power in the super-knowings and had not come to repeated births, assembled there.

9 And again, at an assembly when the Conqueror was coming down from a heaven, there was the second gathering of fifty hundred thousand.

10 That chief disciple of his,[4] approaching the bull of men,[5] approached the Self-Awakened One with four hundred thousand.

8 Therein *had not come to* means had not attained *repeated births*. "Not proceeding[6] in repeated births" is also a reading. That is the very meaning.

9 *Was coming down from a heaven* means was descending from a heaven-world. It should be understood to be in the active voice (of the verb[7]); it is said by changing the voice. Or, *was coming down from a heaven* means was descending from a heaven.[8]

[1] ehibhikkhubhāvena.

[2] Tidiva, normally a name for Tāvatiṁsa. But see comment to ver. 9 below.

[3] See text p. 126.

[4] BvAC, Bv tassa yo, Be, BvAB Sudassano.

[5] BvAC, Bv naravasabhaṁ, Be, BvAB narasabhaṁ.

[6] appavatta. I do not think CPD's "inactive, without action" quite conveys the meaning. The word occurs on text p. 103 in the explanation of "not of double meaning", translated there as "Does not occur".

[7] Normally this would be vorohante, not vorohane as in the verse where the active voice is not used.

[8] tidivorohane ti tidivato otaraṇe.

9 *When the Conqueror* means of the Conqueror.[1] The locative in the sense of a genitive is to be understood.

It is said that our Bodhisatta was then a wheel-turning king.[2] Having heard that a Buddha had arisen in the world, he approached the Lord, heard a talk on Dhamma and, having given his great kingdom which consisted of the four continents together with the seven treasures to the Order of monks with the Buddha at the head, he went forth in the teacher's presence. [**205**] All the people who lived in the continent, taking the produce of the country, performing the duties pertaining to a monastery, constantly gave a great gift to the Order with the Buddha at the head. That teacher too declared of him, "In the future he will be the Buddha named Gotama". Accordingly it was said:

XIII 11 I at that time was lord of the four continents[3], a mover through mid-air was I[4], a wheel-turner[5], very powerful.

13 Bestowing on the Buddha my great kingdom of the four continents and the seven superb Treasures, I went forth in his presence.

14 Monastery-attendants, having gathered together the produce of the countryside, presented the Order of monks with requisites, beds and seats.

15 This Buddha,[6] lord of the ten-thousand, also declared of me: "After thirty thousand eons this one will be a Buddha.

16 When he has striven the striving, carried out austerities . . ." ". . . in the distant future we will be face to face with this one."

17 When I had heard his words all the more did I rejoice. I resolutely determined on the strenuous practice for fulfilling the ten perfections.

18 Having learnt thoroughly the Suttanta and Vinaya and all the ninefold Dispensation of the teacher, I illumined the Conqueror's Dispensation.

[1] jine (loc.) ti jinassa (gen.).
[2] I.e. a universal monarch.
[3] Jambudīpa (India), Pubbavideha, Aparagoyāna, Uttarakuru.
[4] Following the Treasure of the Wheel. At x 13 the Bodhisatta was also an antaḷikkhacara but for a different reason.
[5] One who turned the wheel of government.
[6] BvAC reads so pi maṁ tadā for so pi maṁ buddho.

19 Living diligent therein, developing the Brahma-
development, after reaching perfection in the super-
knowings to the Brahma-world went I.

11 Therein *of the four continents* means of the four great continents with the surrounding continents.

11 *A mover through mid-air* means a mover through the sky following the Treasure of the wheel.

13 *The seven Treasures* means the seven Treasures beginning with the Treasure of the elephant.

13 *Superb* means superb.[1] Or, the meaning is to be understood as "on the superb Buddha."

13 *Bestowing* means giving.

14 *Produce*[2] means what was yielded[3] in the kingdom: the meaning is the income.[4]

14 *Having gathered together* means having made a heap, having collected.

[**206**] 14 *Requisites* means the requisites beginning with robes.

15 *Lord of the ten-thousand* means lord of the ten-thousand world-systems. It should be known that this was said with reference to the field of birth[5]: the Lord (bhagavā) is the lord (issaro) of the unending world-systems.

15 *After thirty thousand eons* means thirty thousand eons hence from now.

And, again,[6] the city of that Lord Sujāta was named Sumaṅgala, the king, his father was named Uggata, his mother was named Pabhāvatī. The two chief disciples were Sudassana and Deva[7], the attendant was named Nārada, the two chief women disciples were Nāgā and Nāgasamālā. The Tree of Awakening was a Great

[1] uttame ti uttamāni.

[2] uṭṭhāna.

[3] uppāda, as above too (just before the verses) can also mean "unusual event" which was here this vast gift of the four continents, etc., so "the yield of the kingdom." But BvA goes on to say "the income".

[4] āya, income, revenue, gain, profit.

[5] See Vism 414 on the 3 Buddha-fields, of birth, of authority, of scope. "The field of birth is limited by the ten-thousand world-spheres that quaked when the Tathāgata took on relinking, and so on".

[6] puna perhaps refers to some of the details mentioned in the opening paragraphs of this Chronicle.

[7] Bv, Be, BvAB Sudeva but BvAC adheres to Deva, both earlier in the Chronicle and ver. 25 below.

Bamboo; they say that the massive trunk lacked hollows[1], was exceedingly delightful, and that the wide-spreading branches were covered with stainless leaves the colour of beryl that gleamed like a peacock's tail. And that Lord's physical frame was fifty cubits in height, the life-span was ninety thousand years. His chief consort was named Sirinandā, the son was named Upasena. He departed riding a thoroughbred steed. And he attained final nibbāna in Sīla-monastery in the city of Candavatī.

XIII 20 Sumaṅgala was the name of the city, Uggata the name of the warrior-noble, Pabhāvatī the name of the mother of Sujāta, the great seer.

25 Sudassana and Deva were the chief disciples. Nārada was the name of the attendant on Sujāta, the great seer.

26 Nāgā and Nāgasamālā were the chief women disciples. That Lord's Tree of Awakening is said to be the Great Velu.[2]

27 And that Tree was sound[3], beautiful, not hollow, leafy, a bamboo that was straight, big, good to look upon, delightful.

28 It grew to a good height as one stem and after that a branch broke out; as the peacock's tail-feathers well tied together, thus shone that Tree.

29 It had neither thorns nor yet a hollow. It was big, the branches outspread, it was not sparse, the shade was dense, it was delightful.

31 That Conqueror was fifty ratanas tall. He was furnished with all the glorious attributes, provided with all the special qualities.

[207] 32 His lustre, equal to the unequalled, streamed forth all round. He was measureless, unrivalled, not to be compared with anything similar.

33 The (normal) life-span lasted then for ninety thousand years. Living so long he caused many people to cross over.

34 Just as the waves in the ocean, just as the stars in the

[1] mandacchiddo, a meaning borne out by acchiddo and n'āpi chiddaṁ in ver. 27, 29.

[2] mahāveḷu. Great Bamboo, probably not the Giant Bamboo.

[3] jāta, Be ghana, thick.

sky, so was the Word (of the Buddha) emblazoned then by arahants.

35 Both that Buddha, equal to the unequalled, and those unrivalled special qualities have all disappeared. Are not all constructions void?

27 Therein *not hollow* means without a hollow. It should be understood as in the contexts "a slim maiden".[1] Some read "the hollow was insignificant".

27 *Leafy* means many leaves. The meaning is that it was loaded with leaves the colours of crystals and gems.[2]

27 *Straight* means not twisted, not crooked.

27 *A bamboo* means a bamboo.[3]

27 *Big* means great all round.

28 (*As*) *one stem* means as one tree in the ground, alone.

28 *Grew to a good height* means grow.[4]

28 *After that a branch broke out*[5] means after that from the bamboo a five-fold branch issuing forth broke out.[5] "After that a branch broke out"[5] is also a reading.

28 *Well tied together* means beautifully tied in the manner of tying (a peacock's) tail-feathers.[6]

28 *Peacock's tail-feathers*[7] means it is to be called a sheaf of peacock's tail-feathers tied (together) and made for warding off the heat.[8]

29 *It had neither thorns*[9] means that on that bamboo-tree were no thorns[9] or parasites[9].

29 *Not sparse* means it was covered with branches that were not sparse.

29 *The shade was dense* means the shade was thick. It is spoken of as "the shade was dense" simply because of the non-sparseness.

[1] anudarā kaññā. Anudara not in CPD or PTC, but see M-W "thin, lank"; lit. without a stomach or a cavity. I have not been able to trace the quotation, if it is meant to be one.

[2] BvAB kācamaṇivaṇṇehi, BvAC marakatamaṇi-. Perhaps mara- should read mora-, peacock?

[3] vaṁso ti veḷu as at SnA 76.

[4] pavaḍḍhitvā ti vaḍḍhitvā.

[5] pabhijjati . . . pabhijjittha . . . pabhijjatha.

[6] BvAC piñjabandhana; BvAB pañcabandhana, see PED s.v. pañca.

[7] morahattha.

[8] Presumably a fan.

[9] kaṇṭakā . . . kaṇṭakino . . . kaṇṭakā. One of the meanings of kaṇṭaka is robber, infestor; hence a parasite.

31 *Was fifty ratanas* means: was fifty cubits.

31 *Furnished with all the glorious attributes* means: furnished with glories in every manner is called "furnished with all the glorious attributes."

31 *Provided with all the special qualities* is merely a synonym for the preceding word.

32 *Measureless* means without measure: measureless because of the impossibility of taking the measure.

32 *Unrivalled:* the meaning is unrivalled by anyone, unique.

32 *With anything similar* means with anything that could be compared.

32 *Not to be compared* means without compare. From the impossibility of saying "Like this and this" the meaning is "not to be compared".

[**208**] 35 *And those special qualities* means: and those special qualities[1]. The meaning is: special qualities beginning with omniscient knowledge. It is said with a change of gender.

Everywhere remaining is quite clear.

Concluded is the Exposition of the Chronicle of the Buddha Sujāta

Concluded is the Twelfth Buddha-Chronicle

XIV THE EXPOSITION OF THE CHRONICLE OF THE BUDDHA PIYADASSIN

And subsequently to Sujāta, a hundred thousand eons prior to now, three Buddhas, Piyadassin, Atthadassin, Dhammadassin, were reborn in one and the same eon.[2] Therein, the teacher named Piyadassin, having fulfilled the perfections, was reborn in Tusita city. Deceasing from there and taking on relinking in the city of Sudhaññavatī in the womb of Queen Candā, whose face[3] resembled the moon (canda), chief consort of the king named Sudassana, after ten months he issued forth from his mother's womb in Varuṇa-pleasaunce. Because a variety of marvels dear

[1] guṇāni ca tānī ti guṇā ca te.

[2] A Vara-eon, see text p. 191.

[3] vadana, not in PED in this sense; see M-W.

to the world were to be seen on his name-taking day, they simply gave him the name Piyadassin (seeing what is dear). He lived the household life for nine thousand years. It is said his three palaces were named Sunimmala[1], Vimala, Giribrahā.[2] There were thirty-three thousand women attending on him with the great Queen Vimalā at the head.

When he had seen the four signs and the prince Kañcana[3] had been born to Queen Vimalā, departing on the Great Departure in a chariot drawn by thoroughbreds, he went forth. A crore of men went forth following his example. When the Great Man, surrounded by these, had engaged in striving for six months, and on the full-moon day of Visākha had partaken of sweet milk-rice given to him by the daughter of the brahman Vasabha in the brahman village of Varuṇa, he spent the day-sojourn in a sāla grove. Accepting eight handfuls of grass given to him by Sujāta, a Naked Ascetic, he approached a Kakudha Tree of Awakening and spread a grass spreading fifty-three cubits in extent. Sitting cross-legged, he pierced omniscient knowledge and uttered the solemn utterance. After he had spent seven weeks there and knew that those who had gone forth following his example were capable of piercing the ariyan Dhamma, he went through the air, descended at Usabhavana pleasaunce near the city of Usabhavatī[4] and turned the Wheel of Dhamma surrounded by the crore of monks. There was then a penetration of Dhamma by a hundred thousand crores. This was the first penetration.

[209] Again, a deva-king named Sudassana lived on Sudassana mountain not far from the city named Subhavatī. He held false views. Every year all the people in Jambudīpa collected a hundred thousand offerings and oblations for him. This deva-king Sudassana while sitting on one and the same seat together with a king of men, received the oblation. Then the Lord Piyadassin thinking, "I will dispel that false view of this deva-king Sudassana", entered his abode at a time when that deva-king had gone to a gathering of yakkhas, ascended a state-couch, and emitting the six-hued rays, sat down resembling the autumn sun on Mount Yugandhara. The devatās who were his followers and attendants having paid

[1] Bv Sunimala.
[2] Bv, Be Giriguhā.
[3] Bv Kañcanaveḷa, also elsewhere. At text p. 214 he is Kañcanāvela.
[4] Ussāvana at Bv xiv 19.

homage to Him of the Ten Powers with garlands, perfumes and unguents stood surrounding him. Then when the deva-king Sudassana returned from the gathering of yakkhas and saw the six-hued rays streaming forth from his own abode, he thought, "Now, such a resplendent glory as this of a blaze of many rays has not before been visible on other days. Who has come in here—a deva or a human being?" Looking round and seeing the Lord sitting and shining with the splendour of the six-hued rays resembling the sun at autumn-time rising over the mountain-crests, he thought, "This shaveling recluse is sitting on the couch of glory surrounded by my retinue". His mind was overcome by anger and he thought, "Indeed, now I will display my own power to him", and he turned that whole mountain into one blazing wreath[1] thinking, "The shaveling recluse must be (burnt to) ashes by this blaze of fire". Looking round and seeing Him of the Ten Powers brightly shining, his glorious physical frame brilliant with the blaze of a multitude of diverse rays, his pure countenance[2] a splendour of beauty, his complexion fair, he thought, "This recluse is immune from burning by fire. Come, I will kill him by overwhelming him with a flood of water", and he created a very deep flood of water in front of his mansion. But even when that flood of water was at the full it did not wet so much as a thread of the Lord's robe as he was seated in that mansion nor as much as a hair[3] of his physical frame. Thereupon the deva-king Sudassana considered, "By *this* the recluse must suffocate[4] and die". But when he had drawn back the water and, looking round, saw the Lord seated surrounded by his own company, shining with the blaze of the multitudinous rays and resembling the moon in autumn-time penetrating fissures in black clouds, not conquering his own rage he thought, "Come, kill him I will" and in anger he rained down a rain of the nine kinds of weapons.[5] But, through the Lord's majesty, all the weapons, turning into wreaths of various kinds of fragrant flowers, extremely pleasing to behold, fell down at the feet of Him of the Ten Powers.

When Sudassana the deva-king saw this wonder he was extremely angry; seizing the Lord's feet in both his hands, and anxious to

[1] BvAC ekajālamālaṁ, BvAB ekajālaṁ.

[2] vadana.

[3] BvAC roma, BvAB loma.

[4] nirassāsa, being without breath or breathing. Not in PED.

[5] Cf. the 9 weapons at text pp. 199, 289, and the 5 at Miln 339.

eject him from his own abode, he sprang aloft[1] and when he had passed over the great sea and arrived on a mountain in the Cakkavāḷa, he thought, "Now, is this recluse alive or dead?" Looking round, he saw him still seated on that same seat, and thought, "Ah, this recluse is of great majesty. *I* am unable to dislodge this recluse from here. If anyone were to know this of me I would be in immense disgrace. [**210**] But as long as no one sees this I can go away, leaving him."

Then Him of the Ten Powers, surveying the character of his thoughts, resolutely determined so that all devas and men saw him. And on that very day a hundred and one kings in the whole of Jambudīpa assembled to give him an offering. These kings of men seeing Sudassana the deva-king seated (there) holding the Lord's feet, thought "Our deva-king is worshipping the feet of the teacher Piyadassin, king of sages. Ah, Buddhas are indeed wonderful, ah, the special qualities of Buddhas are very distinguished" and with minds of faith towards the Lord, they all stood reverencing the Lord raising their clasped hands to their heads. Thereupon the Lord Piyadassin, placing that deva-king Sudassana in the forefront, taught Dhamma. Then ninety thousand crores of devas and men attained arahantship. This was the second penetration.

Again, in Kumuda city which was nine yojanas in extent the Elder Soṇa who, like Devadatta, was inimical to the Buddha, consulted together with Prince Mahāpaduma. When he had had his father murdered he also devised various plans for killing the Buddha Piyadassin[2] but, being unable to do so, he had the mahout of Doṇamukha, king of elephants, summoned and, cajoling him, explained the matter to him: "Now, when that recluse Piyadassin enters this city for almsfood, then set at large the glorious elephant Doṇamukha and let him kill the recluse Piyadassin." Then that mahout, the king's favourite, without thinking of good or bad[3], considered, "This recluse might cause even me to fall from my office[4]", and agreed saying, "So be it."

On the next day, observing the time when Him of the Ten

[1] ukkhipitvā does not mean here, I think, taking (him) up or holding (him) up so much as tossing himself up, rising or raising himself up (into the air).

[2] Cf. the story of Ajātasattu, the parricide, and his attempts to kill the Buddha Gotama.

[3] hitāhitavicāraṇarahita.

[4] ṭhānantara. See Childers; also at DA i 297, DhA i 340.

Powers entered the city and having made the elephant[1] even more intoxicated with a variety of little pieces of food coated with ointments and incense, he sent him, who was glorious among elephants[2] as was the elephant Erāvaṇa[3], to kill the glorious elephant, the elephant of sages. As he was roaming about he approached as if terrifying Antaka.[4] Fine was his forehead[5] and the frontal lobe on his head. He had long sloping flanks[6] like a bow, well spread out straight ears, sweet brown eyes, beautiful back and withers,[7] thick loins, what was hidden between his knees massive, his handsome tusks like ploughshares, his elegant tail blue-black, he was possessed of all the marks, pleasing to behold as is the unfettered sea, his lion-gait graceful and strong, his upper and lower lips both mobile, he was seven-fold firm, and showing signs of rut in seven places.

Then that glorious elephant[8], as though still in rut, having killed elephants, buffaloes, horses, men and women, his physical frame dyed and coloured with the blood of his victims[9], his eyes covered over with an inner blaze, having smashed wagons, windows, pinnacled houses, doorways and portals, wandered about followed by crows, ravens and vultures. When he had broken off the limbs of the buffaloes, men, horses, elephants[10] and so on that he had slain, and was crunching them up like a man-eating yakkha, he saw from afar Him of the Ten Powers coming along surrounded by his company of pupils and he approached the Lord quickly, his speed like that of an eagle in the air. Then the people who lived in the city, their minds filled with fear and terror, getting up on to long-houses, walls, ramparts[11], and on to trees, and seeing (the elephant) rushing[12] towards the Tathāgata uttered the sound of grief, "Ha, ha." [**211**] But some lay-followers began to check him by various means and methods.

[1] Here and below vārana, not nāga.

[2] arivāraṇavāraṇa, cf. text p. 245.

[3] Sakka's elephant, cf. text p. 245.

[4] The End-maker, death, sometimes an epithet of Māra.

[5] Reading -nalāta with BvAB for BvAC's -thala.

[6] suṇḍa taṭa. Not in PED. See M-W s.v. śroṇi-taṭa.

[7] khandhāsana.

[8] dviradavaro. Cf. dirada below, and at p. 288. Not in PED but in Childers.

[9] hata, those he had killed.

[10] dirada.

[11] caya. See M-W s.v. 1 ci, where the several meanings given are all edifices of some kind.

[12] BvAC abhipatantaṁ, BvAB abhidhāvantaṁ.

Then that Buddha-nāga, surveying that elephant-nāga[1] as he was approaching, his heart tranquilly diffusing compassion, pervaded him with loving-kindness. Thereupon that elephant-nāga, knowing his own defect of anger, the springs of his heart made tender by the loving-kindness that pervaded him, unable to stand before the Lord through shame, lay down with his head at the Lord's feet as though he were entering the earth. And while he was lying down thus, his physical frame resembling a mass of darkness, he shone forth like the mass of the unfettered sea near to glorious golden mountain-peaks tinged by the evening light. Seeing the elephant-king[2] lying thus with his head towards the feet of the king of sages, the townspeople, in acclamation shouted out a lion's roar of 'Bravo', their hearts filled with the utmost zest. They honoured him in various ways with garlands of fragrant flowers, with sandal-wood, perfumes, scented powders and adornments. On all sides they waved garments. In the vault of the heavens the drums of the gods resounded. Then the Lord, surveying that glorious elephant[3] lying at his feet like an unfettered mountain-peak, having stroked the glorious elephant's[4] head with the palm of his hand which was adorned with goad, banner, net, chank, and wheel, instructed him by means of a teaching of Dhamma regarding docility of mind:

Listen to what is said about the glorious elephant and follow my words which are bent on weal and welfare. Then, putting away despoiling and addiction to slaughter, attain to peace, a giver of what is pleasant. 85
Lord of elephants, he who harms breathing things because of greed and hatred or confusion for long experiences terrible anguish in Niraya for killing breathing things. 86
Do not do a deed like this again, elephant[5], from negligence or vanity. For making onslaught on breathing things one gains anguish in Avīci enduring for an eon. 87
After experiencing terrible anguish in Niraya, if he goes on to the world of men, repeatedly he is of short life-span, uncomely, cruel, a participant in excessive anguish.[6] 88
And, inasmuch as breathing things are extremely dear to the

[1] hatthi-nāga.
[2] karirājā.
[3] dirada.
[4] gaja.
[5] mātaṅga.
[6] dukkhavisesabhāgī.

great populace, so, beautiful lordly elephant-nāga, knowing that likewise they are dear to another, onslaught on breathing things is to be shunned.

[212] Having found that there are special qualities in hatred and addiction to harming as well as in refraining from onslaught on creatures, (then) shunning onslaught on creatures you may desire[1] happiness in heaven hereafter.

Refraining from onslaught on creatures, well tamed, one becomes dear and liked in this world, and after the breaking up of his body Buddhas speak of him as dwelling in heaven.

No one in the world desires coming to anguish; indeed, everything born seeks only happiness. Therefore, great nāga, putting away harming, develop loving-kindness and compassion all the time.

Then when the glorious tusker, being instructed thus by Him of the Ten Powers, had acquired restraint[2] he was like a pupil possessed of discipline and right behaviour, highly trained. So did the Lord Piyadassin after he had thus tamed the glorious elephant Doṇamukha teach Dhamma there in a gathering of the populace, as did our teacher (after taming) Dhanapāla. Then there was a penetration of Dhamma by eighty hundred thousand crores. This was the third penetration. Accordingly it was said:

XIV 1 After Sujāta was Piyadassin, leader of the world, self-become, difficult to attack, equal to the unequalled, of great renown.

2 And that Buddha of boundless fame shone like the sun. Annihilating all the gloom he turned the Wheel of Dhamma.

3 And under him whose incandescence had no gauge there were three penetrations. The first penetration was by a hundred thousand crores.

4 Sudassana, the deva-king, took pleasure in false view. The teacher, dispelling his false view, taught Dhamma.

5 An assembly of people, without gauge, great, assembled then; the second penetration was by ninety thousand crores.

[1] BvAC icchaya tvaṁ, BvAB icchati ce.

[2] saññа, from saṁ + yamati; cf. Vism 57 asaṁyatassa, v. l. asaññatassa, "of one without restraint".

6 When the charioteer of men had tamed the elephant Doṇamukha there was the third penetration by eighty thousand crores.[1]

In the city of Sumaṅgala the king's son named Pālita and the priest's son, the boy Sabbadassin, were friends. Hearing that the fully Self-Awakened One, Piyadassin, had reached their own city while he was walking on tour, they went out to meet him with their retinues of a hundred thousand crores. When they had heard his Dhamma [**213**] and had given a great gift for seven days, going forth on the seventh day together with the hundred thousand crores on the conclusion of the Lord's benediction for the repasts, they attained arahantship. The Lord recited the Pātimokkha in their midst. This was the first assembly. At a later time at the gathering for Sudassana the deva-king, ninety crores attained arahantship. Surrounded by these, the teacher recited the Pātimokkha. This was the second assembly. Again, eighty crores who had gone forth on the taming of Doṇamukha attained arahantship. The Lord recited the Pātimokkha in their midst. This was the third assembly. Accordingly it was said:

XIV 7 And this Lord Piyadassin had three assemblies. The first was a gathering of a hundred thousand crores.

8 Later, ninety crores of sages gathered together. At the third assembly there were eighty crores.

At that time our Bodhisatta was a brahman youth named Kassapa; he was master of the three Vedas with the legendary tradition as the fifth. When he had heard the teacher's teaching of Dhamma, by means of the sacrifice of a hundred thousand crores, he had a lovely monastery constructed as a monastery for the Order, and was established in the refuges and the five moral habits. Then the teacher declared of him "Eighteen hundred eons from now he will be the Buddha named Gotama." Accordingly it was said:

XIV 9 I at that time was a (brahman) youth[2] named Kassapa, a repeater, expert in the mantras, master of the three Vedas.[3]

[1] 80 hundred thousand given above.
[2] BvAC māṇavo, noted by BvAB which with Bv, Be reads brāhmaṇo.
[3] As at IIA 6, 10.

10 When I had heard his Dhamma I conceived belief. With a hundred thousand crores I constructed a park for the Order.

11 After giving him the park I was exultant, stirred in mind; I undertook the refuges and the five moral habits making myself firm in them.

12 And that Buddha[1] too, as he was sitting in the midst of the Order, declared of me, "After eighteen hundred eons this one will be a Buddha.

13 When he was striven the striving, carried out austerities ..." "... we will be face to face with this one."

14 When I had heard his words all the more did I incline my mind. I resolutely determined on further practice for fulfilling the ten perfections.

[**214**] And that Lord's city was named Sudhañña, the king his father was named Sudatta, his mother the queen was named Sucandā. Pālita and Sabbadassin were the chief disciples. The attendant was named Sobhita, Sujātā and Dhammadinnā were the two chief women disciples. The Tree of Awakening was a Kakudha. The physical frame was eighty cubits in height, the life-span ninety thousand years. Vimalā was the name of his chief consort, the son was named Kañcanāvela. He departed by a chariot harnessed to thoroughbreds. Accordingly it was said:

XIV 15 Sudhañña was the name of the city[2], Sudatta[3] the name of the warrior-noble, Sucandā[4] was the name of the mother of Piyadassin, the teacher.

20 Pālita and Sabbadassin were the chief disciples. Sobhita was the name of the attendant on Piyadassin, the teacher.

21 Sujātā and Dhammadinnā were the chief women disciples. That Lord's Tree of Awakening is said to be the Kakudha.[5]

23 And that Buddha of boundless fame had the thirty-two glorious Marks. Eighty cubits tall, he looked like a king of sāla trees.

[1] tadā above, Buddho at Bv.
[2] Sudhaññavatī at text p. 208 and BvAB, Anoma at Jā i 39.
[3] Sudassana at text p. 208 and BvAB, Sudinna at Jā i 39.
[4] Canda at text p. 208, BvAB, Jā i 39.
[5] Piyaṅgurukkha at Jā i 39.

24 No lustre of fire, the moon and the sun, was like unto the lustre of that great seer who was without an equal.
25 The life-span of this deva of devas was such that the One with vision remained in the world for ninety thousand years.
26 But that Buddha, equal to the unequalled, and those unrivalled pairs have all disappeared. Are not all constructions void?

11 Therein *the refuges and the five moral habits:* the meaning is: the three refuges and the five moral habits.[1]

12 *Eighteen hundred eons* means on the expiry of a thousand and eight hundred eons from now.

23 *Like a king of sāla trees* means he appeared like a king of sāla trees with an evenly rounded trunk[2], exceedingly delightful to look upon when it is in full bloom.

26 *And those pairs* means the couples that are the pairs of chief disciples and so forth.[3]

Everywhere remaining in the verses is quite clear.

Concluded is the Exposition of the Chronicle of the Buddha Piyadassin

Concluded is the Thirteenth Buddha-Chronicle

XV THE EXPOSITION OF THE CHRONICLE OF THE BUDDHA ATTHADASSIN

[215] After the Fully Self-Awakened One, Piyadassin, had attained final nibbāna and his Dispensation had disappeared, and when people's life-spans, which had been of unlimited (duration), had dwindled (and then) increased (again) so that in due course the life-span came to be of a hundred thousand years (in duration), the Buddha named Atthadassin, seer of the highest truth (paramatthadassin), arose in the world. Having fulfilled the perfections he was reborn in Tusita city. Deceasing from there and taking on relinking

[1] saraṇe pañcasīle cā ti tisaraṇāni ca pañcasīlāni cā ti attho.

[2] samavattakkhandha, having shoulders evenly rounded, also one of the 32 Marks of a Great Man; cf. text pp. 124, 204.

[3] Cf. text p. 176.

in the womb of queen Sudassanā, chief consort of the king Sāgara in the extremely resplendent (paramasobhana) city named Sobhana, after ten months he issued forth from his mother's womb in Sucindhana pleasaunce. Even as the Great Man was issuing forth he thought. "The owners of wealth acquired great stores which, laid aside for a very long time, come to a succession of families". On his name-taking day they gave him the name of Atthadassin. He led the household life for ten thousand years. Amaragiri, Suragiri, Girivāhana were the names of his three extremely beautiful palaces. There were thirty thousand women (attendants) with Queen Visākhā at the head.

When he had seen the four signs and the boy named Sela[1] had been born to Queen Visākhā, having mounted a king of horses named Sudassana and departed on the Great Departure, he went forth. Nine crores of men went forth following his example. When the Great Man, surrounded by these, had engaged in striving for eight months, and on the full-moon day of Visākha had partaken of sweet milk-rice brought as an offering to the female nāga Sucindharā by the great populace and given (to him) together with a golden bowl by the female nāga, all of whose physical frame was visible, he spent the day-sojourn in a grove of young sālas which was adorned by a hundred young trees. Towards evening he accepted eight handfuls of kusa-grass given to him by the nāga-king named Dhammaruci, and approaching a Campaka[2] Tree of Awakening he spread a spreading of the kusa-grass fifty-three cubits in extent. Sitting cross-legged, he attained Self-Awakening, uttered the solemn utterance conformably with all Buddhas, and passed seven weeks near the Tree of Awakening itself.

When he had acceded to Brahmā's request for Dhamma and saw that the nine crores of monks who had gone forth with him were capable of piercing the ariyan Dhamma, he went through the air, descended in Anomā pleasaunce near Anomā city, and turned the Wheel of Dhamma there surrounded by these. There was then the first penetration of Dhamma by a hundred thousand crores.

Again, when the Lord, the leader of the world, had gone on tour in the deva-world and was teaching Dhamma there, there was the

[1] Bv xv 16 Sena.

[2] Michelia champaka; Sinh. sapu. A very tall tree with fragrant yellow flowers, it grows only in the tropics, and is related to the jak-fruit tree. In Sri Lanka it grows mostly round Kandy. Its wood is used for furniture after being seasoned for about a month under the mud of a paddy-field.

second penetration by a hundred thousand crores. And when the Lord Atthadassin had entered Sobhana city, as our Lord (entered) Kapila city, and had taught Dhamma, there was then the third penetration of Dhamma by a hundred thousand crores. Accordingly it was said:

[216] XV 1 In that same Maṇḍa-eon[1] Atthadassin of great renown[2], annihilating the great gloom, attained supreme Self-Awakening.

2 On being requested by Brahmā, he turned the Wheel of Dhamma and refreshed with deathlessness the ten-thousand worlds with the devas and men.

3 And under this protector of the world there were three penetrations. The first penetration was by a hundred thousand crores.

4 When the Buddha Atthadassin went on tour among the devas there was the second penetration by a hundred thousand crores.

5 And again, when the Buddha taught in his father's presence, there was the third penetration by a hundred thousand crores.

1 Therein *in that same* means in that same eon. But here a Vara-eon signifies a Maṇḍa-eon. In an eon in which three Buddhas are born, that eon is a Vara-eon, as explained above[3] in the Exposition of the Chronicle of the Buddha Padumuttara. Therefore a Vara-eon is here spoken of as a Maṇḍa-eon.

1 *Annihilating* means annihilating[4], or this is itself the reading.

2 *Being* means being.[5]

2 *With deathlessness* means with the drink of deathlessness for arrival at the fruits of the Ways.

2 *He refreshed* means he refreshed[6]; the meaning is: he invigorated.

2 *The ten-thousand* means the ten-thousand world-system.

4 *On tour among the devas:* the meaning is: on tour in a deva-world for the sake of guiding out the devas.

[1] See text p. 191.
[2] mahāyasa, also at Be, BvAB; narāsabha at Bv.
[3] Text p. 191.
[4] nihantvānā ti nihanitvā.
[5] santo ti samāno.
[6] tappayī ti atappayi.

It is said that in the city of Sucandaka the king's son, Santa, and the priest's son, Upasanta, not having seen essence in the three Vedas for all the time they had studied them, posted four learned and knowledgeable men at the four gateways to the city and said, "Whatever learned recluse or brahman you may see or listen to, come back and tell us about him". And at that time Atthadassin, protector of the world, reached the city of Sucandaka. Then as arranged with them the men went back and announced to them the arrival there of Him of the Ten Powers. Then these, at peace on hearing of the arrival of the Tathāgata, with their retinues of a thousand, cheerful in mind, went out to meet Him of the Ten Powers, immaculate one.[1] When they had greeted him and invited him, they gave a great Unparalleled Gift for seven days to the Order with the Buddha at the head. On the seventh day together with all the men who lived in the city they listened to a talk on Dhamma. It is said that on that day ninety-eight thousand[2] who had gone forth by the 'Come, monk' (formula for) going forth attained arahantship. The Lord recited the Pātimokkha in this company. That was the first assembly.

And when the Lord **[217]** was teaching Dhamma to his own son, the Elder Sela, and had inclined the hearts of eighty-eight thousand, had let them go forth by the 'Come, monk' (formula for) going forth and had caused them to attain arahantship, he recited the Pātimokkha. That was the second assembly.

Again, when he was teaching Dhamma to devas and men at a gathering for the Mahā Maṅgala[3] at the full-moon of Māgha, having caused seventy-eight thousand to attain arahantship, he recited the Pātimokkha. That was the third assembly. Accordingly it was said:

XV 6 And this great seer too had three assemblies of steadfast ones whose cankers were destroyed, stainless, tranquil in mind.

7 The first gathering was of ninety-eight thousand; the second gathering was of eighty-eight thousand.

8 The third gathering was of seventy-eight thousand[4] of those who were freed without substrate (for rebirth remaining), stainless, great seers.

[1] asabala, here an epithet of dasabala.

[2] BvAC 98 hundred thousand, but this is not borne out by ver. 7 below.

[3] See text p. 136.

[4] Bv reads 38,000, aṭṭhatiṁsasahassa.

They say that our Bodhisatta was then considered by people to be a very rich brahman called Susīma in the city of Campaka. Having bestowed all kinds of wealth on the poor, the unprotected, the destitute and beggars and so forth, he went to the Himavant and went forth in the going forth of ascetics. Attaining the eight attainments and the five super-knowings and being of great psychic potency, great majesty, after explaining to the populace the blamelessness and the blameableness of skilled and unskilled states, he came to the Buddha's feet, and stood there.

At a subsequent time when Atthadassin, protector of the world, had arisen in the world and was raining down a rain of the nectar of Dhamma in the midst of the eight companies in the great city of Sudassana, he (Susīma) heard his Dhamma, went to a heaven-world, and brought back from the deva-world flowers of mandārava, lotus, of the Coral Tree and so forth, his visible physical frame showing forth his own majesty. Raining down a rain of the flowers like a great storm-cloud covering the four continents in the four quarters, erecting bowers of flowers all round and golden flower-festooned columns and portals, he honoured Him of the Ten Powers with a canopy of mandārava flowers. And this Lord too declared of him, "In the future he will be the Buddha named Gotama". Accordingly it was said:

XV 9 I at that time was a very severe matted hair ascetic named Susīma, considered the best on earth.

10 When I had brought deva-like flowers of mandārava, lotus and of the Coral Tree from the deva-world, I greatly honoured the Self-Awakened One.

[218] 11 And then[1] he too, Atthadassin, great sage, declared of me: "After eighteen hundred eons this one will be a Buddha.

12 When he has striven the striving . . ." ". . . we will be face to face with this one."

13 When I had heard his words, exultant, stirred in mind, I resolutely determined on further practice for fulfilling the ten perfections.

9 Therein *matted hair ascetic* means a matted hair ascetic has matted hair.

9 *Considered the best on earth* means (he was) considered, estimated thus by even the whole world as best, supreme, glorious.

[1] tadā, Bv buddho.

That Lord's city was named Sobhana, the king his father was named Sāgara, his mother was named Sudassanā. Santa and Upasanta were the two chief disciples. The attendant was named Abhaya. Dhammā and Sudhammā were the chief women disciples. The Tree of Awakening was a Campaka. The physical frame was eighty cubits in height. The lustre of (his) physical frame remained all the time suffusing a yojana all round. The life-span was a hundred thousand years. Visākhā was the name of his chief consort, his son was named Sela. He departed on horseback. Accordingly it was said:

XV 14 Sobhana[1] was the name of the city, Sāgara the name of the warrior-noble, Sudassanā the name of the mother of Atthadassin, the teacher.

22 And that Buddha, equal to the unequalled, eighty cubits[2] tall, shone like a king of sāla trees, like the king of *heavenly bodies* at the full.

23 Countless hundreds of crores of rays from his natural state constantly suffused the ten quarters for a yojana above and below.

24 And that Buddha too, bull of men[3], sage, supreme among all beings, One with vision, remained in the world for a hundred thousand years.

25 Having displayed unrivalled effulgence and shone over the world with the devas, he too attained impermanence like a fire on the consumption of the fuel.

22 Therein *like the king of heavenly bodies at the full* means like the king of stars when his stainless orb is at the full in autumn time.

[219] 23 *From his natural state* means arising on account of his natural state, not on account of resolute determination. As the Lord wished so he could suffuse with radiance even countless hundreds and thousands of crores within the world-system.

23 *Rays* mean rays.[4]

25 *Consumption of the fuel*[5] means like a fire on the destruction of the fuel, on the destruction of the firing[6].

[1] Jā i 39 Sobhita.
[2] BvAC ratana, Bv hattha.
[3] BvAC naravasabho, Bv narāsabho.
[4] raṁsī ti rasmiyo.
[5] upādāna.
[6] indhana, combustibles. See text p. 166.

That Lord too, on the destruction of the four graspings,[1] attained final nibbāna in the element of nibbāna with no substrate (for rebirth) remaining in Anupama city in Anomā monastery. And by resolute determination his relics were dispersed.

The rest of the verses are quite clear in meaning.

Concluded is the Exposition of the Chronicle of the Buddha Atthadassin

Concluded in the Fourteenth Buddha-Chronicle

XVI THE EXPOSITION OF THE CHRONICLE OF THE BUDDHA DHAMMADASSIN

After Atthadassin the Self-Awakened One had attained final nibbāna and an intervening eon had passed, and when the life-spans of beings, which had been unlimited, dwindled gradually so that they were born with life-spans of a hundred thousand years, the teacher named Dhammadassin, bringer of light to the world, guider out of the world's stains of greed and so forth, sole leader of the world, arose in the world. This Lord too, having fulfilled the perfections, was reborn in Tusita city. Deceasing from there, he took on relinking in the womb of Queen Sunandā, chief consort of the king named Saraṇa, refuge (saraṇa) for all the world, in the city of Saraṇa. After ten months he issued forth from his mother's womb in Saraṇa pleasaunce like the full-moon making fissures in the clouds in the rainy season. And even as soon as the Great Man was but issuing forth from his mother's womb unjust practices in the law-books disappeared of their own accord, and only just practices remained. Because of this they gave him the name of Dhammadassin (seeing Dhamma, or, seeing the rightful, the just) on his name-taking day. He lived the household life for eight thousand years. His three palaces were named Araja, Viraja, Sudassana. There were more than a hundred thousand women with Queen Vicikolī[2] at the head.

When he had seen the four signs and the boy named Puññavaḍḍhana had been born to Queen Vicikolī, like a deva-prince who

[1] upādāna.

[2] Bv Vicitoḷī, Be, BvAB -koḷī.

had been delicately nurtured, experiencing bliss like deva-bliss, getting up in the middle watch (of the night) and sitting down on the state-couch, and seeing the alteration in the women now that they were asleep, in a state of thrill he aroused his mind for the Great Departure. Immediately his mind was aroused his palace Sudassana, soaring up into the vault of the heavens, surrounded by a four-factored army, like a second sun and going along like a deva-mansion, [**220**] descended near a red Kuravaka[1] Tree of Awakening and remained there. It is said that the Great Man, accepting yellow robes offered by a Brahmā, went forth and, descending from the palace, remained near it. The palace, going through the air again, came to rest on the earth while keeping the Tree of Awakening within. And the women with their retinues descended from the palace, and stood still after walking at least half a gāvuta. While the women and their attendants and servants, were standing there, all the men went forth following his example. There were a hundred thousand crores of monks.

Then when the Bodhisatta Dhammadassin had engaged in striving for seven days and had partaken of sweet milk-rice given to him by Queen Vicikolī[2], he spent the day-sojourn in Badara-wood. Towards evening he accepted eight handfuls of grass given to him by Sirivaḍḍha, the guardian of a corn-field and, approaching a Bimbijāla Tree of Awakening, he spread a grass-spreading fifty-three cubits in extent. Piercing omniscient knowledge and uttering the solemn utterance, he spent seven weeks there. When he had complied with Brahmā's request and knew that the hundred thousand crores of monks who had gone forth together with him were capable of piercing True Dhamma, he went eighteen yojanas along the road to Isipatana (seers' resort) in only one day surrounded by these and turned the Wheel of Dhamma there. Then was the first penetration of Dhamma by the hundred thousand crores. Accordingly it was said:

XVI 1 In that same Maṇḍa-eon Dhammadassin, of great renown, dispelling that darkness, shone out in the world with the devas.

[1] This tree, called bimbijāla at text pp. 220, 222 and at Bv 19, is the red Amaranth. Below, p. 222 and Jā v 155 rattakuravaka is given as a synonym for bimbijāla. See too Jā i 39, ApA 43: "the Tree of Awakening was a red kuravaka; it is also to be called bimbijāla".

[2] It is not said that this occurred on the day of the Visākha full-moon.

2 And when he of unrivalled incandescence was turning the Wheel of Dhamma there was the first penetration by a hundred thousand crores.

1 Therein *that darkness:* the meaning is: that not considered[1] darkness of confusion.

And when the king named Sañjaya in the city of Tagara had seen the peril in sense-pleasures and the renunciation (of them) as safety he went forth in the going forth of seers. Then ninety crores went forth following his example. Even all these acquired the five super-knowings and the eight attainments. Then the teacher Dhammadassin, seeing their achievement in the qualifications, went through the air and proceeding to the ascetic Sañjaya's hermitage-ground he remained in the air. When he had taught Dhamma suitable to the inclinations of these ascetics, he aroused the vision of Dhamma[2] (in them).That was the second penetration. Accordingly it was said:

XVI 3 When the Buddha Dhammadassin guided away the seer Sañjaya then was the second penetration by ninety crores.

And when Sakka, chief of devas, anxious to hear the Dhamma of Him of the Ten Powers, approached him, then was the third penetration by eighty crores. Accordingly it was said:

[221] XVI 4 When Sakka and his company approached the guider away then was the third penetration by eighty crores.

And when in the city of Saraṇa he let go forth the half-brothers, Prince Paduma and Prince Phussadeva[3] with their retinues, he invited in a pure Invitation[4] in the midst of a thousand crores of monks who had gone forth at the end of those rains. That was the

[1] asaṅkhāta, cf. Jā iv 4, explained arīmaṁsita, not examined, not investigated. Avove the meaning may be that the people had been too confused or ignorant to know how great was this darkness, and accepted it as being natural.

[2] dhammacakkhu, see text p. 33.

[3] DPPN calls these the Buddha's half-brothers. This is very likely as they are called 'Prince', kumāra, but our cty gives no indication that they were related to the Buddha.

[4] One in which all offences, whether seen, heard, or suspected, had been confessed to already, so that the monks taking part in the 'Invitation' were pure in regard to offences, for by the confession of them they had removed them.

first assembly. Again, when the Lord descended from the deva-world there was the second assembly of a hundred crores. And when, in Sudassana-monastery, he had expounded the advantages in the special qualities of the thirteen ascetic practices, he established as chief (in these) the great disciple named Hārita. Then the Lord recited the Pātimokkha in the midst of eighty crores. Accordingly it was said:

XVI 5 And that deva of devas had three assemblies of steadfast ones whose cankers were destroyed, stainless, tranquil in mind.

6 When the Buddha Dhammadassin went to Saraṇa for the rains then was the first gathering of a thousand crores.[1]

7 And again, when the Buddha came from the deva-world to that of men[2], then was the second gathering of a hundred crores.

8 And again, when the Buddha expounded the special qualities of asceticism, then was the third gathering of eighty crores.

Then our Bodhisatta, the Great Being, was Sakka, king of devas. Coming surrounded by devas from two deva-worlds, he honoured the Tathāgata with deva-like perfumes and flowers and so on and with deva-like instrumental music. And that teacher too declared of him: "In the future he will be the Buddha named Gotama." Accordingly it was said:

XVI 9 I at that time was Sakka, fort-shatterer[3]. Greatly I honoured him with deva-like scents, garlands, instrumental music.

10 He too then[4], seated in the midst of devas, declared of me: "After eighteen hundred eons this one will be a Buddha.

11 When he has striven the striving . . ." ". . . face to face with this one."

12 When I had heard his words all the more did I incline my mind. I resolutely determined on further practice for fulfilling the ten perfections.

[1] So Bv, BvAC; a hundred thousand at Be, BvAB.

[2] BvAC eti mānusaṁ; Bv ehi mānuse.

[3] purindada, see MLS ii 52, n. 5. Also meaning a "bounteous giver" as at VvA 171.

[4] BvACB tadā, Bv, Be buddho.

[222] And that Lord's city was named Saraṇa, the king his father was named Saraṇa, his mother was named Sunandā. Paduma and Phussadeva were the chief disciples, the attendant was named Sunetta; Khemā and Sabbanāmā were the two chief women disciples. The Tree of Awakening was a Bimbijāla. And his physical frame was eighty cubits in height, the life-span a hundred thousand years. The queen named Vicikolī was his chief consort, Puññavaḍḍhana was the name of his son. He departed by palace. Accordingly it was said:

XVI 13 Saraṇa was the name of the city, Saraṇa the name of the warrior-noble, Sunandā the name of the mother of Dhammadassin, the teacher.

18 Paduma and Phussadeva were the chief disciples. Sunetta was the name of the attendant on Dhammadassin, the teacher.

19 Khemā and Sabbanāmā[1] were the chief women disciples. That Lord's Tree of Awakening is said to be the Bimbijāla.

21 And that Buddha, equal to the unequalled, eighty cubits tall, shone out with incandescence over the ten-thousand (world-) system.

22 Like a king of sāla trees in full bloom, like lightning in the heavens, like the sun at midday, so did he shine forth.

23 And the life[2] of this one of unrivalled incandescence was similar. The One with Vision remained in the world for a hundred thousand years.

24 Having displayed effulgence, having made a stainless Dispensation, as the moon disappears[3] in the heavens so did he wane out with the disciples.

19 Therein *bimbijāla* means the red kuravaka tree.[4]

21 *Over the ten-thousand (world-) system* means: over the ten-thousand world-system.

[1] Saccanāmā at Bv.

[2] jīvita, life, life-principle, and probably of the same meaning here as āyu, life-span.

[3] Bv reads virocayi, shone forth, a reading which is not at all out of place as other Buddhas are spoken of as waning out in a blaze of glory. Be, BvACB, however, all read cavi, explained below by cuto, fell, deceased and so disappeared, not be born again.

[4] See note to text p. 220.

22 *Like lightning* means like a streak of lightning.

22 *Did he shine forth* means: just as lightning in the heavens and the sun at midday shine forth, thus shone forth this Lord.

23 *Similar* means: his life-span was exactly the same as that of all human beings.[1]

24 *Disappears* means disappeared[2].

[**223**] 24 *As the moon* means like the moon from the heavens he disappeared.

It is said that the Lord Dhammadassin attained final nibbāna in Kesa-park in the city of Sālavatī. In the rest of the verses the meaning is quite clear.

Concluded is the Exposition of the Chronicle of the Buddha Dhammadassin

Concluded is the Fifteenth Buddha-Chronicle

XVII THE EXPOSITION OF THE CHRONICLE OF THE BUDDHA SIDDHATTHA

When the Lord Dhammadassin had attained final nibbāna and that eon had passed and his Dispensation had disappeared, and when a thousand eons and seven hundred eons and six eons had elapsed, ninety-four eons prior to now only one teacher, named Siddhattha, faring for the good of the world[3] and arrived at the highest truth[3], appeared in the world in the one eon.[4] Accordingly it was said:

XVII 1 After Dhammadassin was Siddhattha leader of the world;[5] driving out all gloom, he was like the risen sun then.

The Bodhisatta Siddhattha also, having fulfilled the perfections, was reborn in Tusita abode. Deceasing from there he took on relinking in the womb of the queen named Suphassā, chief consort of the king named Udena in Vebhāra city. After ten months he

[1] Here narasatta. On the whole Buddhas' life-spans were the same as those of their contemporaries.

[2] cavī ti cuto.

[3] Note the play on his name: lok-attha-caro, adhigataparam-attho.

[4] A Sāra-eon, see text p. 191.

[5] BvACB lokanāyako; Bv, nāma nāyako.

issued forth from his mother's womb in Viriya pleasaunce. And when the Great Man was born the enterprises that had been undertaken and longed for by everyone turned out successfully (atthāsiddhi)[1]. Therefore his relations gave him the name of Siddhattha.[2] He lived the household life for ten thousand years. His three palaces were named Kokā, Suppala, Paduma[3]. There were forty-eight thousand women in attendance on him with Queen Somanassā[4] at the head.

When he had seen the four signs and the boy Anupama had been born to Queen Somanassā, he departed at the full moon of Āsāḷhi by a golden palanquin, and having gone to Viriya-pleasaunce, he went forth. A hundred thousand crores went forth following his example. They say that the Great Man together with these engaged in striving for ten months. When, on the full-moon day of Visākha he had partaken of milk-rice given to him by a brahman maiden named Sunettā in the brahman village of Asadisa, [**224**] he spent the day-sojourn in Badara-wood. Towards evening he accepted eight handfuls of grass given to him by Varuṇa, the guardian of a corn-field and, approaching a Kaṇikāra Tree of Awakening, he spread a grass-spreading forty cubits in extent. Sitting cross-legged, having attained omniscience and uttered the solemn utterance, he spent seven weeks there. When he saw that the hundred thousand crores of monks who had gone forth with him were capable of piercing the four truths, going along by an aery path[5] he descended at the deer-sanctuary in Gayā and turned the Wheel of Dhamma for them. Then was the first penetration by a hundred thousand crores. Accordingly it was said:

XVII 2 After he had attained Self-Awakening and was causing the world with the devas to cross over, he rained down from the cloud of Dhamma making the world with the devas cool.

3 And under him whose incandescence had no gauge there were three penetrations. The first penetration was by a hundred thousand crores.

2 Therein *with the devas* means the world with the devas.

[1] atthāsiddhim agamaṁsu.
[2] "Task completed" or successfully carried out.
[3] Bv xvii 14 Kokanudā.
[4] Bv xvii 15 Sumanā.
[5] anilapatha as at text pp. 178, 192.

2 *From the cloud of Dhamma* means from the rain-cloud of a talk on Dhamma.

And in the city of Bhīmaratha, invited[1] by the king named Bhīmaratha, while he was seated in a council-hall built in the middle of the city he smote the drum of deathlessness, filling the ten quarters with his lovely clear melodious voice, a pleasure to hear, extremely sweet, going to the hearts of intelligent people, like an immense consecration, a deep, beautiful voice. Then was the second penetration by ninety crores. Accordingly it was said:

XVII 4 And again, when he smote the drum in Bhīmaratha, then was the second penetration by ninety crores.

And when he was teaching the Chronicle of Buddhas in a gathering of relations in the city of Vebhāra, vision of Dhamma arose to ninety crores. That was the third penetration. Accordingly it was said:

XVII 5 When that Buddha taught Dhamma in the superb city of Vebhāra, then was the third penetration by ninety crores.

In the city of Amara, pleasing to behold, two brothers, Sambahula[2] and Sumitta ruled the kingdom. Then the teacher Siddhattha, seeing the attainment of the qualifications by these kings, going through the vault of the heavens, descended in the centre of the city of Amara, making footprints visible[3] as though he were treading the surface of the earth by walking on it with the soles (of the feet) which were adorned with wheel (-marks). **[225]** When he had arrived in Amara-pleasaunce he sat down on his own extremely delightful flat stone that was cool with compassion.[4] Then the two brother-kings, seeing the footprints of Him of the Ten Powers, followed these and approached Siddhattha, the teacher arrived at the highest truth, the guide of all the world, with his entourage, and having greeted the Lord they sat down surrounding him. The

[1] nimantito, usually meaning invited to a meal.

[2] BvAC Sambahula; BvAB, noticing this as a v. l., reads Sambala, as does the verse on text p. 226, and also Be. Samphala at Bv xvii 18.

[3] padacetiyāni dassetvā footprints left on the ground only by "holy men". Cf. DhA iii 194: "it is said that when Buddhas resolutely determine on a footprint, thinking: Let so-and-so see it, it is to be seen only in a trodden place, and is not seen in any other place."

[4] A play on words here: karuṇāsītale silātale.

Lord taught them Dhamma suitable to their inclinations. When they had heard his talk on Dhamma, being filled with faith, they all went forth and attained arahantship. The Lord recited the Pātimokkha in the midst of these hundred crores of those whose cankers were destroyed. That was the third assembly. Accordingly it was said:

XVII 6 And this supreme among men had three assemblies of steadfast ones whose cankers were destroyed, stainless, tranquil in mind.

7 There were these three occasions of a gathering of stainless ones: of a hundred crores, of ninety, and of eighty crores.

7 Therein *of ninety, and of eighty crores* means there were assemblies of ninety crores and also of eighty crores.

7 *There were these three occasions* means these three were occasions for an assembly.[1] "There were these three occasions"[2] is also a reading.

Then our Bodhisatta was a brahman named Maṅgala in the city of Surasena. Having come to mastery in the Vedas and Vedaṅgas, he bestowed an accumulation of countless crores of wealth on the poor and unprotected and so forth. And as he desired aloofness he went forth in the going forth of ascetics, having attained the meditations and the super-knowings. On hearing that the Buddha named Siddhattha had arisen in the world and was living there, he approached him, reverenced him, and when he had heard his talk on Dhamma he approached, by means of psychic potency, that Rose-Apple Tree after whose rose-apples (jambu) this Rose-apple land (Jambudīpa) is called[3] and fetched fruits from it. He asked Siddhattha the teacher and his entourage of ninety crores of monks to be seated in Surasena-vihāra and, attending on him, refreshed him with the fruits from the Rose-apple Tree. Then the teacher, having partaken of those fruits, declared, "Ninety-four eons from now he will be the Buddha named Gotama". Accordingly it was said:

XVII 8 I at that time was an ascetic named Maṅgala, very

[1] ete āsuṁ tayo ṭhānā ti etāni tīṇi sannipātaṭṭhānāni ahesuṁ.

[2] ṭhānān' etāni tīṇi ahesuṁ.

[3] Cf. Vin i 30.

austere, hard to overcome, endued with powers of the super-knowings.

9 Bringing a fruit from the Rose-apple tree I gave it to Siddhattha. When the Self-Awakened One had accepted it he spoke these words:

10 "Do you see this very severe matted-hair ascetic? Ninety-four eons from now he will be a Buddha.

[226] 11 When he has striven the striving . . ."

12 When I had heard his words all the more did I incline my mind. I resolutely determined on further practice for fulfilling the ten perfections.

8 Therein *hard to overcome* means difficult to attack, or this is itself the reading.

And that Lord's city was named Vebhāra, the king his father was named Udena—and his name was also Jayasena[1], his mother was named Suphassā. The chief disciples were Sambala[2] and Sumitta, the attendant was named Revata. The chief women disciples were Sīvalā and Surāmā. The Tree of Awakening was a Kaṇikāra. The physical frame was sixty cubits in height, the life-span was a hundred thousand years. Somanassā was the name of the chief consort, Anupama the name of the son. He departed in a golden palanquin. Accordingly it was said:

XVII 13 Vebhāra was the name of the city, Udena the name of the warrior-noble, Suphassā the name of the mother of Siddhattha, the great seer.

18 Sambala[2] and Sumitta were the chief disciples. Revata was the name of the attendant on Siddhattha, the great seer.

19 Sīvalā and Surāmā were the chief women disciples. That Lord's Tree of Awakening is said to be the Kaṇikāra.

21 And that Buddha was sixty ratanas high to the sky. Like a golden festooned column[3] he shone forth over the ten-thousand.

22 And that Buddha, equal to the unequalled, unrivalled,

[1] Called this at Jā i 40.

[2] See note to text p. 224.

[3] Cf. xi 27.

matchless, One with vision, remained in the world for a hundred thousand years.

23 Having displayed a far-flung[1] lustre, having caused the disciples to blossom, gracing the attainments[2], he waned out with the disciples.

21 Therein *sixty ratanas* means sixty ratanas in measure high to the sky.

21 *Like a golden festooned column* means looking like a festooned column inlaid with divers jewels and ornamental gold.

21 *He shone forth over the ten-thousand* means he shone forth over the ten-thousand.[3]

23 *Far-flung* means superb, effulgent.

[227] 23 *Having caused to blossom* means: having made them (the disciples) attain the utmost beauty which was a flowering with the flowers of achievement in the meditations, the superknowings, the ways, the fruits.

23 *Gracing* means: himself gracing[4], himself charming.[5]

23 *The attainments* means: with mundane and supermundane attainments and super-knowings.

23 *Waned out* means he waned out in final nibbāna with no clinging (remaining).

And they say that the teacher Siddhattha attained final nibbāna in Anoma-pleasaunce in the city of Kañcanaveḷu.[6] There they erected a cetiya to him made of jewels, four yojanas high.

Everywhere remaining in the verses is quite clear.

Concluded is the Exposition of the Chronicle of the Buddha Siddhattha

Concluded is the Sixteenth Buddha-Chronicle

[1] vipula; Bv vimala, stainless.

[2] Bv vilāsetvā ca samāpattiyā; Be, BvAC vilāsetvā samāpatyā, also BvAB which gives a v. l. varasamāpattiyā.

[3] dasasahassī virocatī ti dasasahassiyaṁ virocati.

[4] vilāsetvā ti vilāsayitvā.

[5] kīḷayitvā; the more usual meaning of to play, sport, amuse oneself, seems rather out of place here.

[6] The golden bamboo.

XVIII THE EXPOSITION OF THE CHRONICLE OF THE BUDDHA TISSA

Subsequently to the Lord Siddhattha there was one eon void of Buddhas. Ninety-two eons ago from now two Buddhas, Tissa and Phussa, were born in one eon[1]. Therein the Great Man named Tissa, having fulfilled the perfections, was born in Tusita city. Deceasing from there he took on relinking in the womb of the queen named Padumā whose eyes were like lotus (paduma)-petals, chief consort of the king named Saccasandha[2] in Khema city. After ten months he issued forth from his mother's womb in Anomā pleasaunce. He led the household life for seven thousand years. His three palaces were named Guhasela[3], Nārisa[4], Nisabha[5]. There were thirty-three thousand women with queen Subhaddā at the head.

When he had seen the four signs and a son, Prince Ānanda, had been born to queen Subhaddā, he mounted the unsurpassed glorious steed named Sonuttara and, having departed on the Great Departure, went forth. A crore of men went forth following his example. Surrounded by these he engaged in striving for eight months. After he had partaken of sweet milk-rice given to him on the full-moon day of Visākha by the daughter of the merchant Vīra in the market-town of Vīra, he spent the day-sojourn in a grove of salaḷa trees.

Towards evening, having accepted eight handfuls of grass brought to him by the guardian of a corn-field named Vijitasaṅgāmaka, he approached an Asana Tree of Awakening and spread a grass-spreading forty cubits in extent. Seated cross-legged, he routed Māra's forces, and after he had arrived at omniscient knowledge he uttered the solemn utterance and spent seven weeks near the Tree of Awakening itself. On seeing that Brahmadeva and Udayana, the two sons of a king in the city of Haṁsavatī, and their entourages were possessed of the qualifications, he went through the air [**228**] and, descending in the deer-sanctuary in the city of

[1] A Maṇḍa-eon.

[2] Recognized as a v. l. in BvAB which, with Bv, Be and text p. 230, reads Janasandha.

[3] Recognized as a v. l. in BvAB which reads Guhā-, as also at Bv.

[4] Bv Nārī; Be, BvAB Nārisaya. BvAB gives Nārisa as a v. l.

[5] BvAB gives v. l. Usabha.

Yasavatī, had the king's sons summoned by the keeper of the pleasaunce. For these and their entourages he turned the Wheel of Dhamma as though, with his sweet beautiful deep voice, clear and carrying, he was making it known to the ten-thousand world-system. Then was the first penetration of Dhamma by hundreds of crores. Accordingly it was said:

XVIII 1 After Siddhattha was Tissa, without an equal, matchless, of unending morality, of boundless fame, highest leader in the world.

2 Dispelling the darkness of gloom, making effulgent the world with the devas, compassionate, great hero, the One with vision arose in the world.

3 His too were unrivalled psychic potency and unrivalled morality and concentration. He, having gone to perfection in everything, turned the Wheel of Dhamma.

4 That Buddha made his pure speech heard in the ten-thousand. At the first teaching of Dhamma hundreds of crores penetrated.[1]

3 Therein *in everything* means he had reached perfection in all things.

4 *In the ten-thousand* means over the ten-thousand.[2]

At a subsequent time the crore of monks who had gone forth with the teacher Tissa had given up living in groups and had gone elsewhere when the Great Man approached the root of the Tree of Awakening. When they heard that the Wheel of Dhamma had been turned by Tissa, the Fully Self-Awakened One, they came to the Yasavatī deer-sanctuary, greeted Him of the Ten Powers, and sat down surrounding him. The Lord taught them Dhamma. Then there was the second penetration of Dhamma by ninety crores. Again, there was the third penetration by sixty crores at the conclusion of the blessings at a gathering for the Mahā-Maṅgala.[3] Accordingly it was said:

XVIII 5 The second was of ninety crores, the third of sixty crores. He released[4] from bondage the men and deities who were present then.

[1] koṭisatāni abhisamiṁsu; Bv koṭisatasahassāni samiṁsu.

[2] dasasahassimhī ti dasasahassiyaṁ.

[3] See text p. 136.

[4] pamocesi; Bv vimocesi.

5 Therein *the second was of ninety crores* means the second penetration was by ninety crores of breathing things.

5 *From bondage* means he set free from bondage by the ten fetters. Now, showing the beings who were set free from their own forms, he said 'Men and deities'.

5 *Men and deities* means men and deities.[1]

It is said that the first assembly was during the rains at the city of Yasavatī when there was an entourage of a hundred thousand arahants who had gone forth. [229] After the prince named Nārivāhana, (the son) of the king named Sujāta, who was well born (sujāta) on both sides, had arrived at the city of Nārivāhana and, with his retinue, had gone to meet the Lord, protector of the world, he invited Him of the Ten Powers with the Order of monks and gave the Unparalleled Gift for seven days. Then, having handed over the kingdom to his own son, he went forth with his retinue by the 'Come, monk' (formula for) going forth in the presence of Tissa, Self-Awakened One, overlord of all the world. They say that that going forth of his was known in all the quarters. Therefore, when the great populace had come after this, they went forth following Prince Nārivāhana's example. Then the Tathāgata recited the Pātimokkha in the midst of ninety hundred thousand monks. That was the second assembly. Again, at a gathering of relations in Khemavatī city, eighty hundred thousand, having gone forth in his presence after they had heard a Dhamma-talk on the Chronicle of Buddhas, attained arahantship. Surrounded by these the Well-farer recited the Pātimokkha. That was the third assembly. Accordingly it was said:

XVIII 6 Tissa, highest leader in the world, had three assemblies of steadfast ones whose cankers were destroyed, stainless, tranquil in mind.

7 The first was a gathering of a hundred thousand[2] whose cankers were destroyed. The second was a gathering of ninety hundred thousand.

8 The third was a gathering of eighty hundred thousand whose cankers were destroyed, stainless, blossoming through freedom.[3]

[1] naramarū ti narāmare. Cf. text pp. 98, 136.

[2] Bv reads a thousand.

[3] pupphitānaṁ vimuttiyā, as at viii 8, and glossed at text p. 175.

Then in the city named Yasavatī the Bodhisatta, being the king named Sujāta, having given away as though they were a faded bundle of grass his rich and prosperous country districts and an accumulation of countless crores of wealth for which he felt no heart's affection, departed, stirred at heart concerning birth and so forth, and went forth in the going forth of ascetics. He was of great psychic potency, of great majesty. When he heard that a Buddha had arisen in the world his physical frame was pervaded by the five kinds of rapture[1]. Approaching the Lord Tissa who was without envy[2], and having reverenced him, he thought, "Come, I will pay homage to the Lord with deva-like blossoms of the mandārava and Coral Tree and so forth". Having thought this he went by means of psychic potency to a heaven-world, entered the Cittalatā Grove and taking deva-like blossoms of lotuses, the Coral Tree and the mandārava and so forth he filled a casket made of silver to the extent of a gāvuta, returned through the vault of the heavens and paid homage to the Lord with the deva-like blossoms. In the middle of a fourfold company he stood holding over the Lord's head a lotus-sunshade that was like a sweetly perfumed sunshade of lotus-filaments, with a jewelled handle, the calixes consisting of gold, the lotus (fan-) leaves consisting of rubies and (other) jewels. Then the Lord declared of him, "Ninety-two eons from now he will be the Buddha named Gotama." Accordingly it was said:

XVIII 9 I at that time was a warrior-noble named Sujāta.
Having abandoned great possessions I went forth in the
going forth of seers.

10 When I had gone forth the leader of the world arose.
Hearing the sound "Buddha" zest arose in me.

11 Taking deva-like flowers of mandārava, lotus, and
Coral Tree flowers in both hands, rustling, I went up to

12 Tissa, highest leader in the world, Conqueror, when he
was surrounded by the four kinds (of companies).
Bringing those flowers, I held them over his head.

13 As he was sitting in the midst of the people he too then[3]
declared of me: "Ninety-two eons from now this one
will be a Buddha.

[1] pīti, rapture or zest. See Vism 143.

[2] apagata-issaṁ Tissaṁ.

[3] tadā, Bv Buddho.

14 When he has striven the striving . . ." " . . . we will be face to face with this one."

15 When I had heard his words all the more did I incline my mind. I resolutely determined on further practice for fulfilling the ten perfections.

10 Therein *when I had gone forth* means when I had reached the status of one who has gone forth.[1] They write in the books, "There being my going forth";[2] this should be understood as a careless (way of) writing.

10 *Arose* means arose.[3]

11 *In both hands* means with both hands.[4]

11 *Taking* means bringing.

22 *Rustling* means as though rustling the bark-garments.[5]

12 *Surrounded by the four kinds* means: surrounded by the four companies meaning, surrounded by warrior-nobles, brahmans, householders and recluses; some read "surrounded by the four vaṇṇas (castes)".[6]

And that Lord's city was named Khema, the warrior-noble who was the father was named Janasandha, the mother was named Padumā. Brahmadeva and Udaya were the chief disciples, the attendant was named Samaha[7]. Phussā and Sudattā were the chief women disciples. That Lord's Tree of Awakening was an Asana. The physical frame was sixty cubits in height, the life-span a hundred thousand years. The name of his chief consort was Subhaddā, the son was named Ānanda. He departed on horseback. Accordingly it was said:

XVIII 16 Khemaka was the name of the city, Janasandha[8] the name of the warrior-noble, and Padumā the name of the mother was Tissa, the great seer.

[231] 21 Brahmadeva and Udaya were the chief disciples.

[1] mayi pabbajite ti mayi pabbajitabhāvaṁ upagate.

[2] mama pabbajitaṁ santaṁ.

[3] upapajjathā ti uppajjittha, referring to "zest".

[4] ubho hatthehī ti ubhohi hatthehi.

[5] Worn by ascetics.

[6] cātuvaṇṇaparivutan ti . . . catuvaṇṇehi parivutan ti paṭhanti keci. I do not know if a difference is meant only in the grammatical usage of -vaṇṇa- and -vaṇṇehi; or if the first vaṇṇa stands for the four companies of warrior-nobles, and so on, as seems more probable, and the second for the four castes as "some", keci, say.

[7] See n. to ver. 21 below.

[8] Saccasandha at text p. 227, where see note.

Samaha[1] was the name of the attendant on Tissa, the great seer.

22 Phussā and Sudattā were the chief women disciples. That Lord's Tree of Awakening is said to be the Asana.

24 That[2] Buddha, Conqueror, was sixty ratanas in height[3]; incomparable, unique, he was to be seen like the Himavant.

25 And the life-span of him of unrivalled incandescence was unsurpassed. The One with vision remained in the world for a hundred thousand years.

26 Having enjoyed great renown, superb, most glorious, best, blazing like a mass of fire he waned out with the disciples.

27 As a cloud by the wind, like frost by the sun, as darkness by a lamp, he waned out with the disciples.

24 Therein *in height* means in tallness.

24 *He was to be seen like the Himavant* means he was to be seen as the Himavant[4], or this itself is the reading. Just as Himavant is a mountain a hundred yojanas in height and can be seen by those standing very far away as being very delightful on account of its height and peacefulness[5], even so was the Lord to be seen also.

25 *Unsurpassed* means not too long, not too short. The meaning is that his life-span was a hundred thousand years.

26 *Superb*, *most glorious*, *best* means: these are synonyms for one another.

27 *Frost* means a particle of ice. As a cloud, frost and darkness are chased away by the wind, by the sun and a lamp, that Lord waned out with the disciples. They say that the Lord Tissa attained final nibbāna in Sunanda-monastery in the city of Sunandavatī. The rest of the meaning is quite clear in the verses.

Concluded is the Exposition of the Chronicle of the Buddha Tissa

Concluded is the Seventeenth Buddha-Chronicle

[1] Recognized as a v. l. in Be. Samaṅga at Bv, Sambhava at Jā i 40.

[2] BvAC so, Bv so pi. [3] BvAC uccattane, Bv uccatarena.

[4] viya dissati . . . va padissati.

[5] sommabhāva, where somma = Skrt. saumya, placid, mild, pleasant, benign, presumably a reference to its woodlands and groves which were suitable for hermits, see e.g. SA i 200, 283, 345; cf. also Miln 283.

XIX THE EXPOSITION OF THE CHRONICLE OF THE BUDDHA PHUSSA

[232] Subsequently to the Lord Tissa when life-spans, having become of unlimited duration, in due course dwindled, increased again and gradually dwindled (again) till people were of life-spans of ninety thousand years, the teacher named Phussa arose in the world in that same eon. Having fulfilled the perfections, he was born in Tusita city. Deceasing from there he took on relinking in the womb of the queen named Sirimā, chief consort of King Jayasena in the city of Kāsi. After ten months he issued forth from his mother's womb in Sirimā-pleasaunce. He led the household life for nine thousand years.[1] It is said that his three palaces were named Garuḷapakkha[2], Haṁsa, Suvaṇṇahārā[3]. There were thirty thousand women in attendance with Kisāgotamī at the head.

When he had seen the four signs and a son named Anupama had been born to Kisāgotamī, having departed on the Great Departure riding a gloriously caparisoned elephant, he went forth. On his going forth a crore of people went forth following his example. Surrounded by these he engaged in striving for six months. Then, getting rid of the crowd, and faring alone for a week he lived increasing the solitary faring. After he had partaken of sweet milk-rice given to him on the full-moon day of Visākha by Sirivaḍḍhā, a merchant's daughter in a certain city, he spent the day-sojourn in a siṁsapā[4] grove.

Towards evening, having accepted eight handfuls of grass given to him by an ascetic[5] named Sirivaḍḍha, he arrived at an Āmalaka Tree of Awakening and spread a grass-spreading thirty-eight cubits in extent. After he had attained complete Self-Awakening and had uttered the solemn utterance he spent seven weeks near the Tree of Awakening. When he saw that the crore of monks who had gone forth together with him were capable of piercing Dhamma, he went through the air, and descending in the deer-sanctuary in the seers' resort in the city of Saṅkassa, he turned the Wheel of

[1] Bv, BvAC give 6,000, but the 9,000 years of Be, BvAB, Jkm accords better with the length of the life-span.

[2] Bv Garuḷa.

[3] Bv -bharā. Other readings -bhārā, -tārā.

[4] Dalbergia sisu.

[5] tāpasa, BvAB giving this as a v. l. for its upāsaka.

Dhamma in their midst. Then was the first penetration by a hundred thousand crores. Accordingly it was said:

XIX 1 In the same Maṇḍa-eon was the teacher Phussa, unsurpassed, incomparable, equal to the unequalled[1], highest leader in the world.

2 When he had dispersed all the gloom and had untangled the great tangle, he rained down the waters of deathlessness refreshing the world with the devas.

3 When Phussa was turning the Wheel of Dhamma during the festival of an asterism[2], there was the first penetration by a hundred thousand crores.

[233] 1 Therein *in the same Maṇḍa-eon* means: an eon in which two Buddhas arise is called above a Maṇḍa-eon[3].

2 *Had untangled* means had unravelled.

2 *The great tangle* means that herein "tangle" is a synonym for craving. That, from arising again and again because of being below and above in the meditational objects among form and so forth, is said to be a tangle like a tangle of what are known as "net-cakes" (with their) clusters of string[4] in the sense of being entwined:[5] that great tangle.

2 *With the devas* means the world with the devas.

2 *Rained down* means shed rain.

2 *Waters of deathlessness*[6] means *refreshing* (the world) he shed rain by means of the waters of a talk on Dhamma which is regarded as deathlessness.

And when in the city of Bārāṇasī the king named Sirivaḍḍha had got rid of his great mass of possessions, he went forth in the going forth of ascetics. Ninety hundred thousand ascetics went forth with him. The Lord taught them Dhamma. Then was the

[1] BvAC asadiso, unique, but Bv, Be, BvAB all asamasamo.

[2] Phussa is also the name of an asterism. This verse could equally well be translated, "When he was turning the Wheel of Dhamma during the festival of the asterism of Phussa." He is supposed to have been born during this asterism, or the festival held then, and was named after it, Mhvu iii 245.

[3] Text p. 191.

[4] suttagumbajālapūvasaṅkhātajaṭā. Ñāṇamoli, Ppn p. 109 suggests that jālapūva at Vism 108 "may be what is now known in Ceylon as 'string-hopper' or something like it". The word jālapūva also occurs at DhA i 319, with v. l. -pūpa.

[5] Or, sewn together, saṁsibbana.

[6] amatambu.

second penetration by the ninety hundred thousand. And when he taught Dhamma to his own son, Prince Anupama, then was the third penetration of Dhamma by eighty hundred thousand. Accordingly it was said:

XIX 4 The second penetration was by ninety hundred thousand.
The third penetration was by eighty hundred thousand.

At a later time in the city of Kaṇṇakujja, the king's son Surakkhita and the priest's son, the boy Dhammasena, together with sixty hundred thousand men went out to meet Phussa, the Fully Self-Awakened One, when he had reached their own city. Having reverenced him and invited him they gave a great gift for seven days, and when they had heard a talk on Dhamma by Him of the Ten Powers,[1] they attained arahantship. The Lord recited the Pātimokkha in the midst of these sixty hundred thousand monks. That was the first assembly. Again, in the city of Kāsi he taught the Chronicle of Buddhas in a gathering of at least sixty kinsfolk of King Jayasena. When they had heard it, fifty hundred thousand went forth by the "Come, monk" (formula for) going forth and attained arahantship. The Lord recited the Pātimokkha in their midst. That was the second assembly. Again, when forty hundred thousand men had heard the Maṅgala-talk at a gathering for the Mahā-Maṅgala,[2] they went forth and attained arahantship. The Wellfarer recited the Pātimokkha in their midst. That was the third assembly. Accordingly it was said:

XIX 5 And Phussa, great seer, had three assemblies of steadfast ones whose cankers were destroyed, stainless, tranquil in mind.
[234] 6 The first was a gathering of sixty hundred thousand; the second was a gathering of fifty hundred thousand.
7 The third was a gathering of forty hundred thousand of those who were freed without clinging (remaining), their relinking cut through.

Our Bodhisatta was then a warrior-noble named Vijitāvin in the

[1] BvAB inserts bhagavati pasīditvā te saparivāro pabbajitvā (being pleased with the Lord, these, with their entourage, having gone forth), and notes the omission at BvAC. Perhaps the sing. saparivāro presents a difficulty because as each prince would probably have had his own retinue the pl. would have been more appropriate.

[2] See text p. 136.

city of Arimanda. Having heard a talk on Dhamma and being pleased with that Lord, he gave him a great gift. Getting rid of his great kingdom, going forth in the Lord's presence he mastered the three Piṭakas. An expert on the three Piṭakas, he gave a talk on Dhamma to the great populace and fulfilled the perfection of Morality. That Buddha too declared of him: "He will be a Buddha." Accordingly it was said:

XIX 8 I at that time was a warrior-noble named Vijitāvin. Abandoning a great kingdom, I went forth in his presence.

9 And this Buddha Phussa, highest leader in the world, also declared of me: "Ninety-two eons from now this one will be a Buddha.

10 When he has striven the striving . . . "

11 . . . for fulfilling the ten perfections.

12 Having learnt thoroughly the Suttanta and Vinaya and all the ninefold Dispensation of the teacher, I illumined the Conqueror's Dispensation.

13 Living diligent therein, developing the Brahma-development, after reaching perfection in the super-knowings to the Brahma-world went I[1].

That Lord's city was named Kāsi[2], the king his father was named Jayasena[3], his mother was named Sirimā. Surakkhita[4] and Dhammasena were the chief disciples. The attendant was named Sabhiya. Sālā and Upasālā[5] were the two chief women disciples. The Tree of Awakening was an Āmalaka. The physical frame was fifty-eight cubits in height, the life-span was ninety thousand years. The chief consort was named Kisāgotamī, his son was named Anupama[6]. He departed riding an elephant. Accordingly it was said:

XIX 14 Kāsika was the name of the city, Jayasena the name of the warrior-noble, and Sirimā the name of the mother of Phussa, the great seer.

[1] For these two last verses cf. text pp. 138, 151, 200.
[2] BvAB Kāsika.
[3] AA i 256 297 Mahinda.
[4] Bv Sukhita.
[5] Bv Cālā Upacālā.
[6] Ānanda at Bv xix 16.

[235] 20 . . . That Lord's Tree of Awakening is said to be the Āmaṇḍa.

22 And that sage was fifty-eight ratanas tall. He shone like him of a hundred rays, like the moon at the full.

23 The (normal) life-span lasted then for ninety thousand years. Living so long he caused many people to cross over.

24 When he had exhorted many beings and had caused many people[1] to cross over, that teacher too, of unrivalled renown, waned out with the disciples.

20 Therein *āmaṇḍa* means an āmalaka tree[2].

24 *When he had exhorted* means having given exhortation, having instructed.

24 *That teacher too, of unrivalled renown* means: that teacher too, of boundless fame. "When he of boundless fame had renounced"[3] is also a reading. The meaning, according to all that is said of him, is that "he, having renounced eminence"[4]. They say that the Lord Phussa attained final nibbāna in Sena[5]-park in Kusinārā. They say that his relics were dispersed.

Everywhere remaining in the verses is quite clear.

Concluded is the Exposition of the Chronicle of the Buddha Phussa

Concluded is the Eighteenth Buddha-Chronicle

XX THE EXPOSITION OF THE CHRONICLE OF THE BUDDHA VIPASSIN

Subsequently to the Buddha Phussa when that eon with an intervening eon[6] had passed, there arose in the world ninety-one eons ago the teacher named Vipassin[7], one thinking over all that was

[1] Be, BvACB bahū jane, Bv mahājane.

[2] āmalaka at text p. 232. MA iv 147 also glosses āmaṇḍa (at M iii 101) by āmalaka. See MLS iii 140, n. 3.

[3] so jahitvā amitayaso.

[4] visesaṁ hitvā.

[5] As at Be, BvACB, Jā, Jkm. But Bv Sona, Thūp 15 Sundara.

[6] sāntarakappa. There are said to be sixty-four divisions in each mahākappa, see CPD s.v. antarakappa.

[7] Cf. Mahāpadāna Sta. (D xiv) which gives Vipassin's "life" and teaching in

known, his intention set on the welfare of others, having insight (vipassin) everywhere[1]. When he had fulfilled the perfections he was born in Tusita abode—an abode profusely illumined by the brilliance of countless jewels. Deceasing from there he took on relinking in the city of Bandhumatī in the womb of Bandhumatī, chief consort of the king named Bandhumā, rich in countless relations (bandhumant). After ten months he issued forth from his mother's womb in the deer-sanctuary at Khema like a full-moon shining untrammelled. And on his name-taking day his kinsmen who were readers of marks **[236]** gave him the name Vipassin, saying: "As well by night as by day he sees what is pure[2] without the darkness that comes from blinking[3], and he sees with broad[4] eyes". Or they say "Vipassin means: constantly investigating he sees[5]". He led the household life for eight thousand years. And his three palaces were named Nanda, Sunanda, Sirimā. There were a hundred thousand and twenty thousand women with Queen Sudassanā at the head. Sudassanā is also called Sutanū.

When, after the eight thousand years, he had seen the four signs and a boy[6] named Samavattakkhandha had been born to Queen Sutanū, departing on the Great Departure in a chariot harnessed to thoroughbreds, he went forth. Eighty-four thousand men went forth following his example. When the Great Man, surrounded by these, had engaged in striving for eight months and on the full-moon day of Visākha had partaken of sweet milk-rice given to him by the daughter of Sudassana, a merchant, he spent the day-sojourn in a sāla grove that was adorned with blossoms.

Having accepted eight handfuls of grass given to him by Sujāta, the guardian of a corn-field, and seeing an adorned Pāṭalī Tree of Awakening[7], he approached it from the southern side. On that day, as that Pāṭalī's trunk[8], of even growth, was fifty ratanas in height and the branches fifty ratanas, it was a hundred ratanas tall. That

---

considerable detail. He is the first of the six Buddhas prior to Gotama recognized there. All are referred to at Divy 333.

[1] Cf. DA 411, Mhbv 11.

[2] *vi*suddhaṁ *pas*sati.

[3] nimesa, blinking; BvAB reads nimmita.

[4] *vi*vaṭehi ca akkhīhi *pas*sati.

[5] *vi*ceyya *pas*sati.

[6] tanaya, offspring.

[7] Cf. DA 415.

[8] Cf. D ii 4.

same day that Pāṭalī was covered everywhere from the roots upwards with flowers of most fragrant scents as though tied in a sheath. A deva-like scent was wafted around. It was not alone in flowering then. All the Pāṭalīs[1] in the ten-thousand world system were flowering too. And not only the Pāṭalīs. In the ten-thousand world-system all the trees, branches[2] and creepers flowered too. And the great ocean, its waters cool and sweet, was covered by lotuses of the five colours and by various kinds of water-lilies. And all[1] the spaces between the ten-thousand world-system were entwined with banners and garlands. Several regions were strewn over with clusters of garlands, various fragrant blossoms hung down, and the surface of the earth was dark with scented incense-powder. Having approached this (Tree) and spread a grass spreading fifty-three cubits in extent, resolutely determining on the energy possessed of four factors, he sat down making the vow: "I will not arise till I am a Buddha". Seated thus he routed Māra's forces with Māra.

When he had come gradually to a mastery[3] of the Way, the four Way-knowledges and, immediately after the Way, the four fruition-knowledges, the four analytical insights, the knowledge of demarcation in the four modes of birth, the knowledge of demarcation in the five bourns, the four confidence-knowledges, the six knowledges not shared (by others) and all the special qualities of Buddhas, his intention was fulfilled. Seated in the cross-legged posture for Awakening, he uttered the solemn utterance thus:

> "Through many a birth in saṁsāra . . . the destruction of cravings*
> Just as the bourn of a blazing spark of fire struck from the anvil, gradually fading, cannot be known,
> so no bourn can be pointed to of those who are rightly freed, through wisdom, have crossed over the bonds and the floods of sense-desires and reached a happiness that moves not."*

[237] Having spent seven weeks near the Tree of Awakening

* See text p. 133.

[1] . . . 1 Given in BvAB, but not in BvAC.
[2] sākhā at DA 415, rambhā, plantains, at BvAB.
[3] hatthagate katvā, made it within his hands, got possession of, come to grips with.

itself, he acceded to Brahmā's request and, surveying the attainment of the qualifications by Prince Khaṇḍa[1], his own half-brother, and by the boy Tissa[1], the priest's son, he went through the air and descended in the deer-sanctuary in Khema[2]. When he had had both these summoned by the keeper of the pleasaunce he turned the Wheel of Dhamma[3] in the midst of these with their retinues. Then was a penetration of Dhamma by innumerable devatās. Accordingly it was said:

XX 1 And after Phussa the Self-Awakened One named Vipassin, supreme among men, One with vision, arose in the world.

2 When he had torn apart all ignorance and had attained supreme Self-Awakening, he set forth to turn the Wheel of Dhamma in the city of Bandhumatī.

3 When the leader was turning the Wheel of Dhamma he awakened both. This was the first penetration, not to be told by number.

2 Therein *had torn apart* means had smashed. The meaning is: had smashed the darkness of ignorance. "Had turned the Wheel in a monastery" is also a reading. "In that monastery" means in the deer-sanctuary at Khema.

2 *He awakened both* means he awakened both Khaṇḍa, his own younger brother, the king's son, and Tissa, the priest's son.

3 *Not to be told by number* means: there was no limit to the counting of the devatās in respect of the penetration.

At a subsequent time he caused Khaṇḍa, the king's son, and Tissa, the priest's son, and the eighty-four thousand monks who had gone forth following his example to drink of the nectar of Dhamma. That was the second penetration. Accordingly it was said:

XX 4 Later, he of boundless fame expounded the truth there. The second penetration was by eighty-four thousand.

[1] Cf. D iii 4, DA 416, 457.

[2] DA 471 says at that time Khema-pleasaunce was a seers' resort, isipatana.

[3] AA i 165 says he taught Dhamma once in every seven years. I believe it is thought, not that he was lazy, but that this was all that was needed. DhA iii 236 says he held Uposatha once in every seven years and the Exhortation he gave on only one day sufficed for seven years. Sikhin and Vessabhū held Uposatha once in every six years. On the long-standing or otherwise of their Brahma-farings see VA 190.

4 Therein *there* means in the deer-sanctuary at Khema.

5 *Eighty-four thousand who had gone forth following the example of the Self-Awakened One* means: herein these men, reckoned as eighty-four thousand, were themselves attendants of Prince Vipassin.

When they had gone[1] early in the morning to attend on the prince, Vipassin, and did not see him, they went away for the morning meal and came back after it asking where the prince was. On hearing that he had gone hence to the pleasaunce-ground they said they would look for him there. As they set out they saw his charioteer returning. He told them that the prince had gone forth. At the very place where they heard this, taking off all their finery, [238] they had themselves clothed with saffron robes from a bazar shop, and having their hair and beards shaved off, they went forth. Having done so, they approached the Great Man and surrounded him. Then the Bodhisatta Vipassin thought: "It is not suitable that while I am engaging in striving I should live in a crowd. As formerly these householders moved about surrounding me, so do they do the same now. What is the use of this crowd?" Feeling dissatisfied with the crowd's society, he thought, 'I will go away this very day'. But he considered again, 'Today is the wrong time. If I were to go away today they would all find out about me. I will go away tomorrow.' And on that day the people living in a village like the village of Uruvelā invited the Great Man together with his company for the morrow. They prepared milk-rice for the Great Man and for those eighty-four thousand. Then on the next day, which was the full-moon day of Visākha, Vipassin the Great Man, after having had the meal in that village together with those people who had gone forth, went to the place where he was staying. Those who had gone forth there, acting as the Great Man had done[2], each entered his own quarters for the night or quarters for the day. And the Bodhisatta, having entered a leaf-hut, thought as he was sitting down: "This is the time to depart". Having departed and closed the door of the leaf-hut, he started off towards the dais round the Tree of Awakening.

They say that those who had gone forth, coming back in the evening to attend on the Bodhisatta, sat down surrounding the leaf-hut. Remarking on how late it had become, they opened

[1] For following passage cf. DA 457.

[2] mahāpurisassa vattaṁ dassetvā.

the leaf-hut but as they did not see him they said, "Now, where has the Great Man gone?" But they did not go after him for they thought, "It seems that the Great Man, wearying of the crowd, wants to be alone, but verily we will see him when he has become a Buddha". And they went off on tour towards the interior of Jambudīpa. Then, hearing that Vipassin had attained Buddhahood and had turned the Wheel of Dhamma, all those who had gone forth with him gathered together in due course in the deer-sanctuary at Khema, in Bandhumatī, the capital. Thereupon the Lord taught them Dhamma. Then was a penetration of Dhamma by the eighty-four thousand monks. That was the third penetration. Accordingly it was said:

XX 5 When they had arrived in the monastery the One with vision taught Dhamma to those eighty-four thousand who had gone forth following the example of the Self-Awakened One.

6 Having gone close and listened when he was speaking (and dwelling) on all aspects, they too went to the glorious Dhamma; this was the third penetration.

5 Therein *eighty-four thousand who had gone forth following the example* (anupabbajuṁ) *of the Self-Awakened One* here means it should be understood that 'Self-Awakened One' is put into the accusative case because of the prefix anu. The meaning is that they went forth after the Self-Awakened One. The rule is to be understood from grammar.[1] "On arrival in the monastery there"[2] is also a reading.

6 *When he was speaking* means when he was uttering.

[239] 6 *Having gone close* means when they had gone near when the gift of Dhamma was being given.

They too means these too, reckoned as the eighty-four thousand who had gone forth and had been Vipassin's attendants.

6 *Went to* means knew his Dhamma. The third penetration was thus by these.

And in the deer-sanctuary at Khema while the Lord Vipassin was seated in the midst of sixty-eight hundred thousand monks who had gone forth following the example of the two chief disciples

[1] See text p. 175.

[2] Apparently tattha replaces tesaṁ in ver. 5: tesaṁ (tattha) ārāmappattānaṁ.

under Vipassin, the Fully Self-Awakened One, he recited this Pātimokkha:

> Patience[1], forbearance[1] is the supreme austerity, nibbāna is (in all ways[2]) supreme, the Buddhas say. For he who injures others is not one "gone forth", nor is one a recluse who is harming another.
> Not doing any evil, accomplishing what is good, cleansing one's own mind[3]: this is the teaching of the Buddhas.
> Not to be one who abuses[4], not to be one who injures[5], and restraint according to the Pātimokkha[6], moderation in eating, and remote bed and seat, and application in the higher thought[7]: this is the teaching of the Buddhas.

And it should be understood that these are the Pātimokkha recital-verses of all Buddhas. This was the first assembly.

Again, the second assembly was after a hundred thousand monks who had gone forth had seen the Marvel of the Double. And when Vipassin's three half-brothers had quietened border disturbances and obtained glorious things with which to attend the Lord, they led him to his own city. Hearing his Dhamma while they were attending on him, they went forth. The Lord, seated in the midst of these eighty thousand in the deer-sanctuary at Khema, recited the Pātimokkha. This was the third assembly. Accordingly it was said:

XX 7 Vipassin, great seer, had three assemblies of steadfast ones whose cankers were destroyed, stainless, tranquil in mind.

8 The first gathering was of sixty-eight hundred[8] thousand. The second gathering was of a hundred thousand monks.

9 The third gathering was of eighty thousand monks. The Self-Awakened One shone out there in the midst of the company of monks.

[1] DA 478 says these are synonyms. These 3 verses are at D ii 49, Dh 184, 183, 185, quoted at DhA iii 237, VA 186. Last verse also at Ud 43. First line at Vism 295. In "The Pātimokkha", transl. Ñāṇamoli Thera, Bangkok 1966, p. 5, this is called "The Ovāda Pātimokkha attributed to the Lord Vipassin".

[2] DA 478 glosses here by sabbākārena.

[3] sacittapariyodapana. DA 478 and DhA iii 237, though not similar in every respect, agree in glossing sa- by attano.

[4] With speech, DA 479, UdA 253.

[5] With body, ibid.

[6] Not transgressing the 7 classes of offence, UdA 253.

[7] Referring to the eight attainments.

[8] Bv omits.

8 Therein *sixty-eight hundred thousand monks* means: a hundred thousand monks with the addition of sixty-eight thousand.

[240] 9 *There* means there in the deer-sanctuary at Khema.

9 *In the midst of the company of monks* means in the midst of the company of monks[1]. "In the midst of his company of monks" is also a reading; the meaning is: in the midst of his company of monks.

Our Bodhisatta was then a nāga-king named Atula, of great psychic potency, of great majesty, and was surrounded by countless hundreds and thousands of crores of nāgas. In order to show reverence to Him of the Ten Powers, to him of unequalled power in moral habit, whose heart was cooled by compassion, and to his retinue, he had a pavilion[2] built for him which looked like the orb[3] of the moon made from jewels, to be regarded as very fine, very choice.[4] On asking him to be seated there, for seven days he gave him a great gift in keeping with his deva-like wealth, and he gave the Lord a chair beautified[5] with all the jewels, very costly, made of gold, profusely illumined by the brilliance of many and various jewels. Thereupon as he (the Lord) was giving him the benediction for the gift of the chair, he declared, "Ninety-one eons from now this one will be a Buddha." Accordingly it was said:

XX 10 I at that time was a nāga-king named Atula, of great psychic potency, meritorious, bearer of light.

11 When I went up to the eldest in the world then, playing on deva-like musical instruments, having surrounded (him) with countless crores of nāgas,

12 having approached Vipassin, the Self-Awakened One, leader of the world, and having invited him, I gave the king under Dhamma a golden seat inlaid with pearls and jewels, embellished with every adornment.

13 As he was sitting in the midst of the Order that Buddha too declared of me: "Ninety-one eons from now this one will be a Buddha.

14 Having departed from the delightful city of Kapila, he

[1] bhikkhugaṇamajjhe ti bhikkuganassa majjhe.
[2] maṇḍapa.
[3] maṇḍala.
[4] maṇḍa.
[5] maṇḍita.

will be a Tathāgata. When he has striven the striving and carried out austerities,

15 After sitting at the root of the Ajapāla Tree and accepting milk-rice there, the Tathāgata will go to the Nerañjarā.[1]

16 And the Conqueror will eat the milk-rice on the bank of the river Nerañjarā and go to the root of the Tree of Awakening by the glorious way prepared.

17 Then, circumambulating the dais of the Tree of Awakening, the unsurpassed one of great renown will awaken to Self-Awakening at the root of an Assattha.

18 His genetrix and mother will be named Māyā, his father, Suddhodana; he will be named Gotama.

[241] 19 Kolita and Upatissa, cankerless, attachment gone, tranquil in mind, concentrated, will be the chief disciples.

20 He by name of Ānanda will attend on this Conqueror[2]. Khemā and Uppalavaṇṇā will be the chief women disciples,

21 cankerless, attachment gone, tranquil in mind, concentrated. That Lord's Tree of Awakening is said to be the Assattha."[3]

22 When I had heard his words all the more did I incline my mind. I resolutely determined on further practice for fulfilling the ten perfections.

10 Therein *meritorious* means meritorious.[4] The meaning is: an accumulation of merit that had been well heaped up.

10 *Bearer of light* means furnished with lustre.

11 *With countless crores of nāgas* means with countless crores of nāgas.[5] The genitive case should be understood in the sense of an instrumental.

11 *Having surrounded* means having surrounded the Lord.

11 *I* demonstrates oneself.

11 *Playing on* means sounding, striking.

12 *Inlaid with pearls and jewels* means arranged with pearls and so forth and various kinds of jewels.

[1] This ver. omitted in BvAC.

[2] BvA Ānando nāma nāmena upaṭṭhissati taṁ jinaṁ; Bv Ānando nām° uppaṭṭhāko upaṭṭhissat° imaṁ jinaṁ.

[3] Cf. ver. 14–21 with IIA 62–69.

[4] puññavanto ti puññavā.

[5] nekānaṁ nāgakoṭīnan ti anekehi nāgakoṭihi, gen. and instr.

12 *Embellished with every adornment* means beautified with decorations made with jewels on the chair, with coral formations[1] and so forth.

12 *A golden seat* means a seat made of gold.

12 *I gave* means I gave.[2]

And the name of that Lord Vipassin's city was Bandhumatī, the king his father was Bandhumā, his mother was named Bandhumatī; Khaṇḍa and Tissa were the chief disciples, the attendant was named Asoka, Candā and Candamittā were the chief women disciples. The Tree of Awakening was a Pāṭalī. The physical frame was eighty cubits in height. The lustre of the physical frame remained suffusing seven yojanas all the time. The life-span was eighty thousand years. His wife was named Sutanū, his son was named Samavattakkhandha; he departed by a chariot harnessed to thoroughbreds. Accordingly it was said:

XX 23 Bandhumatī was the name of the city, Bandhumā the name of the warrior-noble, Bandhumatī was the name of the mother of Vipassin, the great seer.

[242] 28 Khaṇḍa and Tissa were the chief disciples. Asoka was the name of the attendant on Vipassin, the great seer.

29 Candā and Candamittā were the chief women disciples. That Lord's Tree of Awakening is said to be the Pāṭalī.

31 Vipassin, leader of the world, was eighty cubits tall. His lustre streamed forth for seven yojanas all round.

32 That Buddha's life-span was eighty thousand years. Living so long he caused many people to cross over.

33 He released from bondage many devas and men[3], and to the remaining ordinary people he pointed out the Way and what was not the Way.

34 When he had displayed the light and had taught the undying state, blazing like a mass of fire he waned out with the disciples.

35 The glorious psychic potency, the glorious merit, and the Marks that were blossoming[4] have all disappeared. Are not all constructions void?

[1] BvAC pavāḷarūpa, BvAB vāḷarūpa, forms of wild beasts (?).

[2] adās' ahan ti adāsim ahaṁ.

[3] BvA bahū deve manusse ca, Bv bahudevamanussānaṁ.

[4] BvA ca kusumitaṁ, Bv catubhūmikaṁ. Other texts differ.

33 Therein *from bondage* means he freed devas and men from bondage of the fetters of sense-desire and so forth; the meaning is he illuminated[1] (them).

33 *And he pointed out the Way and what was not the Way* means: saying, "This is the Way for arrival at deathlessness, the Way is the middle course exempt from the (false) views of annihilationism and eternalism, this Way is not for bodily fatigue and so forth". The meaning is: *he pointed out* to the rest of the ordinary people.

34 *When he had displayed the light* means: when he had displayed the light of knowledge of the Way.

35 *And the Marks that were blossoming* means that the Lord's physical frame was beautified and flowering with the Mark of the Wheel and so forth.

Everywhere remaining in the verses is quite clear.

Concluded is the Exposition of the Chronicle of the Buddha Vipassin

Concluded is the Nineteenth Buddha-Chronicle

XXI THE EXPOSITION OF THE CHRONICLE OF THE BUDDHA SIKHIN

[243] Subsequently to Vipassin and when that eon had disappeared for fifty-nine eons following on that Buddhas did not arise in the world. Gone[2] was the light of Buddhas. The single kingdom of the defilements, sons of devas and Māras, was without obstacle. But thirty-one eons ago from now two Fully Self-Awakened Ones, Sikhin, like a smokeless crest (of fire) from collected smooth, dry hardwood abundantly sprinkled with ghee, and Vessabhū arose in the world[2].

Then the Lord Sikhin having fulfilled the perfections, was born in Tusita city. Deceasing from there, he took on relinking in the city of Aruṇavatī in the womb of the queen named Pabhāvatī who, of an extremely pleasing golden lustre (pabhā), was the chief consort of the king named Aruṇavata who had extremely good qualities (guṇavata). After ten months had passed he issued forth

[1] vikāseti, made shine, made blossom.

[2] . . . [2] om. in BvAC as noticed by BvAB.

from his mother's womb in Nisabha pleasaunce. And when the soothsayers were naming him they gave him the name Sikhin because his turban (uṇhīsa) stood up like a flame (sikhā).[1] He led the household life for seven thousand years. His three palaces were named Sucandakasiri, Giriyasa, Nārivasabha[2]. There were twenty-four thousand women attending on him with Queen Sabbakāmā at the head.

When he had seen the four signs and the son named Atula of many unrivalled good qualities (guṇagaṇātula) had been born to Queen Sabbakāmā, departing on the Great Departure mounted on the back of a glorious elephant, he went forth. Seventy hundred thousand men went forth following his example. Surrounded by these he engaged in striving for eight months. On the full-moon day of Visākha, getting rid of the society of the company he partook of sweet milk-rice given to him in Sudassana, a market-town, by the daughter of the merchant Piyadassī and spent the day-sojourn in a grove of young acacias.

Having accepted[3] eight handfuls of grass given to him by an ascetic named Anomadassin, he approached a Puṇḍarīka Tree of Awakening[4]. They say that the Puṇḍarīka Tree of Awakening was of the same dimensions as the Pāṭalī[5]. On that very day its trunk was fifty ratanas high, its branches too at least fifty ratanas (high). It was covered with flowers with deva-like perfumes. And not only with flowers, it was thick[6] with fruits too. On one side of it were young fruits, on one side middling sized ones, and one side not over-ripe ones, on one side there hung down here and there (fruits) full of taste, scent and colour as though they were infused with deva-like nutritive essences. It was likewise in the ten-thousand world-systems: flowering trees were beautified with flowers, fruiting trees with fruits.

When he had spread a grass-spreading there twenty-four cubits in extent he sat down in the cross-legged position resolutely determining on the four-factored energy. Seated thus, he routed Māra's forces with Māra over a space of thirty-six yojanas, attained Self-Awakening, uttered the solemn utterance: "Through many a birth

[1] Cf. Mhvu iii 246.
[2] Bv Sucando Giri Vahano.
[3] The usual accompanying words "towards evening" are missing.
[4] Cf. D ii 4.
[5] No doubt referring to Vipassin's Tree, see text p. 236, also DA 416.
[6] BvAC sahito as noticed by BvAB which reads sañchanno.

in saṁsāra", and spent seven weeks near the Tree of Awakening itself. After acceding to Brahmā's request, and seeing that the seventy hundred thousand monks who had gone forth with him had achieved the qualifications, he went by a deva-path and descended in Migācira[1] pleasaunce near the capital Aruṇavatī which had numerous encircling walls (āvaraṇavati). Surrounded by this company of sages, he turned the Wheel of Dhamma in their midst. Then was the first penetration by a hundred thousand crores. Accordingly it was said:

[244] XXI 1 After Vipassin was the Self-Awakened One named Sikhin[2], supreme among men, Conqueror, without an equal, matchless.

2 Having broken asunder[3] Māra's army, attained[4] to supreme Self-Awakening, he turned the Wheel of Dhamma out of compassion for breathing things.

3 As Sikhin, bull (-man)[5] of Conquerors, was turning the Wheel of Dhamma there was the first penetration by a hundred thousand crores.

And again, when he was near Aruṇavatī the capital and had taught Dhamma to Prince Abhibhū[6] and Prince Sambhava with their two retinues, he caused ninety thousand crores to drink of the nectar of Dhamma. That was the second penetration. Accordingly it was said:

XXI 4 And later while the best of the company, the supreme among men, was teaching Dhamma there was the second penetration by ninety thousand crores.

And when at the gateway of the city of Suriyavatī at the root of a champak tree[7] the Lord was performing the Marvel of the Double for crushing and smashing the sectarians and for releasing all people from the bonds and was teaching Dhamma, there was the

[1] BvAB migājina, noticing BvAC's reading.

[2] Be, BvACB Sikhivhayo āsi, Bv Sikhisavhayo nāma.

[3] BvAC pabhinditvā, Bv pamadditvā.

[4] BvAC patvā, Bv patto.

[5] puṅgava as at Vism 78, Mhvu iii 249.

[6] See DPPN s.v. 1 Abhibhū. Referred to at A i 227, Kvu 203, DA 416. Both mentioned at S i 155f.

[7] Michelia champaka.

third penetration by eighty thousand crores. Accordingly it was said:

XXI 5 And while he was displaying the Marvel of the Double to the world with the devas there was the third penetration by eighty thousand crores.

The Lord recited the Pātimokkha in the midst of the hundred thousand arahants who had gone forth together with Abhibhū and Sambhava, the king's son(s). That was the first assembly. He recited the Pātimokkha at a gathering of kinsfolk in the city of Aruṇavatī in the midst of eighty thousand monks who had gone forth. That was the second assembly. He recited the Pātimokkha in the city of Dhanañjaya at the time of 'guiding out' the householder Dhanapālaka[1] in the midst of seventy thousand monks who had gone forth.[2] That was the third assembly. Accordingly it was said:

XXI 6 Sikhin, too, great seer, had three assemblies of steadfast ones whose cankers were destroyed, stainless, tranquil in mind.

7 The first gathering was of a hundred thousand monks; the second gathering was of eighty thousand monks.

[245] 8 The third gathering was of seventy thousand monks; it is unsullied like a lotus grown up in the water.[3]

8 Therein *unsullied* means: as a lotus, born in the water, growing up in the water, is unsullied by the water, so too the assembly of monks, though born in the world was unsullied by the things of the world.

They say that the Bodhisatta was then a king named Arindama in the city of Paribhutta but was somewhere keeping aloof (from society) when the teacher Sikhin with his retinue arrived in the city of Paribhutta. Having gone out of the royal abode to meet him, his heart, eyes and ears filled with serene joy, and together with his retinue having honoured with his head the two lotus-feet of Him of the Ten Powers[4] as he was walking along, he invited Him

[1] No further information about him seems available.

[2] According to DhA iii 236 he recited the Pātimokkha once every 6 years; cf. VA 191.

[3] Cf. A ii 39.

[4] BvAB reads dasabalassa amalacaraṇakamalayugalesu, BvAC dasabalacaraṇakamalayugale. Probably there is a reference to ver. 8 though there paduma is the word used for lotus.

of the Ten Powers. For seven days he gave a great gift in keeping with the faith and the wealth of a ruling family and, having had the store-room for woven cloth opened, he gave costly garments to the Order of monks with the Awakened One at the head. And as he was giving his own glorious elephant which, like the elephant Erāvaṇa[1], was glorious among elephants, being possessed of strength of body and speed and was adorned with garlands of golden netting, its lovely tusks, sheath and tail shining like new gold, its wide mobile ears splendidly gleaming like the kingly moon, he also gave goods that were allowable making them to the same dimensions as the elephant. That teacher too declared of him: "Thirty-one eons from now he will be a Buddha". Accordingly it was said:

XXI 9 I at that time was a warrior-noble named Arindama. With food and drink I refreshed the Order with the Self-Awakened One at the head.

10 After giving many glorious robes—not less than a crore of robes—I gave the Self-Awakened One a caparisoned riding-elephant.

11 Measuring (the dimensions of) the riding-elephant, I presented what was allowable. I fulfilled my purpose which was ever-present and firm.

12 And that Buddha Sikhin, highest leader in the world, also declared of me: "Thirty-one eons from now this one will be a Buddha.

13 Having departed from the delightful city of Kapila[2] . . . "
" . . . we will be face to face with this one."

14 When I had heard his words all the more did I incline my mind. I resolutely determined on further practice for fulfilling the ten perfections.

And that Lord's city was named Aruṇavatī, the king his father was named Aruṇavā, his mother was named Pabhāvatī. Abhibhū and Sambhava were the two chief disciples, the attendant was named Khemaṅkara, the two chief women disciples were Makhilā[3] and Padumā. The Tree of Awakening was a Puṇḍarīka. And his physical frame was seventy cubits in height; the lustre from his

[1] Cf. text p. 210.
[2] See xx 14.
[3] See note to ver. 21 below.

physical frame remained suffusing three yojanas all the time. [246] The life-span was seventy thousand years. His chief consort was named Sabbakāmā, his son was named Atula. Accordingly it was said:

XXI 15 Aruṇavatī was the name of the city, Aruṇavā[1] the name of the warrior-noble, and Pabhāvatī the name of the mother of Sikhin, the great seer.

20 Abhibhū and Sambhava were the chief disciples. Khemaṅkara was the name of the attendant on Sikhin, the great seer.

21 Makhilā[2] and Padumā were the chief women disciples. That Lord's Tree of Awakening is said to be the Puṇḍarīka.

22 Sirivaḍḍha and Canda[3] were the chief attendants. Cittā and Sugattā were the chief women attendants.

23 That Buddha was seventy cubits in height. He of the thirty-two glorious Marks resembled a golden festooned column.

24 The fathom-length halo was a lustre that streamed forth from his body without intermission night and day[4] for three yojanas over all the quarters.

25 This great seer's life-span was seventy thousand years. Living so long he caused many people to cross over.

26 Having made the cloud of Dhamma rain down moistening the world with the devas, attaining to that peace himself, he waned out with the disciples.

27 The minor characteristics with which he was endowed, the thirty-two glorious Marks have all disappeared. Are not all constructions void?

11 Therein *measuring* means gauging by that elephant's dimensions.

11 *Allowable* means: those goods are allowable which are goods it is allowable for monks to accept.

11 *I fulfilled my purpose* means: by the zest of giving I fulfilled my intention and made deep joy arise in me.

[1] So BvAC, S i 155, Jkm 18; Bv, Be, BvAB Aruṇa.

[2] As at BvAC, Be, Jā i 41; Akhilā at Bv; Sakhilā at BvAB.

[3] Be, BvAB Nanda.

[4] BvAC tassa vyāmappabhā kāyā rattindivaṁ atanditā; Bv tūssāpi byāmappabhā kāyā divā rattiṁ nirantaraṁ.

11 *Ever-present and firm:* the meaning is, thinking 'I will give a gift all the time,' because of the gift my intention was (ever-) present and firm.

[247] 21 *Puṇḍarika-tree* means a white mango-tree[1].

24 *Lustre for three yojanas:* the meaning is, the lustre streamed forth for three yojanas.

26 *Cloud of Dhamma* means the rain of Dhamma. A Buddha's cloud is one that rains Dhamma.

26 *Moistening:* the meaning is, moistening, sprinkling with the waters of a talk on Dhamma.

26 *World with the devas* means creatures with the devas.

26 *That peace* means that peace, nibbāna.

27 *The minor characteristics with which he was endowed:* the meaning is that the Lord's physical frame was endowed with the eighty minor characteristics,[2] beginning with the copper-coloured nails, long nails, glossy nails, rounded fingers, and so forth, and was beautified by the thirty-two Marks of a Great Man.

And Sikhin, the Fully Self-Awakened One, waned out in Assa-monastery[3] in the city of Sīlavatī.

Sikhin indeed blazed brilliantly in the world,
Sikhin indeed roared in the on-coming cloud,
Sikhin, great seer, abandoned the firing[4] (for rebirth),
Sikhin indeed is gone, well-gone, to tranquillity.

It is said that the Lord's relics remained as one entirety; they were not dispersed. But the people who lived in the whole of Jambudīpa erected a thūpa three yojanas high, made of the seven kinds of gems and gleaming like a snowy mountain.

The remaining meanings in the verses are quite clear.

Concluded is the Exposition of the Chronicle of the Buddha Sikhin

Concluded is the Twentieth Buddha-Chronicle

[1] setambarukkha as at DA ii 416.

[2] Enumerated Miln-ṭ p. 17.

[3] Assārāma at Be, BvACB, but Dussārāma at Bv, Thūp 16, Jkm 18, perhaps referring to ver. 10 above where the Bodhisatta gave the Buddha dussa, robes.

[4] indhana, fuel, kindling, firewood, as at pp. 166, 219.

XXII THE EXPOSITION OF THE CHRONICLE OF THE BUDDHA VESSABHŪ

And subsequently to the Buddha Sikhin and on the disappearance of his Dispensation, men's life-spans which had been seventy thousand years in duration in due course dwindled till they were of ten years' duration. Increasing again to immeasurable life-spans, in due course these dwindled (again) till they were sixty thousand years in duration. Then the teacher named Vessabhū, his mind conquered, overlord of all the world, self-become[1], arose in the world. And having fulfilled the perfections he was reborn in Tusita city. Deceasing from there he took on relinking in the womb of the virtuous (sīlavatī) Yasavatī, chief consort of the much delighted (supatīta) king named Suppatīta in the city of Anupama[2]. After ten months he issued forth from his mother's womb in Anupama pleasaunce. Immediately on being born he delighted the people by roaring a bull's[3] roar. Therefore on his name taking day they gave him the name of Vessabhū on account of the bull's roar.[4] [248] He led the household life for six thousand years. His three palaces were named Ruci, Suruci, Rativaḍḍhana.[5] There were thirty thousand women in attendance with Queen Sucittā at the head.

When he had seen the four signs and the prince named Suppabuddha had been born to the queen named Sucittā, he went in a golden palanquin to see the pleasaunce and, accepting saffron robes given by devas, went forth. Thirty-seven thousand went forth following his example. Surrounded by these he then engaged in striving for six months. On the full-moon day of Visākha in the market-town of Sucitta he partook of sweet milk-rice given to him by Sirivaḍḍhanā whose appearance was pleasing.

Having spent the day-sojourn in a sāla grove, towards evening he accepted eight handfuls of grass given to him by Narinda, a nāga-king, and approached a Sāla Tree of Awakening[6] circumambulating it. The dimensions of that Sāla Tree were just the same

[1] vijitamanobhū sabbalokābhibhū sayambhū Vessabhū.

[2] BvAB Anoma.

[3] vasabha. Explanations of 3 kinds of bull: vasabha, usabha, nisabha given at SnA 40.

[4] Mhvu iii 246 gives another reason for his name and Mhvs-ṭ i 63 still others.

[5] Vaḍḍhana at Bv xxii 19.

[6] BvAB sālabodhi, BvAC sālavane bodhiṁ.

as those of the Pāṭalī.[1] It must be understood that it was likewise rich in lovely flowers and fruits. Having approached that Sāla Tree, he spread a grass spreading forty cubits in extent. Sitting in the cross-legged position he obtained unobstructed knowledge[2] devoid of the hindrances, all the obstructions dead.[3]

When he had uttered the solemn utterance and had spent seven weeks there, seeing the attainment of the qualifications by his own younger brothers Prince Soṇa and Prince Uttara, he went by deva-path and descended in Aruṇa pleasaunce near the city of Anupama. When he had had the princes summoned by the keeper of the pleasaunce he turned the Wheel of Dhamma in the midst of these with their retinues. Then was the first penetration by eighty thousand crores.

Again, while the Lord was walking on tour in the country teaching Dhamma in this place and that there was a penetration of Dhamma by seventy thousand crores. That was the second penetration. In the city of Anupama itself, breaking the net of (false) views, laying low the banner of the sectarians, shattering conceit and vanity, raising aloft the banner of Dhamma, performing the Marvel of the Double before innumerable companies of men and companies of devas extending for ninety yojanas, and satisfying the devas and men, he refreshed sixty crores with the nectar of Dhamma. That was the third penetration. Accordingly it was said:

XXII 1 In the same Maṇḍa-eon the leader[4] named Vessabhū, without an equal, matchless, arose in the world.

2 Realizing that it was aflame with the fire of passion and was the domain of cravings then,[5] he attained supreme Self-Awakening like an elephant breaking asunder its shackles.

3 When Vessabhū, leader of the world, was turning the Wheel of Dhamma there was the first penetration by eighty thousand crores.

[1] See text p. 236, and cf. p. 243 where the size of the Puṇḍarīka is also said to be the same as that of the Pāṭalī.

[2] Defined Pṭs i 131ff.

[3] A play on words: vigataṁīvaraṇaṁ sabbamatāvaraṇaṁ anāvaraṇañāṇaṁ. In the 2nd compound mata can mean understood as well as dead.

[4] nāyako. Bv reads so jino as noted at Be, BvAB.

[5] Be, BvACB tadā, Bv sadā.

[249] 4 When the eldest[1] in the world, bull of men, was setting out on tour in the realm there was the second penetration by seventy thousand crores.

5 He worked a Marvel driving out a great false view; men and deities of the ten-thousand worlds of men with the devas were gathered together.

6 On seeing the great wonder, astonishing, astounding, sixty crores of devas and men awakened.

2 Therein *aflame* means this entire triple world was on fire.

2 *Fire of passion* means because of passion.

2 *Domain of cravings:* the meaning is, knowing thus: the realm and the occasion of mastery.

2 *Like an elephant breaking asunder its shackles* means: like an elephant breaking through the feeble shackles of a creeper, he attained, he arrived at Self-Awakening.

5 *Of the ten-thousand* means of the ten-thousand.[2]

5 *Men with devas* means in the world of men with the devas.

6 *Awakened* means they awakened.[3]

On the full-moon day of Māgha he recited the Pātimokkha[4] in the midst of the eighty thousand arahants who had gone forth in the gathering with the two chief disciples, Soṇa and Uttara. That was the first assembly. And when the monks, reckoned as thirty-seven thousand, who had gone forth with Vessabhū, overlord of all the worlds, had gone away leaving the crowd behind them, they heard that the Wheel of Dhamma had been turned by Vessabhū, the Fully Self-Awakened One. Arriving in the city named Soreyya they saw the Lord. The Lord taught them Dhamma, and having let them all go forth by the 'Come, monk' (formula for) going forth, he recited the Pātimokkha in a company possessed of the four factors.[5] That was the second assembly. And when the king's son named Upasanta[6] was ruling in the city of Nārivāhana, the Lord went there out of compassion for him. When he heard of the

[1] Bv, Be jeṭṭha; BvAC, as noticed by Be, BvAB seṭṭha, best.
[2] dasasahassī ti dasasahassiyaṁ.
[3] bujjhare ti bujjhiṁsu.
[4] Vessabhū is said to have held uposatha once in every six years, DhA iii 236; see also Vin iii 7ff.
[5] See text pp. 126, 163, 204, 292, 298.
[6] Cf. D ii 6, Upasannaka, a monk.

Lord's arrival he went out with his retinue to meet the Lord. Having invited him, given a large gift, and heard his Dhamma, he went forth, his heart believing. The company, reckoned at sixty thousand, went forth following his example. Together with him they attained arahantship. Surrounded by these the Lord Vessabhū recited the Pātimokkha. That was the third assembly. Accordingly it was said:

XXII 7 Vessabhū, great seer, had three assemblies of steadfast ones whose cankers were destroyed, stainless, tranquil in mind.

8 The first gathering was of eighty thousand monks; the second gathering was of thirty-seven thousand[1].

[250] 9 The third gathering was of sixty thousand monks who had overpassed the fear of ageing and so forth,[2] great seers,[3] own sons[4] (of the Buddha).

The Bodhisatta was then a king named Sudassana, extremely pleasing to look upon (paramapiyadassana) in the city of Sarabhavatī. When Vessabhū, leader of the world, had reached the city of Sarabha and he had heard his Dhamma, then, believing at heart, he brought together his clasped hands which were shining like stainless unsoiled lotus-buds, their ten fingers touching one another,[5] and raised them to his head. After giving a great gift of robes to the Order with the Buddha at the head, he built a scented chamber[6] there for the Lord's residence. Encircling it with a thousand vihāras and making over all kinds and sorts of wealth to the Lord's Dispensation, he went forth in his presence. Possessed of the qualities of right practice, liking the thirteen ascetic practices, delighting in the search for the accessories of Awakening, he dwelt greatly delighting in the Awakened One's Dispensation. And that Lord too declared of him, "In the future thirty-one eons

[1] There is some confusion here. Bv, Be, BvAB give sattatibhikkhusahassa, 70,000 monks, in the verse: but BvAC in the verse and BvACB in the prose portion give sattatiṁsasahassa, 37,000.

[2] BvAC jarādibhayātītānaṁ; Bv -bhayacittānaṁ; Be -bhayabhītānaṁ, BvAB -bhayatītānaṁ.

[3] BvAC mahesino, Bv mahesinaṁ.

[4] "Spiritual" sonship is meant.

[5] Cf. text p. 10. In one of the long compounds above BvAC reads -vikalakuvalayā- and BvAB -vikalakamala-.

[6] Referred to at Divy 333.

from now this one will be the Buddha named Gotama". Accordingly it was said:

XXII 10 The superb Wheel had been turned[1] by that Buddha without an equal. I rejoiced in the going forth when I had heard[2] the excellent Dhamma[3].

11 I at that time was a warrior-noble named Sudassana. Having invited the great hero and given a gift of great value[4], I honoured the Conqueror and the Order with food, drink, with clothing.

12 Having bestowed the great gift, unrelaxing night and day, I went forth in the Conqueror's presence in the going forth that is endowed with special qualities.

13 Endowed with the special quality of right practice, composed in the duties and in morality, seeking for omniscience I delighted in the Conqueror's Dispensation.

14 Having come to faith and zest I reverenced the feet of the teacher[5]. Zest arose for the sake of my Awakening itself.

15 Knowing that I had no intention of turning back[6], the Self-Awakened One spoke thus, "Thirty-one eons from now this one will be a Buddha.

16 Having departed from the delightful city of Kapila . . ."

17 When I had heard his words all the more did I incline my mind. I resolutely determined on further practice for fulfilling the ten perfections.

[251] And that Lord's city was named Anupama, the name of the warrior-noble his father was Suppatīta, his mother was named Yasavatī. Soṇa and Uttara were the two chief disciples, Upasanta was the name of the attendant. Dāmā and Samālā were the chief women disciples. The Tree of Awakening was a Sāla. The physical frame was sixty cubits in height, the life-span sixty thousand years.

[1] BvAC vattitaṁ, Bv vattayiṁ.
[2] BvAC sutvā, Bv sutvāna.
[3] Be, BvAB reverse the positions of this verse and the next.
[4] Bv omits this line.
[5] BvAC, as noted at BvAB, pāde vandāmi satthari; Bv buddhaṁ vandāmi sattharaṁ.
[6] anivattimānasam ñatvā, knowing my purpose of no-turn-back; cf. viii 2 anivattigamanamagga.

His wife was named Sucittā, the son was named Suppabuddha. He departed in a golden palanquin. Accordingly it was said:

XXII 18 Anupama[1] was the name of the city, Suppatīta[2] the name of the warrior-noble, Yasavatī the name of the mother of Vessabhū, the great seer.

23 Soṇa and Uttara were the chief disciples. Upasanta was the name of the attendant on Vessabhū, the great seer.

24 Dāmā[3] and Samālā were the chief women disciples. That Lord's Tree of Awakening is said to be the Sāla[4].

25 Sotthika and Ramma were the chief attendants; Kāligotamī (and) Sirimā[5] were the chief women attendants.

26 He was sixty ratanas tall. He resembled a golden sacrificial pillar. Rays streamed forth from his body like fire at night on a mountain-top.

27 That great seer's life-span lasted[6] for sixty thousand years. Living so long he caused many people to cross over.

28 Having made Dhamma widely famed, having assorted the great populace, and having provided the ship of Dhamma, he waned out with the disciples.

29 All the comely people,[7] the mode of life and the deportment[8] have all disappeared. Are not all constructions void?

10 Therein *the Wheel had been turned* means the Wheel of Dhamma had been turned.

10 *Excellent Dhamma* means Dhamma for further-men.[9]

12 *The going forth that is endowed with special qualities* means: knowing, I went forth.

[1] Bv, Be, BvAB Anoma.

[2] Bv Supatīta, Jkm 18 Pupphavatika.

[3] Be, BvAB Rāmā.

[4] BvAC sālo iti pavuccati, Bv, Be, BvAB mahāsalo ti vuccati.

[5] BvAC Kāligotamī Sirimā, as noted by Be, BvAB which read Gotamī Sirimā c'eva; Bv Gotamī ca Sirimā ca.

[6] Be, BvACB āyu tassa mahesino; Bv āyu vijjati tāvade, the (normal) life-span lasted then.

[7] Be, BvACB sabbajana, Bv mahājana.

[8] iriyāpatha, and at text p. 108, often meaning the four postures of standing, walking, etc.

[9] uttarimanussadhamma, defined at Vin iii 91.

13 *Composed in the duties and in morality* means composed in the duties and in the moral habits;[1] the meaning is: fulfilling each of these, composed.

13 *I delighted* means I greatly delighted.

[252] 14 *Faith and zest* means: having come to faith and to zest.[2]

14 *I reverenced* means I greatly reverenced. The present tense (vandāmi) is to be understood in the sense of the past.

14 *Of the teacher* means: of the teacher[3].

15 *No intention of turning back* means intention of mind of non-faltering.

26 *Resembled a golden[4] sacrificial pillar* means: similar to a golden[5] post.

26 *Streamed forth* means flowed forth from this side and that.

26 *Rays* means rays of his own essence.[5]

26 *Like fire at night on a mountain-top* means the resplendent rays of his body were like a fire on a mountain-top at night.[6]

28 *Having assorted* means having made a classification in respect of exertion and so forth and in respect of stream-entry and so forth.

28 *Ship of Dhamma* means: having provided the ship of Dhamma known as the eight Ways for the sake of crossing over the four floods.[7]

29 *Comely* means comely.[8]

29 *All the people* means all the people;[9] the meaning is: the Fully Self-Awakened One with the Order of disciples.

29 *Mode of life* means mode of life[10]. Everywhere the accusative case is to be understood in the sense of a nominative.

They say that the Lord Vessabhū attained final nibbāna in the

[1] vattasīlasamāhito ti vattesu ca sīlesu ca samāhito.

[2] saddhāpītin ti saddhañca pītiñ ca upagantvā.

[3] sattharī ti sattharaṁ.

[4] hema . . . suvaṇṇa.

[5] Not created by determination, but coming from his physical frame; thus following BvAC sabhāvarasmi rather than BvAB pabhārasmi, lustre and rays, or rays of lustre.

[6] rattiṁ va pabbate sikhī ti rattiyaṁ pabbatamatthake aggi viya raṁsi vijjotitā tassa kāye.

[7] Cf. text p. 91.

[8] dassaneyyan ti dassaneyyo.

[9] sabbajanan ti sabbo jano.

[10] vihāran ti vihāro.

deer-sanctuary Khema in the city of Usabhavatī. And his relics were dispersed.

In the superb city of Usabhavatī the Lord Vessabhū, bull of Conquerors,
Came to be without clinging (to rebirth) remaining in a delightful woodland monastery. 94

Everywhere remaining in the verses is quite clear.

Concluded is the Exposition of the Chronicle of the Buddha Vessabhū

Concluded is the Twenty-first Buddha-Chronicle

XXIII THE EXPOSITION OF THE CHRONICLE OF THE BUDDHA KAKUSANDHA

But after that eon had passed in which Vessabhū, self-become, had attained final nibbāna Conqueror-suns did not arise for twenty-nine eons. In this Bhadda-eon four Buddhas arose. Which four? Kakusandha, Koṇāgamana, Kassapa, our Buddha, and the Lord Metteyya will arise. Thus this eon, praised by the Lord, is called a Bhadda-eon on account of its being much beautified by the arisings of five Buddhas.

Therein, the Lord named Kakusandha, having fulfilled the perfections, was reborn in Tusita city. [253] Deceasing from there, he took on relinking in the womb of the brahman lady named Visākhā, chief consort of the priest named Aggidatta who was instructor in theory and practice[1] to the king named Khemaṅkara in the city of Khemavatī.

And when kings are reverencing, esteeming, venerating, honouring brahmans then Bodhisattas are reborn in a brahman family. And when brahmans are reverencing, esteeming, venerating, honouring warrior-nobles then they arise in a warrior-noble family.[2] They say that brahmans were then being reverenced, esteemed by warrior-nobles; therefore the Bodhisatta, the Great Being, Kakusandha, a bondsman to truth (saccasandha), making

[1] atthadhamma, not in a Buddhist sense here.
[2] Cf. Mhvu iii 247f.

the ten-thousand world-system resound and quiver, arose in a brahman family that was uninvolved in involvements originating in wealth and prosperity. Marvels arose in the manner spoken of above[1]. After ten months he issued forth from his mother's womb in Khema pleasaunce like a glow of fire from a golden flash (of lightning). He led the household life for four thousand years. They say his three palaces were named Suci, Suruci, Rativaḍḍhana[2]. Thirty thousand women were in attendance with the brahman lady Rocanī[3] at the head.

When he had seen the four signs and the unsurpassed (anuttara) prince Uttara had been born to the brahman lady Rocanī[3], having departed on the Great Departure by a chariot harnessed to thoroughbreds, he went forth. Forty thousand went forth following his example. Surrounded by these he engaged in striving for eight months. On the full-moon day of Visākha he partook of sweet milk-rice given to him in the market-town of Sucirindha by the daughter of the brahman Vajirindha and spent the day-sojourn in an acacia grove.

Towards evening, having accepted eight handfuls of grass brought to him by Subhadda, a guardian of a corn-field, he went to a Sirīsa Tree of Awakening, of the dimensions of the Pāṭalī already mentioned[4] which was wafting a deva-like perfume around. Having spread a grass spreading thirty-four cubits in extent, he sat down in the cross-legged position. When he had attained Self-Awakening and had uttered the solemn utterance, he spent seven weeks (there). Seeing that the forty thousand monks who had gone forth with him were capable of piercing the truths in only one day he entered the deer-sanctuary at the seers' resort that was near the city of Makhilā and turned the Wheel of Dhamma in their midst. Then was the first penetration of Dhamma by forty thousand crores. Again, when he had performed the Marvel of the Double at the root of a Great Sāla tree at the gateway to the city of Kaṇṇakujja, he aroused vision of Dhamma in thirty thousand crores. That was the second penetration.

And not far from the city of Khemavatī in a certain dwelling-place for devas[5] there was a yakkha named Naradeva. Reckoned as

[1] See text p. 96ff.
[2] Bv Vaḍḍhana. Be, BvAB call them Kāma Kāmavaṇṇa Kāmasuddhi.
[4] Bv xxiii. 17 Virocamānā, Be Rocinī.
[4] See text p. 236, and cf. pp. 243, 248.
[5] devāyatana.

a man-deva[1], his physical form appearing as human[2], he placed himself in the middle of a desert near a lake whose fragrance was delightful to all people[3], its waters very sweet and cold, the cool waters bearing various kinds of lotuses and water-lilies and, enticing creatures with bunches of the lotuses and water-lilies all ready prepared, he devoured the human beings. [254] When he was on a concealed road, secluded from the concourse of people, he entered some large woods and devoured the creatures that were there. That desert-road was notorious among people. They say that a great crowd, assembling at both sides of the desert, waited to cross over the desert.

Then one day towards dawn Kakusandha, who was without bonds to existence,[4] emerged from an attainment of great compassion, surveyed the world, and saw both that the powerful yakkha Naradeva and the multitude of people were within the net of knowledge. Seeing this, the Lord went across the vault of the heavens and performing many and various marvels that the mass of the people could see, he descended at the abode of that yakkha Naradeva and sat down on his state-couch. Then that man-eating yakkha, seeing that the sun of sages had arrived by a forest-path and was emitting rays of the six hues like the sun encircled by a rainbow, thought, "He of the Ten Powers has come here out of compassion for me". Believing at heart he went with his own retinue of yakkhas to Himavant, the haunt of countless herds of wild animals. When he had gathered the most delightful flowers of various colours and scents growing in the water and on the land, he honoured Kakusandha who was without defects,[5] leader of the world, with garlands, perfumes and unguents as he was sitting on his own couch. Singing songs of praise, he stood paying homage, his clasped hands raised to his head. Thereupon the people, seeing this marvel, gathered together believing at heart and stood surrounding the Lord paying homage. Then the Lord Kakusandha who was devoid of relinking[6], having incited the yakkha Naradeva who was paying him homage, with a vision of the bonds to the fruits of kamma and, having alarmed him with a talk on Niraya,

[1] abhimatanaradeva.
[2] BvAB dissamānamanussasarīra. BvAC omits -manussa-.
[3] BvAB sabbajanasurabhiramassa. BvAC -durabhisarassa.
[4] vigatabhavabandha, word-play on his name.
[5] vigatarandha, another word-play on Kakusandha.
[6] appaṭisandha, another word-play on his name.

he talked on the four truths. Then was a penetration of Dhamma by creatures without measure. This was the third penetration. Accordingly it was said:

XXIII 1 After Vessabhū was the Self-Awakened One named Kakusandha, supreme among men, immeasurable, hard to attack.

2 Having suppressed all becoming, come to (the) perfection(s) through right conduct, like a lion breaking asunder its cage he attained supreme Self-Awakening.

3 When Kakusandha, leader of the world, was turning the Wheel of Dhamma there was the first penetration by forty thousand crores.

4 When he was in mid-air, in the sky, after working the changing Double[1] he awakened thirty thousand crores of devas and men.

[255] 5 When he was expounding the four truths for the yakkha Naradeva, the (number gaining) penetration of his Dhamma was incalculable[2] by computation.

2 Therein *having suppressed* means having abolished.

2 *All becoming* means all the ninefold becoming. Kamma (action) is a sign of resultant becoming.[3]

2 *Come to (the) perfection(s) through right conduct* means: having come to (the) perfection(s) by means of fulfilling all the perfections.

2 *Like a lion breaking asunder its cage* means: as a lion its cage, so the mighty elephant of sages shattered the cage of becoming.

Kakusandha, whose bonds to existence[4] were shattered, had only one assembly of disciples. On the full-moon day of Māgha the Lord recited the Pātimokkha in the deer-sanctuary at the seers' resort near the city of Kaṇṇakujja surrounded by the forty

[1] The Marvel of the Double at text p. 253. This yamaka vikubbana, the changing Double, was a transformation, a marvellous manifestation usually performed through psychic potency by a Buddha or arahants. It probably means simply the Marvel of the Double in all its changing manifestations.

[2] BvAC asaṅkhiya, Bv asaṅkheyyo.

[3] bhavuppatti, cf. Vbh 137 which, under uppattibhava gives the nine kinds of bhava, becoming or existence. Cf. Vism 571f.

[4] bhavabandha, yet another word-play on his name.

thousand arahants who had gone forth with him. Accordingly it was said:

XXIII 6 The Lord Kakusandha had one gathering of steadfast ones whose cankers were destroyed, stainless, tranquil in mind.

7 The gathering then was of forty thousand who had attained the tamed stage by the destruction of the host of canker-enemies.[1]

The Bodhisatta was then a king named Khema. Having given a great gift with bowls and robe-material to the Order with the Buddha at the head, he gave ointment for the eyes and so forth, all medicines.[2] When he had given other requisites for recluses and had heard the Lord's teaching of Dhamma, being believing at heart he went forth in his presence. And that teacher declared, 'In the future, in this same eon, he will be a Buddha' Accordingly it was said:

XXIII 8 I at that time was a warrior-noble named[3] Khema. Having given a considerable gift to the Tathāgata and[4] the Conqueror's sons,

9 having given bowls and robe-material, ointment[5] (for the eyes), wild liquorice[5]—I bestowed all this, very glorious, as he wanted.

10 And that sage Kakusandha, leader of the world[6], also declared of me, "In this Bhadda-eon this one will be a Buddha.

11 Having departed from the delightful city of Kapila . . ."

12 When I had heard his words . . . for fulfilling the ten perfections.

13 Khemavatī was the name of the city. I was named Khema then. Seeking omniscience I went forth in his presence.

[1] āsavāri at Be, BvACB, enemies that were cankers, Bv āsavādi, cankers and so forth.

[2] Therefore not for bodily beautification. See CB, Intr. xlviii.

[3] BvAC nāma, Bv nāmāsi.

[4] Bv omits ca.

[5] añjana madhulaṭṭhika.

[6] Bv, Be, BvAB vināyaka, guider away, BvAC lokanāyaka.

[256] 9 Therein *ointment* (*for the eyes*) means only the familiar one.[1]

9 *Wild liquorice* means a wild stick (of liquorice).[2]

9 *This* means this.[3]

9 *As he wanted* means as he wished.

9 *I bestowed* means: I gave (saying), "May I give?"

9 *Very glorious* means very best. "When he wanted it"[4] is also a reading. The meaning is: I gave him all that he wished. This is more correct.

The name of the city of the Lord Kakusandha who was not slow[5] was Khema. Aggidatta was the name of the brahman his father, Visākhā the name of the brahman lady his mother.[6] Vidhura and Sañjīva were the chief disciples[7]. Buddhija was the name of the attendant.[8] Sāmā and Campā were the chief women disciples. The Tree of Awakening was a Great Sirīsa. The physical frame was forty cubits in height. The lustre of his physical frame streamed forth for ten yojanas all round. The life-span was forty thousand years. And his wife was the brahman lady named Rocanī, his son was named Uttara. He departed by a chariot harnessed to thoroughbreds. Accordingly it was said:

XXIII 14 And the Buddha's father was the brahman named Aggidatta. Visākhā was the name of the mother of Kakusandha, the great seer.[9]

15 There in Khema city dwelt[10] the Self-Awakened One's great clan who were the most glorious and best of men, well-born, of great renown.

20 Vidhura[11] and Sañjīva were the chief disciples. Buddhija was the name of the attendant on Kakusandha, the teacher.

[1] añjana and 5 other kinds allowed at Vin i 203 for curing illnesses affecting the eyes.

[2] madhulaṭṭhikan ti yaṭṭhimadhukaṁ. I cannot distinguish between this doublet. The latter word is also at Mhvs 32.46.

[3] ime tan ti imam etaṁ.

[4] yadā taṁ patthitaṁ for ime taṁ p- of Bv, BvAC.

[5] adandha, another word-play on the name. It seems to mean swift in gaining wisdom, see closing verse of this Chronicle.

[6] D ii 7.

[7] See D ii 4, M i 333 (quoted PṭsA 670), S ii 191.

[8] D ii 6.

[9] Bv, BvAC mahesino, Be, BvAB satthuno, the teacher.

[10] Bv vasi, BvAC vasati.

[11] So at Bv, Be, BvACB, M i 333, S ii 191, MA ii 417. Vidhūra at D ii 4, DA 417, Jā i 42. A Sañjīva is referred to at BvA 26.

21 Sāmā and Campā were the chief women disciples. That Lord's Tree of Awakening is said to be the Sirīsa.

23 That great sage was forty ratanas tall. Golden lustre streamed forth for ten[1] yojanas all round.

24 That great seer's life-span was forty thousand years. Living so long he caused many people to cross over.

[257] 25 Having spread out the shop of Dhamma[2] for (the world of) men and women with the devas, and roaring a lion's roar, he waned out with the disciples.

26 He whose speech possessed eight characteristics[3], and the flawless (things) have all disappeared for ever. Are not all constructions void?

15 Therein *there in Khema city dwelt:* it must be understood that this verse was spoken to show the Lord Kakusandha's city of birth.

15 *Great clan* means: the Lord's father's clan was very high.

15 *Most glorious and best of men* means the most glorious, the best of all men in respect of birth.

15 *Well-born* means very well-born, of superb birth.

15 *Great renown* means great respect[4]. What was that great clan of the Buddha's? *There in Khema city dwelt* is to be regarded as a liaison in the verse.

23 *Ten yojanas all round* means: issuing forth from his physical frame a golden coloured lustre *streamed forth* the whole time for ten yojanas all round.

25 *Shop of Dhamma* means the great shop reckoned as Dhamma.

25 *Having spread out* means: having spread out the shop of Dhamma like a shop full of a variety of merchandise for the sake of selling the merchandise.

25 *For men and women* means: for the sake of arrival[5] of men and women, who could be guided away (from faults), at the

[1] Bv dvādasa, twelve.

[2] Cf. the Buddha Gotama's eight shops at Miln 332ff.

[3] Cf. D ii 211, M ii 140.

[4] Cf. text pp. 152, 160.

[5] adhigama. See The Guide (Ñāṇamoli) p. 126, n. Five kinds at AA i 87: ways, fruits, analytical insights, three knowledges, six super-knowings.

excellence[1] of the jewels of meditation, the attainments, the ways, the fruits.

25 *As*[2] *a lion's roar* means like[3] a lion's roar, roaring a roar of no-fear.

26 *He whose speech possessed eight characteristics* means the teacher had a voice endowed with eight characteristics.

26 *The flawless (things)* means devoid of flaws[4] and so on are the "moral habits, flawless, spotless, without blemish"*, or (it means) flawless, without breach[5] are the pairs of disciples and so on.

26 *For ever* means for good, for all time.

26 *Have all disappeared* means that the teacher and the pairs of disciples and so forth, having reached that whole state of a sage[6], have (now) reached an invisible state.

The Buddha Kakusandha, rid of bonds,[7]
Swift in wisdom[8], all defects gone[9],
A bondsman to the triple world[10], verily a bondsman to truth,[11]
Found his home in Khema wood.[12] 95

Everywhere remaining in the verses is quite clear.

Concluded is the Exposition of the Chronicle of the Buddha Kakusandha

Concluded is the Twenty-second Buddha-Chronicle

* M i 322.

[1] visesādhigama according to PED is "specific attainment", but visesa can also mean excellence, splendour.

[2] Here va, but ca in the verse. [3] viya.

[4] chidda is a hole, rent, tear, and so fig. a flaw.

[5] avivara. vivara is a cleft, fissure, crack. The meaning here is that, with no breaches there was no way in for impurities; or that the chief disciples' Bramha-faring showed no rents, it was untorn.

[6] taṁ sabbaṁ munibhāvaṁ upagantvā.

[7] apetabandha, cf. text p. 254. [8] adandhapañña, cf. text p. 256.

[9] gatasabbarandha, cf. text p. 254.

[10] tilokasandha. Sandha, bondsman, reliable, has not the same sense as bandha, bond, shackle.

[11] saccasandha, as at text p. 253, and probably meaning with AA ii 326 that he joined truth to truth never telling a lie in between.

[12] vāsaṁ akappayittha, a phrase perhaps equivalent to nibbuto as in the concluding Bv verse of this Chronicle: Khemārāmamhi nibbuto, and so perhaps comparable with parinibbāyi and atthaṁgato, went home or set, like the sun.

XXIV THE EXPOSITION OF THE CHRONICLE OF THE BUDDHA KOṆĀGAMANA[1]

And subsequently to the Lord Kakusandha and on the disappearance of his Dispensation when beings were born to a life-span of about thirty thousand years, the teacher named Koṇāgamana, inclining towards[2] the welfare of others, arose in the world.[3] But herein it must be understood that though the life-span had the appearance of a gradual dwindling, the dwindling was not thus, for, having increased, it dwindled (again). How was this? In this same eon the Lord named Kakusandha was reborn in a time when (life-spans lasted) forty thousand years. But, dwindling, the life-span fell to a time of ten years: again, lasting for an incalculable (but) dwindling from that, the life-span endured for a time of about thirty thousand years. It must be understood it was then that the Lord Koṇāgamana arose.

Having fulfilled the perfections he was reborn in Tusita city. Deceasing from there he took on relinking in the city of Sobhavatī[4] in the womb of the brahman lady named Uttarā who was unsurpassed (anuttara) in the qualities of beauty and so forth and was the wife of the brahman Yaññadatta. After ten months he issued forth from his mother's womb in Subhagavatī pleasaunce. As he was being born the (sky-) deva rained down a shower of gold over the whole of this Jambudīpa. So, due to the coming of the gold, they gave him the name of Kanakāgamana[5]. But gradually this name of his was corrupted to the name of Koṇāgamana. He led the household life for three thousand years. And his three palaces were named Tusita, Santusita, Santuṭṭha. There were sixteen thousand women with the brahman lady Rucigattā at the head.

When he had seen the four signs and the son named Satthavāha had been born to the brahman lady Rucigattā, departing on the Great Departure mounted on the back of a glorious elephant, he went forth. Thirty thousand men went forth following his example. Surrounded by these, he engaged in striving for six months. On the full-moon day of Visākha he partook of sweet milk-rice given to him by the daughter of the brahman Aggisona.

[1] BvAC Kona- throughout with exception of concluding verse.

[2] BvAC ponāgamana, BvAB poṇā-; a word-play on the Buddha's name.

[3] BvAB here inserts a passage, not in BvAC, giving some explanation of his name. But BvAC gives sufficient just below.

[4] Cf. D ii 7.

[5] "The coming of (the) gold."

Having spent the day-sojourn in an acacia grove, towards evening he accepted eight handfuls of grass given to him by Tinduka, a guardian of a corn-field, and approached from the right an Udumbara Tree of Awakening. Its dimensions were the same as those of the Puṇḍarīka already mentioned[1] and it was covered with a profusion of fruit. Spreading a grass-spreading twenty cubits in extent, seated in the cross-legged position, he routed Māra's forces, acquired the knowledges of One of the Ten Powers, and uttered the solemn utterance. When he had spent seven weeks (there) he saw that the thirty thousand monks who had gone forth with him had attained the qualifications. Going by a path in the heavens[2] and descending in the deer-sanctuary[3] at the seers' resort near the city of Sudassana, he turned the Wheel of Dhamma in their midst. Then was the first penetration by thirty thousand crores.

Again, when he had performed the Marvel of the Double at the root of a great sāla tree at the gateway to the city of Sundara, he caused twenty thousand crores to drink of the nectar of Dhamma. That was the second penetration. [**259**] When the Lord was teaching the Abhidhamma-piṭaka to gatherings of devatās in the ten-thousand world-systems, having made his own mother, Uttarā, the foremost, there was the third penetration by ten thousand crores. Accordingly it was said:

XXIV 1 After Kakusandha was the Self-Awakened One named Koṇāgamana, supreme among men, Conqueror, eldest in the world, bull of men.

2 When he had fulfilled the ten things he overpassed the wilderness. Cleansing away all stains, he attained supreme Self-Awakening.

3 When the leader Koṇāgamana was turning the Wheel of Dhamma there was the first penetration by thirty thousand crores.

[1] Text p. 243. Cf. p. 248.

[2] BvAB gaganapatha, a path in the heavens; BvAC pavanapatha, a woodland path. This expression has occurred at text p. 254. Perhaps BvAB is the better reading, more analogous to devapatha, text p. 248, and surapatha, text p. 243; also to the more frequent ākāsena, text pp. 161, 167, 198, 203, 208, 215, 227, 232, 237, and anilapatha, aery path, text pp. 178, 192, 224, and gaganatala, text pp. 254, 263. The verb used for the arrival at the desired place is always otaritvā, descended.

[3] Omitted by BvAC.

4 And when he was working the Marvel for crushing the theories of others there was the second penetration by twenty thousand crores.
5 Then the Conqueror, after working the changing (Double),[1] went to a city of the devas. The Self-Awakened One stayed there on an ornamental stone.
6 The sage stayed there for the rains teaching the seven treatises. The third penetration was by ten thousand crores.

2 Therein *when he had fulfilled the ten things* means: when he had fulfilled the ten perfection things.

2 *He overpassed the wilderness* means: he overpassed the wilderness of birth.

2 *Cleansing away* means having cleansed away[2].

2 *All stains* means the three stains of attachment and so forth.

4 *And when he was working the Marvel for crushing the theories of others:* the meaning is when the Lord was working the Marvel.

5 *The changing* means the changing by psychic potency. After working the Marvel of the Double at the gateway to the city of Sundara, (he) *went to a city of the devas (and) stayed there on an ornamental stone.*[3] Why did he stay?

6 *Teaching the seven treatises* means he stayed there teaching the devas the Abhidhamma-piṭaka reckoned as seven treatises.

While the Lord was teaching the Abhidhamma thus there was a penetration by ten thousand crores. Koṇāgamana, coming to the fulfilment of the utterly pure perfections,[4] had only one assembly of disciples.[5] While he was dwelling in Surindavatī pleasaunce near the city of Surindavatī he taught Dhamma to Prince Bhīyasa and to Prince Uttara and to their two retinues of thirty thousand. Having let all these **[260]** go forth by the 'Come, monk' (formula for) going forth, he recited the Pātimokkha in their midst on the full-moon day of Māgha.[6] Accordingly it was said:

[1] Cf. xxiii 4.

[2] pavāhiyā ti pavāhetvā.

[3] The verse reads vasati tattha sambuddho silāyaṁ paṇḍukambale; BvA reads tattha paṇḍukambalasilāyaṁ vasi.

[4] parisuddhapāramīpūraṇāgamana. A word-play on his name.

[5] Cf. D ii 6.

[6] He is said to have held the Observance once in every year, DhA iii 236. See also Vin iii 7f.

XXIV 7 That deva of devas had one gathering only of steadfast ones whose cankers were destroyed, stainless, tranquil in mind.

8 It was a gathering of thirty thousand monks then who had overpassed the floods[1] and were shatterers of mortality.

8 Therein *the floods* means: this is a synonym for the four floods: the flood of sense-desires and so forth. And into whichever these floods pull him down[2], make him sink, for him they exist. 'Of these floods': the genitive[3] should be understood in the sense of an accusative. The meaning is: overpassing the four-fold flood.[4]

8 *Shatterers:* here too this is the same method.

8 *Of mortality* means of mortality.[5]

Our Bodhisatta was then a king named Pabbata in the city of Mithilā. Then, having heard that Koṇāgamana, coming for the going for refuge of all creatures,[6] had reached the city of Mithilā the king, going out with his retinue to meet him, invited Him of the Ten Powers, gave a great gift, and requested the Lord to spend the rains there. Attending on the teacher with the Order of monks for three months, he gave silk from Pattuṇṇa, silk from China, woollen cloth, Kāsi silk, very fine cotton cloth and so forth, very costly and exquisite garments, golden sandals and many other requisites. That Lord too declared of him, "In this same Bhadda-eon this one will be a Buddha". Then the Great Man, on hearing that Lord's declaration, abandoned the great kingdom, and went forth in that Lord's very presence. Accordingly it was said:

XXIV 9 I at that time was a warrior-noble named Pabbata. I was possessed of friends and counsellors, considerable forces and mounts.[7]

10 I went to see the Self-Awakened One and heard the unsurpassed Dhamma. I invited the Order with the Conqueror and gave a gift to my heart's content.[8]

[1] Be, BvACB oghānam atikkantānaṁ; Bv atikkanta-catur-oghānam.
[2] ohananti.
[3] oghānaṁ, gen. pl.
[4] catubbidhe oghe, acc. pl.
[5] maccuyā ti maccuno.
[6] saraṇagatasabbapāṇāgamana, another word-play on his name.
[7] Bv, Be, BvAB anantabalavāhano, BvAC balavāhanam anappakaṁ.
[8] Bv yathicchakaṁ, BvAC yadicchakaṁ.

11 I gave the teacher and the disciples silk from Pattuṇṇa[1], silk from China, Kāsi silk, woollen cloth too, and golden sandals as well.

12 As that sage was sitting in the midst of the Order he too declared of me: "In this Bhadda-eon this one will be a Buddha.

13 Having departed from the delightful city of Kapila . . ."
" . . . face to face with this one."[2]

[261] 14 When I[3] had heard his words all the more did I incline my mind. I resolutely determined on further practice for fulfilling the ten perfections.

15 Seeking omniscience, giving the gift to the supreme among men, I, having renounced a great kingdom, went forth in the Conqueror's presence.[4]

9 Therein *considerable forces and mounts* means many and unending were my forces and mounts beginning with horses and elephants.

10 *To see the Self-Awakened One* means for the sake of seeing the Self-Awakened One.

10 *To my heart's content* means as much as I wished.[5] The meaning is that when the Order with the Buddha at its head had been satisfied with the four kinds of nutriment[6], saying 'Enough, enough' with (a gesture of) the hand they caused it to end.[7]

11 *The teacher and the disciples* means: I gave to the teacher as well as to the disciples.[8]

15 *To the supreme among men* means to the supreme among men.[9]

15 *Having renounced* means having renounced.[10]

[1] BvACB read Pattuṇṇa, Bv Paṭṭunna. Cf. Thūp 17.

[2] Cf. xx 14.

[3] BvAC tassāhaṁ, Bv tassāpi.

[4] Bv tassa santike as noticed at Be which, with BvACB, reads jinasantike.

[5] yadicchakan ti yāvadicchakaṁ. Though the Comy interprets this as referring to the recipients, the above rendering seems to me more in keeping.

[6] Probably referring to what can be eaten, drunk, chewed, savoured, asita pīta khāyita sāyita.

[7] pidahāpetvā. Pidahati is usually to close, shut, cover. Perhaps meaning that the monks signalled by hand that the meal was ended or they covered their bowls with their hands to show that this was so.

[8] satthu sāvake ti satthuno c'eva sāvakānañ ca adāsiṁ.

[9] naruttame ti naruttamassa.

[10] ohāyā ti ohāyitvā.

The Lord Koṇāgamana's city was named Sobhavatī, the brahman his father was named Yaññadatta, the brahman lady his mother was named Uttarā.[1] Bhīyyasa[2] and Uttara were the two chief disciples.[3] Sotthija was the name of the attendant,[4] Samuddā and Uttarā were the chief women disciples. The Tree of Awakening was an Udumbara[5]. The physical frame was thirty cubits in height. The life-span was thirty thousand years, and his wife was the brahman lady named Rucigattā. His son was named Satthavāha. He departed riding an elephant. Accordingly it was said:

XXIV 16 Sobhavatī was the name of the city, Sobha the name of the warrior-noble. The great clan of the Self-Awakened One dwelt there in the city.

17 And the Buddha's father was the brahman Yaññadatta. Uttarā was the name of the mother of Koṇāgamana, the teacher.

22 Bhīyyasa[6] and Uttara were the chief disciples. Sotthija was the name of the attendant on Koṇāgamana, the teacher.

23 Samuddā and[7] Uttarā were the chief women disciples. That Lord's Tree of Awakening is said to be[8] the Udumbara.

[262] 25 That Buddha was thirty cubits in height. As a circlet in a smelting-pot was he thus embellished with rays.

26 The (normal) life-span lasted then[9] for thirty thousand years. Living so long he caused many people to cross over.

27 Having raised up the archway of Dhamma decorated with the streamer of Dhamma, having made a cluster of the flowers of Dhamma, he waned out with the disciples.

[1] D ii 7.
[2] Bv Bhīyyoso, Be, BvAB Bhiyyasa, v. l. Bhīyosa; D ii 4, S ii 191, DA 417 Bhiyyosa; Jā i 43 Bhiyyosa, v. l. -yasa.
[3] D ii 4, S ii 191.
[4] D ii 6.
[5] D ii 4.
[6] See note above.
[7] BvAC ce ti, Bv c°eva.
[8] BvAC pavuccati, Bv vuccati.
[9] BvAC āyu vijjati tāvade, Bv āyu buddhassa tāvade. See CB, Intr. xxxiii.

28 His people, great in grace, (and he) making known the Dhamma of splendour, have all disappeared. Are not all constructions void?

25 Therein *in a smelting-pot* means in a goldsmith's oven.

25 *As a circlet*[1] means like a golden ornament.[2]

25 *Thus embellished with rays* means much embellished, adorned thus with rays.

27 *Having raised up the archway of Dhamma*[3] means having established the cetiya[4] consisting of the thirty-seven things helpful to Awakening.

27 *Decorated with the streamer of Dhamma*[5] means decorated with the banner of the four true things.

27 *Having made a cluster of the flowers of Dhamma* means having made a cluster of garlands and flowers consisting of Dhamma.[6] Having established the shrine of Dhamma[7] for the homage of the populace who were standing on the dais of the shrine of insight,[8] the teacher attained final nibbāna with the Order of disciples.

28 *Great in grace* means attained to the grace of great psychic potency.

28 *His* means that Lord's.

28 *People* means the people who were disciples.

28 *Making known the Dhamma of splendour:* the meaning is that, like the Lord, the making known of the supermundane things[9] have all disappeared.

[1] kambu as at Jā iv 18, 130, VvA 167.

[2] suvaṇṇanekkha, cf. M iii 102. See MLS iii 141, n. 2 for further references.

[3] Dhammaceti, where ceti seems to mean arch or archway, that by which one enters, suitable here.

[4] cetiya, shrine. Possibly the ceti (of last note) is merely an abbreviation. At the same time one has to remember dhammacetiya at M ii 124f., which appears to mean testimony to or word of respect for Dhamma. See MLS ii 307, n. 1.

[5] Dhammadussa, cloths as a streamer, cf. xxv 44.

[6] Cf. the Buddha's flower-shop, Miln 332.

[7] Dhammacetiya.

[8] vipassanā-cetiyaṅgana. Transl. very tentative.

[9] lokuttaradhamma could also mean the Dhamma of the supermundane.

Happily, Koṇāgamana, devoid of cankers,
Great seer, coming (to make) breathing things desireless,[1]
Coming of a pure lineage,[1] dwelt
In a remote forest known as Splendour[2]. 96

Everywhere remaining in the verses is quite clear.

Concluded is the Exposition of the Chronicle of the Buddha Koṇāgamana

Concluded is the Twenty-third Buddha-Chronicle

XXV THE EXPOSITION OF THE CHRONICLE OF THE BUDDHA KASSAPA

[263] Subsequently to Koṇāgamana and when his Dispensation had disappeared, beings' life-spans which had been thirty thousand years in duration gradually dwindled to life-spans of ten years, increasing again to immeasurable life-spans. Again dwindling, when creatures were born with life-spans of twenty-thousand years the teacher named Kassapa, protector of countless men[3], arose in the world. Having fulfilled the perfections, he was re-born in Tusita city. Deceasing from there he took on relinking in the womb of the brahman lady named Dhanavatī[4] of abundant good qualities (vipulaguṇavatī), (wife of) the brahman Brahmadatta[4] in the city of Bārāṇasī. After ten months he issued forth from his mother's womb in the deer-sanctuary at the seers' resort.

They gave him the name of Boy Kassapa[5] in accordance with

[1] Two more word-plays on his name: vikāmapāṇāgamano, visuddhavaṁsāgamano.

[2] Sirināmadheyya.

[3] anekamanussapo, a word-play on the name Kassapa. Meaning of -po obscure, partly because we do not know the exact transl. of the name Kassa-pa, or even if it is divisible thus; if not, the clan then would be Kassapa-gotta; see also DPPN ii 477, n. 4. It is possible, however, to take the above compound as derived from Skrt. pṛī, to fill; to fulfil; to sate, satisfy, refresh; to cherish, nourish; to protect, and therefore perhaps as an abbreviation of pāla, guardian, protector, keeper. Cf. Childers, bhūmipāla, a king.

[4] D ii 7.

[5] Kassapakumāra. Kumāra is not 'prince' here as he was brahman.

his clan[1]. He led the household life for two thousand years. His three palaces were Haṁsavā, Yasavā, Sirinanda.[2] There were forty-eight thousand women in attendance on him with the brahman lady named Sunandā at the head.

When he had seen the four signs and the son named Vijitasena had been born to the brahman lady Sunandā, a thrill arising (in his mind), he thought, "I will depart on the Great Departure". Then, immediately upon his reflection, a palace, spinning like a potter's wheel, soared up into the vault of the heavens surrounded by countless hundreds of men like a most lovely moon[3] surrounded by a host of stars, as though adorning the vault of the heavens, as though making clear the might of merit, and as though drawing away the eyes of the people, and as though itself yearning for the tree-tops it went along and came to rest on the ground with a Nigrodha Tree of Awakening in the centre.

Then the Bodhisatta, the Great Being, taking his stand on the earth, carrying a banner of arahants given by devas, went forth. His dancing-women, descending from the palace and going half a gāvuta along a road sat down with the retinue making an encampment.[4] Then all who had come with him, excepting the retinue of women, went forth. They say the Great Man, surrounded by these, engaged in striving for seven days, partook on the full-moon day of Visākha of sweet milk-rice given to him by the brahman lady Sunandā, and spent the day-sojourn in an acacia grove.

Towards evening he accepted eight handfuls of grass brought to him by Soma, the guardian of a corn-field, and, approaching the Nigrodha Tree of Awakening he spread a grass-spreading fifteen cubits in extent. Seated there he attained complete Self-Awakening, uttered the solemn utterance and spent seven weeks. When he saw that the crore of monks who had gone forth with him had attained the qualifications, he went through the vault of the heavens, descended in the deer-sanctuary at the seers' resort near Bārāṇasī and, surrounded by them, turned the Wheel of Dhamma there. **[264]** Then was the first penetration of Dhamma by twenty thousand crores. Accordingly it was said:

[1] gottavasena. See also SnA 285f. where Tissa addressed Kassapa by his clan (-name), gottena ālapati.

[2] Bv Haṁsa Yasa Sirinanda; BvAC Sirinandana.

[3] karanikara.

[4] BvAC senānivesa, BvAB senāsannivesa.

XXV 1 After Koṇāgamana was the Self-Awakened One named Kassapa[1], supreme among men, king under Dhamma, bringer of lustre.

2 Cast aside was his family fortune; giving away in charity to supplicants much food, (both) beverages and soft food[2], and fulfilling his purpose, (he went forth) like a bull breaking down its tethering post and attained supreme Self-Awakening.

3 When Kassapa, leader of the world, was turning the Wheel of Dhamma there was the first penetration by twenty thousand crores.

2 Therein *cast aside* means left behind, thrown off, renounced.

2 *Family fortune* means family house. The meaning is: thrown off, as though it were grass, what was very difficult to give up: limitless masses of property, hoards of countless thousands of crores of wealth gleaming like the abode of him of a thousand eyes.

2 *To supplicants* means giving to supplicants.[3]

2 *Tethering post* means cow-stall. As a bull breaks down a cow-stall, thus too the great Man, breaking down the bondage to house as he liked, on the occasion he wished, attained full Self-Awakening.

Again, when the teacher was walking on tour for four months in the countryside there was the second penetration by ten thousand crores. And when, at the gateway to the city of Sundara, performing the Marvel of the Double at the root of an Asana tree, he taught Dhamma. Then was the third penetration of Dhamma by five thousand crores. Again, having performed the Marvel of the Double, there was a deva-hall named Sudhammā in the abode of the Thirty-Three, an abode difficult of conquest by enemies of the gods—seated there teaching the seven treatises of the Abhidhamma-piṭaka so that the devatās of the ten-thousand world-system might learn them with his own mother, the lady Dhanavatī, at the head, he caused three thousand devatās to drink of the nectar of Dhamma. Accordingly it was said:

[1] Mentioned at KhA 203, PvA 21 in extension of the story given there about the Buddha Phussa. DhA iii 236 says he held uposatha once in every 6 months. See also Vin iii 7ff.

[2] Be, BvACB bahv° annapānabhojanaṁ; Bv bahunaṁ pānabhojanaṁ.

[3] yācake ti yācakānaṁ datvā.

XXV 4 When for four months the Buddha was walking on tour in the world there was the second penetration by ten thousand crores.

5 When he had worked the changing Double[1] and had proclaimed[2] the element of knowledge there was the third penetration by five thousand crores.

6 He expounded Dhamma there in the Sudhammā (Hall) in a delightful deva-city; the Conqueror awakened three thousand crores of devas.

[265] 7 Later, at a teaching of Dhamma to the yakkha Naradeva, the penetrations by these were incalculable by computation.

4 Therein *for four months* means for four months,[3] or this itself is the reading.

4 *Was walking* means walked.

5 *When he had worked the changing Double* means when he had worked the Marvel of the Double.

5 *Element of knowledge* means the nature of omniscient knowledge; they also say the element of all-knowledge.

5 *Proclaimed* means expounded to the populace.

6 *Sudhammā* means that in the abode of the Thirty-Three there is a Hall named Sudhammā; seated there is the meaning.

6 *Dhamma* means Abhidhamma.

7 They say that there was a yakkha then named Naradeva, a man-deva vanquished by the majesty (of the Buddha), of great authority[4], a yakkha of great psychic potency like the yakkha Naradeva spoken of above[5]. In a certain city in Jambudīpa, if a king's physical form were of such a kind, he, being an insatiable eater of flesh, fashioned a tone of voice and a physical appearance of that kind, killed and devoured that king, and acquired the kingdom with the women's quarters. And it was said he was a scoundrel with women. But when these skilful clever women discovered, "This is not our king, this is a non-human being", then

[1] Cf. xxiii 4, xxiv 5.

[2] Bv, Be, BvAB pakittayi, BvAC pakāsayi.

[3] catumāsan ti cātumāse.

[4] mahesakkha. Cf. Cp II 8 1 where the reading mahesakkho is explained at CpA 161 by mahāparivāra, having a great following, as also at AA iii 183. But nothing is said of this above.

[5] Perhaps at text p. 253f.

he, feeling shamed (at their discovery), devoured them all and went off to another city. In this way the yakkha Naradeva used to feed upon human beings. But when he came towards the city of Sunanda and the inhabitants saw him, terrified by the fear of dying they left their own city and fled in all directions. Then Kassapa, Him of the Ten Powers, seeing these people fleeing, stood in front of the yakkha Naradeva. Naradeva roared a fearsome roar, a shout at the deva of devas who stood still, but as he was unable to arouse fear in the Lord he went to him for refuge and asked a question. When he had answered the question and had tamed him and while he was teaching him Dhamma there was a penetration by the men and deities who were present beyond the ways of computation. Accordingly, at the beginning (of the verse) it was said: *To the yakkha Naradeva.*

7 *Later, at a teaching of Dhamma* means later, at a teaching of Dhamma.[1]

7 *By these* means by these[2], or this itself is the reading.

And the Lord Kassapa had only one assembly of disciples.[3] Tissa was the name of a priest's son in the city of Bārāṇasī.[4] As he had seen the splendour of the Marks on the physical frame of Kassapa when he was the Bodhisatta and had heard his father talking (about them), he had thought, "Undoubtedly this one, departing on the Great Departure, will be a Buddha. I, having gone forth in his presence, will get free from the anguish of saṁsāra." So, having gone to the Himavant which abounded in hosts of sages who had faith, he went forth in the going forth of ascetics. There were twenty thousand ascetics in his entourage. **[266]** Later, when he had heard that Kassapakumāra had departed and had attained full Self-Awakening, he came with his entourage and with his entourage went forth in the Lord Kassapa's presence by the 'Come, monk' (formula for) going forth and he attained arahantship. The Lord Kassapa recited the Pātimokkha in that gathering on the full-moon day of Māgha. Accordingly it was said:

[1] apare dhammadesane ti aparasmiṁ dhammadesane.

[2] etesānan ti etesaṁ. Referring to the men and deities mentioned just above.

[3] Cf. D ii 6, Jā i 43.

[4] Said at SnA i 280 to have been born on the same day as Kassapa and a friend from early boyhood. See this whole SnA passage commenting on the opening verse, Sn 239, of the Āmagandhasutta; it tells the episodes mentioned above in greater detail.

XXV 8 That deva of devas had one gathering only of steadfast ones whose cankers were destroyed, stainless, tranquil in mind.

9 It was a gathering of twenty thousand monks then, of steadfast ones who, by modesty and morality, had overpassed those who still had attachment.[1]

9 Therein *of (those) who had overpassed those who still had attachment:* the meaning is of all whose cankers were destroyed (who) had overpassed ordinary people, stream-entrants and so forth.

9 *Of steadfast ones who, by modesty and morality*[2] means of such-like ones who, by modesty and by morality[3].

The Bodhisatta was then a brahman named Jotipāla[4], master of the three Vedas, familiar with (the examination of) ground and sky. He was a friend of Ghaṭīkāra, a potter. Approaching the teacher together with him, he heard his talk on Dhamma and went forth in his presence. Putting forth energy, he mastered the three Piṭakas and, through the practice of the observances, illumined the Buddha's Dispensation. And that teacher too declared of him. Accordingly it was said:

XXV 10 I was then the brahman[5] Jotipāla, a famous repeater[6], expert in the mantras, master of the three Vedas.

11 I had reached perfection in (the science of) the Marks, in the legendary tradition and the obligatory duties (of a brahman). I was skilled in the (signs of) earth and sky[7], a sorcerer[8], experienced.[9]

[1] BvAC atikkantarāgavantānaṁ, Be, BvAB atikkantabhavantānaṁ, Bv abhikkantabhagavantānaṁ.

[2] hirisīlena.

[3] hiriyā ca sīlena ca.

[4] Cf. M ii 46ff., S i 34f., Jā i 43, Ap 301, Miln 221, UdA 265, Mhvu Transl. i 265ff.

[5] BvAC ahaṁ tena samayena. Bv, Be, BvAB ahaṁ tadā māṇavako.

[6] Here and next verse, cf. A ii 6.

[7] Cf. D i 9.

[8] katavijja, which may mean "lore (or spells, charms) laid up", or one who has acquired knowledge, is scientific, a philosopher.

[9] Bv anāvayo, Be anavayo noticing BvAC anāmayo (which means "hardy"). I follow Be. See CPD s.v. anavaya.

12 Ghaṭīkāra was the name of the Lord Kassapa's attendant, respectful, deferential[1], he waned out in the third fruition.[2]

13 Ghaṭīkāra, taking me with him, approached Kassapa the Conqueror. When I had heard his Dhamma I went forth in his presence.

14 Being one who put forth energy, proficient in all the observances, I fell away in none; I fulfilled the Conqueror's Dispensation.

[267] 15 Having learnt thoroughly all the ninefold Dispensation of the Conqueror[3] as far as it had been uttered by the Buddha, I illumined the Conqueror's Dispensation.

16 When he had seen the wonder of mine that Buddha too declared, "In this Bhadda-eon this one will be a Buddha.

17 Having departed from the delightful city of Kapila . . ."

31 When I had heard his words, exultant, stirred in mind[4], I resolutely determined on further practice for fulfilling the ten perfections.

32 Thus I, faring on (in saṁsāra), avoiding wrong conduct, engaged in austerities for the sake of my Awakening itself.[5]

11 Therein *skilled in the* (*signs of*) *earth and sky* means skilled in examinings of the earth and in astronomical lore as to the wheeling stars.[6]

12 *Attendant* means attendant.[7]

12 *Deferential* means deferential.[8]

12 *Waned out* means was guided out or flowed out[9].

[1] Jotipāla, as Bodhisatta, on the other hand, was rude to the Buddha Kassapa, see M Sta. 81. Therefore when later he was the Bodhisatta Gotama he had to spend as many as six years performing austerities before he gained Awakening.

[2] Cf. M ii 52.

[3] BvAC jinasāsana, Bv satthasā-, the teacher's.

[4] BvAC haṭṭho saṁviggamānaso, as at e.g. text pp. 170, 176, followed above. Bv, Be, BvAB bhiyyo cittaṁ pasādayiṁ, all the more did I incline my mind.

[5] Cf. xxii 14.

[6] joticakkācāre jotivijjāya.

[7] upaṭṭhāko ti upaṭṭhāyako. Cf. Divy 426 for upasthāyaka.

[8] sappatisso ti sappatissayo.

[9] vissuta cannot have the PED meaning of renowned or famous here, for here it seems to be a synonym of nibbuta. It may be a Pali form of Skrt vi-sruta from vi-sru, to flow forth or away, stream, trickle; or it may mean dried up (with reference to the kilesas).

12 *In the third fruition:* the locative case (denoting) cause or reason[1]; the meaning is he waned out because of arrival at the third fruition.

13 *Taking* means having taken.

14 *In all the observances* means: in the lesser observances, in the principal observances.[2]

14 *Proficient* means skilled: skilled in fulfilling these.

14 *I fell away in none* means he explained he fell away nowhere or in any place from moral habits or concentration, the attainments and so forth, saying, "It did not come to pass that I fell away in any circumstances". "I fell away in none"[3] is also a reading. It has the same meaning.

14 *As far as*[4]*:* this is an expression of demarcation; the meaning is: as much as.[5]

15 *Uttered by the Buddha* means the word of the Buddha.

15 *I illumined*[6] means I made shine[6], I expounded.

16 *The wonder of mine* means my right practice; the meaning is that when the Lord Kassapa had seen the astonishing wonder not shared by others.

32 *Faring on* means faring on in saṁsāra.

32 *Wrong conduct:* the meaning is that wrong conduct is not to be done[7], it is improper[8].

The city where the Lord Kassapa was born was named Bārāṇasī, his father was the brahman named Brahmadatta, his mother was the brahman lady named Dhanavatī of the highest good qualities (paramaguṇavatī). Tissa and Bhāradvāja were the chief disciples[9], **[268]** Sabbamitta was the name of the attendant.[10] Anulā and Uruvelā were the chief women disciples. The Tree of Awakening was a Nigrodha. The physical frame was twenty cubits in height, the life-span was twenty thousand years. His wife and chief

[1] nimittasattamī. See Intr. p. xxxiii f.

[2] Said to be 80 mahāvatta at MA iii 30. There are also the duties or observances of a pupil towards his preceptor, see Vin i 44ff., VA v 977ff.

[3] na koci instead of na kvaci.

[4] yāvatā.

[5] yāvatakaṁ. This has same meaning as yāvatā.

[6] sobhayim . . . sobhesim (caus.).

[7] akattabbaṁ.

[8] akaraṇīya, also meaning "not to be done", "should not be done".

[9] Cf. D ii 5.

[10] Ibid. 6.

consort was named Nandā, his son was named Vijitasena. He departed by means of a palace. Accordingly it was said:

XXV 33 Bārāṇasī was the name of the city, Kikī the name of the warrior-noble. The great clan of the Self-Awakened One lived there in the city.

34 And the Buddha's father was the brahman Brahmadatta. Dhanavatī was the name of the mother[1] of Kassapa, the great seer.

39 Tissa and Bhāradvāja were the chief disciples. Sabbamitta was the attendant on Kassapa, the great seer.

40 Anulā and Uruvelā[2] were the chief women disciples. That Lord's Tree of Awakening is said to be the Nigrodha.

42 That Buddha was twenty ratanas in height. He was like a streak of lightning, like the moon encircled by celestial bodies.

43 That seer's life-span was twenty thousand years. Living so long he caused many people to cross over.

44 Having created the pond of Dhamma, given moral habit as a perfumed ointment, having dressed in the streamer of Dhamma[3], he arranged[4] the chaplet of Dhamma[3].

45 When he had placed the stainless mirror of Dhamma before the populace he said, "Let those wishing for nibbāna see my ornaments."

46 Giving the armour[5] of moral habit, wearing the coat of mail of the meditations, having put on the hide of Dhamma and given the supreme armature[6],

47 having given the shield of mindfulness, the sharp lance of knowledge, having given the glorious sword of Dhamma (and) moral habit for crushing (wrong) association,

48 having given the ornament of the threefold knowledge, the four fruitions as a garland for the forehead, having

[1] Bv, Be, BvAB Dhanavatī nāma janikā, BvAC mātā Dhanavatī nāma.
[2] Bv Anuḷā Uruveḷā.
[3] Cf. xxiv 27.
[4] BvAC vibhajjiya, Bv virājiya. Cf. M i 364 virājeti, S ii 255 vighajeti.
[5] kañcuka.
[6] sannāha.

given the decoration of the six super-knowings, the flowers of Dhamma worn on one's person,

[269] 49 having given the white sunshade of True Dhamma for warding off evil, having created a flower of no-fear[1], he waned out with the disciples.

50 And this Fully Self-Awakened One, immeasurable, difficult to attack, and this jewel of Dhamma, well-taught[2], a come-and-see thing,

51 and this jewel of the Order, faring along rightly, unsurpassed, have all disappeared. Are not all constructions void?

42 Therein *like a streak of lightning* means as lightning embedded[3] in a storm-cloud.

42 *Like the moon encircled by celestial bodies* means as the full-moon surrounded by a circlet[4] of celestial bodies.

44 *Having created the pond of Dhamma* means having himself created the pond of the Dhamma of mastery.[5]

44 *Having given moral habit as a perfumed ointment* means: having given perfumed ointment for the sake of ornamenting the continuity of mind known as the four utterly purified moral habits.[6]

44 *Having dressed in the streamer of Dhamma*[7] means: having dressed in a pair of outer cloaks known as states of conscience and shame.[8]

44 *He arranged the chaplet of Dhamma* means: having arranged, having planned a chaplet of blossoms of the thirty-seven things helpful to Awakening.

[1] BvAC māpayitv' abhayaṁ, Bv māpetvā abhayaṁ.

[2] BvAC svākkhāto, Bv svākhyāto.

[3] saṇṭhita, fixed, established.

[4] parivesa. Cf. M-W s.v. parivesha, a circle, circlet, wreath, crown; the circumference of a circle; the disk of the sun or moon; a halo round the sun or moon.

[5] pariyatti has the 2 meanings of mastery and scripture. At DA 21, MA ii 107, Asl 23 it is of 3 kinds.

[6] catupārisuddhisīla. As at e.g. A ii 194f., Jā iii 291, DhA iv 111, AA i 87, ii 66 91, 133: (control) by the Pātimokkha is one sīla, then there are control over the faculties, complete purity of mode of livelihood, and of what is based on the requisites; cf. Miln 336. Different at AA iv 57, 60. It seems that complete purity of body, speech, thought and mode of livelihood is chiefly meant.

[7] Cf. xxiv 27.

[8] Defined Dhs 30, 31.

45 *Stainless mirror of Dhamma:*[1] the meaning is, the stainless mirror is known as the way of stream-entry; having placed the mirror of Dhamma on the bank of the pond of Dhamma for the populace for the sake of (their) reflecting on blameable, blameless, skilled and unskilled states.

45 *Before the populace* means for the populace.[2]

45 *Those wishing for nibbāna* means they walk the stainless way of stream-entry making for the dissolution of all unskilled stains, and are wishing for the undying, unconstructed, distressless, utterly peaceful, unchanging nibbāna. The meaning is, *let those see* this *ornament* shown by me in the way spoken of. "Let those greatly wishing for nibbāna see my ornament" (alaṅkara) is also a reading. It has the same meaning. Ornament (alaṅkara) is said making (the vowel) short.[3]

46 *Armour of moral habit* means the armour consisting of the five moral habits, the ten moral habits, the four utterly purified moral habits[4].

46 *Wearing the coat of mail of the meditations* means binding on the coat of mail of the meditations as tetrads and pentads.[5]

46 *Having put on the hide of Dhamma* means having put on the hide known as mindfulness and clear consciousness.

46 *Having given the supreme armature* means having given, having made a supreme armature of the energy that is possessed of the four factors.[6]

47 *Having given the shield of mindfulness* means having given the protection of the shield of the four applications of mindfulness for protecting against attachment and so forth, hatred, enemies and evil.[7]

47 *The sharp lance of knowledge* means that, because of its being able to penetrate, it is the sharp lance of the knowledge of insight—the meaning is: the glorious lance sharp for the knowledge of insight; the meaning is, making for impoverishing the strength of

[1] Cf. D ii 93, S v 357.
[2] mahājane ti mahājanassa
[3] Normally alaṅkāra.
[4] See above, note on 44, and cf. text p. 123.
[5] A reference to the 4 jhānas sometimes being extended to five.
[6] See text pp. 8, 83, 133, 142, 161, 172, 177, 236, 243.
[7] This compound could also be translated: for protection against the evil and enemies which are attachment and so forth, hatred.

the defilements, it was established for him who is an earnest student of yoga.[1]

[270] 47 *Having given the glorious sword of Dhamma* means having given the glorious sword of wisdom in the Way(s), a weapon for that earnest student of yoga, sharp at the edge, from the (whet-)stone of energy.

47 *Moral habit for crushing (wrong) association:* the meaning is the ariyan supermundane morality for the sake of crushing association with the defilements, for the sake of suppressing defilements.

48 *Having given the ornament of the threefold knowledge* means having given the ornament consisting of the threefold knowledge.

48 *The four fruitions as a garland for the forehead*[2] means having made the four fruitions into a head-ornament[3].

48 *The decoration of the six super-knowings* means: having given the six super-knowings for the sake of making an adornment, for the sake of a decoration.

48 *The flowers of Dhamma worn on one's person* means making a garland of the blossoms known as the nine supermundane states.

49 *Having given the white sunshade of True Dhamma for warding off evil* means having given complete purity, the sunshade of escape to freedom[4] warding off the heat of all unskill.

49 *Having created a flower of no-fear:* the meaning is, having made a flower that is the eightfold Way leading to the city of No-fear.[5]

It is said that the Lord Kassapa attained final nibbāna in Setavyā pleasaunce in Setavyā city in the Kāsi kingdom. It is said that his relics were not dispersed. The people[6] inhabiting the whole of Jambudīpa, having assembled and for the external finish using golden bricks each worth a crore and inlaid with jewels, and for the internal filling (bricks) each worth half a crore, doing the plaster-work with red arsenic and the binding-work with sesame oil, built a thūpa a yojana in height.[7]

[1] BvAC kilesabalanidhanakaraṁ yogāvacaraṁ, BvAB -karasamatthaṁ vā yogāvacarayodhavaraṁ.

[2] āvela.

[3] vataṁsaka.

[4] vimuttisesacchatta; taking sesa as one of the meanings of Skrt. śesha.

[5] Abhayapura, equivalent to nibbāna.

[6] As at Thūp 17; cf. text p. 141.

[7] MA ii 122f. tells of the difference of opinion among the people as to the size of the thūpa and the material to be used for its construction. Eventually it was

And the Lord Kassapa, his duty done,
Acting solely for the welfare of all creatures,
In the deer-sanctuary in the king of Kāsi's city
Lived bringing bliss to the world. 97

Everywhere remaining in the verses is quite clear.

Concluded[1] is the Exposition of the Chronicle of the Buddha Kassapa
in the Commentary on the Chronicle of Buddhas
called Clarifier of Sweet Meaning

As far as here the Exposition of the Chronicle of the twenty-four Buddhas is concluded[1] in all ways

XXVI THE EXPOSITION OF THE CHRONICLE OF THE BUDDHA GOTAMA

As now we have come in due course to the Exposition of the Chronicle of our Buddha this then is its Exposition. Therein: Our Bodhisatta, performing an act of merit in the presence of twenty-four Buddhas beginning with Dīpaṅkara, has come after four incalculables and a hundred thousand eons in addition. [271] Now after[2] the Lord Kassapa there has been no other Buddha excepting this Fully Self-Awakened One[3]. Thus the Bodhisatta received the declaration in the presence of twenty-four Buddhas beginning with Dīpaṅkara. And, having combined these that are the eight things by means of making (his) resolve at the feet of Dīpaṅkara:

> Human existence, attainment of the (male) sex, cause, seeing a Teacher, going forth, attainment of the special qualities, an act of merit, will-power—by combining these eight things the aspiration succeeds,[4]

---

decided it should be quadrangular in shape and a king, his son, a general and a merchant were each made responsible for one of the faces. But money was short. The lay-devotee, Sorata, a non-returner, went all over Jambudīpa to collect from the people and sent the proceeds to the site of the thūpa. This became completed, but Sorata, on his way back to reverance it, was murdered by thieves in the forest that came to be known as Andhavana, Blind Men's Grove, because they could not believe he had no money with him.

[1] BvAC samattā, BvAB niṭṭhitā.

[2] orābhage, on the near side.

[3] I.e. the Buddha Gotama.

[4] As at IIA 59; cf. CpA 16.

and exerting himself,

"Come, I will examine the things making a Buddha, here and there"[1],

and thinking:

"Examining, I saw then the first perfection, that of Giving"[2],

and fulfilling those things seen as making a Buddha beginning with the perfection of Giving, he came from (his) individuality as Vessantara. And as he was coming those advantages of the resolves made (by Bodhisattas[3]) were lauded[4]:

Thus men who are endowed with all the factors are assured of Awakening even if the long journey in saṁsāra is of hundreds of crores of eons.
They do not arise in Avīci nor yet in the spaces between the worlds; they are not departed beings[5] consumed by constant craving[6], tormented by hunger and thirst.[6]
They are not even tiny creatures arising in a bad bourn. When born among men they are not born blind.
They have no deficiency in hearing, nor are they dumb or paralyzed; they are not born as women nor as hermaphrodites or eunuchs. Men assured of Awakening are not included (in these classes).
Released are they from offences which bring immediate results; the suitable places for them to visit[7] are pure in every respect.
Beholding the efficacy of kamma they do not follow false views.
Even though dwelling in the heavens they will not arise in a non-conscious state; no cause exists for (rebirth) among the devas of the Pure Abodes.[8]

[1] IIA 116. [2] IIA 117.
[3] Not in BvAC, but in BvAB and Jā i 44.
[4] Jā i 44f., CpA 330, Jkm 20 for the following verses.
[5] kālakañjaka, a kind of asura, non-god; cf. D ii 259, iii 7, DA 510, 789, 820.
[6] nijjhāmataṇhā khuppipāsa; cf. Miln 294, KhA 214.
[7] gocara; given this meaning at NdI 474, also the 4 satipaṭṭhāna.
[8] There is no return from birth in these Pure Abodes, suddhāvāsa; perhaps better Abodes of the Pure or of the Purified. It is the only state of being in which our Bodhisatta had no recollection of being reborn, M i 82; apparently only non-returners are born here, see MR and Ill, p. 131, n. 61. Perhaps I may be allowed to add that shortly before his untimely death Professor K. N. Jayatilleke told me he hoped to work out a connexion between the Pure Abodes and the conceptions of the Pure Land form of Buddhism.

Good men, bent on Departure, dissociated from repeated existence, walk the world over fulfilling all the perfections for its welfare. 104

[272] He came, having arrived at these advantages. Coming thus, while he was alive in the individuality of Vessantara he said:

This earth, though incognizant, not knowing pleasure or pain, yet quaked seven times at the power of my giving.[1] 105

And having done great merits so that there were quakings of the great earth thus, he deceased from there[2] on the completion of the life-span and was reborn in Tusita abode.

And while the Bodhisatta was living in Tusita abode[3] there arose what is known as a Buddha-tumult.[4] For three Tumults arise in the world, that is to say: an Eon-tumult, a Buddha-tumult, a Wheel-Turner-tumult. Therein "after a hundred thousand years there will be the end of the eon"[5] means that the devas known as Lokabyūha, of the sensual sphere, with their heads bared, their hair dishevelled, with piteous faces, wiping away their tears with their hands, clad in red cloth and wearing their dress in great disarray, travel up and down the haunts of men, making the announcement, "Friends, friends, after a hundred thousand years from now there will be the end of the eon. This world will be annihilated, even the great ocean will dry up, and this great earth and Sineru, king of mountains, will be burnt up and annihilated. The annihilation of the world will be as far as the Brahma-world. Develop loving-kindness, friends, develop compassion, sympathetic joy, equanimity, friends; care for your mothers and fathers, honour the elders of your clan." This is called the Eon-tumult.

The devatās who are the guardians of the world, thinking, "After a thousand years an omniscient Buddha will arise in the world", go about proclaiming, "After a thousand years from now friends, a Buddha will arise in the world". This is called the Buddha-tumult.

[1] See Vessantara Jātaka (No. 547), and Miln 113ff.

[2] Birth as Vessantara.

[3] Here begins Avidure-nidāna, Jā i 47f. I have drawn extensively on RhD's trans. in The Jātaka, London 1880, p. 58ff. for the following material.

[4] Referred to at text p. 141.

[5] kappuṭṭhāna. From here to the end of the devas' speech below, also at Vism 415.

Devatās thinking, "After a hundred years a wheel-turning king will arise", go about proclaiming, "After a hundred years from now, friends, a wheel-turning king will arise". This is called the Wheel-Turner-tumult.

When they have heard about the Buddha-tumult from those (devas) the devatās of the entire ten-thousand world-systems assembling together, knowing that the being named so-and-so will be a Buddha, approach him and request him; and while they are requesting him, they request that his former portents[1] may arise. And then too all those from each world-system, having assembled together in one world-system together with the Four Regent Devas, Sakka, the Suyāma, Santusita, Vasavatti (devas) and the great Brahmās, went to Tusita-abode and into the presence of the Bodhisatta of whom the portent was of arising and deceasing[2], and entreated him saying, "Friend, you have fulfilled the ten perfections. While you were fulfilling them, you did not fulfil them aspiring to attainment as Sakka, Brahmā and so forth but you fulfilled them for Buddhahood aspiring for omniscience for the sake of helping the world across:

[273] This is the time for you; great hero, arise in the womb of a mother.
Helping men with the devas to cross over, may you awaken to the undying state".[3]

Then the Great Being[4], being requested thus by the devatās, but not giving them an assurance, simply investigated the five great investigations according to the demarcations by time, continent, district, family, (length of) the mother's life-span.

As to this,[5] first he investigated the time: "Is it the time or is it not the time?" For if the length of the life-span has increased to more than a hundred thousand years, it is not the time. Why? For then the birth, ageing and dying of beings are not manifest, and there is no teaching of the Dhamma of Buddhas that is freed from the three characteristic marks, so that when they are talking to these (people) about impermanence, anguish and no-self, they say "Whatever is this they are talking about?" and think it should

[1] See text p. 95ff.
[2] uppannacutinimittassa; other MSS give -cuticittassa.
[3] Verse at i 67. See above, text p. 53.
[4] Cf. text p. 54 for the 5 investigations.
[5] Cf. the following with text p. 54.

neither be listened to nor believed. Consequently there is no penetration. This being so it is a Dispensation not leading out. Therefore this is not the (right) time. Nor is it the (right) time when the duration of the life-span is less than a hundred years. Why? Then beings are abounding in defilements. Exhortation given to those who are abounding in defilements does not persist after the occasion of the exhortation but vanishes quickly like a streak drawn on water. Therefore this too is not the (right) time. The (right) time is when the duration of the life-span is less than a hundred thousand years and more than a hundred years. As the duration then was a hundred years, so the Great Being saw that it was the time when he should be reborn.

Then, investigating the continent, he investigated the four continents with the surrounding (islands), and thought, "There are three continents in which Buddhas are not reborn, they are reborn only in Jambudīpa", and he saw the continent.

Next, he thought, "Jambudīpa is great indeed, ten thousand yojanas in extent. Now, in which district are Buddhas reborn?" And investigating the region he saw the Middle District and came to the conclusion, "It is there, in the city of Kapilavatthu, that I should be reborn."

Next, investigating the family, he thought, "Buddhas are not reborn either in a vessa family or in a sudda family. But they are reborn either in a warrior-noble family or in a brahman family whichever is then of the higher repute in the world. At the present time the warrior-noble family is of the higher repute in the world. I will be reborn therein. The king named Suddhodana will be my father", and he saw the family.

Next, investigating the mother, he thought, "A Buddha's mother is not a wanton or a drunkard. On the contrary, for a hundred thousand eons she has fulfilled the perfections; never since her birth has she torn the five moral habits. And this queen named Mahāmāyā is such a one. She shall be my mother". And then, thinking what would be the extent of her life-span, he saw it would be for ten months and seven days.

So that when he had investigated this fivefold great investigation in this way saying "It is the time, dear sirs, for my Buddhahood", and after giving an assurance to the devas he dismissed those devatās, saying, "You may depart", and entered Nandana Grove in Tusita city surrounded by the devatās of Tusita (abode).

In all the deva-worlds there is likewise a Nandana Grove. The devatās there said to him, "Deceasing from here, may you go to a good bourn", and [274] they went about reminding him of a prior occasion when he had done a skilled deed. So now, when he was surrounded by those devatās who were going about there reminding him of what was skilled, deceasing, he took on relinking in the womb of Mahāmāyā under the asterism of Uttarāsāḷhā.

At the moment that the Great Man took on relinking in his mother's womb the whole of the ten-thousand world-system quaked with one accord and the thirty-two former portent-signs appeared. When the Bodhisatta had thus taken on relinking, four devaputtas, sword in hand, kept guard over his mother to shield her from harm. No thoughts of passion for men arose in the Bodhisatta's mother for, attained to the highest degree of control[1], she was happy and unwearied. And she saw the Bodhisatta in her own womb as clearly as (one sees) a white thread passed through a transparent gem. But as the womb where a Bodhisatta has dwelt is like the interior of a cetiya and can be neither made use of nor occupied by another, so the Bodhisatta's mother, having done her (kammic) time, was reborn in Tusita city a week after the Bodhisatta was born. Moreover, other women give birth some before, some after ten months, some sitting down, some lying down. Not so the mother of a Bodhisatta. For she, having carried a Bodhisatta in her womb for (exactly) ten months, gives birth while she is standing. This is regulation for the mother of a Bodhisatta.

When Queen Mahāmāyā had carried the Bodhisatta in her womb for ten months she felt herself far gone with child. Wishing to go to her family home, she told the great King Suddhodana: "Sire, I want to go to the city of Devadaha." The king assented saying, "So be it", and from Kapilapura as far as the city of Devadaha he had the direct way levelled and decked out with plantain trees, well filled water-jars, flags and banners. Seating the queen in a new golden palanquin of great splendour he sent her away with a great retinue.

Between the two cities and used by the inhabitants of both there was a grove of "Good Omen" sāla trees called Lumbinī Grove. At that time, from the roots up to the topmost branches all was one mass of bloom. Among the branches as well as among the flowers

[1] lābhagga, where lābha, often gain, can have the sense of taking captive here "passion", rāga. Abh 778 includes the meaning "subduing".

there were the most delightfully sweet warblings of birds that were flying about, pleased and happy, enjoying themselves. When the queen beheld this Grove which in beauty resembled Nandana Grove she was minded to disport herself in the sāla grove.

Adorned, extremely thrilling to young people,
Like a woman garlanded, her limbs ornamented,
Always garlanded with bees in the form of eyes of people,
So shone Lumbinī like a ravishing beauty.[1] 106

The ministers told the king and taking the queen entered Lumbinī Grove. She, going up to the root of a "Good Omen" sāla, [275] wanted to take hold of a branch of its straight and evenly rounded trunk that was adorned with flowers, fruits and sprouts. That branch of the sāla, not feeble, with a love of people in its heart, bent down of it own accord till it came within reach of her hand. Then with the utmost delight she took hold of that branch of the sāla tree with her right hand which was shining with a bracelet made of new gold, her fingers rounded like a lotus-leaf, her nails long and copper-coloured. When the queen had taken hold of that branch of the sāla, standing there she shone forth like the crescent of a new moon that had torn fissures in dark clouds, and like the lustre of a flame recently lit, and like the devīs of Nandana Grove. She immediately began to feel the labour-pains. Then the populace, standing before the mother, drew a curtain around her and retired. While she was standing and holding the branch of the sāla she was delivered. At that very moment the four Great Brahmās came bringing a golden net and, receiving the Bodhisatta on that golden net, they stood before the mother and said, "Be joyful, lady, a mighty son has been born to you".

And though other beings on issuing forth from the mother's womb issue forth smeared with disagreeable, impure matter, it was not so with the Bodhisatta. Stretching out his hands and feet he issued forth erect from his mother's womb, shining like a gem placed on a silken cloth, pure, clean, not smeared with any impurity. Yet, even though this was the case, two showers of water came down from the sky in honour of the Bodhisatta and the Bodhisatta's mother and brought refreshment to the physical frame of the Bodhisatta and to his mother.

Then from the hands of the Brahmās who, standing, had

[1] Verse not included in Jātaka-nidāna.

received him on the golden net the four Great Kings received him on a cloth of black antelope skins, soft to the touch, considered to be of good omen[1]; from their hands people received him on a roll of fine cloth. On leaving the hands of the people he stood upon the ground surveying the eastern quarter. The various thousands of world-systems were a single open space. Devas and mankind there, paying homage to him with perfumes, flowers, garlands and so forth, said, "Great Man, there is no one like unto you here, how then a greater?" When he had surveyed the ten quarters thus, not seeing one like himself he took seven strides facing northward. As he was walking on the ground thus, he did not go through the sky, he went like an unclothed (ascetic), not like one who was clothed, and he went like a boy, not as one who was in his sixteenth year; but, to the populace he was walking as though through the sky and as though he were deckt out and adorned and as though he were in his sixteenth year. Then, at the seventh step he stood still, and at once sending forth his noble voice, he roared the lion's roar, "I am the highest in the world."

In three of his individualities the Bodhisatta, immediately on issuing forth from his mother's womb, had sent forth his voice: in his individuality as Mahosadha[2], in his individuality as Vessantara[3], and in this individuality.[4]

They say that in his individuality as Mahosadha, Sakka, king of devas, came as he was issuing forth from his mother's womb and having placed essence of sandalwood in his hand went away, and that he issued forth with this in his fist. So his mother asked him, "What is it you are holding as you come, dear?" "A medicinal plant, mother". Thus, because he came holding a medicinal plant (osadha), they gave him the name of Osadhakumāra (Medicinal Plant Child).[5]

[1] maṅgala-sammata. See A. B. Keith, Relig. and Philosophy of the Veda and Upanishads, p. 301f.: "The wearing of the black antelope skin is a practice which is especially enjoined on the brahman student, and it is natural to see in it some special connexion with the power to be derived from wearing such a skin . . . the choice of a black skin also suggests that the idea of making the wearer invisible to the demons may have something to do with the use . . . antelope hide is the one worn by the student who is in a special condition of religious communion with the divine."

[2] Jā No 546.

[3] Jā No 547.

[4] Cf. Jā vi 485.

[5] Jā vi 331f.

[276] And in his individuality as Vessantara, when he was issuing forth from his mother's womb he issued forth stretching out his right arm, saying, "Is there anything in this house, mother? I would give a gift." His mother replied, saying, "You are born into a wealthy family, dear" and taking her son's hand in hers she placed it on a bag containing a thousand.[1]

In this individuality he roared this lion's roar. Thus did the Bodhisatta send forth his voice in three individualities even as he was issuing forth from his mother's womb. And at the moment of birth the thirty-two former portent-signs appeared. At the time when our Bodhisatta was born in Lumbinī Grove there were also born the lady who was Rāhula's mother, Channa, Kāḷudāyin the minister, Ājānīya the elephant-king, Kanthaka the horse-king, the great Tree of Awakening, and the four treasure-urns of which one was one gāvuta in size, one half a yojana, one three gāvutas, and one a yojana. These are called the seven Connatal ones.[2]

The inhabitants of the two cities took the Great Man and went off to the city of Kapilavatthu. On that same day the assemblies of devas in the abode of the Thirty-Three, exultant and elated, waving garments and so forth, rejoiced saying, "The son of the great king Suddhodana of the city of Kapilavatthu is seated at the root of a Tree of Awakening. He will be a Buddha."

At that time the ascetic named Kāladevala[3], one who had acquired the eight attainments, was a confidant of the great king Suddhodana. When he had finished his meal and had gone to the abode of the Thirty-Three for the day-sojourn and was seated there during the day-sojourn he saw those devatās rejoicing, elated in mind. And he asked, "Why are you rejoicing, elated in mind, joyous at heart? Tell me the reason." Those devatās said: "Friend, a son is born to King Suddhodana. When he has sat on the dais round the Tree of Awakening and has become a Buddha he will turn the Wheel of Dhamma. We will be able to see his infinite beauty and Buddha's grace. For this reason we are elated." When the ascetic had heard their words, descending from the

[1] Cf. Jā vi 485.

[2] This list shows some discrepancies in the names compared with other lists at text pp. 131, 298, and RhD. Bud. Birth Stories, p. 68, n. The 4 treasure-urns have to be counted as one item. Ajānīya hatthirājā is mentioned nowhere but here in BvA, and seems to be in place of Ānanda. BvAB in a note notices BvAC's Ājānīya, but omits hatthirājā. See Intr. p. xliv f.

[3] Cf. Sn. 679fl., SnA ii 483ff. for the following, also Mhvu ii 30ff.

deva-world, a bejewelled world most delightful to behold, he entered the dwelling of the lord of men and sat down on the appointed seat. Then he said to the king who had received him in a friendly way, "Sire, they say a son has been born to you. May we have an opportunity to see him?"

The king, having commanded that he (the baby) be adorned and decorated, fetched him (for him) to pay homage to the ascetic Devala. But the Great Man's feet, turning round like a flash of lightning in an untrammelled rent in the clouds, came to rest on the ascetic's matted hair. For in this individuality there was no one to be reverenced by the Bodhisatta. Then the ascetic, rising from his seat, held up his clasped hands to the Bodhisatta. When the king saw this wonder he reverenced his own son. The ascetic, on seeing the Bodhisatta's attainment of the Marks, and having considered, "Will he or will he not be a Buddha?" knew by his own knowledge of the future that without a doubt he would be a Buddha, and he smiled thinking, "This is a marvel among men." Then, reflecting on whether or not he would have the opportunity to see him when he had become a Buddha, he perceived that he would not. For "Doing my (kammic) time before then, I will be reborn in the formless sphere so that even if a thousand Buddhas came I would not be able to awaken." And [277] he wept at the thought, "Indeed it will be a great loss to me that I will not get the opportunity to see such a marvel among men as this." And when the people saw this they asked, "Our master, who was laughing just now has begun to weep again. What is it, revered sir? Is there to be some stumbling-block for our young master?" The ascetic said, "There is no stumbling-block for him. Without a doubt he will be a Buddha." "Then why are you weeping?" He said, "I will not get the opportunity to see such a marvel among men as this when he has become a Buddha. Indeed it will be a great loss for me. I weep, grieving for myself."

Then on the fifth day, having washed the Bodhisatta's head and paid reverence, they said, "We will choose a name".[1] They perfumed the royal abode with the four kinds of scents[2], strewed the five articles of honouring with puffed rice as the fifth[2] and had milk-rice prepared undiluted with water. Having invited eight hundred brahmans, masters of the three Vedas, and having seated

[1] Following Jā i 55 gaṇhissāma against text's -āmi.
[2] See text p. 84.

them in the royal abode, they gave them the sweet milk-rice, and paying reverence, said, "Now, what will he be?" and asked them to read the marks. Eight of the brahmans among these, beginning with Rāma[1], were readers (of marks). Seven of these, holding up two fingers, declared, "Endowed with these marks he will be a wheel-turning king living in a house (or), going forth, a Buddha." But a boy among them all, a brahman named Koṇḍañña of that clan, seeing the Bodhisatta's attainment of the glorious Marks, holding up one finger only, declared thus: "There is no reason for him to stay in a house; he will certainly be a Buddha, drawing back the veil (from the world)." And on choosing a name for him they gave him the name of Siddhattha on account of his accomplishment for the welfare of all the world[2].

Then these brahmans, going each to their own homes, addressing their sons, spoke thus, "We are old. Whether or not we witness the attainment of omniscience by the son of the great King Suddhodana, do you, having gone forth under him, go forth in his Dispensation after he has attained omniscience." Then these seven persons, having remained for the rest of their life-spans, went on according to kamma. The brahman youth Koṇḍañña was healthy.

Then the king asked them, "Having seen what will my son go forth?" "When he has seen four former portent-signs." "And what are they?" "An old man, an ill man, a dead man, and one who had gone forth." The king saying, "From now on do not let such things come near my son", placed a guard at every gāvuta in the four quarters to prevent an old man and so forth from coming into the boy's range of vision.

On that day, in that place, at an assembly of eighty thousand families of relations each one dedicated one son saying, "Let this one become either a Buddha or a king, we are each giving a son. If he becomes a Buddha he will go about surrounded only by recluses who are warrior-nobles; if he becomes a wheel-turning king he will go about surrounded only by young men who are warrior-nobles."

Then the king appointed nurses who were without any blemishes and were endowed with the utmost beauty for the Great Man. The Bodhisatta grew up in great splendour and luxury[3] with an un-

[1] Names are given at Jā i 56, ver. 270.
[2] sabbalokatthasiddhikarattā.
[3] sirisamudaya.

ending retinue. Then, one day there was the king's ploughing festival. On that [**278**] day the king went to a place to plough at the ploughing festival with a great and magnificent retinue. There the king took a golden plough for the high festival; the counsellors and so forth took silver ploughs. On that day a thousand ploughs were yoked. And the nurses, having surrounded the Bodhisatta, said while they were seated, "Let us see the king's prowess", and they went out from within the curtain. Then the Bodhisatta, looking about on this side and that but seeing no one, got up quickly and, sitting in the cross-legged position controlling his in-breathing and out-breathing, entered on[1] the first meditation. The nurses delayed a little moving about among the solid and soft foods. The shadow of the rest of the trees turned, but the shadow of that rose-apple tree remained just where it was, circular in form. Then it occurred to the nurses, "The young master is all alone", and hurriedly raising the curtain-wall and searching, they saw him seated in the splendid cross-legged position and went to tell that marvel to the king. The king went hurriedly, paid homage to his son, and said, "This is a second homage for you, dear".

So, in due course the Great Man came to be sixteen years of age. The king had three palaces built for the Bodhisatta, suitable for the three seasons, named Ramma, Suramma, Subha. One was of nine storeys, one of seven storeys, one of five storeys, but though there was a difference in the number of storeys the three palaces were equal in height. Then the king thought, "My son has come of age. Having unfurled the sunshade[2] I will see success for the kingdom." And he said, "My son, who has come of age, has sent messages of sorrow. I will have him established in sovereignty. Let all the young girls who have come of age in their own houses enter this house." When they had heard the king's message they[3] said, "The prince, though endowed with every beauty, knows no craft whatever; he will not be able to maintain a wife; we will not give him our daughters". The king, hearing of this turn of events, went into his son's presence and told him the turn of events. The Bodhisatta said, "What craft must I display?" "My dear, you must string the bow that requires the strength of a thousand men."[4]

[1] Lit. produced, nibbattesi.
[2] Presumably, the sunshade of state, part of the royal regalia.
[3] Obviously meaning the parents.
[4] Cf. Jā vi 38.

"Well then, do have it fetched". The king had the bow fetched and gave it to him. The Great Man strung that bow (with the strength of a) thousand men, took it down (with the strength of a) thousand men, and having had a quiver of arrows brought and sitting down as though in the cross-legged position, twirling the bow-string in his toes, drawing it, and even stringing the bow with his toes, holding the shaft in his left hand and drawing with his right hand, he raised the bow-string. The whole city was aware it was rising up. And when they had said, "What noise is this?" they said, "The (sky-) god is thundering." But others said, "Do you not know? The (sky-) god is not thundering. This is the sound of the bow-string after Prince Aṅgīrasa has strung the bow with the strength of a thousand (men)". Immediately the Sakyans heard that they were satisfied and elated in mind.

Then the Great Man said, "What must be done?" "With an arrow[1] one must pierce a sheet of iron eight finger-breadths thick." **[279]** When he had pierced that he said, "What else must be done?" They said, "One must pierce a plank of asana-wood four finger-breadths thick".[2] When he had pierced that he said, "What else must be done?" They said, "One must pierce a plank of fig-wood twelve finger-breadths[3] thick." When he had pierced that he said, "What else must be done?" Then they said, "Wagons of sand." The Great Being pierced through a wagon of sand and a wagon of straw, he made an arrow[4] enter into the water for a distance of one usabha[5] and into the dry ground for a distance of eight usabhas. Then they said, "One must pierce a hair of a horse's tail by the indicating sign of an egg-plant." "Well then, have an egg-plant fastened a yojana away." When he had spoken thus they had a hair of a horse's tail fastened to the indicating sign of an egg-plant a yojana away. He let fly an arrow round the six quarters under cover of a storm-cloud in the dark of the night. When it had gone for the distance of the yojana and had split the hair of the horse's tail he made it enter the earth. But, indeed, not even all this craft that the Great Man displayed to the world on that day alone was the whole of its extent.

Then the Sakyans, adorning their own daughters, sent them off.

[1] kaṇḍa here.

[2] For these feats of archery cf. Sarabhaṅga-jātaka, Jā v 131.

[3] Here vidatthi, a span (of 12 finger-breadths); above the word is aṅgula.

[4] kaṇḍa.

[5] A measure of length = 140 cubits.

There were forty thousand dancing-women. And the queen Rāhula's mother, was the chief consort. The Great Man, like a deva-prince surrounded by youthful gods, amusing himself with the instrumental music of the females, and enjoying great luxury, stayed in one of those three palaces according to whichever season it was.

Then one day the Bodhisatta, wanting to go to a pleasure-ground, said to a charioteer, "Harness a chariot, I will see the pleasure-ground." He answered, "So be it" in assent. After he had decorated a glorious chariot of great value, lovely to behold like the chariot of the sun, its pole and fender[1] glorious, beautiful, strong, the rims of the wheels and the naves very strong, the front part of the shafts studded with glorious gold, silver, pearls and jewels, the sides of the rims of the wheels arranged with glittering fresh gold and silver, resplendent with intertwined ropes of various fragrant flowers, and after he had harnessed four state horses from Sindh, thoroughbreds, resembling the moon in colour or white lotus flowers and having the speed of the wind or of an eagle, he informed the Bodhisatta. The Bodhisatta mounted that glorious chariot which resembled a deva's mansion and went off towards the pleasaunce.

Then the devatās thought, "The time for Prince Siddhattha's full Self-Awakening is near. We will show him the former portent-signs." They did this by making one devaputta display a physical form that was feeble with age, the teeth decayed, the hair of the head grey, the limbs crooked, tottering along holding a stick. Only the Bodhisatta and the charioteer saw him. Then the Bodhisatta asked exactly in the way handed down in the Mahāpanāda Sutta[2], "Charioteer, what is this man called that even his hair is not like that of others?" On hearing his words, he said, "Shame indeed then upon birth in that the ageing of what is born is evident!" And turning back from there, troubled at heart, he reached the palace. The king asked, "Why did my son turn back?" "Because he saw an old man, sire." Thereupon the king, his mind in a turmoil, [**280**] established a guard every half-yojana.

Again, when the Bodhisatta was going to the pleasaunce one day

[1] varūtha, not in PED. "A sort of wooden ledge or fender fastened round a chariot as a defence against collision," M-W., and Childers.

[2] Mahāpanāda-jātaka, at Jā ii 331. BvAC also reads Mahāpanāda, BvAB and Jā i 59 Mahāpadāna, see D ii 21ff. of the Buddha Vipassin.

and saw an ill man created by those same devatās, he asked in the same way as before. Turning back, troubled at heart, he regained the palace. When the king heard[1] this he dispatched dancers thinking, "They will put a stop[2] to his going forth[3]"; he increased the guard establishing it at distances of three gāvutas all round.

Again[4], when the Bodhisatta was going to the pleasaunce one day he saw one who had done his (kammic) time, likewise created by those same devatās. Having asked in the same way as before, troubled at heart, he turned back and regained the palace. When the king had asked the reason for his return, he again increased the guard establishing it at a distance of a yojana all round.

Again, when the Bodhisatta was going to the pleasaunce one day he saw one who had gone forth properly dressed, properly clothed[5]. He asked the charioteer, "What is this one called, good charioteer?" Though the charioteer, owing to the absence of any trace whatever of a Buddha[6], did not know either one who had gone forth or the special qualities of one who had gone forth, nevertheless, through the majesty of the devatās, said; "Sire, this is called one who has gone forth", and he praised to him the special qualities of going forth. Thereupon the Bodhisatta, having aroused a liking for going forth, went to the pleasaunce that day.

Bodhisattas of long life-spans saw the old man and so forth one by one at the end of every hundred years. But because our Bodhisatta had arisen at a time when life-spans were short he saw them gradually one by one as he was going to the pleasaunce after (every) four months. The Dīgha-reciters say that as he was going (to the pleasaunce) he saw the four portent-signs on one day. Sporting there during the day-time, enjoying the delights of the pleasaunce, bathing in the state lotus-pool, at the setting of the sun he sat down on a stone slab of state wanting to have himself adorned. Then as Sakka, chief of devas, was considering the state of his (the Bodhisatta's) mind, Vissakamma, a deva-putta, came at his command and, looking just like his barber, adorned him with deva-like adornments. When he was adorned with all adornments

[1] BvAC sutvā, BvAB pucchitvā.

[2] bhinnaṁ karissanti.

[3] BvAC pabbajjaṁ, BvAB pabbajāya mānasam.

[4] BvAC omits this "portent-sign" in error.

[5] sunivattha, dressed properly as to his inner and upper robes; and supāruta, clothed properly as to his outer cloak.

[6] Buddhappāda.

and the brahmans each showed brilliance on the musical instruments and when, with manifold utterances, they had made him hear, among the auspicious things heard, their shouts of praise and auspicious utterances beginning with the words, "Conquer, rejoice!" he mounted a glorious chariot that was adorned with all adornments.

At that time the great King Suddhodana heard that Rāhula's mother had given birth to a son and he sent a message to say, "Convey[1] (my) elation to my[2] son". When the Bodhisatta heard this he said, "Rāhula is born, a bond is born". When the king had asked what his son had said and had heard what it was, he said, "From now on let my grandson be Prince Rāhula, however."

And the Bodhisatta, mounted on that glorious chariot, entered the city with a great retinue (and) with exceeding charm and splendid pomp. At that time a warrior-noble maiden named Kisāgotamī, beautiful and not lean[3], was on the upper storey of a glorious palace; seeing the beauty of the Bodhisatta as he was entering the city, full of zest and happiness, she uttered this solemn utterance:

Tranquil[4] indeed is that mother,
Tranquil indeed is that father,
Tranquil indeed is that wife
Of whom one such as this is the lord.*

[**281**] The Bodhisatta thought as he heard her, "Sweet-sounding are the words she makes me hear. I, seeking nibbāna[5], am moving about. This very day, renouncing my household life, it behoves me, having gone forth after the Departure, to seek nibbāna. Let this be her teacher's fee". And from his neck he loosened an exceedingly lovely string of pearls worth a hundred thousand and had it sent to Kisāgotamī. She, filled with happiness, thought, "Prince Siddhattha being in love with me sends me a present." But the Bodhisatta, entering an exceedingly delightful palace with

* Frequent, e.g. at Jā i 60, DhA i 85, ApA 65, Asl 34, UJ 127.

[1] BvAC pavedatha, BvAB nivedetha.
[2] BvAC omits.
[3] akisā, in spite of her name, which means Thin Gotamī.
[4] nibbuta, waned out, at peace, tranquil, happy.
[5] Jā i 61, ApA 66 give one to understand that nibbāna is the waning out of the fires of passion and so forth, and of the defilements of conceit, false view, etc.

great pomp and splendour, reclined on a state-couch. Immediately beautiful young women, their faces glorious and pleasing, resembling the full moon, their lips[1] and wearing apparel like the fruit of a bimba[2] (-tree), their lovely teeth[3] regular, even, white and stainless, their eyes black, their hair braided, their dark eyebrows arched like beautiful curving lotus-stalks, their breasts evenly shaped like the beautiful ruddy goose, their girdles studded with lovely fresh gold and silver and glorious jewels, their sloping hips massive and strong, their pairs of broad (feet) resembling an elephant's[4], skilled in dancing, singing, music, resplendent like young goddesses, glorious young women—with sweet cries they took up musical instruments, surrounded the Great Man, and set to work on delightful dancing, singing and music. But because the Bodhisatta was detached in mind from the defilements he took no delight in the dancing and singing and so forth and fell asleep in a moment.

When they saw him they said: "He for whose sake we set to work dancing and so forth has gone to sleep. For whose sake are we now playing?" And covering the musical instruments they were holding they lay down. The scented oil lamps burnt on. When the Bodhisatta had woken up and was sitting cross-legged on his couch he saw those women sleeping like forms in a cemetery, their musical instruments and possessions strewn about, some foaming at the mouth, their cheeks and limbs wet with perspiration, some grinding their teeth, some talking confusedly, some with mouths agape, some with their garments in disarray, their private parts uncovered, their hair come loose and tangled. When the Great Being saw the change in them, all the more did his mind find no delight in sensual pleasures.

There arose in him the utmost loathing for even that adorned and decorated glorious palace, splendid as the abode of him of the thousand eyes, which seemed like a cemetery of carrion full of abandoned dead bodies and ordure[5]. The three becomings rose up

[1] dasana, given as teeth in PED, must mean lips here. Red lips are a mark of female beauty.

[2] Momordica monadelpha, a species of amaranth, gold or red in colour.

[3] dasana.

[4] karikarasannibhoruyugalā.

[5] kuṇapa as corpse could only be a synonym for mata-sarīra, "dead bodies" or forms. The idea of an āmakasusāna, "cemetery of carrion" is that, among other things, it is evil-smelling. Cf. IIA 21, 23 for kuṇapa as ordure.

like houses in flames. An utterance broke from him, "How oppressive it is, indeed how terrible!" and he bent his mind intensely to the going forth: "This very day I must depart on the Great Departure", and arising from the state-couch and going close to the door, he said, "Who is here?" Channa, who was lying with his head on the threshold, said, "It is I, young master, Channa". "Today I want to depart on the Great Departure. Quickly saddle a very swift horse without telling anyone". Saying "Very good, sire", he took horse-trappings, went to the stables where scented oil lamps were burning, [282] and saw the glorious steed Kanthaka, a noble slayer[1], standing on a delightful piece of ground under a canopy of great-flowered jasmine. He saddled Kanthaka, thinking, "This is the very state-horse to saddle for my young master's Departure today." Even while he was being saddled the horse knew, "This saddling is very tight; it is not like the saddling on other days at the time of going to sport in the pleasaunce. Undoubtedly the young master is departing on the Great Departure today" and, elated in mind, he neighed a mighty neigh. The sound of it would have resounded over the whole of Kapilapura had not the devatās impeded it and let no-one hear.

The Bodhisatta thinking, "I will just see my son", went from where he was standing to the apartments of Rāhula's mother and opened the door of the room. At that time a scented oil lamp was burning in the room. Rāhula's mother was asleep on a glorious couch which was completely strewn over with a mass of different kinds of jasmine[2] and was resting her hand on her son's head. Stopping with his foot on the threshold the Bodhisatta looked and thought, "If I lift the princess's[3] hand and take up my son the princess will awaken, and that will be a stumbling block to my Departure. Only when I have become a Buddha will I come back and see my son."

Coming down from the palace-terrace and going to the horse he spoke thus, "Good Kanthaka, do you today carry me through this one night; when, in consequence of this I have become a Buddha, I will help the world with the devas to cross over." Thereupon, leaping up he mounted Kanthaka's back. Kanthaka was eighteen

[1] arimanthaka. See text p. 6.

[2] Lit. with at least an ammaṇa measure of great-flowered jasmine, Arabian jasmine and so on.

[3] devī, meaning a queen, lady, female deva.

cubits in length from his neck and of proportionate height. He was beautiful, swift and strong, in colour resembling a clean chank. Then the Bodhisatta, riding on the back of the glorious steed, telling Channa to hold on to the horse's tail, arrived at the city's great gateway at midnight. But the king then, as before, in order to prevent the Bodhisatta from going away had had each of the two gateways closed by a thousand (men) and had set up a guard there of many men. The Bodhisatta, it is said, had the strength of a hundred thousand crores counted in men, and of a thousand crores counted in elephants.[1] Therefore he thought, "Should the gateway not open today, then, seated on Kanthaka's back, with Channa holding on to his tail, pressing Kanthaka with my thighs, I will get away, jumping the ramparts." But Channa and Kanthaka simply thought thus, "The devatās who inhabit the gateway opened it."

At that moment Māra the Malign arrived, thinking, "I will turn back the Great Being" and, standing in the vault of the heavens, he said,

"Do not depart, great hero. In seven days from now the deva-
like treasure of the Wheel will certainly appear to you. 107

You will rule over the great continents and the two thousand smaller islands surrounding them. Turn back, good sir." The Great Being said, "Who are you?" "I am Vasavattin". [283] He said:

"I, Māra, know the nature of my deva-like Wheel.[2] I have no
use for sovereignty. Go away, Māra, do not you be here. 108
For I will be a Buddha, a guider out for the world, making even
the entire ten-thousand world-system resound (with joy)". 109

Then and there he disappeared.

At the age of twenty-nine the Great Man who had in his hand a wheel-turner's empire throwing it aside with indifference as though it were a blob of spittle, at the full-moon of Āsāḷha during the asterism of Uttarāsāḷha departed from the royal abode that had the pomp and glory of a wheel-turner's. But when he had departed from the city he wanted to look upon it. At the very thought that

[1] Cf. text p. 42.

[2] I follow a v. l. instead of BvAC's jānām'ahaṁ mahārāja mayham dibbācakkassa sambhavaṁ, in which the Bodhisatta addresses Māra as mahārāja, great king.

part of the ground immediately revolved like a potter's wheel. Even as it stood still after the Great Being had seen Kapilapura he pointed out a place for a cetiya "Where was Kanthaka's Stopping" on that part of the ground. And making Kanthaka face towards the way to be travelled, he set forth in great pomp and magnificent splendour. Then as the Bodhisatta was going along devatās in front of him held sixty hundred thousand torches, likewise behind him, sixty hundred thousand on his right side, likewise on his left side. More devatās, surrounding him, went along reverencing him with fragrant blossoms, roots, wreaths, sandalwood and scented powders and beautiful flags and banners. And countless were the deva-like songs and the musical instruments they played.

Going along in this pomp and splendour the Bodhisatta, in that one night traversing three territories, going thirty yojanas along a road, arrived at the bank of the river Anomā. Then the Bodhisatta, stopping at the river-bank, asked Channa, "What is this river called?" "It is called Anomā,[1] sire." "May my going forth be perfect[2] too" he said, and touching[3] the horse with his heel he gave it a signal.[4] Leaping the stretch of eight usabhas[5], the horse stood still on the opposite bank of the river. The Bodhisatta dismounted from his back, and standing on the sandy bank which resembled a mass of pearls, he addressed Channa, saying, "Good Channa, you go, taking my ornaments as well as Kanthaka. I will go forth". Channa said, "I will go forth too, sire."

"It is not for you to go forth. You must go straight back", and having refused him three times, he entrusted his ornaments as well as Kanthaka to him, and thought, "The hair of my head is not suitable for a recluse. I will cut it off with this sword". And taking a glorious and extremely sharp sword in his right hand and holding his topknot, together with his diadem, in his left hand, he cut them off. His hair was only two finger-breadths (long) and, curling from the right, lay close to his head. For as long as he lived his hair was of the same length. His beard was in proportion, and there was no need to shave his hair or beard (ever) again.

When the Bodhisatta was holding his topknot, together with his diadem, he thought, "If I am to become a Buddha let them remain

[1] Cf. pp. 6, 54.
[2] anoma, peerless, perfect, illustrious.
[3] ghaṭento, lit. uniting the horse with his heel.
[4] saññaṁ adāsi as at Jā vi 302.
[5] A linear measure.

in the sky; if not, let them fall to the ground", [284] and he threw them up into the sky. The diadem that was tied to the topknot rose into the sky to the distance of a yojana and remained there. Then Sakka the deva-king looking round with deva-like vision received it in a casket for jewels a yojana high and established a cetiya called Diadem (Cūḷāmaṇicetiya) in the abode of the Thirty-Three. As it was said:

> Having cut off the glorious perfumed topknot, the highest among men threw it up into the air. The one of the thousand eyes, Vāsava[1], received it with reverence in a glorious golden casket.

Again the Bodhisatta thought, "These garments of materials from Kāsi[2] are not suitable for me as a recluse." Then Ghaṭīkāra, the Great Brahmā who formerly had been a friend of his in the time of the Buddha Kassapa, because of the friendship that had not been impaired during the one interval between the Buddhas, thought, "My friend is departing today on the Great Departure. I am going along and am taking a recluse's requisites for him".[3]

> Three robes and a bowl, razor, needle, and girdle, with a water-strainer—these eight are for a monk intent on earnest endeavour." 110

And he gave these eight recluse's requisites that he had brought.

After clothing himself in the banner of an arahant[4] and choosing a garb that was supreme for the going forth, the Great Man dismissed Channa with the words, "Channa, in my name tell my parents that I am well." Then Channa, honouring the Great Man and circumambulating him keeping his right side towards him, set off. But Kanthaka, hearing the Bodhisatta's bidding as he was talking to Channa, thought, "Never again now will I see my master" and going out of his sight, unable to bear the sorrowful separation he died of a broken heart. He was reborn as a devaputta named Kanthaka in a most lovely abode of gods in the abode of the Thirty-Three. His arising is to be taken from the Vimalatthavilāsinī, the Commentary on Vimānavatthu[5]. At first Channa's grief had been but single. (But now) oppressed by the second grief of Kanthaka's death, he returned in anguish, weeping and lamenting.

[1] One of Sakka's names.

[2] Kāsi, or Bārāṇasī, was famous then as now for its beautiful silks, muslins and fine cloth.

[3] Cf. SnA ii 382, VvA 314.

[4] The yellow robe of a monk.

[5] VvA 314.

But the Bodhisatta, having gone forth, spent seven days in the bliss of going forth in a mango-grove called Anupiya there in that self-same place. Then, guarding his glorious yellow robes like the autumn moon at the full guarding the evening lustre illuminating the clouds and, even though he was alone, shining forth as though he were surrounded by countless people, making as it were the drink of deathlessness available for forest-dwelling beasts and birds, faring alone like a lion, the lion of men, walking with the measured gait of an elephant, in only one day walked the earth for thirty yojanas and crossing the river Ganges which was untrammelled, for the waves that had risen had subsided[1], [**285**] he entered the city called Rājagaha, a glorious and lovely royal residence (rājagaha) resplendent with a mass of shining treasures. Having entered, he walked for alms in successive order[2].

And at the sight of the Bodhisatta's beauty that entire city was thrown into a commotion as was this city when Dhanapāla entered it, or as is a deva-city when a chief of the asuras enters it. As the Great Man was walking for alms the inhabitants of the city, full of zest and happiness at the sight of his beauty, astonished, were perplexed at heart[3] on seeing the Bodhisatta. One of these men spoke thus to another, "Is it not the full-moon, good sir, that is coming to the world of men aglow with escaping from the peril of Rāhu?" Another spoke thus to him, "What are you saying, my good man? When have you ever before seen the full-moon coming to the world of men? Is it not rather the deva Kāma who with blossoms and banners, bringing fire[4], has come to sport with our great king and the citizens, having seen their extreme grace and splendour?" Another, smiling at him, spoke thus, "What now, good sir, are you out of your mind? Surely Kāma as a physical form was utterly burnt up by the fire of the lord's anger.[5] This is

[1] uttuṅgataraṅgabhaṅgaṁ asaṅgaṁ Gaṅgaṁ, cf. text pp. 6, 56. Uttuṅga not in PED, but see M-W.

[2] sapadānaṁ, i.e. not missing out a house or choosing only the better looking ones; for in respect of the houses the almstour should be continuous, uninterrupted, see Vin iv 191f. in Sekhiya 33.

[3] This seems to be the meaning of the compound dassanāvajjitahadayā.

[4] vesantaram ādāya. Meaning of vesantara is doubtful. Vesanta is fire, M-W. Or is it a misreading for Vasantaṁ, Vasanta being Kāma's commander-in-chief?

[5] The legend is that Siva, the lord, was once pierced by an arrow shot by Kāma which was meant both to arouse him to love and to break his meditation. "A lightning flash of anger broke from Siva's third or middle eye . . . and the

him of the thousand eyes, lord of gods, who has come here thinking it was Amarapura[1]." Then another, laughing slightly, said, "What are you speaking about, good sir? The difficulties in what was said last are: where are his thousand eyes, where his thunder-bolt, where Erāvaṇa?[2] Undoubtedly this is Brahmā who, knowing the laziness of the brahman people, is coming to stimulate them (to learn) the Vedas and Vedaṅgas and so forth." When they had all disparaged this then one (of them) spoke thus: "This is neither the full-moon nor Kāma, nor even him of the thousand eyes and not even Brahmā. This is the leader of the world, the teacher, a marvel among men."[3]

While the citizens were discussing in these ways, the king's men, having gone back, related the event to King Bimbisāra, "Your majesty, now is this a deva or a heavenly musician or is it a nāga-king or a yakkha who is walking for alms in our city?" Having heard them, the king, standing on the terrace of the palace, saw the Great Man and his mind was filled with marvel and wonder. He commanded the king's men, "Go, good sirs, and investigate. Should it be a non-human being, departing from the city it will disappear; should it be a devatā it will go off through the sky; should it be a nāga-king it will go off plunging into the earth; should it be a man he will make use of almsfood as he receives it."

The Great Being, his sense-faculties tranquil, his mind tranquil, looking ahead no more than a plough's length, and as though a cynosure of the eyes of the great populace because of the beauty of his appearance, gathered enough food of a mixed nature to keep himself going and, departing from the city by the gateway at which he had entered, he sat down facing eastwards in the shadow of the Paṇḍava mountain, considered the nutriment and perseveringly made use of it.[4] Thereupon the king's men returned and related the event to the king.

---

body of Kāma, the very vision of Charm Irresistible, was reduced to ashes", H. Zimmer, Philosophies of India, New York, 1951, p. 141.

[1] Sakka's city. At Mhvs 80 5 called Amarāvatī.

[2] Two of Siva's attributes; Erāvaṇa is his elephant.

[3] Or, a marvellous man, acchariya-manussa, said of the Tathāgata at A i 22, of Buddhas at Jā i 277. Cf. acchariya-purisa above, text p. 276f.

[4] Jā i 66 says it turned his stomach and made as if it would come out of his mouth. I have the impression, but cannot find supporting evidence, that to the end of his life the Buddha found his food rough and coarse and disagreeable but persisted in eating it—for he had found starvation etc. did not lead to Awakening, see below, text p. 286, also text p. 6 above.

Hearing what the messengers said, the king, overlord of Magadha, hard to equal[1], the elect of Meru and Mandāra, the elect of beings, Bimbisāra, with (those) ignorant people quickly departed then from the city full of the excitement of seeing the Bodhisatta on account of his special qualities.[**286**] Going along towards Mount Paṇḍava, getting down from the vehicle, he went into the Bodhisatta's presence, obtained his permission,[2] and sat down on a stone-slab cool with the affinity (existing) between relations[3]. Pleased with the Bodhisatta's posture, he made over to him all the suzerainty. The Bodhisatta said, "I, sire, have no use either for desires for property or for desires for the defilements. I am departing, aspiring for paramount Self-Awakening". The king, though asking in many a way but not gaining his consent, said, "Assuredly you will be a Buddha, and after you have become a Buddha you must come back to my kingdom first." And he entered the city.

Then when the glorious king of men had gone to Rājagaha, the city, the glorious royal residence, the glorious king of mountains,[4] the glorious king of sages, gone (like) the king of beasts, was gone, well-gone. 11

Then the Bodhisatta, walking on tour, gradually approached Āḷāra Kālāma and Uddaka Rāmaputta. But when he had acquired (their) attainments he thought, "This is not the way to Awakening" and, wanting to strive the striving, he went on to Uruvelā without having found satisfaction in that development of the attainments. Thinking, "This is indeed a delightful stretch of land",[5] and taking up his dwelling there he strove the great striving. The four sons of the brahmans who were readers of marks and the brahman Koṇḍañña[6], five who had gone forth, were walking for alms through villages, market-towns and capital cities when they came

[1] duranusāra, difficult to conform to(?). This word and the 2 following, Merumandārasāro sattasāro, are plays on the name Bimbisāra. Cf. text p. 6 for other and similar epithets and for this para. in general.

[2] katānuñño.

[3] bandhujanasinehasītala. Gotama and Bimbisāra were both khattiyas. They had been friends in their youth and their fathers had been friends, Mhvs-ṭ 137.

[4] girirājavara. Rājagaha has the alternative name Giribbaja. Here a better reading would be Giribbajavare, in the glorious Giribbaja.

[5] As at M i 167.

[6] See text p. 277.

upon the Bodhisatta there. Then for six years while he was striving the striving they kept near him attending on him with all manner of services such as sweeping his cell and so forth, thinking "Now he will be a Buddha, now he will be a Buddha."

But the Bodhisatta thinking, "I will engage on austerities to the end"[1], subsisted on only one grain of sesamum or rice and so forth[2] and even fasted entirely. A devatā, bringing a nutritive essence, infused it into the pores of his skin. But because of his being without food his body became exceedingly emaciated, the body which had been of a golden hue became dark and the thirty-two Marks of a Great Man were obliterated. Then the Bodhisatta, having gone to the extreme[3] of austerities thought, "But this is not the Way to Awakening", and walking for almsfood in villages and market-towns so as to eat substantial nutriment, he obtained it. Then his thirty-two glorious Marks were restored and his body was golden-coloured.

Then the group of five monks thought, "Though he has been engaging in austerities for six years he has not been able to penetrate omniscience. Now that he is walking for almsfood through villages, market-towns and capital cities and is obtaining substantial nutriment what will he be able to do? He is living in abundance, is wavering in striving, what is he to us?" Abandoning the Great Man they went to the seers' resort near Bārāṇasī.

Then on the full-moon day of Visākha the Bodhisatta arrived at the market-town of Senānī[4] near Uruvelā; in the house of a landowner in Senānī[4] there was a girl named Sujātā. **[287]** Having accepted a golden bowl and partaken of the sweet milk-rice infused with deva-like nutritive essence that was given by her, who was filled with joyousness, from the bank of the Nerañjarā he threw it upstream and awakened the sleeping nāga-king Kāla. Then the Bodhisatta, after making a day-sojourn in a delightful sāla-grove which was dark in appearance, beautifully adorned with fragrant blossoms, went in the evening towards the Tree of Awakening by a way adorned by devatās. Devas, nāgas, yakkhas, siddhas[5]

[1] koṭippatta, until the end, i.e. nibbāna, is reached. Perhaps the same as koṭigata, cf. Nd2 436, rather than "extreme" of PED of similar passage at Jā i 67.

[2] Probably, daily is meant.

[3] Here, *anta*.

[4] BvAB reads Sena.

[5] An accomplished one; see MQ i 168 (Miln 120) where these all appear to be ones who made successful asseverations of truth.

and so forth paid homage to him with garlands, perfumes and unguents.

At that time a brahman named Sotthiya, a grass-cutter, came along from the opposite direction carrying grass; knowing the aspect of a Great Man, he gave him eight handfuls of grass. Accepting the grass, the Bodhisatta approached an Assattha Tree of Awakening resembling a hill of black collyrium, like one's own heart in a net of darkness, its shade cool (like) the coolness of compassion, not overcrowded by flocks of birds, as though dancing adorned with its massive branches, as though, fanned by gentle breezes, it was exhilarated with zest, as though resplendent among hosts of trees[1], (and) having thrice circumambulated the Assattha, king of trees,[2] standing at the north-east side he grasped those grasses by the tips and scattered them. At once there was a fourteen cubit (place for) sitting cross-legged. And it was as if those grasses were lines drawn by an artist.

Just as the Bodhisatta was seated there on the grass-spreading that was fourteen cubits in extent, sprouts of the Tree of Awakening, falling down, shone (like) coral arranged on a golden plate. As the Bodhisatta was sitting like that, the deva-putta, Vassavatimāra, thinking, "Prince Siddhattha wants to pass beyond my sphere, but I will not give it to him now to pass beyond it", told this matter to Māra's forces, and departed together with Māra's forces. It is said that that army of Māra stretched twelve yojanas ahead of Māra, likewise on the left side and on the right, but behind him, standing above the rim of the mountains surrounding the world it was nine yojanas in height. And the sound of its shoutings was heard from a thousand yojanas away like the sound of the earth splitting open.

At that time Sakka[3], king of devas, was standing and blowing on his conch named Vijayuttara. It is said that that conch was about one hundred and twenty cubits (long). Pañcasikha, the deva-putta who was a heavenly musician, bringing a yellow lute[4] made of vilva wood and three gāvutas in length, stood playing on it and singing songs connected with good omens. Suyāma, king of devas stood holding a deva-like fly-whisk that was splendid as the moon, three gāvutas in length, and fanning himself very pleasantly. And Brahmā Sahampati stood holding over the Lord a white sun-

[1] taru. [2] duma.

[3] Cf. Mhvs xxxi 78, 82f. for the devas mentioned in this paragraph.

[4] Given by Sakka to Pañcasikha, SnA 394; also cf. Vism 392.

shade three yojanas in extent, like a second full-moon. Mahākāla, too, the nāga-king, surrounded by eighty thousand relations, stood honouring the Great Being, sending forth hundreds of praises. In the ten-thousand world-systems the devatās stood sending forth applause while paying homage to him with manifold fragrant blossoms, wreaths, incense, scented powders and so forth.

Then when Māra [**288**] the deva-putta, had mounted Girimekhala, a noble elephant[1], a hundred and fifty yojanas in height, resembling a mountain-peak, extremely lovely to behold, the glorious trappings inlaid with gems, he created a thousand arms and with a firm grasp seized hold of various weapons. Māra's company, too, going along carrying on high a variety of swords, axes, arrows, daggers and bows, clubs, javelins[2], spikes, barbed darts, lances and stones, cudgels, spears, lances[3], wheels, discs, (uttering) sounds like those made by lions, birds, sarabha-deer, tigers, monkeys, snakes, cats, owls, (uttering) sounds (like those made by) buffaloes, spotted deer, horses, elephants [4] and so forth, and with terrifying, hideous, revolting bodies, with bodies like men, yakkhas, pisācas, they[5] went to the Great Being, the Bodhisatta, as he was seated in the open air at the root of the Tree of Awakening and, surrounding him, stood looking towards Māra's vicinity. Then, as Māra's forces were approaching the dais round the Tree of Awakening not even one of those—Sakka and so forth—was able to remain. Each fled in the direction he was facing. And Sakka, king of devas, on fleeing, put the conch Vijayuttara on his back and stood on the outer rim of the mountains surrounding the world. The Great Brahmā, placing the white sunshade on the summit of the mountains surrounding the world, simply went to the Brahma-world. Kāla, the nāga-king, throwing aside all his relations, plunged into the earth and going to the Mañjerika nāga-abode which was five hundred yojanas in extent, lay down covering his face with his hands. Not even one devatā was capable of remaining there. The Great Man sat quite alone like Great Brahmā in the empty mansion.[6] "Now Māra will come" he thought, and

[1] Cf. text p. 8, which reads arivāraṇa varavāraṇa, which perhaps is the right reading for arivāraṇavāraṇa above.

[2] BvAC hali, BvAB phāla; see PED s.v. phāla.

[3] kappaṇa, M-W s.v. karpaṇa, a kind of lance or spear.

[4] dirada, see text p. 210.

[5] I.e. Māra's company.

[6] D i 17.

at once there appeared unpleasing bad portents in manifold forms.

> At the time when the battle between the kinsman of the careless and the kinsman of the three worlds was in progress torches went out all around and the quarters, dark with smoke, were terrible. ||
>
> Even this[1] that is incognizant, but as though cognizant, quivered with the oceans and various things it supported like a creeper in the wind, like a woman desiring separation even from her lord. ||
>
> The waters and seas were in commotion, the rivers ran[2] only against the current, the tops of the mountains crashed down to earth splitting together many a tree. ||
>
> A fierce wind raged all round, tumultuous was the noise of destruction; a terrible darkness went with the sun as he roamed in the heavens like a headless corpse. ||
>
> Thus extremely unpropitious, unpleasing, and terrible was it for birds that were hiding. At the coming of Māra there were indeed countless bad portents all round. ||
>
> **[289]** But the company of devas, seeing that he indeed wanted to destroy that deva of devas, being compassionate, made the sound 'Alas, alas' together with the female deities. ||
>
> Like an eagle in the midst of birds, like a lion, supreme in the midst of beasts, the one of great renown sat in the midst of Māra's forces, confident, without fear. ||

Then Māra thought, "When I have terrified Siddhattha I will make him flee". But, unable to make the Bodhisatta flee by the nine downpours[3]: by wind, rain, a rain of missiles, a rain of rocks, then[4] burning charcoal, hot ashes, sand, mud, darkness—furiously angry in mind, he had Māra's company commanded, saying, "Why do you, sirs, stand still? Make it evident that he is not accomplished,[5] seize him, cut him, shackle him, make

[1] The earth.

[2] vahiṁsu, drew (away) (?).

[3] This is the same list as at SnA 224 and Jā i 73. But above, the first compound, *vātavassaṁ*, must be taken as standing for two downpours (cf. *vātavassāhi* at PvA 55) so as to bring the total to nine, and not as one downpour in spite of the next 2 compounds, *paharaṇāvassaṁ* and *pāsāṇavassaṁ*, each standing for one downpour. Another 9-fold downpour, rather different, occurs at text. p 199.

[4] puna.

[5] Siddhatthamasiddhattaṁ. Cf. asiddhattā at Vism 509.

him flee", and himself seated on Girimekhala's back, twirling an arrow with one hand, he approached the Bodhisatta and said, "Good Siddhattha, rise from the cross-legged position". And Māra's company worked very terrible oppression on the Great Being.

But the Great Being, by the might of his own perfections of patience, loving-kindness, energy, wisdom and so forth, having shattered even those forces of Māra together with Māra, having recollected former habitations during the first watch (of the night), purified deva-like vision during the middle watch, towards evening entered on knowledge according to the method of conditions[1] customary to all Buddhas. When by in-breathing and out-breathing, making this the basis itself, he had achieved the four meditations, increasing insight, by following the Way he had discovered, flinging aside all the defilements by means of the fourth Way, penetrating all the special qualities of a Buddha, he uttered the solemn utterance customary to all Buddhas "Through many a birth in saṁsāra . . . the destruction of cravings." As the Lord was seated after having uttered it, it occurred to him, "I, by reason of this cross-legged position during the hundred thousand eons and the four incalculables through which I have run, will not rise from my cross-legged position, the cross-legged position of heroes where I am sitting, till my intentions have been fulfilled". He sat there for seven days entering upon the attainments which numbered countless hundred thousands of crores. In reference to this it was said, "Then the Lord sat in the one cross-legged position for seven days experiencing the bliss of freedom."*

Then a reasoning arose to certain devas, "Now, surely there is still something to be done by Siddhattha today in that he does not abandon his posture in the cross-legged position." Then the teacher, knowing the devatās' reasoning and for the sake of allaying their reasoning, rising above the ground, displayed the Marvel of the Double. Having allayed thus the devatās' reasoning by this Marvel, he stood to the northern side facing slightly towards the east of where he had been sitting cross-legged. He thought, "Indeed, omniscient knowledge has been pierced by me when I

* Vin i 1. Cf. VA 957, UdA 51f.

[1] paccayākāra, referring to the "chain" of Conditioned Genesis.

was in this cross-legged position", [290] and he passed seven days surveying with steadfast gaze the place of the cross-legged position for it was the place of his attainment of the perfections that he had fulfilled during the four incalculables and the hundred thousand eons. That place received the name Animisacetiya "Cetiya of the Steadfast Gaze". Then having created the Walk stretching from west to east between the place where he had stood and that where he had sat cross-legged, he passed seven days walking up and down on the Jewel-Walk. That place received the name Ratanacetiya "Jewel Cetiya".

In the fourth week devatās created Ratanaghara "Jewel-House" to the north-west of the Tree of Awakening. Seated there in the cross-legged position he passed seven days thinking out the Abhidhamma-piṭaka. That place received the name Ratanaghara-cetiya "Cetiya of the Jewel-House".

Thus, having passed exactly four weeks near the Tree of Awakening, in the fifth week he approached Ajapāla's Banyan from the root of the Tree of Awakening. And he sat just there thinking out Dhamma and experiencing the bliss of freedom.

Having passed seven days there he went on to the root of the Mucalinda. There, because of the onset of seven days of rainy weather, he passed a week, experiencing the bliss of freedom, with the coils of Mucalinda, the nāga-king, wrapped seven times around him as a protection against the cold and so forth as though he were staying comfortably in the Scented Chamber. Then he approached the Rājāyatana (tree) passing a week there. There too he sat for exactly a week experiencing the bliss of freedom. Up to now seven weeks had been completed. In this space of time there had been no need for the Lord either to rinse his mouth or to attend to his physical frame or to bathe; he spent the time simply in the bliss of the fruits. Then at the end of the seven weeks, on the forty-ninth day, the teacher rinsed his mouth with tooth-wood from an ironwood tree and with water brought by Sakka, chief of devas, from Lake Anotatta. He sat just there at the root of the Rājāyatana (tree).

At that time two merchants, named Tapassu and Bhalluka, were encouraged by a devatā who was a blood-relation of theirs to give nutriment to the Lord. Taking rice-cakes and honey-balls, they approached the Lord and stood there saying, "May the Lord accept this nutriment out of compassion". Because of the disappearance of the bowl that had been given by the deva[1] on the very day he had accepted the milk-rice, the Lord thought, "Tathāgatas do not receive food in the hands. Now, how shall I receive this?" Then the Four Great Regents, knowing the Lord's thoughts, brought from the four quarters four bowls made of sapphire.[2] The Lord refused these. So they brought four bowls made of stone the colour of kidney-beans. Having accepted (these) simply out of compassion for these four devaputtas, making them into one, receiving the nutriment into that new bowl made of stone and making use of it, the Lord gave the benediction. Those two merchant-brothers, going to the Buddha and Dhamma for refuge, became lay-followers using the two-fold formula.

The teacher, returning to the Ajapāla Banyan sat down at the root of the banyan. No sooner was he seated there and was reflecting on the profundity of the Dhamma at which he had arrived than, **[291]** as is the custom of all Buddhas, he thought, "This is the Dhamma at which I have arrived".[3] And the reasoning arose (to him) that he had no kind of desire to teach Dhamma to others. Then Brahmā Sahampati, saying "Indeed, sir, the world is lost", taking from among the ten-thousand world-systems Sakka, Suyāma, Santusita, (the devas who) delight in creating, those who delight in the creation of others, and the Great Brahmās, he went into the teacher's presence and requested a teaching on Dhamma in the way beginning, "Reverend sir, may the Lord teach Dhamma."

Then the teacher, giving him an assurance, thought, "To whom should I first teach Dhamma?" Knowing that Āḷāra and Uddaka had done their (kammic) time, he thought, "The group of five monks was very useful to me", and reasoning carefully about the group of five and reflecting, "Now, where are they staying at present?" and knowing, "In the deer-sanctuary near Bārāṇasī, he thought, "Going there, I will turn the Wheel of Dhamma". But when he had stayed for a few days walking for alms in the vicinity of the dais of the Tree of Awakening itself, he thought, "On the full-moon day of Āsāḷha I will go to Bārāṇasī", and taking bowl and robe he went eighteen yojanas along the road. Seeing the exultant Naked Ascetic named Upaka on the highway and having

[1] This must refer to Sujātā's golden bowl which she had been taking to the tree-devatā but gave to the Bodhisatta instead, see e.g. text pp. 7, 287.

[2] indanīlamaṇimaya as at DA 244.

[3] For the following cf. Vin i 4ff.

pointed out to him his own Buddha-status, he arrived at the seers' resort in the evening of that same day.

But the group of five, seeing the Tathāgata coming in the distance, made a bond to the effect that, "This, friends, is the recluse Gotama who is coming; he has reverted to a life of abundance, his body is rounded, he is joyful at heart, he is the colour of gold. We will not greet him but only make ready a seat". The Lord, knowing the disposition of their minds, concentrating on a mind of loving-kindness capable of suffusing all creatures in general suffused them in particular with a mind of loving-kindness. Suffused by the Lord's mind of loving-kindness, these, unable to adhere to their own bond, greeted the Tathāgata as he came ever nearer and did all the proper duties. Then the Lord, informing them of his own Buddha-status, sat down on the glorious Buddha-seat that had been made ready. While the asterism of Uttarāsāḷha was in progress and he was surrounded by eighteen crores of brahmans, addressing the group of the five Elders he taught the Discourse of the Turning of the Wheel of Dhamma.[1] Of these, Aññākoṇḍañña, ordering his knowledge in conformity to the teaching, at the end of the Discourse was established together with the eighteen crores of brahmans in the fruit of stream-entry. Accordingly it was said:

XXVI 1 I at the present time am the Self-Awakened One[2] Gotama, one who advances the glory of the Sakyans. When I had striven the striving I attained supreme Self-Awakening.

2 On being requested by Brahmā I turned the Wheel of Dhamma. The first penetration was by eighteen crores.

1 Therein *I* demonstrates self.

1 *At the present time* means in this time.[3]

[292] 1 *One who advances the glory of the Sakyans*[4] means one who advances the glory of the Sākiyan clan. "A Sakyan great-man"[4] is also a reading.

[1] Vin i 10.

[2] Be, BvACB sambuddha, Bv buddha.

[3] etarahī ti asmiṁ kāle. The meaning of etarahi is clearly not the same as idāni and the word should not be translated as "now". Rather is it opposed to atīte, in the past. See text p. 293, comment on ver. 11, 12.

[4] Sakyavaddhano . . . Sakyapuṅgavo. Lit. puṅgava is a bull.

1 *The striving* is called (right) conduct.[1]

1 *When I had striven* means when I had exerted myself, endeavoured, engaged in austerities.

2 *By eighteen crores:* the meaning is that at the talk of the Discourse of Turning the Wheel of Dhamma at the seers' resort in the deer-sanctuary near Bārāṇasī there was the first penetration by eighteen crores of brahmans headed by the Elder Aññākoṇḍañña.

Now the Lord, having talked about a past, said, talking about a future penetration:

XXVI 3 And subsequently when I was teaching in a gathering of men and deities[2] there was the second penetration, not to be told by number.

3 Therein *in a gathering of men and deities* means that at a time after that at a gathering for the Mahāmaṅgala in the midst of devas and men in the ten-thousand world-systems, at the conclusion of the Maṅgala-sutta[3] *there was* (ahu) *the second penetration*, meaning "there will be" (hessati), by devas and men going beyond the way of counting. Though the future tense should be used, *was* was spoken in the past tense on account of its effect on the ear[4] or owing to a change of tense. And henceforth for other similar phrases[5] this is the method. Again, at the teaching of the Discourse on the Exhortation to Rāhula[6] he made beings beyond the way of counting to drink of the drink that is the nectar of penetration. That was the third penetration. Accordingly it was said:

XXVI 4 Here, at the present time, when I myself exhorted[7] my son there was the third penetration, not to be told by number.

It is said that the Lord had only one assembly of disciples. It was an assembly of one thousand two hundred and fifty of these: of a thousand matted hair ascetics under Uruvela-Kassapa (and his

[1] But see definitions at text pp. 78, 94, 139.

[2] BvAC desente naramarūnaṁ samāgame; Be, BvAB desente naradevatasamāgame; Bv desento naradevasamāgamo.

[3] See text p. 136.

[4] Read sotapatitattā.

[5] Or, tenses, vacana.

[6] Probably the Cūḷa-Rāhulovādasutta, M Sta 147.

[7] BvAC uses future tense, Bv, Be, BvAB aorist.

brothers)[1], and of two hundred and fifty under the two chief disciples.[2] Accordingly it was said:

XXVI 5 I had only one assembly of disciples, great seers; it was a gathering of one thousand two hundred and fifty monks.

5 Therein *I had one* means I had only one[3].

5 *Of one thousand two hundred and fifty* means of twelve hundred and of fifty in addition.

5 *It was of monks* means it was of monks.[4]

And the Lord recited the Pātimokkha in the midst of these in an assembly having the four factors[5]. Then the Lord, pointing out his own procedure, spoke beginning:

XXVI 6 Shining, stainless, in the midst of the Order, like the jewel granting all desires I give everything that is aspired after.

[**293**] 6 Therein *shining* means shining with the splendour of a Buddha.

6 *Stainless* means gone was the dust of attachment and so forth and of the defilements.

6 *Like the jewel granting all desires* means that he said, "As the cintāmaṇī[6] so too am I a giver of all desires; I give all the variety of mundane and super-mundane happiness that is wished for and aspired after."

Now, pointing out the aspirations aspired after he spoke beginning:

XXVI 7 To those longing for fruition, to those seeking to get rid of the craving for becoming I expound the four truths out of compassion for breathing things.

7 Therein *fruition* means the fourfold fruition beginning with the fruition of stream-entry.

[1] Vin i 24.
[2] Ibid. 42.
[3] eko ˀsī ti eko va āsi. Bv reads eko va.
[4] bhikkhūnˀ āsī ti bhikkhūnaṁ āsi.
[5] Cf. text pp. 126, 163, 169, 294, 249, 298.
[6] A fabulous gem supposed to yield its possessor all desires—a philosopher's stone. At VvA 32 a deed of merit is likened to it and to the tree that grants all desires, kapparukkha. To be distinguished from cintāmaṇī as a vijjā, science.

7 *To those seeking to get rid of the craving for becoming* means: to those abandoning the thirst for becoming, to those anxious to abandon the thirst for becoming.

7 *Out of compassion* means out of mercy.

Now, pointing out the penetration during the expounding of the four truths, he spoke beginning "by tens and twenties of thousands".

8 *By tens and twenties of thousands* means by tens of thousands and by twenties of thousands.

8 *By ones and twos* means in the way beginning thus.

The ninth and tenth verses are quite clear.

11, 12 In the eleventh and twelfth verses *now at the present time* means that both phrases (idān' etarahi), because they lend themselves (to this) as they are one in meaning, are said (together) like purisapuggalā. Or, *now* means: since I have arisen; *at the present time* means: while (I am) teaching Dhamma.

11 *Without having attained their purpose* means without having attained the fruits of arahantship.

12 *The direct ariyan Way* means the ariyan eightfold Way.

12 *Delighting in* means commending.

12 *Will awaken* means: in the future they will pierce, which means they will conduct themselves by, the Dhamma of the four truths.

12 *The stream of saṁsāra* means the ocean of saṁsāra.[1]

Now pointing out his own natal city and so forth, he spoke beginning:

> 13 My city is Kapilavatthu, King Suddhodana is my father, my genetrix and mother is known as Queen Māyā.
>
> 14 I lived the household life for twenty-nine years.[2] The three superb palaces were Ramma, Suramma, Subhaka.[3]
>
> 15 There were forty thousand beautifully adorned women. Yasodharā[4] was the name of my wife, Rāhula the name of my son.

[1] BvACB saṁsārasaritan ti saṁsārasāgaraṁ. Bv saṁsārasaritā narā, Be saṁsārasaritaṁ gatā.

[2] Line alters in Bv and Be.

[3] Bv Rāma Surāma Subhata. BvAC has v. l. Sucandaka Kokanada Koñcaya; Jkm 27 reads Canda Kokanuda Koñca.

[4] Bv Bhaddakaccā, Be, BvAB, Jkm 27 Bhaddakaccānā; Jkm also calls her Rāhulamātā and BvAB Yasodharā in the prose following the verses. See DPPN

[294] 16 After I had seen the four signs I departed on horseback. For six years I engaged in striving, difficult to do.

17 The Conqueror's Wheel was turned[1] in the seers' resort near Bārāṇasī. I, Gotama the Self-Awakened One, am the refuge for all breathing things.

18 The two monks, Kolita and Upatissa, are the chief disciples. Ānanda is the name of the attendant attending closely upon me.

19 The nuns Khemā and Uppalavaṇṇā are the chief women disciples. Citta and Haṭṭhāḷavaka are the chief lay attendants.

20 Nandamātā and Uttarā are the chief laywomen attendants. I attained supreme Self-Wakening at the root of an Assattha.

21 The lustre of my fathom-deep halo always rises sixteen cubits high. Now at the present time the (normal) life-span is a brief hundred years.

22 Living so long I am causing many people to cross over, having established the torch of Dhamma (and) the awakening of the people who come after.

23 But I, in no long time, together with the Order of disciples, will wane out entirely here like a fire on the consumption of the fuel.

And my three palaces, named Ramma, Suramma, Subha, had nine storeys, seven storeys, five storeys (respectively). There were forty thousand dancing-women. Yasodharā was the name of my chief consort. When I had seen the four signs I departed on the Great Departure on horseback. Then, having striven the striving for six years, on the full-moon day of Visākha I partook of sweet milk-rice given by Sujātā, the graceful[2] daughter of Senānī, a land-owner in the market-town of Senānī near Uruvelā. Having passed the day-sojourn in a sāla-grove, towards evening I accepted eight handfuls of grass given by Sotthiya, a grass-cutter, and approached the root of the Assattha Tree of Awakening. Routing

---

s.v. Rāhulamātā; E. J. Thomas, Life of Buddha, pp. 49f., 59; Et. Lamotte, Le Traité de la Grande Vertu de Sagesse, II 1001.

[1] BvAC jinacakkaṁ pavattitaṁ, Bv, Be cakkaṁ pavattitaṁ mayā.

[2] sampasādajāta can also mean serene, trustful, propitious.

Māra's forces there, I declared to all,[1] "I am attained to Self-Awakening".

23 Therein *together with the Order of disciples* means together with the Order of disciples.[2]

23 *I will wane out entirely* means I will wane out entirely.[3]

23 *Like a fire on the consumption of the fuel* means like a fire; as a fire on the destruction of the firing[4] **[295]** wanes out lacking in fuel[5], so too will I entirely wane out lacking in grasping.[5]

24 *Body with the glorious special qualities*[6] means this body with special qualities[7]: the six knowledges not shared (with others).

24 *And those of unrivalled incandescence* means these pairs of chief disciples and so forth whose incandescence is unique.

24 *And these ten powers* means: and these ten powers of the physical frame.

25 *Will disappear* means: all these[8], spoken of as mentioned[9], will disappear, will be lost[10].

25 *Are not all constructions void?* means: herein *are not* is a particle in the sense of assent. *Void* means void, empty, being without the essence of the permanent, the essence of the stable. "For everything of which I am constructed[11], being liable to destruction, liable to decay, liable to the cessation of dispassion is impermanent owing to (its) non-existence; it is anguish because it is hard pressed by arising and so forth; it is not-self owing to (one's having) it not under subjection[12]". Therefore, having shown the three characteristic marks that are in the constructions, having

[1] sabbaṁ vyākāsi could also mean "I declared (it) all."

[2] saddhiṁ (om. in error in Ee of BvAC) sāvakasaṅghato ti saddhiṁ sāvakasaṅghena.

[3] parinibbissan ti parinibbāyissāmi.

[4] ind(h)anakkhayena.

[5] nirūpādāna means both lack of fuel and of grasping. The meaning is that where there is no grasping after, in particular, bhava, existence, there is no fuel remaining for a new birth, no attachment to it, no holding on to it. Cf. text pp. 166, 219.

[6] BvAC guṇdharavaradeho; Bv guṇavaradeho; Be, BvAB guṇadhāraṇo deho, where the reading is due perhaps to attraction by the next word, asadhāraṇañāṇāni.

[7] guṇadharo, or, bearing special qualities.

[8] BvAB etāhi, BvAC vuttāni.

[9] I.e. in ver. 24.

[10] BvAC nassissanti, BvAB vinass-.

[11] sabbam me saṇkhataṁ. Cf. M i 500, S ii 26.

[12] avasavattana, cf. MA i 73, UdA 236.

increased insight, he arrived at the undying, the unconstructed, the immovable, nibbāna. "This is now our instruction, our teaching for you: Go forward with diligence.[1]"

It is said that on the conclusion of the teaching the minds of a thousand crores of devatās were freed from the cankers without grasping, and that those who were established in the remaining ways and fruits were beyond the ways of counting. Thus the Lord, having spoken even the entire Chronicle of Buddhas arranged by eon, name, birth and so forth as he was walking up and down on the Jewel-Walk in the sky, having caused his relations to honour him[2], descended from the sky and sat down on the glorious Buddha-seat that had been made ready. And as the Lord, protector of the world, was sitting down there was a gathering of (his) relations who had attained to the training[3]. They all sat down, their minds one-pointed. Then a great storm-cloud rained down a lotus rain[4]. At that moment the water went roaring down. It wetted only him who wanted to get wet. Not even as much as a drop fell on the physical frame of him who did not want to get wet. Everyone who saw this was filled with wonder and astonishment and set going the talk, "Ah, wonderful, astonishing".[5] When he had heard this the teacher said, "Not only now did lotus-rain rain down at a gathering of (my) relations. It rained down in the past too". He spoke the Vessantara-jātaka[6] because of this need arisen.[7] The teaching of Dhamma came with the need (for it). Then the Lord, rising from his seat, entered the vihāra.

XXVII 1 *Immeasurable eons ago there were four guiders away* means that the eighteen verses beginning thus[8] were established

[1] D ii 156.

[2] See text p. 24f. From here to almost the end of the paragraph is also part of the Intr. to Vessantara-jātaka (No 547, vol. vi 479). Much shorter at DhA iii 163.

[3] BvACB sikhāppatto, as noticed at Jā vi 479 which reads sikkhā-.

[4] Cf. Jā i 88, KhA 164 where pokkharavassa also has this property of wetting only those who want to get wet but not those who want to keep dry. The word occurs also at DhA iii 163.

[5] Referring to Bv i 27.

[6] Jā No 547.

[7] aṭṭhuppatti, see text p. 64.

[8] These verses appear in No xxvii, the "Miscellancy of the Buddhas" which, following the Chronicle of Gotama, consists of 20 verses. At the end of the eighteenth verse Morris remarks that "here the Buddhavaṁsa rightly ends". Not only were two verses added in xxvii, but the whole of No xxviii on the Distri-

by the recensionists and should be understood as Envoi Verses. Everywhere remaining in the verses is quite clear.

Concluded is the Exposition of the Chronicle of the
Buddha Gotama
in the Commentary on the Chronicle of Buddhas
called Clarifier of Sweet Meaning

Concluded is the twenty-fifth Buddha-Chronicle

THE EXPOSITION OF DIFFERENCES BETWEEN THE BUDDHAS

[**296**] And now eight differences[1] between the twenty-five Buddhas who have been designated in this whole *Chronicle of Buddhas* must be spoken of. What are the eight[2]? Difference in (the length of the) life-span, difference in height, difference in family, difference in (the time required for) the striving, difference in (the extent of) the rays, difference in the vehicle, difference in the Tree of Awakening, difference in (the size of the spreading for) the cross-legged position.

Therein difference in (the length of the) life-span means that some were of long life-span, some of short life-span. So, in this respect these nine Buddhas were of a life-span of a hundred thousand years: Dīpaṅkara, Koṇḍañña, Anomadassin, Paduma, Padumuttara, Atthadassin, Dhammadassin, Siddhattha, Tissa. These eight Buddhas were of a life-span of ninety thousand years: Maṅgala, Sumana, Sobhita, Nārada, Sumedha, Sujāta, Piyadassin, Phussa. And these two Buddhas were of a life-span of sixty thousand years: Revata, Vessabhū. The Lord Vipassin was of a life-span of eighty thousand years. These four Buddhas were of a life-span of seventy, forty, thirty, twenty thousand years respectively: Sikhin, Kakusandha, Koṇāgamana, Kassapa. Our Lord was of a life-span of a hundred years. Even among Buddhas whose merits were accumulated and who were furnished with kammas

bution of the Relics. BvA does not comment on any of these. Instead, in the following Section it recounts the differences between the Buddhas.

[1] Cf. the five at text, p. 130.

[2] Eight also, but somewhat differently given, at SnA 407f.

conducing to long life-spans, on account of the world-period the length of the life-span was without measure. This is called difference[1] in the life-span of the twenty-five Buddhas.[2]

Difference in height means that some were tall, some short. So, in this respect the measure of the physical frame of the Buddhas, Dīpaṅkara, Revata, Piyadassin, Atthadassin, Dhammadassin, Vipassin was eighty cubits in height. The body of Koṇḍañña, Maṅgala, Nārada, Sumedha was eighty-eight cubits in height. The physical frame of Sumana was ninety cubits in height. The physical frame of the Buddhas Sobhita, Anomadassin, Paduma, Padumuttara, Phussa was fifty-eight cubits in height. The physical frame of Sujāta was fifty cubits in height. Siddhattha, Tissa, Vessabhū were sixty cubits in height. Sikhin was seventy cubits in height. Kakusandha, Koṇāgamana, Kassapa were respectively forty, thirty, twenty cubits in height. Our Lord was eighteen cubits in height. This is called difference in the height of the twenty-five Buddhas.

Difference in family means that some were born in a warrior-noble family, some in a brahman family. The Fully Self-Awakened Ones Kakusandha, Koṇāgamana, Kassapa were born in a brahman family, the remaining twenty-two Fully Self-Awakened Ones in a warrior-noble family. This is called difference in family of the twenty-five Buddhas.

Difference in (the time required for) the striving means that the striving engaged in by Dīpaṅkara, Koṇḍañña, Sumana, Anomadassin, Sujāta,[3] Siddhattha, Kakusandha[4] was for ten months. By Maṅgala, Sumedha, Tissa, Sikhin it was for eight months. By Revata for seven months. By Sobhita for four months[5]. By Paduma, Atthadassin, Vipassin it was for half a month. By Nārada, Padumuttara, Dhammadasin, Kassapa **[297]** it was for seven days. By Piyadassin, Phussa, Vessabhū, Koṇāgamana it was for six months. Our Buddha's engagement in striving was for six years. This is called difference in (the time required for) the striving.

Difference in (the extent of) the rays means: it is said that the rays from the physical frame of Maṅgala, Fully Self-Awakened

[1] BvAC vemattatā throughout, BvAB vemattaṁ.

[2] BvAB adds pañcavīsatiya buddhānaṁ here and for the next two cases where Buddhas differ.

[3] Bv xiii 23: nine months.

[4] Bv xxiii 18: eight months.

[5] Bv vii 19: seven days.

One, remained suffusing the ten-thousand world-system. The Buddha Padumuttara's were of twelve yojanas. The Lord Vipassin's were of seven yojanas. Of Sikhin the measure was three yojanas. Of the Lord Kakusandha it was ten yojanas. Of our Lord it was merely a fathom all round. Of the remainder it is undetermined. This difference in (the extent of) the rays is called dependent on the inclination—that lustre of his physical frame suffused as far as he wished. But there is no difference between any of them in the special qualities acquired. This is called difference in the (extent of) the rays.

Difference in the vehicle means that some departed riding an elephant, others departed variously by horse, chariot, foot, palace, palanquin. In this respect Dīpaṅkara, Sumana, Sumedha, Phussa, Sikhin, Koṇāgamana departed riding an elephant. And Koṇḍañña, Revata, Paduma, Piyadassin, Vipassin, Kakusandha by means of a chariot. Maṅgala, Sujāta, Atthadassin, Tissa, Gotama on horseback. Anomadassin, Siddhattha, Vessabhū by means of a palanquin. Nārada on foot. Sobhita, Padumuttara, Dhammadassin, Kassapa departed by palace. This is called difference in the vehicle.

Difference in the Tree of Awakening means that the Tree of Awakening of the Lord Dīpaṅkara was the Kapitthana[1]. The Tree of Awakening of Koṇḍañña was the lovely Sāla. The Tree of Awakening of Maṅgala, Sumana, Revata, Sobhita was the Nāga. The Tree of Awakening of Anomadassin was the Ajjuna. The Tree of Awakening of Paduma, Nārada was the Great Soṇa. The Tree of Awakening of Padumuttara was the Salaḷa. Of Sumedha the Nīpa. Of Sujāta the Veḷu. Of Piyadassin the Kakudha. Of Atthadassin the Campaka Tree. Of Dhammadassin the Kuravaka[2] Tree. Of Siddhattha the Kanikāra. Of Tissa the Asana. Of Phussa the Āmalaka[3] Tree. Of Vipassin the Pāṭalī Tree. Of Sikhin the Puṇḍarīka Tree. Of Vessabhū the Sāla Tree. Of Kakusandha the Sirīsa Tree. Of Koṇāgamana the Udumbara Tree. Of Kassapa the Nigrodha. Of Gotama the Assattha. This is called difference in the Tree of Awakening.

Difference in (the size of) the spreading[4] for the cross-legged

[1] So BvAC; kapītana at BvAB, Feronia elephantum. His Tree is given as pipphalī at IIB 214. See text p. 129, pipphalī ti pilakkhakapitthanarukkha. For these Trees see CB, Intr. xliff. and EC 13ff., notes.

[2] BvAB rattakarūvaka.

[3] BvAC āmala.

[4] Cf. this list with that giving the heights of the Buddhas, text p. 296.

position means that for Dīpaṅkara, Revata, Piyadassin, Atthadassin, Dhammadassin, Vipassin it was fifty-three cubits[1]. For Koṇḍañña, Maṅgala, Nārada, Sumedha it was fifty-seven cubits.[2] For Sumana (the size of the spreading for the) cross-legged position was sixty cubits.[3] For Sobhita[4], Anomadassin, Paduma, Padumuttara, Phussa it was thirty-eight cubits. For Sujāta thirty-two cubits[5]. For Siddhattha, Tissa, Vessabhū forty cubits. For Sikhin thirty-two cubits[6]. For Kakusandha twenty-six cubits[7]. For Koṇāgamana twenty cubits. For Kassapa fifteen cubits. For Gotama (the size of) the spreading for the cross-legged position was fourteen cubits. This is called difference in (the size of) the spreading for the cross-legged position.

And for all Buddhas there are four unalterable places[8]: **[298]** unalterable for all Buddhas is the cross-legged position for Awakening in one place only; the turning of the Wheel of Dhamma in a seers' resort in a deer-sanctuary is also unalterable; the placing of the first footstep at the gateway of the city of Saṅkassa at the time of descending from the devas is also unalterable; the positions for the four legs of the bed in the Scented Chamber in Jetavana are unalterable. And the vihāra whether it be small or large indeed does not alter, only the city alters[9].

We showed the demarcation of those born simultaneously with our Lord and the demarcation of the asterisms[10]. It is said that these seven were born simultaneously together with our omniscient Bodhisatta: Rāhula's mother, the Elder Ānanda,[11] Channa, Kanthaka, the treasure-urn(s)[12], the great Tree of Awakening, Kāḷudāyin. This is demarcation by simultaneous birth.

[1] Ninety for Dīpaṅkara, text p. 83.

[2] Fifty-eight, fifty-eight, fifty-eight, twenty respectively at text pp. 133, 142, 183, 197.

[3] Thirty at text p. 153.

[4] No cross-legged position mentioned in Comy. on Sobhita's Chronicle.

[5] Thirty-three at text p. 203.

[6] Thus the same as Sujāta's. Text p. 243 gives twenty-four.

[7] Thirty-four at text p. 253.

[8] Cf. text p. 131.

[9] *vijahati*, alters, or leaves the place where are the legs of the bed. Clearly, the vihāra must be where they are so cannot move or alter. But the city, though always attached to the vihāra, may be at different points of the compass, N.S.E. or W. of the vihāra (which can vary in size but not in position) and thus of the bed. I have followed the reading at BvAB: vihāro na vijahati yeva nagaraṁ para vijahati.

[10] See text p. 131.

[11] BvAC omits.

[12] *nidhikumbho* here, *-bhā* at text p. 131.

And under the asterism of Uttarāsāḷha the Great Man descended into his mother's womb, departed on the Great Departure, turned the Wheel of Dhamma, performed the Marvel of the Double. Under the asterism of Visākha he was born and was fully Self-Awakened and attained final nibbāna. Under the asterism of Māgha there was the assembly of his disciples and the relinquishing of the life-span's concomitants. And under the asterism of Assayuja the descent from the devas. This is demarcation by asterisms.

Now we will explain what is regulation for all Buddhas but not shared by others. What is regulation for Self-Awakened Ones is exactly thirty-fold. That is to say: (1) on descending into his mother's womb the Bodhisatta is aware of its being his last existence; (2) the cross-legged position in the mother's womb facing outwards; (3) the standing position of the Bodhisatta's mother when she is giving birth; (4) issuing forth from the mother's womb only in a forest; (5) the feet being placed on a golden cloth, taking seven steps facing north, surveying the four quarters, roaring a lion's roar; (6) the Great Departure of the Great Beings after they have seen the four signs and a son has been born; (7) taking up the banner of an arahant[1], having gone forth, (then) engaging in striving for (at least) seven days according to all the demarcations given above;[2] (8) on the day of reaching Self-Awakening the partaking of milk-rice; (9) arrival at omniscient knowledge while seated on a grass-spreading; (10) preparation for the meditational practice of in-breathing and out-breathing; (11) the shattering of Māra's forces; (12) while still in the cross-legged position for Awakening, beginning with the three knowledges, acquisition of the special qualities beginning with the knowledges not shared (by others); (13) the spending of seven weeks close to the Tree of Awakening itself; (14) a Great Brahmā's request for the teaching of Dhamma; (15) the turning of the Wheel of Dhamma in a seers' resort in a deer-sanctuary; (16) on the full-moon day of Māgha the recital of the Pātimokkha in an assembly having the four factors; (17) regular dwelling in a place in the Jetavana; (18) the performance of the Marvel of the Double at the gateway to the city of Sāvatthī; (19) the teaching of Abhidhamma in the abode of the Thirty-Three; (20) the descent from the deva-world at the gateway to the city of Saṅkassa; (21) constantly

[1] I.e. the yellow robe as at text p. 284.
[2] Text p. 296.

attaining the attainments of the fruits; (22) surveying people who could be guided out in two meditations; (23) laying down a rule of training when a matter had arisen; (24) telling a Jātaka (-story) when a need had arisen[1]; (25) speaking the *Chronicle of Buddhas* in a gathering of relations; (26) giving a friendly welcome to incoming monks; (27) spending the rains where invited and not leaving without asking for permission; (28) every day carrying out the duties for before a meal, for after a meal, for the first, middle, last watches (of the night); (29) partaking of the flavour of meat on the day of the final nibbāna[2]; (30) the final nibbāna after having attained the twenty-four hundred thousand crores of attainments. **[299]** These, thirty exactly, are regulation for all Buddhas.

In respect of all Buddhas, no one is able to make a stumbling-block to the four requisites presented specially (to any one of them.) No one is able to make a stumbling-block to the life-span. Accordingly it was said: "It is impossible, it cannot come to pass that one should deprive a Tathāgata of life by aggression".* No one is able to make a stumbling-block to the thirty-two Marks of a Great Man (or) to the eighty minor characteristics. No one is able to make a stumbling-block to the Buddha-rays. These are called the four things not causing stumbling-blocks.[3]

Thus (lit. to this extent, so far) is accomplished the Commentary on the *Chronicle of Buddhas* adorned by various methods explained through appropriate words.
The Commentary on the Buddhavaṁsa was done by me taking indeed the way of the Ancient Commentaries which make clear the meaning of the Pali (text).
Eschewing proliferation, making clear the sweet meaning every-way—hence (its name) "The Clarifier of the Sweet Meaning."[4]
On the land purified by the flowing of the waters of the Kāvīra,

* Vin ii 194.

[1] aṭṭhuppatti, text p. 64.

[2] This would make it appear as if the sūkaramaddava, of which the Buddha Gotama's last meal consisted, was boar's flesh, pork, rather than "truffles" as sometimes has been suggested. See Intr. p. xxxix.

[3] See Miln 157 where the 4 stumbling-blocks that cannot be made are to the Lord's receiving a gift made specially for him, to his rays, omniscience, and life-principle, *jīvita*.

[4] Madhuratthappakāsinī, an alternative title to Madhuratthavilāsinī as the name of BvA.

in the delightful port of Kāvīra crowded with various men and
women, 122
In the vihāra with diverse charming walls and gates built by
pious Kaṇhadāsa[1] of gentle words, 123
In the delightful Godhāsalilasampāta,[2] with no encumbrance
from bad people, which is blissful and where there is joy of
solitude, 124
Dwelling there in the eastern building, exceedingly cool, was the
Commentary on the *Chronicle of Buddhas* made by me. 125
As this Commentary has come to a successful conclusion without
obstruction, may the pious aspirations of people likewise come
to a successful conclusion without obstruction on their way[3]. 126
Whatever amount of merit was wished for by me in doing this
Commentary on the *Chronicle of Buddhas*, ever by the power of
that may the world attain the ultimate goal (i.e. Nibbāna),
stable, permanent and peaceful. 127

Thus is concluded the Commentary on the Chronicle of Buddhas called Clarifier of Sweet Meaning[4]

The Elder (*thera*) renowned by the name Buddhadatta pronounced by his teachers, having done the Commentary,
Clarifier of Sweet Meaning, 128

[1] Skt. Kṛṣṇadāsa.

[2] Probably a palicized local name. Cf. the Siṃhala village name Attanagalla, palicized as Hatthavanagalla.

[3] Readings of this verse at BvAC and BvAB differ. BvAC reads:

Yathā vaṇṇanā ᵓyaṁ gatā sādhu siddhiṁ
vinā antarāyaṁ tathā dhammayuttā
janānaṁ vitakkā vinā cᵓantarā va
ᵓntarāyena siddhiṁ gamissantu sādhu.

And BvAB:

Yathā Buddhavaṁsassa saṁvaṇṇanā ᵓyaṁ
gatā sādhu siddhiṁ vinā antarāyaṁ
tathā dhammayuttā janānaṁ vitakkā
vināvantarāyena siddhiṁ vajantu.

[4] BvAB inserts this at the very end, and has two verses here, not in BvAC, as follows:

vinassantu rogā manussesu sabbā
pavassantu devā pi vassantakāle
sukhaṁ hotu niccaṁ paraṁ nārakā pi
visākhāpāyātā vipasā bhavantu.
surā accharānaṁ gaṇādīhi saddhaṁ
ciraṁ devaloke sukhaṁ cānubhontu
ciraṁ thātu dhammo munindassa loke
sukhaṁ lokapālā mahiṁ pālayantu.

[300] And leaving this book (manuscript) beneficial to the succession of teachers, alas! went under the power of death because of transitoriness. 12

Thus, in regard to portions for recital[1] there are 26 portions for recital; in regard to parts[2] there are 6,500 parts; in regard to syllables[3] there are 203,000 syllables.

[1] A *bhāṇavāra* consists of 8000 syllables.

[2] A *gantha* consists of 32 syllables.

[3] *akkhara* (syllable): the unit of pronunciation of a vowel alone or a vowel with a consonant. Buddhappiya says that the *akkharas* will not cease to exist (*nakkharantī ti akkharā*, *Rūpasiddhi*, ed. Paññāsekhara, Colombo, 1933, p. 2) by using them in writing. Hence they are called *akkharas*. Signification is well known by *akkhara* (*Attho akkharasaññāto*, *Kaccāna*, ed. Revata, Colombo, 1923, p. 1). The metre (*chanda*) is the harmonious order of *akkharas* (*akkharaniyamo chandam*, *Bālāvatāra*, ed. Dharmārāma, Kälaṇiya, 1948, p. 8).

Literary Work Measure:

8 syllables	= "foot", quarter of a verse or sentence
4 "foots" or quarters or 32 syllables	= verse or part
250 parts	= portion for recital, i.e. 8000 syllables.

I am indebted to Ven. Dr H. Saddhatissa for the 3 notes above and the Literary Work Measure.

Indexes

Abbreviations used in these Indexes

Ads. Atthadassin, Ano. Anomadassin, Dhd. Dhammadassin, Dīp. Dīpaṅkara, Gtm. Gotama, Kak. Kakusandha, Kas. Kassapa, Kṇḍ. Koṇḍañña, Koṇ. Koṇāgamana, Mṅg. Maṅgala, Nār. Nārada, Pdm. Paduma, Phs. Phussa, Piy. Piyadassin, Pmt. Padumuttara, Rev. Revata, Sbh. Sobhita, Sdh. Siddhattha, Skh. Sikhin, Smdh. Sumedha, Suj. Sujāta, Sum. Sumana, Tss. Tissa, Ves. Vessabhū, Vip. Vipassin.

a. attendant, as. ascetic, B. Buddha, br. brahman, Bs. Bodhisatta, c.a. chief attendant, c.d. chief disciple, c.w.a. chief woman attendant, c.w.d chief woman disciple, cy. city, d. deva, d.k. deva-king, dtr. daughter, e. elephant, f. father, g.c.f. guardian of a corn-field, h. horse, k. king, m. mother, mct. merchant, mk-t. market town, mt. mountain, my. monastery, n. nāga, n.a. naked ascetic, n.k. nāga-king, p. palace, pk. park, pr. prince, s. son, u.m. universal monarch, vge. village, w. wife, y. yakkha.

I. INDEX OF WORDS

[Figures in heavy type indicate that the word is commented on]

above (*uddha*) **45** **151**
across (*tiriya*) **45**
act of merit (*adhikāra*) 3 **132** **133** 387
adorned with . . . trinkets (*āmutta . . . ābharaṇa*) **265**
advance (*abhikkamati*) **148**
afflicted (*addita*) **154**
aflame (*āditta*) **355**
age, feeble with (*jarājajjara*) 400
aggregates (*khandha*) **233** 266 276; *see also* category
aim (*attha*) **200** **245**
air (*ambara*) 59
all (*sabba*) **66** **290**; beings (*s-satta*) **27**; best of (*s-seṭṭha*) **66**
allowable (*kappiya*) 350 **351**
alms (food): (*bhikkhā*) 410; (*piṇḍa*) 10 155 248 408 f. 411
analytical insights (*paṭisambhidā*) 176 191 211 224 267 338
and (*ca*) 267; and too (*pi ca*) 74
anger and courtesy (*kopānunaya*) **162**
anguish (*dukkha*) 102 175 379 390 424; destruction of **94**
animals, wild (*miga*) 178 259 362
annihilationism (*uccheda*) 346
Antecedents (*nidāna*) 6 ff. 181
approval (*tayā*) **157**
anu, a gram. prefix 129 341
apertures (*chidda*), nine **108**
arahant 72 211 227 235 243 f. 251 270 273 328 349 355 363; banner of (*-dhaja*) 120 376 407 429; -ship 28 33 f. 133 169 180 f. 183 195 f. 210 f. 213 220 227 233 235 252 257 268 f. 275 295 303 307 312 323 328 334 356 379 421
are not (*nanu*) **423**
arising (*upapatti*) **148**
armature (*sannāha*) **385**

army (*senā*) 232 241 264 316
around (*vitthata*) **45**
arrival (*adhigama*) 366
arrow(s): (*kaṇḍa*) 399; (*sara*) 415, quiver of (*sarāsana*) 399
articles of honouring (5 kds. *lājapañcama*) 123 396
as: (*va*) **262 367**; (*yathā*) **104**; (*yathā hi*) **202**; as far as (*yāvatā*) **147 151 382**; as long as (*yāva*) **219**; as many as (*yāvatā*) **165**; *see also* like
ascetic (*tāpasa*) 115 278 317 332 f. 347 379 396; going forth of (*t-pabbajjā*) 313 323 329 333 379; matted hair (*jaṭila*) 5 **136**
ascetic quality (*dhutaguṇa*) **74** 318 356
aspiration (*paṇidhāna*) 255; (*patthanā*) li 16 132 ff. 137 167 **169** 205 f.
aspired to (*patthita*) **89** 169 420
assembly (*sannipāta*): of disciples 178 180 f. 196 213 379 419; four-factored 180 227 235 244 295 355 420 429
assonance xl ff.
assorted, having (*vibhajitvā*) **359**
assured, -ly (*dhuva*) **149**
asterism (*nakkhatta*) 82 116 188 392 405 418 428 f.
astonishing (*abbhuta*) **59**
astounding (*lomahaṁsana*) **59 60 85**
astronomical lore (*jotivijjā*) 381
attachment (rāga) **147 154** 173 370 **380** 385; a. hatred, confusion (*dosa, moha*) 127
attainment(s) (*samāpatti*) 13 86 110 121 123 133 174 **176** 197 216 223 f. 270 313 317 **325** 367 395 410 415 430; *see* cessation *and* compassion; (*sampatti*) 94
austerities (*dukkara*) 10 411 419
avoid (*vivajjati*) **155 169**
Awakened One, Self- (*sambuddha*) 4 6 58 188 205 346 350 429
Awakening (*bodhi*) 12 83 f. **89** 116 131 **151 169 170 209 294** 337 388; Gtm's residences after xxvii xxxii 4 f.; accessories of (*b-sambhāra*) 356; constituents of (*bojjhaṅga*) 195; knowledge of 208; maturing for **152** 162; 37 things pertaining to 195 223 374 384; way to 411
Awakening, Self- (*sambodhi*) 24 33 77 **83** f. 89 122 f. 125 130 133 151 168 196 203 **217** 222 241 286 310 332 347 355 361 376 f. 379 400 410 423 429
Awakening, Trees of (*bodhi-rukkha*) xlvii xlix f. 121 150 177 184 191 f. 201 205 221 229 232 238 240 275 277 285 310 314 316 319 321 324 326 f. 330 332 335 337 f. 340 345 347 350 361 365 368 373 376 427; Gtm's xliv xlvii l 6 f. 12 ff. 80 83 134 188 208 395 411 ff. 416 f. 422 428 f.; *see also* trees

balanced (*tulābhuta*) **159 162**
bamboo (*vaṁsa, veḷu*) **299**
banner (*dhaja*) **57**; *see also* arahant
bark-garment (*vākacīra*) **113** 127 330
baseless (*asaṁvuta*) **41**
be, to (*hetuye*) 104; is (*atthi*) **103**; must be (*hehiti*) **103**; was (*ahu*) **48 419**; was (*āsi*) **165**; was (is) not (*na hoti*) **147**; will be (*hessati*) 419; there are (*santi*) **18**
becoming(s) (*bhava*) **104** 153 **154 233**; again- (*puna-*) 23 102 127; all, every (*sabba-bh-*) 154 **156 363**; three **132** 234 **249** 403; bonds of 223; cage of (*bh-pañjara*) 363; craving for (*bh-cchanda*) 421; height of **242**; prison of 103; release from **104**; repeated (*bhavābhava*) 295 389; non- (*vibhava*) **104 233**
bed, legs of (*mañcapāda*) 188 428
bees: (*ali*) 231 393; (*bhamara*) 137 259
beings (*sattā*) **19** 81; abodes of (*s-āvāsa*) 132; aggregation of (*s-kāya*) 78; all (*sabba-s*) **27**; birth etc. of 390; (*pajā*) **60**
below (*adho*) **45 151**
benediction (*anumodana*) 31 170 ff. 197 216 243 253 270 289 307 343 417
best (*seṭṭha*) **313 366**
binding-work (*udakakicca*) 203 386
birth (*jāti*) 3 **83 104** 131 240 274 329 366 400 424; field of 297; wilderness of 370; (*yoni*) 191 267 338
blaze (*jalati*) **68 72**
blissful (*ānandita*) **42**
blossom: to make (*pupphāpeti*) **325**; -ing (*pupphita*) 252; *see also* flower
Bodhisatta(s) 81 f. 111 116 133 137 f. 141 143 f. 147 151 162 166 ff. 197

205 f. 215 281 360 376 401; city, father of 3 184; mother of a 3 184 **185** 392 429; occasions for rebirth of 360; their sacrifices (*cāga*) 215; Gtm. 8 ff. 188 f. 387–415
bodily eye (*maṁsacakkhu*) 49 f.
body: (*deha*) bearer of last (*antimadehadhārin*) **23**; with the special qualities **423**; (*kāya*) **109** 426, gem-like **239**
bond, -age (*bandhana*) **248** **328** **346** **348** **355** (shackles)
books, manuscripts (*potthaka*) ix ff. 330
border-country (*paccantadesavisaya*) **124**
bourn(s) (*gati*): five 191 267 238
bow (*dhanu*) 398 f.; -string (*jiya*) 399
bowl (*patta*) 9 14 33 417; golden 11 411
brahman(s) 4 100 **101** f. 210 212 236 360 f. 396 f. 402 409 f. 418 f.; family 187 360 390 426; guise of a 206 215
branch (*sākhā*) **299** 337 f. 347
bringer of light (*jutindhara*) **22** **344**
broad of shoulder (*usabhakkhandha*) **176** **294**
Buddha 1 10 36 69 78 88 125 f. 132 f. 138 147 f. 168 170 177 197 202 210 228 243 253 296 338 343 350 364 379 395 ff. 401 404 ff. 410 f. 420; -hood, -status li 82 88 f. 93 130 132 134 137 143 150 177 200 237 245 267 341 390 f. 418; -eye 49 241 250; -rays 268; -seat 192 418 428; -seed 137 f. **141**; -thing **237**; -Tumult 203 389 f.; cetiya of 206; cloud of **170**; grace of 69 127; knowledge(s) of 40 63 f. **78** **169** 191 **266**; light of 208 346; majesty of 86; mother of 81 f. 391; power of 4 **40** **41**; power of psychic potency **40** **64** f.; power of wisdom **40**; rebirth of 81 f. 390 f.; special qualities of 30 40 52 66 77 121 241 266 270; things making 131 134 **150** 151–62 200; word of **200** 216 **222** 382
Buddhas 1 f. 11 52 63 170 188 f. 208 303 326 333 346 387 391; common to 15; customary to 293 310 415 417; disciples of 70 133; differences among 187 425–30; natal city of 185; non-stumbling blocks for 430; physical frame of 205; past **93**; plane of **167** 171; practice of 193 208; range of 70; recital verses of 342; regulation for 429 f.; special qualities of 60 69 85 **167** 188 249 276 f. 303 338 387 427 429; teaching of 342; unalterable places for xxvii xxxii 188 428; utterance of 148 245; void of 247 274 285 326; word of 185 222
buddhas by and for themselves (*pacceka-b.*) 6 66 70 88 133 171 276
bull (*usabha*) 177 377; of men (*narāsabha*) **58** **68**; -'s roar (*vasabhanāda*) 353
"burners-up" (*tapassī*) **253**

cakkhu xxi f.; *deva-* xvi; *See* eye
calamities, all (*sabbītiyo*) **169**
cankers (*āsava*), destroyed, waned (*khīṇāsava*) 5 35 **69** 70 120 123 126 **129** 137 182 196 200 202 253 269 288 323 380 424; destruction of (*ā-kkhaya*) 40 131
cardinal faculties (*indriya*) **195**
carpenter, guise of a (*vaḍḍhakivaṇṇa*) 214
case(s): gram. (*vacana*) xxxii ff. 54 58 69 72 79 83 85 99 106 122 124 129 142 144 149 151 163 166 175 177 183 200 237 246 249 268 281 290 296 341 344 359 371 382; (*vibhatti*) 259
cast aside (*sañchaḍḍita*) **377**
category (*khandha*) 121 141 191 205; *see also* aggregates
cause (*hetu*) **133**
celebrated (*nikiḷita*) **93**
cessation: attainment of (*nirodhasamāpatti*) 235 260 f.; talk on (*n-kathā*) 226
cetiya 120 202 206 232 264 284 325 374 406 f.
chair (*pīṭha*) 343
changing, the (*vikubbana*) **370** **378**
characteristics: 80 minor 62 86 127 185 **352**; no stumbling block to 430
chariot (*ratha*) 400 402 427; of the sun (*ravi-r.*) 400; drawn by thoroughbreds (*ājañña-r.*) 190 232 238 256 301 308 337 345 361 365; -eer 400 f.
chief (*agga*) 74 f.; proclaimed (*a-nikkhitta*) **74**

children (*dāraka*) 206
circlet (*kambu*) **374**; (*parivesa*) 384
city (*nagara*) 3 **223**; of birth (*jāta-n*) 184 366 382 421
clap the hands (*apphoṭheti*) **61**
clear eyed (*pasannanetta*) **286**
clinging(s) (*upadhi*) **292** (4 kds.); no c. (*anupādā*) 325
cloth (*dussa*) **281**
"Come, monk" (*ehibhikkhu*) formula: 29 33 f. 180 211 f. 227 235 243 f. 251 258 f. 270 279 f. 294 f. 312 328 334, 355 370 379
commended (*vaṇṇita*) **75** **76**
Commentary 49 77; Old ix f. xvi xxiii 430
company (*parisā*) 33 329 **330** (4 kds.)
compared, not to be (*anūpama*) **300**
compassion (*anukampā*) **20** 355 362 416 f. **421**; (*karuṇā*) 305 322 343 389; attainment of great (*mahā-k*) 287 362
compassionate for the world's welfare (*lokahitānukampaka*) **55** **56**
composed (*samāhita*) **359**
co-natals (*sahajātāni*) xxxii xliii l 188 395 428
concentration (*samādhi*) **63** **67** 71 126 141 182 222 f. 240 248; like Meru **194**; unending **257**
conditions (*paccaya*) 121 191 205 220 266 275 415
conduct (*cariya*) 79; right (*caraṇa*) **22** 126; wrong (*anācāra*) **382**
confidences (*vesārajja*): the four 4 263 267 338
conquered (*nijjinitvā*) **223**
Conqueror (*jina*) **53** **56** **122** **166** **170** **200**
conscience (*hiri*) **225**
constellations (*nakkhatta*) **146**
constructions (*saṅkhāra*) 181 **220** **262** 266; are void (*ritta*) **186** 255 **423**
continent(s) (*dīpa*) 81 **297** 313 390 f. 405
continuous (*nirantara*) **224**
Coral tree, *see* pāricchattaka, *s.v.* trees
Council, first 16 21; Khandhaka on 16
count, to (*gaṇeti*) **219**
craft (*sippa*) 398 f.
craving (*taṇhā*) 132 333
crops (*dhañña*) **101**
cross-legged (*pallaṅka*) 12 f. **143** 147 188 205 221 248 256 *passim* 398 412 415 f. 428 f.; difference in size of the spreading for sitting 427
cross over to (*tarati* and other verbal parts) 80 f. 134 **177** **186**; helper across (*tāraka*) **280**; helping to (*tārayanta*) **80**
crowd (*gaṇa*) 92 121 332 340 f. 355
curable (*satekiccha*) **76**

darkness (*andhakāra*) 43 45 **317** 339
deathlessness, the undying (*amata*) 10 174 209 222 **250** **311** 346 385 424; city of **223**; drink of (*a-pāna*) 4 408; drum of **222** 322; pool of 269; waters of (*a-ambu*) **333**
deceasing (*cuti*) **148**
declaration (*vyākaraṇa*) 3 138 141 143 216 371 387
declare (*vyākaroti*) 197 244
deed (*kamma*) 207
deer-sanctuary (*migadāya*) 4 f. 27 188 321 326 f. 332 337 339 ff. 360 f. 363 369 375 f. 417 ff. 428 f.
defect (*dosa*) 105 ff. 110 **111** **112** **113** 173
defilements (*kilesa*) 12 71 81 105 f. 130 **131** 172 175 219 223 253 **266** 346 386 391 403 410 415
demarcation (*pariccheda*) 2 f. 6 93 186 188 191 205 390 428 f.
dense (*tibba*) **43**; (*sanda*) **299**
depart, to (*nikkhamati*) 321 324
Departure (*nekkhamma*) 3 109 113 240 389 402; the Great xxx xlix 8 134 188 204 231 247 256 272 275 285 293 301 310 315 326 332 337 347 361 368 376 379 404 407 422 429
dependent origination (*paṭiccasamuppāda*) 13 81
desert (*kantāra*) 362
designation (*paṇṇatti*) 209
deva(s) **36** **44** **54** 120 f. **129** **142** 145 167 170 178 184 190; -abode 168; -city 54; -dancers 59; -king 31; -like (*dibba*) 14 **54** 121 **169** 214 247 318 400 f.; -like vision 13 50 **75** 275 407 415; -mansion 275 316 400; -prince 231 315; *-putta* 195 223 392 417; city of 408; descent from 188 318 428 f.; dwelling-place for 361; by purification 178; worlds of (*sade-*

vakā) **43**; of the 4 Great Kings 41 **173** 390 417; of the Thirty-three 54 f. 173; Yama's 55; various 41 ff. **55** **56**; man-d. 362; with d. (*sadevakā*) **85** **93** **131** **132** **141** **159** **167** 186 **321** **333** **352** **355** 391; -*dhīta* (female devas) 59 n.
devatā 8 13 **59** 81 f. 84 116 **129** 138 148 f. 165 168 190 195 204 210 226 265 301 339 369 377 389 f. 391 f. 395 400 f. 404 ff. 409 411 413 415 f. 424; tree-d. 11
deviate (*okkamati*) **159**
Dhamma 1 8 10 14 ff. 19 27 35 51 *passim*. **166** 174 192 195 ff. 207 ff. **212** 222 232 234 ff. 241 250 **378** 390 417; archway of (-*ceti*) 374; banner of (-*dhaja*) 354; body of (-kāya) 62 f.; bridge of (-setu) **274**; chaplet of (-*mālā*) **384**; city of (-*nagara*) 225; cloud of (-*megha*) **322** **352**; conch of (-*saṅkha*) **222**; drum of (-*bheri*) 225; flowers of (-*puppha*) **374** **386**; hide of (-*camma*) **385**; incandescence of (-*teja*) **164** 165; mirror of (-*ādāsa*) **385**; nectar of (-*amata*) 177 f. 222 226 279 313 339 348 354 369 377; pond of (*taḷāka*) **384** 385; rain of 121 **279** 352; ship of (-*nāvā*) 130 **132** **359**; shop of (-*āpaṇa*) 224 **266**; shrine of (-*cetiya*) 374; streamer of (-*dussa*) **374** **384**; sword of (-*khagga*) **386**; speakers on 76; teaching of 424; torch of (-*okkā*) **207** **220**; vision of 288 317 322 361; Wheel of (-*cakka*) 33 77 121 ff. 125 131 177 188 233 241 250 256 264 267 278 286 293 301 316 324 327 332 339 341 348 354 f. 358 361 369 376 395 417 429; turning the Wheel of (-*ppavattana*) **65** **84** 116 **195** 222 417 428 f.; of splendour (*siri*-) **374**; excellent **358**; Dh. protects 207
Dhamma, True (*saddhamma*) 223 f.; city of 316; white sunshade of (-*paṇḍaracchatta*) **386**
dialect(s) (*bhāsa*) 100
diamond (*vajira*) **266**
differences (*vematta*) among Buddhas, *see* Buddhas
difficult to attack (*durāsada*) **194** 324
diligent (*appamatta*) **201** **225**
dirt (*raja*) **161**
disappear: will 423; -ed (*antarahita*) **255** **367**
disciples (*sāvaka*): ariyan 22; great 88; pairs of 367; pairs of chief 423; two chief 3 88 254 f. 341 355 420; shared by 6; one assembly of 370 419 429; assemblies of 3
discourse: delivery of (*suttanikkhepa*) 4 kds. 96; suitable **51**
Dispensation (*sāsana*) 18 31 **184** f. 189 **200** 203 218 220 231 239 263 274 285 292 309 320 353 356 368 375 380 391 397
district (*desa*) 81 390 f.
disturbed (*upadduta*) **166**
double meaning (*dvejjhavacana*) **149** **158**
doubt (*kaṅkhā*) 13 **70** **77**
downpour (*vassavuṭṭhi*) 9 kds. 288 414
drum(s) (*cammāvanaddha*) **59**
dry land (*thala*) **144**
dust (*mala*) **161**; little (*apparaja*) **19**

earth: (*dharaṇī*) **82** **194** 338; (*mahī*) 292; (*medinī*) **164** **202**; (*paṭhavī*) 15 31 **42** 157 161 164 167 172 194 214 f. 240 278 305 316 322 389 399 409 412 ff.; -quake, -quaking, trembling 31 79 84 f. 116 122 131 163 f. 206 389; (*vasudhā*) **164**; (*vasudharā*) 197
earth and sky, skilled in (the signs of) (*bhummantaḷikkhe kusala*) **381**
egg-plant (*vātiṁgaṇa*) 399
elated, exultant, joyous (*haṭṭhatuṭṭha pamodita*) **125**
elements (*dhātu*) **233**
elephant(s): (*dirada*, *dvi*-) 304 413; (*dantī*, tusked) 306; (*gaja*) 305; riding an 332; (*hatthin*) 120 163 350 372 405; mounted on (-*yāna*) 187 221 229 285 290 335 347 368 373 427; the ten 63 f.; (*kari*) 305 f.; (*mātaṅga*) 305 408; (*nāga*) 305, like a *n*- **355**; (*vāraṇa*) 205 304 350; of sages (*munikuñjara*) 363
elsewhere (*aññatra*) **163**
embellished (*bhūsita*) **345**
endeavour (*dhiti*) **243** **281**
endures (*sahati*) 157
energy (*viriya*) 88 138 156 **225** 243 281 380 386; four factored (*caturaṅga*-) 12 121 191 205 232 248 256 275 338 347 385; sluggish (*alīna*-) **156**

enumerations of kinds xix f.
eon(s) (*kappa*) x 3 13 **97** 134 189 f. 200 203 236 239 247 274 **276** f. 285 300 311 315 320 326 332 336 346 356 360 364 368 387 f. 415 f. 424; -tumult 389; Void, Non-void 276 f.; end of an 389
equal (*sama*) **83** **143**; to the unequalled (*asamasama*) **63** **271**; without e. (*asama*) **141** **161** **222** **257**; unequalled (*asama*) **64**
essential nature (*sabhāva*) **220** 224
eternalism (*sassata*) 346
evil (*pāpaka*) **104**; warding off e. (*-nivāraṇa*) 386
exertion (*ugghaṭita*) 359
exhortation (*ovāda*) 81 199 **246** 336 391
exhorter (*ovādaka*) **280**
explain (*pakāseti*) **195**
eye (*akkhi*, *cakkhu*) 215; of knowledge (*ñāna-c.*) 49 (5 kds.); of wisdom (*pañña-c.*) 50; bodily (*maṁsa-c.*) 50

faith (*saddhā*) 323
fame (*yasa*) **248** **292**; wide f. **266**; *see* renown
family (*kula*) 81 390 f.; -fortune (*k-mūla*) **377**; differences in among Buddhas 425
fare along (*paṭipajjati*) **95**
far-flung (*vipula*) **42** **45** **325**
festival (*samajja*) 180
festooned column (*agghi*, *agghiyasaṅkāsa*) **230** **262** **273** 313 **325**
fetter (*saññojana*) 346
fire (*aggi*) 179 246 262 **423**; threefold **104**; (*dahana*) 202; (*sikhī*) **262**; column of (*dhūmaketu*) **220**
firing (*indhana*) 239 314 352 423
five-hued (*pañcavaṇṇika*) **56**
flame (*sikhā*) 347
flawless (*acchidda*) **367**
flood(s) (*ogha*) 4 132 359 **371**
flowers (*puppha*) 56 **386**; various (*vicittā*) **145**; flower(ed) (*pupphanti*) **144**; are flowering (*pupphitanti*) **144**; fully f. (*supupphita*) **182**; flowering ones (*pupphina*) **169**
"folds" (*vidha*) xx ff.
following (*yasa*) **193**; having a (*gaṇī*) **76**; with a (*saparijjana*) **271**; *see also* host, retinue
foot (*pāda*) 277; on (*padasā*) 117 264 272 427; -prints 322; -step 188 428; feet 9 179
for (*hi*) **36** 223
ford (*tittha*) 137
forest: (*aṭavī*) 287 f.; (*pavana*) **170** **246** 258 **259**
form (*rūpa*) **62** 233 f.; -lessness (*a-*) 233 f.; -less sphere (arūpabhāva) 396
former **166**; f. event, faring (*pubbacariya*) 206 211; habitations (*p-nivāsa*) 13 40 80 **93** 121 191 205 275 415
formula, twofold (*dvevācaka*) 417
fostered (*paribhāvita*) **202**
freedom (*vimutti*) **63** 68 126 **252** **257**; bliss of 13 f. 415 f.; essence of 263; escape to 386; (*mutti*) **154**
frost (*ussāva*) **331**
fruit, fruition (*phala*) 209 367 382 **386** **420**; of arahantship 257; of no-return 270; of recluseship 176; bliss of 14 416; the four 191 195; supreme (4 kds.) **176**
fuel (*upādāna*) **239** 246 262 **314** 423; *see also* graspings

gandhabba(s) 142
garland for the forehead (*āvela*) **386**
gauged, not to be (*atuliya*) **202**
gavapāna 215 ff.
gāvuta 395 401 412
gems (*ratana*) 203 214 232 253 264 269 352; *see also* jewels, treasures
gender, gram. (*liṅga*) xxxvii 61 100 104 144 155 176 227 234 239 266 279 287 300
generation (*pajā*) **20**
gift (*dāna*) 31 f. 170 ff. 197 211 215 f. 228 234 f. 243 f. 253 270 281 289 296 307 334 f. 341 343 350 352 356 364 371 395; Unparalleled Great 123 197 312 328
girls (*dārikā*) 398
give, to (*dadāti*) **218**; giver (*dātā*) 32; giving (*dāna*) 31 206, advantage in 172; perfection of 200 388
gloom (*tamas*) **43** **207** **209** 220 **257**; fourfold 57
go forth, to (*pabbajati*) 34 80 **133** 180 216 232 235 240 258 295 f. 307 328 **330** 340 f. 349 406; gone forth, one (*pabbajita*) 401 410

god (*sura*) 178 210 305; non-g. (*asura*) **142** 210
going forth, the (*pabbajjā*) 210 221 328 401 404 407; bliss of (*-sukha*) 408; *see also* ascetic(s), seer(s)
gold, golden (*kanaka*) 368; shower of (*-vassa*) 368; (*su(o)vaṇṇa*) 11 **53 359**; -coloured (*s-vaṇṇa*) 127
grace (*vilāsa*) **374**
graduated talk (*ānupubbī-kathā*) 211
grammar, grammatical science (*sadda-sattha*) xiv xxxii ff. 37 163 252 341; gram. construction (*siddhi*) 36; *see also* rule, word (*sadda*)
grammarian (*akkharacintaka*) 101; (*saddavidū*) 151 249
grasping, without (*anupādāya*) 424
graspings (*upādāna*) 315 423; *see also* fuel
grass-spreading (*tiṇasanthara*) 121 427 ff.
great hero (*mahāvīra*) **61**
guard, a (*ārakkha*) 397 400 f. 405
guide out, away (*vineti*) 179 268 366 430; guider out, away (*vināyaka*) **48 107** 315 405 424; guiding out 269 288 311 349
guise (*vaṇṇa*), of a: brahman 206 215; carpenter 214

hair (*kesa*) 211 232 400 406; (*loma*) 268 288 302; of a horse's tail (*vāla*) 399
halo (*raṁsi*) 62 68 86 127 187; *see also* rays
hand, palm of (*karatala*) 305
hands clasped (*katañjali*) 8 **18 129**; clasped hands (*añjali*) 15 211 303 356 362 396
happiness (*sukha*) **104 143** 420; deva-like 204; (*somanassa*) 206
headless corpse (*kavandha*) 414
heat, element of (*tejodhātu*) 202
heaven(s) (*gagana*) **72** 192 195 202 208 240 f. 264 273 316 320 322 329 362 376 405 414; (*sagga*) 130 174, talk on (*s-kathā*) 173, -world 313 329
heavenly body (*uḷu*) **202 230 273 314**
height (*pamāṇa*), differences among Buddhas 426
here (*idha*) **18**
hermitage (*assama*) **111** 270
hindrances (*nīvaraṇa*) 111 176 354
hold sway, to **198** 200
hollow, not (*acchidda*) 299
honoured by devas and men (*deva-manussapūjita*) **48**
horse(s) (*assa*) 372; -back (*-yāna*) 218 310 314 422 427
host, leading the great (*mahāgaṇī*) **72**; *see* following
householder (*gihīliṅga*) 133
human existence (*manussatta*) **132**

I (*ahaṁ*) **40 344 418**; (*me*) **122**
ideational element (*dhamma-dhātu*) **151**
illness (*roga*) **169**
illumined (*sobhayim*) **382**
immeasurable (*appameyya*) **193**
impermanence (*anicca*) 205 220 233 255 266 390
imperturbable (*asaṅkhobbha*) **202 249**
in-breathing and out-breathing (*ānā-pāna*) 240 266 276 398 415 429
incalculable (*asaṅkheyya*) 13 **78 98** 134 190 200 203 220 236 239 247 263 274 368 387 415 f.
incandescence (*tejo*) **193 257**; of Dhamma **164** 165; intense **286**; those of unrivalled **423**; -ent **248**
incomparable (*anuttama*, *anupama*) **237 257**
indeed (*ve*) **129**
individuality (*attabhāva*) 14 394 ff.
inflection (*vibhatti*), gram. 104 143
initiate(s) (*sekkhā*) 182 **183** 223 273
insight (*vipassanā*) 191 223 276 415 424; knowledge of (*-ñāṇa*) 385; shrine of (*-cetiyaṅgana*) 374; talk on 181; having (*vipassin*) 337
instruction (*anusāsanī*) **51** 52; (*anu-siṭṭhi*) **246**
instructor (*viññāpaka*) **280**
instrumental music (*turiya*) 214 228 240 318 400
intentional lie (*musāvāda*) 158
investigation (*vilokana*) 81 116 204 390 f.
"Invitation" (*pavāraṇā*) 181 227 244 258 317
"invite" (*pavāreti*) 5 28 31 181 244 259
island (*dīpa*) **57**

jaw, mighty in (*mahāhanu*) **176**
jewel(s) (*ratana*) **41 51 53** 54 247 284

jewel(s) (*cont.*)
337 343; made of (*r-maya*) 14 **53** 325; the three 31; *see also* gems, treasures
jewel granting all desires (*maṇī sabbakāmada*) **420**
journey (*gamana*) 34
joyous (*pamodita*) **54 55**

kamma 1 132 f. 249 362 f. 397
karavīka, bird **92**
kaṭhina robe-material 258 288
keci, *see* "some"
king(s) 303 360 378 397; 4 Great 394; 4 Regent 390
kingdom (*rajja*) 296 328 335 371 378
knowledge (*ñāṇa*) **230 257**; element of (*-dhātu*) **378**; eye of (*-cakkhu*) 49; lance of (*-kuntima*) **385**; net of (*-jāla*) 362; power of 63 f.; like the heavens (*gagana*) **194**; of One of the Ten Powers (*dasabala-*) 369; not shared (*asādhāraṇa-*) 40 191 267 338 423 429; (*vijjā*) three: 174 **176** 241 248 256 263 f. **386** 429; (with *caraṇa*) **21**
koraṇḍa (flower) **73**

lair(s) (*āsaya*) **146**
lamp (*dīpa*) **57** 220 234
law-books (*satthapotthaka*) 315
lay-follower (*upāsaka*), using the 2 fold formula, 417
leader (*nāyaka*) **193**
leaf-hut (*paṇṇasālā*) 110 **111** 113 f. 340
leafy (*pattika*) **299**
legendary tradition (*itihāsa*) **102**
life (*jīvita*) 206; in doubt (*j-saṁsaya*) **236**
life-span (*āyu*) 81 f. 116 187 190 203 205 210 216 218 220 f. 229 231 238 f. 245 254 f. 261 263 272 283 290 292 297 308 f. 315 319 324 332 335 353 357 365 368 373 375 382 389 ff. 397 401; difference in length of Buddhas' 425 f.; of Bs's mother 81 390 f.; relinquishing of 188 429; no stumbling-block to 430
light (*āloka*) 44 f. 346; bearer of (*jutindhara*) **344**
lightning (*vijju*) **320**; flash of, streak of **202** 320 **384** 396
like (*iva*) **73 277 367** (*va*); (*yathā*) **68 239 262**; inasmuch as (*yathā*) **61**; as (*yathā*) **73**; (*viya*) 367
lion (*sīha*) 156 176 258 363; -jawed (*-hanu*) **294**; -'s roar (*-nāda*) 121 260 **367** 394 f. 429
liquorice, wild (*madhulaṭṭhika*) **365**
look after, to (*paricarati*) **282**
Lord, the (*bhagavā*) **52**
loss (*vyasana*) 94
lotus (*kamala*): -buds (*k-makula*) 15 211; -feet (*-yugala*) 349; -grove (*-vana*) 11 220; womb of a (*-gabbha*) 207; (*komala*) 278; (*kumuda*) 400; (*kuvalaya*) 232 264, -buds (*-makula*) 356; (*paduma*) 313 329 349; rain of (*-vassa*) 275 f.; (*uppala*) 9; lotus-rain (*pokkhara-vassa*) 424
loveliness (*kalyāṇa*) **104**
loving-kindness (*mettā*) 82 117 **161** 305 389 418
low, high, middling (*hina-m-ukkaṭṭha-majjhima*) **151 155**
lustre (*pabhā*) 11 32 187 204 f. 208 230 **262** 272 f. 284 314 344 ff. 350 365 f.; streamed forth **254** 352
lutes (*vīṇā*) xxxix 61; Pañcasikha's 412

ma (syllable) 89 149 151 176 255
magnificent (*uḷāra*) **44**
main-street (*mahāvīthi*) **224**
male sex (*purisaliṅga*) 133
mark of a hundred merits (*satapuññalakkhaṇa*) **49**
Marks (*lakkhaṇa*) 397; thirty-two 9 **54** 62 68 86 100 102 127 179 185 211 n. 213 269 346 352 379 396 411; no stumbling-block to 430; 3 characteristic 81 86 220 235 390 423; readers of (*l-pāṭhaka*) 204 337 (*l-paṭiggāhaka*) 397 410
marvel (*pāṭihāriya*, *pāṭihīra*) 30 **44** 51 (3 kds.) **52** 116 137 143 190 204 221 231 233 240 247 274 300 361 f. 398; of Making the Worlds Bright (*lokappasādana*) **70**; of unveiling the World (*lokavivaraṇa*) 257
Marvel of the Double (*yamaka-p*) xxxii 5 13 45 ff. 49 66 178 188 195 210 226 242 250 257 268 293 342 348 354 361 369 f. 377 f. 415 428
master(y) (*vasin*) **52** 126 **143** 283 355; -ies 52 (5 kds.)

matchless person (*appaṭipuggala*) **26**
meal of the 4 sweet things (*catumadhurabhojana*) 216
measureless (*appamāṇa*) **300**
meat, flavour of (*maṁsarasa*) xxxix 430
medicine (*bhesajja*) 216 364
meditation(s) (*jhāna*) 45 52 55 f. **67** 101 121 126 **143** 240 323 325 367 415; the first 18 398; the fourth 45 191 266 276; two 430; unbroken (*aparihīna*) 197 216; bliss of 14; coat of mail (*-kavaca*); delight of (*-rati*) **123**
men: and deities (*naramarū*) **141** **195** **328** 379 **419**; with devas (*sadevaka*, *sadeva-mānusa*) **36** **80** 137 **159**
merit (*puñña*) 9 11 214 240 247; accumulation of 9; doers of **100**; might of (*-anubhāva*) 376
mind (*mānasa*), stirred in **128**
mindfulness (*sati*) 182 201 223 385; applications of 195 **224**; shield of (*-phalaka*) **385**
mire (*kalala*) 127 **130** 132 134 143
moment (*khaṇa*) **60** **129**
monks (*bhikkhu*) 316 f.; group of five 27 410 f. 417 f.; in-coming 430; newly ordained 216
moon (*canda*) **68** **72** 116 126 f. 137 179 192 204 f. 232 239 268 275 278 280 291 294 300 315 337 343 350 393 408 f.; as the **320** **384**; lustre of 208; orb of **55**; (*karanikara*) 376; (*rajanikara*) 240 253 302 403 408 412; (*sasin*) 400
morality, moral habits (*sīla*) **63** 68 71 126 141 **152** 153 (4 kds.) 172 ff. **175** 182 222 f. 248 **283** 307 **309** 343 359 380 **384** **386** 391; armour of (*-kañcuka*) **385**; like the ocean **194**; talk on 172 f.
mover through mid-air (*antaḷikkhacara*) **297**
multiple meanings xxiv ff.
musical instrument(s): (*kākali*) 259; (*tāḷāvacara*) 259; (*turiya*) 60–1 **145** 403

nāga 42 48 71 141 f. 411; -abode 413; -king 228 267 f. 343 353 409
nasal sound (*anussāra*) 18 106
nibbāna 57 83 f. 95 102 f. **104** 105 130 209 222 f. 249 352 402 424; city of 105 107 172 f. 223 f.; element of 315; wishing for **385**; final n. (*pari-n*) xxxix 3 7 16 182 188 f. 202 f. 218 220 246 263 274 283 285 298 309 315 320 325 331 336 359 361 374 386 429 f.
Niraya(s) 45 279 362
no-fear (*abhaya*) 367 **386**; city of 386
no-self (*anattā*) 390 423
non-human beings (*amanussa*) 178 409
non-returner (*anāgāmin*) 29
not (*na*) **36** **273**; (particle) 146
now at the present time (*idān'etarahi*) **421**
number, gram.: change of (*vacanavipariyāsa*) 219
nurses (*dhātī*) 397 f.
nutriment (*āhāra*) 372 (4 kds.) 409 411 416 f.
nutritive essence (*oja*) 121 204 221 347 411

observances, all (*vattāvatta*) **382**
observance day (*uposathadivasa*) 180
obstructions (*āvaraṇa*) 354
ocean (*sāgara*) **276** 414; (*samudda*) 389
oil-press (*telayanta*) **164**
ointment (for the eyes) (*añjana*) 364 **365**
omniscience, omniscient knowledge (*sabbaññutā*, *s-ñāṇa*) 13 16 83 f. 169 f. 209 221 232 264 301 316 321 326 378 390 397 411 415 429
Order (*saṅgha*): of disciples (*sāvaka-s*) 213 374 **423**; of monks (*bhikkhu-s*) 32 138 170 179 197 234 f. 243 f. 253 260 267 281 289 296 307 312 328 330 356 364 371 f.
ordure (*kuṇapa*) **108**; various **103**
ornament (*alaṅkāra*) **385**
"others" (*aññe*) xi xxxix
outer cloak (*sāṭaka*) **112**
overturned (*adhokata*) **151** **152**

pair (*yuga*) **254** **309**
palace (*pāsāda*) 3: of Dhd. 316 319 427; of Gtm. 398 400 402 f. 422; of Kas. 376 383 427; of Pmt. 275 427; of Sbh. 240 f. 245 254 275 427
palanquin (*sivikā*) 247 254 321 324 353 358 392 427
patience (*khamana*) **194**

Pātimokkha 180 196 213 235 243 250 258 269 f. 280 295 307 312 318 323 328 334 342 349 355 f. 363 370 379 420 429; Great 235; recital verses 342
pavilion (*maṇḍapa*) 14 16 214 f. 253 269 343
peace (*khema*) **352**
peacock's tail-feathers (*morapattha*) **299**
penetration (*abhisamaya*) of Dhamma 3 81 177 f. 181 **182** 184 f. 209 f. 212 226 234 f. 242 f. 250 256 264 267 ff. 278 f. 286 288 293 301 303 306 310 f. 316 f. 321 f. 327 f. 333 f. 339 341 348 f. 354 361 363 369 f. 376 f. 379 391 419 421; (*paṭivedha*) 84 246 332 (piercing)
perfections (*pāramī*) 13 16 23 (the ten) 79 f. 89 ff. (the ten) 138 150–63 165 ff. 190 203 221 237 239 247 255 263 274 284 f. 292 300 309 315 320 326 332 337 346 353 360 368 370 (the ten) 375 390 (the ten) 391 416; 3 kds. 89 162 f.; 4 kds. 415; of Giving 200 388; of Morality 335; of Wisdom 88; the utterly pure 370; come to (*pāramiṅgata*) **363**
physical frame (*sarīra*) 10 f. 22 f. 32 204 206 f. 215 218 ff. 245 254 261 268 272 278 283 f. 287 290 297 305 308 310 313 f. 319 324 330 335 345 f. 350 ff. 357 365 f. 373 379 382 393 400 416 423 ff.
Piṭakas, three 197 335 380
pity, one with (*kāruṇika*) **66**
plaster-work (*mattikākicca*) 203 386
play on, to (*vajjeti*) **344**
pleasaunce (*uyyāna*) 400 f.
ploughing festival (*vappamaṅgala*) 398
pool (*taḷāka*) 105; of the Undying (*amatantala*) 105 **106**
populace (*mahājana*) **186**
portent (-signs) (*pubbanimitta*) 116 ff. 122 138 **144** 203 390 392 394 397 400 f.
portents, bad (*dunnimitta*) 414
possessed of (*sampanna*) **21**
powers (*bala*) **195**; *see also* Buddha
pride (*mada*) **94** 95
prison (*andughara*) **154**; (*bandhanāgāra*) 153 f.
prone (*avakujja*) **130**
prostration, fivefold (*pañcapatiṭṭhita, patiṭṭhitapañcaṅga*) 11 142
psychic potency (*iddhi*) 33 35 **51** 52 78 126 f. **143** **182** **186** 211 228 253 313 323 329 343 370 374 378; bases of 195; display of (*i-vikubbana*) 78; power of **37** ff. 292
pupils, duties of (*antevāsika-vatta*) 208
pure, impure (*sucī, a-*) **157**
purpose (*mānasa*) **183** **351** **421**

qualifications (*upanissaya*) 176 179 208 211 232 241 250 267 278 317 322 326 348 354 369 376
question (*pañha*) 379; *pucchā* 88 (5 kds.); questioning (*paripucchanta*) **155**

radiance (*ābhā*) **44** 45
rain(s) (*vassa*) 28 196 293 317 430; of gold (*kanaka-*) 368; of weapons (9 kds.) 302; -residence (*-āvāsa*) 180 258 371; lotus- (*pokkhara-*) 424; *saṅkhāra-* 267
rain down (*abhivassati*) **333**
raining (*vassante*) **250** **251** **279** 312 f.; downpours (9 kds.) 288 414
ratana, linear measure **300**
rays (*raṁsi*) 3 206 268 301 f. **314** **359** 362; differences in extent of 426 f.; no stumbling-block to 430; him of a hundred **54** **246** **294**; *see also* halo
"reading(s)" (*pāṭha*) xvii ff. 40 f. 43 ff. 48 56 59 70 72 f. 76 80 94 108 125 128 130 f. 136 142 ff. 146 149 151 154 ff. 159 ff. 165 ff. 175 177 184 186 200 202 209 212 223 237 239 242 246 249 f. 252 255 257 260 ff. 268 271 279 281 295 299 311 323 f. 331 336 339 341 343 365 378 f. 382 385 418
recensionists (*saṅgītikārakā*) 21 35 41 71 92 425
recluse (*samaṇa*) 179 397 405 f.; -ship (*sāmañña*) 24 **175** 224 233
recipient of offerings (*āhutīnaṁ paṭiggaha*) **136**
redundancy (*punarutta*) 55 125
refuge(s) (*saraṇa*) 30 **174** 179 228 236 244 268 283 289 307 **309** 371 379 417
relics (*dhātu*) 202 283 315 336 352 360 386

relinking (*paṭisandhi*) 80 102 116 122 131 190 204 221 231 240 247 255 263 274 285 292 300 309 315 320 326 332 337 346 353 392
remove (*vinodeti*) **166**
renown (*yasa*) **230** **336** **366**; *see* retinue
repeater (*ajjhāyaka*) **101**
repugnance (*paṭigha*) **157**
requisites (*paccaya*) 218 **297** 430; (*parikkhāra*) 120 211 243 364 407
resolute determination (*adhiṭṭhāna*) 37 f. 45 65 162 167 f. 314 f.
resolve (*abhinīhāra*) 6 8 23 86 **88** 93 130 134 387 f.; (*paṇidhi*) 269
retinue (*yasa*) **186** **220**; *see also* fame, following, renown
rise and fall (*udayabbaya*) 121 191
river (*jhāra*) 146; (*nadī*) 414
robe(s), r-material (*cīvara*) 216 281 356 364; (*kāsāya*) 232; pair of (*dussayuga*) 228; upper (*uttarā-saṅga*) 123 236 f.
rock, a (*sela*) **160**
rule, gram. (*lakkhaṇa*) xxxv f. 129 163 252 341
rule of training (*sikkhāpada*) 430
rustling (*dhunamāna*) **330**

sacrifice(s) (*cāga*) 213; (*pariccāga*) (5 kds.) 79; to (*pariccajati*) 206
sacrificial post (*yūpa*) **359**
sadda, *see* word
safety-blessing (*sotthi*) **169**
saṁsāra 20 172 274 379 382 388; delivery from **94**; ocean of 57; sea of 130 225; stream of **132** **273** **421**
sandal-wood, red (*lohitacandana*) 270
scent (4 kds.) (*catujātigandha*) 123 396
sea (*samudda*) 57 170 199 249 414; end to end of **198** 200; (*jaladhara*) 305; *see* ocean
seasons (*utuvassa*) **159**
sectarian (*titthiya*) 195 210 226 **282** 283 348 354
seer(s) (*isi*) **77** **141** 168; going forth of (*-pabbajjā*) 270 317; resort (*-patana*) 4 f. 188 332 361 363 369 375 f. 411 419 428 f.
self-become (*sayambhū*) **72**
sense-pleasure (*kāma*) 317 403
sequence of meanings (*anusandhi*) (3 kds.) 87
shade (*chāyā*) **299**
shine (*sobhati*) **186** 382; forth (*upa-s*) **184**
shining (*virocamāna*) 420
shoulder, broad of (*usabhakkhandha*) **176** **294**
sign(s) (*liṅga*) 147; (*nimitta*), four **122** 123 190 204 221 231 240 247 256 264 275 285 301 310 315 326 332 337 347 353 361 368 376 397 400 f. 421 429
silent (*nissadda*) **144**
simile (*upamā*) 194
skill (*kusala*): jewel of (*-ratana*) 223; roots of (*-mūla*) 192; un- 386
skilled (*kusala*) **73** 152 313 392; things (*-dhamma*) (10 kds.) 175; and un-skilled (*k-ākusala*) 385 f.
sky (*ākāsa*) 45 **59** 124 **130** 168 **249** 275 393 f. 407 409 424; *see also* space
slight (*tanu*) **147**
smelting-pot (*ukkāmukha*) **374**
so few only (*ettakā yeva*) **163**
solitary faring (*ekacariya*) 332
"some" (*keci*) xi f. xxxix 20 40 f. 49 60 98 112 200 217 220 226 230 266 291 299 330
soothsayers (*nemittakā*) 347
sorrow (*soka*) **94**
sound, to (*abhiravati*) **145**
sound(s) (*sadda*). ten **98** f.
space (*ākāsa*) **78** **147** 194; *see also* sky
speaker (*kathika*) **76**
special qualities (*guṇa*) 12 17 65 f. 102 110 **111** **113** **114** **133** 138 152 172 193 f. 235 **237** 280 318 410; body with the **423**; *see also* Buddha, Buddhas
splendour (*tāpa*) **170**
stain(s) (*mala*) **370**; -less (*vi-*) **69** **200** **202** **420**
stairway (*sopāna*) 172 f.
star (*tāra*, *tāraka*) **146** 186 192 202 205 232 278 291 376; king of 314
stationary and mobile (*thāvara-jaṅ-gama*) xxxviii 82 172
steadfast one(s) (*tādin*) **22** 196
steed, thoroughbred (*turaṅga*) 293 298 326
stirred in mind (*saṁviggamānasa*) **128**
storm-cloud (*megha*) **74**
straight (*uju*) 299
stream (*savantī*) **144**

stream: -entrant(s) (*sotāpanna*) 195 220 380; -entry (*sotāpatti*) 28 30 180 359 385 418 420
stream forth (*niccharati*) **359 366**
street (*vīthi*) 224
striving (*padhāna*) xxx n. 3 80 **115** 120 **136** 187 190 192 **200** 204 221 232 240 247 256 264 275 285 293 301 310 316 321 326 332 337 340 347 353 361 368 376 **419** 429; to strive the s. 110 134 410 f.; right 195; time required for 426; wavering in (*p-vibbhanta*) 411
stumbling-blocks (*antarāya*) 4 not affecting Buddhas 430
sugar-cane mill (*ucchuyanta*) **164**
sun (*divasakara*) 11 22 240 285 302 316 362; (*ravi*) 414; chariot of 400; (*suriya*) 12 **68** 138 192 204 f. 227 235 268 301 320; lustre of 208; as the setting **220**
sunshade (*chatta*) 398 413
superb being (*sattuttama*) **47**
super-knowing(s) (*abhiññā*) 45 68 110 ff. 115 122 127 133 174 **176** 180 **182** 197 216 224 270 313 317 323 325 **386**; power in **252**
supermundane states (*lokuttara-dhamma*) 386
support (*patiṭṭhā*) **57**
suppose that (*yannūna*) **103**
supreme (*uttama*) 89; among men (*dipadut-*) **57**, (*narut-*) **37**, (*purisut-*) 103
sword (*asi*) 9 232 264; (*khagga*) 406

taints, without (*anaṅgana*) **252**
tall stature (*brahā*) **287**
tamed (*danta*) **71**; taming (*dama*) 127
tangle (*jaṭa*) **333**; untangled (*vijaṭetvā*) **333**
tasks done (*katakicca*) **69**
Tathāgata x xv 1 4 f. 17 **23** ff. 33 45 f. 59 61 63 ff. 76 129 143 167 211 312 328 417 f.; strength (*bala*) of 63 f. 405
teach (*deseti*) **19**
teacher (*ācariya*) 107, succession of 6; (*satthā*) **48 57** 65 367, seeing a **133**
tense, gram. (*vacana*) xxxvi 144 f. 149 176 359 419
ten-thousand, the **53 141** 177 230 **297 311 319 355**; was brilliant (*virocati*) **273**
tethering post (*ālaka*) **377**
that (*yaṁ*) **78**
these (*te*), those (*ye*) **225**
thief (*cora*) **109**
thing (*dhamma*) **237**; eight (*aṭṭha-*) 130 132 134 387; supermundane (*lokuttara-*) 374; ten (*dasa-*) **170 370**
thorns (*kaṇṭaka*) 299
thoroughbred (horses) 400
thronged (*samākula*) **292**
throw out, to (*nicchubhati*) **283**
thūpa 352 386
time (*kāla*) 81 390 f. 418; (*samaya*) **159 183**; present (*etarahi*) **418 420**
torch (*ukkā*) **207 272** 406 414
Treasure: the Elephant 297; the Jewel 291; the Wheel 199 210 f. 297 405
treasure(s) (*ratana*) 101 **144**; seven **100** 296 f.; *see also* jewel
treasure-urns (*nidhikumbhā*) xliv ff. 188 395 428
tree(s) (*rukkha*) 83 178 209 243 398; root of a **114** 210; of lamps, lights (*dīpa-*) **68 185**; (*taru*) 414
Trees, named in Pali.*
- ajjuna* 245 248 427
- āmalaka* 332 335 427
- āmanda* 336
- amba (mango) 226; -grove 408
- asana* 243 250 326 330 427; -plank of 399
- asoka 143
- assakaṇṇa 143
- assattha* xlvii l 134 f. 198 210 412 427
- bimba 403
- bimbijāla* 316 **319**
- campaka* 210 243 310 314 427
- cittapāṭalī (trumpet-flower) 242
- jambu (rose-apple) 323 398
- kakudha* 243 301 308 427
- kaṇikāra* 321 324 427
- kapitthana* 427
- karavīra 243
- khadira (acacia): -grove 347 361 369 376
- kiṁsuka 126

* Signifies Tree of Awakening; *see* CB xli ff. for these and some other trees.

koviḷāra 54
kuravaka* 316 319 427
mandārava **129** 169 313 329
nāga* 14 218 221 229 232 238 241 243 245 348 416 427
nīgrodha* (banyan) 10 14 134 376 382 427
nīpa **130** 285 290 427
panasa 243
pāricchattaka (Coral tree) **54** 86 169 178 186 210 242 266 313 329
pāṭalī* xlix f. 337 f. 345 347 354 361 427
pilakkhakapitthana 185 n.
pipphalī* 184 **185**
puṇḍarīka* xlix f. 347 350 **352** 369 427
punnāga 243
sāla* 67 f. 164 **186** 191 **201** 293 353 f. 357 361 369 393 427; -grove 121 191 232 248 275 285 293 301 337 353 369 392 f. 411 422; king of **309**
saḷala* **130** 275 283 326 427
sahakāra 243
setamba 352 n.
sirīsa (acacia) l 178 361 365 427
soṇa* 256 261 264 **265** 266 272 427
udumbara* l 369 373 427; plank of 399
vakula 243
vaṁsa, veḷu* (bamboo) 293 298 299 427
true things, four (*catusaccadhamma*) 19 f. 24 374
truth: the highest, ultimate (*paramattha*) 175 320 322
truths (*sacca*) (the four) 24 85 93 **209** 222 246 286 288 321 361 363 421; Dhamma of 293; juice of (*-rasa*) **209**
tumults (*kolāhala*) 389 (3 kds.)
turn back, to (*nivattati*) **86** **148**; no intention to (*anivattimānasa*) **359**; going to the no-turn-back (*anivattigamana*) **249**

undisturbed (*nirākula*) **144**
undying, the: *see* deathlessness
unending (*ananta*) **249** **257** **266**
unexcelled (*anadhivara*) 18
universal monarch (*cakkavattin*) 80 198 ff. 202 210 276; gem of **291**
unknown (*aññāta*) 16 130 **131**
unrivalled (*atula*) **210** **230** **300** (*-iya*); u. incandescence **423**
unsullied (*anupalitta*) **349**
unsurpassed (*anuttara*) **41** **331**
upadhi xix xxi 292 n.
upright (*uju*) **287**
usabha, linear measure 399 406
utterance, solemn (*udāna*) 13 191 205 221 232 241 248 256 264 276 286 293 301 310 316 321 326 332 338 347 354 361 369 376 402 415

vehicle (*yāna*) differences in 427
verse(s) li f. 181
victory's joy (*jayasumana*), a plant 12 123 126
vihāra xxvii 3 188 243 356 424 428
vision, one with (*cakkhumā*) **49** ff. **166**; deva(-like) 13 50 **75** 80 191 205 275 407 415
viveka xix xxi
voice (*vāca*) 394 f.; (*sara*) sweet **92** 322 327; gram. (*kāraka*) 36 295
void (*ritta*) **186** 255 **423**; *see also* constructions, eons
vowel (*anussara*) 236 385

warrior-noble (*khattiya*) 360 397; family (*-kula*) 187 360 391 426
watch of the night (*yāma*) 13 80 121 191 241 248 256 264 275 316 415 430
water, 399; flood of (*udakogha*) 302; showers of (*u-dhāra*) 393
waves (*ūmī*) 219
Way, the (*magga*) 83 **95** 104 106 109 121 169 175 209 f. **249** 266 276 338 **346** 386 415 **421**; bridge of 274; fruits of 311; ship of 225; -knowledges 338; the fourth 415; names for 106; ariyan eight-fold 175
ways, the 195 367 424; fruits of 137 174 233; the eight 132 359 421; the four 81 174 176 191 233 424
weapons (*āyudha, āvudha*) 302 (9 kds.) 413 (various)
went to (*gantvā*) **341**
what (*kiṅ*) **78**
Wheel (*cakka*) 61 211; -follower 235 **236**; -mark **61** f. **73** 322 346; -turner **264** 296 397 405; -tumult 389 f.; potter's 275 376 406; *see also* treasure

wilderness (*kantāra*) **370**
will-power (*chandatā*) **134**
winds, rough (*bhusavāta*) **160**
wisdom (*paññā*) 68 71 126 141 222 235 248 386; *see also* perfection; great **67**; (*buddhi*) 79
wise one (*dhīra*) **68**
women (*itthi*) 378
wonder (*acchariya*) **382** 396
wonderful (*accheraka*) **43 44 58**
word (*pāvacana*) **184**
word (*sadda*) xxiii ff.; construction of a (*-siddhi*) 36 f.; the word *ādi-* ("and so forth") 98, *sādhu-* xxiii f. **71**; *va-* 277[1]
words not in PED xxxvii ff.
world(s) (*loka*) 45 **143**; of beings 18; of the devas **43**; of men 43 45 408; chief in (*-adhipati*) **17**; highest in (*-agga*) 394; knower of (*-vidū*) **135**; leader of (*-nāyaka*) **51 85** 409; protector of (*-nātha*) **66 200** 280; things of (*-dhamma*) 202 (8 kds).; welfare of 10 **55 56 93** 397; freed from (*l. muccitvā*) **170**; spaces between (*lokantarikā*) **43** 44 117; drawing away the veil from (*vivatta-cchad(d)a*) 10 269 397; three 17 44 414
world-system(s), -spheres, -element (*cakkavāḷa, lokadhātu*): ten-thousand 15 35 45 **52 53 54 58 78 79** 83 **85** 86 116 122 138 **141** 143 148 **149** 165 167 187 195 203 ff. 207 218 220 226 230 276 **297** 338 347 361 377 390 392 394 405 413 417 419; great thousand, thirty thousand 58
write, writing (*lekhā*) 330

yak-cow (*camarī*) 152 **153**
yakkha(s) 48 141 165 179 f. 184 206 287 f. 301 f. 361 f. 378 f. 409 411; -general 253
yoga, earnest student of (*yogāvacara*) 386
yojana 33 43 **177** 192 199 202 f. 211 214 216 243 254 264 272 284 291 314 316 325 331 345 347 350 352 354 365 f. 391 395 399 401 406 ff. 412 f. 417; half- 395 400

zenith (*nabha*) **41 59** 72 **130**
zest (*pīti*) 60 (5 kds.) **94** 126 128 **143** 206 215 **217** 329 (5 kds.)

II. INDEX OF PALI PROPER NAMES

Abhaya a. Ads. 314
Abhibhū c. d. Skh. 348 ff.
Abhidhamma (-piṭaka) 13 178 210 212 242 250 369 f. 377 f. 416 429
Aciravatī river 173
Aggidatta f. Kak. 360 365
Aggisona br. 368
Ājānīya e.k. xliv f. 395
Ajapāla banyan tree 14 f. 416 f.
Ajātasattu k. xlviii li 16 303 n.
Akaniṭṭha (devas) 42 56 70 86 242
Ākaṅkheyya-sutta 96
Ālakamanda d. cy. 100
Āḷāra Kālāma 10 18 410 417
Āḷavaka y. 4 48 288
Āḷavī cy. 4
Amara, Amaravatī cy. (1) of Bs. Smdh. 96 **98 101** 109 137 178 (2) in Kṇḍ's time 192 (3) in Sdh's time 322 (4) of Sakka 100 137 409
Ambaṭṭha Discourse 21
Amitā c.w.d. Pmt. 283
Ānanda (1) a. Gtm. xliv f. xlvii f. 16 134 f. 188 197 428 (2) f. Pmt. 279 283 (3) s. Tss. 326 330
Ancients, the: *see* Porāṇā
Aṅga-Magadha 5 35
Aṅgarāja a. Sum. 229
Aṅgārāma 229
Aṅgīrasa (name of Gtm.) 399

[1] For more examples of sadda as 'word', see above, p. xxiv.

Animisaya cetiya 13 416
Aññā-koṇḍañña 28 77 418 f.
Anoma (1) c. d. Ano. 253 (2) a. Sbh. 245 (3) mk-t. 221 (4) n. a. 248
Anomā (1) m. Nār. 263 272 (2) cy. 310 (3) river 9 80 406
Anomadassin (1) B. 189 247–55 **248** 425 ff. (2) as. 347
Anotatta, lake 14 416
Antaka (end-maker) 304
Anulā c.w.d. Kas. 382
Anupama (1) s. Phs. 332 334 f. (2) s. Sdh. 321 324 (3) s. Sum. 221 229 (4) cy. 315 353 f. 357 (5) mct. 221 248 (6) n. a. 221 (7) vge. 248
Anupamā mct's d. 221
Anupiya, mango-grove 408
Anurāja pr. 211
Anuruddha (1) Elder xlviii 75 77 (2) a. Kṇḍ. 201
Aparagoyāna 199
Arimanda cy. 335
Aruṇavā f. Skh. 346 350
Aruṇavatī cy. 346 348 ff.
Asadisa vge. 321
Āsāḷha, month 27 82 116 321 405 471
Asama (1) f. Pdm. 255 261 (2) c. d. Sbh. 241 245
Asamā (1) m. Pdm. 255 261 (2) c.w.d. Pmt. 283
Asoka a. Vip. 345
Asokā c.w.d. Mṅg. 218
Assayuja, asterism 188 429
Atideva Bs. 236
Atthadassin B. 189 300 309–15 425 ff.
Atthasālinī xxxi 181
Atula (1) Bs. 228 343 (2) s. Skh. 347 351
Avīci 45 86 388

Badara-wood 316 321
Bakkula, Elder 38
Bamboo grove (Veḷuvana) 31 33
Bandhumā f. Vip. 337 345
Bandhumatī (1) m. Vip. 337 345 (2) cy. 337 341 345
Bārāṇasī 4 f. 27 333 375 f. 379 382 411 417 419
Bāvari xlvii n.
Bhadda c. d. Kṇḍ. 201
Bhaddā c.w.d. Rev. 237
Bhadda-eon 200 267 f. 360 371
Bhaddasāla c. d. Nār 269 272
Bhallika mct. 15 416
Bhāradvāja c. d. Kas. 382
Bhāvittatta (1) c. d. Sum. 222 228 (2) k. 258
Bhayabherava Discourse 21
Bhīmaratha (1) cy. 322 (2) k. 322
Bhīyasa c. d. Koṇ. 370 373
Bimbisāra k. 10 29 ff. 409 f.
Birth-story (Jātaka) 430; Cūḷasutasoma 90, Ekarāja 91, Khantivāda 91, Lomahaṁsa 92, Mahājanaka 90, Mahānāradakassapa 30, Mahāsutasoma 91, Mūgapakkha 91, Saṅkhapāla 89, Sasapaṇḍita 89, Sattubhattaka 90, Sivi 215, Vessantara 97 n. 424
Bojjhaṅga saṁyutta 96
Brahmā(s) **17** 31 56 58 80 120 f. 127 143 145 177 184 192 208 222 232 241 250 256 267 278 286 293 310 316 339 348 390 393 409; Mahā- 17 f. 27 31 390 413 417 429
Brahmā Sahampati 8 15 ff. **18** 20 27 49 412 f. 417
Brahma: -abidings 218; -worlds 120 197 f. 216 226 389 413
Brahmadatta f. Kas. 375 382
Brahmadeva (1) c. d. Rev. 237 (2) c. d. Tss. 326 330
Brahmāyu xlvii n.
Buddhadatta, BvA "compiler" vi ix f. xxx f. xxxv lii 431
Buddhaghosa vi ff. xxiii f.
Buddhasīha 2
Buddhavaṁsa 69 f. 86 88 93 ff.; *see also* Chronicle of Buddhas
Buddhija a. Kak. 365

Campā (1) c.w.d. Kak. 365 (2) cy. 255 261
Campaka cy. 313
Canda (1) a. Kṇḍ. 201 (2) my. 196 201 f.
Candā (1) m. Piy. 300 308 (2) c.w.d. Vip. 345
Candamāṇava br. 198
Candamittā c.w.d. Vip 345
Candārāma 196 201
Candavatī cy. 196 247 253 298
Cariyāpiṭaka 92
Channa, charioteer xliv f. xlviii f. 80 188 395 404 ff. 428

Chronicle of Buddhas (*Buddhavaṁsa*) xxix 1 ff. 5 8 96 f. 181 269 279 322 328 334 424 f. 430; cty. on 2 f. 6 96 189 430 f.; see *Buddhavaṁsa*
Citta cy. 210
Cittakūṭa mt. 231
Cittalatā Grove 329
Cūḷāmaṇi-cetiya 407

Dāmā c.w.d. Ves. 357
Deva c. d. Suj. 293 297
Devadatta li 303
Devadaha cy. 392
Deva-grove 192
Devakūṭa mt. 288
Devala (1) c. d. Pmt. 278 283 (2) as. 396, *see* Kāla-
Devatāsaṁyutta 96
Dhammā c.w.d. Ads. 314
Dhammadassin B. 189 300 315–20 425 ff.
Dhammadāyāda-sutta (Heirs of Dhamma) 97
Dhammadinnā c.w.d. Piy. 308
Dhammaguṇa park 243
Dhammaka (1) a. Ano. 254 (2) mt. 110 **111** 170
Dhammapāla vi f. ix f. xiv n. xxiii xxxi
Dhammaruci n. k. 310
Dhammasena (1) c. d. Mṅg. 212 218 (2) c. d. Phs. 334 f.
Dhanañjaya cy. 349
Dhanapāla e. 48 306 408
Dhanapālaka (layman) 349
Dhanavatī m. Kas. 375 377 382
Dhaññavatī (1) mct's dtr. 256 (2) cy. 256 263 272
Dīgha-reciters 401
Dīpaṅkara B. xxi lii 6 93 115 f. 119 ff. 130 134 f. 137 141 148 f. 167 170 175–89 193 387 425 ff.; Chronicle of 190 204
Discourse on: Burning (*Ādittapariyāya*) 29; Exhortation to Rāhula (*Rāhulovāda-sutta*) 96 178 419; Marks of Non-self (*Anattalakkhaṇa-sutta*) 28; Turning the Wheel of Dhamma (*Dhammacakkappavattana-sutta*) 28 96 192 208 418 f.
Doṇa n. k. 267 f.
Doṇamukha e. l 303 306 f.; verses to 305

Erāvaṇa e. 304 350 409

Gaṇḍamba, tree 210
Ganges 9 173 267 269 f. 408
Gayā 321
Ghaṭīkāra, potter 380 407
Ghosita, householder 39
Girimekhalā, Māra's e. 12 413 415
Gosiṅga wood 258
Gotama (1) B. xxix f. xlvii ff. li 12 ff. 134 165 197 216 236 253 260 270 289 296 307 313 318 323 329 357 387–425; last meal xxxix 429 (2) Bs. xxx xxxii xliii ff. li 8 ff. 188 f. 236 387–415; powers of psychic potency 35; relations of 4 f. 34 ff. 40 45

Haṁsavaha h. 293
Haṁsavatī cy. 274 279 283 326
Hārita (1) Brahmā 232 (2) disciple 318
Himavant 11 168 270 313 **331** 362 379

Isidatta k. 251

Jambudīpa 31 81 180 199 203 256 263 283 292 301 303 341 352 368 378 386 391
Janasandha f. Tss. 330; *see* Saccasandha
Jaṭika (Jaṭila) Bs. 281
Jaṭilaka, householder 39
Jayasena (1) f. Phs. 332 334 f. (2) a. Sbh. 242 245 (3) f. Sdh. 324 (*see* Udena (1))
Jetavana 188 428 f.
Jeṭṭha, month 196
Jewel-Walk 4 13 35 49 51–95 416 424
Jotipāla (1) Bs. xxx 380 (2) archer xxx
Jumnā 173

Kakusandha B. l 187 189 360–7 368 425 ff.
Kāla n. k. 11 48 411 413
Kāladevala, as. 395 f.
Kāḷudāyin xliv f. xlviii 5 33 f. 188 395 428
Kāma, deva 408 f.
Kañcana, -āvela s. Piy. 301 308
Kañcanapabbata (Golden Mountain) **228**
Kañcanaveḷu cy. 325
Kaṇṇakujja cy. 334 361 363

Kanthaka h. xxxi xliv f. xlix 9 80 188 395 404 ff. 428
Kapilapura. K-vatthu 4 f. 8 35 66 77 134 311 391 f. 395 404 406
Kāsi (1) cy. 332 334 f. 407 (2) k-dom 386
Kassapa (1) B. xxx 18 93 187 189 360 375–87 407 425 ff. (2) Bs. 307 (3) Bs. 375 379 (4) the Boy (Kumāra-K.) 74 76 375 379 (5) Great (Mahā-K.) xlviii **74** f. (6) of Uruvelā 29 f. 74 419 (7) others 74
Khaṇḍa c. d. Vip. 339 345
Khandhaka 77; on the Council 16: on Schism 75
Khāṇukoṇḍañña, Elder 39
Khara y. 48
Kharadāṭhika y. 206
Khema Bs. 364
Khema(-ka, -vatī) cy 326 328 330 337 339 ff. 360 f. 365
Khemā (1) c.w.d. Dhd. 319 (2) c.w.d. Gtm. 134 f. 198
Khemaṅkara (1) a. Skh. 350 (2) k. 360
Kisāgotamī (1) w. Phs. 332 335 (2) maiden 402
Kolita c. d. Gtm. 134 f. 197
Koṇāgamana B. 1 187 189 360 368–75 425 ff.
Koṇḍañña (1) B. 93 189–203 207 425 ff. (2) br. 397 410
Kusinārā cy. 336
Kosambī 4
Kumbhakaṇṇa y. 287
Kumuda cy. 303
Kurundī viii f.
Kūṭadantasutta 57

Lokabyūha devas 389
Lumbinī grove 392 ff.

Madhurindhara k. 251
Magadha 10 410
Māgha, month 180 188 213 280 312 355 363 370 379 429
Mahā-(Mūla-) aṭṭhakathā viii ff. xxxix
Mahā-Mahinda vii f.
(*Mahā-*)*Maṅgala-sutta* 195 251 312 327 334 419
Mahā-Māyā m. Gtm. 82 134 197 391 ff.
(Mahā-)Moggallāna 52 **74** 255
Mahāniddesa 22
Mahāpaccarī viii f.
Mahāpaduma pr. 303
Mahāpanāda Sutta 400
Mahāvihāra viii f. xxxi xlvii 2
Mahī river 173
Mahosadha Bs. 90 394
Makhilā (1) w. Sbh. 240 245 (2) c.w.d. Skh. 350 (3) cy. 361
Makuṭacetiya 120
Maṇḍa-eon 276 f. 285 n. 292 294 311 **333**
Mandāra Hill 10 409
Maṅgala (1) B. 187 189 203–20 425 ff. (2) Bs. 323
Mañjerika, n.-abode 413
Māra(s) 12 80 115 121 184 191 205 221 223 232 241 248 256 264 274 f. 285 293 326 338 346 f. 369 405 412 ff. 422 429
Medhaṅkara B. 93 188 f.
Mekhala cy. 212 221 227 f. 235 243
Meṇḍaka mct. 39
Meru, mt. 53 **194** 196 214 274 409
Metteyya B. xlvi 360
Middle Fifty (*Majjhima-paṇṇāsaka*) 22
Mithilā cy. 278 ff. 371
Mucalinda n. k. 14 416

Nāgā c.w.d. Suj. 297
Nāgasamālā c.w.d. Suj. 297
Nakula mk-t. 285
Nakulā (1) c.w.d. Sbh. 245 (2) mct's dtr. 285
Nālāgiri e. li 48 n.
Nanda (1) a. Dīp. 187 (2) pk. 187
Nandā c.w.d. Dīp. 184; *see* Sunandā
Nandana Grove 171 391 ff.
Nanduttarā s. Nār. 264 268 272
Nārada (1) B. xii 189 247 263–74 425 ff. (2) a. Suj 297 (3) mt. 178 ff. (4) y. 179
Naradeva y. li (1) 361 f. (2) 378 f.
Narinda n. k. 353
Nārivāhana (1) cy. 328 355 (2) pr. 328
Nerañjarā 11 134 f. 411
Nigrodha's pk. 4 8 35
Nisabha c. d. Ano. 253

Osadhakumāra Bs. 394
Osadhī (1) cy. 250 231 (2) star **158 159**

Pabbata Bs. 371
Pabhāvatī (1) m. Skh. 346 350 (2) m. Suj. 292 297
Paduma (1) B. 189 247 255–62 425 ff. (2) c. d. Dhd. 317 319
Padumā (1) w. Dīp. 187 (2) c.w.d. Skh. 350 (3) m. Tss. 326 330
Padumuttara B. 189 274–84 285 425 ff.; Chronicle of 311
Pālita (1) a. Mṅg. 218 (2) c. d. Piy. 307 f.
Pañcasikha, heavenly musician 42
Paṇḍara h. 204
Paṇḍava mt. 10 409 f.
Paribhutta cy. 349
Pārileyyaka (1) e. 48 (2) forest 4
Paṭṭhāna 13
Phagguna, month 5 34
Phaggunī c.w.d. Nār. 272
Phussa (1) B. 189 326 332–6 425 ff. (2) month 5
Phussā c.w.d. Tss. 330
Phussadeva c. d. Dhd. 317 319
Piyadassin (1) B. l lii 189 300–9 425 ff. (2) mct. 347
Pokkharasādi xlvii n.
Porāṇa, Porāṇaṭṭhakathā (the Ancients) x f. xvii li 23 n. 24 n. 25 n. 26 n. 52 277
Pubbavideha 199
Punabbasumitta s. Smdh. 285 290
Puṇṇa (1) Mantānī's son 76 **77** (2) br. 77
Puṇṇā, slave 11
Punnavaḍḍhana s. Dhd. 315 319
Pure Abodes (Suddhāvāsa) 120 143 388

Rādhā c.w.d. Pdm. 261
Rādhavatī cy. 251
Rāhu 68 408; freed from **170**
Rāhula s. Gtm. xlvii 80 402; *see also Discourse* on
Rāhulamātā m. Rāhula and w. Gtm. xliv xlvii 188 395 400 402 404 428
Rājagaha 4 f. 9 f. 16 29 31 33 f. 66 77 408 410
Rājāyatana, tree 14 416
Rāma br. 397
Rāmā c.w.d. Smdh. 290
Ramma(vatī) (1) cy. Dīp. 116 119 123 f. 126 130 137 f. 164 167 170 174 184 (2) cy. Kṇḍ. 190 201 (3) cy. Pdm. 256 f. 261 (4) cy. Rev. 236
Ratanacaṅkamanacetiya 13
Ratanacetiya 416
Ratanagharacetiya 14 416
Revata (1) B. 189 203 231–9 425 ff. (2) a. Sdh. 324
Rocanī w. Kak. 361 365
Rose-apple Land (Jambudīpa) 323
Rucī(devī) w. Kṇḍ. 190 201
Rucigattā w. Koṇ. 368 373
Rucinandā mct's dtr. 275

Sabbadassin c. d. Piy. 307 f.
Sabbakāma c. d. Smdh. 290
Sabbakāmā w. Skh. 347 351
Sabbamitta a. Kas. 382
Sabbanāmā c.w.d. Dhd. 319
Sabhiya a. Phs. 335
Saccakāli (1) brother Smdh. 286 (2) c. d. Smdh. (? Sabbakāma, q.v.) 290
Saccasandha f. Tss. 326; *see* Janasandha
Sādhudevī mct's dtr. 232
Sāgara (1) f. Ads. 310 314 (2) a. Smdh. 290
Sāgata a. Dīp. 184
Sahaka, Elder 18
Sahampati: *see* Brahmā Sahampati
Sakka d. k. 14 f. 80 111 120 127 n. 184 192 n. 214 f. 227 232 244 n. 264 317 f. 390 394 401 407 412 f. 416 f.
Sakyan(s) 8 35 399; glory of 418; "great-man" 418
Sāla c. d. Pdm. 257 f. 261
Sālā c.w.d. Phs. 335
Sālavatī cy. 320
Sāmā c.w.d. Kak 365
Samaha a. Tss. 330
Samālā c.w.d. Ves. 357
Sāmavatī, laywoman 39
Samavattakkhandha (1) s. Dīp. 177 (2) s. Vip. 337 345
Samavattakkhandha Usabha-kkhandha s. Dīp. 177
Samba(hu)la c. d. Sdh. 322 324
Sambhava (1) a. Rev. 237 (2) c. d. Skh. 348 ff.
Samuddā c.w.d. Koṇ. 373
Saṁyutta-reciters 278
Sañjaya k. 317
Sañjīva (1) c. d. Kak. 365 (2) Elder 38
Saṅkassa cy. 188 227 332 428 f.
Santa c. d. Ads. 312 314

Santusita (1) Bs. as d. k. 79 (2) d. k. 15 390 417
Sarabha(vatī) cy. 356
Sarada as. 278
Sāra-eon 276 f.; -maṇḍa eon 276 f.
Sarabhū, river 173
Saraṇa (1) f. Dhd. 315 319 (2) c. d. Smdh. 286 290 (3) c. d. Sum. 222 228 (4) cy. 315 317 319
Saraṇaṅkara B. 93 189
Sarassatī, river 173
Sāriputta (General under Dhamma) 1 6 8 38 52 66 **67** f. 71 **73** 77 86 f. 92 97 112 255
Sātāgiri y. 48
Satthavāha s. Koṇ. 368 373
Sāvatthi 5 f. 429
Scented Chamber (Gandhakuṭi) 14 126 188 416 428
Sela (1) s. Ads. 310 312 314 (2) br. xlvii n.
Senaka Bs. 90
Senānī mk-t. 10 411 422
Setavyā cy. 386
Siddhattha (1) B. 189 320–5 425 ff. (2) Gtm. 35 397 400 402 412 414 f.
Sīhakumāra s. Sbh. 240 245
Sikhin B. xlix 189 346–52 425 ff.
Sīlavatī cy. 352
Simile of the Child's Flesh (Puttamaṁsūpama) 97
Sindh 400
Sineru mt. **53** 120 232 264 389
Sirimā (1) w. Ano. 247 254 (2) m. Phs. 332 335 (3) m. Sum. 221 228
Sirinandā w. Suj. 293 298
Sirinandana (1) cy. 293 (2) mct. 293
Sirivaḍḍha (1) as. 332 (2) cy. 208 (3) g.c. f. 316 (4) k. 333 (5) n. a. 285
Sirivaḍḍhā mct's dtr. 332
Sirivaḍḍhanā, a girl 353
Sīvala s. Mṅg. 204 218
Sīvalā (1) c.w.d. Mṅg. 218 (2) c.w.d. Sdh. 324
Sobhana cy. 310 f. 314
Sobhavatī cy. 368 373
Sobhita (1) B. 189 239–46 f. 425 ff.; Chronicle of 254 275 (2) a. Piy. 308
Soma g. c. f. 376
Somanassā w. Sdh. 321 324
Soṇa (1) c. d. Ves. 354 f. 357 (2) Elder 303
Soṇā c.w.d. Sum. 229
Sonuttara h. 326
Soreyya cy. 251 355
Sotārāma my. 245
Sotthija a. Koṇ. 373
Sotthiya, grass-cutter 12 412
Sri Lanka vii ff.
Subhadda (1) c. d. Kṇḍ. 196 201 (2) g. c. f. 361
Subhaddā (1) c.w.d. Rev. 237 (2) w. Tss. 326 330
Subhavatī cy. 250 301
Sucandaka cy. 312
Sūciloma y. 48
Sucindhara br. 196
Sucindharā, *nāgī* 310
Sucirindha mk-t. 361
Sucitta mk-t. 353
Sucittā w. Ves. 353 358
Sudassana (1) Bs. 356 (2) p. Dhd. 316 (3) f. Piy. 300 (*see* Sudatta) (4) c. d. Suj. 293 295 297 (5) cy. 119 242 285 f. 288 290 369 (6) d. k. 301 ff. 307 (7) h. 310 (8) mct. 337 (9) mk-t. 347 (10) mt. 180 301 (11) my. 174 (12) pk. keeper 264
Sudassanā (1) m. Ads. 310 (2) w. Rev. 231 238 (3) w. Vip. 337 (*see* Sutanū)
Sudatta (1) f. Piy. 300 308 (*see* Sudassana) (2) f. Smdh. 285 290 (3) f. Sum. 221 228
Sudattā (1) m. Smdh. 285 290 (2) c.w.d. Tss. 330
Suddhodana f. Gtm. 33 f. 36 82 134 197 391 f. 395 397 402
Sudeva (1) Dīp. 184 f. (2) c. d. Mṅg. 212 218 (3) f. Nār. 263 272
Sudhamma (1) f. Sbh. 239 f. 245 (2) cy. 239 245
Sudhammā (1) c.w.d. Ads 314 (2) m. Sbh. 239 245 (3) d-hall 377 **378**
Sudhammavatī cy. 294
Sudhaññavatī cy. 231 235 237 300 308
Sujāta (1) B. 189 285 292–300 425 ff. (2) Bs. 244 329 (3) c. d. Pmt. 278 283 (4) k. 328 f. (5) g. c. f. 337 (6) n. a. 301
Sujātā (1) m. Kṇḍ. 190 201 (2) m. Pmt. 274 283 (3) c.w.d. Piy. 308 (4) c.w.d. Sbh. 245 (5) of Senānī 10 f. 134 411 422
Sumana (1) B. 189 203 221–30 f. 425 ff. (2) Bs. 221 (3) a. Pmt. 283

Sumanā (1) c.w.d. Ano. 254 (2) w. Smdh. 285 290
Sumaṅgala (1) c. d. Dīp. 184 (2) cy. 293 297 307
Sumedha (1) B. 189 285–92 294 425 ff. (2) Bs. 96–170 181 (3) f. Dīp. 184
Sumedhā m. Dīp. 178 184
Sumitta (1) c. d. Sdh. 322 324 (2) n. a. 275
Sunanda (1) f. Kṇḍ. 190 201 (2) cy. 379 (3) my. 177 (4) n. a. 293 (5) u. m. 210 f. (6) vge. 190
Sunandā (1) c.w.d. Dīp. 184 (2) m. Dhd. 315 319 (3) w. Kas. 376 383
Sunandaka n. a. 191
Sunandavatī cy. 226 243 331
Sundara cy. 369 f. 377
Sundarī c.w.d. Ano. 254
Sunetta (1) a. Dhd. 319 (2) c. d. Sbh. 241 245
Sunettā br. girl 321
Suphassā m. Sdh. 320 324
Suppabuddha s. Ves. 353 358
Suppatīta f. Ves. 353 357
Suppatiṭṭhita 11
Surabhi cy. 210
Surādhā c.w.d. Pdm. 261
Surakkhita c. d. Phs. 334 f.
Surāmā (1) c.w.d. Sdh. 324 (2) c.w.d. Smdh. 290
Surasena cy. 323
Surinda, vihāra 243
Surindavatī cy. 370
Suriyavatī cy. 348
Suruci (1) Bs. 213 (2) vge. 213
Susīma Bs. 313
Sutanū w. Vip 337 345 (*see* Sudassanā (3))
Suttanta **200**
Suttapiṭaka 200
Suyāma: devas 390; d-k. 15 412 417

Tagara cy. 317
Taṇhaṅkara B. 93 188 f.
Tapassu mct. 15 416
Tapovana 113
Thirty-Three (Tāvatiṁsa): abode of 4 178 210 232 242 250 264 293 377 f. 395 407 429; devas of 53 f. 173; (Tidasa) 192 232; (Tidiva) 172 295
Thullakoṭṭhita cy. 269.
Tinduka g. c. f. 369
Tissa (1) B. 189 326–31 425 ff. (2) c. d. Dīp. 184 (3) c. d. Kas. 379 382 (4) c. d. Vip. 339 345
Tissā c.w.d. Kṇḍ. 201
Titthika n. a. 256
Triple Gem 174 f.
Tusita xlviii 6 79 f. 116 190 203 221 231 239 247 255 263 274 285 292 300 309 315 320 326 332 337 346 353 360 368 375 389 ff.

Udaya(na) c. d. Tss. 326 330
Uddaka (Rāmaputta) 10 18 410 417
Udena (1) f. Sdh. 320 324 (2) a. Sum. 228 (3) k. 196
Uggata (1) f. Suj. 292 297 (2) k. 243
Ujjeni cy 275
Upaka n. a. 27 417
Upakāri cy. 288
Upāli, Elder 76 f.
Upasāla c. d. Pdm. 257 261
Upasālā c.w.d. Phs. 335
Upasanta (1) c. d. Ads. 312 314 (2) a. Ves. 355 357
Upasena s. Suj. 293 298
Upasoṇā c.w.d. Sum. 229
Upatissa c. d. Gtm. 134 f. 197
Upatissā c.w.d. Kṇḍ. 201
Upavāna, Upavāraṇa s. Ano. 247 254
Uppalavaṇṇā c.w.d. Gtm. 134 f. 198
Uruvelā (1) c.w.d. Kas. 382 (2) cy. 5 10 29 340 410 f. 422
Usabhakkhandha s. Dīp. 187
Usabhavatī cy. 258 301 360
Uttara (1) Bs. 289 (2) s. Kak. 361 365 (3) c. d. Koṇ. 370 373 (4) f. Mṅg. 204 218 (5) s. Pmt. 275 283 (6) c. d. Ves. 354 f. 357 (7) cy. 204 218 234 f. (8) mct. 205 (9) n. a. 205 (10) vge. 205
Uttarā (1) c.w.d. Koṇ. 373 (2) m. Koṇ. 368 f. 373 (3) c.w.d. Nār. 272 (4) m. Mṅg. 204 218 (5) w. Pdm. 256 261 (6) donor to Mṅg. 205 (6) laywoman 39
Uttarakuru 199 270
Uttara-madhurā pk. 204
Uttarārāma 213
Uttarāsāḷha, asterism 82 116 188 392 405 418 429

Vajirindha br. 361
Vaṅka mt. 206

Vappa, Elder 28
Vara-eon 276 f. 311
Varuṇa (1) a. Ano. 254 261 (2) c. d. Rev. 231 235 ff. (3) g. c. f. 321 (4) vge. 301
Varuṇārāma 233
Varuṇindhara n. a. 232
Vasabha br. 301
Vāsava (Sakka) 407
Vasavatti devas 390
Vasavattī p. Pmt. 275
Vasavattin (Māra) 405 412
Vāseṭṭha a. Nār. 272
Vassakamma, d-putta 120
Vasudattā w. Pmt. 275 283
Vaṭaṁsikā w. Sum 221 229
Vatthu-sutta 96
Vebhāra (1) cy. 320 322 324 (2) mt. 16 280
Vedas 100 ff. 213 307 312 323 380 396 409
Vedaṅgas 323 409
Verañjā 4
Verocana n. k. 269
Vesālī 4 7
Vessabhū B. l 189 346 353–60 425 ff.
Vessantara 6 79 f. 116 190 205 388 f. 394 f.
Vicikolī w. Dhd. 315 f. 319
Vidhura c. d. Kak. 365
Vijayuttara, Sakka's conch 412 f.
(Vi)jitamitta c. d. Nār. 269 272
Vijitasaṅgāmaka g. c. f. 326
Vijitasena (1) s. Kas. 376 383 (2) s. Kṇḍ. 190 196 201
Vijitasenā w. Nār. 263 f. 272
Vijitāvin (1) Bs. 196 ff. (2) Bs. 334
Vimalā w. Piy. 301 308
Vimalatthavilāsinī cty on Vv. 407
Vimānavatthaṭṭhakathā xxxi 407
Vinaya-piṭaka 76 98 **200**
Vipassin B. xlix 23 189 336–46 425 ff.
Vipula f. Rev. 231 237
Vipulā m. Rev. 231 237
Vīra (1) mct. 326 (2) mk-t. 326
Visākha, asterism, month 10 80 121 188 190 205 208 221 232 247 256 264 275 285 293 301 310 321 326 332 337 340 347 353 361 368 376 411 422 429
Visākhā (1) w. Ads. 310 314 (2) m. Kak. 360 365 (3) laywoman xlvii n.
Vissakamma, d-putta 111 401
Visuddhimagga ix xxii f.
Vulture Peak mt. 66 ff.

Yaññadatta f. Koṇ. 368 373
Yasa 28
Yasavā f. Ano. 247 253
Yasavatī w. Mṅg. 204 218 (2) m. Ves. 353 357 (3) cy. 327 ff.
Yasodhara br. 196
Yasodharā (1) m. Ano. 247 253 (2) w. Gtm. xlvii 422 (3) mct. dtr. 190
Yugandhara mt. 22 137 197 227 301